Collector
Plates

THE OFFICIAL®
PRICE GUIDE TO
Collector
Plates

Gene Ehlert

FIFTH EDITION

House of Collectibles
New York, New York 10022

©1988 Random House, Inc.

This is a registered trademark of Random House, Inc.

All rights reserved under International and
Pan-American Copyright Conventions.

Published by: The House of Collectibles
                 201 East 50th Street
                 New York, New York 10022

Distributed by Ballantine Books, a division of Random House, Inc., New York and simultaneously in Canada by Random House of Canada Limited, Toronto.

Manufactured in the United States of America

Library of Congress Catalog Card Number: 82-82256

ISBN: 0-876-37361-9

Fifth Edition: February 1988

10 9 8 7 6 5 4

For my "women"—
Linda, Annie, and Elizabeth.

Table of

Contents

Acknowledgments xi

Special Acknowledgments xii
    Collectors' Information Bureau xv

Market Review 1
    Today's Hottest Plates and Artists, as Compiled by Our Panel of
        Experts 4

What is a Collector Plate? 6

The History of Collector Plates 13

Approaches to Collecting 20

Investing in Collector Plates 26

Buying and Selling Collector Plates 29
    Sources of Supply 30
    Buying Direct From the Manufacturers 32
    Buying From Plate Dealers 33
    Buying by Mail Order 35
    Buying From Flea Markets and Secondhand Shops 37
    Buying at Auction 38
    Buying From Other Collectors 41
    Buying and Selling Through the Bradford Exchange 42

Selling Your Plates 43
Selling by Auction...................................... 46

Fakes and Imitations................................ 47

How to Display Your Plates 50

Caring for Your Plates 54
Packing for Shipment.................................. 55
Insurance.. 56

Artist Interviews 58
Sandra Kuck 58
John McClelland 61
Gregory Perillo 63
Donald Zolan 65

A Gallery of Artists................................. 69
Roger Akers 69
Sy and Dorothea Barlowe 69
Lenore Béran.. 70
Ben Black 71
Alan Brunettin 71
Carl Romanelli 72
Ted DeGrazia 73
Edna Hibel 74
Rusty Money.. 75
P. Buckley Moss 76
Don Ruffin 76
D. L. "Rusty" Rust.................................... 77
Red Skelton... 77
Irene Spencer.. 78
Abigail Williams 79

Manufacturers: A Few Histories 81
Anna-Perenna Porcelain, Inc........................... 81
Bareuther... 82
Bing and Grondahl 83
Fenton Art Glass Company............................. 84
Frankoma Pottery 85
Pemberton & Oakes.................................... 86
Rockwell Museum...................................... 86
Royal Copenhagen..................................... 87

Glossary 89

Publications 94

1987 NALED List of Dealer Members 96

1987 Canadian Limited Edition Dealer Members 109

How to Use This Book 114

Collector Plate Listings 115

Acknowledgments

A special thanks to Galina Kolev and Donna Jordan for their assistance in the production of this book. The author would also like to thank all of the people quoted in this edition for their time and efforts, especially Paul Stark of Design Galleries. In addition, the help provided by Ginny Sexton, Manager of Public Relations at the Bradford Exchange, in securing photos for the book was invaluable. The time and assistance of Sandy Forgach of Collectibles etc. in Brown Deer, Wisconsin, and the advice, at the earliest stages of this book, from Joyce Pearce of Lowell, Massachusetts, are truly appreciated.

We would like to thank the following for supplying photos for this book: Collectors' Information Bureau; Bradford Exchange; Anna-Perenna Inc.; Armstrong's; Bing & Grondahl; Carmel Collection; Carson Mint; Chinese Fine Arts; Christian Bell Porcelain; Christian Fantasy Collectibles; Enesco Imports; R. J. Ernst; Evergreen Press; Fine Arts Marketing; Flambro Imports; Gartlan USA; Gorham Co.; Dave Grossman Designs; Hamilton Collection; Edna Hibel Corp.; Historic Providence Mint; Incolay Studios Inc.; Lenox China; Limoges; Limoges-Turgot; Modern Masters; Pemberton & Oakes, Ltd.; Reco International; Norman Rockwell Museum; Roman Inc.; Royal Doulton; Royal Orleans; Sports Impressions; D. H. Ussher; Vague Shadows; Wedgwood.

Special
Acknowledgments

The author would like to offer a special note of thanks to Diane Carnevale and the Collectors' Information Bureau. The Bureau's generosity in allowing the use of its price listings in this book is very much appreciated. The assistance and patience of Diane Carnevale in this regard was truly invaluable.

The following list of manufacturers and their series was graciously provided for this book by the Collectors' Information Bureau:

American Artists, The Horses of Fred Stone, Family Treasures; *American Rose Society,* All-American Rose; *Anna-Perenna,* Uncle Tad's Cats, Flowers of Count Bernadotte; *Anri,* Ferrandiz Children; *Arabia of Finland,* Kalevala; *Armstrong's/Crown Parian,* The Three Graces, Statue of Liberty, Reflections of Innocence, Lovable Kittens, Huggable Puppies, The Buck Hill Bears, Companions, The Signature Collection, Happy Art Series; *Portraits of Childhood,* Freddie the Freeloader, American Folk Heroes, Freddie's Adventures; *Artists of the World,* Holiday, Children, Children, autographed, Children of Aberdeen; *Bareuther,* Christmas, Danish Church; *Belleek Pottery,* Christmas, Irish Wildlife; *Berlin Design,* Christmas, Historical, Holiday Week of the Family Kappelmann; *Bing & Grondahl,* Christmas, Jubilee 5-Year Cycle, Mother's Day, Children's Day, Moments of Truth, Statue of Liberty, Christmas in America; *Blue River Mill,* Once Upon a Barn; *Boehm Studios, Edward Marshall,* Egyptian Commemorative; *Curator Collection,* Masterpieces of Rockwell, Rockwell Americana, Rockwell Trilogy, Simpler Times, Special Occasions, Masterpieces of Impressionism, Magical Moment, Playful Pets, The Tribute, Nursery Pair, On the Road, The Great Trains, Becker Babies, Portraits, Sailing Through History, Curator Gift Editions; *D'Arceau Limoges,* Christmas; *Duncan Royale,* History of Santa Claus I; *Enesco,* Inspired

Thoughts, Mother's Love, Christmas Collection, Joy of Christmas, The Four Seasons, Open Editions, Christmas Love; *R. J. Ernst Enterprises,* Women of the West, A Beautiful World, Seems Like Yesterday, Turn of the Century, Hollywood Greats, Commemoratives, Classy Cars, Star Trek, Star Trek: The Commemorative Collection, Elvira; *Fairmont China,* Spencer Special, Famous Clowns; *Fenton Art Glass,* American Craftsman Carnival; *Flambro Imports,* Emmett Kelly, Jr.; *Fleetwood Collection,* Christmas, Royal Wedding, Statue of Liberty; *Frankoma Pottery,* Annual Christmas, Birthday, Teenagers of the Bible, Madonna; *Fukagawa,* Warabe No Haiku; *Gartlan USA,* Pete Rose Platinum Edition, The Round Tripper, George Brett Gold Crown Collection, Roger Staubach Sterling Collection; *Ghent Collection,* April Fool Annual, American Bicentennial Wildlife; *Goebel (Germany),* M. I. Hummel Collectibles—Annual, M. I. Hummel Collectibles—Anniversary, M. I. Hummel—Little Music Makers, Goebel Collectors Club Exclusive—Celebration; *Gorham Collection,* Christmas 1974–1985, Christmas 1986–1987, A Boy and His Dog Four Seasons, Young Love Four Seasons, Four Ages of Love, Grandpa and Me Four Seasons, Me and My Pals Four Seasons, Grand Pals Four Seasons, Going On Sixteen Four Seasons, Tender Years Four Seasons, A Helping Hand Four Seasons, Dad's Boys Four Seasons, Old Timers Four Seasons, Life with Father Four Seasons, Old Buddies Four Seasons, Bas Relief, Single Issues, Boy Scout, Presidential, Four Seasons Landscapes, Gallery of Masters, Barrymore, Pewter Bicentennial, Vermeil Bicentennial, Silver Bicentennial, China Bicentennial, Remington Western, Moppet Plates—Christmas, Moppet Plates—Mother's Day, Moppet Plates—Anniversary, Julian Ritter, Fall in Love, Julian Ritter—Single Issues, Julian Ritter, To Love a Clown, Christmas/Children's Television Workshop, Pastoral Symphony, Encounters, Survival and Celebrations, Charles Russell, Gorham Museum Doll, Time Machine Teddies, Lewis & Clark Expedition—Trailblazers of Northwest; *Grande Copenhagen,* Christmas; *Hackett American Collector,* Endangered Species, Playful Memories; *Hamilton Collection,* The Greatest Show on Earth, Japanese Floral Calendar, Portraits of Childhood, Utz Mother's Day, Single Issues, Summer Days of Childhood, Birds of Prey, Eternal Wishes of Good Fortune, Gardens of the Orient, Chinese Symbols of the Universe, A Garden of Verses, Flower Festivals of Japan, Tale of Genji, Passage to China, Chinese Blossoms of the Four Seasons, A Child's Best Friend, A Country Summer, The Little Rascals, The Japanese Blossoms of Autumn, Star Wars, Noble Owls of America, Butterfly Garden; *Hampton House,* Single Issue; *Haviland,* Twelve Days of Christmas; *Haviland & Parlon,* Tapestry I, Tapestry II, Christmas Madonnas; *Hibel Studios,* Arte Oval, The World I Love; *Hutschenreuther,* Gunther Granget, The Glory of Christmas, Enchantment, Arzberg; *Incolay Studios,* Romantic Poets; *International Silver,* Bicentennial; *Jensen, Svend,* Christmas, Mother's Day; *Kaiser,* Oberammergau Passion Play, Christmas, Memories of Christmas, Mother's Day,

Anniversary, Great Yachts, Garden and Song Birds, King Tut, Feathered
Friends, Happy Days, Egyptian, Four Seasons, Romantic Portraits, On the
Farm, Classic Fairy Tales Collection, Dance, Ballerina, Dance, Children's
Prayer, Famous Horses, Traditional Fairy Tales, Racing for Pride and Profit,
Bird Dog, Childhood Memories, Harmony and Nature, Woodland Creatures,
Water Fowl, Wildflowers, Famous Lullabies, Bicentennial, The Graduate;
Knowles, Edwin M., Wizard of Oz, Gone with the Wind, Cstari Grandparent,
Americana Holidays, Annie, The Four Ancient Elements, Biblical Mothers,
Hibel Mother's Day, Friends I Remember, Father's Love, The King and I,
Encyclopaedia Britannica Birds of Your Garden, Frances Hook Legacy,
Hibel Christmas, Upland Birds of North America, Oklahoma!, Sound of
Music, American Innocents, J. W. Smith Holiday, Living With Nature—
Jerner's Ducks, Lincoln Man of America, Portraits of Motherhood; *Konigs-
zelt, Bavaria,* Hedi Keller Christmas; *Lenox,* Boehm Birds, Boehm Wood-
land Wildlife, The Confederacy, Boehm Birds/Young America, Colonial
Christmas Wreath, Butterflies and Flowers, Nature's Nursery, Lenox Christ-
mas Tree, The Confederacy Collection, American Wildlife; *Lihs Lindner,*
Christmas; *Maruri USA,* Eagle; *Mingolia/Home Plates,* Christmas, Copper
and Enamel, Christmas, Porcelain; *Nostalgia Collectibles,* Shirley Temple
Collectibles, Shirley Temple Collectibles, autographed, Shirley Temple Clas-
sics; *Pickard,* Lockhart Wildlife, Annual Christmas, Children of Renoir,
Mother's Love, Children of Mexico; *Porsgrund,* Christmas Annual; *Reco
International,* The World of Children, Mother Goose, The McClelland Chil-
dren's Circus Collection, Becky's Day, Games Children Play, The Grandpar-
ent Collector's Plates, Little Professionals, Days Gone By, A Childhood
Almanac, Mother's Day Collection, A Children's Christmas Pageant, The
Barefoot Children, The Sophisticated Ladies Collection, The Springtime of
Life, Vanishing Animal Kingdoms, Arabelle and Friends, Arta Christmas,
Arta Mother's Day, Bohemian Annuals, Americana, Dresden Christmas,
Four Seasons, Western, Great Stories from the Bible; *Reece, Maynard,*
Waterfowl; *Reed and Barton,* Audubon; *River Shore,* Famous Americans,
Remington's Bronze, Della Robbia, Norman Rockwell Single Issue, Baby
Animals, Rockwell Four Freedoms, Grant Wood Single Issue, Rockwell
Vignette, Rockwell Cats, Rockwell/Good Old Days, Timberlake Christmas
after Christmas, Favorite American Songbirds, Lovable Teddies; *Rockwell
Museum,* American Family I, Christmas, American Family II; *Rockwell
Society,* Christmas, Mother's Day, Heritage, Rockwell's Rediscovered
Women, Rockwell's Light Campaign, Rockwell's American Dream, Coloni-
als—The Rarest Rockwells, A Mind of Her Own; *Royal Cornwall,* Creation,
Creation Calhoun Charter Release; *Roman, Inc.,* The Masterpiece Collec-
tion, A Child's World, Frances Hook Collection—Set I, Frances Hook Col-
lection—Set II, Petty Girls of the Ice Capades, The Ice Capades Clown,
Roman Memorial, Roman Cats, The Magic of Childhood, Frances Hook

Legacy, The Lord's Prayer, The Sweetest Songs, Fontanini Annual Christmas; *Rorstrand,* Christmas; *Rosenthal,* Christmas, Wiinblad Christmas, Nobility of Children, Oriental Gold, Classic Rose Christmas; *Royal Bayreuth,* Christmas; *Royal Copenhagen,* Christmas, Mother's Day, The Motherhood Collection; *Royal Devon,* Rockwell Christmas, Rockwell Mother's Day; *Royal Orleans,* Pink Panther Christmas Collection, Dynasty; *Royal Orleans/ Hoyle Products,* Nostalgia Magazine Covers; *Royal Worcester (Great Britain),* Doughty Birds; *Royal Worcester (United States),* The American History, Currier & Ives, Fabulous Birds, Christmas, Water Birds of North America, Kitten Classics; *Schmid (Germany),* Christmas, Mother's Day; *Schmid (Japan),* Peanuts Christmas, Disney Christmas, Disney Mother's Day, Davis Country Pride, Davis Cat Tales, Davis Special Edition, Davis Christmas, Ferrandiz Music Makers Porcelain, Ferrandiz Wooden Birthday, Juan Ferrandiz Porcelain Christmas, Paddington Bear/Musician's Dream, Raggedy Ann Christmas, A Year with Paddington Bear, Peanuts Mother's Day, Peanuts Valentine's Day, Peanuts World's Greatest Athlete, Peanuts Special Edition, Raggedy Ann Valentine's Day, Raggedy Ann Annual, Raggedy Ann Bicentennial, Walt Disney Special Edition; *Seeley's Ceramic Service,* Old French Doll Collection; *Spode,* American Song Birds; *U.S. Historical Society,* Annual Stained Glass & Pewter Christmas, The Christmas Carol, Great American Sailing, Annual Spring Flowers; *Vague Shadows,* The Chieftains, The Plainsmen, The Professionals, Pride of America's Indians, Legends of the West, Chieftains 2, Child Life, Indian Nations, The Storybook Collection, Perillo Santa's, The Princesses, Nature's Harmony, Arctic Friends, The Plainsmen Series—Bronze, Motherhood, The War Ponies, The Thoroughbreds, Special Issues, The Arabians; *Val St. Lambert,* Annual Old Masters, American Heritage; *Viletta China,* Disneyland; *Wedgwood, Enoch,* Christmas, Mother's Day, Blossoming of Suzanne, Eyes of the Child, Calendar, Child's Christmas, Children's Story, Queen's Christmas, Child's Birthday, Peter Rabbit Christmas, Bicentennial, Cathedrals Christmas, Portraits of First Love, Street Sellers of London, The Legend of King Arthur, Christmas Traditions, Valentine, Statue of Liberty; *Wildlife Internationale,* Sporting Dog, Old Family.

COLLECTORS' INFORMATION BUREAU

WHAT IS THE CIB?

The contemporary limited-edition field has shown extraordinary growth over the past 15 years. And with this growth, collectors find it challenging to stay abreast of the latest developments in plates, figurines, bells, graphics, steins, and dolls. To help meet this need, a group of limited-edition manufacturers and marketers formed Collectors' Information Bureau (CIB) in 1982. The CIB is a not-for-profit business league whose purpose is to provide current market prices, facts, and interesting feature material for collectors in the United States, Canada, and beyond. For further information, contact Diane Carnevale, Executive Director, 2059 Edgewood S.E., Grand Rapids, Michigan 49506.

WHO ARE THE CIB'S MEMBERS?

With current dues-paying enrollment of 30 Regular and Associate Members, CIB represents many of the world's most respected names in limited editions and collectibles. Regular Members market limited-edition items of their own, while Associate Members provide materials, accessories, and/or manufacturing facilities for marketers or collectors.

WHAT SERVICES DOES THE CIB PROVIDE?

- *Collectibles Market Guide & Price Index*, published by the Collectors' Information Bureau. A comprehensive book with more than 200 pages of lively, well-reported, and well-written material about the collectibles field, it includes history, trends, background articles, features on today's top artists, products, and manufacturers, and an exceptionally fine reference section. What's more, the book contains the 40-page "CIB Price Index to Plates, Figurines, Bells, Graphics, Steins and Dolls." This index covers thousands of products, including valuable identifying information as well as current quotes obtained via interviews with the CIB's panel of 27 dealers. CIB dealers include the most knowledgeable secondary market traders in America and are well dispersed geographically. Retail price: $13.95.

- Price Index in *Collectors Mart* Magazine. As it is updated twice yearly, the CIB Price Index is printed in *Collectors Mart* magazine, which carries a guaranteed circulation of 50,000. What's more, the index is available in this form at major collectors' shows. CIB also provides a regular column on collectibles in each issue of *Collectors Mart*.

Market Review

There seems to be general agreement among the plate experts we contacted that, after a few slow years of readjustment within the field, plates are coming back again! It's a volatile marketplace, and even as this is written, inflationary pressures are building, somewhat similar to those that fueled the "boom years" in plates back in the late 1970s and early 1980s. As a general rule, collectibles of all kinds tend to appreciate in value more rapidly as interest rates rise and inflation takes hold. Our economy is a cyclical one, and many economists feel that after the 1988 presidential and congressional elections, no matter who wins, federal deficit spending and the international trade imbalance will catch up with us, bringing inflation and a recession of some degree.

As Susan K. Jones, former executive director and currently special consultant at the Collectors' Information Bureau, says, "If inflation continues, it can't help but favorably impact the investment potential of limited-edition plates." Buddy Savetz, co-owner of Limited Edition, a well-respected plate dealership in Merrick, New York, agrees: "If inflation comes back strong, the plate as a collectible will be seen again as a hedge."

The overall national economy seems primed for a plate resurgence, but what about the fuel—the buyers and investors themselves? We sampled opinion from around the country to get some answers. Out on the West Coast, Jim Woodward organizes the California Plate and Collectibles Show every year in Pasadena. "We've just had a very successful show out here, with over sixteen thousand in attendance," he said recently. "We're very optimistic now. This was always a hotbed of plate activity, but interest dipped out here in southern California for a couple years. Now it seems we've turned the corner, and the enthusiasm is on its way back." Lance Klass, marketing director at Pemberton & Oakes, a major manufacturer of plates in Santa Barbara, California, concurs: "We're coming out of a slump in the market. It's stronger now than in the last few years." Joyce Zielinski, show coordinator at the prestigious International Plate and Collectibles Show held annually in South Bend, Indiana, added, "I don't know if it will ever be like the incredible boom of the late seventies and early eighties again, but it's steady, with a good age mix now, which could be pointing to an upsurge. It's a little too soon to tell just how big this could be."

This sense of cautious excitement was the common denominator we found all over the country. Susan Elliott, formerly editor at *Plate Collector* magazine and recently named to the same position at *Collector's Mart* magazine: "Plates are coming back. I just returned from the West Coast, and things are humming there like they haven't been in several years. You can feel the enthusiasm returning." Susan K. Jones: "Plates are on an upswing. You can feel it here in the upper Midwest as well. The economy has been affected by more working women within the marketplace. These dual incomes have allowed for more discretionary spending in many families, and this has translated into more plate collectors."

Another indicator of good times ahead is the fact that many more young people than ever before are becoming interested in collecting plates for art and investment. Arlene Young, owner of Strawberry House, a plate retail shop in the Chicago suburb of Mundelein, Illinois, has noticed the change: "When I started this business back in 1970, almost all of my customers were women in their fifties. Now I have a lot in the twenty-five to thirty-five age bracket. They were given plates as presents when they were children and have grown up with them around the house. Now they own their own homes and are buying their own plates, new issues and secondary market pieces as well."

This broadening of the market has also been evident in the greater number of men who are buying collector plates. Many editions have come out featuring sports stars and more male-oriented subjects to appeal to this wider market. Baseball notables like Reggie Jackson, Steve Garvey, and Pete Rose have been featured on popular issues, along with basketball superstar Larry Bird and race car legend Richard Petty. The automobiles themselves have appeared as well, with classic sports cars such as the Corvette being big favorites. Several plate series have been issued by Christian Bell Porcelain of Canada featuring steam locomotives from the past, and several artists have portrayed famous aircraft and events from aviation history. These traditionally male subject areas had been virtually ignored for many years, but healthy price appreciation of plates such as the Reggie Jackson issue have fueled a reexamination of the potential in these subjects.

Many other people have been drawn to plates in the last few years by celebrities and by television/motion picture themes. Knowles China has issued successful "Gone with the Wind" and "Wizard of Oz" series, which have been joined by a host of others, including Marilyn Monroe, James Dean, and John Wayne portraits, as well as plates on "Dynasty" characters and a commemorative on the television series "M*A*S*H."

Traditionally, the most successful subject matter of collector plates has been apple pie and motherhood. Small children and cuddly animals have been the mainstays. But a change of focus is beginning to appear. Other than celebrity and pop culture plates, the newest phenomenon is nature plates. Limited-edition prints and duck stamps featuring the works of wildlife artists have been produced and collected for years. These have been most popular in the south and southwest but now are beginning to gain interest in the rest of the country as well. Both the Top Plate Under $50, "Brave And Free" by Gregory Perillo, and the Top Plate Over $50, "Freedom Flight" by Mario Fernandez, as awarded at the 1987 California Plate Show, featured eagles as subjects. Fernandez had previously taken honors at 1985's major shows with "Courtship Flight," yet another plate featuring eagles. Many other renowned wildlife artists have entered the world of plate art of late, including Bart Jerner, Richard Lowe, Terry Redlin, Roger Tory Peterson, and Kevin Daniel, just to name a few.

Another factor that has expanded and changed the market is the pricing of collector plates at issue. There seems to be a sharp definition developing in plates now. There are the plates that come out in editions of 10,000 or less and generally cost $50 and above. On the other hand, there are the issues limited by the number of firing days, the exact number of which you'll never know. These plates are less expensive, in the $19 to $40 range, and seem to be bringing a lot of new people into the fold. You would think that these plates with no specific production amount would never appreciate, but some do surprisingly well. For example, some of the Rockwell Society issues have gained a great deal in market value though initially very modestly priced and with an unknown quantity produced. As Paul Stark, owner of Design Galleries in Wilkes-Barre, Pennsylvania, and author of "Limited Edition Collectibles: Everything You'll Ever Need to Know," explains: "The critical factor in the collector market is the law of supply and demand. The edition size of a collectible really doesn't matter, as long as it does not exceed its demand."

Plate collectors are still buying complete series, with the first in a series likely to be the most valuable on the secondary resale market. When the series contains more than four plates, there is less likelihood of a buyer wanting the complete set unless it's a Christmas or Mother's Day issue. Annual holiday series often become a tradition and are purchased every year as gifts. These collections can become quite valuable over time but are less frequently traded because of personal attachments.

Nearly everyone agrees that today's collector is more pragmatic and conservative than ever before. They are also more knowledgeable and continue to educate themselves by reading the books and periodicals that are available. These more sophisticated buyers have forced many shoddy manufacturers of inferior plates out of the marketplace and have reduced the field to a group far more conscious of providing quality art on quality porcelain or other material at a reasonable price. This competition should raise the investment potential of many plates, though all responsible parties involved recommend buying art you like and want to display rather than merely trying to turn a profit. That way you win even if the plate never appreciates measurably on the secondary market.

TODAY'S HOTTEST PLATES AND ARTISTS, AS COMPILED BY OUR PANEL OF EXPERTS

Susan Elliott: After a recent trip to California, Susan singled out Greg Perillo's "Brave And Free," Mario Fernandez's "Wings Of Freedom," and Rob Sauber's "Brides Series." Top artists to look for are Sandra Kuck, Jan Hagara, Pat Buckley Moss, and Irene Spencer.

Paul Stark: With wildlife and western themes invading the east,

Perillo and Fernandez are top sellers. Sandra Kuck stays very popular, as well as the all-time marathon champion, Norman Rockwell, who seems to continue indefinitely. Paul also claims Edna Hibel plates always do well, and that sport personality plates—signed—are becoming very popular.

Lois Felder: Owner of The Village Plate Collector in Cocoa, Florida, she has a tremendous track record of picking award winners and was right on the money again this year, predicting "Brave and Free" to win awards at the California show in late April. She also feels that Edna Hibel's Mother's Day plates and anything by Sandra Kuck will also do well.

Susan K. Jones: She agrees with everyone else that Reco International's Sandra Kuck and Fountainhead's Mario Fernandez are tops right now, issuing quality plates one after the other. She also foresees more cute animals than ever before.

Arlene Young: She still sees a lot of interest in children as subjects, but "scenery" plates are the hottest at the moment. Knowles's "Birds Series" by Kevin Daniels and Ray Day's "Once upon a Barn" series are very strong too, along with hardy perennial Norman Rockwell; everybody's pick, Sandra Kuck; and Edna Hibel.

Joyce Zielinski: Cat themes and nostalgia are big in Indiana, and interest in "bird plates" is growing daily, especially Terry Redlin's plates from Hadley House. Pat Buckley Moss from Anna-Perenna Co. and Bing & Grondahl had popular Christmas editions; Schmid's Lowell Davis and Ray Day from Blue River Mill continue successfully with their rural Americana.

Somewhat like investing in stocks, bonds, or other commodities, excellent appreciation in value can sometimes be realized by picking an unknown artist from a new company and trusting that others will realize your "wisdom." However, more prudent advice for those looking for a financial advantage comes from Lance Klass of Pemberton & Oakes, who counsels that "the best bet for a plate to appreciate is good art on quality porcelain, and a good track record of the artist and the manufacturer." Perhaps the best advice of all is simply to buy what you like, display it well, and just enjoy it.

What is a
Collector Plate?

Tracing its beginnings to the 1895 blue and white porcelain Christmas plate by Bing and Grondahl, the limited-edition plate is here to stay. It has weathered the storms of flooded markets, slipshod, opportunistic manufacturers, and wildly fluctuating economic conditions. Indeed, 8½ million people around the globe buy them, ranking collector plates third behind stamps and coins as the most collected objects in the world today.

Limited-edition plates are made in every shape, size, subject matter, and material imaginable. It is in the word *imagination* that we hold the key to the future of collector plates. There are no limits to the field, as technology and artistic creativity continue to merge, constantly producing innovations in both the aesthetic and production phases.

The unifying element in this field is found in the concept of the limited edition itself. Editions are limited in several ways. The number of plates produced is restricted, or the number of days in which to produce them is. In addition, some plates are limited by subscription date; that is, the number of plates produced is determined by how many orders for the plate are received by a certain deadline. Finally, some editions are simply canceled by the manufacturer, and no more are produced.

This information is usually recorded on the back of each plate, along with the backstamp, which is the trademark of the manufacturer. Other information that may be found includes the name of the plate, the series, the artist, and the date it was made. Sometimes plates are even hand-numbered in the order in which they were produced.

Why do 8½ million people around the world buy collector plates? One has only to see the plates themselves to understand instantly the popularity of this relatively young collectible field. Every type of subject imaginable is portrayed, and as new themes and styles are created, they immediately find their way to the face of a plate.

Beautiful horses running in the wind, a child gazing up adoringly at his mother, Snoopy and Charlie Brown engaged in a battle of wits—all of these things and more make up the subject matter that appears on today's collector plates. These plates are produced on every possible topic in order to appeal to the collector that lurks in all of us. Probably no other collectible has the tremendous range of subjects that the collector plate field has. One of the most dominant themes is that of the wonderful world of children in all of their infinite, playful variety. We have all been children, so when we see these touching reminders of our own youth we make a very pleasant association. Even the most diehard noncollectors are hard pressed not to respond to a childhood scene that parallels their own.

Animal lovers are also taken care of by the manufacturers of collector plates. Every animal and bird you can think of can be found immortalized on a plate. The depictions can vary from traditional, realistic, Audubon-like renditions to comic relief caricatures.

If you are a student of art on a limited budget, there are plates done by famous fine artists available to you. Indeed, most plate collectors display their plates as artwork and derive the same sense of pleasure and satisfaction from them that they would from original paintings. However, the pleasure is heightened by the knowledge that the prices are vastly different for the two. A lovely plate can be bought for $25 to $85, whereas an important painting of the same genre would run to thousands of dollars. As an added bonus, these plates can appreciate at a phenomenal rate. Consider that the "Los Ninos" plate by Ted DeGrazia was issued in 1976 by Artists of the World for $35 and now brings as much as $1,800 on the secondary market. That's not a bad return on a $35 investment! You can also compare limited-edition plates with limited-edition prints. Both are produced by fine artists in a limited edition, both have investment potential, and both are aesthetically pleasing in the process. The affordability of collector plates gives it quite an edge over prints, however.

People get into plate collecting in many indirect ways. Perhaps a couple receives a plate as a wedding gift. They may decide to commemorate their anniversary by adding a new plate to their collection each year. There are many anniversary plates issued to satisfy this specific market. Perhaps you collect circus memorabilia. A friend sees the Emmett Kelly plate while shopping for your birthday gift and decides it would be just the present for you. Often plates find their way into people's lives because they collect the subject depicted on a particular plate. Collectors of antique dolls can hardly be expected to resist the Seely Doll series, each of which depicts one of the classic antique dolls. Norman Rockwell fans have dozens of plates to choose from, as the works of the late illustrator are one of the most popular subjects for collector plates. Do you love to collect Hummel figurines? Then you probably have at least a few of the Hummel Annual plates by Anri or Schmid. Perhaps you loved John Wayne, Marilyn Monroe, Henry Fonda, or Elvis Presley. You can find a plate depicting your particular hero on today's market.

Just how are these plates produced? Few people probably understand how ceramic limited-edition plates are made. Obviously, the artist does not paint each plate individually, but how is the original painting reproduced onto a ceramic plate? The answer is, by means of a ceramic decal. But before you turn up your nose, dispel any preconceived notions about decals you might have. Ceramic decals bear no resemblance to bumper stickers or to the old-fashioned fruit and flowers your grandmother decorated her kitchen cabinets with. The making of a ceramic decal is a very involved, highly artistic, and extremely technical process that generally takes a year or two from the planning stage to the end result, which is the finished plate.

First of all, the artist meets with the producer to discuss the concept for the plate or series. The artist then, in his or her own way, produces the original painting from which a decal will be produced. To do this, the artist often uses a matte that precisely outlines the shape of the plate.

At this point the producer must meet with the decal manufacturer he or she has chosen. There are many key decisions to be made at this crucial stage. One of the most important decisions is the choice of a method for making the decal. There are three basic techniques that can be used: screen printing, offset lithography, or litho/screen combination. Each of these methods has its advantages and disadvantages, and it is crucial to select the process best suited to the special requirements presented by the original artwork.

Screen printing produces opaque colors, and varying the amount of color can also produce a textured look. However, extremely fine detail work and subtle shading cannot be adequately achieved using this process.

Offset multicolored lithography, on the other hand, permits extremely fine detail and tonal gradations. This is possible because of the basic premise of lithography, which is the use of tiny dots of color. The dots can vary in size and in distance from each other, thus permitting delicate shading. However, its high cost and lack of certain colors, including white, make it less than desirable for some projects.

If neither of these two processes individually will produce the desired results, then a combination of the two is used. This is referred to as litho/screen combination printing. Screen-printed colors are added to a lithographic decal when brightness is needed. An example of this would be using a silkscreen white for highlighting on a predominantly offset decal. Sometimes waves or clouds are best presented in silkscreen, which gives them a heavier appearance, a sense of depth.

Color chemists become involved at this point. They are experts in knowing how the various ceramic colors will fire on the different blank plates available. The color chemist is responsible for choosing the various colors that will match the original painting, but unlike the artist, he or she is restricted by the printing process chosen. When the color chemist has completed this task, the process moves to the making of the color transparency. A series of negatives is made by photographing the original artwork, using various filters and screens. From these negatives the color separations are made.

Here's the time for yet another decision. There are basically two major approaches to be considered. The first is a four-color, camera-separation process that is similar to that used in the printing of magazines. In essence, the color separation is a photographic positive of one color. The difference is that in ceramic decals the colors are not totally transparent and a true magenta is not available. As a consequence, the results are not as true to the original as they are in nonceramic printing, from the standpoint of both color and detail. This is why in many cases a decision has to be made: whether to use the above-mentioned process, utilize a traditional hand-separation method, or go to a combination of the two, using additional "picked colors" to improve on the standard process.

The hand-separation method is considerably more time-consuming, sometimes taking several months to complete. Separate "boards" must be made for each color, from six or seven to as many as thirty or more. A "proofing" process of transferring individual color dot patterns from a metal plate to special composition paper is arduous as well. This hand-separation method produces an unparalleled richness of color but does move away somewhat from the artist's original colors. Each method has its advantage, so sometimes a combination of techniques is used. For instance, skin tones of a child may be done by hand while the rest of the image is done by the camera process. All of this requires an expertise gained by experience, knowing what each decision will mean when the final product goes to the oven for firing.

In essence, the color separation is a photographic positive of one color. For example, in the four-color process there are four sheets of clear acetate, and each one contains a portion of the total image done in varying shades of one color, which is applied in dots. The colors used are yellow, magenta (red), cyan (blue), and black. When these sheets are layered on top of each other and precisely aligned, the desired image and colors appear. The coloration of each sheet must be perfect if the original artwork is to be faithfully reproduced.

The industry has developed computerized scanners that scan the original artwork and print the color separations. The result, although not as accurate as the work of a skilled color separator, offers future promise.

The printing plates are made from each color separation. The printing of the decal itself is a very arduous procedure. Special paper that has a very shiny, smooth film on one side is used. This paper will dissolve when dipped in water prior to transferring the decal to the blank plate for firing. Decal paper is also unique in that it will always lie perfectly flat, permitting the layers of colored ceramic powder to be precisely applied.

The blank sheets of decal paper are then placed in an offset printing press and are individually printed with a very thin layer of varnish, the pattern of which is determined by the color separation. The sheet then goes to a dusting machine, where the special ceramic color powder is applied. When fired, this powder "paints" the plate. Only the varnished areas hold the powder, and only one color per day can be printed. The decals are reinserted each day, and new color is added until each decal is completed. If the plate requires twenty colors, it will take twenty days to print the decals alone. They are constantly checked throughout the printing process for correct alignment of the colored powder. The different colors must be perfectly aligned so that there will be no overlapping of color or gaps in the design on the finished plate. When all of the colors have been applied to the decal, it is sealed with a thin top layer of clear lacquer. This lacquer is organic and dissolves without a trace during the firing of the plate. Its only job is to hold the colors in place while the decal is transferred to the blank ceramic plate.

David Jacobs of Design Point Decal, Inc., of New Hyde Park, New York, a leading decal manufacturer that includes Pemberton & Oakes and The Hamilton Collection among its clients, puts it all in perspective:

> Producing the ceramic transfer is perhaps the most difficult, time-consuming and exacting art form in the world. No one has yet invented an automated, mechanical, or photographic method that can satisfactorily reproduce an artist's original hand-painted design, decoration, or image on a ceramic transfer. Unlike painting or printing on paper or canvas, in which the final results of color are immediately evident, the printing of the ceramic transfer gives no valid indication of its final colors until it is actually fired in the kiln. Even after ceramic decals emerge from the press, the final colors are not evident and are haunted by the unknown judge— how the decal will fire in the kiln. The ceramic decal is plagued with so many natural and man-made variations that its creation has been described as involving 10,000 times more headaches than printing with a standard four-color process.

> Ceramic transfers get their color from finely ground particles of metallic salts and oxides, which are mixed with powdered glass and flux and suspended in a carrying agent, a transparent plastic material known as plexigum. During the firing process, the carrying agent burns off and the layers of metal oxides fuse to the ceramic or glass surface attaining, for the first time, their true and immutable color.

> Since the ceramic colors are really metal oxides, they are highly sensitive to the variations in their natural state and to the humidity, firing, and other human factors in their manufacturing process. There is no guarantee that, despite years of empirical data, any given ceramic color will consistently achieve the desired hue. Compounding the problem is that each ceramic color will react differently depending upon the chemical composition of the glaze and whether the composition of the ceramic object is hard paste or soft porcelain, earthenware or some other form of pottery.

When the decals are finished, they are sent to the plate manufacturer, where they will be dipped in water and transferred to the blank, back-stamped plates for firing. If everyone along the way has done his or her job perfectly, the finished plate will be a true reproduction of the original painting. The process is very exacting, as some plates require several firings. Hand-decorated detail work may also be done at this time, such as application of gold borders around the edge of the plate.

Of course, limited-edition plates are made in many other ways, utilizing many different materials. However, the vast majority are made with ceramic decals, and understanding this very complicated procedure gives us an added appreciation for the finished plate.

Although the majority of limited-edition plates are made from pottery or porcelain with glazed finishes, this is by no means the only material used. Wedgwood makes its plates with unglazed stained jasperware, which features applied white bas-relief figures in a classical motif. Studio di Volteradici executes its sculpted plates in ivory alabaster. Incolay Studios has come up with a new material made from crushed rock with a marble-like appearance. Lalique of France uses lead crystal with etched details. The Franklin Mint, River Shore, Danbury Mint, and Reed and Barton, to name a few, produce sculpted metal plates made from gold, silver, pewter, or damascene. Another new material, toriart, was devised by the House of Anri. It consists of wood resin that is molded and hand-painted in bright colors. One of the most unusual plates introduced recently is the exquisite stained glass plate "Old Ironsides," produced by the United States Historical Society. The stained glass portion is surrounded by a polished pewter rim. It has been acclaimed by collectors and has already made a permanent place for itself in the plate world.

The diversity of material, theme, size, shape, and price of limited-edition plates is no doubt responsible for the tremendous popularity of this collectible field. Welcome to the wonderful world of collector plates!

The History of Collector Plates

Although decorative plates have been fascinating people for centuries, the hobby of collecting is only a fairly recent occurrence. Elaborate designs on plates are known to exist even in the third and fourth centuries, with an ornamental plate called "The Paris Plate." Through the centuries, discoveries have been made that have laid the foundation for the production of the first collector plate. The initial discovery was perfecting the process for making porcelain in China. When the formula was finally learned in Europe, the making of fine ceramic wares began. Decorating these wares to add appeal soon became a concern of the manufacturers. This led to a major discovery at one of the oldest porcelain factories in Denmark. Arnold Krog, the director of Royal Copenhagen, in 1888 perfected what is known today as the underglazing process. Underglazed decoration was produced by dipping an object into a transparent glaze after it had been painted in cobalt blue glaze. The two glazes fused to produced a fuzzy blue and white surface.

Many other porcelain factories in Europe produced small sets of decorative plates or small editions of commemorative issues in honor of celebrated guests in their countries. These specimens, although limited in their production size, were only the forerunners of collector plates. They didn't qualify as *limited* by today's standards. The production size was limited initially, but if enough people requested the item, the manufacturer would produce more. These plates prepared the public for a phenomenon that continues today.

There was a custom in Denmark for many years, as the story goes, of the wealthy giving gifts to their servants at Christmastime. To celebrate the holidays, they would fill plates with cakes and cookies to take to their servants. Each year that the custom was practiced the plates became more and more decorative, until the plates themselves were the objects more valued by the receivers. They would even hang them up as decoration throughout the holidays. In 1895 Harald Bing, of the Bing & Grondahl factory, decided to produce a decorative plate to be used in this custom. He wanted to expand his current line of production with a novelty giftware item. The plate, which is considered the first true *collector plate,* carried a design of the Copenhagen skyline in winter. It was named "Behind the Frozen Window," and it carried an inscription of the date 1895. The swishes of white against a blue background were a design by Franz August Hallin. Though the company did not plan this plate as a series, the use of a date made it convenient to issue another Christmas plate for 1896. Sales of the 1895 plate satisfied expectations, and Bing & Grondahl has been issuing Christmas plates ever since. This is the longest series of collector plates and is also the largest in terms of the number of plates produced. It is certainly the most challenging and costly for a hobbyist to assemble, though by no means impossible.

Naturally, Bing & Grondahl was not at first attempting to cater to *collectors.* Its 1895 Christmas plate was conceived as an interesting decorative piece, an appropriate gift for the holiday, and possibly a keepsake for the recipient. It was novel in that the concept was new, and the reaction of customers could not be predetermined. The number of people who bought this plate when it was first issued is estimated at around four hundred. It was a new product and was successful enough for Bing & Grondahl to continue issuing new designs each year.

However, there was no floodtide of imitators. In fact, most of the earliest series to follow were short-lived. Rorstrand of Sweden began producing a series of plates in 1904 that lasted for 22 years. Another Norwegian company, Porsgrund, issued a Christmas plate in 1909, but it was the only one issued. A German manufacturer called Rosenthal put Christmas plates on the market between 1905 and 1909. Hutschenreuther and KPM-Berlin also produced early plates, but both of these survived only a few years. It was not until 1908 that another Danish company brought out a successful Christmas series, which still continues. Royal Copenhagen and the success of its Christmas plates roughly paralleled that of Bing & Grondahl. This was of course hampered by the war in 1914 to 1918. Materials became some- what scarce, which caused a slowdown in production. Buying also slowed because few people could afford to buy luxury items in Europe. Both world wars caused widespread economic depression. The Christ- mas plates were considered simply curios. No one could foresee the complexity of buying, selling, and trading that occurs today.

The first plate issued as something more than giftware was made by Lalique, a French glassworks company. In 1965 Lalique an- nounced its intention of producing an *annual* plate. Unlike the earlier manufacturers, who had made no special concessions to collectors, Lalique proclaimed that its first plate would be limited not only in length of time produced but in *actual number*. Here was something new, which suddenly broadened the horizon of plate making. Lalique produced just two thousand specimens of the 1965 plate, a thousand of which were placed in the hands of U.S. distributors and the rest sold in other parts of the world. This in itself said a great deal. Lalique was apparently well aware that the concept of a *collector plate in limited edition* would win more favor in America than anywhere else. The issue price was set at $25.

The venture was a resounding success, and for the next several years the porcelain trade and related industries bubbled with specula- tion on what might come next. Lalique kept producing annual plates, as did the old-line firms, and all the while collector interest built. As early as 1968 collectors were combing the market for 1965 Lalique plates, and when found they carried a price four times the original price. Values were rising on the old European plates, too, which had nòt been manufactured with any announced limit on quantities. The secondary market was at this time a paradise for any willing buyer or any investor with the slightest foresight. Half-century-old plates, whose numbers in existence had vastly diminished over the years, could be picked up for reasonable amounts. Even if they had doubled and tripled in price, they were at a mere fraction of the levels they hold today. And this was less than twenty years ago! Collector publications were laden with ads seeking to buy and sell the 1965 Lalique plate. No other plate issued up to that time had generated so much collect- ing activity. Some observers cynically commented on inflated prices that were sure to go down, leaving owners holding overpriced, hard- to-sell items. Just the reverse happened; prices continued going up the following year and the year after, eventually reaching over $1,800.

What happened to the 1965 Lalique annual on the collector market had much more influence on other plate manufacturers than the year-by-year sales figures for subsequent Lalique plates. Here was proof in a nutshell that the American public would respond favorably to high-quality limited-edition plates, not only favorably but in great numbers and with a sort of passion. They were not scared off by big prices. In fact, they seemed encouraged by them. As the price of the 1965 Lalique went up and up, so did the demand. Lalique's plate shot to stardom after starting off with a high $25 issue price, while $2 and $3 plates sparked no great interest. There was no doubt that, with the way so attractively paved, other manufacturers would soon be able to duplicate the Lalique success.

The next important step toward building the present-day collector-plate market came in 1969. In that year the most prestigious earthenware company in Great Britain inaugurated a series of Christmas plates. Wedgwood, with roots dating to the eighteenth century, was a legend of the industry. It was not a porcelain maker. (It is certainly significant that the major contributors to the development of the collector-plate market, Lalique and Wedgwood, were not in the porcelain business!) Wedgwood produced jasperware, an earthenware with an almost satiny texture but without glaze. The year 1969 marked its two-hundredth anniversary, and this was the chief reason for issuing a dated annual plate. During those two centuries Wedgwood had manufactured every imaginable sort of product in jasper, basalt, and other materials, including statues, plaques, busts, and miscellaneous ornaments. Its first annual plate was in blue with a white sculptured likeness of Windsor Castle. It reads: "Christmas 1969."

With its background, Wedgwood was certainly collector-conscious. It planned its entry into the annual market with collectors in mind. And it really did more in terms of drawing other companies into the field than did Lalique or any of its predecessors. Just like the 1965 Lalique plate, the Wedgwood plate's price was set at $25. Wedgwood did not give a figure for production, and it has never been learned just how many specimens of its 1969 plate were distributed. But although it was not promoted as a limited edition in that sense, Wedgwood assured its customers that they would indeed be owning an item of some exclusivity. After production had ceased, the company destroyed the mold and thereby rendered further production, authorized or unauthorized, impossible. Here was a promise to the public that no previous manufacturer had made.

Demand soon exceeded supply, and specimens were not long reaching the secondary market. During 1970 the price went up and topped at $240. The pace of buying and selling, especially in the United States, and the rate of price increases exceeded that of the Lalique 1965 plate on the secondary market.

Several dozen companies soon began advertising their production of collector plates, and this activity proved very beneficial to the market. With more and more plates coming out, there was another kind of buyer entering the market: the hobbyist who wanted to collect and wanted (at that early stage, anyway) to get one of everything that existed. Since this was a new collecting field, it was impossible to judge its potential. America was unquestionably a nation of collectors. There were doubters who felt that collecting enthusiasm simply would not continue to grow. It did and surprisingly quickly.

A very innovative step was taken the following year by the Franklin Mint of Franklin Center, Pennsylvania. This organization had been operating since 1964 but at first had dealt mainly in commemorative medals and other numismatic items. The first Franklin Mint Christmas plate carried a design by Norman Rockwell, who was specially contracted by the firm to create this design. It was produced not in ceramic but sterling silver, thereby capturing the collector market from several distinct angles. For those who collected Rockwell, it was a must. Buyers came also from the ranks of silver investors, and of course from among those who were by now interested generally in collector plates. With that kind of varied appeal its success was assured, even at the very high issue price of $100—the most expensive collector plate issued to that time. Fearing that the price might place it out of reach for the average buyer, and also that the concept of a colorless plate would not necessarily be appealing, some gift shops hesitated to order it. Those who put confidence in the 1970 Franklin plate were well rewarded. It did extremely well; and when it reached the secondary market, its value jumped wildly. Thereafter, Franklin Mint became one of the leaders of the plate industry, offering collectors' editions in not only silver but also porcelain and crystal. The scope of Franklin Mint's plate production has become so extensive that many collectors now specialize exclusively in the works of this company.

The early 1970s was a period of intense activity for plate collecting, which molded the hobby into its present proportions. Collector magazines and the general press began giving coverage to plate collecting, and specialized publications for the hobby made an appearance. Shows were held, clubs and associations founded. The number of manufacturers issuing plates and the types of plates offered on the market multiplied at an unprecedented rate: collector editions in glass, silver, pewter, wood, and other materials followed. On the secondary market, competition between hobbyists and investors drove some values to great heights. Prices changed so rapidly that dealers could scarcely keep current tabs on them, making published advertisements obsolete a few weeks after release. Naturally, this state of affairs brought about some confusion and in some ways was counterproductive to the hobby. Fortunately, the problems that arose in this hectic period were effectively dealt with before causing any long-term harm. Chief among them was the controversy over use of the term "limited edition." It became apparent that some manufacturers, while labeling their plates limited editions, had produced them in very large quantities—the editions were either not truly limited, or limited to such high numbers that the edition carried no exclusivity. There was a certain amount of bandwagoning, or quick entry into the field, by manufacturers whose standards of quality were lower than those of most specimens seen before. It was inevitable that this should occur, and the circumstances invited it. It appeared to anyone watching the market in the years from 1970 to 1972 (and, similarily, today's market) that investment buyers had lost all sense of reason and were pumping huge sums of money into anything called limited edition—not just plates but medals, prints, statuettes, and other items. Serious collectors were using judgment in their buying, but even they were at somewhat of a disadvantage because of the newness of the hobby. They could not help but be influenced by the wild movement of prices. Many certainly felt justified in paying $300 or $400 for a plate whose issue price had been one-tenth that much. Waiting could have meant paying an even higher figure or watching the price soar completely out of reach. If collectors alone had been in the market, or collectors plus a minor sprinkling of investors, things would not have reached the panic level. Prices would have advanced but at a slower and steadier pace. The market would have been more stable, and the slower growth would have allowed more time for all concerned (including the dealers) to plan their course of action. As things stood, many people bought in a rush and sold in a rush. By 1973 so many plates were coming back on the market that supply began to exceed demand. Prices decreased on a number of editions, including plates of real quality that did not deserve to get caught up in this tornado of speculation and profiteering. Plate collecting had been called a "fad," a passing fancy from which the public would soon turn, and the first indication of market weakness was seized on as proof of these assertions. But actually, the events of 1973 were the best thing that could have happened to the hobby. They shook plate collecting out of the fantasy world in which it had been led by speculators and profiteers and brought it back to earth, opening the way for serious collectors, fair-minded dealers, and responsible manufacturers to take over. Some manufacturers went out of business; chiefly, these were the firms whose plates had been bought by investors but that had attracted only a minimal hobbyist following. Some plate prices dipped by 50 percent or more within the calendar year. Once again, these were mainly editions that had no special claim on the collector's attention, whose prices had risen out of all proportion to their quality, originality, or edition size. The sudden dose of reality drove home a clear message: plate collecting was not going to be a paradise for quick-buck artists and entrepreneurs. It was shaping itself into an activity of genuine prestige, where quality and reputation carried weight and the inferior product or questionable sales approach would be recognized as such. This reorganization of the market caused some pain and financial loss to many individuals, but it carried so good a lesson—one that extended even beyond plates into other hobbies—that the serious collectors uniformly applauded it.

Approaches
to Collecting

The beginner's approach to plate collecting is, inevitably, to buy what appeals to him or her usually with a view toward decoration more than engaging in a hobby. This tends to be the case with hobbies in general; but it is even more so with plates, as their visual charms attract many people who have no intention of "collecting." Also, collector plates are frequently given as gifts, and many individuals are nudged along the path to collecting in that fashion. No decision is made to collect, much less how to collect. The person knows only that he or she enjoys plates.

There is so much satisfaction for beginners in buying plates that appeal to their aesthetic senses, that they rarely look deeper. Certainly they know about the plate hobby, and they know that hobbyists are buying in a more sophisticated way. They have heard of the various refinements of plate collecting—it would be hard to live in today's world and not have heard of them. Many of these individuals do not develop into full-blown collectors. On their next visit to the gift shop, or wherever they buy plates, it may be a gilt candlestick or a framed tapestry that excites their attention. They have an "eye" for decorative quality and for art and could develop into masterful plate collectors—but they lack the collecting flame or drive.

But some of them do graduate into serious collecting, sooner or later. Their purchases are made with more discrimination and a sense of real direction. They acquire knowledge along with their plates. They learn to look, not with the starry-eyed longing of a child looking at ice cream or the methodical precision of a decorator who wants a certain shade of green; they start thinking about artists and artistic quality. And after becoming a serious collector, they inevitably think of whether a plate is merely gift shop ware or something special and magical.

By then the beginning collector has done perhaps a great deal of buying, most of it in a very nonselective way, and owns many pretty plates, which certainly beautify his or her home. Possibly they have even increased in value since they were purchased. But rather than being the nucleus of a collection, the odds are quite good that they are nothing more than miscellaneous plates—a gift shop assortment. And at that point one will undoubtedly begin reproaching oneself for not becoming serious in buying sooner.

To the majority of collectors, a sense of direction is a necessary ingredient in their hobby. This is becoming all the more true today, when the number of available plates has so enormously increased. No one can own them all, or even a tenth of them. One cannot approach the hobby like Britannia embracing the world. So then, the logical alternative is to choose some aspect of the hobby, segregate these plates from the rest, and focus all attention on them.

This is called *specializing*. Still it is very fitting. Serious collectors specialize by turning their eyes, emotions, and checkbooks toward one class of plates. The chosen group becomes, for that person, the hobby; and one disciplines oneself to treat all other plates as nonexistent. By so doing collectors bring themselves many advantages, eliminating confusion and quickly becoming experts on one type of plate, much more rapidly than they could become expert on all plates. Each acquisition, regardless of price, is significant because it complements what is already owned. It fits like a piece in a puzzle. Perhaps best of all, when (and if) the times arrives for selling, one is likely to find buyers more enthusiastic about one's collection than if it were mixed and miscellaneous.

In choosing a suitable specialty, various considerations should be taken into account. Some of these involve the plates themselves, but more revolve around the hobbyist's personality, tastes, and financial circumstances. It is advisable that a beginner or prospective collector become thoroughly acquainted with plates before getting into the batter's box. False starts on collections are usually made because the individual is not aware of the variety of plates that exist on the market. This book ought to help, and it will certainly furnish the necessary education on plate collecting and the current plate market; but seeing plates in a book is not equal to seeing them in person. An excellent approach for any beginner would be to visit the shops, as a browser rather than a buyer, with one's mind firmly against buying anything. The more shops that can be visited before doing any buying, the better.

The obvious considerations for the beginner are money and space. One can hardly buy what one cannot afford, nor display a large collection in a confined area. Hobbyists with ample finances and space can allow their imaginations to roam free. But those with limitations in either of these directions are not seriously handicapped. Outstanding collections of plates have been assembled by hobbyists on tight budgets and those living in cramped apartments. More planning is necessary in these cases; but hobbyists forced to use care, who must make every dollar and inch of wall space count, often make the best purchases because of this. They do no impulsive spending, and they put together a collection in which real pride can be taken.

It will probably be smartest, at the outset, to figure up a plate budget that can be worked into a usual budget—a certain sum that can be set aside weekly and left to accumulate until it has grown sufficiently to make a purchase. Beginners are sometimes in a rush to buy and spend all they have. This is understandable. When one starts a collection and has nothing, the natural desire is to see it grow and thereby satisfy oneself that progress is being made. Stop to realize, though, that good collections have been worked on for years by their owners, in many instances at a very leisurely pace. Acquisitions were made here and there, and each acquired plate was enjoyed and admired, not bought in a panic just to watch the accumulation build. Quite likely you will have dry spells in your collecting when money is needed for other purposes or, for one reason or another, time passes without any fresh acquisitions. This gives one the opportunity to slow down and reflect on what one already owns and perhaps to appreciate it even more.

Collectors have different philosophies and motivations. Some of them prefer working toward a specific goal. This is the common approach in stamp and coin collecting: filling out a set or series. It can be applied just as well to plates, in many different ways. The most obvious, of course, is to build a set of plates issued as a set, and another is to make a collection of annual plates (which is known as a *series collection*). It is fairly simple, in set or series collecting, to judge what the total expenditure will be. One cannot gauge this with complete accuracy, as prices could change somewhat before the collection is completed. By the same token a close estimate can be made of the length of time needed for completion. One can choose a short set in the low price range and complete it fairly quickly, or select one of the long-running annual plates and set up a greater challenge. Of course, the longer it takes to complete a collection, the more uncertainty there is about the total cost involved. The market could rise substantially along the way. This, however, should not be regarded as a deterrent. Quite the reverse, if one is building a collection whose components rise rapidly in value, one automatically owns a good investment and is not apt to be sorry about the situation.

There is yet another factor to be weighed. In set collecting, one can build upward to the complete set and know when it is attained. Series collecting is slightly different if the series is still in progress. To maintain a completed series collection as truly *complete*, the new releases must be added—and of course this ought to be done as soon as possible, when they can be bought at the issued price.

Unfortunately, some collectors (well in the minority) take a very negative approach while building a set or series collection. Their attention is so firmly riveted on *completion* that they make the hobby a hard and cold businesslike exercise. They do not really enjoy themselves. They miss the fun and satisfaction of collecting because their minds are constantly on the plates they don't own rather than the ones they do. For these individuals we would have to say that set or series collecting is unwise.

One may need a goal to work toward in collecting, but the goal need not necessarily be completing a set or group. It could be, for example, to represent the works of as many important artists as possible in one's collection.

Another method of collecting is by manufacturer, an approach that has many adherents. This is certainly the oldest way to collect plates, as persons living in European towns, where plates were made, bought those of local manufacture. With so many companies now producing collector plates, the choice is boundless. If the hobbyist's choice is a large company that has issued numerous plates and continues to do so, the goal will probably not be actual completion. Rather, the hobbyist will strive for a good representation of the company's works, leaning toward the issues which have special appeal for him or her. These may comprise the efforts of favorite artists or issues showing subjects of a topical interest. Collecting by manufacturer is a rather advanced way of collecting, but there is no reason why it cannot be suitable for a beginner. The *investment* aspect of such a collection is, of course, very apparent, since values of collector plates tend to change *by company* much more than by individual issues. There are exceptions to this statement, but in general it has held true during the past decade or more of plate collecting. One reason is surely the concentration of hobbyist interest on manufacturers.

Harmony is perhaps the chief attraction of a manufacturer collection. All of the plates represented in such a collection, while they may differ in artist and subject and even in size, have common roots, and their relationship is unmistakable. They "go together," and this "going together" not only adds to their visual charm but to their cash value. When such an assemblage is sold, it will invariably fetch a strong price. It can be sold to a specialist dealer who makes a practice of stocking the products of that company and has waiting buyers.

Of course, some selectivity is called for in manufacturer collecting, as in all approaches to the collector-plate hobby. The thinking hobbyist will want to select a manufacturer with solid reputation—one whose plates are universally recognized for quality, both of subject themes and execution, and one whose plates are not produced in numbers which exceed the demand for them. This does not necessarily mean going automatically for the companies with the highest-priced plates. Some firms whose plates fall in the moderate price range are certainly worthy of collecting. Whether a European or American manufacturer is chosen makes little difference, so long as its products are readily available in this country. One point that the collector ought to consider is the *possible fluctuation in availability* with some European plates. It sometimes happens that quantities of an older foreign plate reach the U.S. market and temporarily upset the domestic selling price. This should not be any real hazard but is worth reflecting on.

The only real "warning" we would give, in manufacturer collecting, would be to avoid firms that are very new or about which little is known. Products of a brand-new firm are always in the questionable category. They might represent excellent bargains if broad collecting interest develops in that firm's plates.

Yet another collecting approach is by artist. The hobbyist may have a favorite artist whose works are featured on plates; or he or she may, by studying the available selection of plates, be drawn to a certain artist or artists. Artist collecting is a basic and sound approach, especially as collector plates are really prints in which ceramic substitutes for paper. The hobbyist need not apologize for being more interested in the artist than in the plate itself, because, in a sense, the artist is the plate: his or her reputation and skills give the plate most of its value and all of its physical beauty.

Investing in Collector Plates

Investment in collectors' items reached a record pace in the late 1970s and early 1980s. Plates have attracted even more attention than most collectibles because of their limited-edition status and the fact that prices on *some* plates advance very quickly. Investment in plates has not been at an even pace and occasionally has had an effect of temporarily upsetting the market. This occurred in 1973, when numerous investors sold plates they had been holding for two or three years, and many prices dropped as a result. Today things have stabilized somewhat, and the ups and downs due to investor buying and selling are rarely in evidence. Current investors are more selective in their buying and are holding longer before selling. This is healthy for the market as a whole because it takes many plates out of circulation for an extended period of time and adds to their scarcity. It makes them more desirable not only for investors but for hobbyists as well.

There is definitely the opportunity to profit by investing in collector plates. This requires knowledge of plates and the plate market and of basic investment principles. It isn't as simple as going out and buying a random selection of plates, then putting them away for a certain length of time. Some plates have better investment characteristics than others.

First of all, in buying for profit, one must understand what constitutes *profit*. Selling for more than you paid does not necessarily result in a profit. The length of holding time must be figured in. For example, let us presume you buy a plate for $70 today and sell it for $100 five years later. This may look like a profit, but it really isn't. While the five years passed, inflation reduced the dollar's buying power by at least 50 percent (assuming inflation holds at around 10 percent annually). So the $100 you receive won't buy as much as the $70 you originally spent. You actually lost money instead of making a profit. This is why shopkeepers aim for quick sales. The longer something takes to sell, the more it must be sold for to realize the same kind of return. If your plate is not rising in value faster than the rate of inflation, if cannot be a profitable investment, regardless of how high its value eventually goes. Also, consider the fact that you would be buying at retail and probably selling at wholesale when the time comes to cash in your investment. In selling to a dealer, you will not obtain the full retail price. Therefore, your plates need to register a very dramatic price increase, in the neighborhood of 25 percent per year or more, to be sold profitably. Some plates do this well; some do even better. There have been cases of plates tripling in value in less than a year after their release. But plates in general do not make a 25 percent annual increase, so the investor must choose them very carefully and have a little luck as well.

As an investor, you have the option of purchasing newly issued editions as they come out and paying the issue price. You can also buy older plates that are now selling for more than their issue price. Buying older items has something to be said for it, since the older plates have already shown indications of their investment potential. If a plate has moved up 20 percent to 30 percent in price within six months of being sold out, it stands a fair chance of doing just as well, or better, over the next several years. A newly issued plate, even though you can acquire it for the base minimum price, could stagnate at the issue price for a year or two before starting its upward movement. Public reaction is sometimes difficult to forecast. Even the most knowledgeable experts misjudge the popularity of plates on some occasions. There have been many instances of editions that drew little attention when they first came on the market but rose rapidly in value thereafter. Others perhaps showed all of the favorable signs for investment but just did not catch on as expected.

There are some basic guidelines that apply when attempting to forecast future price movement. These, however, are very loose and flexible according to current market changes:

- Since many collectors buy their plates by artist, a new edition of plates by an artist with an established collector following is usually considered favorable for investment. This becomes less so, however, if the artist's work has been used in plate form to the degree of saturating the market.

- The edition size plays some role in investment potential, if other qualities are favorable. A low-edition plate by an unknown artist would not generally be considered attractive for investment.

- Topical themes of very popular interest can affect a plate's investment potential. Here again, the overall characteristics of the edition must be weighed, such as the artist, the edition size, and reputation of the issuing company.

Buying and Selling Collector Plates

Some general advice can be given on buying and selling collector plates, but each reader will need to modify these comments based on his or her own objectives, whether strictly collecting, investing, or becoming a collector and a dealer.

You *can* make a profit buying and selling collector plates. But if profit is your chief motive, your approach needs to be different from that of a hobbyist or simply a "fan" of collector plates. Plates that appeal to you may have to be passed by occasionally because they do not offer attractive profit potential. Also, just the reverse is true. If you are buying for profit, you may acquire some editions that are not among your personal favorites. This is not to say, however, that your private collection, built entirely for enjoyment, cannot result in a cash gain. Many collections that were assembled without the slightest intention of reselling have been sold profitably. Circumstances in the market at the time you buy and sell are a key factor. So too is the care and selectivity with which your plates are acquired. Certain types of collections are more apt to return a profit than others. This has little to do with their size or the total sum of capital put into them. It's largely a matter of how attractive the collection is to a dealer in terms of its resale to the public. Collections focusing on popular editions of the major plate manufacturers are always in the favorable category for resale. They can be sold more easily to a dealer and for a higher percentage of their current retail value. Miscellaneous collections can also arouse interest from the dealers. Topical collections tend to fall into that category, which may be worthwhile for the topical hobbyist to consider. If you collect cats on plates, you may build a very appealing collection. A dealer may be tempted to pay even higher if his clientele includes a customer with similar topical interests.

An artist collection is sometimes a miscellaneous collection. Quite often, the artist will design a complete series for a single company. Then besides that series, he or she may do another series for another company. If your collection includes plates from each series, then you have a miscellaneous collection. If the artist is popular with hobbyists, most dealers will welcome the opportunity to buy such a collection. They may already have standing orders from their customers for some of the plates included. You will find ads in hobbyist publications from dealers seeking to buy certain artist's plates, regardless of manufacturer. Of course, this sort of thing occurs most often with the in-demand artists.

SOURCES OF SUPPLY

The major sources of supply for collector plates are the specialist dealers and general gift shops, and of course the manufacturers themselves, many of whom sell directly to the public. Collector plates are also found in a wide variety of other outlets: antique shops, second-hand shops, antique shows and conventions, auction sales of all kinds, "country" and "estate" sales, flea markets, garage sales, advertisements in the collector publications and in local newspapers. If you want to buy collector plates, you will find them readily available, regardless of where you live. The local selection can always be supplemented by mail-order purchases. Hence, the collector living in a remote rural area has just as good an opportunity to buy as those surrounded by neighborhood dealers. Of course, there are great differences you will encounter between buying from one type of source rather than from another. The prices may be quite different from one to the next, and so may be the selection. Dealers offering the best selections tend to charge the full market prices or very close to them, whereas "bargains" many times turn up in locations where just a few plates are found. In this respect, you have a distinct advantage over many other hobbyists. If a coin collector or an antique enthusiast finds an item selling for half or less the usual value, the possibility of *fakes* is apparent. Unless the individual is very experienced and can confidently make his own appraisals, he does not know whether the object is indeed a "find" or a worthless reproduction. Fakes, as such, have not invaded the world of collector plates. This is not to say that buying should be done haphazardly without proper examination of the item. While authenticity may not be in question, there are other points to consider: the physical condition and the correct identification. Some plates are very similar to others while being totally different editions with different market values. Titles may be nearly identical, and they may reproduce the work of the same artist. This is why the often-repeated saying, "The back of a plate tells more about it than the front," is well worth remembering. So make sure you check the back of the plate for the manufacturers' marks, series, name, and edition size. You won't want to be surprised after you get the plate home.

One of the undeniable lures of plate collecting is combing about through small shops, flea markets, and other possible sources of bargains. Bargains occur at off-the-beaten-path sources for various reasons. In some cases, the sellers are not aware of current market values and have acquired collector plates from individuals who likewise were unaware of their values. Perhaps this happens with plates more frequently than with most collector's items. If a noncollector received a plate as a gift in the early 1970s when the hobby was not yet totally off the ground, he or she might not be informed of its current value, thinking of it merely as a pretty decoration. When selling the plate, the individual may be perfectly satisfied to receive $5 or $10 for an item that actually is worth $100 or more. The dealer to whom it is sold will probably know about the collector-plate hobby, and know vaguely that some plates are valuable, but may not have reference material on hand to check out values if he or she runs a small second-hand shop or other neighborhood business. Having made the purchase for $10, the owner does not hesitate to sell for $20 and double his or her money, even though the plate could have a much better sales potential.

Finding bargains is certainly exciting. However, if you have some specific goal in your collecting, such as completing an artist collection or building up a full set of one manufacturer's series, chance bargains will need to be supplemented with purchases from the regular plate trade. It can be exasperating to continually look for a plate and not find it. The hope of saving some money on it, when and if eventually found, is really not worth the effort for many hobbyists. They would much prefer to pay the full retail value and order the plate from a well-stocked supplier. In the final analysis, the approach to take when

buying is whatever suits *you.* Some collectors have a more adventur-
ous spirit than others, more free time, and more mobility. They enjoy
the chase as much as the capture. We would recommend that you
study and investigate the various sources of supply and form your own
opinions.

BUYING DIRECT FROM THE MANUFACTURERS

Some manufacturers sell their plates directly to the public. Orders are
taken from advertisements placed in magazines and from announcements sent to collectors on the company mailing list. If you respond
to a manufacturer's magazine ad, you will be placed on its mailing list
and receive announcements of future editions. You are also likely to
receive announcements from manufacturers with whom you have
never done business. You may be puzzled at how they knew you were
interested in collector plates. The manufacturers do not randomly
solicit names from the phone book, since the percentage of potential
plate buyers in the general population is too small to make this
worthwhile. What they sometimes do is swap customer names and
addresses between one manufacturer and another. One manufacturer
trades names of 500 of its customers for 500 of another company's
customers. Also, the manufacturers frequently sell their mailing lists,
with the result that a name from one maker's list gradually gets on
almost every maker's list. Few collectors object to this. They want to
receive the announcements and keep fully informed on every new
issue. Of course, you cannot buy every plate offered to you. But you
would be well advised to *save all literature received* from manufacturers even if you have no intention of buying their plates. Serious
hobbyists maintain filing systems for manufacturers' announcements
and brochures. This material could be very useful to you in the future
for checking the value progress of a particular item. There is really
no better way to keep informed about the plate market than to
compare these manufacturers' announcements with the offerings
of dealers.

The most important step in buying from a manufacturer is to be
sure of what you're ordering. Read the description carefully. Notice
the size, material, type of decoration, and all other pertinent information. Plates pictured in brochures are not always shown in the actual
size. If marked "reduced," this could mean that the actual plate is

twice as large as the photograph or very slightly larger. Many times you will find a precise statement of the diameter in the promotional text. Keep in mind also that sales brochures and announcements are sometimes printed before any actual specimens of the plate exist. The photos they carry are not of the plates to be delivered but of a master or "dummy" model that has been prepared strictly for use in advertising. The actual plates should be very nearly identical to the photograph, but sometimes there is a minor variation. As far as the colors are concerned, these will not reproduce 100 percent accurately in the photograph. Even if the photograph is excellent in quality, which most of those in plate brochures are, it will not catch every nuance or subtle tonal quality of the colors. Do not expect the plate to look precisely like the photograph. Many times the colors may be sharper and richer. Also, be attentive to any imperfections in the plate. The time to act is right at that moment. Contact the company and return the plate immediately for a replacement that has no flaws.

There may be a slight delay in receiving your plate, particularly if ordered from a "time deadline" announcement. Veteran collectors have learned to use patience and not begin watching the mail a week after posting their orders. If you have not received it after six to eight weeks of placing your order, and no indication is given in the announcement of the expected mailing date, you can drop a note to the company's sales division.

When your plate is received, *save the box.* This will add slightly to its collector value in the future. Also *save all literature* that may accompany it.

BUYING FROM PLATE DEALERS

Here we are speaking of the primary dealers who either make a specialty of plates or for whom plates make up a large portion of their stock and trade. They include plate dealers and gift shops, some of whom deal exclusively in newly issued editions and some of whom sell new editions along with secondary-market items (those that are no longer available from the manufacturer). Selling issues that are no longer being produced is really the lifeblood of many plate dealers because there are more of these plates and the markup is usually higher between the dealer's cost price and selling price. Therefore, these plates are more profitable for the dealers to handle. A dealer selling a current plate must stay fairly close to the manufacturer's announced price. Often he or she will undercut the suggested retail price a bit for the sake of competing against other dealers. Having bought the plate at the established wholesale level, this leaves the dealer only a modest profit margin. Secondary-market items present more flexibility. The dealer buys them not from a wholesaler charging a set price but mostly from the public, and the price is negotiated sale by sale. Dealers not only have more leeway in buying but in selling, too. If the plate is in demand they can charge over the original issue price. There is not much incentive with these items to undercut the competition because the competition is not selling for any standard price.

The larger dealers try to maintain as comprehensive a stock as possible of the most popular editions and series. They cannot keep everything on hand at all times because the pace of buying and selling does not permit this. They may be slightly overstocked on a plate at one time and out of stock at another, depending on whether the buyers are outnumbering the sellers. As more and more editions come on the market, as they do constantly, the task of keeping "something for everybody" grows more challenging. Some dealers have already begun to specialize, and this will probably be a common practice in the future. So if you're looking for a plate issued by one of the smaller or more obscure manufacturers, you may need to inquire from several dealers before finding one who handles the plates of that maker.

Browsing in a plate shop, especially one that is well-stocked, is a treat for any collector. You will see some plates that you were not aware existed, and the rest will look quite different "in person" from pictures in books or brochures. In most cases, the selling price will be marked alongside each plate on a card. This refers to *that plate only* and does not necessarily mean that another plate from the same series is being sold for the same price. It is a common occurrence that plates from the same series, after reaching the secondary market, sell for different prices. One or two pieces, usually the first edition from the series, become more popular than the rest. But because prices vary in a given shop on plates of the same series, that does not mean that they vary throughout the trade. Unless you make comparisons between the shops or keep up on the trade by subscribing to collector periodicals, you may not be in a position to know this. The shopkeepers will not tell you which plates they've overstocked.

If you want a certain plate and do not find it displayed in the shop, *ask* for it. In many shops, there is space to display only a portion of the stock. The dealer may have many other plates in a back room or cellar. Possibly a consignment has just arrived and is in the process of being unpacked. The plate you want may go on display the very next day. When dealers do not have the plate you want, they may (according to their style of doing business) be willing to take your name and address, order it, and notify you when they acquire it. With the kind of connections that most dealers have these days, they can get just about any plate you want in a very short time. But they must have the assurance that you'll take it once they get it. You could tell the dealer that you're interested in buying if it's in your price range. And then quote a price. If the price you state is too low, this could hurt your chances of getting the plate. Chances are the dealer will be buying the plate from another dealer and then adding on a margin of profit, or "commission." Therefore, the price could end up being higher than you would pay by finding that same plate in a shop. Whether this is a sound way to acquire plates hinges completely on your own point of view. It has convenience to be said for it, and perhaps that compensates for paying a slightly higher amount.

If the dealer issues a list, pick one up before you leave and study it at home. It may be somewhat obsolete by the time it's in your hands because many of the plates are probably already sold. But it's useful for comparing against the lists and advertisements of other dealers to see just how the shop does in its overall pricing practices.

If you order a plate from a dealer, when it comes in, examine your purchase for scratches or other damage before paying. If a plate is in a sealed box, open the box and make your inspection *in the shop,* not at home. It may not be easy or even possible to return a plate after you've bought it.

BUYING BY MAIL ORDER

Collector plates are sold by mail by large specialist dealers (often the very same ones who run shops), by general dealers in collector's items, and by private collectors. The hobbyist publications contain page after page of advertisements by individuals selling through the mail. Some list all of their available plates and prices in their advertisements. Others ask you to send in your "want list." And there are even some who list their available plates without attaching prices to them.

Instead, they ask for bids from the public. This form of selling (auctions) is discussed later.

Mail-order buying is a very satisfactory way of adding to your collection. It gives you a far greater choice of what you can buy and from whom you can buy. The whole sphere of collector plates from the oldest to the newest is brought directly within your grasp by buying through mail order. Any slight disadvantages that may be involved, such as delays in the mail, do not offset the positive factors.

One big plus of mail-order buying is that the offerings of many sellers are before you at the same time. They can be compared against each other to find the best prices. Comparing prices in retail shops is not nearly this easy. Unless the plate you're seeking is very scarce, two or more dealers—probably dozens—will be offering it at the same time. The prices are sure to be slightly different, at the least, from one seller to the next. One dealer may be a private collector, another an investor, another a regular dealer. Their cost prices are different, so their selling prices are different. Also, the terms they offer, as far as returns are concerned, for example, may likewise be different. So the seller offering the lowest price is not automatically the one from whom you should buy.

Admittedly, mail order is more suitable for the buyer who knows what he or she wants and not the beginner who is unfamiliar with plates. If you are a beginner, shop browsing is probably the best course to take, since this enables you to see many different plates and get the "feel" of them. If you have never seen a certain plate and are unaware of what it looks like, there is not much point in ordering it by mail. It could prove very different from your expectations.

Always read the ads and lists carefully before placing an order. A well-prepared ad or list gives the name of the manufacturer as well as the series and plate name; it may also provide information on the artist and the year of issue and the size. To save space, some dealers omit portions of this information. In extreme cases, everything is omitted except the title. Take care in ordering from such an ad or list because the plate you order might not be the one you think it is! This is particularly true if the stated price is far different from the figure at which it normally sells. It might be the same scene by the same artist but in a smaller size. There is absolutely no way of knowing for sure unless you contact the seller and ask for specifics.

The rush with which lists are prepared and published prevents any kind of standard arrangement. Therefore, you will need to read the list from top to bottom to find out exactly what it contains.

Do not pay much attention to the promotional "blurbs" in lists or ads. Dealers may state in all honesty that their price is the lowest for a particular plate or series. They may have believed it to be the lowest in the trade when they were preparing their lists or ads. But there is no way they can know about the ads and lists being prepared *at the same time* by other dealers. Some of these may show the same item at a lower price. The more ads you read and the more lists you receive, the better will be your capability of judging the really good buys.

BUYING FROM FLEA MARKETS AND SECONDHAND SHOPS

Collector plates *do* turn up at these locations—perhaps not in quite the same quantity as they did a few years ago, but they're certainly available. Sometimes a collector plate will be offered alongside ordinary table plates for the same price! You may not get *that* lucky, but if you comb the nonprimary sources you will definitely encounter many, many bargains. Plates are still coming on the market from the hands of noncollectors and other uninformed owners. They just drift around until someone spots them. The level of "plate awareness" on the part of the general public is not overly high, but it's growing. Annual plates are more apt to be recognized as potentially valuable even by a noncollector because they carry a date. A plate that does not bear a date will often be considered just a pretty household decoration. Once again you will need to know the values, to see whether or not you're getting a bargain.

The basic problem with plates sold by secondhand shops and other nonprimary outlets is that they're usually no longer in the original box, and they may be scratched or otherwise marred. If the seller is unaware of their collector status, he or she may not handle them carefully. It's vital to make a careful examination before buying and satisfy yourself about the condition. There is not much possibility of returning anything bought in this fashion.

Don't ask for plates at a nonprimary source, whether it be a flea market or shop. Find them yourself. An expression of interest on the buyer's part has a tendency to raise the price, since the sums asked by sellers are not nearly as firm as in the primary market. They will ask for whatever they feel they can get.

BUYING AT AUCTION

Auction selling is becoming more and more commonplace in the plate business. Most sales are in the "mail bid" category. Some floor sales are held, and collector plates are also included in general estate sales, art auctions, and rural sales. Auction buying is very appealing to many plate collectors. The competition itself and the showlike atmosphere of auctions can be exhilarating. Even if you fail to get the desired plates, you have probably been better entertained at an auction than by browsing in shops. And at the very least, you have learned some valuable information about the workings of auctions and strategies used by bidders. At the present time there are no floor sales (that is, public auctions with in-person bidding) devoted exclusively to collector plates. As the hobby continues to grow, they will almost certainly come about. The mail-bid plate sales are thriving, and undoubtedly some of their promoters will begin turning to floor selling.

The great attraction of auction sales is that they present the possibility of buying under normal retail prices. Anyone bidding at an auction, whether mail-bid or floor-sale, could get lucky and buy a $100 plate for $50 or $60. This is not a rare occurrence. In a typical auction of 200 or 300 plates, there will be several dozen selling below the usual market price. There are also many selling at about the normal retail, and some (though the beginner finds this hard to understand) going for higher sums than they bring in dealers' shops.

Auction results are not predictable. A plate may sell for much more or much less than was expected. Even the operators of auction sales have difficulty forecasting prices. It all depends on who attends the sale and who bids through the mail, and what sort of competition develops for each lot. The level of competition is never even because each bidder has his or her own aims and purposes. One bidder comes just to bid on the plates of a certain manufacturer. Another is a topical collector and wants the half dozen railroad-motif plates included in the sale. Yet another is a Rockwell collector, and another needs a certain Hummel Christmas plate to complete a collection. Some of the bidders are dealers, executing orders for customers or buying for their own stock. It's inevitable, in any large sale, that some lots draw little or no bidder interest and that others become the target of heated competition. There may be two bidders at the sale who have made up their minds to get Lot No. 16. This may be a plate that both have tried unsuccessfully to find in the shops and perhaps have placed bids on in previous auctions, only to come up short. This time, they resolve, they will spare nothing to have it. When two determined bidders clash on any lot, the price will very likely balloon over the plate's normal retail value. The successful bidder may or may not have second thoughts afterward, chastising himself for overspending, especially if he soon thereafter finds the same plate in a shop, selling for much less. But there are many auction buyers who readily pay more than the "book" values without guilt feelings. When this is an isolated case, it does not affect the market value. If the same plate begins to top its market value regularly, when it comes up for auction, the market value will rise.

Dealers keep a careful watch on auction sale results. Prices realized at auctions are always taken into account when dealers decide how much they can pay in buying or charge in selling. Most of the "trends" in plate collecting become apparent at auction before showing themselves elsewhere. To say that the auctions make the market is much more accurate than to say the market makes the auctions. So it is very important for collectors to keep up with the auction scene, regardless of how much bidding they intend to do. This can easily be accomplished by subscribing to the collector periodicals, which carry auction lists for mail-bid sales and also advertisements of floor sales. Lists and catalogs for auction sales can be obtained by writing to the auction houses. Usually a subscription fee is charged that includes not only the catalogs but lists of prices realized, which you will receive two or three weeks after each sale. These show the sums at which every item in the sale sold. The lists of results also show which items were "passed" (not sold), and that too can be revealing.

Every collector plate in existence may come up for auction sooner or later. The more recent and common ones are auctioned repeatedly, sometimes with several specimens in the same auction. Most auctions consist of items from the stocks of dealers. This is especially true of the mail-bid sales, quite a few of which are actually run by plate dealers. By offering some of their plates for bidding, they open up a new market for them and draw more collector interest. Of course, dealers who run sales will not sell any of their plates for less than the cost price. If the only bids received for a certain lot fall below the cost, or are only marginally above it, dealers will reject them and return the plate to their regular retail stock. They will, however, sell plates at auction for less than the full retail prices, as long as the prices are not ridiculously low. Dealers know that auction bidders like to get bargains and that without bargains there would be very little appeal for auction sales.

With public or floor sales you will have the opportunity to examine each lot before bidding on it. Every auction has a presale exhibit, in which all of the lots are placed on view and can be handled. It is certainly a good idea to do this if you live near the gallery. Use the catalog to keep a record of the items you want to bid on and the maximum limit of your bids. Deciding on your bid limits *before* the sale is much wiser than waiting until the competition unfolds. You have the chance to deliberate coolly and calmy before you are under the influence of the auction itself.

How much should you bid? The usual advice is "Bid what the lot is worth to you." This should probably be amended to read, "Bid what the lot is worth to you, in light of the alternatives." First of all, would you really be happy owning a $50 plate for which you paid $100? Second, what are the chances of finding it on the regular retail market, and, when found, how much is the price likely to be? If you keep in touch with the dealers (who will only be too glad to keep in touch with you), you will have repeated opportunities to buy almost any plate you need. The price may rise somewhat but probably not to the point where you would be justified in making a desperate lunge at an auction specimen. Most serious collectors, those who have experience in auction buying and are fully confident of their actions, limit their bids to 10 percent over the normal retail value. In most cases, they bid less than this. Quite often, they will bid only two-thirds of the normal retail value. This is a perfectly logical bid for a plate that is abundant on the market and can be purchased from any dealer. If you fail to get it, what have you really lost? You can always go out and buy it from a dealer.

Look over the catalog carefully to see how the sale is set up. There may be "minimum bids" for some or all of the lots. This is more apt to be the case in a mail-bid sale than at a public auction. If a minimum bid is stated, you are at liberty to bid that amount if you wish—there is no obligation to bid higher. However, the chances are quite good that someone else will also be bidding the minimum bid. So if you really want the item, it would be wise to bid slightly more. Instead of a minimum bid, an "estimate price" might be stated. These are used simply for the aid of bidders who might be unsure about values. The lots could sell for more or less than the estimated prices. Experienced collectors do not gauge their bids strictly according to these estimates;

they verify the values from dealers' lists and other sources. Sometimes the "estimated prices" in an auction catalog tend to be rather high.

The disadvantage in bidding by mail is that you can't watch the results. You don't find out about them until after the sale. When bidding in person, you might decide to adjust your bids on some lots, based on your success or failure in bidding on other lots. For example, say there are ten lots in a sale that interest you. If you bid on the first five that come up and get them all, you might want to quit at that point. Some mail-bid auctioneers will permit you to place a "total limit" on your bids. To do this, you list your bids in the normal fashion, then, at the bottom of the bid sheet, write (for example), "Please limit total purchases to $100." This lets you bid on more lots than you really could afford to buy, with the assurance that you won't be receiving a staggering auctioneer's bill.

Read the catalog descriptions carefully to be sure you know exactly what you're bidding on. Sometimes the descriptions in an auction catalog are set up a bit differently from those in a dealer's list.

When you bid in a mail sale, it may be as long as two weeks after the sale before you receive the auctioneer's invoice. Don't assume that your bids were unsuccessful if word is not received immediately. Of course, you can call the auction house and find out sooner if you prefer. Wait until the day after the sale to call, since the employees will be extremely busy on sale day.

BUYING FROM OTHER COLLECTORS

You might be able to buy below market values by dealing with other collectors or noncollector owners of plates. This usually involves some expense, however. Unless you know of individuals with plates to sell, they may not be easily found without running advertisements. Ads can be placed in your local newspaper or in the collector publications, or both. Hometown ads are often very effective, especially in localities where there are no plate shops. Anyone in these areas who has plates to sell is glad to find a willing buyer nearby. Swapping with other collectors is also a possibility. Plate hobbyists don't swap as much as stamp and coin collectors do because they rarely have duplicates to trade. They may, however, have switched from one field of interest to another within the plate hobby and would rather swap their no longer needed plates than sell them.

BUYING AND SELLING THROUGH THE
BRADFORD EXCHANGE

No information guide in this field would be complete without reference to the Bradford Exchange, the world's largest trading center for limited-edition collector plates. Founded in 1962, this titan of the collectibles industry certainly lives up to its stated function, "to facilitate the buying and selling of collector's plates."

The Bradford Exchange, with its international headquarters in the Chicago suburb of Niles, Illinois, serves several functions. First and foremost, they operate a high-tech "stock exchange" where over 13,000 plate transactions take place daily over toll-free telephone lines. In 1986 collectors' plates with a total value of over $100 million were traded on the exchange floors, and over 3 million collectors were served through seven worldwide offices.

The primary highlight of the Exchange is the computerized trading floor and *Instaquote* trading system, the only one of its kind in the collectibles industry. The trading system enables plate collectors to receive up-to-the-second information on prices, to place buy and sell orders by toll-free telephone, and to receive immediate confirmations of transactions while still on the telephone.

There is no fee for listing a plate on the Exchange. Buyers are charged a commission of 4 percent on purchases over $100, or $4 on plates priced less than $100. Bradford also guarantees confirmed sales. The seller receives the asking price minus a commission of 30 percent.

In addition, plate collectors can receive market information and trade on approximately 5,000 over-the-counter plates that are not

J. Roderick MacArthur,
founder of the Bradford
Exchange.

listed on the Exchange. To reach the Bradford Exchange trading floor, call toll-free 1-800-323-8078 (Illinois residents call collect 312-966-1900). The Exchange is open Monday through Friday from 8 A.M. to 5:30 P.M. Central Time.

The Bradford Exchange is one of the industry's largest marketers of plates. Through arrangements with such heavyweights as Knowles China, Rockwell Society of America, Studio Dante di Volteradici, and others, they maintain a strong position in the sales of new issues.

They also produce the major periodical within the plate field. Their *Plate World* magazine is a slick, four-color, bimonthly compendium of plate news and information, unmatched in the field. More information on this publication is contained in our section on magazines and periodicals.

Also at its headquarters building is The Bradford Museum of Collector's Plates, the world's largest permanent exhibit of limited-edition plates. Included are more than 1,300 porcelain, crystal, china, and wooden plates produced by more than sixty manufacturers from twelve countries. This collection has been estimated to be worth more than $250,000. It is located at The Bradford Exchange, 9333 Milwaukee Avenue, Niles, Illinois 60648; (312) 966-2770.

The publicity, public relations, and information value of the efforts of the Bradford Exchange over the years defies the setting of a dollar estimate, but suffice it to say that without Bradford's unflagging support, the limited-edition plate phenomenon would never have approached its current status in the world of collecting.

SELLING YOUR PLATES

There are various approaches to take in selling. Collector plates are reasonably easy to sell. It's just a matter of whom you want to sell to and when. You probably will never be in the position of wanting to sell your plates and being unable to find a buyer. Dealers (to mention one class of potential buyers) have to buy plates to replenish their stock. They much prefer to buy secondary-market editions from the public than from other sources of supply. In fact, it's largely the general public selling to dealers that keeps the secondary market going. This is an important advantage that plate collectors have over some other hobbyists. When you go to sell your plates, there will be no questions raised about their authenticity or "grade," assuming, of course, that they haven't been damaged while in your possession. This is far different from the situation faced by coin hobbyists who want to sell their coins. They may be told that their coins are overgraded and not worth the sum they paid for them, or that several are fakes. Also, since plates have established market values, both you and the dealer know how much they're worth. This makes it much easier to arrive at a mutually satisfactory price.

The thought of selling your plates is probably the last thing on your mind if you're actively collecting. However, the continual buying and selling keeps the market strong. Of course, some of these plates that return to the market are sold by investors. They were bought originally for the purpose of holding until the value doubled or tripled. Sales by investors are carefully planned, and this is the best way to sell if your circumstances permit. A fast or "forced" sale, made in a hurry because cash is needed for some emergency, usually results in a loss. Still, even in these cases, it's very handy to have plates around! You can raise money on them almost instantly, if need be, which is more than can be said for most objects in the average home. Also, even if you do take a loss on them in a rush sale, it will be a much smaller loss than on a car, jewelry, or other things you could sell. In this respect, plates are truly an investment, even if you don't buy them with investing in mind.

Whether or not you can make a profit on your plates when selling them to a dealer will depend on the current market value. If you bought a plate at $90 when it was issued and the average retail price has now reached $300, you will have no trouble profiting. A dealer may give you around $200 for it, possibly even more if it's a really hot item for which he or she gets many requests. On the other hand, if your plate has not advanced very much in value, a dealer's buying price will probably represent a loss for you. Naturally, dealers do not base their buying prices on the original issued prices but on the amounts attained by each plate on the secondary market. It's all a matter of how much the dealers feel they can get when they sell the plates, and how long it will take to sell them.

Various other factors also influence the price. A dealer who is overstocked on a particular plate will either decline to purchase it or offer a slightly lower sum than usual. Dealers do not care to build up overly large stocks of any single plate unless there is reason to believe its value will be rising in the near future. If the dealer is totally out of stock on the plate or plates you want to sell, he or she might be tempted to pay a bit more. This is why it usually pays to talk with several dealers before accepting an offer. The offers you receive will vary somewhat from one dealer to the next.

In the advertisements run by dealers in hobbyist plate publications, buying prices are often stated. In fact, many of the ads are set up to show buying and selling prices for all the listed plates. You may be surprised at the comparatively small "spread" between each dealer's buying and selling price, sometimes as little as 20 percent. Do not assume, however, that dealers' buying prices are equally high on items *not* listed in ads. The advertised plates are usually those in which the dealer specializes and has the most calls for. They may pay 60 percent of the normal retail price for plates that are not on their "most wanted" list. Only on rare occasions do the offers from established dealers fall below 60 percent of the average market value. When dealers make low offers, it is usually because they feel a plate is overpriced on the current market and are anticipating a decrease in price. Another dealer may feel entirely differently and be willing to pay you much more.

If you sell a plate that has just recently gone out of production, dealers will not express great interest in it. The market value at that point will probably be the issued price and nothing more. And some dealers will not be willing to buy because they purchased quantities of the plate at wholesale and still have remaining stock. In a year the situation could be very different. The longer you hold your plates before selling, the more likely you are to receive a satisfactory price. Just imagine the prices you could get on plates bought in the late 1960s and early 1970s if you sold them on the present market!

You can sell to a dealer by mail or by taking your plates to the shop. When selling by mail, send the dealer a list of the plates you want to sell and wait to receive a reply before shipping them. On your list, state the manufacturer, artist, series name, individual plate titles, and sizes. Do not include prices on your list. The dealer probably already has established buying prices for these plates and your figures would be meaningless.

A critical phase in selling by mail is to pack your plates securely for shipment, and insure them for their full value. If the value exceeds the limit for postal insurance, use a commercial delivery service such as United Parcel Service.

SELLING BY AUCTION

Auctioneers who sell plates will accept your specimens for inclusion in their sales. You can often do better selling by auction than selling outright. Of course, there is no guarantee of this. Auction selling involves some uncertainty. There's the chance of doing very well (obtaining the full retail value in some cases) or experiencing a disappointing sale. Some auctioneers will let you place minimum selling prices on your plates to prevent them from going for ridiculously low prices. However, they will not allow reserves higher than about 60 percent of the normal retail value, since the auction company makes no money. In fact, it loses money on lots that have to be returned to their owners. Whether to sell by auction or to a dealer is a choice the individual must make based on his or her circumstances. When cash is needed in a hurry, selling outright to a dealer is the logical route because auction selling is not quick. From the time your plates are consigned for sale until the date payment is received, three or four months might elapse. Some auctioneers will make a cash advance on a really large, valuable collection, but the advance is generally only a small fraction of the estimated value.

Material sold on consignment is auctioned on a commission basis. The auction house receives a certain percentage of the price on each lot. Most houses work with a percentage of around 20 percent, though some charge as much as 30 percent. Usually the company's overhead costs determine the size of percentage; an auctioneer who publishes illustrated catalogs will normally work with a higher commission rate. However, this is not necessarily unfavorable for the owner, since these big houses with attractive catalogs nearly always get better prices for the items they sell. Even if you pay a commission that is 5 percent or 10 percent higher than somewhere else, you could still come out better.

When items are accepted for sale by an auctioneer, both you and the auctioneer sign your names to a consignment contract. The contract carries all of the terms involved in the sale. It specifies the date on which your plates will be sold, the rate of commission, the date on which you can expect to receive payment (usually 30 days after the auction), and other details. Read the contract thoroughly before signing it, and ask questions about anything that isn't clear. Keep your copy of the contract until you receive payment for your merchandise.

Fakes and Imitations

The hobby of collecting, no matter what area you choose, is constantly being plagued by producers of fakes and counterfeits who are only out to deceive the collector and to make an easy dollar. The plate collector, however, is luckier than the hobbyist who buys stamps, antiques, coins, or most other items. While these hobbies are rampant with fakes, doctored material, and various questionable items, the field of plate collecting has few hidden traps for the unwary. Actual fakes are very rare on the United States market in spite of rising prices and the corresponding increase in temptation for counterfeiters. In fact, the field is virtually free of fakes, and we should probably count ourselves lucky.

This does not mean, however, that the inexperienced buyer should not continue to be cautious. There are certain pitfalls for the buyer of plates. With a little insight and know-how, you can become informed and can easily avoid them.

Any manufactured object of quality that proves successful on the market will always draw inexpensive imitations. This is true of cars, clothing, anything—and plates are no different. If the public will rush to buy a plate issued for $50, there is a great incentive for a manufacturer to produce a plate with less quality and sell it for $5 or $10. The assumption, of course, is that many purchasers of collector plates are not connoisseurs or even *collectors* but are simply charmed into buying by the physical qualities of the plate. Could they not just as well be charmed by a less expensive article that could be made and sold in hundreds of thousands rather than in a limited edition?

This is precisely what is happening today. Gift shops are being inundated with plates that have the appearance of collector plates but that are nothing more than facsimiles of them. They do not carry the designs of noted artists, or if they do, the designs are poorly reproduced. Overall workmanship is not up to the standard of collector plates. The edition is not limited. In fact, these imitations are just the reverse of a limited-edition collector plate; production is overwhelmingly high, and quality is very low.

If you are a novice in this field of collecting, the first thing for you to recognize is that every plate you find in a shop is not necessarily a collector plate. When attractively displayed among collector plates, imitations may be deceiving. They may be the same size as the better-quality plates. They may be just as colorful most of the time. When you handle them, they feel about the same to you. But if you want a true collector plate, don't be fooled by these characteristics. If you want the added quality, go into the shop prepared. We hope this book will help you acquire the knowledge that will enable you to make a wise choice. Become familiar with the names of companies that make collector plates and with their backstamps or hallmarks. Learn to recognize the styles and the signatures of your favorite artists. Backstamps and signatures are two important assurances that what you buy is authentic and not an imitation.

Many imitations are made in Hong Kong or Japan. Their designs are similar to themes on collector plates, but they are imported in huge quantities, large enough to saturate the market with as many or more plates than the manufacturer thinks he can sell. This material, although not a limited production, obviously sells; otherwise the producers and dealers would not profit.

The question is not whether a plate is a forgery. As we have discussed, this is virtually nonexistent. Basically, it boils down to whether you want to collect limited-edition plates or just hang a pretty plate on your wall for decoration. If you are interested only in collector plates, then your best protection is to do your buying only in the shops in your area that specialize in this. By dealing with reputable professionals you will save yourself a lot of problems. Do not expect to find a valuable collector plate in the dime store or large discount store. The plates you will find there may be decorative, but they will not be limited-edition plates that may possibly appreciate in value. The key is to view collecting plates as you would view collecting fine art. You would never expect quality artwork to be cheaply reproduced and sold at bargain-basement prices. Which bring us to the most important point of all: It is of the utmost importance to educate yourself in this field. Subscribe to the various fine collector-plate periodicals, which are a treasure trove of invaluable information to both the novice and the advanced collector.

Once you have learned to spot designers' styles and manufacturers' hallmarks, you can easily avoid imitations. But the number-one rule still is, buy what you like!

How to Display
Your Plates

One facet of collecting plates that tends to fascinate and delight hobbyists is the seemingly endless ways to display them. A well-displayed collection can add appeal to any room and can be a source of pleasure for the collector. Plates are one group of collectibles whose beauty is recognized and admired by all. Visitors to your home need not be collectors to be impressed with your display. There are many ways to display, and with your own imagination and creative talents you can effectively and beautifully arrange them in whatever space you have available.

There are three basic places to display a group of plates: on a wall, in a cabinet, or in individual stands on top of furniture. The first of these, wall hanging, is a very popular means of display and is easily adaptable to either a small or large collection. Wooden frames and metal hangers can be purchased in many gift shops and plate stores to help you display your collection. Wooden frames are available in many colors, sizes, and shapes to fit any specimen. A very effective way to show a series is in multiple frames—wooden frames with velvet backgrounds that hold more than one plate. Some of these frames have glass fronts. The glass may help you keep your specimens cleaner, but it may detract from brilliant colors if the glass itself is not kept free from dust.

There are two types of metal wall hangers. The first consists of two individual plastic or rubber-coated wires, each with a U-shape, that hooks the plate at the top and bottom. The two ends of each U are bent to clip over the edge and are the only part of the hanger that is visible from the front. The top and bottom wires are held in place by two springs. The hanger is attached to the plate from the back by clipping the bottom wire prongs over the edge and then stretching the springs until you can hook the top wire prongs into place. The top wire then has a slight bend, which allows you to hang the plate over a nail or hook.

The second type of hanger consists of two half-circle wires that also hook over the top and bottom of the plate. The wires, which are joined together at the center of the hanger, are shorter in length than the diameter of the plate. To attach this hanger, situate it in the center of the plate and then stretch all four ends outward until they reach the rim. Then hook the four prongs over the edges. Another wire attached to the hanger then allows you to hang the plate over a nail or hook.

Many collector plates can be hung on a wall without using store-bought hangers. Some manufacturers provide you with two holes in the foot rim on the back of the plate. Wire or string can be threaded through each hole and then tied. However, you must allow enough slack in the wire so that it can be draped over a nail or hook. But before you place the wire over a hook, be sure to double-check that the knots are securely tied.

If your collection is fairly small and not likely to grow at a rapid pace, cabinet storage may be suitable. If possible, use a cabinet with glass-panel doors. These can be very expensive when newly purchased but can sometimes be found on the secondhand furniture market for a fairly reasonable price. You may encounter a display cabinet with a lighting attachment, which is usually a fluorescent bulb placed at the top. These normally have glass shelves rather than wooden ones so that light can travel throughout the entire cabinet. It is best that a display cabinet used for plates not have wheels at the base. One on wheels will move if it is slightly bumped, possibly knocking down some plates. When arranging items in a cabinet, don't overcrowd the shelves. Leave at least 2 inches of space between each plate for easier viewing. Don't trust plates to stand by propping them against the back wall. They may stand temporarily, but any slight trembling of the floor may dislodge them. Instead, use plate stands or racks, which are available at most gift shops and specialty plate stores.

One type of stand is made of twisted wire about the thickness of coat-hanger wire. When using these, be very careful that you don't scratch the plate. A second type is made of molded plastic with a groove to hold the bottom of the plate. They are inexpensive and serve the purpose perfectly. If you buy holders in quantity, you may even be able to purchase them at a discount. You may also find them secondhand at flea markets or garage sales.

If you use a glass-front cabinet for displaying your collection, you will have a distinct advantage over a wall display: your plates will take much longer to collect dust. Plates displayed uncovered on a wall may need to be wiped every week or more often, but only the glass front of the cabinet will have to be dusted that often.

Metal or plastic stands can also be used to place specimens on tables, mantels, or any flat surface you want to display them on. They can be very decorative and add to the design of the plate, or very plain, in clear plastic, so that every part of the plate can be seen. If you display your plates in this way, take the time to consider how susceptible they are to damage that could result from children or pets.

Once you've decided where you want to display your collection, then the fun part really begins. The possibilities of combinations for displays are endless, so here are a few suggestions to consider. From here, use your imagination and enjoy!

You may want to accent your collection or just a few plates with other items that correspond in topic, basic design, or era of artistic style. If Hummel annuals and anniversary issues are in your collection, try accenting them with other items made by Goebel, such as figurines, wall plaques, and fonts. If you own one of the candleholders, lamp bases, or music boxes, this will also add variety to your display and may be just perfect for a baby's room.

If you are one of those enthusiasts who collect topically, a good variety can stem from this also. Ceramic puppies, puppies on hooked rugs, tapestries, and even paintings can make an attractive display for any room you choose. Or if flowers are your hobby, try arranging vases of home-grown flowers to go with your display. Dried or silk flowers can also add variety to your collection. Maybe you could even place your favorite teddy bear on a table next to your plates that depict children playing with *their* favorite toys.

If you have many items made by a single manufacturer, these too can be displayed together. Collector plates of jasperware can attractively be shown in a china or curio cabinet with the many other wares made by Wedgwood. Royal Copenhagen has a Mother and Child Series in plates as well as in figurines. The design of the first plate, a mother and baby robin, was taken directly from figurines. Both have the same soft look from the underglazed design and would create a very impressive combination.

Another good way to add variety to your display is to supplement it with works in other media by the same artist. This is a more costly means of variety, but many times hobbyists who collect an artist's work acquire paintings, lithographs, or serigraphs first, and later they are attracted to plates by finding the same designs on ceramic that they found in the other media.

So get started! Take time to choose the right colors and styles for *you*. Coordinate your favorite pieces to create a display that any collector would be proud of. Then share your decorated rooms with others, but most of all, *enjoy them yourself!*

Caring for
Your Plates

Collector plates require minimum care and attention. There are only a few basic rules to learn in storing and preserving your collection. It is true that plates, like all ceramic objects, will break if dropped, but aside from this they are quite sturdy in terms of resistance to deterioration and can endure for a very, very long time. The proof of this can be seen in art museums, where pottery three thousand and four thousand years old is displayed. Much of this is archeological ware, buried beneath the ground for ages upon ages. Yet it has remained intact for the most part and still survives today.

The objective for you to establish is to maintain your plates in exactly the same condition as when you acquired them. Some thought and preventive maintenance will do all that is necessary, because a plate is more easily kept from harm than restored after damage or deterioration.

The way plates are stored will play a major role in their preservation. With safe storage there is virtually no need for anything further, aside from an occasional cleaning to remove the inevitable accumulation of dust.

It may be necessary to wash your plates occasionally, but do this only for ceramic with a glazed surface. A simple wiping with a damp cloth will remove surface dust if it has not been allowed to build up too long. Wiping surfaces that are not glazed may only rub the dirt into the more porous surface and give the appearance of being ingrained or stained. This type of ware must instead be dusted often, so as not to allow dust to build up. If washed or dusted with care, there should be no accidents, and the plates will be much the better for it. You would do well to wash your plates as soon as they show evidence of needing it, because the task only becomes challenging as dust builds up.

Collector plates can be washed in lukewarm water with mild soap, not in hot water and not with ordinary dish detergents. These may be too harsh and might remove some of the delicate surface banding or highlights. For wiping, use a soft cloth. Don't wipe hard, and take care that your fingernails don't come into contact with the plate. It's also wise to remove rings before doing this job. Don't wash collector plates under running water but in a basin, first with soapy water and then clear water. It may be necessary to rinse them several times. Wash the backs as well as the fronts, and the edges too—but go particularly easy on the edges if these carry any gold banding. Gold edges are the most vulnerable area of a plate.

After washing, dry your plate with another soft cloth, one that will not leave lint particles. You may want to use thick paper towels instead, to prevent lint remnants, but discard each towel as soon as it becomes thoroughly wet and use another dry one.

Some types of common grease stains can be successfully removed. The procedure in removing grease stains (or attempting to) is to use soap and water as outlined above but concentrate wiping in the area of the stain. Periodic checks must be made during the cleaning procedure to measure your progress. You do not want to keep wiping longer than is necessary. On the other hand, grease stains that appear to have vanished in the washing process sometimes reappear after the plate is dry. The water camouflages them. Rather than wiping too much, it is best to dry the plate and see how it has come out. Then wash again if necessary.

PACKING FOR SHIPMENT

The dread of every plate collector is moving to a new home, which means taking down plates, packing them, and waiting to see if all survive the trip intact. There is very little danger in transporting plates or even in shipping them through the mail, if ordinary precautions are taken. Dealers mail plates regularly and seldom encounter breakage. When sending plates by mail or by any commercial carrier, it is usually best to pack one plate per container. You can pack more than one in a container, but the risk of breakage increases somewhat with each additional plate because you then have the danger of the plates damaging each other in addition to being damaged by external forces. Assuming you are packing one plate per container, you will want to begin with a sturdy box that is at least 3 inches larger on all sides than the plate. In other words for a plate 10 inches in diameter, the ideal box would measure 16 inches by 16 inches. The box should be about 2 inches deep and preferably closed on the top and bottom, with a flap-type opening on one end. This is better than a box on which the lid is removable. In any event the box must be good and strong. If it's flexible at all, it may not be safe enough to do the job. The first step is to wrap the plate in several layers of tissue paper, securing it with cellotape. Then wrap in layers of newspapers, again sealing with cellotape. This is just the beginning to provide a cushioning and protection against scraping. The next step is to place a sheet of very heavy cardboard (about the same thickness as the walls of the box) on each side of the plate. These sheets of cardboard should be nearly as large as the box so that they will fit inside tightly. Having done this, tape the edges of the cardboard sheets together to form a sandwich, enclosing the plate inside them. (You may need to use a stronger tape than cellotape for this.) Then wrap it up in layers of newspaper until it becomes so thick that it will just barely fit in the box. Insert it in the box and seal the end flap shut with strong tape. The plate should then travel safely, but it is still smart to insure the parcel and obtain a receipt for it. Mark the parcel "Fragile."

INSURANCE

As with any other valued possession, the time to act on the possibility of theft, vandalism, fire, or accidental breakage of your collector plates is now, not when the damage has been done and it's too late. Each insurance company has a somewhat different way of tackling the problem, and the terminology may vary as well, so the best first step is to contact your own agent or company and find out where you stand already.

Plates are considered "fine arts" according to the criteria of most companies, satisfying the definition of "rarity, historic value and artistic merit." This generally makes them eligible to be included in either a Personal Articles floater to existing homeowner's coverage, under a separate Fine Arts policy, or as a Fine Arts floater.

If you plan to include them on your regular homeowner's policy, make sure that they are on a separate schedule, otherwise the best you could hope for would be reimbursement up to a set maximum amount of about $1,000 for the entire lot. If you have an extensive collection, this could work out to only a fraction of their actual value.

To establish the value of your plates, some insurance companies are willing to rely on values set by a respected source such as this book, Bradex market values, or those of the Collectors' Information Bureau. Other insurers may insist on an independent appraisal. Most plate retailers will perform this service for a fee, which will vary from appraiser to appraiser. Each plate should be valued separately in writing, and make sure to keep a copy of the appraisal, perhaps even an extra copy in a location outside your own home, just in case. Fine arts losses are always paid at the value scheduled. Generally, they are subject to an annual review, when new acquisitions can be added. Unless you've made a substantial addition to your collection within the year's period, don't worry about your plates purchased within that time frame. Recent plates are automatically covered to approximately 25 percent to 30 percent of their value as long as receipts are retained.

Artist Interviews

SANDRA KUCK

Sandra Kuck, one of America's most honored plate artists, currently lives in Old Bethpage, New York, with her husband, John, a retired police detective, and their two children. She has garnered a number of awards, including 1983 Plate of the Year for "Sunday Best," and Plate Artist of the Year in both 1986 and 1987, as chosen by the National Association of Limited Edition Dealers.

Q: Were you always interested in art, even as a child?
A: Yes. I always doodled a lot, but I never took it seriously, I always thought I'd be a doctor or a lawyer when I grew up. My high school teachers realized I had a gift and would let me out of regular art classes, allowing me to do my own projects. By the end of my senior year I had quite a portfolio from these projects, and an artist from my neighborhood began encouraging me to pursue it more seriously.

Q: Did you attend art school?
A: When I was about ten, we moved to California; after high school I went to UCLA as an art major. They were very much into abstract art at the time, but I preferred the representational style. So after a year I decided to go to New York to attend the Art Students' League school in Manhattan. A friend persuaded me to go there by saying that I'd find more people in New York with

Artist Sandra Kuck.

interests similar to mine, and he was right. It also worked out well because that's where I met my husband. He's always been very encouraging about my career as an artist, and after our children were born, he would often take care of them when I needed time to paint.

Q: What artists have influenced you the most?
A: When I was younger, I spent a lot of time copying the works of Rembrandt. Then I became fascinated by the Impressionists because of their use of color. And of course, Thomas Eakins for his incredibly realistic art. Now I'm in love with John Singer Sargent. I really admire the charm and prettiness of the Impressionists and Realists.

Q: How did you get started in limited-edition plates?
A: The people at Reco International were on the lookout for artists who were painting children, and they saw some some of my work at a gallery in Garden City, New York. I didn't know

anything about plates at the time. I found it difficult to paint for plates because I was trying to create what I thought somebody else would like, that is, not being true to myself. But I realized that in order for it to work for my audience, it first has to work for me.

Q: Do you have to think differently when designing and painting for plates—round as opposed to square or rectangular?
A: Yes, it's quite different. The composition has to be perfect. Because of its small size, you have to be able to look at it and understand it immediately. It must have a clear focal point to grab the viewer. This concept was difficult to master at first, but I've grown into it.

Q: You specialize in plates with children as subjects. How do you get from the initial idea to the finished product?
A: First, I sketch the idea out to get a basic picture in my mind. Then I go looking for costumes, mostly in antique shops, that I feel have the right look. The next step is to find the right models. For these I usually scout around the neighborhood for little girls, usually ones under five years old who get along well with each other. I don't use a lot of boys because at that age they don't really like girls and are less outgoing. They also don't like getting into the costumes that I pick. Then we get the children into the right setting, and my husband takes photos. These I look at later and then make my final sketches.

Q: What's your favorite plate of all you've done?
A: I'm always very critical of my own work, but I have a special fondness for "Sunday Best." It's the only plate that my own daughter ever appeared on. She's the little blond girl in the picture, and now that she's sixteen, it's a sentimental look back for me.

Q: Are there any new ideas in the planning stages for future plate issues?
A: I've been giving some thought lately to perhaps doing a series on young women, a change of pace for me in the plate field. I also hope to be able to spend more time doing sculpture, an art form that I really love.

JOHN McCLELLAND

When I'd last spoken to John McClelland, he was living in New Canaan, Connecticut, near New York City. Since then he and his wife have moved back to his roots in Georgia, though not exactly home again. A native of Atlanta, he's now four hours away in Savannah on Skidaway Island, one of the newly developed sea islands once accessible only by boat from the mainland.

Q: Why back down south, John?
A: The cold had gotten in my bones one too many times, and I'm too old to shovel. We had lived up in Connecticut for thirty-five years and decided it was time to move.

Q: You always wanted to be an artist, didn't you?
A: Oh yes, there was never a question. But not just an artist. I wanted to be an illustrator for the magazines: pretty girls, handsome men, and all that. I decided to go straight to art school after high school, but my father insisted that I attend college for at least one year. It turned out to be good advice. I went to Auburn University in Alabama and enjoyed it so much in their art program that I stayed an extra year. It was excellent training and was a real advantage when I did go to art school in New York the next year.

Q: Then World War II came along?
A: Yes, I was drafted into the army, where I got a lucky assignment. They sent me to a unit in San Antonio, Texas, where I illustrated training manuals for pilots, navigators, and bombardiers. The army couldn't find enough artists, so one of my duties was to go up to New York to oversee civilian illustrators who were helping us out. That's when I was offered a job by one of the studios. After the war I got into magazine work by the connections I made at the studio.

Q: Which magazines did you do illustrations for?
A: Oh, all of them: *Woman's Day, Collier's, Ladies' Home Journal, Cosmopolitan, McCall's.* That lasted for several years, but then television came along. People read fewer short stories, and advertising fell off. The magazines were hurting, jobs became more

scarce, and I started doing more portrait work. Just before the war I'd studied with a fine portrait artist named Jerry Farnsworth at his summer studio on Cape Cod. I could already paint pretty well, but he taught me color. I learned more from him than from anyone else. I did portrait work for years in New York and still do quite a few today for Portraits South in Raleigh, North Carolina.

Q: When did you start doing plates?

A: I was contacted by Heio Reich of Reco International in 1976. He'd seen some covers I'd been doing for Christmas gift catalogs that the Miles Kimball Company put out, and he liked what he saw, I guess. At the time I didn't even know people collected plates, but I've always liked a challenge, something new.

Q: Are plates much different from other kinds of art you've done?

A: To some degree. I have to be very conscious of the roundness in composing the plate. The images have to flow around and carry the viewer's eye around with them. I also learned that when I portray something with a sharp edge to it, that it must be done with a lot of contrast; otherwise it can look a little too soft when it gets onto the finished plate. It has something to do with the firing process, and I try to keep this in mind while I'm working. The reproduction on our plates has improved so much recently that it's not much of a consideration anymore.

Q: Who are some of your favorite artists?

A: There are so many: Degas for his color and pastels, Thomas Eakins for those incredible skin tones that seem so alive. Being a portrait artist myself, I greatly admire Gainsborough. And lately I've come to love the work of Matisse, who probably wouldn't be big on plates but whose economy of strokes is fascinating.

Q: How about your own work? Which plate have you been most proud of?

A: One of my big favorites is "Little Miss Muffet." I always visualize what the finished product will look like and then paint toward that end. That plate came out closer to what I had planned than any other I've ever done.

John is currently embarked on a new hobby, playing the piano, and had to excuse himself to go practice for his afternoon lesson with a lady down the road. "I hope she gives me a new song this week," he said, "I'm getting awfully bored with 'Camptown Races.'" That's John McClelland, who laughingly refers to himself as "America's oldest living plate artist," off to take on another challenge, always looking for something new.

GREGORY PERILLO

Gregory Perillo, one of America's premier plate artists, has been exclusively with Richard Habeeb's Vague Shadows, Ltd. since 1977. Throughout the years of this association with Vague Shadows, Mr. Perillo has garnered first place awards in all major categories: Artist of the Year (NALED, 1982); Figurine of the Year (NALED, 1982); Plate of the Year (both Silver, Chalice Award and first place NALED Award, 1987); and Plate World Reader Survey (Plate of the Year, 1987).

Artist Gregory Perillo.

Mr. Perillo, a giant among plate artists, and a specialist in art of the American West, was born and raised on Staten Island in New York City. The son of poor, immigrant parents, he grew up speaking Italian before learning English in the New York public schools. Though his family struggled financially in their adopted country, they imparted to their son a burning love of art and a strong interest in American history. Greg's grandfather was an accomplished artist, and his father, though not possessing the same God-given talent, was a history buff, who nurtured his son's interest in the subject with tales of the American Indians. "Most of the stories were true," Greg recalled, "but some, I'm sure, he spiced up to keep me interested."

Though a high school dropout at age seventeen, Greg had been since early childhood a prolific and promising artist. Without the finances for traditional art supplies, his mother would iron the creases out of shopping bags for his canvas and brew an extra cup of espresso coffee for his paints. As an avid boxing fan and an undefeated amateur ex-fighter himself, it's no wonder that "with only one basic color for paint and canvas, the great Joe Louis, the 'Brown Bomber' himself, became one of my favorite subjects." He feels now that the lack of varied colors at his disposal made him more aware of and sensitive to the subtleties of tone so important to an artist.

After a stint in the navy, "where I really grew up," Greg earned his high school diploma and attended several art schools in New York City under the G.I. Bill. Like most art students he frequented the city's art galleries, and while at one of his favorites, the Grand Central, he became enthralled with the work of one of the great painters of the American West, W. R. Leigh. "I did figures pretty well by then but couldn't quite get western landscapes the way I wanted them," said Perillo. "After all, I'd only seen them in books and in the movies." So off he went to Arizona, where he finally met his idol. Leigh was fascinated by the young New Yorker—"He thought I sounded like one of the Bowery Boys"—and became his teacher and mentor, the two becoming lifelong friends.

Coincidentally, it was while displaying his gallery paintings at a show in Prescott, Arizona, in 1976 that Perillo became involved in the field of limited-edition plates. With the works of such notables as Norman Rockwell, John Clymer, and Frank McCarthy also in the competition, Perillo was approached by a man who predicted that one of Greg's paintings, "Amigos," would win the juried award as the best at the exhibition. To Greg's astonishment, the prediction came true.

And it was only a few weeks later that he received a phone call from the very same man, Bud Kern, the founder of Kern Collectibles, who wanted permission to feature another of Greg's paintings, "Apache Girl," on a limited-edition plate. Perillo's first reaction was "My painting on a dish?" When Kern persisted, Perillo finally agreed, and his incredible career "in the round" had begun. He went on to become one of America's premier plate artists, garnering the field's highest award in 1983, Plate Artist of the Year.

Today, at an amazingly fit fifty-two, he still lives on Staten Island, in a truly lavish dream house that he and his wife, Mary, recently designed. "It's like my own Disneyland," he said. For the past four years, first as a hobby, and now as an art form in itself, Greg has been a self-proclaimed "dancing fanatic," and when it came time to make up the blueprints, his new-found obsession wasn't forgotten. He built the home around his own disco dance floor, "the flashiest and most exciting you can possibly imagine." As a matter of fact, when not working at his easel, finishing up one of his award-winning sculptures, exhibiting his works at galleries from Paris to Beverly Hills to Israel, or personally meeting his legions of fans at one of the big plate shows, Greg says, "That's where you'll find me, relaxing, but still working hard, out on the dance floor."

DONALD ZOLAN

Donald Zolan has been named "Favorite Living Plate Artist" three years in a row by *Plate World* magazine's annual nationwide reader's survey, something that has never occurred before. It's being called a phenomenon in the world of limited-edition plates. Each year the Bradford Exchange selects its prestigious Plate of the Year award, for the "plate on the secondary market which has appreciated the most in the previous year." For 1987 the winner was Donald Zolan's "Erik and the Dandelion," featuring the artist's own five-year-old son. What's so amazing about recognition for this plate is the fact that this was Zolan's first; it was released in 1978! It's not that recognition hasn't come his way before—after all, he did win the same prize in 1979 for "Sabina in the Grass," a portrait of his daughter—but being awarded such an honor for a plate produced nearly a decade ago has never happened before.

And all of this from a man who specializes in works featuring

Artist Donald Zolan.

children, or "little people" as Zolan calls them. Zolan, by the way, worked for twelve years at *Playboy* magazine!

Donald Zolan always figured he had a special talent. He came from a family of artists and, with his brother Richard, became the fifth generation to put brush to canvas. Born and raised in Brookfield, Illinois, about forty-five miles southwest of the Windy City, he garnered his first art scholarship at the precocious age of ten, to the prestigious Art Institute of Chicago. Others followed, culminating in a full scholarship to the American Academy of Art after high school.

After a short stint as a commercial artist, he joined *Playboy* as an apprentice on key line assembly. He stayed with Hefner's organization for twelve years through positions as head designer and associate picture editor. It was there that he developed his particular skills in photography, which would prove so valuable in the preliminary design phase of his plates.

While at the magazine, he continued painting in his off hours and

Donald Zolan's version of "Music Man" Donald Duck, which he drew while only four years old.

had many works displayed at local galleries in Chicago. It was at one of these, Merrill-Chase, that his work was first seen by John Hugunin, then president of Bradford, who in 1976 signed Zolan to be the first artist for his own fledgling plate company, Pemberton & Oakes, to be based in Santa Barbara, California.

Zolan has had various influences on his artistic career, including the renowned commercial artist Haddon Sunblom of Coca-Cola Santa Claus fame, with whom he served as an apprentice. He feels that the greatest impact, however, has come from those Old Masters Rembrandt and Rubens. Don still utilizes some of Rembrandt's time-honored techniques of paint preparation and toning of the canvas, which have achieved the desired effects of light and shadow since the seventeenth century.

An interesting sidelight of Zolan's career was his flirtation with becoming a physician. While working as an x-ray orderly for a year, he attended art classes with a plastic surgeon. The doctor was impressed by Zolan's sketch of a person's lip and asked if he could use it as a model for an operation on a young girl with a harelip. This was the first of many collaborations between the two, who became lifelong friends. Zolan began to think that plastic surgery might be a career to follow, but was dissuaded by his friend, who finally convinced him to pursue his great artistic gift rather than become a "technician."

Donald Zolan's
precocious artwork at
the age of four.

Donald moved from Illinois about a year and a half ago and is currently living in Carmel, California. He feels that the change in character of the sunlight along the Pacific coast has had a considerable impact on his paintings. "I'm using brighter colors now and a larger open pallet. The effect is really noticeable, and the response has been great," he says. Plans to move yet again are in the works, and before long he expects to be in the San Diego area, with yet another change in light on the way.

Like other artists we've spoken to who often paint children, Zolan's first step is to take a series of photographs of his subject. "Little people don't stay still long enough to really focus on them." Then he does a cartoon or color sketch of what the final piece will resemble and shows it to John Hugunin, with whom he shares "the closest creative relationship I've ever had with anyone." With suggestions in mind, he stretches a square, double-primed Belgian linen canvas, which is then "aged" for three or four days. When the canvas is ready, he draws a plate-size circle in the middle, and a new Zolan creation is on the way.

Donald Zolan is one of the happiest and friendliest people you'll ever meet. "This is all fun for me," he says convincingly, and should you ever run across him at one of the plate shows he regularly attends, be careful—a bit of his enthusiasm for life and art is sure to rub off.

A Gallery of Artists

ROGER AKERS

Roger Akers has won increasing recognition for his work in the collector's plate medium and in the more traditional fine-art sculptural media: laminated wood, clay, and polyester resin. His works are widely exhibited in the United States, and he has received numerous awards at important Midwestern shows, including Best of Show at the 1981 Excellence in Woodcarving exhibit in Chicago. Among his favorite commissions are the 1974 Coin of the Year for the American Numismatic Association and a bust of John F. Kennedy.

Major galleries now display Akers's fine-art pieces, and his work has been selected by the Illinois Arts Council as part of its permanent museum collection. He has already begun to make his mark in the collector's plate medium with his works for the Incolay Romantic Poets Collection. Now his work for The Love Sonnets of Shakespeare Series—the logical next step in Akers' artistic career—can only enhance still further the national reputation of this rising young sculptor.

SY AND DOROTHEA BARLOWE

Sy and Dorothea Barlowe began their careers in the 1940s at New York's Museum of Natural History. And in 1950, four years after their marriage, they began working as free-lance illustrators. Over the years they have done features for such noted publications as *The New York Times* and *Newsday*. Their work has been honored not only in awards but with exhibits at the Society of Illustrators in New York and Expo '67 in Montreal. Together the Barlowes have illustrated nature books for some of the largest publishing houses in America. In addition Dorothea and Sy Barlowe have contributed illustrations to several Audubon Society guides and to the *Audubon Society Encyclopedia of North American Birds* and other reference books. They have shared their knowledge and expertise by having taught at the Parsons School of Design in New York. In all things of nature there is something marvelous, and through the art of Dorothea and Sy Barlowe untold thousands are able to enjoy the beauty nature has to offer. For the past twenty-nine years, the Barlowes have lived on Long Island. They have two children—Amy, a concert violinist, and Wayne, an award-winning illustrator himself.

LENORE BÉRAN

From her studio in Van Nuys, California, Lenore Béran creates paintings and mosaics that have made her very popular in the collector market today. "Little Blue Horse" may be the most famous of her mosaic collages that has been adapted to a collector plate. It was the first in a series produced by Brindle Fine Arts.

Béran, who studied art with Hal Reed and Ron Labyorteaux, has more than learned the basics of composition, color harmony, and structure, but these are the aspects that make her art more than just a pretty picture. She is known for her versatility in the field. She is an artist, sculptor, and printmaker. She has created fragile, almost ethereal oil-wash paintings; bright, richly colored mosaics; and bold and powerful bronze sculptures. Her paintings have been displayed throughout the United States and Canada.

Brindle Fine Arts has produced three plate series designed by Béran: Fantasy in Motion, Moods of the Orient, and The Lenore Béran Special. She is a confident and disciplined artist who will continue to produce many more paintings and mosaics. One day there may be more subjects for collector plates to add to her collection, which is now so much admired by the public.

BEN BLACK

Ben Black came to the field of collector plates with his first design released in 1982 in the Behind the Painted Masque Series by Royal Doulton. However, he is not new to the world of art. His career as an artist began before World War II after he graduated from Massachusetts College of Art. He has worked as an art director for a Boston advertising agency and has contributed works to such magazines as *The New Yorker, The Saturday Evening Post,* and *Reader's Digest.*

Black combines and balances colors, textures, and patterns to create many different kinds of art. His portraits often reveal great expressions of human feelings, reflecting a celebration of life. His still lifes are a colorful, mosaic-like mixture of designs from different ethnic and cultural backgrounds. Many of Black's works can be viewed in collections in cities all over the world, including England, Italy, and Brazil.

Using the designs of Black's first venture into ceramics, Royal Doulton is promoting a new technique in collector plates with two distinct aspects. First, the plate is outwardly curved for better viewing and easier hanging. This camber shape is sure to be a success in the market. The second aspect, which will be very interesting to art hobbyists, is an interview with the artist on cassette tape. "The Sound of Art," as Royal Doulton calls it, accompanies the first issue in the series. It is truly a unique way for the collector to get to know his favorite artist.

Ben Black, a veteran of the arts for about forty years, is making an impact in the plates field and, with the help of Royal Doulton, is making great innovative steps in bringing the artist closer to the enthusiasts who have respected and loved his works for years.

ALAN BRUNETTIN

Alan Brunettin is a young artist who is beginning to make a very definite mark on the American art scene. His recent success in national art competitions (in the categories of drawing and painting), as well as his commission from Incolay Studios to execute the Voyage of Ulysses series, suggests a rare range of talent and an enormous artistic vitality.

Brunettin's own reflections on his art confirm his appetite for new challenges, but they also reveal a deep and abiding respect for artistic tradition:

"Art is my life, my primary means of expression, so of course I investigate the possibilities inherent in many media—sculpture, painting, drawing, even photography. I appreciate their nuances; each one touches a different part of me. But expression is not a simple thing; it's a relationship between the medium—the wealth of traditional knowledge about painting or sculpture—and the artist himself. I'm still learning in many areas; at this stage in my career my art is a voyage of discovery. Maybe that's why the figure of Ulysses is so appealing to me. But his voyage ended; he found his way home. I'm not sure yet where my artistic home will be, but I do believe that my work on the Voyage of Ulysses is helping me to find it."

In a sense, however, Alan Brunettin does know his artistic home—he grew up in it. His best work in all media remains close, in spirit, to the precepts and practice of his father, the celebrated sculptor Alfred Brunettin. The elder Brunettin exhibited his welded and cast-bronze abstract constructions in Europe and designed major medallion series for Lincoln Mint and Hamilton Mint. Alan did much more than talk art with his father; he learned as artists traditionally learn—by doing. For nine years Alan Brunettin worked as his father's apprentice, playing an increasingly independent role in the execution of important commissions.

"In the old days there was a large element of craftsmanship in art," Mr. Brunettin recalls. "You learned at the master's knee. And that's what I did. My father was a stern teacher, very strict. He did expressionistic pieces himself; he wouldn't let me do them. 'Master the human figure first,' he would say, 'then you will have the skills to express yourself.' He brought me up on Michelangelo and Rodin and the Greek classics—the Apollo Belvedere.

"In a sense, 'The Isle of Circe' and the other Voyage of Ulysses plates express my gratitude both to classical Greek sculpture and to the lessons my father taught me."

CARL ROMANELLI

Carl Romanelli is the seventh generation of a family that originated in Florence, Italy, and has given famous sculptors to the world, father teaching son, since 1840.

Surpassing in this instance even the works of his famous father, Carlo Romanelli, Carl Romanelli is in his turn noted for his bronze of the nineteenth-century theologian, John Henry Cardinal Newman, which is on permanent display at the Vatican in Rome.

Aside from his Vatican statue, numerous monumental pieces and heroic statues bear his signature in collections throughout the world.

Working in collaboration with the artisans of Incolay Studios of California, Mr. Romanelli brings intact his seven-generation Florentine precision to the creation of his first collector's plate, "Antony and Cleopatra."

TED DeGRAZIA

On September 17, 1982, the art world suffered a tragic loss. Ted DeGrazia, truly a legend in his own time, passed away, leaving behind a rich treasure of art and humanity. The grizzly, animated, prolific former miner spent his life in the desert of Arizona, where he lived and worked among his Indian friends. Shunning the trappings of wealth, DeGrazia lived a simple life in the shadow of his beloved Superstition Mountains. He painted the Indian children he loved in his own inimitable style, always taking time out to chat with the many visitors who came to see him. He lived and worked at the DeGrazia Gallery in the Sun outside Tucson. This complex served as home, studio, and gallery. He built the studio by hand with help from Indian friends. Never a man to hold back, DeGrazia would speak his mind on any subject, much to the delight and chagrin of those who came into contact with him. And whoever did that always went away a friend.

DeGrazia took the entire world by storm in 1960 when his charming painting "Los Ninos" was chosen to be depicted on the UNICEF Christmas card that year. In 1976 he began his annual children series and in 1977 issued the first plate in his annual holiday series. These plates feature somber, dark-eyed Indian children and are painted with bold impressionistic strokes in bright colors. His Indian angels are haloed and winged, carrying a staff topped with a blazing star. In the DeGrazia memorial plate painted by his close friend, artist Larry Toschik, DeGrazia's head and shoulders appear superimposed on his beloved Superstition Mountains at sunset while a DeGrazia angel lights the way to heaven. Indeed, Ted DeGrazia, a truly original man of the people, has achieved immortality through the gift of his art to the world.

EDNA HIBEL

Edna Hibel is one of America's most widely acclaimed contemporary artists. Her recognizable and highly individualized style has earned her an international reputation as a painter and lithographer of extraordinary humanity, sensitivity, and technical virtuosity.

Born in Boston in January, 1917, she began her formal artistic training as a private student of the noted portrait painter Gregory Michaels. Following graduation from high school, she studied at the Boston Museum School of Fine Arts under the direction of Karl Zerbe and Alexander Jacovleff. It was there she was awarded the prestigious Ruth B. Sturtevant Traveling Fellowship in 1939. One year later the Boston Museum of Fine Arts purchased one of her

Artist Edna Hibel.

paintings for its permanent collection, making her the youngest living artist so honored by a major American museum.

In 1969 the distinguished Craig Collection of Hibel art went on public display, bringing the perspective of time to Edna's public exhibitions. From the time of her involvement as organizer of the first Boston Arts Festival in 1954, through her 1976 receipt of the New England Region of Hadassah's Citizen's Award, she has maintained her determination to make art the vehicle for enriching the lives of men and women everywhere.

Hibel's first designs displayed in ceramic plates were the Mother's Day and Mother and Child Series for Royal Doulton. The six plates of a mother and child, each from a different cultural background, showed Hibel's versatility in portraying the sensitivity and warmth of human life. She has displayed similar characteristics in plate series made by Rosenthal, Hutschenreuther, and her own Hibel Studio. She is truly an artist loved by collectors; many of her plate designs have jumped in value. She is currently the hottest artist on the market of collector plates.

The Hibel Museum of Art in Palm Beach, Florida, was opened in January 1977 and marked an unprecedented recognition of her unique role in contemporary art. The only museum in the United States devoted to the works of a living woman artist, the Hibel Museum of Art demonstrates both the beauty and the importance of Hibel's masterful works.

RUSTY MONEY

Conjure up beautiful impressionistic visions of the turn of the century in luscious colors and you are immediately in the world of artist Rusty Money. This Californian paints from memory as she relives her own dreamlike childhood, dressing up in her Gibson girl grandmother's antique clothes. The attic was a magical place for Rusty, and those days permanently imprinted her as an incurable romantic. In her four series for R. J. Ernst Enterprises, Ms. Money conveys all the nostalgic charm of the turn of the century as revealed in the names of the series: Seems Like Yesterday, Turn of the Century, Mommie and Me, and My Fair Ladies. A plate artist since 1981, Rusty Money was an overnight sensation in the plate world with "Stop and Smell the Roses," the first issue in her Seems Like Yesterday series.

P. BUCKLEY MOSS

The Amish and Mennonite plates and paintings by P. Buckley Moss have become extremely popular since their introduction in 1978. Patricia Buckley Moss was born in Staten Island, New York, in 1933. When she was ten years old, a serious automobile accident kept her out of school for a year, giving her unlimited time for drawing and painting.

Her portfolio was shown to Margaret Meade, then the principal of Washington Irving High School in Manhattan. An exception was made for her to attend classes there. Four years later, P. Buckley Moss was awarded a scholarship by the Cooper Union and subsequently graduated in Fine Arts and Design.

In the early 1960s she moved to Virginia's Shenandoah Valley. A friendship with the Mennonites developed that led to her various paintings of their life-styles.

The combination of unique style, talent, and goodwill that her plates and paintings evoke has already earned her an important place in contemporary American art and has made her a favorite of plate collectors everywhere.

DON RUFFIN

"Navajo Lullaby," "Inner Peace," "Sun Kachina"—each of these simple names reveals a lot about the artist who created them, Don Ruffin. He was born in Arizona and raised near an Indian reservation. It was there his long and warm relationship with the Maricopa and Pima Indians began. Many subjects of his paintings are the natives of Southwest America and their traditions. Another feature seen from the names is Ruffin's involvement in nature and humanity. He has painted landscapes, the sea, flowers, and the people of the Southwest and Mexico. An artist, a sculptor, and a teacher, he was frequently sought for seminars in both the United States and other countries. There was variety in what he painted, but Ruffin made one characteristic constant. He believed that the "feeling" that went into his work was very important and that it must "come from the soul."

The joining of nature and the spirit of man *is* Don Ruffin's paintings. He viewed it this way: "Painting is a metaphysical thing. The mind sees, the spirit reveals, the hand paints." Because collectors know that new works will never be produced due to Ruffin's death in

1977, they have learned to enjoy his existing paintings more thoroughly. The success of these will be felt each time an old man or a little child sees his work as Ruffin experienced it.

D. L. "RUSTY" RUST

D. L. Rust was born in Erie, Pennsylvania, in 1932. He worked in various fields of art, from grocery store signs as a high school student in the 1950s to book jacket illustrations. He moved to Florida in 1954 and still resides with his family in Sarasota. In his studio are several loose-leaf notebooks filled with photos of his portrait work. The portraits range from smiling cherubic little girls to serious business executives and plump fiftieth-anniversary couples. Active both nationally and internationally in fine arts, he has to his credit more than four hundred commissioned portraits, mostly of prominent persons.

Rust met Emmett Kelly in 1962 and has painted his clowns in limited paintings of 250 each. He immortalized his good friend, America's most famous clown—and his unforgettable sad-faced clown character, "Weary Willie"—in a portrait so accurate that it has been purchased by the Smithsonian Institution in Washington, DC, and will be on display at the National Portrait Gallery.

RED SKELTON

Born July 18, 1913, two months after the death of his father, Red Skelton put his talents to work at age ten. In May 1923 he joined a medicine show, and since that time his comedy creations have been a part of tent shows, minstrels, circuses, burlesques, Mississippi showboats, motion pictures, radio, and vaudeville. Red holds a record twenty consecutive years on television and even now is on the verge of launching a new career in video tape cassettes and presentation of his re-runs.

Red has starred in forty-eight motion pictures and has written nearly five thousand musical selections, many of which have been played and recorded by such as Arthur Fiedler, Van Cliburn, David Rose, and the London Philharmonic Symphony Orchestra. In addition, he has written sixty-four symphonies, which have been performed by the Las Vegas Symphony, Anthony Movella, Thomas Mancini, and the Palm Springs Desert Symphony Orchestra.

In his spare time, Red paints in oil, has done limited-edition plates, does pastel pencil drawings, and bookbinds. He also gardens—Bonsai trees are his specialty—and has had a rose named in his honor.

A prolific writer, Red has authored more than four thousand short stories and has published full-length books: *Red Skelton In Your Closet* and *Red Skelton's Gertrude and Heathcliff.* He also has three story–coloring books: *Clown Alley, The Big Fellows,* and *Frog Follys.* He soon plans on publishing his *Twenty Christmas Stories* with his own illustrations, along with *The True Scrooge.*

Red is one of the few entertainers alive today who has had the honor of being a guest and entertainer of seven United States presidents—Roosevelt, Truman, Eisenhower, Kennedy, Johnson, Nixon, and Ford. He has also received private audiences with three popes—Pope Pius XII, Pope John, and Pope Paul. Not bad for a thirty-third-degree Mason.

His Pledge of Allegiance has won him forty-two awards and has twice been read into the *Congressional Record.* Other honors bestowed on Red include awards from the American Legion, the American Freedom Foundation, and the United Conference of Christians and Jews. He holds doctorate degrees from Boston's Emerson College, Indiana's Vincennes University, and Indiana State University. Among his most recent honors is the Cecil B. DeMille Award for outstanding contributions to the entertainment industry, presented to him by the Hollywood Foreign Press Association at its annual Golden Globe Awards program, and a Command Performance at Royal Albert Hall, London, on March 20, 1984.

Though his life has been filled with personal tragedy, Red Skelton is as dedicated to comedy as the most monastic monk is to religion. For laughter is part of Red's religion and, as he puts it, "God's children and their happiness are my reasons for being."

IRENE SPENCER

Veteran plate artist Irene Spencer is one of the shining stars of the collector plate realm. This lady has a very colorful background, having once been an elephant trainer in the circus, among other things. Originally from Chicago, the petite Ms. Spencer now lives and works in the beautiful hill country of Vista, California. She is renowned for her portraits of exquisitely beautiful women and children and has been a plate artist since the Franklin Mint issued her first annual Mother's Day plate in 1972. Extremely prolific, Irene Spencer has produced over a dozen new plates since 1972. These include her Franklin Mint Mother's Day series of five plates, Gorham's 1975 "Dear Child" and 1976 "Promises to Keep," Fairmont's 1977 "Patient Ones," 1978 "Yesterday, Today and Tomorrow," 1978 "Hug Me," 1978 "Sleep Little Baby," and Pickard's Symphony of Roses series—1982, "Wild Irish Rose" and 1983, "Yellow Rose of Texas."

ABIGAIL WILLIAMS

It began in the early 1900s. That's when Abbie Williams's great-grandparents honeymooned in East Boothbay, Maine. From that point on the family spent summer vacations in this picturesque coastal town, a tradition that was well established by the time Abbie was born in northern New Jersey. Following her schooling there, Abbie was an undergraduate in illustration at Moore College of Fine Arts in Philadelphia. Several of her works remain there on permanent display.

In the early 1970s, Abbie moved to the Boothbay region permanently. There she met the lady who was to be one of the greatest influences in the direction and pursuit of her art career: Frances Hook. Perhaps it was an inherent kinship between the two artists that accounts for the close friendship that developed from their first meeting. Hours would pass as Frances and Abbie discussed art and how they might pursue it together. For well over a year, Abbie was a private student of Frances Hook.

Abbie's artistic philosophy and technique were nurtured and refined. Her commissions expanded from capturing private residences on canvas to portraits. Her work can be found in homes from New England to New Mexico, and beyond, as far as Algiers and Venezuela. Many of Abbie's commissions have arisen from private showings in New York and gallery shows, including the Abacus in Boothbay, the Margot Moore Shop (Camden, Maine), and The Brick House Gallery, Boothbay's Art Foundation.

Abbie's work also has been widely published by such companies as Standard Publishing and *Down East* magazine. And she is under contract with Roman, Inc., for the creation of collectibles and giftware. Her work includes two series of collector plates (The Magic of Childhood and The Lord's Prayer) and musical figurines.

Abbie's work on future projects is now so extensive that she is unable to honor all of the portrait commissions she receives. What spare time she does have is devoted to her two sons. The people close to her and her artwork are, in Abbie's words, "my whole life—I really couldn't ask for a better life than I have."

Manufacturers:
A Few Histories

ANNA-PERENNA PORCELAIN, INC.

Anna-Perenna Porcelain, Inc., is an international firm specializing in fine art on limited-edition collector plates. Offerings of this firm are made of the finest hard-paste porcelain, created in a tradition dating back many generations.

The firm was founded in 1977 by Klaus D. Vogt, former president of Rosenthal, U.S.A. Vogt was fascinated by the possibilities of fine art on fine porcelain and left Rosenthal to pursue this new art medium with his own firm.

The name Anna-Perenna is derived from the Roman goddess of spring. From her name the English words for "annual" and "perennial" also stem. This international firm required a name that could be pronounced easily in English, German, and French, and Anna-Perenna filled the bill. Even more appropriately, this goddess was also the protectorate of the arts.

Anna-Perenna Porcelain has commissioned some of the world's most celebrated and unique artists to create original artwork for collector plates. Each Anna-Perenna artist submits paintings "in the round," and as near to the actual size of the plate as possible, as Vogt stresses that this is the only way to achieve fidelity in the creation of multicolor art on porcelain plates.

Anna-Perenna artists include Count Lennart Bernadotte, creator of a collection inspired by his Island of Mainau; Ken Danby, Canadian Reflections of Youth Series artist; Thaddeus "Uncle Tad" Krumeich, creator of numerous cat-subject plates; Frank Russell and Gertrude

Barrer, who introduced the triptych concept to the plate world; actress-turned-artist Elke Sommer; Margaret Kane, creator of the unique Masquerade Fantasy plates; and Pat Buckley Moss, artist for American Silhouettes, who also has been painting an annual Christmas plate series since 1985. Moss's plate "Wedding Joy" is the first and only plate ever to have been voted Plate of the Show at both plate collectors' fairs in 1986, in April in Pasadena, California, and in July in South Bend, Indiana. Also in the roster are Canadian-Indian master artist Norval Morrisseau, cartoonist-turned-plate-artist Al Hirschfeld, and Nori Peter, famous for her Eskimo subjects.

BAREUTHER

In 1867 a German sculptor founded a porcelain factory in Waldsassen, Bavaria. Johann Matthaeus Ries, with one small porcelain kiln and one anular brick kiln, began producing dinnerware, vases, and giftware. The factory grew and flourished but was sold in 1884 by Ries's son to Oskar Bareuther. The porcelain factory, called Bareuther, has since grown into one of the world's leading factories.

In 1967, to celebrate Bareuther's one-hundredth anniversary, the company issued the first in a series of Christmas plates. Each plate in the series, which still continues today, is decorated in cobalt blue underglaze with an inscription of the year and "Weihnachten." The artist for the first issue was Hans Mueller, who was himself a son of a Bareuther artist. He joined the factory in 1952 as an artist after studying at the Porcelain Academy in Selb. He was promoted to chief designer in 1968.

Since the Christmas Series was so widely accepted, Bareuther released in 1969 the first issues in a Mother's Day Series and a Father's Day Series. These are also done in underglazed cobalt blue with inscriptions "Muttertag" and "Vatertag." A Thanksgiving Day Series was started in 1971, with the first issue titled "First Thanksgiving." To commemorate the first ten years of the very successful Christmas Series, a "Jubilee Plate" was issued in 1977.

Today the Bareuther factory enjoys much popularity with hobbyists in the collectors' market. They continue to produce a new issue each year in their three collector plate series, fine dinnerware and giftware items that are exported to at least thirty countries. The factory's seven hundred employees include sixty painters and sixty printers, who strive to keep Bareuther items as highly respected and valued as they have been for over one hundred years.

BING AND GRONDAHL

When Frederick Grondahl, a porcelain modeler, and Meyer and Jacob Bing, merchant brothers, joined in 1853 to form a porcelain factory, one of today's most widely recognized companies was born. They began their production of bisque plaques the next year from designs by a well-known Danish sculptor named Thorwaldsen. Within ten years their production was such that they decided to add figurines and dinnerware to their line.

With the advent of underglazing by Arnold Krog of Royal Copenhagen, a new aspect of porcelain design began to be experimented with in the Bing and Grondahl factory. The process was much popularized at the World Exhibition in Paris in 1900 by a painter named Willumsen. For years only the "Copenhagen blue" was used to color porcelain wares, but Bing and Grondahl later discovered that other colors, such as black, brown, green, and flesh tones, could withstand the intense heat of a high-gloss firing.

In 1895 Harald Bing decided to make a decorative plate for Christmas. His idea was, first of all, for a functional plate, but he also wanted to add some decoration to an old Danish custom. Traditionally, the wealthy would bring gifts of plates of cakes and cookies to their servants in celebration of the holiday. The plates became more and more decorative through the years. To carry on the tradition, Bing designed a blue and white snow scene that, although intended for practical use, became the first "collectible" plate.

The 1895 plate showed the Copenhagen skyline from "Behind a Frozen Window." The swishes of white against the blue background, as designed by Franz August Hallin, beautifully depicted a Danish winter. Many issues since have also pictured Danish landscapes and have shown designs of the Christmas and religious holiday.

Other than Christmas plates, Bing and Grondahl has produced Mother's Day and Olympic plates and commemorative issues. But the same quality has applied to each item in its line of production. For instance, the hours of hand labor painstakingly used in producing one figurine would add up to weeks of artists' and craftsmen's skillful work.

Today, the quality of Bing and Grondahl products is assured to any buyer by the traditional three-tower backstamp. It depicts the towers used in the coat of arms of the city of Copenhagen. The factory, located in the heart of the city, uses several tons of clay daily in producing its artware, dinnerware, and figurines. Some 1,300 workers skillfully monitor and produce about 10 million pieces each year. Its line of production also includes bells, cameos for jewelry, thimbles, and even high-voltage insulators. The kinds of items are widely varied, but careful inspections take place, and the quality remains consistent throughout all facets of production at the Bing and Grondahl porcelain factory.

FENTON ART GLASS COMPANY

In 1905 two brothers, John and Frank Fenton, opened a glass-decorating business in Martins Ferry, West Virginia, called the Fenton Art Glass Company. In a short time the business, although relatively small, began to appear as a threat of competition to the companies who were supplying Fenton with glass "blanks" for decoration. Consequently, the companies soon refused to deliver any more glass. Within the next two years, the Fenton brothers decided to alleviate the problem by producing their own glass.

The plant, now located in Williamstown, drew skilled glassworkers—one in particular who worked with colors and helped teach other glassworkers to make carnival glass. Many variations have been produced through the years by Fenton because of the many glass treatments that were tried and perfected by craftsmen. Colors were added: caramel slag, or chocolate glass; Burmese, a greenish-yellow shade; milk glass, white and opaque; and Vasa Murrihina, a transparent glass with suspended flakes of mica that appear as silver or gold.

With these innovative ideas put to practice, the company, as a natural step of succession, entered the collector plate market. Fenton had already gained a reputation for their glasswares and were being sought by collectors all over. So in 1970 the first issue in the American Craftman Series was released. The series was created to honor the craftsmen who built America, and the first issue was appropriately titled "Glassmaker." Also in 1970, the Christmas in America Series began with the first issue, "Little Brown Church in the Vale," produced in carnival, blue satin, and brown glass.

The Fenton Art Glass Company is still producing decorative plates and offers designs from their own artists in the decorating department as well as scenes from Currier & Ives. The products made today are different from those first pieces produced in 1907, but all are quality wares from the Fenton Art Glass Company.

FRANKOMA POTTERY

In 1927 a young man of twenty-three moved from Chicago to Norman, Oklahoma, to become an instructor of art and ceramics at the University of Oklahoma. Because of his involvement in studies and geological surveys of the Oklahoma clays, John Frank set a goal to open the first pottery there to produce wares made only from Oklahoma clays. He founded the Frankoma Pottery in 1933, and with one kiln, a butter churn to mix the clay, and fruit jars of glaze, he began making pottery for everyday uses. A clay from Ada was originally used, but on discovering a red-burning clay in Sapula, Frank chose this clay to be the substance from which all Frankoma pottery is made.

Frank and his wife, Grace Lee, struggled through some hard times trying to make their pottery a success. They had grown into a small factory by 1938, when they moved to Sapula to further their studies on clays. The next years were hard, and with their seven employees the Franks developed a once-fired process, where the clay and glaze are fired at the same time as the maturing point of the clay. The rugged, everyday earthenware was durable and beautiful with its bright-colored glazes, but the Frank family decided to try something new.

In 1965 Frank designed a decorative plate that became the first Christmas plate annually produced in America. Inspired by the Christmas story, Frank chose "Good Will Toward Men" as the title of this first in a series that still continues today. A Della Robbia white glaze has a unique affect on each Christmas theme shown in bas-relief. Another series titled Teenagers of the Bible was started in 1973, and a Madonnas Series was designed by Grace Lee. Each issue for each series is produced for one year, and then the mold is destroyed on Christmas Eve.

Since Frank's death in 1973, his daughter Joneice has continued designing the two series originally designed by her father. The Frankoma Pottery today produces about 375 pieces of earthenware pottery, artware, and sculptures. It continues to fill the public's need for the colorful and durable earthenware pottery.

PEMBERTON & OAKES

Pemberton & Oakes Galleries entered the limited-edition field in 1977 to provide high-quality, affordable art to American art collectors. To begin the company's entry into this field, President John Hugunin selected Chicago-based artist Donald Zolan, who had displayed a remarkable ability to capture real-life children in situations that showed the wonder and joy of early childhood.

Pemberton & Oakes issued its first limited-edition plate, the famous "Erik and Dandelion" by Donald Zolan, in 1978. Zolan began winning Favorite Living Plate Artist awards, in addition to Plate of the Year accolades in both the United States and Canada.

"I wanted to see what would happen," Hugunin recalls, "if we pushed the level of plate quality as high as possible and yet kept a tight ceiling on both price and quantity. The result has been a string of award-winning plates that has sold out rapidly and then appreciated even more rapidly on the secondary market. I get letters all the time from collectors who bought their Zolan plates because they were touched by the art but who are also pleased as punch that their plates are worth a whole lot more than they paid for them."

Pemberton & Oakes has also produced major series of collector plates by artists Robert Anderson and Shell Fisher, and it produces the annual "Nutcracker Ballet" plate, which depicts a scene from Tchaikovsky's immortal Christmas ballet.

Pemberton & Oakes is located in beautiful Santa Barbara, California, and welcomes visitors to its gallery. Hours are 9 A.M. to 5 P.M., Monday through Friday. On display are many of the original Zolan oil paintings that formed the basis for his most famous plates, new Zolan works that have yet to be represented in porcelain, and a permanent exhibit of Zolan plates, prints, and figurines. For more information, call or write Pemberton & Oakes Ltd., 133 E. Carrillo Street, Santa Barbara, CA 93101; (805) 963-1371.

ROCKWELL MUSEUM

In 1975 Donald and Marshall Stoltz opened a museum of the largest and most complete exhibit of the works of one of America's best-known artists. Norman Rockwell was the artist who told a pictorial history, clearly and with great detail, of the life of the typical American.

Rockwell was born in 1894, and as early as age five he began drawing. Although he never finished high school, he studied at Chase School of Art and at the National Academy of Art. He also received a degree, a doctorate in Fine Arts, from the University of Vermont. Rockwell's illustrations and paintings reflect a sense of real life, as if he had frozen a moment of life just so he could reproduce it to every exact detail. He gained the American people's attention, if not their hearts, with his illustrations for the covers of the *Saturday Evening Post* and *Boy's Life*.

The Norman Rockwell Museum in Philadelphia represents the reality of a dream after the Stoltz brothers had collected Rockwell's works for over thirty years. In 1978 a selection of twelve works was chosen to portray moments of American life on collector plates. Production of the American Family Series began, and what was originally meant to be a collection of only twelve expanded into a whole new series called American Family Series II. Then, after Rockwell died that same year, a special plate was issued titled "Rockwell Remembered," to pay tribute to his meaningful career.

Since then Rockwell's works have been the subjects of many plates made by the Museum and by many other companies. However, the Museum marks each piece they produce with a seal of authenticity. This seal is round and carries the Museum's name and a silhouette of Rockwell.

A celebration of his life is carried on by the Museum and the Stoltz brothers. The words of Marshall Stoltz express the respect and love for Rockwell illustrations that much of America feels today: "Norman Rockwell was a master at his craft. No one captured America like Rockwell."

ROYAL COPENHAGEN

In the early 1770s a Dane named Frantz Heinrich Muller founded the oldest porcelain factory in Denmark. Four years later, when the company was granted royal privileges, it was named Royal Copenhagen, as it is known today. In 1867 the firm lost its royal status, but this didn't stop its success. When Arnold Krog became the company's director in 1885, he began developing a technique that proved to be a great asset to the field of ceramics.

Royal Copenhagen wares are perhaps best known for a soft appearance common to many plates and figurines. This process, known as underglaze painting, was perfected by Krog in 1888. The method of dipping an object into a transparent glaze after it has been colorfully painted sparked great interest in factories all over Europe. Carving a mold to develop the artist's design in relief worked very well with the underglazed effect to create a unique design since made famous by Royal Copenhagen.

Many companies have used the underglazing process, but a highly recognizable trademark distinguishes Royal Copenhagen from the rest. It consists of three wavy blue lines. Each stands for one of the principal Danish waterways: the Sound, The Great Belt, and The Little Belt. Although there have been minor variations, the trademark has remained steady, just as the quality of its products has. Royal Copenhagen has traditionally drawn talented sculptors and artists to create the right effect for each of its products: the delicacy of porcelain, the sturdiness of stoneware, and the bright colors of faience.

Since its first Christmas plate was produced in 1908, the factory has designed collector plates for eighty years. The company employs 1,700 workers, craftsmen, and technicians. The factory's painters alone comprise 650 of these. Each person does his job in creating Christmas, Mother's Day, historical, and special issue plates. Each strives to continue the traditions that were set many years ago by the original skilled artisans of the Royal Copenhagen porcelain factory.

Glossary

Alabaster. A fine-grained, somewhat translucent kind of gypsum stone or a mottled kind of calcite that is found in marble. (See also Ivory Alabaster.)

Annual. A term used to describe an item issued once a year, or yearly. When used as a series name, *annual* usually means the series is not a commemorative or a holiday issue.

Art Deco. A classical style of art that emphasized symmetrical and rectilinear shapes, such as the cylinder and the rectangle. It was popular from the 1920s to the 1940s in Europe and the United States.

Art Nouveau. A style of art popular in the 1890s and until about 1920. It emphasized decoration rather than form, expressing this often in a whiplash curve and lines of floral and leaflike designs.

Backstamp. A printed or incised symbol or logo, usually found on the underside of an object, that gives some or all of the information on the object's origin, such as the name of the producer, sponsor, or artist, the title, issue date, number of sequence, and artist's signature.

Banding. A term used to describe hand application of metals, such as gold and silver, to the rim of an item.

Baroque. A French word meaning an irregular shape. It was used to describe a style of art popular in the seventeenth and eighteenth centuries. Baroque art was characteristically displayed by dynamic movements, exaggerated ornamentation, bold contrasts, and massive forms.

Basalt. A dense, fine-grained black volcanic stone. Wedgwood introduced black basalts for ornamental and useful wares.

Bas-Relief. A method of decoration on an object in which the design is raised above a background. This is produced either by pouring a liquid mixture into a mold or by applying to a background an already formed design.

Bisque or **Biscuit.** A name applied to any pottery item that has been fired in a kiln once but has not been glazed.

Body. The clay or mixture of substances combined to make any pottery ware.

Bone Ash. The powder produced when animal bones, usually those of oxen, are crushed and ground. It is an ingredient in bone china that makes it appear whiter and more translucent.

Bone China or **Bone Porcelain.** Ceramic wares that are pure white due to added bone ash. It is softer than hard-paste porcelain but more durable than soft-paste porcelain.

Camber. A shape that has a slightly convex-curved surface. The first camber-shaped collector plate was issued in 1982 by Royal Doulton.

Cameo. A carving in relief that has a color contrasting with its background.

Carnival Glass. Inexpensively produced glass made primarily from 1900 to 1925. Items made of carnival glass were originally used as fair prizes. This glass is iridescent and is produced in many colors.

Ceramic. Any ware or work of a potter or any object made from baked clay.

Certificate of Authenticity. A written statement received when an object is bought that assures the origin and sequence number of an edition.

China. A term originally used for all wares produced in China. It is now used in reference to any hard, vitreous, or glassy ceramic consisting of kaolin, ball clay, china stone, feldspar, and flint.

Cinnabar. A bright red mineral found in hydrothermal deposits of volcanic regions. It is the principal ore of mercury and mercuric sulfide.

Cobalt. A steel-gray metallic element used as a pigment in glazes and tin-enamels. The most common use is in cobalt blue glaze.

Crazing. A mesh of cracks in the glaze on a piece of pottery; also called *crackle* if found in Chinese porcelains.

Crystal. A very clear, brilliant glass of fine quality, well suited for prism cuts by refracting light. Full lead crystal contains at least 24 percent lead.

Damascene. A method of decorating by filling inlaid designs with gold or copper, perfected by Reed & Barton.

Delftware. Tin-glazed earthenware that was originally developed in Delft, Holland.

Dresden. A term often used as synonymous with Meissen porcelain. Dresden and Meissen were two cities in East Germany that produced porcelain. The first porcelain produced outside China was discovered by Johann Friedrich Bottger in the Dresden factory in 1709.

Earthenware. Any pottery that is not vitrified. It is the largest kind of pottery, including delftware, faience, and majolica.

Edition. The total number produced of one design in a series.

Electroplating. Method of covering one metal with another by electrolysis.

Embossing. A method of decoration with raised designs, produced either in a mold or with a stamp.

Enamel. A glassy substance with mineral oxides fused to a surface for decoration.

Engraving. A method of decoration produced by cutting into a surface with tools or acids.

Etching. A method of decoration produced by using acid to cut a design. The surface to be decorated is first covered with a wax; then the acid eats into the areas left bare or carved out with a needle.

Faience. A type of earthenware covered in a tin glaze. Faience is increasingly being used to mean the same as delftware and majolica. The difference is that the Delft faience uses a more refined clay. The name comes from an Italian town called Faenza.

Feldspar. A kind of crystalline rock from which kaolin, one of the main components of porcelain and china, is formed when the rock decomposes.

Fire. The process of heating a piece of clay to high temperatures, transforming it into porcelain or pottery.

Flow Blue. The name given to pottery blue underglaze designs because of the slight fuzziness resulting from glazing over the color blue.

Glaze. A liquid compound that, when fired on a ceramic piece, becomes a glasslike surface. It is used to seal the surface so that it is nonabsorbent and resistant to wear.

Glost Fire. A process of firing in a kiln to fuse the glaze.

Hallmark. A stamped or incised mark identifying the manufacturer.

Hard-Paste Porcelain. A vitreous ceramic made primarily of kaolin, or china clay, and petuntse, which is china stone. It is somewhat translucent and when tapped should ring. When chipped, it will have a shell-like or conchoidal shape to the chip.

Incising. A method of cutting into the surface of an object for decoration.

Incolay Stone. A material from which Incolay Studios produces art objects that look like cameos. The process for making it is kept secret by the Studio, but it is known that it contains some quartzlike minerals.

Inlaid. A kind of decoration produced by etching into a surface and then filling the etched-out areas with another substance, usually silver or gold.

Iridescence. The intermingling of colors as in a rainbow or as seen in mother-of-pearl. This may be produced by alkaline glazes on ceramic wares.

Ivory Alabaster. A type of fine-grained nontranslucent gypsum, which may acquire a patina with age.

Jasperware. A hard, unglazed stoneware produced by Wedgwood originally in 1775. Color is added to a naturally white body by mixing in metallic oxides. Pale blue is the most common.

Kaolin. A fine white clay, also called china clay, used to produce china and porcelain.

KPM. The abbreviation for Koenigliche Porzellan Manufacture.

Kiln. An oven in which ceramic pieces are fired.

Limited Edition. A term used to describe an item that is produced for a period of time or in a particular amount previously decided on by the manufacturer.

Lead Crystal. (See Crystal.)

Luster. A film covering an item made of silver, copper, gold, or platinum pigment reduced from an oxide for decoration.

Majolica. Any tin-glazed earthenware from Italy.

Mold. The form that shapes ceramic pieces of art. The object is formed either by pressing clay into the mold or by pouring a liquid clay formula into the mold, and the excess water is absorbed, leaving a hardened shape.

Overglaze. An enameled design painted on top of a fired glaze and then fired again at a lower temperature for permanence.

Parian. A hard-paste porcelain named after parian marble. It is a vitrified china that can be fired at a lower temperature, allowing for a greater variety of possible colors for designs.

Pentuntse. A fusible component of hard-paste porcelain.

Porcelain. A fine, hard, white, vitrified material that is generally fired at about 1400 degrees Celsius. Its chief components are kaolin and pentuntse, and when fired they produce a translucent material that will ring when tapped.

Pottery. A general name given to all ceramic wares. In the present market, it sometimes refers only to earthenware, not including porcelain or any ceramic with a vitrified surface.

Queen's Ware. An earthenware developed by Wedgwood for Queen Charlotte of England in 1765. It is cream in color and is also called white ware.

Relief Decoration. A design that is raised above a background. This is produced either by pouring a liquid clay mixture into a mold or by applying an already formed design to an object.

Satin Glass. Art glass made with a matte finish rather than a polished finish.

Soft-Paste Porcelain. A porcelain made of white firing clay and silicate, a ground-up mass of glass, sand, or broken china. This very translucent material is also called artificial porcelain and is generally fired at about 1100 degrees Celsius.

Stoneware. A name that applies to all vitrified and nonporous pottery, except porcelain.

Terra Cotta. The name used for clay fired without glaze. This type of clay is more often formed by a potter than by a sculptor, who produces earthenware.

Tin Glaze. A dense lead glaze that is colored white and made opaque by adding ashes of tin. It may also be colored by adding metallic oxides.

Toriart. A method of molding wood shavings into a solid form, perfected by the House of Anri. The forms may then be carved to carry a design or may already have a relief design from the mold.

Translucence. A property of some ceramics in which light can be seen through an object that is not transparent.

Triptych. A set of three paintings with a common theme, usually religious, connected together and often used as an altarpiece.

Underglaze. A method in which colors are painted on ceramic bisque, which is then dipped in glaze and fired a second time.

Vitreous or **Vitrification.** The condition of a ceramic object when fired that results in a glassy and impermeable surface.

Publications

PLATE WORLD. If you're a serious plate collector or would like to become one, this bimonthly (six times per year) publication from the Bradford Exchange is a must. It's a slick, full-color, well-designed magazine with enough news and views on plates to satisfy even the most avid enthusiast. Regular features include

- articles on and interviews with artists, retailers, manufacturers, collectors, etc.
- features on plate series and themes
- plate collecting tips
- comprehensive information on new plate issues
- a question-and-answer column to answer specific reader queries
- current price quotes on hotly traded plates from the Bradford Exchange trading floor

Subscription rates: $19.50 per year, $21.50 outside the U.S. Subscription address: Plate World, Circulation Service Center, P.O. Box 1085, Skokie, IL 60076; (312) 647-7124. Editorial offices: Plate World, 9200 N. Maryland Ave., Niles, IL 60648. Editor: Alyson Sulaski Wyckoff.

COLLECTORS MART. Billed as the "Magazine of Art Collectibles," this quarterly magazine covers a wide range of limited-edition collectibles. Plates are featured, though not nearly as comprehensively as in *Plate World*. Dolls, prints, figurines, and teddy bears are also included regularly. In May 1987 a new editor, Susan Elliott, was brought aboard. Susan previously edited *Plate Collector* magazine, *Plate World*'s major competitor until it ceased publication in 1986. Collectors' Information Bureau price listings of many limited-edition items are included twice yearly.

Subscription rates: $12 per year. Subscription and editorial address: WEB Publications, Inc., P.O. Box 12830, Wichita, KS 67277; (316) 722-9750. Editor: Susan Elliott.

COLLECTOR EDITIONS. Another magazine that covers plates to some degree but also features dolls, figurines, art glass, etc. It has more of a giftware feel to it than the others and a high advertising-to-editorial ratio.

Subscription rates: $14 per year; published quarterly, in March, June, September, and November. Subscription address: Collector Editions, 95 Rockwell Road, Marion, OH 43305; (614) 383-3141. Editorial address: Collector Communications Corp., 170 Fifth Avenue, 12th Floor, New York, NY 10010; (212) 989-8700. Editorial Director: Krystyna Poray Goddu.

COLLECTORS NEWS. This is a monthly tabloid newspaper that has a section each issue on collector plates. Most of the editorial content appears to be press releases from plate manufacturers.

Subscription rates: $15.97 per year; outside U.S., $22.47 in U.S. funds. Subscription address: Collectors News, P.O. Box 156, Grundy Center, IA 50638; (319) 824-5456. Editor: Linda Kruger.

ANTIQUE TRADER. This weekly tabloid newspaper has been around since 1957 and covers a wide range in the antique and collectibles field. There are brief, incomplete listings on new plate issues and some occasional editorial on the subject; filled with classifieds for all types of collector items.

Subscription rates: $22 per year for 52 weekly issues. Subscription address: The Antique Trader, P.O. Box 1050, Dubuque, IA 52001; (319) 588-2073.

1987 NALED List
of Dealer Members

Accents
Carol Backhus
1412 Loop 336 West
Conroe, TX 77304
(409) 756-7704

Accent on Collectibles
Rosalie Brown
12002 N.E. Glisan
Portland, OR 97220
(503) 253-0841

A Country Mouse
Dorothy Smith
7940 W. Layton
Milwaukee, WI 53220
(414) 281-4210

Andrew's Limited Editions
Mark & Pat Andrews
Box 20743, Garfield Ave. S.
Minneapolis, MN 55420
(612) 888-8511

Apple Tree East
Ron Schuster
4447 Buffalo Road
Erie, PA 16510
(814) 898-1789

Aracoma Drug Gift Galleries
George Kostas
305 Stratton
P.O. Box 507
Logan, WV 25601
(304) 752-3811

Armstrong Enterprises
David Armstrong
150 East Third Street
Pomona, CA 91766
(714) 623-6464

Bartom Imports
Betty Sterk
435 Ridge Road
Munster, IN 46321
(219) 836-2115

Bee Hive Gifts, Inc.
Richard & Elsie Bolinger
358 W. North Boo
Burns Harbor, IN 46304
(219) 787-8745

Bergstrand's
John & Eunice Bergstrand
200 N. Central Avenue
Straus Mall
Valley City, ND 58072
(701) 845-4252

Betty Jeans
Betty Bauman–Jean Ziolkowski
2082 W. Main St.
Norristown, PA 19403
(215) 539-4563

Betty's Collectibles Ltd.
Betty Farris
2204 Riverside Dr.
Harlingen, TX 78550
(512) 423-8234

Blevins Plates & Things
Larry Blevins
Georgia Street Plaza
301 Georgia Street
Vallejo, CA 94590
(707) 642-7505

Bodzer's Collectibles
Dolly Bodzer
White Marsh Mall
8200 Perry Hall Blvd.
Baltimore, MD 21236
(301) 529-0200

The Bradford Exchange
Peter Howard
9301 Milwaukee Ave.
Niles, IL 60648
(312) 966-2770

C C Collectibles
Bill & Ceil Hays
702 Huntington Pike
Rockledge, PA 19111
(215) 663-1202

The Calico Butterfly
Franklin Stephenson
6030 Hickory Ridge Mall
Memphis, TN 38115
(901) 362-8121

Caravan Gifts & Photo
Judy Achey
614 Fenton Square
Fenton, MI 48430
(313) 629-4212

Card & Gift Gallery
Ronald Schwartz
1163 E. Ogden
Naperville, IL 60540
(312) 355-2225

Carol's Gift Shop
Marge & Joe Rosenberg
17601 S. Pioneer Blvd.
Artesia, CA 90701
(213) 924-6335

Carousel Gifts
Wanda Nasses
4550-86 E. Cactus Road
Phoenix, AZ 85032
(602) 953-1429

Cellar Antiques
Robert Sadoff
1611 Keith St.
Baraboo, WI 53913
(608) 356-5118

Century Coin Service
Earl Leach
2473 Sun Valley Ct.
Green Bay, WI 54304
(414) 494-2719

Ceramica Gift Gallery
Shlomo Tsadok
1009 Avenue of the Americas
New York, NY 10018
(212) 354-9216

The Chalet Collectors Gallery
Howard & Christine Hemmerling
7024 27th St. West
Tacoma, WA 98466
(206) 564-0326

Cherie's Gallery
Harold & Cherie Hilgenberg
1234 W. Lake St.
Hanover Park, IL 60103
(312) 830-1110

The Clock Man Gallery
Ruth & Bruce Wally
Poughkeepsie Plaza, Route 9
Poughkeepsie, NY 12601
(914) 473-9055

Collectible Cottage
Diane Hollis
2530 Snow Rogers Rd.
P.O. Box 511
Gardendale, AL 35071
(205) 631-2413

Collectible Heirlooms
Laura Anderson
271 Pasadena Town Square
Pasadena, TX 77506
(713) 473-2820

Collectibly Yours
Rhea Mikes
38 East Rt. 59
Spring Valley, NY 10977
(914) 425-9244

Collectors Corner
Agnes Petzold
109 Route 101 A
Amherst, NH 03031
(603) 883-5880

Collectors Emporium
Steve & Illona Bloom
600 Meadowland Parkway
Secaucus, NJ 07094
(201) 863-2977

Collector's Galleria, Inc.
Katherine Evans
Sutter Place Mall
5221 S. 48th St.
Lincoln, NE 68516
(402) 483-5620

Collector's Gallery
Jo Lynn Powell
7115 Blanco, Suite 112
San Antonio, TX 78216
(512) 341-7222

Collector's Gift Gallery
Sue Cox
700 S.E. Chkalov Dr. Suite 11
Vancouver, WA 98684
(206) 256-6963

Commemorative Imports
Daryl Moeller
Rt. 2, Box 129
Ireton, IA 51027
(712) 278-2024

Coppola's
Louise Dosdourian
P.O. Box 1309
630 Grand Ave.
Carlsbad, CA 92008
(619) 729-0256

Crown Card & Gift Shop
Laura Cohen
Moorestown Mall
Moorestown, NJ 08057
(609) 235-3526

Crystal Fair
Mary Mamut
725 S. Adams Rd.
Birmingham, MI 48011
(313) 642-3660

Dare to Be Different
Alice Jensen
159 & Cedar Rd.
Route 6, Box 367
Lockport, IL 60441
(815) 838-8642

Dave & Janelle's
Janelle Patrick
543 18th S.E.
Mason City, IA 50401
(515) 423-6377

Davern's Gifts, Inc.
Maggi Davern
117 Loehmann's Plaza
St. Paul, MN 55113
(612) 636-1716

David's of Kingwood
David White
4321 Kingwood Dr.
Kingwood, TX 77345
(713) 360-3402

DeLuca's Gallery of Collectibles
Joanne & Joe DeLuca
Stage House Village
Scotch Plains, NJ 07076
(201) 322-7750

Design Galleries
Paul & Flori Stark
Wyoming Valley Mall
Wilkes-Barre, PA 18702
(717) 822-6704

Diamond Jewelry Co.
Beverly Levin
Cobb Place No. 5
800 Ernest Barrett Pkwy.
Kennesaw, GA 30144
(404) 428-6170

Double L Collectibles & Gifts
Mrs. L. H. Harris
1455 West 14 Mile Rd.
Madison Heights, MI 48071
(313) 588-9494

Down's Collector's Showcase
William Spray
2200 S. 114th St.
Milwaukee, WI 53227
(414) 327-3300

Eloise's Collectibles
Eloise Parks
9395 Richmond Avenue
Houston, TX 77063
(713) 783-3611

The Emporium
Lucretia Biddle
611 E. 23 St.
Panama City, FL 32405
(904) 785-2737

Especially Unlimited
Wren & Elaine Harper
800 D'Olive St
P.O. Box 1108
Bay Minette, AL 36507
(205) 937-2883

European Imports
Edward Delgau
Oak Mill Mall, European Village
7900 N. Milwaukee Ave.
Niles, IL 60648
(312) 967-5253

Eva Marie
Eva Simmons
1915 S. Catalina Ave.
Redondo Beach, CA 90277
(213) 375-8422

Marianne K Festersen Plates &
  Antiques
Marianne Festersen
701 N. 72 Ave.
Omaha, NE 68114
(402) 393-4454

Fifth Avenue Gallery
Nick Kreiman
Liberty Tree Mall
Danvers, MA 01923
(617) 922-0490

Figurine World
Judy Koch
Lake Forest Mall
701 Russell Ave.
Gaithersburg, MD 20877
(301) 977-3997

Forte Olivia
Olive Matthews
675 S. Glendora Ave.
West Covina, CA 91790
(213) 962-2588

Fox's Gifts & Collectables
Genevra Fox
6948 Fifth Ave.
Scottsdale, AZ 85251
(602) 947-0560

The Gallery
Jean Gibbs
Roosevelt Mall
Jacksonville, FL 32210
(904) 384-2929

Gazebo Gifts/Mercury Florists
Edwin Wilson Jr.
293 Newmarket North
Newport News, VA 23605
(804) 826-5748

Gems In Glass
Barrett & Carmen Lasher
1157 Green St.
Iselin, NJ 08830
(201) 283-1586

Genna's
John & Kathy Genna
29092 Van Dyke
Warren, MI 48093
(313) 573-4542

Georgia's Gift Gallery
Michelle Suttle, Michael McCarty
615 N. Mill St.
Plymouth, MI 48170
(313) 453-7733

Gift Garden
Tri Gupta
498 Euclid Square Mall
Euclid, OH 44132
(216) 289-0116

Gifts du Jour
Joann Fourish
4 Larchmont Centre
Rt. 38 & Ark Road
Mount Holly, NJ 08060
(609) 234-2044

Gillespie Jeweler Collectors Gallery
Leighton Gouck
1774 Main St.
Northampton, PA 18067
(215) 261-0882

Glomar Ltd.
Gloria & Marshall Burns
9530 April Rd.
Miami, FL 33157
(305) 238-3884

The Gold Shoppe
Bob Bianchi
Rainier Place
4009 Tacoma Mall Bvld., Suite 2
Tacoma, WA 98409
(206) 473-4653

Grandmother's Corner Gallery
Dana Swain
120 W. Dayton St., Suite A2
Edmonds, WA 98020
(206) 789-0747

Great Temptations
Ann & Winfield Scott
917 N. Glynn St.
Fayetteville, GA 30214
(404) 461-1657

Haddad's Gifts, Inc.
Robert & Beverly Haddad
Logan Square Shopping Center
3222 S. Logan
Lansing, MI 48910
(517) 882-8334

Hall of Cards & Books
Robert Sones
2232 S. Eleventh St.
Niles, MI 49120
(616) 684-5115

Hawke Hollow
Char Hawks
106 S. Riverview
Bellevue, IA 52031
(319) 872-5467

Heirloom Jewelers
George Jones
219 E. State St.
Centerville, IA 52544
(515) 856-5715

Heirlooms of Tomorrow
Pearl Finkelstein
2178½ N.E. 123 St.
North Miami, FL 33181
(305) 899-0920

Hickory House
Karl Wilz
819 North Court
Ottumwa, IA 52501
(515) 682-8391

Hollywood Limited Editions
W. G. Freudenberg III
6990 Central Park Ave.
Lincolnwood, IL 60645
(312) 673-3250

The Hourglass
Randy Blue–Helen Stallbaumer
4600 W. Kellogg Towne West
  Square
Wichita, KS 67209
(316) 942-0562

E. W. Hunt Imports
Ernestine Hunt
2136 Center Ave.
P.O. Box 387
Bay City, MI 48708
(517) 892-6639

Island Treasures
Betty Caggiano–Jo Franklin
2845 Richmond Ave.
Staten Island, NY 10314
(718) 698-1234

International House
Larry Agins
Lakeview Plaza
15802 LaGrange Road
Orland Park, IL 60462
(312) 349-3366

It's A Small World
Anne Napolitano
827 Annadale Road
Staten Island, NY 10312
(718) 984-7510

J & J Collectibles
Doris & Henry Scheid
9250 N. 43rd Avenue #20
Glendale, AZ 85302
(602) 242-4243

J & L Collectibles
Judy Baker & Lyn Gay
Beacon Plaza
111 D Bullard Parkway
Tampa, FL 33617
(813) 985-0483

Jeri's Hallmark
Charlene Cram
230 Virginia
Crystal Lake, IL 60014
(815) 459-8926

Joy's Lamplight Shoppe
Don Parker
5480 E. Avon Road
Avon, NY 14414
(716) 226-3341

Karen's Collector Corner
Karen Hood
East 13817 Sprague Suite 6A
Spokane, WA 99216
(509) 924-5687

The Kent Collection
Reda Walsh
2223 S. Monaco Parkway
Willa Monaco Center
Denver, CO 80222
(303) 753-9600

Kiefer's Galleries Limited
John & Ray Kiefer
26 S. LaGrange Road
LaGrange, IL 60525
(312) 354-1888

Kiefer's Gallery of Cresthill
Kitty Kiefer
2364 Plainfield Rd.
Cresthill, IL 60435
(815) 744-4547

Kings Gallery of Collectables
Cornelia & King Minister
1912 W. Colorado Ave.
Colorado Springs, CO 80904
(303) 636-2828

L & L Gifts
Leonard & Lucinda Brester
1720 N. Bell
Fremont, NE 68025
(402) 727-7275

Lena's Gift Gallery
Judy Lena
137 E. 4th Ave.
San Mateo, CA 94401
(415) 342-1304

The Leonard Gallery
Cheryl Cohen
1067 E. Columbus Ave.
Springfield, MA 01105
(413) 733-9492

The Limited Edition
Ruth Wolf
2170 Sunrise Highway
Merrick, NY 11566
(516) 623-4400

Limited Plates
Karen Henry–Evelyn Bruce
313 Main St.
Collegeville, PA 19426
(215) 489-7799

Little Shop on the Portage
Mary Asmus
330 W. Main
Woodville, OH 43469
(419) 849-3742

Lorrie's Collectibles
Lorrie Church
3107 Eubank N.E. Suite 34
Albuquerque, NM 87111
(505) 292-0020

Louise Marie's Fine Gifts
Louise Grutzeck
186 S. "K" Street
Livermore, CA 94550
(415) 449-5757

Lynn's & Company
Lois Knaack
17 S. Dunton
Arlington Heights, IL 60005
(312) 870-1188

McCrystal's Crystals & Collectibles
Maureen Schellorn–Cathleen
  McCrystal
260 Deer Park Ave.
Babylon, NY 11702
(516) 587-8823

McHugh's Gifts & Collectibles
Don & Shirley Humes
3822 14th Ave.
Rock Island, IL 61201
(309) 788-9525

McNamara's of Boca Raton
David McNamara
1107 Galdes Plaza, 2200 Glades
  Rd.
Boca Raton, FL 33431
(305) 395-2343

Marg's Mania
Paul & Margaret Norfolk
6900 Nashville Rd.
Lanham/Seabrook, MD 20706
(301) 552-2425

Marylyn's Collectibles
Marylyn Knoner
9862A Metro Parkway East
Phoenix, AZ 85051
(602) 943-0438

Matawan Card & Gift
John & Maryann Buglino
Rt. 34 & Lloyd Road
Matawan, NJ 07747
(201) 583-9449

Nasser's, Inc.
Maurice Nasser
New London Shopping Center,
   Rt. 1
New London, CT 06320
(203) 443-6523

North Hill Gift Shop
Betty McKenney
255 E. Tallmadge Ave.
Akron, OH 44310
(216) 535-4811

Northern Lights
Peter Clark
1560 Fourth St.
San Rafael, CA 94901
(415) 457-2884

Notes-A-Plenty Gift Shoppe
John & Mary Krauss
The Waystation, Fulper Rd.
Flemington, NJ 08822
(201) 782-0700

Nyborg Castle Gifts & Collectibles
Bea Nyborg
Virginia Hills Shopping Center
6662 Alhambra Ave.
Martinez, CA 94553-0888
(415) 930-0200

Oakwood Cards & Gifts
Ralph Freid
Oaktree Rd. & Wood Ave.
Edison, NJ 08820
(201) 549-9494

Odyssey
Basil & Linda Janavaras
1675 Mankato Mall
Mankato, MN 56001
(507) 388-2004

Old Wagon Gifts
Don & Liz Peseux
Colts Town Plaza
41 Rt. 34 South, P.O. Box 238
Colts Neck, NJ 07722
(201) 780-6656

P M Collectibles
Myron & Patricia Nigh
10875 N. Wolfe Road
Cupertino, CA 95014
(408) 725-8858

Pat's Place
Patricia Pettyjohn
11035 Tronwood Rd.
San Diego, CA 92131
(619) 271-8117

Paul's Economy Pharmacy
Rhoda Turkowitz
169 Richmond Ave.
Staten Island, NY 10302
(718) 442-2924

Peppermill Collectables
Ver Handler–Helen Powell
1101 Candace Lane
LaHabra, CA 90631
(213) 691-2315

The Plate Cottage
Frank & Margaret Weiskopf
430-1 N. Country Rd.
St. James, NY 11780
(516) 862-7171

The Plate Lady
Lenore Crawford Gearns
16347 Middlebelt Road
Livonia, MI 48154
(313) 261-5220

The Plate Lady of Opera
Jan Patterson
601 Van Ness Ave.
San Francisco, CA 94102
(415) 673-1491

Plates Etc.
Carol Hastie
8050 Chase Dr.
Arvada, CO 80003
(303) 426-7785

Plates 'N Things
Lucille Wasmer
2013 Carolyn Terrace
Valdosta, GA 31601
(912) 244-0777

The Present Peddler
Lynn Nichols
9532 S.W. Washington Sq.
Portland, OR 97223
(503) 639-2325

Raphael Galleries Ltd.
Ralph & Gertrude Plotkin
3200 Las Vegas Blvd. S.
Las Vegas, NV 89109
(702) 732-9523

Raven's Hallmark Cards
Robert & Arlene Raven
3568 Tyler Mall
Riverside, CA 92503
(714) 688-2454

Red Cross Pharmacy, Inc.
Kris Busch
146 Walnut St.
Spooner, WI 54801
(715) 635-2117

Rochelle's Fine Gifts
Rochelle Pfaff
344 Franklin Park Mall
Toledo, OH 43623
(419) 472-7673

Rocking Horse Gift Shoppe
Lisa Vereneck
At The Crossroads
Bakerstown, PA 16059
(412) 443-0450

Rosemary's Collectibles
Rosemary & Ronald Bunes
19158 Fort
Riverview, MI 48192
(313) 479-0494

Rosemary's Place, Inc.
George & Rosemary Schessler
144 Marina Dr.
Long Beach, CA 90803
(213) 430-4992

Rummel's Village Guild
Helene Rummel
1859 Montebello Town Center
Montebello, CA 90640
(213) 722-2691

Rystad's Limited Editions
Dean Rystad
1013 Lincoln Ave.
San Jose, CA 92125
(408) 279-1960

Sandalmar
Sandra Romano
Mesa Plaza
2319 Bridge Ave.
Point Pleasant, NJ 08742
(201) 892-5599

Saville's Limited Editions
Mayne Saville
Northway Mall
1128 McKnight Rd.
Pittsburgh, PA 15237
(412) 366-5458

Saxony Imports
Albert Shmalo
38 W. 5th St.
Cincinnati, OH 45202
(513) 621-7800

Schnitzelbank Woodcarving Shop
Judy Humpert
545 S. Main St.
Frankenmuth, MI 48734
(517) 652-8331

Schultz Gift Gallery
Mildred Schultz
219 Kaiser St.
P.O. Box 598
Pinconning, MI 48650
(517) 879-3110

Schumm Pharmacy & Gifts
Thomas & Diane Schumm
504 S. Main St.
Rockford, OH 45862
(419) 363-3630

Seefeldt Gallery
Charles & Edith Seefeldt
Pavilion Place
1655 W. Co. Rd. B2
Roseville, MN 55113
(612) 631-1397

Shropshire Curiosity Shop
Edna Samara
600 Main Street
Shrewsbury, MA 01545
(617) 842-4202

The Side Door
Winifred Slack
4094 S. Washington Rd.
McMurray, PA 15317
(412) 941-3750

Sir Richard Tobacco Shoppe
Adrienne Teuschen
Edison Mall
Ft. Myers, FL 33901
(813) 936-6660

Sir Timothy of Stratford
Timothy Buckley
Stratford Square
Bloomingdale, IL 60108
(312) 980-9797

Something So Special
Diane Tureson
1617 N. Alpine Rd.
Rockford, IL 61107
(815) 226-1331

Stage Crossing Gifts & Collectibles
Harold & Virginia Schwartz
5800 Stage Road
Bartlett, TN 38134
(901) 372-4438

Stage Road Interiors
R. David Mauk
101 W. Main
Jonesborough, TN 37659
(615) 753-6116

Stanley's Gifts
Max & Jean Kelso
Hilltop Plaza
Clovis, NM 88101
(505) 769-0007

Stones Hallmark Shops
David Stone
2508 S. Alpine
Rockford, IL 61108
(815) 399-4481

Stovall's
Carolina Canales
412 North Star Mall
San Antonio, TX 78216
(512) 344-8921

Strawberry House
Arlene Young
229 Banbury Rd.
Mundelein, IL 60060
(312) 566-8149

Strohl's Limited Editions
Daris & Garland Strohl
118 N. Morgan St.
Shelbyville, IL 62565
(217) 774-5222

Sunshine House Collectibles
Joan & Hirshel Parrish
914 18th St.
Plano, TX 75074
(214) 424-5015

Suzanne's Collectors Gallery
Suzanne Stoll
Rt. 1, Box 131, Spring River Rd.
Miami, OK 74354
(918) 542-3808

Swiss Miss Shop
Tom & Pepper Dugdale
8455 Highway 24
P.O. Box 10
Cascade, CO 80809
(303) 684-9679

Tannenbaum Shoppe
Arlene Wagner
645 Front St.
Leavenworth, WA 98826
(509) 548-7014

Today's Pleasure Tomorrow's Treasure
Linda Matrafailo
93B Hessinger Lare Rd.
Jeffersonville, NY 12748
(914) 482-3690

Tomorrow's Treasures
Vivian Mullen
3310 W. Fox Ridge
Muncie, IN 47368
(317) 284-6355

Tomorrow's Treasures
Shirley & George Kraus
2456 Conowingo Rd.
Bel Air, MD 21014
(301) 836-9075

The Tower Shop
Robert Flynn
17 E. Burlington
Riverside, IL 60546
(312) 447-5258

Viking Import House
Pat Owen
412 S.E. 6th St.
Fort Lauderdale, FL 33301
(305) 763-3388

Village Gift Shop
Rose Ann Narchus
2333 Niagara Falls Blvd.
Tonawanda, NY 14120
(716) 691-4425

Village Plate Collector
Lois Felder
217 King St.
P.O. Box 1118
Cocoa, FL 32922
(305) 636-6914

Walter's Collectibles
William Walter
1647 East Main St.
Plainfield, IN 46168
(317) 839-2954

Washington Square Limited
Helen Yanek
605 Christiana Mall
Newark, DE 19702
(302) 453-1776

Watson's
Winnie Watson Sweet
135 E. Michigan St.
New Carlisle, IN 46552
(219) 654-3550

Wee House of Collectibles
Dolly & Joe Buzer
372 Camino De Estrella
San Clemente, CA 92672
(714) 496-8811

Weston's Limited Editions
Hermine & Arthur Weston
105 Monmouth St.
Red Bank, NJ 07701
(201) 747-8220

The Wilson Gallery of Collectibles
Bill Wilson
2080 Stonington Ave.
Hoffman Estates, IL 60195
(312) 882-5111

Wishing Well
Victor Peles
3050-64 N. 5th St. Highway
Reading, PA 19605

Zaslow's Fine Collectibles
Marlene & Irv Zaslow
Strathmore Shopping Center
Matawan, NJ 07747
(201) 583-1499

1987 Canadian Limited Edition Dealer Members

The following is a list of Canadian limited edition dealers supplied to the House of Collectibles by Fred Knight, treasurer of the Canadian Association of Limited Edition Dealers.

Allan's Collectibles
601 Dundas Street
Woodstock, Ontario
N4S 1C9
Attention: Allan Hilderlay

Avenue Jewellers Ltd.
873 Portage Avenue
Winnipeg, Manitoba
R2C 2G3
Attention: Boris Romanow

Bakerosa
188 Deer Park Circle
London, Ontario
N6H 3C1
Attention: Art and Sheila
  Baker

Bargoon Palace
10154 Yonge Street
Richmond Hill, Ontario
L4C 1T6
Attention: Don Levitt

Blue Jay Collectables
160 Main Street S. (Brampton
  Mall)
Brampton, Ontario
L6W 2E1
Attention: Bill and Judi Dann

Browsers Nook
360 George Street N.
Peterborough, Ontario
K9H 7E7
Attention: Angie Hochley

Central Flowers & Gifts
3237 Kalum Street
Terrace, British Columbia
V8G 2N3
Attention: Sheila Jackson, Linda
  McBean

Charles House of Plates
P.O. Box 160, 39 Main Street
Bloomfield, Ontario
K0K 1G0
Attention: Charles and Reta
  Scoyne

Chornyj's Hadke
884 Queen Street E.
Sault Ste. Marie, Ontario
P6A 2B4
Attention: Anthony Chornyj

Colonial Plates
7 Water Street
St. Mary's, Ontario
N0M 2V0
Attention: Claudia and Doug
  Forster

Comyn Collectibles
Box 6616, Station "J"
Ottawa, Ontario
K2A 3Y7
Attention: Alex Cumming

Dania Unique Inc.
3350 Fairview St.,
Burlington, Ontario
L7N 3L5
Attention: Willy Kjarsgaard, Asta
  Ostergaard

Distinctive Collectibles
P.O. Box 178
Selkirk, Manitoba
R1A 2B2
Attention: Elsie Wyspinski

Durand Diamonds & Jewels Ltd.
1 Stadium Shopping Centre
Calgary, Alberta
T2N 2V2
Attention: Hazel Durand

Excelsior Jewellers Ltd.
24C South Second Avenue
Williams Lake, B.C.
V2G 1H6
Attention: Joe Amaral

Fraser's Classic Collectables
P.O. Box 212, Station "M"
Toronto, Ontario
M6S 4T3

G. Smith's Jewellery Stores Inc.
P.O. Box 74
Cayuga, Ontario
N0A 1E0
Attention: Gwen Smith

Homestead Gift Shop
R.R. 2, 3905 Rte. 147
Lennoxville, Quebec
J1M 2A3
Attention: Bev Musty

Huffman's Antiques
R.R. 4, Hwy. 2
Belleville, Ontario
K8N 4Z4
Attention: Ruth Huffman

Hyette's Giftware Ltd.
3156 Mussery Drive
Prince George, B.C.
V2N 2S9
Attention: Larry Hyette, Ann
  Sherba

K & R Collectibles
795 Delaware Avenue
Sudbury, Ontario
P3A 3X5
Attention: Keith and Ruth Godin

Kay's Place
14 Gibbons Street
Oshawa, Ontario
L1J 4X7
Attention: Kay and Fred Knight

King's Hut Treasures
22 Charing Cross Street
Brantford, Ontario
N3R 2H2
Attention: Alfreda Trupp

Lee's Jade & Opals Ltd.
3563-232nd Street
R.R. 12, Langley B.C.
V3A 7B9

McIntosh & Watts Ltd.
2425 Holly Lane
Ottawa, Ontario
K1V 7P2
Attention: John McIntosh

Middaugh's Collectibles
45 Albert Street
Clinton, Ontario
N0M 1L0
Attention: Marlene Armstrong

Mitchell & Jewell Ltd.
4812 Gaetz Avenue
P.O. Box 388,
Red Deer, Alberta
T4N 5E9

Model Drug Store (1973) Ltd.
32 Birch St., P.O. Box 190
Chapleau, Ontario
P0M 1K0
Attention: Irene P. MacNeil

Oak Bay Florist Ltd.
#115, 2515-90th Avenue S.W.
Oak Bay Plaza, Calgary, Alta.
T2V 0L8
Attention: Nola Merchant

Ostrander's Jewellers
Fairview Park Shopping Centre
Kitchener, Ontario
N2C 1X1
Attention: Barry Chiswell

Pedden's Collector Plates
R.R. 6
Strathroy, Ontario
N7G 3H7
Attention: Dorothy Pedden

Plates Unlimited
129 McCannel Street
Regina, Saskatchewan
S4R 3T9
Attention: Peter Stom

Plato's Collector Plates
12-10015-82nd Avenue
Edmonton, Alberta
T6E 1Z2
Attention: Percy Connell

Precious Plates 'N Things
108 Brock St. N.
Whitby, Ontario
L1N 4H2
Attention: Pat Schleiffer

Queensbury Collectibles Ltd.
708 Queensbury Avenue
North Vancouver B.C.
V7L 3V8
Attention: Betty Dully

Randall's Book Store
52 Walton Street
Port Hope, Ontario
L1A 1N1
Attention: Mel Talbot

Reflections on Plates
13389-72nd Avenue
Surrey, B.C.
V3W 2N5
Attention: Jackie Schwark

Rick's Velvet Interiors Inc.
2603 West Railway
Abbotsford, B.C.
V2S 2E3
Attention: Rick Peters

*Rob McIntosh China & Crystal
   Shops*
Cornwall Square, 1 Water St. E.
Cornwall, Ontario
K6H 6M2
Attention: Rob and Barb
   McIntosh

Rock & Rail Gift Shop
Box 172
Mindemoya, Ontario
P0P 1S0
Attention: Mrs. Willie Keller

Shabsove's The Collector's Gallery
81 Auriga Drive
Nepean (Ottawa) Ontario
K2E 7V7
Attention: Mr. Shabsove

Shortreed Stationery
181 St. Andrew St. W.
Fergus, Ontario
N1M 1N6
Attention: Jerry and Gladys
   Shortreed

Stairway to Collectables
130 Garafraxa Street S.
Durham, Ontario
N0G 1R0
Attention: George Benninger,
   Rosemary Ringler

Stein Bros. Collectibles
20472 Fraser Highway
Langley, B.C.
V3A 4G2
Attention: Christine Steinmann,
   Manfred Steinmann

Sussex Antiques
435 East Columbia Street
New Westminster B.C.
V3L 3X4
Attention: Don and Pat Peters

The Challenge
R.R. 3
Colborne, Ontario
K0K 1S0
Attention: Eileen Hughes

The Country Collection
R.R. 3
Pakenham, Ontario
K0A 2X0
Attention: Myrlak Levi

The Plate Connection
2016 Sherwood Drive
Sherwood Park, Alberta
T6E 3X3
Attention: Martin and Joan Smee

The Red Pelican
225 Fairview Drive
Brantford, Ontario
N3R 7E3
Attention: Pat Rivait

The Site of the Green Ltd.
R.R. 1
Dundas, Ontario
L9H 5E1
Attention: Ian Campbell, Linda
  Campbell

Timeless Treasures
2684 Midland Avenue
Agincourt, Ontario
M1S 1R7
Attention: Maynard Dacey

Vi's Glass & China
51 Wilson Street, W.
Ancaster, Ontario
L9G 1N1
Attention: Vi Brennan

How to Use
This Book

The plates are listed first by manufacturer, arranged alphabetically. They are further broken down by series, also alphabetically. Year of issue is followed by plate title, production quantity, the price the plate was issued at, and the current value. The reader may note an XX marking, where the date should be, in various listings. This means the year of issue is unknown.

An index is provided at the back of this book to help locate a particular plate, listed by artist and manufacturer.

Collector Plate Listings

ACCENT ON ART

United States

	Issue Price	Current Value
MOTHER GOOSE SERIES		
☐ **1978** **Jack and Jill,** artist: Oscar Graves, production quantity 5,000	59.50	80.00
NOBILITY OF THE PLAINS SERIES		
☐ **1978** **The Comanche,** artist: Oscar Graves, production quantity 12,500	80.00	80.00
☐ **1979** **Moving Day,** artist: Oscar Graves, production quantity 3,500	80.00	80.00

COUNT AGAZZI

Italy

CHILDREN'S HOUR SERIES		
☐ **1970** **Owl,** production quantity 2,000	12.50	12.50
☐ **1971** **Cat,** production quantity 2,000	12.50	12.50
☐ **1972** **Pony,** production quantity 2,000	12.50	12.50
☐ **1973** **Panda,** production quantity 2,000	12.50	12.50

		Issue Price	Current Value
EASTER SERIES			
☐ 1971	**Playing The Violin,** production quantity 600	12.50	12.50
☐ 1972	**At Prayer,** production quantity 600 . . . . , . .	12.50	12.50
☐ 1973	**Winged Cherub,** production quantity 600 . .	12.50	12.00
FAMOUS PERSONALITIES SERIES			
☐ 1968	**Famous Personalities,** production quantity 600	8.00	8.00
☐ 1970	**Famous Personalities,** production quantity 1,000	12.50	12.00
☐ 1973	**Famous Personalities,** production quantity 600	15.00	15.00
FATHER'S DAY SERIES			
☐ 1972	**Father's Day,** production quantity 144	35.00	35.00
☐ 1973	**Father's Day,** production quantity 288	19.50	20.00
MOTHER'S DAY SERIES			
☐ 1972	**Mother's Day,** production quantity 144 . . .	35.00	35.00
☐ 1973	**Mother's Day,** production quantity 720 . . .	19.50	20.00
SINGLE RELEASES			
☐ 1969	**Apollo II,** production quantity 1,000	17.00	17.00
☐ 1973	**Peace,** production quantity 720	12.50	12.50

ALLISON AND COMPANY

United States

LATE TO PARTY			
☐ 1982	**Piece of Cake,** artist: Betty Allison, production quantity 12,500	35.00	35.00
☐ 1983	**Cheese Please,** artist: Betty Allison, production quantity 12,500	35.00	35.00
☐ 1983	**Toast to a Mouse,** artist: Betty Allison, production quantity 12,500	35.00	35.00
NATURE'S BEAUTY SERIES			
☐ 1981	**Winter's Peace,** artist: Betty Allison, production quantity 7,500	70.00	72.00
☐ 1982	**Summer's Joy,** artist: Betty Allison, production quantity 7,500	70.00	72.00

AMERICAN ARTISTS

United States

	Issue Price	Current Value
CATS FOR CAT LOVERS SERIES		
☐ **1987 Romeo and Juliet,** artist: Susan Leigh, quantity: N/A	**29.50**	**30.00**
FAMILY TREASURES SERIES		
☐ **1981 Cora's Recital,** artist: R. Zolan, production quantity 18,500	**39.50**	**39.50**
☐ **1982 Cora's Tea Party,** artist: R. Zolan, production quantity 18,500	**39.50**	**39.50**
☐ **1983 Cora's Garden Party,** artist: R. Zolan, production quantity 18,500	**39.50**	**39.50**
FEATHERED FRIENDS SERIES		
☐ **1982 Parakeets,** artist: Linda Crouch, production quantity 19,500	**29.50**	**30.00**
FLOWER FANTASIES		
☐ **1985 Spring Blossoms,** artist: Donald Zolan, production quantity: 15 firing days	**24.50**	**35.00**
THE HORSES OF FRED STONE SERIES		
☐ **1982 Patience,** artist: Fred Stone, production quantity 9,500	**55.00**	**110.00**
☐ **1982 Arabian Mare and Foal,** artist: Fred Stone, production quantity 9,500	**55.00**	**110.00**
☐ **1982 Safe and Sound,** artist: Fred Stone, production quantity 9,500	**55.00**	**70.00**
☐ **1983 Contentment,** artist: Fred Stone, production quantity 9,500	**55.00**	**70.00**
☐ **1983 Black Stallion,** artist: Fred Stone, production quantity 9,500	**49.50**	**85.00**
☐ **1983 Andalusian,** artist: Fred Stone, production quantity 9,500	**49.50**	**63.00**
☐ **1984 Man O'War,** artist: Fred Stone, production quantity 9,500	**65.00**	**85.00**
☐ **1984 Secretariat,** artist: Fred Stone, production quantity 9,500	**65.00**	**80.00**
☐ **1985 John Henry,** artist: Fred Stone, production quantity 9,500	**65.00**	**75.00**
☐ **1985 Seattle Slew,** artist: Fred Stone, production quantity 9,500	**65.00**	**65.00**

	Issue Price	Current Value

MOTHER AND CHILD CATS SERIES

☐ **1983 Kitty Love,** artist: Phyllis Hollands-Robinson, production quantity 19,500 . . . . .   **29.50**   **30.00**

NOBLE TRIBES SERIES

☐ **1983 Algonquin,** artist: Donald Zolan, production quantity 19,500 . . . .   **49.50**   **65.00**

☐ **1984 Sioux,** artist: Donald Zolan, production quantity 19,500 . . . .   **49.50**   **65.00**

SATURDAY EVENING POST COVERS SERIES

☐ **1983 Santa's Computer,** artist: Scott Gustafson, production quantity: 15 firing days **29.50**   **35.00**

ZOE'S CATS SERIES

☐ **1985 The Sniffer,** artist: Zoe Stokes, production quantity 12,500 . . . .   **29.50**   **30.00**

☐ **1985 Waiting,** artist: Zoe Stokes, production quantity 12,500 . . . .   **29.50**   **30.00**

☐ **1985 Sunshine,** artist: Zoe Stokes, production quantity 12,500 . . . .   **29.50**   **30.00**

☐ **1985 Tarzan,** artist: Zoe Stokes, production quantity 12,500 . . . .   **29.50**   **30.00**

SINGLE ISSUES

☐ **1984 Going to Grandma's House,** artist: Donald Zolan, production quantity 15,000 . . . .   **29.50**   **35.00**

☐ **1986 May Queen,** artist: Zoe Stokes, production quantity: 21 firing days **29.95**   **30.00**

☐ **1987 The Shoe,** artist: Fred Stone, production quantity 9,500 . . . .   **75.00**   **80.00**

AMERICAN COMMEMORATIVE

United States

SOUTHERN LANDMARK SERIES

☐ **1973 Monticello,** production quantity 9,800 . . . . .   **43.00**   **96.00**

☐ **1973 Williamsburg,** production quantity 9,800 . .   **43.00**   **96.00**

☐ **1974 Beauvoir,** production quantity 9,800 . . . . . .   **43.00**   **88.00**

☐ **1974 Gabildo,** production quantity 9,800 . . . .   **43.00**   **88.00**

		Issue Price	Current Value
☐ 1975	**Hermitage,** production quantity 9,800	**43.00**	**80.00**
☐ 1975	**Oak Hill,** production quantity 9,800	**43.00**	**80.00**
☐ 1976	**Governor Tyron's Place,** production quantity 9,800	**43.00**	**70.00**
☐ 1976	**Montpelier,** production quantity 9,800	**43.00**	**70.00**
☐ 1977	**Elmscourt,** production quantity 9,800	**43.00**	**60.00**
☐ 1977	**Ashland,** production quantity 9,800	**43.00**	**61.00**
☐ 1978	**Mt. Vernon,** production quantity 9,800	**43.00**	**61.00**
☐ 1978	**White House,** production quantity 9,800 . .	**43.00**	**50.00**
☐ 1979	**Curtis Lee,** production quantity 9,800	**43.00**	**50.00**
☐ 1979	**Drayton Hall,** production quantity 9,800 . .	**43.00**	**43.00**
☐ 1980	**Ft. Hill,** production quantity 9,800	**43.00**	**43.00**
☐ 1980	**Liberty Hall,** production quantity 9,800 . . .	**43.00**	**43.00**

AMERICAN CRYSTAL

United States

CHRISTMAS SERIES

☐ 1970	**Christmas**	**17.50**	**20.00**
☐ 1971	**Christmas**	**12.00**	**15.00**
☐ 1972	**Christmas**	**12.00**	**15.00**
☐ 1973	**Christmas**	**17.00**	**20.00**

MOTHER'S DAY SERIES

☐ 1971	**Mother's Day**	**8.00**	**10.00**
☐ 1972	**Mother's Day,** production quantity 2,000 . .	**12.00**	**15.00**
☐ 1973	**Mother's Day**	**23.00**	**25.00**

SINGLE RELEASES

☐ 1969	**Astronaut**	**17.50**	**20.00**

AMERICAN EXPRESS

United States

AMERICAN TREES OF CHRISTMAS SERIES

☐ 1976	**Douglas Fir,** production: one year	**60.00**	**62.00**
☐ 1977	**Scotch Pine,** production: one year	**60.00**	**62.00**

BIRDS OF NORTH AMERICA SERIES

☐ 1978	**Saw-Whet Owls,** production quantity 9,800	**38.00**	**40.00**

		Issue Price	Current Value
☐ 1978	**Bobwhite Quail,** production quantity 9,800	38.00	40.00
☐ 1978	**October Cardinals,** production quantity 9,800	38.00	40.00
☐ 1978	**Long-Eared Owl,** production quantity 9,800	38.00	40.00
☐ 1978	**Eastern Bluebirds,** production quantity 9,800	38.00	38.00
☐ 1978	**American Woodcock,** production quantity 9,800	38.00	38.00
☐ 1978	**Ruffed Grouse,** production quantity 9,800	38.00	38.00
☐ 1978	**House Wren,** production quantity 9,800 ...	38.00	38.00

FOUR FREEDOMS SERIES

☐ 1976	**Freedom of Worship,** production: one year	37.50	38.00
☐ 1976	**Freedom from Want,** production: one year	37.50	38.00
☐ 1976	**Freedom from Fear,** production: one year ..	37.50	38.00
☐ 1976	**Freedom of Speech,** production: one year ..	37.50	38.00

ROGER TORY PETERSON

☐ 1981	**Bob-o-Link,** production quantity limited by subscription............................	55.00	57.00
☐ 1982	**Blue Bird,** production quantity limited by subscription............................	55.00	57.00
☐ 1982	**Mocking Bird,** production quantity limited by subscription..........................	55.00	57.00
☐ 1982	**Scarlet Tanager,** production quantity limited by subscription........................	55.00	57.00
☐ 1982	**Robin,** production quantity limited by subscription............................	55.00	57.00
☐ 1982	**Blue Jay,** production quantity limited by subscription............................	55.00	57.00
☐ 1982	**Cardinal,** production quantity limited by subscription............................	55.00	57.00
☐ 1982	**Wood Thrush,** production quantity limited by subscription...........................	55.00	57.00
☐ 1982	**Baltimore Oriole,** production quantity limited by subscription.....................	55.00	57.00
☐ 1982	**Rose-Breasted Grosbeak,** production quantity limited by subscription..............	55.00	57.00
☐ 1982	**Barn Swallow,** production quantity limited by subscription..........................	55.00	57.00
☐ 1982	**Flicker,** production quantity limited by subscription............................	55.00	57.00

AMERICAN HERITAGE

United States

AFRICA'S BEAUTIES	Issue Price	Current Value
☐ 1983 **Elephant Family,** artist: Douglas Van Howd, production quantity 5,000	65.00	67.00
☐ 1984 **Zebra Family,** artist: Douglas Van Howd, production quantity 5,000	65.00	65.00

AMERICA'S HERITAGE OF FLIGHT

☐ 1983 **Kitty Hawk,** artist: Allen Adams, production quantity 5,000	39.50	41.00

AMERICAN SAIL

☐ 1983 **Down Easter in a Squall,** artist: Edward Ries, production quantity 5,000	39.50	41.00
☐ 1983 **Young America,** artist: Edward Ries, production quantity 5,000	39.50	41.00

BATTLE WAGONS

☐ 1982 **General Quarters,** artist: Edward Ries, production quantity 5,000	39.50	41.00
☐ 1983 **Last Cruise,** artist: Edward Ries, production quantity 5,000	39.50	41.00

CELEBRITY CLOWNS SERIES

☐ 1982 **Emmett,** artist: John Helland, production quantity 12,500	50.00	52.00
☐ 1982 **Judy,** artist: John Helland, production quantity 12,500	50.00	52.00
☐ 1982 **Jimmy,** artist: John Helland, production quantity 12,500	50.00	52.00
☐ 1982 **The Shark** (Charlie Chaplin), artist: John Helland, production quantity 12,500	50.00	52.00

CRAFTSMAN HERITAGE

☐ 1983 **Decoy Maker,** artist: Ray Orosz, production quantity 5,000	39.50	41.00
☐ 1983 **Sailmaker,** artist: Ray Orosz, production quantity 5,000	39.50	41.00

EQUESTRIAN LOVE

☐ 1983 **Arabian Destiny,** production quantity 5,000	39.50	41.00

		Issue Price	Current Value

LIL' CRITTERS

| ☐ 1982 | Inquisitive, artist: Allen Adams, production quantity 10,000 . . . . | 40.00 | 42.00 |

SAWDUST ANTICS

| ☐ 1983 | Emmett's Eight Ball, artist: John Helland, production quantity 5,000 . . . . | 50.00 | 52.00 |
| ☐ 1983 | Emmett with a Bang, artist: John Helland, production quantity 5,000 . . . . | 50.00 | 52.00 |

VANISHING WEST

| ☐ 1982 | Hellbent, artist: David Miller, production quantity 7,500 . . . . | 60.00 | 61.00 |
| ☐ 1983 | Cold Trail, artist: David Miller, production quantity 5,000 . . . . | 60.00 | 61.00 |

AMERICAN HOUSE

United States

SINGLE ISSUES

| ☐ 1972 | Landing of Columbus, production quantity 1,500 . . . . | 100.00 | 100.00 |
| ☐ 1972 | Landing of Columbus, production quantity 1,000 . . . . | 250.00 | 250.00 |

AMERICAN LEGACY

United States

CHILDREN TO LOVE

| ☐ 1982 | Wendy, artist: Sue Etem, production quantity 10,000 . . . . | 60.00 | 125.00 |
| ☐ 1982 | Jake, artist: Sue Etem, production quantity 10,000 . . . . | 60.00 | 72.00 |

HOLIDAYS AROUND THE WORLD

| ☐ 1984 | Elysa's Christmas, artist: Ignacio Gomez, production quantity 12,500 . . . . | 39.50 | 40.50 |

SPECIAL HEART SERIES

| ☐ 1982 | Reaching Together, artist: Sue Etem, production quantity 40,000 . . . . | 35.00 | 37.00 |

		Issue Price	Current Value
☐ 1983	**Love in Your Heart,** artist: Sue Etem, production quantity 40,000	**35.00**	**37.00**

WALTER BRENNAN SERIES

☐ 1983	**Grampa,** artist: Walter Brennan, Jr., production quantity 10,000	**60.00**	**60.00**
☐ 1984	**To Kiss a Winner,** artist: Walter Brennan, Jr., production quantity 10,000	**45.00**	**45.00**

AMERICAN ROSE SOCIETY

United States

ALL-AMERICAN ROSE SERIES

		Issue Price	Current Value
☐ 1975	**Oregold,** production quantity 9,800	**39.00**	**142.00**
☐ 1975	**Arizona,** production quantity 9,800	**39.00**	**142.00**
☐ 1975	**Rose Parade,** production quantity 9,800 ...	**39.00**	**137.00**
☐ 1976	**Yankee Doodle,** production quantity 9,800	**39.00**	**135.50**
☐ 1976	**America,** production quantity 9,800	**39.00**	**135.50**
☐ 1976	**Cathedral,** production quantity 9,800	**39.00**	**135.50**
☐ 1976	**Seashell,** production quantity 9,800	**39.00**	**135.50**
☐ 1977	**Double Delight,** production quantity 9,800	**39.00**	**115.00**
☐ 1977	**Prominent,** production quantity 9,800	**39.00**	**115.00**
☐ 1977	**First Edition,** production quantity 9,800 ...	**39.00**	**115.00**
☐ 1978	**Color Magic,** production quantity 9,800 ...	**39.00**	**107.00**
☐ 1978	**Charisma,** production quantity 9,800	**39.00**	**107.00**
☐ 1979	**Paradise,** production quantity 9,800	**39.00**	**89.00**
☐ 1979	**Sundowner,** production quantity 9,800	**39.00**	**89.00**
☐ 1979	**Friendship,** production quantity 9,800	**39.00**	**89.00**
☐ 1980	**Love,** production quantity 9,800	**49.00**	**80.00**
☐ 1980	**Honor,** production quantity 9,800	**49.00**	**80.00**
☐ 1980	**Cherish,** production quantity 9,800	**49.00**	**80.00**
☐ 1981	**Bing Crosby,** production quantity 9,800 ...	**49.00**	**75.00**
☐ 1981	**White Lightnin',** production quantity 9,800	**49.00**	**75.00**
☐ 1981	**Marina,** production quantity 9,800	**49.00**	**75.00**
☐ 1982	**Shreveport,** production quantity 9,800	**49.00**	**69.00**
☐ 1982	**French Lace,** production quantity 9,800 ...	**49.00**	**69.00**
☐ 1982	**Brandy,** production quantity 9,800	**49.00**	**69.00**
☐ 1982	**Mon Cheri,** production quantity 9,800	**49.00**	**49.00**
☐ 1983	**Sun Flare,** production quantity 9,800	**49.00**	**69.00**
☐ 1983	**Sweet Surrender,** production quantity 9,800	**49.00**	**55.00**
☐ 1984	**Impatient,** production quantity 9,800 ......'	**49.00**	**55.00**
☐ 1984	**Olympiad,** production quantity 9,800	**49.00**	**55.00**

		Issue Price	Current Value
☐ 1984	**Intrigue,** production quantity 9,800	**49.00**	**58.00**
☐ 1985	**Showbiz,** production quantity 9,800	**49.50**	**49.50**
☐ 1985	**Peace,** production quantity 9,800	**49.50**	**49.50**
☐ 1985	**Queen Elizabeth,** production quantity 9,800	**49.50**	**49.50**

ANNADOR TRADING COMPANY

Canada

SINGLE ISSUE

☐ 1987	**The Apprentice,** artist: Nori Peter, production quantity 7,500	**45.00**	**45.00**

ANNA-PERENNA

Germany

AMERICAN SILHOUETTES COLLECTION I—THE CHILDREN SERIES

☐ 1981	**Fiddlers Two,** artist: P. Buckley Moss, production quantity 5,000	**75.00**	**77.00**
☐ 1982	**Mary with the Lambs,** artist: P. Buckley Moss, production quantity 5,000	**75.00**	**77.00**
☐ 1982	**Waiting for Tom,** artist: P. Buckley Moss, production quantity 5,000	**75.00**	**77.00**
☐ 1982	**Ring Around the Rosie,** artist: P. Buckley Moss, production quantity 5,000	**75.00**	**77.00**

AMERICAN SILHOUETTES COLLECTION II—THE FAMILY SERIES

☐ 1982	**Family Outing,** artist: P. Buckley Moss, production quantity 5,000	**75.00**	**77.00**
☐ 1982	**John and Mary,** artist: P. Buckley Moss, production quantity 5,000	**75.00**	**77.00**
☐ 1982	**Homemakers A-Quilting,** artist: P. Buckley Moss, production quantity 5,000	**75.00**	**77.00**
☐ 1984	**Leisure Time,** artist: P. Buckley Moss, production quantity 5,000	**75.00**	**77.00**

		Issue Price	Current Value
AMERICAN SILHOUETTES COLLECTION III—VALLEY LIFE SERIES			
☐ 1982	**Frosty Frolic,** artist: P. Buckley Moss, production quantity 5,000	75.00	77.00
☐ 1982	**Hayride,** artist: P. Buckley Moss, production quantity 5,000	75.00	77.00
☐ 1983	**Sunday Ride,** artist: P. Buckley Moss, production quantity 5,000	75.00	77.00
☐ 1984	**Market Day,** artist: P. Buckley Moss, production quantity 5,000	75.00	77.00
ANNUAL PLATE SERIES			
☐ 1984	**Noel, Noel,** artist: P. Buckley Moss, production quantity 5,000	69.00	69.00
ARCTIC SPRING SERIES			
☐ 1983	**Patience,** artist: Nori Peters, production quantity 9,500	75.00	77.00
BASHFUL BUNNIES SERIES			
☐ 1981	**Spring's Surprise,** artist: Mary Ellen Wehrli, production quantity 15,000	62.50	65.00
☐ 1982	**Summer's Sunshine,** artist: Mary Ellen Wehrli, production quantity 15,000	62.50	65.00

Frosty Frolic, artist: P. Buckley Moss.

Hayride, artist:
P. Buckley Moss.

		Issue Price	Current Value
☐ 1982	**Fall's Frolic,** artist: Mary Ellen Wehrli, production quantity 15,000	62.50	65.00
☐ 1983	**Winter's Wonder,** artist: Mary Ellen Wehrli, production quantity 15,000	62.50	65.00

BIRDS OF FANCY SERIES

☐ 1978	**Firebird,** artist: Dr. Irving Burgues, production quantity 5,000	110.00	102.00

CAPRICIOUS CLOWNS SERIES

☐ 1981	**Clowns and Unicorns,** artist: Margaret Kane, production quantity 9,800	95.00	90.00
☐ 1981	**Masquerade Party,** artist: Margaret Kane, production quantity 9,800	95.00	90.00

CHILDREN OF MOTHER EARTH SERIES

☐ 1983	**Spring,** artist: Norval Morrisseau, production quantity 2,500	250.00	252.00
☐ 1983	**Summer,** artist: Norval Morrisseau, production quantity 2,500	250.00	252.00
☐ 1983	**Autumn,** artist: Norval Morrisseau, production quantity 2,500	250.00	252.00
☐ 1983	**Winter,** artist: Norval Morrisseau, production quantity 2,500	250.00	252.00

		Issue Price	Current Value

ENCHANTED GARDENS SERIES

☐ **1978 June Dream,** artist: Carol Burgues, production quantity 5,000 . . . . **75.00** **65.00**

☐ **1978 Summer Day,** artist: Carol Burgues, production quantity 5,000 . . . . **95.00** **100.00**

FLORAL FANTASIES SERIES

☐ **1978 Empress Gold,** artist: Carol Burgues, production quantity 5,000 . . . . **110.00** **92.00**

FLOWERS OF COUNT BERNADOTTE

☐ **1982 The Iris,** artist: Count Lennart Bernadotte, production quantity 17,800 . . . . **75.00** **95.00**

☐ **1983 Carnation,** artist: Count Lennart Bernadotte, production quantity 17,800 . . . . **75.00** **95.00**

☐ **1983 Lily,** artist: Count Lennart Bernadotte, production quantity 17,800 . . . . **75.00** **75.00**

☐ **1983 Freesia,** artist: Count Lennart Bernadotte, production quantity 17,800 . . . . **75.00** **75.00**

☐ **1984 Orchid,** artist: Count Lennart Bernadotte, production quantity 17,800 . . . . **75.00** **75.00**

☐ **1984 Rose,** artist: Count Lennart Bernadotte, production quantity 17,800 . . . . **75.00** **75.00**

☐ **1984 Tulip,** artist: Count Lennart Bernadotte, production quantity 17,800 . . . . **75.00** **90.00**

☐ **1984 Chrysanthemum,** artist: Count Lennart Bernadotte, production quantity 17,800 . . . . . . **75.00** **75.00**

GOLDEN OLDIES SERIES

☐ **1986 My Merry Oldsmobile,** artist: Thaddeus Krumeich, production unannounced **39.50** **39.50**

HAPPY VILLAGE SERIES

☐ **1983 Spring—Spring Picnic,** artist: Elke Sommer, production quantity 5,000 . . . . **55.00** **57.00**

☐ **1983 Summer—On the Pond,** artist: Elke Sommer, production quantity 5,000 . . . . **55.00** **57.00**

☐ **1983 Autumn—Harvest Dance,** artist: Elke Sommer, production quantity 5,000 . . . . **55.00** **57.00**

☐ **1983 Winter—Snow Kids,** artist: Elke Sommer, production quantity 5,000 . . . . **55.00** **57.00**

My Merry Oldsmobile, artist: Thaddeus Krumeich.

	Issue Price	Current Value
INTERNATIONAL MOTHER LOVE SERIES		
☐ 1979 **Gesa und Kinder,** artist: Edna Hibel, production limited	195.00	195.00
☐ 1980 **Alexandra und Kinder,** artist: Edna Hibel, production limited	195.00	195.00
JOYS OF MOTHERHOOD SERIES		
☐ 1979 **Gesa and Children,** production quantity 5,000	165.00	165.00
☐ 1980 **Alexandra and Children,** production quantity 5,000	175.00	180.00
MASQUERADE FANTASIES SERIES		
☐ 1981 **The Masquerade Party,** artist: Margaret Kane, production quantity 9,800	95.00	100.00
☐ 1981 **Clowns and Unicorns,** artist: Margaret Kane, production quantity 9,800	95.00	95.00
ORIENTAL TRANQUILITY SERIES		
☐ 1978 **Chun Li at Pond,** artist: Dr. Irving Burgues, production quantity 5,000	100.00	82.00
☐ 1979 **Ming Tao on Path of Faith,** artist: Dr. Irving Burgues, production quantity 5,000	110.00	105.00

	Issue Price	Current Value

REFLECTIONS OF YOUTH

☐ **1984** **The Swimmers,** artist: Ken Danby, production quantity 9,500	75.00	77.00

RHYTHM AND DANCE SERIES

☐ **1983** **Ballroom,** artist: Al Hirschfeld, production quantity 5,000	29.50	31.00
☐ **1983** **Pas de Deux,** artist: Al Hirschfeld, production quantity 5,000	29.50	31.00
☐ **1983** **Swing,** artist: Al Hirschfeld, production quantity 5,000	29.50	31.00
☐ **1983** **Jazz,** artist: Al Hirschfeld, production quantity 5,000	29.50	31.00
☐ **1983** **Aerobics,** artist: Al Hirschfeld, production quantity 5,000	29.50	31.00
☐ **1983** **Cake Walk,** artist: Al Hirschfeld, production quantity 5,000	29.50	31.00
☐ **1983** **Charleston,** artist: Al Hirschfeld, production quantity 5,000	29.50	31.00
☐ **1983** **Strut,** artist: Al Hirschfeld, production quantity 5,000	29.50	31.00

ROMANTIC LOVE SERIES

☐ **1979** **Romeo and Juliet,** artist: Frank Russell and Gertrude Barrer, production quantity 7,500	95.00	95.00
☐ **1980** **Lancelot and Guinevere,** artist: Frank Russell and Gertrude Barrer, production quantity 7,500	95.00	95.00
☐ **1981** **Helen and Paris,** artist: Frank Russell and Gertrude Barrer, production quantity 7,500	95.00	95.00
☐ **1982** **Lovers of Taj Mahal,** artist: Frank Russell and Gertrude Barrer, production quantity 7,500	95.00	95.00

TRIPTYCH SERIES

☐ **1978** **Byzantine Triptych,** artist: Frank Russell and Gertrude Barrer, production quantity 5,000	325.00	325.00
☐ **1980** **Jerusalem Triptych,** artist: Frank Russell and Gertrude Barrer, production quantity 5,000	350.00	350.00

UNCLE TAD'S CAT SERIES

☐ **1979** **Oliver's Birthday,** artist: Thaddeus Krumeich, production quantity 5,000	75.00	190.00

Jerusalem Triptych,
artist: Frank Russell
and Gertrude Barrer.

		Issue Price	Current Value
☐ 1980	**Peaches and Cream,** artist: Thaddeus Krumeich, production quantity 5,000	**75.00**	**85.00**
☐ 1981	**Princess Aurora, Queen Of The Night,** artist: Thaddeus Krumeich, production quantity 5,000	**80.00**	**80.00**
☐ 1981	**Walter's Window,** artist: Thaddeus Krumeich, production quantity 5,000	**85.00**	**85.00**

Princess Aurora, Queen
of the Night, artist:
Thaddeus Krumeich.

Walter's Window, artist:
Thaddeus Krumeich.

UNCLE TAD'S HOLIDAY CATS SERIES	Issue Price	Current Value
☐ 1982 **Jingle Bells,** artist: Thaddeus Krumeich, production quantity 9,800	75.00	77.00
☐ 1983 **Pollyanna,** artist: Thaddeus Krumeich, production quantity 9,800	75.00	77.00
☐ 1984 **Pumpkin,** artist: Thaddeus Krumeich, production quantity 9,800	75.00	77.00

Jingle Bells, artist:
Thaddeus Krumeich.

Perry, Buttercup and
Blackeyed Susan, artist:
Thaddeus Krumeich.

		Issue Price	Current Value
☐ 1985	**Perry, Buttercup and Blackeyed Susan,** artist: Thaddeus Krumeich, production quantity 9,800	**75.00**	**75.00**

UNCLE TAD'S TICK TOCK SERIES

		Issue Price	Current Value
☐ 1982	**Hickory, Dickory,** artist: Thaddeus Krumeich, production quantity 5,000	**150.00**	**155.00**

ANRI

Italy

CHRISTMAS SERIES

		Issue Price	Current Value
☐ 1971	**St. Jakob in Groden,** artist: J. Malfertheiner, production quantity 10,000	**37.50**	**125.00**
☐ 1972	**Pipes at Alberobello,** artist: J. Malfertheiner, production: one year	**45.00**	**130.00**
☐ 1973	**Alpine Horn,** artist: J. Malfertheiner, production: one year	**45.00**	**400.00**
☐ 1974	**Young Man and Girl,** artist: J. Malfertheiner, production: one year	**50.00**	**95.00**
☐ 1975	**Christmas in Ireland,** artist: J. Malfertheiner, production: one year	**60.00**	**225.00**

		Issue Price	Current Value
☐ 1976	**Alpine Christmas,** artist: J. Malfertheiner, production: one year	65.00	130.00
☐ 1977	**Heiligenblut,** artist: J. Malfertheiner, production quantity 6,000	65.00	185.00
☐ 1978	**Klocker Singers,** artist: J. Malfertheiner, production quantity 6,000	80.00	140.00
☐ 1979	**Moss Gatherers,** production quantity 6,000	135.00	175.00
☐ 1980	**Wintry Churchgoing,** production quantity 6,000	170.00	168.00
☐ 1981	**Santa Claus in Tyrol,** production quantity 6,000	165.00	170.00
☐ 1982	**The Star Singers,** production quantity 6,000	165.00	165.00
☐ 1983	**Unto Us a Child Is Born,** production quantity 6,000	165.00	165.00
☐ 1984	**Yuletide in the Valley,** production quantity 6,000	165.00	165.00

FATHER'S DAY SERIES

☐ 1974	**Alpine Father and Children,** production quantity 5,000	35.00	100.00
☐ 1975	**Alpine Father and Children,** production quantity 5,000	45.00	95.00
☐ 1976	**Sailing,** production quantity 5,000	50.00	100.00
☐ 1977	**Cliff Gazine,** production quantity 5,000 ...	60.00	90.00

FERRANDIZ ANNUAL SERIES

☐ 1984	**Pastoral Journey,** artist: Juan Ferrandiz, production quantity 2,000	170.00	170.00
☐ 1985	**A Tender Touch,** artist: Juan Ferrandiz, production quantity 2,000	170.00	170.00

FERRANDIZ CHRISTMAS SERIES

☐ 1972	**Christ in the Manger,** artist: Juan Ferrandiz, production quantity 2,500	35.00	230.00
☐ 1979	**The Drummer,** artist: Juan Ferrandiz, production quantity 4,000	120.00	175.00
☐ 1980	**Rejoice,** artist: Juan Ferrandiz, production quantity 4,000	150.00	160.00
☐ 1981	**Spreading the Word,** artist: Juan Ferrandiz, production quantity 4,000	150.00	150.00
☐ 1982	**The Shepherd Family,** artist: Juan Ferrandiz, production quantity 4,000	150.00	150.00
☐ 1983	**Peace Attend Thee,** artist: Juan Ferrandiz, production quantity 4,000	150.00	150.00

FERRANDIZ MOTHER'S DAY SERIES	Issue Price	Current Value
☐ **1972 Mother Sewing,** artist: Juan Ferrandiz, production: one year	35.00	200.00
☐ **1973 Mother and Child,** artist: Juan Ferrandiz, production: one year	40.00	150.00
☐ **1973 Christmas,** artist: Juan Ferrandiz, production quantity unknown	40.00	225.00
☐ **1974 Holy Night,** artist: Juan Ferrandiz, production: one year	50.00	100.00
☐ **1975 Flight into Egypt,** artist: Juan Ferrandiz, production: one year	60.00	95.00
☐ **1976 Mary and Joseph,** artist: Juan Ferrandiz, production: one year	60.00	100.00
☐ **1976 Tree of Life,** artist: Juan Ferrandiz, production: one year	60.00	60.00
☐ **1976 Girl with Flowers,** artist: Juan Ferrandiz, production quantity 4,000	65.00	185.00
☐ **1978 Leading the Way,** artist: Juan Ferrandiz, production quantity 4,000	77.50	180.00
☐ **1974 Mother Holding Child,** artist: Juan Ferrandiz, production: one year	50.00	150.00
☐ **1975 Mother and Dove,** artist: Juan Ferrandiz, production: one year	60.00	150.00
☐ **1976 Mother Knitting,** artist: Juan Ferrandiz, production: one year	60.00	200.00
☐ **1977 Girl and Flowers,** artist: Juan Ferrandiz, production: one year	65.00	125.00
☐ **1978 The Beginning,** artist: Juan Ferrandiz, production quantity 3,000	77.50	150.00
☐ **1979 All Hearts,** artist: Juan Ferrandiz, production quantity 3,000	120.00	170.00
☐ **1980 Spring Arrivals,** artist: Juan Ferrandiz, production quantity 3,000	150.00	165.00
☐ **1981 Harmony,** artist: Juan Ferrandiz, production quantity 3,000	150.00	150.00
☐ **1982 With Love,** artist: Juan Ferrandiz, production quantity 3,000	150.00	150.00

FERRANDIZ WEDDING SERIES

☐ **1972 Boy and Girl Embracing,** artist: Juan Ferrandiz, production: one year	40.00	145.00
☐ **1973 Wedding Scene,** artist: Juan Ferrandiz, production: one year	40.00	95.00
☐ **1974 Wedding,** artist: Juan Ferrandiz, production: one year	48.00	48.00

		Issue Price	Current Value
☐ 1975	**Wedding,** artist: Juan Ferrandiz, production: one year	60.00	60.00
☐ 1976	**Wedding,** artist: Juan Ferrandiz, production: one year	60.00	60.00

FERRANDIZ WOODEN BIRTHDAY SERIES

☐ 1973	**Birthday Boy,** artist: Juan Ferrandiz, production: one year	10.00	10.00
☐ 1973	**Birthday Girl,** artist: Juan Ferrandiz, production: one year	15.00	15.00
☐ 1973	**Birthday Boy and Girl,** artist: Juan Ferrandiz, production: one year	20.00	20.00
☐ 1974	**Birthday Boy,** artist: Juan Ferrandiz, production: one year	22.00	22.00
☐ 1974	**Birthday Girl,** artist: Juan Ferrandiz, production: one year	22.00	22.00

MOTHER'S DAY SERIES

☐ 1972	**Alpine Mother and Children,** production quantity 5,000	35.00	50.00
☐ 1973	**Alpine Mother and Children,** production quantity 5,000	45.00	55.00
☐ 1974	**Alpine Mother and Children,** production quantity 5,000	50.00	55.00
☐ 1975	**Alpine Stroll,** production quantity 5,000	60.00	65.00
☐ 1976	**Knitting,** production quantity 5,000	60.00	65.00

SARAH KAY ANNUAL SERIES

☐ 1984	**A Time for Secrets,** artist: Sarah Kay, production quantity 2,500	120.00	120.00
☐ 1985	**Carousel Magic,** artist: Sarah Kay, production quantity 2,500	120.00	120.00

ANTIQUE TRADER

United States

BIBLE SERIES

☐ 1973	**David and Goliath,** production quantity 2,000	10.75	11.00
☐ 1973	**Moses and Golden Idol,** production quantity 2,000	10.75	11.00

		Issue Price	Current Value
☐ 1973	Noah's Ark, production quantity 2,000	10.75	11.00
☐ 1973	Samson, production quantity 2,000	10.75	11.00

CHRISTMAS SERIES

☐ 1971	Christ Child, production quantity 1,500 ...	10.95	11.00
☐ 1972	Flight into Egypt, production quantity 1,500	10.95	11.00

C. M. RUSSELL SERIES

☐ 1971	Bad One, production quantity 2,000	11.95	13.00
☐ 1971	Discovery of Last Chance Gulch, production quantity 2,000	11.95	13.00
☐ 1971	Doubtful Visitor, production quantity 2,000	11.95	13.00
☐ 1971	Innocent Allies, production quantity 2,000	11.95	13.00
☐ 1971	Medicine Man, production quantity 2,000	11.95	13.00

CURRIER & IVES SERIES

☐ 1969	Baseball, production quantity 2,000	9.00	9.00
☐ 1969	Franklin Experiment, production quantity 2,000	9.00	9.00
☐ 1969	Haying Time, production quantity 2,000 ..	9.00	9.00
☐ 1969	Winter in Country, production quantity 2,000	9.00	9.00

EASTER SERIES

☐ 1971	Child and Lamb, production quantity 1,500	10.95	12.00
☐ 1972	Shepherd with Lamb, production quantity 1,500	10.95	12.00

FATHER'S DAY SERIES

☐ 1971	Pilgrim Father, production quantity 1,500	10.95	12.00
☐ 1972	Deer Family, production quantity 1,000 ...	10.95	12.00

MOTHER'S DAY SERIES

☐ 1971	Madonna and Child, production quantity 1,500	10.95	12.00
☐ 1972	Mother Cat and Kittens, production quantity 1,000	10.95	12.00

THANKSGIVING SERIES

☐ 1971	Pilgrims, production quantity 1,500	10.95	12.00
☐ 1972	First Thanksgiving, production quantity 1,000	10.95	12.00

ARABIA OF FINLAND

Finland

CHRISTMAS ANNUAL SERIES	Issue Price	Current Value
☐ 1978 **Inland Village Scene,** production: one year	49.00	50.00
☐ 1979 **Forest Village Scene,** production: one year	72.00	75.00
☐ 1980 **Seaside Village Scene,** production: one year	79.00	80.00
☐ 1981 **Christmas Plate,** production: one year	87.00	90.00
☐ 1982 **Christmas Plate,** production: one year	95.00	95.00

COMMEMORATION SERIES

	Issue Price	Current Value
☐ 1973 Production: rare	20.00	68.00
☐ 1974 Production: rare	20.00	68.00

KALEVALA SERIES

	Issue Price	Current Value
☐ 1976 **Vainomoinen's Sowing Song,** artist: Raija Uosikkinen, production quantity 1,996	30.00	230.00
☐ 1977 **Aino's Fate,** artist: Raija Uosikkinen, production quantity 1,008	30.00	30.00
☐ 1978 **Lemminkainen's Chase,** artist: Raija Uosikkinen, production quantity 2,500	39.00	40.00
☐ 1979 **Kullervo's Revenge,** artist: Raija Uosikkinen, production: one year	39.50	40.00
☐ 1980 **Vainomoinen's Rescue,** artist: Raija Uosikkinen, production: one year	45.00	65.00
☐ 1981 **Vainomoinen's Magic,** artist: Raija Uosikkinen, production: one year	49.50	49.50
☐ 1982 **Joukahainen Shoots the Horse,** artist: Raija Uosikkinen, production: one year	55.50	55.50
☐ 1983 **Lemminkainen's Escape,** artist: Raija Uosikkinen, production: one year	60.00	90.00
☐ 1984 **Lemminkainen's Magic Feathers,** artist: Raija Uosikkinen, production: one year	49.50	90.00
☐ 1985 **Lemminkainen's Grief,** artist: Raija Uosikkinen, production: one year	60.00	60.00

ARIZONA ARTISAN

United States

CHRISTMAS SERIES

	Issue Price	Current Value
☐ 1974 **Mexican Christmas,** production: one year ..	20.00	20.00
☐ 1975 **Navajo Christmas,** production: one year ...	20.00	20.00

	Issue Price	Current Value
THANKSGIVING SERIES		
☐ 1975 **Navajo Thanksgiving,** production: one year	15.00	15.00

ARLINGTON MINT

United States

	Issue Price	Current Value
CHRISTMAS SERIES		
☐ 1972 **Hands in Prayer,** production: one year	125.00	95.00

ARMSTRONG'S/CROWN PARIAN

United States

	Issue Price	Current Value
AMERICAN FOLK HEROES		
☐ 1983 **Johnny Appleseed,** artist: Gene Boyer, production: 50 days	35.00	40.00
☐ 1984 **Davy Crockett,** artist: Gene Boyer, production: 50 days	35.00	35.00
☐ 1985 **Betsy Ross,** artist: Gene Boyer, production: 50 days	35.00	35.00
BEAUTIFUL CATS OF THE WORLD SERIES		
☐ 1979 **Sheena,** artist: Douglas Van Howd, signed, production quantity 5,000	60.00	80.00
☐ 1979 **Sheena's Cubs,** artist: Douglas Van Howd, signed, production quantity 5,000	60.00	62.00
☐ 1980 **Elisheba,** artist: Douglas Van Howd, signed, production quantity 5,000	65.00	68.00
☐ 1980 **Elisheba's Cubs,** artist: Douglas Van Howd, signed, production quantity 5,000	65.00	68.00
☐ 1981 **Atarah,** artist: Douglas Van Howd, signed, production quantity 5,000	60.00	63.00
☐ 1982 **Atarah's Cubs,** artist: Douglas Van Howd, signed, production quantity 5,000	60.00	63.00
BUCK HILL BEAR SERIES		
☐ 1986 **Tiddlywink and Pixie,** artist: Robert Pearcy, production quantity 10,000	29.50	29.50
☐ 1986 **Rebecca and Friend,** artist: Robert Pearcy, production quantity 10,000	29.50	29.50

Tiddlywink and Pixie, artist: Robert Pearcy.

Rebecca and Friend, artist: Robert Pearcy.

		Issue Price	Current Value
COMPANIONS SERIES			
☐ 1986	**All Bark and No Bite,** artist: Robert Pearcy, production quantity 10,000	**29.50**	**29.50**
FREDDIE THE FREELOADER SERIES			
☐ 1979	**Freddie in the Bathtub,** artist: Red Skelton, production quantity 10,000	**55.00**	**200.00**

All Bark and No Bite,
artist: Robert Pearcy.

		Issue Price	Current Value
☐ 1980	**Freddie's Shack,** artist: Red Skelton, issued quantity 10,000	60.00	150.00
☐ 1981	**Freddie on the Green,** artist: Red Skelton, issued quantity 10,000	60.00	150.00
☐ 1981	**Love That Freddie,** artist: Red Skelton, issued quantity 10,000	60.00	85.00

FREDDIE'S ADVENTURES SERIES

☐ 1982	**Captain Freddie,** artist: Red Skelton, production quantity 15,000	60.00	150.00
☐ 1982	**Bronco Freddie,** artist: Red Skelton, production quantity 15,000	60.00	62.50
☐ 1983	**Sir Freddie,** artist: Red Skelton, production quantity 15,000	62.50	62.50
☐ 1984	**Gertrude and Heathcliffe,** artist: Red Skelton, production quantity 15,000	62.50	62.50

HAPPY ART
(Crown Parian)

☐ 1981	**Woody's Triple Self-Portrait,** artist: Walter Lantz, production quantity 10,000	39.50	39.50
☐ 1983	**Gothic Woody,** artist: Walter Lantz, production quantity 10,000	39.50	39.50
☐ 1984	**Blue Boy Woody,** artist: Walter Lantz, production quantity 10,000	39.50	39.50

Gertrude and
Heathcliffe, artist: Red
Skelton.

		Issue Price	Current Value
HUGGABLE PUPPY SERIES			
☐ **1984**	**Take Me Home,** artist: Robert Pearcy, production quantity 10,000	29.50	29.50
☐ **1985**	**Oh How Cute,** artist: Robert Pearcy, production quantity 10,000	29.50	29.50
☐ **1985**	**Puppy Pals,** artist: Robert Pearcy, production quantity 10,000	29.50	29.50
☐ **1986**	**Who, Me?,** artist: Robert Pearcy, production quantity 10,000	29.50	29.50

LOVABLE KITTENS			
☐ **1983**	**The Cat's Meow,** artist: Robert Pearcy, production quantity 10,000	29.50	29.50
☐ **1984**	**Purr-Swayed,** artist: Robert Pearcy, production quantity 10,000	29.50	29.50
☐ **1985**	**The Prince of Purrs,** artist: Robert Pearcy, production quantity 10,000	29.50	29.50
☐ **1986**	**Pet, And I'll Purr,** artist: Robert Pearcy, production quantity 10,000	29.50	29.50

MOMENT OF NATURE SERIES			
☐ **1980**	**California Quail,** artist: John Ruthven, production quantity 5,000	39.50	40.00
☐ **1981**	**Chickadee,** artist: John Ruthven, production quantity 5,000	39.50	40.00

Woody's Triple
Self-Portrait, artist:
Walter Lantz.

Gothic Woody, artist:
Walter Lantz.

Blue Boy Woody, artist:
Walter Lantz.

Take Me Home, artist: Robert Pearcy.

Oh How Cute, artist: Robert Pearcy.

Who, Me?, artist: Robert Pearcy.
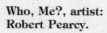

The Cat's Meow, artist:
Robert Pearcy.

Purr-Swayed, artist:
Robert Pearcy.

	Issue Price	Current Value
☐ **1981** **Screech Owls,** artist: John Ruthven, production quantity 5,000	**39.50**	**40.00**

The Prince of Purrs, artist: Robert Pearcy.

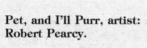

Pet, and I'll Purr, artist: Robert Pearcy.

	Issue Price	Current Value
NORTH AMERICAN BIRDS		
☐ **1984 California Quail,** artist: Jon Roberton, production quantity 7,500	**60.00**	**62.00**
PORTRAITS OF CHILDHOOD		
☐ **1983 Miss Murray,** artist: Sir Thomas Lawrence, production quantity 7,500	**65.00**	**65.00**

	Issue Price	Current Value
☐ 1984 **Master Lambton,** artist: Sir Thomas Lawrence, production quantity 7,500	65.00	65.00

REFLECTIONS OF INNOCENCE SERIES

	Issue Price	Current Value
☐ 1984 **Me and My Friend,** artist Miguel Paredes, production quantity 10,000	37.50	37.50
☐ 1985 **My Rain Beau,** artist Miguel Paredes, production quantity 10,000	37.50	37.50
☐ 1986 **Rowboat Rendezvous,** artist Miguel Paredes, production quantity 10,000	37.50	37.50
☐ 1987 **Hatching a Secret,** artist Miguel Paredes, production quantity 10,000	37.50	37.50

SPORTING DOGS SERIES

	Issue Price	Current Value
☐ 1980 **Decoys, Labrador Retriever,** artist: John Ruthven, production quantity 5,000	55.00	56.00
☐ 1981 **Dusty,** artist: John Ruthven, production quantity 5,000	55.00	56.00
☐ 1981 **Rummy,** artist: John Ruthven, production quantity 5,000	55.00	56.00
☐ 1982 **Scarlet,** artist: John Ruthven, production quantity 5,000	55.00	56.00

Master Lambton, artist:
Sir Thomas Lawrence.

**Me and My Friend,
artist: Miguel Paredes.**

**My Rain Beau, artist:
Miguel Paredes.**

**Rowboat Rendezvous,
artist: Miguel Paredes.**

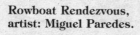

	Issue Price	Current Value
STATUE OF LIBERTY SERIES		
☐ **1985** **The Dedication,** artist: Alan D'Estrehan, production quantity 10,000	39.50	39.50
☐ **1986** **The Immigrants,** artist: Alan D'Estrehan, production quantity 10,000	39.50	39.50
☐ **1986** **Independence,** artist: Alan D'Estrehan, production quantity 10,000	39.50	39.50
☐ **1986** **Re-Dedication,** artist: Alan D'Estrehan, production quantity 10,000	39.50	39.50
THE THREE GRACES SERIES		
☐ **1985** **Thalia,** artist: Michael Perham, production quantity 7,500	49.50	49.50
☐ **1986** **Aglia,** artist: Michael Perham, production quantity 7,500	49.50	49.50
☐ **1987** **Euphrosyne,** artist: Michael Perham, production quantity 7,500	49.50	49.50
WELLS FARGO COLLECTION SERIES		
☐ **1979** **Under Surveillance,** artist: McCarty, production quantity 10,000	65.00	65.00
☐ **1979** **Promised Land,** artist: McCarty, production quantity 10,000	65.00	65.00

The Dedication; The Immigrants; Independence; Re-Dedication, artist: Alan D'Estrehan.

		Issue Price	Current Value
☐ **1982**	**Wintersong,** artist: McCarty, production quantity 10,000	**65.00**	**65.00**
☐ **1983**	**Turning the Lead,** artist: McCarty, production quantity 10,000	**65.00**	**65.00**

SINGLE RELEASES

		Issue Price	Current Value
☐ **1978**	**Affection,** artist: Rosemary Calder, production quantity 7,500	**60.00**	**62.00**
☐ **1978**	**Sweet Dreams,** artist: James Daly, production quantity 7,500	**55.00**	**58.00**
☐ **1979**	**Crow Baby,** artist: Penni Anne Cross, production quantity 7,500	**55.00**	**58.00**
☐ **1979**	**Reve de Ballet,** artist: Julian Ritter, production quantity 7,500	**55.00**	**58.00**
☐ **1980**	**Navajo Madonna,** artist: Olaf Weidhorst, production quantity 7,500	**65.00**	**68.00**
☐ **1981**	**Paiute Pals,** artist: Penni Anne Cross, production quantity 7,500	**60.00**	**62.00**
☐ **1982**	**Buon Natale,** artist: Valentino Garavani, production quantity 7,500	**300.00**	**310.00**
☐ **1983**	**Big Sister's Buckskins,** artist: Penni Anne Cross, production quantity 7,500	**55.00**	**60.00**
☐ **1983**	**Seventy Years Young,** artist: Red Skelton, production quantity 10,000	**85.00**	**87.00**

**Seventy Years Young,
artist: Red Skelton.**

Freddie the Torchbearer, artist: Red Skelton.

		Issue Price	Current Value
☐ **1984**	**Navajo Nanny,** artist: Penni Anne Cross, production quantity 7,500	55.00	60.00
☐ **1984**	**Freddie the Torchbearer,** artist: Red Skelton, production quantity 10,000	62.50	62.50
☐ **1985**	**Pete Rose,** artist: Rod Schenken, production quantity 9,000	45.00	45.00

ARTA

Austria

CHRISTMAS SERIES

☐ **1973**	**Nativity—in Manger,** production quantity 1,500	50.00	70.00

MOTHER'S DAY SERIES

☐ **1973**	**Family with Puppy,** production quantity 1,500	50.00	70.00

ARTISTS OF THE WORLD

United States

THE ANTHONY SIDONI SERIES	Issue Price	Current Value
☐ **1982** **The Little Yankee,** artist: Anthony Sidoni, production quantity 15,000	**35.00**	**36.00**
☐ **1983** **Little Satchmo,** artist: Anthony Sidoni, production quantity 15,000	**40.00**	**40.00**

CHILDREN OF ABERDEEN SERIES

	Issue Price	Current Value
☐ **1979** **Girl with Little Brother,** artist: Kee Fung Ng, production: one year	**50.00**	**50.00**
☐ **1980** **The Sampan Girl,** artist: Kee Fung Ng, production: one year	**50.00**	**60.00**
☐ **1981** **Girl with Little Sister,** artist: Kee Fung Ng, production: one year	**55.00**	**55.00**
☐ **1982** **Girl with Seashells,** artist: Kee Fung Ng, production: one year	**60.00**	**65.00**
☐ **1983** **Girl with Seabirds,** artist: Kee Fung Ng, production: one year	**60.00**	**60.00**
☐ **1984** **Brother and Sister,** artist: Kee Fung Ng, production: one year	**60.00**	**75.00**

Girl with Little Brother, artist: Kee Fung Ng.

		Issue Price	Current Value

THE CHILDREN OF DON RUFFIN SERIES

☐ 1980	**Flowers for Mother,** artist: Don Ruffin, production quantity 5,000	50.00	52.00
☐ 1981	**Little Eagle,** artist: Don Ruffin, production quantity 5,000	55.00	57.00
☐ 1982	**The Lost Moccasins,** artist: Don Ruffin, production quantity 7,500	60.00	62.00
☐ 1982	**Security,** artist: Don Ruffin, production quantity 7,500	60.00	62.00
☐ 1984	**Americans All,** artist: Don Ruffin, production quantity 7,500	60.00	62.00

THE DEGRAZIA CHILDREN OF THE WORLD SERIES

☐ 1976	**Los Ninos,** artist: Ted DeGrazia, production quantity 5,000	35.00	1800.00
☐ 1976	**Los Ninos,** artist: Ted DeGrazia, signed, production quantity 500	100.00	1500.00
☐ 1977	**White Dove,** artist: Ted DeGrazia, production quantity 5,000	40.00	220.00
☐ 1977	**White Dove,** artist: Ted DeGrazia, signed, production quantity 500	100.00	190.00
☐ 1978	**Flower Girl,** artist: Ted DeGrazia, production quantity 9,500	45.00	190.00
☐ 1978	**Flower Girl,** artist: Ted DeGrazia, signed, production quantity 500	100.00	140.00
☐ 1979	**Flower Boy,** artist: Ted DeGrazia, production quantity 9,500	45.00	190.00
☐ 1979	**Flower Boy,** artist: Ted DeGrazia, signed, production quantity 500	100.00	140.00
☐ 1980	**Little Cocopah Indian Girl,** artist: Ted DeGrazia, production quantity 9,500	50.00	140.00
☐ 1980	**Little Cocopah Indian Girl,** artist: Ted DeGrazia, signed, production quantity 500 ...	100.00	130.00
☐ 1981	**Beautiful Burden,** artist: Ted DeGrazia, production quantity 9,500	50.00	130.00
☐ 1981	**Beautiful Burden,** artist: Ted DeGrazia, signed, production quantity 500	100.00	375.00
☐ 1981	**Merry Little Indian,** artist: Ted DeGrazia, production quantity 9,500	55.00	150.00
☐ 1981	**Merry Little Indian,** artist: Ted DeGrazia, signed, production quantity 500	100.00	375.00
☐ 1983	**Wondering,** artist: Ted DeGrazia, production quantity 10,000	60.00	110.00

		Issue Price	Current Value
☐ 1984	**Pink Papoose,** artist: Ted DeGrazia, production quantity 10,000	**65.00**	**110.00**
☐ 1985	**Sunflower Boy,** artist: Ted DeGrazia, production quantity 10,000	**65.00**	**110.00**

THE DON RUFFIN SERIES

		Issue Price	Current Value
☐ 1976	**Navajo Lullaby,** artist: Don Ruffin, production quantity 9,500	**40.00**	**90.00**
☐ 1976	**Navajo Lullaby,** artist: Don Ruffin, signed, production quantity 500	**100.00**	**230.00**
☐ 1977	**Through the Years,** artist: Don Ruffin, production quantity 5,000	**45.00**	**150.00**
☐ 1978	**Child of the Pueblo,** artist: Don Ruffin, production quantity 5,000	**45.00**	**80.00**
☐ 1979	**Colima Madonna,** artist: Don Ruffin, production quantity 5,000	**50.00**	**55.00**
☐ 1980	**Sun Kachima,** artist: Don Ruffin, production quantity 5,000	**50.00**	**55.00**
☐ 1981	**Inner Peace,** artist: Don Ruffin, production quantity 5,000	**55.00**	**60.00**
☐ 1982	**Madonna of the Cross,** artist: Don Ruffin, production quantity 5,000	**60.00**	**62.00**
☐ 1983	**Navajo Princess,** artist: Don Ruffin, production quantity 5,000	**60.00**	**60.00**
☐ 1983	**Security,** artist: Don Ruffin, production quantity 7,500	**60.00**	**62.00**
☐ 1984	**Americans All,** artist: Don Ruffin, production quantity 7,500	**60.00**	**62.00**

ENDANGERED BIRDS SERIES

		Issue Price	Current Value
☐ 1976	**Kirtland's Warbler,** production quantity 5,000	**195.00**	**200.00**
☐ 1976	**American Eagle,** production quantity 5,000	**195.00**	**200.00**
☐ 1977	**Peregrine Falcon,** production quantity 5,000	**200.00**	**200.00**

THE HOLIDAY SERIES

		Issue Price	Current Value
☐ 1976	**The Festival of Lights,** artist: Ted DeGrazia, production quantity 9,500	**45.00**	**250.00**
☐ 1976	**Festival of Lights,** artist: Ted DeGrazia, signed, production quantity 500	**100.00**	**750.00**
☐ 1977	**Bell of Hope,** artist: Ted DeGrazia, production quantity 9,500	**45.00**	**100.00**
☐ 1977	**Bell of Hope,** artist: Ted DeGrazia, signed, production quantity 500	**100.00**	**300.00**

		Issue Price	Current Value
☐ 1978	**Little Madonna,** artist: Ted DeGrazia, production quantity 9,500	**45.00**	**130.00**
☐ 1978	**Little Madonna,** artist: Ted DeGrazia, signed, production quantity 500	**100.00**	**350.00**
☐ 1979	**The Nativity,** artist: Ted DeGrazia, production quantity 9,500	**50.00**	**140.00**
☐ 1979	**The Nativity,** artist: Ted DeGrazia, signed, production quantity 500	**100.00**	**450.00**
☐ 1980	**Little Pima Drummer,** artist: Ted DeGrazia, production quantity 9,500	**50.00**	**100.00**
☐ 1980	**Little Pima Drummer,** artist: Ted DeGrazia, signed, production quantity 500	**100.00**	**450.00**
☐ 1981	**A Little Prayer—The Christmas Angel,** artist: Ted DeGrazia, production quantity 9,500	**55.00**	**100.00**
☐ 1981	**A Little Prayer—The Christmas Angel,** artist: Ted DeGrazia, signed, production quantity 500	**100.00**	**420.00**
☐ 1982	**Blue Boy,** artist: Ted DeGrazia, production quantity 10,000	**60.00**	**100.00**
☐ 1982	**Blue Boy,** artist: Ted DeGrazia, signed, production quantity 96	**100.00**	**unknown**
☐ 1983	**Heavenly Blessings,** artist: Ted DeGrazia, production quantity 10,000	**65.00**	**85.00**
☐ 1984	**Navajo Madonna,** artist: Ted DeGrazia, production quantity 10,000	**65.00**	**100.00**
☐ 1985	**Saguaro Dance,** artist: Ted DeGrazia, production quantity 10,000	**65.00**	**120.00**

THE PROWLERS OF THE CLOUDS SERIES

☐ 1981	**First Light—Great Horned Owl,** artist: Larry Toschik, production quantity 5,000	**55.00**	**57.00**
☐ 1981	**His Golden Throne—Screech Owl,** artist: Larry Toschik, production quantity 5,000	**55.00**	**57.00**
☐ 1982	**Freedom's Symbol—The Bald Eagle,** artist: Larry Toschik, production quantity 5,000	**60.00**	**62.00**
☐ 1982	**Freedom's Champion—The Golden Eagle,** artist: Larry Toschik, production quantity 5,000	**60.00**	**62.00**

SWEETHEART SERIES

☐ 1984	**We Believe,** artist: Rusty Money, production quantity 10,000	**40.00**	**40.00**

	Issue Price	Current Value

THE VEL MILLER SERIES

☐ **1982 Mama's Rose,** artist: Vel Miller, production quantity 15,000 . . . . **35.00** **36.00**

☐ **1983 Papa's Boy,** artist: Vel Miller, production quantity 15,000 . . . . **40.00** **42.00**

WOODLAND FRIENDS SERIES

☐ **1983 Spring Outing—Whitetail Deer,** artist: Larry Toschik, production quantity 5,000 . . . . **60.00** **60.00**

☐ **1984 No Rest for the Night Shift,** artist: Larry Toschik, production quantity 5,000 . . . . **60.00** **60.00**

☐ **1984 Spring Outing,** artist: Larry Toschik, production quantity 5,000 . . . . **60.00** **60.00**

THE WORLD OF GAME BIRDS SERIES

☐ **1977 Mallards—Whistling In,** artist: Larry Toschik, production quantity 5,000 . . . . **45.00** **82.00**

☐ **1978 Maytime—Gambel Quail,** artist: Larry Toschik, production quantity 5,000 . . . . **45.00** **46.00**

☐ **1979 American Autumn—The Ring Necked Pheasant,** artist: Larry Toschik, production quantity 5,000 . . . . **50.00** **51.00**

☐ **1980 November Journey—Canada Geese,** artist: Larry Toschik, production quantity 5,000 . . **50.00** **51.00**

SINGLE ISSUES

☐ **1977 The Statesman,** artist: Don Ruffin, production quantity 3,500 . . . . **65.00** **40.00**

☐ **1977 The Clown Also Cries,** artist: Don Ruffin, production quantity 7,500 . . . . **65.00** **62.00**

SPECIAL RELEASE

☐ **1983 DeGrazia and His Mountain,** artist: Larry Toschik, production quantity 15,000 . . . . . . **65.00** **70.00**

☐ **1984 Little Girl Paints DeGrazia,** artist: Ted DeGrazia, production quantity 12,500 . . . . **65.00** **65.00**

ART WORLD OF BOURGEAULT

United States

ROYAL LITERARY SERIES

☐ **1986 John Bunyan Cottage,** artist: Robert Bourgeault, production quantity 4,500 . . . . **60.00** **60.00**

		Issue Price	Current Value
☐ **1987**	**Thomas Hardy Cottage,** artist: Robert Bourgeault, production quantity 4,500	65.00	65.00

SINGLE ISSUES

☐ **1986**	**Rose Cottage,** artist: Robert Bourgeault, production quantity 1,500	150.00	150.00
☐ **1986**	**Anne Hathaway Cottage,** artist: Robert Bourgeault, production quantity 500	250.00	250.00

AVONDALE

United States

CAMEOS OF CHILDHOOD

☐ **1978**	**Melissa,** artist: Frances Taylor Williams, production quantity 23,050	65.00	67.00
☐ **1979**	**First Born,** artist: Frances Taylor Williams, production quantity 12,000	70.00	72.00
☐ **1980**	**Melissa's Brother,** artist: Frances Taylor Williams, production quantity 8,400	70.00	72.00
☐ **1981**	**Daddy and I,** artist: Frances Taylor Williams, production quantity 10,000	75.00	76.00

CHRISTMAS ANNUAL SERIES

☐ **1981**	**. . . And the Heavens Rejoiced,** artist: Frances Taylor Williams, production quantity 6,500	90.00	90.00
☐ **1982**	**. . . And There Came the Wisemen,** artist: Frances Taylor Williams, production quantity 6,500	90.00	90.00
☐ **1983**	**The Shepherd,** artist: Frances Taylor Williams, production quantity 6,500	90.00	95.00

MOTHER'S DAY

☐ **1982**	**A Ribbon for Her Hair,** artist: Frances Taylor Williams, production quantity 6,500 . . .	75.00	76.00
☐ **1984**	**Just Like Mother,** artist: Frances Taylor Williams, production quantity 6,500	75.00	76.00

MYTHS OF THE SEA SERIES

☐ **1979**	**Poseidon,** artist: Gregg Appleby, production quantity 15,000	70.00	72.00
☐ **1981**	**Maiden of the Seappleby,** production quantity 10,000	75.00	77.00

	Issue Price	Current Value

TRIBUTES TO THE AGELESS ARTS SERIES

	Issue Price	Current Value
☐ 1979 **Court Jesters,** artist: Almazetta, production quantity 10,000	70.00	72.00

WORLD OF DANCE SERIES

	Issue Price	Current Value
☐ 1979 **Prima Ballerina,** artist: Almazetta, production quantity 15,000	70.00	72.00

AYNSLEY

Great Britain

A CHRISTMAS CAROL SERIES

	Issue Price	Current Value
☐ 1979 **Mr. Fezziwig's Ball,** production: one year	30.00	32.00
☐ 1980 **Marley's Ghost,** production: one year	36.00	38.00

SINGLE ISSUES

	Issue Price	Current Value
☐ 1969 **Prince of Wales,** production quantity 1,000	50.00	50.00
☐ 1970 **The Mayflower,** production quantity 1,000	35.00	35.00
☐ 1973 **1,000 Years of English Monarchy,** production quantity 1,000	30.00	30.00

B & J ART DESIGNS

United States
(See also Carson Mint)

OLD-FASHIONED CHRISTMAS SERIES

	Issue Price	Current Value
☐ 1983 **Carol,** artist: Jan Hagara, production quantity 15,000	45.00	47.00

OLD-FASHIONED COUNTRY SERIES

	Issue Price	Current Value
☐ 1984 **Cristina,** artist: Jan Hagara, production quantity 20,000	39.00	39.00
☐ 1985 **Laurel,** artist: Jan Hagara, production quantity 15,000	42.50	42.50

YESTERDAY'S CHILDREN SERIES

	Issue Price	Current Value
☐ 1978 **Lisa and the Jumeau Doll,** artist: Jan Hagara, production quantity 5,000	60.00	95.00

		Issue Price	Current Value
☐ 1979	**Adrianne and the Bye-Lo Doll,** artist: Jan Hagara, production quantity 5,000	60.00	92.00
☐ 1980	**Lydia and the Shirley Temple Doll,** artist: Jan Hagara, production quantity 5,000	60.00	77.00
☐ 1981	**Melanie and the Scarlett O'Hara Doll,** artist: Jan Hagara, production quantity 5,000	60.00	62.00

BAREUTHER

Germany

CHRISTMAS SERIES

☐ 1967	**Stiftskirche,** artist: Hans Mueller, production quantity 10,000	12.00	100.00
☐ 1968	**Kapplkirche,** artist: Hans Mueller, production quantity 10,000	12.00	35.00
☐ 1969	**Christkindlemarkt,** artist: Hans Mueller, production quantity 10,000	12.00	15.00
☐ 1970	**Chapel in Oberndorf,** artist: Hans Mueller, production quantity 10,000	12.50	15.00
☐ 1971	**Toys for Sale,** artist: Hans Mueller (from drawing by L. Ricter), production quantity 10,000	12.75	15.00
☐ 1972	**Christmas in Munich,** artist: Hans Mueller, production quantity 10,000	14.50	33.00
☐ 1973	**Sleigh Ride,** artist: Hans Mueller, production quantity 10,000	15.00	15.00
☐ 1974	**Black Forest Church,** artist: Hans Mueller, production quantity 10,000	19.00	19.00
☐ 1975	**Snowman,** artist: Hans Mueller, production quantity 10,000	21.50	21.50
☐ 1976	**Chapel in the Hills,** artist: Hans Mueller, production quantity 10,000	23.50	23.50
☐ 1977	**Story Time,** artist: Hans Mueller, production quantity 10,000	24.50	32.00
☐ 1978	**Mittenwald,** artist: Hans Mueller, production quantity 10,000	27.50	31.00
☐ 1979	**Winter Day,** artist: Hans Mueller, production quantity 10,000	35.00	30.00
☐ 1980	**Mittenberg,** artist: Hans Mueller, production quantity 10,000	37.50	39.00
☐ 1980	**Walk in the Forest,** artist: Hans Mueller, production quantity 10,000	39.50	39.50

		Issue Price	Current Value
☐ 1982	**Bad Wimpfen,** artist: Hans Mueller, production quantity 10,000	**39.50**	**39.50**
☐ 1983	**Night Before Christmas,** artist: Hans Mueller, production quantity 10,000	**39.50**	**39.50**
☐ 1984	**Zeil on the River Main,** artist: Hans Mueller, production quantity 10,000	**42.50**	**42.50**
☐ 1985	**Winter Wonderland,** artist: Hans Mueller, production quantity 10,000	**42.50**	**42.50**

DANISH CHURCH SERIES

☐ 1968	**Roskilde Cathedral Fe,** artist: unannounced, production: one year	**12.00**	**27.00**
☐ 1969	**Ribe Cathedral,** artist: unannounced, production: one year	**12.00**	**25.00**
☐ 1970	**Marmor Kirken,** artist: unannounced, production: one year	**13.00**	**13.00**
☐ 1977	**Budolfi Kirken,** artist: unannounced, production: one year	**15.95**	**23.00**
☐ 1978	**Haderslav Cathedral,** artist: unannounced, production: one year	**19.95**	**17.00**
☐ 1979	**Holmens Church,** artist: unannounced, production: one year	**15.30**	**20.00**

FATHER'S DAY SERIES

☐ 1969	**Castle Newschwanstein,** artist: Hans Mueller, production: one year	**10.50**	**55.00**
☐ 1970	**Castle Pfalz,** artist: Hans Mueller, production: one year	**12.50**	**20.00**
☐ 1971	**Ejby Church,** artist: unannounced, production: one year	**13.00**	**16.00**
☐ 1972	**Kalundborg Kirken,** artist: unannounced, production: one year	**13.00**	**22.00**
☐ 1973	**Grundtvig Kirken,** artist: unannounced, production: one year	**15.00**	**20.00**
☐ 1974	**Broager Kirken,** artist: unannounced, production: one year	**15.00**	**20.00**
☐ 1975	**St. Knuds Kirken,** artist: unannounced, production: one year	**20.00**	**20.00**
☐ 1976	**Osterlas Kirken,** artist: unannounced, production: one year	**20.00**	**22.00**
☐ 1971	**Castle Heidelberg,** artist: Hans Mueller, production: one year	**12.75**	**23.00**
☐ 1972	**Castle Hohenschwangau,** artist: Hans Mueller, production: one year	**14.50**	**23.00**

		Issue Price	Current Value
☐ 1973	**Castle Katz,** artist: Hans Mueller, production: one year	15.00	30.00
☐ 1974	**Wurzburg Castle,** artist: Hans Mueller, production: one year	19.00	52.00
☐ 1975	**Castle Lichtenstein,** artist: Hans Mueller, production: one year	21.50	33.00
☐ 1976	**Castle Hohenzollern,** artist: Hans Mueller, production: one year	23.50	32.00
☐ 1977	**Castle Eltz,** artist: Hans Mueller, production: one year	24.50	28.00
☐ 1978	**Castle Falkenstein,** artist: Hans Mueller, production: one year	27.50	28.00
☐ 1979	**Castle Reinstein,** artist: Hans Mueller, production quantity 2,500	35.00	30.00
☐ 1980	**Castle Cochem,** artist: Hans Mueller, production quantity 2,500	37.50	40.00
☐ 1981	**Castle Gutenfels,** artist: Hans Mueller, production quantity 2,500	39.50	42.00
☐ 1982	**Castle Zwingerberg,** artist: Hans Mueller, production quantity 2,500	39.50	40.00
☐ 1983	**Castle Launstein,** artist: Hans Mueller, production quantity 2,500	39.50	39.50
☐ 1984	**Castle Nuenstein,** artist: Hans Mueller, production: one year	42.50	44.00

MOTHER'S DAY SERIES

		Issue Price	Current Value
☐ 1969	**Mother and Children,** artist: Ludwig Richter, production quantity 5,000	10.50	75.00
☐ 1970	**Mother and Children,** artist: Ludwig Richter, production quantity 5,000	12.50	28.00
☐ 1971	**Mother and Children,** artist: Ludwig Richter, production quantity 5,000	12.75	20.00
☐ 1972	**Mother and Children,** artist: Ludwig Richter, production quantity 5,000	15.00	20.00
☐ 1973	**Mother and Children,** artist: Ludwig Richter, production quantity 5,000	15.00	20.00
☐ 1974	**Musical Children,** artist: Ludwig Richter, production quantity 5,000	19.00	35.00
☐ 1975	**Spring Outing,** artist: Ludwig Richter, production quantity 5,000	21.50	25.00
☐ 1976	**Rocking the Cradle,** artist: Ludwig Richter, production quantity 5,000	23.50	25.00
☐ 1977	**Noon Feeding,** artist: Ludwig Richter, production quantity 5,000	24.50	28.00

		Issue Price	Current Value
☐ 1978	**Blind Man's Bluff,** artist: Ludwig Richter, production quantity 5,000	27.50	30.00
☐ 1979	**Mother's Love,** artist: Ludwig Richter, production quantity 5,000	37.50	40.00
☐ 1980	**The First Cherries,** artist: Ludwig Richter, production quantity 5,000	37.50	40.00
☐ 1981	**Playtime,** artist: Ludwig Richter, production quantity 5,000	39.50	43.00
☐ 1982	**Suppertime,** artist: Ludwig Richter, production quantity 5,000	39.50	43.00
☐ 1983	**On the Farm,** artist: Ludwig Richter, production quantity 5,000	39.50	39.50
☐ 1984	**Village Children,** artist: Ludwig Richter, production quantity 5,000	42.50	42.50

MURILLO, ESTEBAN SERIES

☐ 1972	**Beggar Boys Playing Dice**	42.00	45.00
☐ 1972	**Boys Eating Melons and Grapes**	42.00	45.00
☐ 1972	**Fruit Vendors Counting Money**	12.00	45.00
☐ 1972	**Boys Eating Pastry**	12.00	45.00

THANKSGIVING SERIES

☐ 1971	**First Thanksgiving,** production quantity 2,500	13.50	35.00
☐ 1972	**Harvest,** production quantity 2,500	14.50	20.00
☐ 1973	**Country Road in Autumn,** production quantity 2,500	15.00	20.00
☐ 1974	**Old Mill,** production quantity 2,500	19.00	20.00
☐ 1975	**Wild Deer in Forest,** production quantity 2,500	21.50	25.00
☐ 1976	**Thanksgiving on Farm,** production quantity 2,500	23.50	28.00
☐ 1977	**Horses,** artist: Hans Mueller, production quantity 2,500	24.50	28.00
☐ 1978	**Apple Harvest,** artist: Hans Mueller, production quantity 2,500	27.50	30.00
☐ 1979	**Noontime,** artist: Hans Mueller, production quantity 2,500	35.00	38.00
☐ 1980	**Longhorns,** artist: Hans Mueller, production quantity 2,500	37.50	40.00
☐ 1981	**Gathering Wheat,** artist: Hans Mueller, production quantity 2,500	39.50	40.00
☐ 1982	**Autumn,** artist: Hans Mueller, production quantity 2,500	39.50	42.00

	Issue Price	Current Value
☐ **1983 Harrow,** artist: Hans Mueller, production quantity 2,500	**39.50**	**39.50**
☐ **1984 Farmland,** artist: Hans Mueller, production quantity 2,500	**42.50**	**42.50**

BARTHMANN

Germany

CHRISTMAS SERIES

☐ **1977 Mary with Child,** production quantity 300	**236.00**	**240.00**
☐ **1978 Adoration of Child,** production quantity 500	**326.00**	**330.00**
☐ **1979 Holy Mother of Kasanskaja,** production quantity 500	**361.00**	**360.00**
☐ **1980 Holy Mother by Kykos,** production quantity 500	**385.00**	**390.00**

BAYEL OF FRANCE

France

BICENTENNIAL SERIES

☐ **1974 Liberty Bell,** production quantity 500	**50.00**	**50.00**
☐ **1975 Independence Hall,** production quantity 500	**60.00**	**60.00**
☐ **1976 Spread Eagle,** production quantity 500	**60.00**	**60.00**

EAGLE SERIES

☐ **1974 Eagle Head,** production quantity 300	**50.00**	**55.00**
☐ **1974 Eagle in Flight,** production quantity 300 ..	**50.00**	**55.00**

FLOWERS SERIES

☐ **1972 Rose,** production quantity 300	**50.00**	**55.00**
☐ **1973 Lilies,** production quantity 300	**50.00**	**55.00**
☐ **1973 Orchid,** production quantity 300	**50.00**	**55.00**

BEACON PLATE MANUFACTURING

United States

PACE SETTERS SERIES

☐ **1987 Frederick Douglass,** artist: unannounced, production quantity 2500	**53.50**	**55.00**

BELLEEK POTTERY

Great Britain

CHRISTMAS SERIES	Issue Price	Current Value
☐ 1970 **Castle Caldwell,** artist: unannounced, production quantity 7,500	25.00	85.00
☐ 1971 **Celtic Cross,** artist: unannounced, production quantity 7,500	25.00	40.00
☐ 1972 **Flight of the Earls,** artist: unannounced, production quantity 7,500	30.00	44.00
☐ 1973 **Tribute to Yeats,** artist: unannounced, production quantity 7,500	38.50	62.00
☐ 1974 **Devenish Island,** artist: unannounced, production quantity 7,500	45.00	210.00
☐ 1975 **The Celtic Cross,** artist: unannounced, production quantity 7,500	48.00	59.00
☐ 1976 **Dove of Peace,** artist: unannounced, production quantity 7,500	55.00	55.00
☐ 1977 **Wren,** artist: unannounced, production quantity 7,500	55.00	55.00

IRISH WILDLIFE SERIES

	Issue Price	Current Value
☐ 1978 **A Leaping Salmon,** artist: unannounced . . .	55.00	72.00
☐ 1979 **Hare at Rest,** artist: unannounced	58.50	66.00
☐ 1980 **The Hedgehog,** artist: unannounced	66.50	66.50
☐ 1981 **Red Squirrel,** artist: unannounced	78.00	78.00
☐ 1982 **Irish Seal,** artist: unannounced	78.00	78.00
☐ 1983 **Red Fox,** artist: unannounced	85.00	85.00

ST. PATRICK'S DAY SERIES

	Issue Price	Current Value
☐ 1986 **St. Patrick Banishing the Snakes from Ireland,** artist: Fergus Cleary, production quantity 10,000	75.00	75.00

BENGOUGH

Canada

CHRISTMAS SERIES

	Issue Price	Current Value
☐ 1972 **Charles Dickens Christmas Carol,** production quantity 490	125.00	130.00

	Issue Price	Current Value

NORTHWEST MOUNTED POLICE SERIES

☐ 1972 **1898 Dress Uniform,** production quantity
1,000 .... **140.00** **140.00**
☐ 1972 **First Uniform,** production quantity 1,000 ... **140.00** **140.00**

ROYAL CANADIAN POLICE SERIES

☐ 1972 **Order Dress,** production quantity 1,000 ... **140.00** **140.00**

BERLIN DESIGN

Germany

CHRISTMAS SERIES

☐ 1970 **Christmas in Bernkastel,** artist: unannounced, production quantity 4,000 .... **14.50** **135.00**
☐ 1971 **Christmas in Rothenburg,** artist: unannounced, production quantity 20,000 ...... **14.50** **35.00**
☐ 1972 **Christmas in Michelstadt,** artist: unannounced, production: one year **15.00** **50.00**
☐ 1973 **Christmas in Wendelstein,** artist: unannounced, production: one year **20.00** **40.00**
☐ 1974 **Christmas in Bremen,** artist: unannounced,
production: one year **25.00** **25.00**
☐ 1975 **Christmas in Dortland,** artist: unannounced,
production: one year **30.00** **72.50**
☐ 1976 **Christmas in Augsburg,** artist: unannounced,
production: one year **32.00** **32.00**
☐ 1977 **Christmas in Hamburg,** artist: unannounced,
production: one year **32.00** **32.00**
☐ 1978 **Christmas in Berlin,** artist: unannounced,
production quantity 20,000 .... **36.00** **65.00**
☐ 1979 **Christmas in Greetsiel,** artist: unannounced,
production quantity 20,000 .... **47.50** **62.50**
☐ 1980 **Christmas in Mittenberg,** artist: unannounced, production quantity 20,000 ...... **50.00** **60.00**
☐ 1981 **Christmas Eve in Hahnenklee,** artist: unannounced, production quantity 20,000 ...... **55.00** **57.50**
☐ 1982 **Christmas Eve in Wasserberg,** artist: unannounced, production quantity 20,000 ...... **55.00** **55.00**
☐ 1983 **Christmas in Oberndorf,** artist: unannounced, production quantity 20,000 ...... **55.00** **55.00**
☐ 1985 **Christmas in Ramsau,** artist: unannounced,
production quantity 20,000 .... **55.00** **55.00**

	Issue Price	Current Value

FATHER'S DAY SERIES

☐ 1971 **Brooklyn Bridge on Opening Day,** production quantity 12,000	14.50	20.00
☐ 1972 **Continent Spanned,** production quantity 3,000	15.00	37.00
☐ 1973 **Landing of Columbus,** production quantity 2,000	18.00	40.00
☐ 1974 **Adorn's Balloon,** production: one year	25.00	37.00

HISTORICAL SERIES

☐ 1975 **Washington Crossing the Delaware,** production: one year	30.00	40.00
☐ 1976 **Tom Thumb,** production: one year	32.00	35.00
☐ 1977 **Zeppelin,** production: one year	32.00	35.00
☐ 1978 **Benz Motor Car Munich,** production quantity 10,000	36.00	36.00
☐ 1979 **Johannes Gutenberg at Mainz,** production quantity 10,000	47.50	48.00

HOLIDAY WEEK OF THE
FAMILY KAPPELMANN

☐ 1984 **Monday,** production quantity limited	33.00	40.00
☐ 1984 **Tuesday,** production quantity limited	33.00	33.00
☐ 1985 **Wednesday,** artist: Detlev Nitschke, production quantity limited	33.00	33.00
☐ 1985 **Thursday,** production quantity limited	35.00	35.00
☐ 1985 **Friday,** production quantity limited	35.00	35.00
☐ 1986 **Saturday,** production quantity limited	35.00	35.00
☐ 1986 **Sunday,** production quantity limited	35.00	35.00

MOTHER'S DAY SERIES

☐ 1971 **Grey Poodles,** production quantity 20,000	14.50	25.00
☐ 1972 **Fledglings,** production quantity 10,000	15.00	25.00
☐ 1973 **Duck Family,** production quantity 5,000 . . .	16.50	40.00
☐ 1974 **Squirrels,** production quantity 6,000	22.50	40.00
☐ 1975 **Cats,** production quantity 6,000	30.00	40.00
☐ 1976 **Deer,** production quantity 6,000	32.00	34.00
☐ 1977 **Storks,** production quantity 6,000	32.00	35.00
☐ 1978 **Mare and Foal,** production quantity 6,000	36.00	40.00
☐ 1979 **Swans with Cygnets,** production quantity 6,000	47.50	50.00
☐ 1980 **Goat Family,** production quantity 6,000 . . .	55.00	58.00
☐ 1981 **Dachshund and Puppies,** production: one year	50.00	55.00

BETOURNE STUDIOS

France

JEAN-PAUL LOUP CHRISTMAS SERIES	Issue Price	Current Value
☐ 1971 **Noel,** production quantity 300	125.00	1000.00
☐ 1972 **Noel,** production quantity 300	150.00	700.00
☐ 1973 **Noel,** production quantity 300	175.00	500.00
☐ 1974 **Noel,** production quantity 400	200.00	500.00
☐ 1975 **Noel,** production quantity 250	250.00	500.00
☐ 1976 **Noel,** production quantity 150	300.00	600.00

MOTHER'S DAY SERIES

	Issue Price	Current Value
☐ 1974 **Mother and Child,** production quantity 500	250.00	1200.00
☐ 1975 **Mother's Day,** production quantity 400 ...	285.00	300.00
☐ 1976 **Mother and Child,** production quantity 250	300.00	600.00

BING & GRONDAHL

Denmark

BICENTENNIAL SERIES

☐ 1976 **E Pluribus Unum,** production: one year ...	50.00	50.00

CARL LARSSON SERIES

☐ 1977 **Flowers on Windowsill,** set of 4, production quantity 7,500	150.00	150.00
☐ 1977 **Breakfast Under Big Birch,** set of 4, production quantity 7,500	150.00	150.00
☐ 1977 **Yard and Warehouse,** set of 4, production quantity 7,500	150.00	150.00
☐ 1977 **Kitchen,** set of 4, production quantity 7,500	150.00	150.00
☐ 1978 **First Born,** set of 4, production quantity 7,500	150.00	150.00
☐ 1978 **Room for Mother and Children,** set of 4, production quantity 7,500	150.00	150.00
☐ 1978 **Portrait of Inga-Maria Thiel,** set of 4, production quantity 7,500	150.00	150.00
☐ 1978 **Iduna,** set of 4, production quantity 7,500	150.00	150.00
☐ 1979 **Forestry,** set of 4, production quantity 7,500	150.00	150.00
☐ 1979 **Cutting Grass,** set of 4, production quantity 7,500	150.00	150.00
☐ 1979 **Potato Harvest,** set of 4, production quantity 7,500	150.00	150.00
☐ 1979 **Fishery,** set of 4, production quantity 7,500	150.00	150.00

		Issue Price	Current Value

CARL LARSSON MINIATURE PLATE SERIES

		Issue Price	Current Value
☐ 1986	The Flower Window, production quantity 15,000	15.00	15.00
☐ 1986	Lunch Under the Birch Tree, production quantity 15,000	15.00	15.00
☐ 1986	Winter and the Old Barn, production quantity 15,000	15.00	15.00
☐ 1986	Mama's Room, production quantity 15,000	15.00	15.00
☐ 1986	Iduna's New Dress, production quantity 15,000	15.00	15.00
☐ 1986	Working in the Woods, production quantity 15,000	15.00	15.00
☐ 1986	Harvest, production quantity 15,000	15.00	15.00
☐ 1986	Potato Harvest, production quantity 15,000	15.00	15.00
☐ 1986	Fishing, production quantity 15,000	15.00	15.00
☐ 1986	Opening Day of the Crayfish Season, production quantity 15,000	15.00	15.00
☐ 1986	Azalea, production quantity 15,000	15.00	15.00
☐ 1986	Apple Harvest, production quantity 15,000	15.00	15.00

CAT PORTRAIT SERIES

		Issue Price	Current Value
☐ 1987	Manx and Kittens, artist: Angela Sayer, production quantity 14,500	39.50	40.00
☐ 1987	Persian and Kittens, artist: Angela Sayer, production quantity 14,500	39.50	40.00
☐ 1987	Somali and Kittens, artist: Angela Sayer, production quantity 14,500	39.50	40.00
☐ 1987	Burmese and Kittens, artist: Angela Sayer, production quantity 14,500	39.50	40.00

CHILDREN'S DAY SERIES

		Issue Price	Current Value
☐ 1985	The Magical Tea Party, artist: C. Roller, production: less than one year	24.50	26.00
☐ 1986	A Joyful Flight, artist: C. Roller, production: less than one year	26.50	28.00
☐ 1987	The Little Gardeners, artist: C. Roller, production: one year	29.50	29.50

CHRISTMAS IN AMERICA SERIES

		Issue Price	Current Value
☐ 1986	Christmas Eve in Williamsburg, artist: J. Woodson, production: less than one year	29.50	29.50

		Issue Price	Current Value
CHRISTMAS SERIES			
☐ 1895	**Behind the Frozen Window,** artist: Franz August Hallin, production: one year	.50	3600.00
☐ 1896	**New Moon,** artist: Franz August Hallin, production: one year	.50	1475.00
☐ 1897	**Sparrows,** artist: Franz August Hallin, production: one year	.75	1100.00
☐ 1898	**Roses and Star,** artist: Fanny Garde, production: one year	.75	600.00
☐ 1899	**Crows,** artist: Dahl Jensen, production: one year	.75	900.00
☐ 1900	**Church Bells,** artist: Dahl Jensen, production: one year	.75	810.00
☐ 1901	**Three Wise Men,** artist: S. Sabra, production: one year	1.00	500.00
☐ 1902	**Gothic Church Interior,** artist: Dahl Jensen, production: one year	1.00	300.00
☐ 1903	**Expectant Children,** artist: Margarethe Hyldahl, production: one year	1.00	150.00
☐ 1904	**Frederiksberg Hill,** artist: Centhinka Olsen, production: one year	1.00	127.50
☐ 1905	**Christmas Night,** artist: Dahl Jensen, production: one year	1.00	135.00
☐ 1906	**Sleighing to Church,** artist: Dahl Jensen, production: one year	1.00	90.00
☐ 1907	**Little Match Girl,** artist: E. Plockross, production: one year	1.00	120.00
☐ 1908	**St. Petri Church,** artist: Povi Jorgensen, production: one year	1.00	85.00
☐ 1909	**Yule Tree,** artist: Aarestrup, production: one year	1.50	96.00
☐ 1910	**The Old Organist,** artist: C. Ersgaard, production: one year	1.50	90.00
☐ 1911	**Angels and Shepherds,** artist: H. Moltke, production: one year	1.50	75.00
☐ 1912	**Going to Church,** artist: Einar Hansen, production: one year	1.50	81.00
☐ 1913	**Bringing Home the Tree,** artist: T. Larsen, production: one year	1.50	98.00
☐ 1914	**Amalienborg Castle,** artist: T. Larsen, production: one year	1.50	75.00
☐ 1915	**Dog Outside Window,** artist: Dahl Jensen, production: one year	1.50	120.00
☐ 1916	**Sparrows at Christmas,** artist: J. Bloch Jorgensen, production: one year	1.50	67.50

		Issue Price	Current Value
☐ 1917	**Christmas Boat,** artist: Achton Friis, production: one year	1.50	75.00
☐ 1918	**Fishing Boat,** artist: Achton Friis, production: one year	1.50	90.00
☐ 1919	**Outside Lighted Window,** artist: Achton Friis, production: one year	2.00	75.00
☐ 1920	**Hare in Snow,** artist: Achton Friis, production: one year	2.00	75.00
☐ 1921	**Pigeons,** artist: Achton Friis, production: one year	2.00	60.00
☐ 1922	**Star of Bethlehem,** artist: Achton Friis, production: one year	2.00	57.00
☐ 1923	**The Hermitage,** artist: Achton Friis, production: one year	2.00	57.00
☐ 1924	**Lighthouse,** artist: Achton Friis, production: one year	2.50	70.00
☐ 1925	**Child's Christmas,** artist: Achton Friis, production: one year	2.50	78.00
☐ 1926	**Churchgoers,** artist: Achton Friis, production: one year	2.50	68.00
☐ 1927	**Skating Couple,** artist: Achton Friis, production: one year	2.50	115.00
☐ 1928	**Eskimos,** artist: Achton Friis, production: one year	2.50	65.00
☐ 1929	**Fox Outside Farm,** artist: Achton Friis, production: one year	2.50	80.00
☐ 1930	**Town Hall Square,** artist: H. Flugenring, production: one year	2.50	96.00
☐ 1931	**Christmas Train,** artist: Achton Friis, production: one year	2.50	85.00
☐ 1932	**Life Boat,** artist: H. Flugenring, production: one year	2.50	95.00
☐ 1933	**Korsor-Nyborg Ferry,** artist: H. Flugenring, production: one year	3.00	72.00
☐ 1934	**Church Bell in Tower,** artist: Immanuel Tjerne, production: one year	3.00	75.00
☐ 1935	**Lillebelt Bridge,** artist: Ove Larsen, production: one year	3.00	60.00
☐ 1936	**Royal Guard, Amalienborg,** artist: Ove Larsen, production: one year	3.00	78.00
☐ 1937	**Arrival of Christmas Guests,** artist: Ove Larsen, production: one year	3.00	75.00
☐ 1938	**Lighting the Candles,** artist: Immanuel Tjerne, production: one year	3.00	112.00

		Issue Price	Current Value
☐ 1939	Old Lock-Eye, The Sandman, artist: Immanuel Tjerne, production: one year	3.00	172.00
☐ 1940	Christmas Letters, artist: Ove Larsen, production: one year	4.00	165.00
☐ 1941	Horses Enjoying Meal, artist: Ove Larsen, production: one year	4.00	330.00
☐ 1942	Danish Farm, artist: Ove Larsen, production: one year	4.00	150.00
☐ 1943	Ribe Cathedral, artist: Ove Larsen, production: one year	5.00	160.00
☐ 1944	Sorgenfri Castle, artist: Ove Larsen, production: one year	5.00	120.00
☐ 1945	Old Water Mill, artist: Ove Larsen, production: one year	5.00	130.00
☐ 1946	Commemoration Cross, artist: Margrethe Hyldahl, production: one year	5.00	84.00
☐ 1947	Dybbol Mill, artist: Margrethe Hyldahl, production: one year	5.00	85.00
☐ 1948	Watchman, artist: Margrethe Hyldahl, production: one year	5.50	75.00
☐ 1949	Landsoldaten, artist: Margrethe Hyldahl, production: one year	5.50	80.00
☐ 1950	Kronborg Castle, artist: Margrethe Hyldahl, production: one year	5.50	150.00
☐ 1951	Jens Bang, artist: Margrethe Hyldahl, production: one year	6.00	112.50
☐ 1952	Thorvaldsen Museum, artist: Borge Pramvig, production: one year	6.00	84.00
☐ 1953	Snowman, artist: Borge Pramvig, production: one year	7.50	96.00
☐ 1954	Royal Boat, artist: Kjeld Bonfils, production: one year	7.00	105.00
☐ 1955	Kaulundborg Church, artist: Kjeld Bonfils, production: one year	8.00	108.00
☐ 1956	Christmas in Copenhagen, artist: Kjeld Bonfils, production: one year	8.50	144.00
☐ 1957	Christmas Candles, artist: Kjeld Bonfils, production: one year	9.00	165.00
☐ 1958	Santa Claus, artist: Kjeld Bonfils, production: one year	9.50	108.00
☐ 1959	Christmas Eve, artist: Kjeld Bonfils, production: one year	10.00	127.50
☐ 1960	Village Church, artist: Kjeld Bonfils, production: one year	10.00	180.00

		Issue Price	Current Value
☐ 1961	**Winter Harmony,** artist: Kjeld Bonfils, production: one year	10.50	96.00
☐ 1962	**Winter Night,** artist: Kjeld Bonfils, production: one year	11.00	85.00
☐ 1963	**Christmas Elf,** artist: Henry Thelander, production: one year	11.00	105.00
☐ 1964	**Fir Tree and Hare,** artist: Henry Thelander, production: one year	11.50	50.00
☐ 1965	**Bringing Home the Tree,** artist: Henry Thelander, production: one year	12.00	58.00
☐ 1966	**Home for Christmas,** artist: Henry Thelander, production: one year	12.00	45.00
☐ 1967	**Sharing the Joy,** artist: Henry Thelander, production: one year	13.00	48.00
☐ 1968	**Christmas in Church,** artist: Henry Thelander, production: one year	14.00	30.00
☐ 1969	**Arrival of Guests,** artist: Henry Thelander, production: one year	14.00	27.00
☐ 1970	**Pheasants in Snow,** artist: Henry Thelander, production: one year	14.50	19.50
☐ 1971	**Christmas at Home,** artist: Henry Thelander, production: one year	15.00	20.00
☐ 1972	**Christmas in Greenland,** artist: Henry Thelander, production: one year	16.50	20.00
☐ 1973	**Country Christmas,** artist: Henry Thelander, production: one year	19.50	27.00
☐ 1974	**Christmas in the Village,** artist: Henry Thelander, production: one year	22.00	22.00
☐ 1975	**Old Water Mill,** artist: Henry Thelander, production: one year	27.50	27.50
☐ 1976	**Christmas Welcome,** artist: Henry Thelander, production: one year	27.50	27.50
☐ 1977	**Copenhagen Christmas,** artist: Henry Thelander, production: one year	29.50	29.50
☐ 1978	**Christmas Tale,** artist: Henry Thelander, production: one year	32.00	32.00
☐ 1979	**White Christmas,** artist: Henry Thelander, production: one year	36.50	42.00
☐ 1980	**Christmas in Woods,** artist: Henry Thelander, production: one year	42.50	42.00
☐ 1981	**Christmas Peace,** artist: Henry Thelander, production: one year	49.50	49.50
☐ 1982	**Christmas Tree,** artist: Henry Thelander, production: one year	54.50	54.50

		Issue Price	Current Value
☐ 1983	**Christmas in the Old Town,** artist: Henry Thelander, production: one year	**54.50**	**54.50**
☐ 1984	**The Christmas Letter,** artist: Edward Jensen, production: one year	**54.50**	**54.50**
☐ 1985	**Christmas Eve at the Farmhouse,** artist: Edward Jensen, production: one year	**54.50**	**54.50**
☐ 1986	**Silent Night, Holy Night,** artist: Edward Jensen, production: one year	**54.50**	**54.50**
☐ 1987	**The Snowman's Christmas Eve,** artist: Edward Jensen, production: one year	**59.50**	**59.50**

COMPOSERS OF CLASSICAL MUSIC SERIES

		Issue Price	Current Value
☐ 1979	**Beethoven,** production: one year	**37.50**	**38.00**
☐ 1980	**Bach,** production: one year	**37.50**	**38.00**
☐ 1981	**Brahms,** production: one year	**37.50**	**38.00**
☐ 1982	**Chopin,** production: one year	**37.50**	**38.00**
☐ 1983	**Haydn,** production: one year	**37.50**	**38.00**
☐ 1984	**Edvard Grieg,** production: unannounced . . .	**37.50**	**38.50**

GENTLE LOVE SERIES

		Issue Price	Current Value
☐ 1985	**Joanna and Jon,** artist: A. H. Cooper, production quantity 9,500	**45.00**	**45.00**
☐ 1985	**Alexandra and Amy,** artist: A. H. Cooper, production quantity 9,500	**45.00**	**45.00**
☐ 1985	**Ingrid and Lisa,** artist: A. H. Cooper, production quantity 9,500	**45.00**	**45.00**
☐ 1985	**Elizabeth and David,** artist: A. H. Cooper, production quantity 9,500	**45.00**	**45.00**

HANS CHRISTIAN ANDERSEN SERIES
(Ghent Collection)

		Issue Price	Current Value
☐ 1979	**Thumbelina,** production quantity 7,500	**42.50**	**45.00**
☐ 1979	**Princess and the Pea,** production quantity 7,500	**42.50**	**45.00**
☐ 1979	**Wild Swans,** production quantity 7,500	**42.50**	**45.00**
☐ 1980	**Emperor's New Clothes,** production quantity 7,500	**42.50**	**45.00**
☐ 1980	**Little Mermaid,** production quantity 7,500	**42.50**	**45.00**
☐ 1980	**Nightingale,** production quantity 7,500	**42.50**	**45.00**

	Issue Price	Current Value

HERITAGE SERIES

☐ 1976 **Norseman,** production quantity 5,000 ..... 30.00 32.00
☐ 1977 **Navigators,** production quantity 5,000 ..... 30.00 32.00
☐ 1978 **Discovery,** production quantity 5,000 ..... 39.50 42.00
☐ 1979 **Exploration,** production quantity 5,000 .... 39.50 42.00
☐ 1980 **Helmsman,** production quantity 5,000 ..... 45.00 48.00

JUBILEE FIVE-YEAR CHRISTMAS SERIES

☐ 1915 **Frozen Window,** artist: Franz August Hallin, production: one year 3.00 225.00
☐ 1920 **Church Bells,** artist: Fanny Garde, production: one year 4.00 60.00
☐ 1925 **Dog Outside Window,** artist: Dahl Jensen, production: one year 5.00 300.00
☐ 1930 **The Old Organist,** artist: C. Ersgaard, production: one year 5.00 225.00
☐ 1935 **Little Match Girl,** artist: E. Plockross, production: one year 6.00 1000.00
☐ 1940 **Three Wise Men,** artist: S. Sabra, production: one year 10.00 2000.00
☐ 1945 **Royal Guard Amalienborg Castle,** artist: T. Larsen, production: one year 10.00 150.00
☐ 1950 **Eskimos,** artist: A. Friis, production: one year 15.00 180.00
☐ 1955 **Dybbol Mill,** artist: Margarethe Hyldahl, production: one year 20.00 210.00
☐ 1960 **Kronborg Castle,** artist: Margarethe Hyldahl, production: one year 25.00 90.00
☐ 1965 **Churchgoers,** artist: A. Friis, production: one year 25.00 39.50
☐ 1970 **Amalienborg Castle,** artist: T. Larsen, production: one year 30.00 35.00
☐ 1975 **Horses Enjoying Meal,** artist: O. Larsen, production: one year 40.00 50.00
☐ 1980 **Happiness over Yule Tree,** artist: Aarestrup, production: one year 60.00 60.00
☐ 1985 **Lifeboat at Work,** artist: H. Flugenring, production: one year 65.00 65.00

MOMENTS OF TRUTH SERIES

☐ 1984 **Home Is Best,** artist: Kurt Ard, production quantity limited 29.50 31.50
☐ 1984 **The Road to Virtuosity,** artist: Kurt Ard, production quantity limited 29.50 35.00

		Issue Price	Current Value
☐ 1985	**First Things First,** artist: Kurt Ard, production quantity limited	29.50	35.00
☐ 1985	**Unfair Competition,** artist: Kurt Ard, production quantity limited	29.50	35.00
☐ 1986	**Bored Sick,** artist: Kurt Ard, production quantity limited	29.50	35.00
☐ 1986	**First Crush,** artist: Kurt Ard, production quantity limited	29.50	32.00

MOTHER'S DAY SERIES

		Issue Price	Current Value
☐ 1969	**Dogs and Puppies,** artist: Henry Thelander, production: one year	9.75	400.00
☐ 1970	**Bird and Chicks,** artist: Henry Thelander, production: one year	10.00	30.00
☐ 1971	**Cat and Kitten,** artist: Henry Thelander, production: one year	11.00	15.00
☐ 1972	**Mare and Foal,** artist: Henry Thelander, production: one year	12.00	19.50
☐ 1973	**Duck and Ducklings,** artist: Henry Thelander, production: one year	13.00	20.00
☐ 1974	**Bear and Cubs,** artist: Henry Thelander, production: one year	16.50	20.00
☐ 1975	**Doe and Fawns,** artist: Henry Thelander, production: one year	19.50	19.50
☐ 1976	**Swan Family,** artist: Henry Thelander, production: one year	22.50	25.00
☐ 1977	**Squirrel and Young,** artist: Henry Thelander, production: one year	23.50	25.00
☐ 1978	**Heron,** artist: Henry Thelander, production: one year	24.50	25.00
☐ 1979	**Fox and Cubs,** artist: Henry Thelander, production: one year	27.50	37.50
☐ 1980	**Woodpecker and Young,** artist: Henry Thelander, production: one year	29.50	40.50
☐ 1981	**Hare and Young,** artist: Henry Thelander, production: one year	36.50	36.50
☐ 1982	**Lioness and Cubs,** artist: Henry Thelander, production: one year	39.50	39.50
☐ 1983	**Raccoon and Young,** artist: Henry Thelander, production: one year	39.50	39.50
☐ 1984	**Stork and Nestlings,** artist: Henry Thelander, production: one year	39.50	39.50
☐ 1985	**Bear and Cubs,** artist: Henry Thelander, production: one year	39.50	39.50

Raccoon and Young,
artist: Henry Thelander.

		Issue Price	Current Value
☐ 1986	**Elephant with Calf,** artist: Henry Thelander, production: one year	**39.50**	**39.50**
☐ 1987	**Sheep with Lambs,** artist: Henry Thelander, production: one year	**42.50**	**42.50**

MOTHER'S DAY FIVE-YEAR JUBILEE SERIES

☐ 1979	**Dog and Puppies,** artist: Henry Thelander, production: one year	**55.00**	**55.00**
☐ 1984	**Swan with Cygnets,** artist: Henry Thelander, production quantity unannounced	**65.00**	**65.00**

OLYMPIC GAME SERIES

☐ 1972	**Olympiad—Munich,** production: one year	**20.00**	**22.50**
☐ 1976	**Olympic Montreal,** production: one year . .	**29.50**	**32.00**
☐ 1980	**Moscow by Night,** production: one year . . .	**43.00**	**45.00**

SEASONS REMEMBERED SERIES

☐ 1983	**The Wildflowers of Summer,** artist: Verner Munch, production quantity 10,000	**35.00**	**35.00**
☐ 1983	**Autumn Showers,** artist: Verner Munch, production quantity 10,000	**35.00**	**35.00**
☐ 1983	**The Promise of Spring,** artist: Verner Munch, production quantity 10,000	**35.00**	**35.00**

		Issue Price	Current Value
☐ 1983	**The Winter of the Snowman,** artist: Verner Munch, production quantity 10,000	35.00	35.00
☐ 1984	**The Wildflowers of Summer,** artist: Verner Munch, production quantity 7,500	35.00	35.00
☐ 1984	**Autumn Showers,** artist: Verner Munch, production quantity 7,500	35.00	35.00
☐ 1984	**The Promise of Spring,** artist: Verner Munch, production quantity 7,500	35.00	35.00
☐ 1984	**The Winter of the Snowman,** artist: Verner Munch, production quantity 7,500	35.00	35.00

STATUE OF LIBERTY

☐ 1986	**Statue of Liberty,** artist: unannounced, production quantity 10,000	60.00	75.00

SUMMER AT SKAGEN SERIES

☐ 1986	**Summer Evening,** production quantity limited	34.50	35.00
☐ 1987	**Luncheon at Kroyer's,** production quantity limited	34.50	35.00

WINDJAMMERS SERIES

☐ 1980	**Danmark,** artist: James Mitchell, production quantity 10,000	95.00	100.00
☐ 1980	**Eagle,** artist: James Mitchell, production quantity 10,000	95.00	100.00
☐ 1981	**Gladan,** artist: James Mitchell, production quantity 10,000	95.00	100.00
☐ 1981	**Gorch/Fock,** artist: James Mitchell, production quantity 10,000	95.00	100.00
☐ 1982	**Amerigo Vespucci,** artist: James Mitchell, production quantity 10,000	95.00	100.00
☐ 1982	**Christian Radich,** artist: James Mitchell, production quantity 10,000	95.00	100.00

SINGLE RELEASES

☐ 1978	**Madonna,** production quantity 10,000	45.00	48.00
☐ 1978	**Seagull,** production quantity 7,500	75.00	72.00
☐ 1980	**Viking,** production quantity 10,000	65.00	68.00

Amerigo Vespucci and Christian Radich, artist: James Mitchell.

BLUE DELFT

Netherlands

CHRISTMAS SERIES	Issue Price	Current Value
☐ 1970 **Drawbridge Near Binnehof,** production: one year	12.00	25.00
☐ 1971 **St. Lauren's Church,** production: one year	12.00	25.00
☐ 1972 **Church at Bierkade,** production: one year	12.00	16.00
☐ 1973 **St. Jan's Church,** production: one year	12.00	16.00
☐ 1974 **Dingeradeel,** production: one year	13.00	16.00
☐ 1975 **Maassluis,** production: one year	13.00	16.00
☐ 1976 **Montelbaanstower,** production: one year ...	15.00	16.00
☐ 1977 **Harbour Tower of Hoorn,** production: one year	19.50	22.50
☐ 1978 **Binnenpoort Gate,** production: one year ...	21.00	22.50

CHRISTMAS STORY SERIES

	Issue Price	Current Value
☐ 1982 **The Angel Gabriel Foreboding Maria**	35.00	37.00

FATHER'S DAY SERIES

	Issue Price	Current Value
☐ 1971 **Francesco Lana's Airship,** production: one year	12.00	32.00
☐ 1972 **Dr. Jonathan's Balloon,** production: one year	12.00	28.00

MOTHER'S DAY SERIES	Issue Price	Current Value
☐ 1971 **Mother and Daughter of the 1600s,** production: one year	12.00	14.00
☐ 1972 **Mother and Daughter of the Isle of Urk,** production: one year	12.00	14.00
☐ 1973 **Rembrandt's Mother,** production: one year	12.00	14.00

SINGLE RELEASES

☐ 1972 **Olympiad**	12.00	16.00
☐ 1972 **Apollo 11**	6.00	9.00

BLUE RIVER MILL

United States

ONCE UPON A BARN SERIES

☐ 1986 **Mail Pouch Barn,** artist: Ray Day, production quantity 5,000	45.00	45.00
☐ 1986 **Rock City Barn,** artist: Ray Day, production quantity 5,000	45.00	45.00
☐ 1987 **Meramec Caverns Barn,** artist: Ray Day, production quantity 5,000	45.00	45.00
☐ 1987 **Coca-Cola Barn,** artist: Ray Day, production quantity 5,000	45.00	45.00

BOEHM, LINDA

EGYPTIAN TREASURES OF TUTANKHAMEN SERIES

☐ 1977 **The Headdress,** production quantity 5,000	50.00	50.00
☐ 1978 **The Mummy Collar,** production quantity 5,000	50.00	50.00

BOEHM STUDIOS, EDWARD MARSHALL

Great Britain

AWARD-WINNING ROSES SERIES

☐ 1979 **Peace Rose,** artist: Boehm Studio Artists, production quantity 15,000	45.00	100.00
☐ 1979 **White Masterpiece Rose,** artist: Boehm Studio Artists, production quantity 15,000	45.00	75.00

		Issue Price	Current Value
☐ 1979	**Tropicana Rose,** artist: Boehm Studio Artists, production quantity 15,000	**45.00**	**65.00**
☐ 1979	**Elegance Rose,** artist: Boehm Studio Artists, production quantity 15,000	**45.00**	**55.00**
☐ 1979	**Queen Elizabeth Rose,** artist: Boehm Studio Artists, production quantity 15,000	**45.00**	**55.00**
☐ 1979	**Royal Highness Rose,** artist: Boehm Studio Artists, production quantity 15,000	**45.00**	**55.00**
☐ 1979	**Angel Face Rose,** artist: Boehm Studio Artists, production quantity 15,000	**45.00**	**55.00**
☐ 1979	**Mr. Lincoln Rose,** artist: Boehm Studio Artists, production quantity 15,000	**45.00**	**55.00**

BANQUET OF BLOSSOMS AND BERRIES SERIES
(The Hamilton Collection)

		Issue Price	Current Value
☐ 1982	**Winter Holiday Bouquet,** artist: Boehm Studio Artists, production quantity 15,000	**62.50**	**62.50**
☐ 1982	**Thanksgiving Bouquet,** artist: Boehm Studio Artists, production quantity 15,000	**62.50**	**65.00**
☐ 1982	**School Days Bouquet,** artist: Boehm Studio Artists, production quantity 15,000	**62.50**	**65.00**
☐ 1982	**Indian Summer Bouquet,** artist: Boehm Studio Artists, production quantity 15,000	**62.50**	**65.00**
☐ 1982	**Mid-Summer Bouquet,** artist: Boehm Studio Artists, production quantity 15,000	**62.50**	**65.00**
☐ 1982	**Autumn Bouquet,** artist: Boehm Studio Artists, production quantity 15,000	**62.50**	**65.00**

BOEHM OWL COLLECTION

Note: Some plates were sold at below market test prices. Current market value reflects authorized issue price.

		Issue Price	Current Value
☐ 1980	**Boreal Owl,** artist: Boehm Studio Artists, production quantity 15,000	**45.00**	**75.00**
☐ 1980	**Snowy Owl,** artist: Boehm Studio Artists, production quantity 15,000	**45.00**	**62.50**
☐ 1980	**Barn Owl,** artist: Boehm Studio Artists, production quantity 15,000	**45.00**	**62.50**
☐ 1980	**Saw Whet Owl,** artist: Boehm Studio Artists, production quantity 15,000	**45.00**	**62.50**
☐ 1980	**Great Horned Owl,** artist: Boehm Studio Artists, production quantity 15,000	**45.00**	**62.50**

	Issue Price	Current Value
☐ 1980 **Screech Owl,** artist: Boehm Studio Artists, production quantity 15,000	45.00	62.50
☐ 1980 **Short-Eared Owl,** artist: Boehm Studio Artists, production quantity 15,000	45.00	62.50
☐ 1980 **Barred Owl,** artist: Boehm Studio Artists, production quantity 15,000	45.00	62.50

BUTTERFLIES OF THE WORLD SERIES

☐ 1978 **Monarch and Daisy,** production quantity 5,000	62.00	62.00
☐ 1978 **Red Admiral and Thistle,** production quantity 5,000	62.00	62.00

BUTTERFLY SERIES

☐ 1975 **Blue Mountain Swallowtails,** production quantity 100	450.00	450.00
☐ 1975 **Jezabels,** production quantity 100	450.00	450.00
☐ 1976 **Comma with Loops,** production quantity 100	450.00	450.00
☐ 1976 **African Butterflies,** production quantity 100	450.00	450.00
☐ 1976 **Solandras Maxima,** production quantity 100	450.00	450.00

EGYPTIAN COMMEMORATIVE SERIES

☐ 1978 **Tutankhamen,** production quantity 5,000 . .	125.00	170.00
☐ 1978 **Tutankhamen,** hand-painted, production quantity 225	975.00	975.00

EUROPEAN BIRD PLATES SERIES

☐ 1973 **Swallow,** production quantity 4,319	50.00	50.00
☐ 1973 **Chaffinch,** production quantity 4,319	50.00	50.00
☐ 1973 **Coal Tit,** production quantity 4,319	50.00	50.00
☐ 1973 **Tree Sparrow,** production quantity 4,319 . .	50.00	50.00
☐ 1973 **Kingfisher,** production quantity 4,319	50.00	50.00
☐ 1973 **Gold Crest,** production quantity 4,319	50.00	50.00
☐ 1973 **Blue Tit,** production quantity 4,319	50.00	50.00
☐ 1973 **Linnet,** production quantity 4,319	50.00	50.00

FANCY FOWL SERIES

☐ 1974 **Pair,** production quantity 85	2000.00	2000.00

FAVORITE FLORAL SERIES

☐ 1978 **Clematis,** production quantity 2,500	58.00	58.00
☐ 1978 **Rhododendron,** production quantity 2,500	58.00	58.00
☐ 1979 **Boehm Orchid,** production quantity 2,500	58.00	58.00

		Issue Price	Current Value
☐ 1979	**Yellow Rose,** production quantity 2,500 ...	**58.00**	**58.00**
☐ 1980	**Spider Orchid,** production quantity 2,500 ..	**58.00**	**58.00**
☐ 1980	**Dahlia,** production quantity 2,500	**58.00**	**58.00**

FLOWER SERIES

☐ 1975	**Lilies,** production quantity 100	**450.00**	**490.00**
☐ 1975	**Passion Flowers,** production quantity 100	**450.00**	**490.00**
☐ 1975	**Double Clematis,** production quantity 100	**450.00**	**490.00**

GAMEBIRDS OF NORTH AMERICA SERIES

☐ 1984	**Ring-Necked Pheasant,** artist: Boehm Studio Artists, production quantity 15,000	**62.50**	**62.50**
☐ 1984	**Bob White Quail,** artist: Boehm Studio Artists, production quantity 15,000	**62.50**	**62.50**
☐ 1984	**American Woodcock,** artist: Boehm Stud. Artists, production quantity 15,000	**62.50**	**62.50**
☐ 1984	**California Quail,** artist: Boehm Studio Artists, production quantity 15,000	**62.50**	**62.50**
☐ 1984	**Ruffed Grouse,** artist: Boehm Studio Artists, production quantity 15,000	**62.50**	**62.50**
☐ 1984	**Wild Turkey,** artist: Boehm Studio Artists, production quantity 15,000	**62.50**	**62.50**
☐ 1984	**Willow Partridge,** artist: Boehm Studio Artists, production quantity 15,000	**62.50**	**62.50**
☐ 1984	**Prairie Grouse,** artist: Boehm Studio Artists, production quantity 15,000	**62.50**	**62.50**

HARD FRUIT SERIES

☐ 1975	**Plums,** production quantity 100	**450.00**	**450.00**
☐ 1975	**Pears,** production quantity 100	**450.00**	**450.00**
☐ 1975	**Peaches,** production quantity 100	**450.00**	**450.00**
☐ 1975	**Apples,** production quantity 100	**450.00**	**450.00**

HONOR AMERICA SERIES

☐ 1974	**American Bald Eagle,** production quantity 12,000	**85.00**	**85.00**

HUMMINGBIRD COLLECTION SERIES

Note: Some plates were sold at below market test prices. Current market value reflects authorized issue price.

		Issue Price	Current Value
☐ 1980	**Calliope Hummingbird,** production quantity 15,000	62.50	75.00
☐ 1980	**Broadtail Hummingbirds,** production quantity 15,000	62.50	62.50
☐ 1980	**Rufous Flame Beaver Hummingbird,** production quantity 15,000	62.50	62.50
☐ 1980	**Steamer-Tail Hummingbird,** production quantity 15,000	62.50	62.50
☐ 1980	**Blue-Throated Hummingbird,** production quantity 15,000	62.50	62.50
☐ 1980	**Crimson-Topas Hummingbird,** production quantity 15,000	62.50	62.50
☐ 1980	**Brazilian Ruby,** production quantity 15,000	62.50	62.50

JUDAIC COMMEMORATIVE SERIES

☐ 1979	**Blue,** production quantity 1,500	45.00	45.00
☐ 1978	**Rose/Gold,** production quantity 75	555.00	550.00

LIFE'S BEST WISHES SERIES
(The Hamilton Collection)

☐ 1982	**Longevity,** artist: Boehm Studio Artists ...	75.00	75.00
☐ 1982	**Happiness,** artist: Boehm Studio Artists ...	75.00	75.00
☐ 1982	**Fertility,** artist: Boehm Studio Artists	75.00	75.00
☐ 1982	**Prosperity,** artist: Boehm Studio Artists ...	75.00	75.00

MINIATURE ROSES SERIES
(The Hamilton Collection)

☐ 1982	**Toy Clown,** artist: Boehm Studio Artists, production: 28 days	39.50	46.00
☐ 1982	**Rise n'Shine,** artist: Boehm Studio Artists, production: 28 days	39.50	46.00
☐ 1982	**Cuddles,** artist: Boehm Studio Artists, production: 28 days	39.50	46.00
☐ 1982	**Puppy Love,** artist: Boehm Studio Artists, production: 28 days	39.50	46.00

THE MUSICAL MAIDENS OF THE IMPERIAL DYNASTY SERIES

☐ 1984	**The Flute,** production quantity 15,000	65.00	65.00

ORIENTAL BIRDS SERIES

☐ 1975	**Bluebacked Fairy Bluebirds,** production quantity 100	400.00	400.00

		Issue Price	Current Value
☐ 1975	**Azure-Winged Magpies,** production quantity 100	**400.00**	**400.00**
☐ 1976	**Golden-Fronted Leafbird,** production quantity 100	**400.00**	**400.00**
☐ 1976	**Golden Throated Barbet,** production quantity 100	**400.00**	**400.00**

PANDA SERIES

☐ 1982	**Panda, Harmony,** production quantity 5,000	**65.00**	**65.00**
☐ 1982	**Panda, Peace,** production quantity 5,000	**65.00**	**65.00**

ROSE PLATE COLLECTION SERIES
(The Hamilton Collection)

☐ 1979	**Angel Face Rose,** production quantity 15,000	**45.00**	**50.00**
☐ 1979	**Peace Rose,** production quantity 15,000	**45.00**	**48.00**
☐ 1979	**Queen Elizabeth Rose,** production quantity 15,000	**45.00**	**48.00**
☐ 1979	**Tropicana Rose,** production quantity 15,000	**45.00**	**48.00**
☐ 1979	**White Masterpiece Rose,** production quantity 15,000	**45.00**	**48.00**
☐ 1980	**Elegance Rose,** production quantity 15,000	**45.00**	**48.00**
☐ 1980	**Royal Highness Rose,** production quantity 15,000	**45.00**	**48.00**
☐ 1980	**Mister Lincoln Rose,** production quantity 15,000	**45.00**	**48.00**

ROSES OF EXCELLENCE SERIES

☐ 1981	**The Love Rose,** artist: Boehm Studio Artists, production: one year	**62.00**	**85.00**
☐ 1982	**White Lightnin',** artist: Boehm Studio Artists, production: one year	**62.00**	**72.00**
☐ 1983	**Brandy,** artist: Boehm Studio Artists, production: one year	**62.50**	**62.50**
☐ 1983	**Sun Flare,** artist: Boehm Studio Artists, production: one year	**62.50**	**62.50**

SEASHELL SERIES

☐ 1975	**Violet Spider Conch,** production quantity 100	**450.00**	**450.00**
☐ 1975	**Rooster Tail Conch,** production quantity 100	**450.00**	**450.00**
☐ 1976	**Orange Spider Conch,** production quantity 100	**450.00**	**450.00**
☐ 1976	**Cheragra Spider Conch,** production quantity 100	**450.00**	**450.00**

		Issue Price	Current Value
SOFT FRUIT SERIES			
☐ 1975	**Loganberries,** production quantity 100	**450.00**	**450.00**
☐ 1976	**Cherries,** production quantity 100	**450.00**	**450.00**
☐ 1976	**Strawberries,** production quantity 100	**450.00**	**450.00**
☐ 1976	**Grapes,** production quantity 100	**450.00**	**450.00**

TRIBUTE TO AWARD-WINNING ROSES
(Hamilton Collection)

		Issue Price	Current Value
☐ 1983	**Irish Gold,** artist: Boehm Studio Artists, production quantity 15,000	**62.50**	**62.50**
☐ 1983	**Handel,** artist: Boehm Studio Artists, production quantity 15,000	**62.50**	**62.50**
☐ 1983	**Queen Elizabeth,** artist: Boehm Studio Artists, production quantity 15,000	**62.50**	**62.50**
☐ 1983	**Elizabeth of Glamis,** artist: Boehm Studio Artists, production quantity 15,000	**62.50**	**62.50**
☐ 1983	**Iceberg,** artist: Boehm Studio Artists, production quantity 15,000	**62.50**	**62.50**
☐ 1983	**Mountbatten,** artist: Boehm Studio Artists, production quantity 15,000	**62.50**	**62.50**
☐ 1983	**Silver Jubilee,** artist: Boehm Studio Artists, production quantity 15,000	**62.50**	**62.50**
☐ 1983	**Peace,** artist: Boehm Studio Artists, production quantity 15,000	**62.50**	**62.50**

TRIBUTE TO BALLET SERIES
(The Hamilton Collection)

		Issue Price	Current Value
☐ 1982	**Nutcracker,** artist: Boehm Studio Artists, production quantity 15,000	**62.50**	**67.00**
☐ 1982	**Firebird,** artist: Boehm Studio Artists, production quantity 15,000	**62.50**	**67.00**
☐ 1982	**Don Quixote,** artist: Boehm Studio Artists, production quantity 15,000	**62.50**	**67.00**
☐ 1982	**La Bayadere,** artist: Boehm Studio Artists, production quantity 15,000	**62.50**	**67.00**

WATER BIRDS SERIES

		Issue Price	Current Value
☐ 1981	**Canada Geese,** artist: Boehm Studio Artists, production quantity 15,000	**62.50**	**75.00**
☐ 1981	**Wood Ducks,** artist: Boehm Studio Artists, production quantity 15,000	**62.50**	**62.50**
☐ 1981	**Hooded Mergansers,** artist: Boehm Studio Artists, production quantity 15,000	**62.50**	**62.50**
☐ 1982	**Ross' Geese,** artist: Boehm Studio Artists, production quantity 15,000	**62.50**	**62.50**

		Issue Price	Current Value
☐ 1982	**Common Mallards,** artist: Boehm Studio Artists, production quantity 15,000	62.50	62.50
☐ 1982	**Canvas Backs,** artist: Boehm Studio Artists, production quantity 15,000	62.50	62.50
☐ 1982	**Green-Winged Teals,** artist: Boehm Studio Artists, production quantity 15,000	62.50	62.50
☐ 1982	**American Pintails,** artist: Boehm Studio Artists, production quantity 15,000	62.50	62.50

WOODLAND BIRDS OF AMERICA SERIES

☐ 1984	**Downy Woodpecker with Flowering Cherry Blossoms,** production: limited	75.00	75.00

BOHEMIA

Czechoslovakia

MOTHER'S DAY SERIES

☐ 1974	**Mother's Day,** production quantity 500 . . .	130.00	155.00
☐ 1975	**Mother's Day,** production quantity 500 . . .	140.00	160.00
☐ 1976	**Mother's Day,** production quantity 500 . . .	150.00	160.00

BONITA

Mexico

MOTHER'S DAY

☐ 1972	**Mother with Baby,** artist: Raul Anguiano, production quantity 4,000	75.00	85.00

BORSATO

MASTERPIECE SERIES

☐ 1978	**Serenity,** production quantity 5,000	75.00	68.00
☐ 1978	**Titian,** production quantity 5,000	75.00	68.00

PLAQUES SERIES

☐ 1973	**Golden Years,** production quantity 750	1450.00	1750.00
☐ 1974	**Tender Musings,** production quantity 250	1650.00	1900.00

BOYS TOWN

United States

SINGLE ISSUE	Issue Price	Current Value
☐ **1986** **Rev. Edward J. Flanagan, Founder of Boys Town,** artist: Michael Engstrom, production quantity 5,000	32.00	32.00

BRANTWOOD COLLECTION

United States

HOWE CHRISTMAS SERIES

☐ **1978** **Visit from Santa,** production: one year	45.00	48.00

JOHN FALTER CHRISTMAS SERIES

☐ **1979** **Christmas Morning,** artist: John Falter, production quantity 5,000	25.50	25.00

LITTLE CLOWN SERIES

☐ **1979** **Going to Circus,** production quantity 5,000	29.50	32.00

MARIEN CARLSEN MOTHER'S DAY SERIES

☐ **1978** **Jennifer and Jenny Fur,** production: one year	45.00	48.00
☐ **1979** **Football Brothers,** production quantity 5,000	45.00	48.00

ROCKWELL MOTHER'S DAY SERIES

☐ **1979** **Homecoming,** production quantity 20,000 . .	39.50	42.00

SINGLE RELEASE

☐ **1978** **Tribute to Rockwell,** production: one year	35.00	38.00

BRAYMER HALL

United States

AMERICAN FOLK ART SERIES

☐ **1982** **Spring Celebration,** artist: Fred Wallin, production quantity 10,000	24.50	26.00
☐ **1982** **Summer Bounty,** artist: Fred Wallin, production quantity 10,000	24.50	26.00

	Issue Price	Current Value
CHILDHOOD SONATAS SERIES		
☐ **1981 Serenade,** artist: Frank Palmieri, production quantity 15,000	**28.50**	**30.00**
☐ **1982 Prelude,** artist: Frank Palmieri, production quantity 15,000	**28.50**	**30.00**
☐ **1982 Caprice,** artist: Frank Palmieri, production quantity 15,000	**28.50**	**30.00**
YESTERDAY DREAMS SERIES		
☐ **1983 Swing Quartet,** artist: Jack Appleton, production quantity 5,000	**50.00**	**52.00**
☐ **1984 Sleigh Belles,** artist: Jack Appleton, production quantity 5,000	**50.00**	**52.00**
SINGLE ISSUE		
☐ **1982 How Do I Love Thee?,** artist: Rob Sauber, quantity 19,500	**39.95**	**40.00**

BRENTWOOD FINE ARTS

United States

NOSTALGIC MEMORIES SERIES		
☐ **1984 First Game,** artist: Marilyn Zapp, production quantity 12,500	**39.50**	**40.00**

BRIANT, PAUL AND SONS

United States

CHRISTMAS SERIES		
☐ **1971 Fruits of Spirit,** production quantity 350 . .	**125.00**	**115.00**
☐ **1972 Labour of Love,** production quantity 700 . .	**100.00**	**107.00**
☐ **1973 Annunciation**	**100.00**	**105.00**
EASTER SERIES		
☐ **1972 The Last Sacrifice,** production quantity 500	**85.00**	**82.00**
SEVEN SACRAMENTS		
☐ **1982 The Gift of the Spirit,** artist: Terry Clark, production quantity 2,000	**110.00**	**110.00**

BRIARCREST

United States

	Issue Price	Current Value
TOYS FROM THE ATTIC SERIES		
☐ **1982 This Ole Bear Chauncey James,** artist: Janet Tuck, production: 10 days	45.00	47.00

BRIMARK LTD.

United States

YETTA'S HOLIDAYS SERIES

☐ **1986 Christmas Blocks,** artist: Carol-Lynn Rossel Waugh, production quantity: unannounced	29.50	30.00

BRINDLE FINE ARTS

United States

EXPRESSIONS SERIES

☐ **1979 Quiet Eyes,** artist: Claude Hulce, production quantity 3,000	60.00	62.00

FANTASY IN MOTION SERIES

☐ **1978 Little Blue Horse,** artist: Lenore Béran, production quantity 3,000	75.00	72.00
☐ **1979 Horse of a Different Color,** artist: Lenore Béran, production quantity 3,000	75.00	77.00

LENORE BÉRAN SPECIAL SERIES

☐ **1980 Homage,** artist: Lenore Béran, production quantity 2,500	125.00	127.00

MOODS OF THE ORIENT SERIES

☐ **1978 Softly, the Sun Sets,** artist: Lenore Béran, production quantity 4,000	75.00	75.00
☐ **1980 Tranquil Morn,** artist: Lenore Béran, production quantity 3,000	75.00	75.00

THOSE PRECIOUS YEARS SERIES

☐ **1980 Little Curt and Friend,** production quantity 3,000	60.00	60.00

BYDGO

CHRISTMAS SERIES	Issue Price	Current Value
☐ **1969 Shepherdess and Sheep,** production quantity 5,000	**10.00**	**10.00**
☐ **1970 Clumsy Hans,** production quantity 5,000 ..	**10.00**	**10.00**
☐ **1971 The Flying Trunk,** production quantity 5,000	**10.00**	**10.00**
☐ **1972 Chinese Nightingale,** production quantity 5,000	**10.00**	**10.00**

CABOCHON—CONTEMPORARY ORIGINALS, INC.

United States

NANCY DOYLE'S CANDY GIRLS

	Issue Price	Current Value
☐ **1983 Rebecca,** artist: Nancy Doyle, production quantity 15,000	**50.00**	**50.00**

CALIFORNIA PORCELAIN, INC.

United States

BEST OF SASCHA SERIES

	Issue Price	Current Value
☐ **1979 Flower Bouquet,** artist: Sascha Brastoff, production quantity 7,500	**65.00**	**68.00**

NOW IS THE MOMENT SERIES

	Issue Price	Current Value
☐ **1984 Be Still,** artist: Carolyn Blish, production quantity 12,500	**35.00**	**35.00**

SEED OF THE PEOPLE SERIES

	Issue Price	Current Value
☐ **1984 Keenah, The Strong One,** artist: Carolyn Blish, production quantity 10,000	**29.95**	**30.50**

VANISHING ANIMALS SERIES

	Issue Price	Current Value
☐ **1979 Asian Monarch,** artist: Gene Dieckhoner, production quantity 7,500	**40.00**	**53.00**
☐ **1979 Snow Leopards,** artist: Gene Dieckhoner, production quantity 7,500	**45.00**	**53.00**
☐ **1980 Pandas,** artist: Gene Dieckhoner, production quantity 7,500	**45.00**	**48.00**
☐ **1981 Polar Bears,** artist: Gene Dieckhoner, production quantity 7,500	**50.00**	**53.00**

	Issue Price	Current Value
SINGLE ISSUE		
☐ **1983 Koala,** artist: Gene Dieckhoner, production quantity 5,000	**29.95**	**30.50**

CANADIAN COLLECTOR PLATES

Canada

CHILDREN OF THE CLASSICS

☐ **1982 Anne of Green Gables,** artist: Will Davies, production quantity 15,000	**78.00**	**78.00**
☐ **1983 Tom Sawyer,** artist: Will Davies, production quantity 15,000	**78.00**	**78.00**

DAYS OF INNOCENCE

☐ **1982 Butterflies,** artist: Will Davies, production quantity 15,000	**78.00**	**78.00**
☐ **1983 He Loves Me,** artist: Will Davies, production quantity 15,000	**78.00**	**78.00**

DISCOVER CANADA SERIES

☐ **1979 Sawmill—Kings Landing,** artist: Keirstead, production quantity 10,000	**98.00**	**350.00**
☐ **1980 Quebec Winter,** artist: Krieghoff, production quantity 10,000	**125.00**	**150.00**
☐ **1981 Before the Bath,** artist: Paul Peel, production quantity 10,000	**125.00**	**125.00**
☐ **1982 The Grist Mill, Delta,** artist: Keirstead, production quantity 10,000	**125.00**	**125.00**
☐ **1982 Anglican Church at Magnetawan,** artist: A. J. Casson, production quantity 10,000	**125.00**	**125.00**
☐ **1983 Majestic Rockies,** production quantity 10,000	**125.00**	**130.00**
☐ **1983 Habitants Driving the Sleigh,** production quantity 10,000	**125.00**	**125.00**
☐ **1984 Autumn Memories,** production quantity 10,000	**125.00**	**125.00**
☐ **1984 After the Bath,** production quantity 10,000	**125.00**	**125.00**

CAPO DI MONTE

Italy

CHRISTMAS SERIES	Issue Price	Current Value
☐ 1972 **Cherubs,** production quantity 500	55.00	92.00
☐ 1973 **Bells and Holly,** production quantity 500 ..	55.00	58.00
☐ 1974 **Christmas,** production quantity 1,000	60.00	62.00
☐ 1975 **Christmas,** production quantity 1,000	60.00	62.00
☐ 1976 **Christmas,** production quantity 250	65.00	68.00

MOTHER'S DAY SERIES

	Issue Price	Current Value
☐ 1973 **Mother's Day,** production quantity 500 ...	55.00	68.00
☐ 1974 **Mother's Day,** production quantity 500 ...	60.00	68.00
☐ 1975 **Mother's Day,** production quantity 500 ...	60.00	68.00
☐ 1976 **Mother's Day,** production quantity 500 ...	65.00	68.00

CARMEL COLLECTION

United States

COUNTRY FRIENDS SERIES

	Issue Price	Current Value
☐ 1983 **Meeting at the Fence,** artist: Helen Rampel, production quantity 15,000	45.00	45.00

FAMOUS PARADES SERIES

☐ 1983 **Macy's Thanksgiving Parade,** artist: Melanie Taylor Kent, production: one year	39.50	40.00

FIRST PERFORMERS SERIES

☐ 1983 **Darling Diana,** artist: Elizabeth Maxwell, production quantity 19,500	39.50	40.00

JOY OF CHRISTMAS SERIES

☐ 1983 **Christmas Delight,** artist: Jerome Walczak, production quantity 19,500	39.50	40.00

MEMORIES OF THE HEART SERIES

☐ 1984 **Petals,** artist: Elizabeth Maxwell, production quantity 15,000	28.50	28.50

Petals, artist: Elizabeth Maxwell.

CARSON MINT

United States

AMERICA HAS HEART SERIES	Issue Price	Current Value
(B & J Art Designs)		
☐ **1980 My Heart's Desire,** artist: Jan Hagara, production: one year	**24.50**	**135.00**
☐ **1981 Hearts and Flowers,** artist: Jan Hagara, production: one year	**24.50**	**40.00**
☐ **1982 The Hearty Sailor,** artist: Jan Hagara, production: one year	**28.50**	**30.00**
☐ **1983 Shannon's Sweetheart,** artist: Jan Hagara, production: one year	**28.50**	**30.00**

THE BEAR FEATS SERIES		
☐ **1983 Teddy Bear Picnic,** artist: Susan Anderson, production quantity 15,000	**37.50**	**37.50**
☐ **1984 On the Beach,** artist: Susan Anderson, production quantity 15,000	**37.50**	**37.50**

BIG TOP SERIES		
☐ **1981 The White Face,** artist: Edward J. Rohn, production: 60 days	**28.50**	**30.00**

On the Beach, artist: Susan Anderson.

		Issue Price	Current Value
☐ **1982**	**The Tramp,** artist: Edward J. Rohn, production: 60 days	**28.50**	**30.00**

HOLLYWOOD SQUARES SERIES

		Issue Price	Current Value
☐ **1979**	**Peter Marshall,** production: 100 days	**28.50**	**32.00**
☐ **1980**	**George Gobel,** production: 100 days	**28.50**	**30.00**

THE LITTLEST SERIES

		Issue Price	Current Value
☐ **1982**	**The Littlest Stocking,** artist: June Colbert, production quantity 12,500	**29.50**	**30.00**
☐ **1983**	**Littlest Santa,** artist: June Colbert, production quantity 12,500	**29.50**	**30.00**

MAGIC AFTERNOONS SERIES

		Issue Price	Current Value
☐ **1980**	**Enchanted Garden,** artist: Jo Anne Mix, production quantity 5,000	**39.50**	**40.00**
☐ **1981**	**The Delightful Tea Party,** production quantity 5,000	**39.50**	**40.00**

	Issue Price	Current Value
MOMENTS IN TIME SERIES		
☐ **1979 Freedom Flight,** production quantity 5,000	**55.00**	**56.00**
NATURE'S CHILDREN SERIES		
☐ **1982 Candice,** artist: Don Price, production quantity 12,500	**29.50**	**30.00**
☐ **1983 Cory,** artist: Don Price, production quantity 12,500	**29.50**	**30.00**
OLD-FASHIONED MOTHER'S DAY SERIES (B & J Art Designs)		
☐ **1979 Daisies from Mary Beth,** artist Jan Hagara, production: one year	**38.00**	**80.00**
☐ **1980 Daisies from Jimmy,** artist Jan Hagara, production: one year	**37.50**	**80.00**
☐ **1981 Daisies from Meg,** artist Jan Hagara, production: one year	**37.50**	**40.00**
☐ **1982 Daisies for Mommie,** artist Jan Hagara, production: one year	**37.50**	**40.00**
TO MOM WITH LOVE SERIES		
☐ **1983 A Basket of Love,** artist: Cynthia Knapton, production quantity 15,000	**37.50**	**37.50**

CARTIER

France

	Issue Price	Current Value
CATHEDRAL SERIES		
☐ **1972 Chartres Cathedral,** production quantity 12,500	**50.00**	**68.00**
☐ **1974 Chartres Millous,** production quantity 500	**130.00**	**160.00**

CASTLETON CHINA

United States

	Issue Price	Current Value
AVIATION SERIES (American Historical)		
☐ **1972 Amelia Earhart,** production quantity 3,500	**40.00**	**62.00**

	Issue Price	Current Value
☐ 1972 **Charles Lindbergh,** production quantity 3,500	**40.00**	**42.00**

BICENTENNIAL SERIES
(Shenango)

☐ 1972 **A New Dawn,** production quantity 7,600 ..	**60.00**	**62.00**
☐ 1972 **Turning Point,** production quantity 7,600 ..	**60.00**	**62.00**
☐ 1973 **Silent Foe,** production quantity 7,600	**60.00**	**62.00**
☐ 1973 **The Declaration,** production quantity 7,600	**60.00**	**62.00**
☐ 1973 **The Star-Spangled Banner,** production quantity 7,600	**60.00**	**62.00**
☐ 1973 **USS Constitution,** production quantity 7,600	**60.00**	**62.00**
☐ 1974 **One Nation,** production quantity 7,600	**60.00**	**62.00**
☐ 1974 **Westward Ho,** production quantity 7,600 ..	**60.00**	**62.00**

NATURAL HISTORY SERIES
(American Historial)

☐ 1973 **Painted Lady,** production quantity 1,500 ..	**40.00**	**42.00**
☐ 1973 **Roseate Spoonbill,** production quantity 1,500	**40.00**	**42.00**

SINGLE RELEASE

☐ 1976 **General Douglas MacArthur,** production quantity 1,000	**30.00**	**32.00**

CATALINA PORCELAIN

United States

ESCALERA'S CHRISTMAS SERIES

☐ 1982 **Special Delivery,** artist: Rudy Escalera, production quantity 19,500	**32.50**	**32.50**

CERTIFIED RARITIES

United States

INDIAN DANCER SERIES

☐ 1978 **Eagle Dancer,** artist: Don Ruffin, production quantity 2,500	**300.00**	**305.00**
☐ 1979 **Hoop Dancer,** artist: Don Ruffin, production quantity 2,500	**300.00**	**305.00**

		Issue Price	Current Value
POSTAL ARTISTS SERIES			
□ 1978	**Colias Eurydice,** artist: Stanley Galli, production quantity 15,000	60.00	62.00
□ 1979	**Euyphydryas Phaeton,** artist: Stanley Galli, production quantity 7,500	60.00	60.00

RENAISSANCE MASTERS SERIES

□ 1978	**Alba Madonna,** production quantity 15,000	55.00	38.00
□ 1979	**Pieta,** production quantity 5,000	55.00	55.00

CHILMARK

United States

FAMILY CHRISTMAS SERIES

□ 1978	**Trimming the Tree,** production quantity 10,000	65.00	68.00

HOLY NIGHT SERIES

□ 1979	**Wisemen,** production quantity 10,000	65.00	66.00

IN APPRECIATION SERIES

□ 1978	**Flowers of Field,** production quantity 10,000	65.00	66.00

TWELVE DAYS OF CHRISTMAS SERIES

□ 1979	**A Partridge in a Pear Tree,** artist: R. Lamb, J. Nussbaum, production quantity 10,000 ..	89.50	90.50

CHRISTIAN BELL PORCELAIN

Canada

THE AGE OF STEAM SERIES

□ 1981	**Symphony in Steam,** artist: Theodore Xaras, production quantity 15,000	65.00	260.00
□ 1982	**Brief Encounter,** artist: Theodore Xaras, numbered, production quantity 15,000	65.00	100.00
□ 1983	**No Contest,** artist: Theodore Xaras, numbered, production quantity 15,000	65.00	95.00
□ 1983	**Timber County,** artist: Theodore Xaras, production quantity 15,000	65.00	90.00

		Issue Price	Current Value
AMERICAN STEAM			
□ **1982**	**Hiawatha,** artist: Ted Xaras, production quantity 15,000	**65.00**	**65.00**
□ **1983**	**Hittin' the Diamond,** artist: Ted Xaras, production quantity 15,000	**65.00**	**65.00**
□ **1984**	**Morning at the Depot,** artist: Ted Xaras, production quantity 15,000	**65.00**	**65.00**
□ **1984**	**Winter on the Boston & Maine,** artist: Theodore Xaras, production quantity 15,000 . . .	**65.00**	**65.00**
□ **1985**	**On the Horsehoe Curve,** artist: Ted Xaras, production quantity 15,000	**65.00**	**65.00**
COPELAND REMEMBERS SERIES			
□ **1986**	**Possession Is . . .,** artist: Eric Copeland, production quantity N/A	**65.00**	**65.00**
GREAT ATLANTIC LINERS SERIES			
□ **1987**	**R.M.S. Queen Mary,** artist: Ted Xaras, production quantity N/A. Prices not available at press time	—	—
LAST SPIKE CENTENNIAL			
(Two-Plate Series)			
□ **1986**	**Spiral Tunnel,** artist: Ted Xaras, production quantity 7500	**135.00**	**145.00**
□ **1986**	**Big Hill,** artist: Ted Xaras, production quantity 7500	**135.00**	**145.00**
MEN OF THE RAILS			
□ **1982**	**Engineer,** artist: Ted Xaras, production: less than one year	**39.50**	**42.00**
□ **1983**	**Pullman Porter,** artist: Ted Xaras, production: less than one year	**39.50**	**42.00**
□ **1983**	**Conductor,** artist: Ted Xaras, production: less than one year	**39.50**	**42.00**
□ **1983**	**Night Operator,** artist: Ted Xaras, production: less than one year	**39.50**	**42.00**
PRESERVING A WAY OF LIFE SERIES			
□ **1980**	**Making Way for Cars,** production quantity 5,000	**60.00**	**62.00**
□ **1980**	**Atop Hay Wagon,** production quantity 5,000	**60.00**	**62.00**
□ **1982**	**Sugarbush,** artist: Peter Etril Snyder, hand-numbered, production quantity 10,000	**65.00**	**67.00**

Sugarbush, artist: Peter
Etril Snyder.

		Issue Price	Current Value
☐ 1982	**Fishing for Redfin,** artist: Peter Etril Snyder, production quantity 10,000	**65.00**	**67.00**
☐ 1982	**Wheat Harvest,** artist: Peter Etril Snyder, production quantity 10,000	**65.00**	**67.00**
☐ 1982	**Returning from the Village,** artist: Peter Etril Snyder, production quantity 10,000	**65.00**	**67.00**
☐ 1986	**The New Horse,** artist: Peter Snyder, production quantity 10,000	**65.00**	**65.00**

VANISHING AFRICA SERIES

☐ 1983	**The Sentinel,** artist: Douglas Manning, production quantity 15,000	**75.00**	**75.00**

THE WILD NORTH SERIES

☐ 1983	**Emperor of the North,** artist: Douglas Manning, production quantity 15,000	**75.00**	**75.00**

CHRISTIAN FANTASY COLLECTIBLES

United States

CHRISTIAN FANTASY SERIES

☐ 1985	**The Legend of the Prayer Bear I,** artist: Tim Hildebrandt, production quantity 5,100	**50.00**	**50.00**

			Issue Price	Current Value
☐	1986	**The Legend of the Prayer Bear II,** artist: Tim Hildebrandt, production quantity 5,100	**50.00**	**50.00**
☐	1987	**The Legend of the Prayer Bear III,** artist: Tim Hildebrandt, production quantity 5,100	**50.00**	**50.00**

THE FANTASY COOKBOOK SERIES

			Issue Price	Current Value
☐	1986	**Picnic in the Woods,** artist: Tim Hildebrandt, production quantity 7,100	**50.00**	**50.00**
☐	1987	**The Magical Lagoon,** artist: Tim Hildebrandt, production quantity 7,100	**50.00**	**50.00**
☐	1987	**A Dwarf Celebration,** artist: Tim Hildebrandt, production quantity 7,100	**50.00**	**50.00**
☐	1987	**The Wizard's Magical Feast,** artist: Tim Hildebrandt, production quantity 7,100 .·...	**50.00**	**50.00**
☐	1987	**A Stew Pot,** artist: Tim Hildebrandt, production quantity 7,100	**50.00**	**50.00**
☐	1987	**The Mermaid's Hidden Waterfall,** artist: Tim Hildebrandt, production quantity 7,100	**50.00**	**50.00**
☐	1987	**Tiny Celebration,** artist: Tim Hildebrandt, production quantity 7,100	**50.00**	**50.00**
☐	1987	**The Enchanted Realm of Zir,** artist: Tim Hildebrandt, production quantity 7,100	**50.00**	**50.00**

REALMS OF WONDER SERIES I

			Issue Price	Current Value
☐	1986	**Wizard's Glade,** artist: Tim Hildebrandt, production quantity 9,100	**50.00**	**50.00**
☐	1987	**Mermaid's Grotto,** artist: Tim Hildebrandt, production quantity 9,100	**50.00**	**50.00**
☐	1987	**Ice Palace of the Fairies,** artist: Tim Hildebrandt, production quantity 9,100	**50.00**	**50.00**
☐	1987	**Mushroom Village of the Elves,** artist: Tim Hildebrandt, production quantity 9,100	**50.00**	**50.00**
☐	1987	**Forest of the Unicorn,** artist: Tim Hildebrandt, production quantity 9,100	**50.00**	**50.00**
☐	1987	**The Elven Fortress (Pegasus),** artist: Tim Hildebrandt, production quantity 9,100 .·...	**50.00**	**50.00**
☐	1987	**The Water Nixie,** artist: Tim Hildebrandt, production quantity 9,100	**50.00**	**50.00**
☐	1987	**Dwarves,** artist: Tim Hildebrandt, production quantity 9,100	**50.00**	**50.00**

REALMS OF WONDER SERIES II

			Issue Price	Current Value
☐	1987	**Wizard's Steed,** artist: Tim Hildebrandt, production quantity 9,100	**50.00**	**50.00**

The Legend of the
Prayer Bear I, artist:
Tim Hildebrandt.

The Legend of the
Prayer Bear II, artist:
Tim Hildebrandt.

The Legend of the
Prayer Bear III, artist:
Tim Hildebrandt.

Picnic in the Woods,
artist: Tim Hildebrandt.

Wizard's Glade, artist:
Tim Hildebrandt.

		Issue Price	Current Value
☐ 1987	**Sea Lord of Lamuria,** artist: Tim Hildebrandt, production quantity 9,100	50.00	50.00
☐ 1987	**Council of the Elves,** artist: Tim Hildebrandt, production quantity 9,100	50.00	50.00
☐ 1987	**Fairies II,** artist: Tim Hildebrandt, production quantity 9,100	50.00	50.00

Santa Daydreams,
artist: Tim Hildebrandt.

	Issue Price	Current Value
SANTA'S NIGHT OUT SERIES		
☐ **1986 Santa Daydreams,** artist: Tim Hildebrandt, production quantity 9,100	**50.00**	**50.00**

CHINESE FINE ARTS CO. INC.

United States

THE EIGHT IMMORTALS SERIES		
☐ **1979 Li T'ieh-Kuai—Poverty,** signed and dated by sculptor, production quantity 300	**175.00**	**175.00**

CLEVELAND MINT

United States

DA VINCI SERIES		
☐ **1972 Last Supper,** production quantity 5,000 . . .	**150.00**	**95.00**

Li T'ieh-Kuai—Poverty.

COLLECTOR'S WEEKLY

United States

AMERICAN SERIES	Issue Price	Current Value
☐ **1971 Miss Liberty,** production quantity 500	**12.50**	**16.00**
☐ **1972 Miss Liberty,** production quantity 900	**12.50**	**16.00**
☐ **1973 Eagle,** production quantity 900	**9.75**	**12.00**

CONTINENTAL MINT

United States

TOM SAWYER SERIES

☐ **1976 Taking His Medicine,** production quantity 5,000	**60.00**	**62.00**
☐ **1977 Painting Fence,** production quantity 5,000	**60.00**	**62.00**
☐ **1978 Lost in Cave,** production quantity 5,000 ...	**60.00**	**62.00**
☐ **1979 Smoking Pipe,** production quantity 5,000 ..	**60.00**	**62.00**

SINGLE RELEASE

☐ **1979 Butter Girl,** production quantity 5,000	**60.00**	**62.00**

CREATIVE WORLD

United States

	Issue Price	Current Value

AESOP'S FABLES SERIES

☐ **1979** **The Fox and the Grapes,** production quantity
9,750 .... 85.00 · 86.00

FOUR SEASONS SERIES

☐ **1972** **Fall,** silver plate, production quantity 2,000 · 75.00 · 76.00
☐ **1972** **Fall,** sterling silver, production quantity
2,000 .... 125.00 · 125.00
☐ **1973** **Spring,** silver plate, production quantity
2,300 .... 75.00 · 76.00
☐ **1973** **Spring,** sterling silver, production quantity
750 .... 125.00 · 125.00
☐ **1974** **Summer,** silver plate, production quantity
300 .... 75.00 · 76.00
☐ **1974** **Summer,** sterling silver, production quantity
750 .... 125.00 · 125.00
☐ **1973** **Winter,** silver plate, production quantity
2,000 .... 75.00 · 76.00
☐ **1973** **Winter,** sterling silver, production quantity
2,250 .... 125.00 · 125.00

IMMORTALS OF EARLY AMERICAN LITERATURE SERIES

☐ **1978** **Village Smithy,** artist: Roger Brown, production quantity 15,000 .... 50.00 · 28.00
☐ **1979** **Rip Van Winkle,** artist: Roger Brown, production quantity 15,000 .... 55.00 · 58.00

LIVING DOLLS SERIES

☐ **1982** **Eriko and Noriko,** artist: David Smiton, numbered, production quantity 9,500 ..... 49.50 · 50.50
☐ **1983** **Ingrid and Ingemar,** artist: David Smiton, production quantity 9,500 .... 49.50 · 50.50

PRIZE COLLECTION

☐ **1982** **Family Cares,** artist: unknown, handnumbered, production quantity 12,500 .... 45.00 · 46.00
☐ **1983** **Wind in the Frolic,** artist: unknown, production quantity 12,500 .... 45.00 · 46.00

		Issue Price	Current Value
ROCKWELL SERIES			
☐ 1978	**Looking Out to Sea,** artist: Roger Brown, production quantity 15,000	**50.00**	**66.00**
☐ 1978	**Yankee Doodle,** artist: Roger Brown, production quantity 15,000	**50.00**	**26.00**
☐ 1979	**Girl at the Mirror,** artist: Roger Brown, production quantity 15,000	**55.00**	**56.00**
WAGS TO RICHES SERIES			
☐ 1982	**Benji the Movie Star,** artist: Murray Karn, numbered, production quantity 19,500	**29.50**	**30.00**
☐ 1982	**Benji and Tiffany,** artist: Murray Karn, numbered, production quantity 19,500	**29.50**	**30.00**
☐ 1983	**Merry Christmas Benji,** artist: Murray Karn, production quantity 19,500	**29.50**	**30.00**
☐ 1984	**Benji's Barber Shop Blues,** artist: Murray Karn, production quantity 19,500	**35.00**	**35.00**

CRISTAL D'ALBRET

France

FOUR SEASONS SERIES			
☐ 1972	**Summer,** production quantity 1,000	**65.00**	**110.00**
☐ 1973	**Autumn,** production quantity 1,000	**75.00**	**95.00**
☐ 1974	**Spring,** production quantity 1,000	**75.00**	**170.00**
☐ 1975	**Winter,** production quantity 1,000	**88.00**	**155.00**
SINGLE RELEASE			
☐ 1972	**Bird of Peace,** production quantity 3,700 . .	**88.00**	**155.00**

CROWN DELFT

Netherlands

CHRISTMAS SERIES			
☐ 1969	**Man by Fire,** production: one year	**10.00**	**28.00**
☐ 1970	**Two Sleigh Riders,** production: one year . .	**10.00**	**20.00**
☐ 1971	**Christmas Tree,** production: one year	**10.00**	**16.00**
☐ 1972	**Baking for Christmas,** production: one year	**10.00**	**14.00**

		Issue Price	Current Value
FATHER'S DAY SERIES			
☐ 1970	**Father's Day,** production: one year	**10.00**	**12.00**
☐ 1971	**Father's Day,** production: one year	**10.00**	**14.00**
☐ 1972	**Father's Day,** production: one year	**10.00**	**14.00**
☐ 1973	**Father's Day,** production: one year	**10.00**	**14.00**
MOTHER'S DAY SERIES			
☐ 1970	**Sheep,** production: one year	**10.00**	**15.00**
☐ 1971	**Stork,** production: one year	**10.00**	**14.00**
☐ 1972	**Ducks,** production: one year	**10.00**	**14.00**
☐ 1973	**Mother's Day,** production: one year	**10.00**	**14.00**

CURATOR COLLECTION

United States

		Issue Price	Current Value
THE BECKER BABIES SERIES			
☐ 1983	**Snowpuff,** artist: Charlotte Becker, production limited	**29.95**	**29.95**
☐ 1984	**Pals,** artist: Charlotte Becker, production limited	**29.95**	**29.95**
☐ 1984	**Smiling Through,** artist: Charlotte Becker, production limited	**29.95**	**29.95**
CLASSIC CIRCUS SERIES			
☐ 1983	**The Favorite Clown,** artist: unknown, production quantity 17,500	**39.95**	**39.95**
GIFT EDITION			
☐ 1982	**The Wedding,** artist: Rob Sauber, production quantity: unannounced	**37.50**	**37.50**
☐ 1984	**Happy Birthday,** artist: Rob Sauber, production quantity: unannounced	**37.50**	**37.50**
☐ 1985	**All Adore Him,** artist: Rob Sauber, production quantity: unannounced	**37.50**	**37.50**
☐ 1985	**Home Sweet Home,** artist: Rob Sauber, production quantity: unannounced	**37.50**	**37.50**
☐ 1986	**The Anniversary,** artist: Rob Sauber, production quantity: unannounced	**37.50**	**37.50**
☐ 1986	**Sweethearts,** artist: Rob Sauber, production quantity: unannounced	**37.50**	**37.50**
☐ 1986	**The Christening,** artist: Rob Sauber, production quantity: unannounced	**37.50**	**37.50**

All Adore Him, artist:
Rob Sauber.

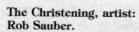

The Christening, artist:
Rob Sauber.

		Issue Price	Current Value
☐ 1987	**Motherhood,** artist: Rob Sauber, production quantity: unannounced	37.50	37.50
☐ 1987	**Fatherhood,** artist: Rob Sauber, production quantity: unannounced	37.50	37.50
☐ 1987	**Sweet Sixteen,** artist: Rob Sauber, production quantity: unannounced	37.50	37.50

Motherhood, artist: Rob
Sauber.

Fatherhood, artist: Rob
Sauber.

		Issue Price	Current Value
THE GREAT TRAINS SERIES			
☐ **1986**	**Santa Fe**, artist: Jim Deneen, production quantity 7,500	35.00	35.00
☐ **1986**	**Twentieth Century Ltd.**, artist: Jim Deneen, production quantity 7,500	35.00	35.00
☐ **1986**	**Empire Builder**, artist: Jim Deneen, produc- tion quantity 7,500	35.00	35.00

		Issue Price	Current Value
MAGICAL MOMENTS SERIES			
☐ **1981**	**Happy Dreams,** artist: Bessie Pease Gutmann, production: less than one year	29.95	70.00
☐ **1981**	**Harmony,** artist: Bessie Pease Gutmann, production: less than one year	29.95	60.00
☐ **1981**	**His Majesty,** artist: Bessie Pease Gutmann, production: less than one year	29.95	29.95
☐ **1982**	**Waiting for Daddy,** artist: Bessie Pease Gutmann, production: less than one year	29.95	29.95
☐ **1982**	**Thank You God,** artist: Bessie Pease Gutmann, production: less than one year	29.95	29.95
☐ **1983**	**Lullaby,** artist: Bessie Pease Gutmann, production: less than one year	29.95	29.95

MASTERPIECES OF IMPRESSIONISM SERIES

☐ **1980**	**Woman with a Parasol,** artist: Claude Monet, production quantity 17,500	35.00	50.00
☐ **1981**	**A Young Mother Sewing,** artist: Mary Cassatt, production quantity 17,500	35.00	35.00
☐ **1981**	**Sara in Green Bonnet,** artist: Mary Cassatt, production quantity 17,500	35.00	35.00
☐ **1982**	**Margot in Blue,** artist: Mary Cassatt, production quantity 17,500	35.00	35.00

MASTERPIECES OF ROCKWELL SERIES

☐ **1980**	**After the Prom,** artist: Norman Rockwell, production quantity 17,500	42.50	90.00
☐ **1981**	**The Challenger,** artist: Norman Rockwell, production quantity 17,500	50.00	50.00
☐ **1981**	**Girl at the Mirror,** artist: Norman Rockwell, production quantity 17,500	50.00	75.00
☐ **1982**	**Missing Tooth,** artist: Norman Rockwell, production quantity 17,500	50.00	50.00

MASTERPIECES OF THE WEST SERIES

☐ **1980**	**Texas Night Herder,** artist: Frank Tenny Johnson, production quantity 17,500	35.00	35.00
☐ **1981**	**Indian Trapper,** artist: Frederic Remington, production quantity 17,500	35.00	35.00
☐ **1982**	**Cowboy Style,** artist: William R. Leigh, production quantity 17,500	35.00	35.00
☐ **1982**	**Indian Style,** artist: Gregory Perillo, production quantity 17,500	35.00	70.00

	Issue Price	Current Value

MOTHER'S LOVE SERIES

☐ **1984** **Contentment,** artist: Norman Rockwell, production quantity 7,500 . . . . | 35.00 | 35.00

NURSERY PAIR

☐ **1983** **In Slumberland,** artist: Charlotte Becker, production limited . . . . | 25.00 | 25.00

☐ **1983** **The Awakening,** artist: Charlotte Becker, production limited . . . . | 25.00 | 25.00

ON THE ROAD SERIES

☐ **1984** **Pride of Stockbridge,** artist: Norman Rockwell, production limited . . . . | 35.00 | 35.00

PLAYFUL PETS SERIES

☐ **1982** **Curiosity,** artist: John Henry Dolph, production quantity 7,500 . . . . | 45.00 | 45.00

☐ **1982** **Master's Hat,** artist: John Henry Dolph, production quantity 7,500 . . . . | 45.00 | 45.00

PORTRAITS SERIES

☐ **1986** **Chantilly,** artist: John Eggert, production quantity limited . . . . | 24.50 | 24.50

PORTRAITS OF AMERICAN BRIDES SERIES

☐ **1987** **Caroline,** artist: Rob Sauber, production: 10 days . . . . | 29.50 | 29.50

☐ **1987** **Jacqueline,** artist: Rob Sauber, production: 10 days . . . . | 29.50 | 29.50

☐ **1987** **Elizabeth,** artist: Rob Sauber, production: 10 days . . . . | 29.50 | 29.50

☐ **1987** **Emily,** artist: Rob Sauber, production: 10 days . . . . | 29.50 | 29.50

☐ **1987** **Meredith,** artist: Rob Sauber, production: 10 days . . . . | 29.50 | 29.50

☐ **1987** **Laura,** artist: Rob Sauber, production: 10 days . . . . | 29.50 | 29.50

☐ **1987** **Sarah,** artist: Rob Sauber, production: 10 days . . . . | 29.50 | 29.50

☐ **1987** **Rebecca,** artist: Rob Sauber, production: 10 days . . . . | 29.50 | 29.50

Caroline, artist: Rob
Sauber.

	Issue Price	Current Value
ROCKWELL AMERICANA SERIES		
☐ **1981 Shuffleton's Barbershop,** artist: Norman Rockwell, production quantity 17,500	75.00	100.00
☐ **1982 Breaking Home Ties,** artist: Norman Rockwell, production quantity 17,500	75.00	75.00
☐ **1983 Walking to Church,** artist: Norman Rockwell, production quantity 17,500	75.00	75.00
SAILING THROUGH HISTORY SERIES		
☐ **1986 Flying Cloud,** artist: Kipp Soldwedel, production quantity: unannounced	29.50	29.50
SIMPLER TIMES SERIES		
☐ **1984 Lazy Daze,** artist: Norman Rockwell, production quantity 7,500	35.00	35.00
☐ **1984 One for the Road,** artist: Norman Rockwell, production quantity 7,500	35.00	35.00
SPECIAL OCCASIONS SERIES		
☐ **1981 Bubbles,** artist: Frances Tipton Hunter, production: less than one year	29.95	29.95
☐ **1982 Butterflies,** artist: Frances Tipton Hunter, production: less than one year	29.95	29.95

		Issue Price	Current Value
ROCKWELL TRILOGY SERIES			
☐ **1981**	**Stockbridge in Winter I,** artist: Norman Rockwell, production: less than one year ..	35.00	35.00
☐ **1982**	**Stockbridge in Winter II,** artist: Norman Rockwell, production: less than one year ..˙	35.00	35.00
☐ **1983**	**Stockbridge in Winter III,** artist: Norman Rockwell, production: less than one year ..	35.00	35.00
TRIBUTE SERIES			
☐ **1982**	**I Want You,** artist: James Montgomery Flagg, production limited	29.95	29.95
☐ **1982**	**Gee, I Wish I Were a Man,** artist: Howard Chandler Christy, production limited	29.95	29.95
☐ **1983**	**Soldier's Farewell,** artist: Norman Rockwell, production limited	29.95	29.95

DANBURY MINT

United States

		Issue Price	Current Value
BICENTENNIAL SILVER SERIES			
☐ **1973**	**Boston Tea Party,** production quantity 7,500	125.00	125.00
☐ **1974**	**First Continental Congress,** production quantity 7,500	125.00	125.00
☐ **1975**	**Paul Revere's Ride,** production quantity 7,500	125.00	125.00
☐ **1976**	**Declaration of Independence,** production quantity 7,500	125.00	125.00
☐ **1977**	**Washington at Valley Forge,** production quantity 7,500	125.00	125.00
☐ **1978**	**Molly Pitcher,** production quantity 7,500 ..	125.00	125.00
☐ **1979**	**Bon Homme Richard,** production quantity 7,500	125.00	125.00
CHRISTMAS SERIES			
☐ **1975**	**Silent Night,** production: less than one year	24.50	25.00
☐ **1976**	**Joy to the World,** production: less than one year	27.50	28.50
☐ **1977**	**Away in the Manger,** production: less than one year	28.50	28.50
☐ **1978**	**The First Noel,** production: less than one year	29.50	31.00
CURRIER & IVES SILVER SERIES			
☐ **1972**	**The Road Winter,** production quantity 7,500	125.00	126.00

		Issue Price	Current Value
☐ 1973	**Central Park Winter,** production quantity 7,500	**125.00**	**126.00**
☐ 1974	**Winter in the Country,** production quantity 7,500	**125.00**	**126.00**
☐ 1975	**American Homestead,** production quantity 7,500	**125.00**	**126.00**
☐ 1976	**American Winter Evening,** production quantity 7,500.............................	**135.00**	**136.00**
☐ 1977	**Winter Morning,** production quantity 7,500	**135.00**	**136.00**

GREAT AMERICAN MASTERPIECES SILVER SERIES

☐ 1975	**Mona Lisa,** production quantity 7,500	**125.00**	**125.00**
☐ 1975	**The Last Supper,** production quantity 7,500	**135.00**	**135.00**
☐ 1976	**Sunflower,** production quantity 7,500	**135.00**	**135.00**
☐ 1976	**Blue Boy,** production quantity 7,500	**135.00**	**135.00**

MICHELANGELO CRYSTAL SERIES

☐ 1977	**Pieta,** production: less than one year	**75.00**	**76.00**
☐ 1978	**Holy Family,** production: less than one year	**75.00**	**76.00**
☐ 1978	**Moses,** production: less than one year	**75.00**	**76.00**
☐ 1979	**Creation of Adam,** production: less than one year	**75.00**	**76.00**

MICHELANGELO SILVER SERIES

☐ 1973	**Creation of Adam,** production quantity 7,500	**125.00**	**141.00**
☐ 1973	**Pieta,** production quantity 7,500	**125.00**	**141.00**
☐ 1973	**Moses,** production quantity 7,500	**125.00**	**141.00**
☐ 1973	**Holy Family,** production quantity 7,500 ...	**125.00**	**141.00**

PEWTER SERIES

☐ 1977	**Christmas Carol**	**27.50**	**28.50**

SINGLE RELEASES

☐ 1977	**Official America's Cup,** production: less than one year	**20.00**	**22.50**
☐ 1977	**Tall Ships,** production: less than one year	**21.00**	**22.50**
☐ 1977	**Queen's Silver Jubilee,** production: less than one year	**85.00**	**86.00**

D'ARCEAU LIMOGES

France

	Issue Price	Current Value
CAMBIER FOUR SEASONS SERIES		
□ **1978 La Jeune Fille d'Ete,** artist: Guy Cambier, production quantity 15,000	105.00	122.00
□ **1979 La Jeune Fille d'Hiver,** artist: Guy Cambier, production quantity 15,000	105.00	106.00
□ **1980 La Jeune Fille du Printemps,** artist: Guy Cambier, production quantity 15,000	105.00	106.00
□ **1980 La Jeune Fille d'Automne,** artist: Guy Cambier, production quantity 15,000	105.00	126.00

CHRISTMAS SERIES		
□ **1975 La Fruite en Egypte,** artist: Andre Restieau, production: unannounced	24.32	35.00
□ **1976 Dans la Creche,** artist: Andre Restieau, production: unannounced	24.32	30.00
□ **1977 Le Refus d'Hèbergement,** artist: Andre Restieau, production: unannounced	24.32	30.00
□ **1978 La Purification,** artist: Andre Restieau, production: one year	26.81	30.00
□ **1979 L'Adoration des Rois,** artist: Andre Restieau, production: one year	26.81	37.00
□ **1980 Joyeuse Nouvelle,** artist: Andre Restieau, production: one year	28.74	29.00
□ **1981 Guides par L'Etoile,** artist: Andre Restieau, production: one year	28.74	30.00
□ **1982 The Annunciation,** artist: Andre Restieau, production: one year	30.74	45.00

LES FEMMES DU SIÈCLE		
□ **1976 Scarlet en Crinoline,** artist: Francois Ganeau	14.80	38.00
□ **1976 Sarah en Tournure,** artist: Francois Ganeau	19.87	32.00
□ **1976 Colette,** artist: Francois Ganeau	19.87	31.00
□ **1977 Lea,** artist: Francois Ganeau	19.87	31.00
□ **1977 Albertine,** artist: Francois Ganeau, production: one year	22.74	27.00
□ **1977 Daisy,** artist: Francois Ganeau, production: one year	22.74	27.00
□ **1977 Marlene,** artist: Francois Ganeau, production: one year	22.74	26.00
□ **1978 Helene,** artist: Francois Ganeau, production: one year	22.74	26.00

The Annunciation,
artist: Andre Restieau.

		Issue Price	Current Value
☐ 1978	**Sophie,** artist: Francois Ganeau, production: one year	22.74	47.00
☐ 1979	**Francoise,** artist: Francois Ganeau, production: one year	22.74	47.00
☐ 1979	**Brigitte,** artist: Francois Ganeau, production: one year	22.74	47.00

JOSEPHINE AND NAPOLEON SERIES

☐ 1984	**L'Emperatrice Josephine,** production quantity limited	29.32	30.50
☐ 1984	**Bonaparte Traversant les Alpes,** production quantity limited	29.32	30.50
☐ 1984	**The Meeting,** production quantity limited	29.32	30.50

LAFAYETTE LEGACY SERIES

☐ 1973	**The Secret Contract,** artist: Andre Restieau, production quantity: unannounced	14.82	15.00
☐ 1973	**North Island Landing,** artist: Andre Restieau, production quantity: unannounced	19.82	20.00
☐ 1974	**City Tavern Meeting,** artist: Andre Restieau, production quantity: unannounced	19.82	20.00
☐ 1974	**Battle of Brandywine,** artist: Andre Restieau, production quantity: unannounced	1982	20.00
☐ 1975	**Message to Franklin,** artist: Andre Restieau, production quantity: unannounced	19.82	23.00

		Issue Price	Current Value
☐ 1975	**Siege at Yorktown**, artist: Andre Restieau, production quantity: unannounced	**14.82**	**15.00**

LES NOELS DE FRANCE SERIES

| ☐ 1986 | **The Magical Window**, artist: Jean-Claude Guidou, production: 150 firing days ...... | **28.47** | **50.00** |

LES SITES PARISIENS DE LOUIS DALI SERIES

☐ 1979	**L'Arc de Triomphe**, artist: Louis Dali	**22.94**	**24.00**
☐ 1980	**La Cathedrale Notre Dame**, artist: Louis Dali	**22.94**	**27.00**
☐ 1981	**La Place de la Concorde**, artist: Louis Dali	**22.94**	**27.00**
☐ 1981	**L'Église Saint-Pierre et le Sacré-Coeur de Montmartre**, artist: Louis Dali	**22.94**	**27.00**
☐ 1982	**Le Marché Aux Fleurs et la Conciergerie**, artist: Louis Dali, production: one year	**26.83**	**27.00**
☐ 1982	**La Pointe du Vert Galant**, artist: Louis Dali, production: one year	**26.83**	**27.00**
☐ 1983	**Le Jardin des Tuileries**, artist: Louis Dali, production: one year	**26.83**	**27.00**
☐ 1983	**Le Moulin Rouge**, artist: Louis Dali, production: one year	**26.83**	**27.00**
☐ 1983	**Le Pont Alexandre**, artist: Louis Dali, production: one year	**26.83**	**27.00**
☐ 1983	**L'Opera**, artist: Louis Dali, production: one year	**26.83**	**27.00**
☐ 1983	**La Tour Eiffel**, artist: Louis Dali, production: one year	**26.83**	**27.00**
☐ 1983	**L'Hotel de Ville de Paris**, artist: Louis Dali, production: one year	**26.83**	**27.00**

LES TRES RICHES HEURES SERIES

☐ 1979	**Janvier,** artist: Jean Dutheil, production: one year	**75.48**	**76.00**
☐ 1980	**Avril**, artist: Jean Dutheil, production: one year	**75.48**	**76.00**
☐ 1981	**Aout**, artist: Jean Dutheil, production: one year	**75.48**	**76.00**
☐ 1982	**Juin**, artist: Jean Dutheil, production: one year	**75.48**	**76.00**
☐ 1984	**Mai**, artist: Jean Dutheil, production: one year	**75.48**	**76.00**

Mai, artist: Jean
Dutheil.

DAUM

France

		Issue Price	Current Value
ART NOUVEAU SERIES			
☐ 1979	**Water Lilies,** production quantity 4,000 ...	125.00	126.00
☐ 1980	**Lily Pond,** production quantity 4,000	150.00	151.00
☐ 1981	**Swan,** production quantity 4,000	170.00	171.00
FAMOUS MUSICIANS SERIES			
☐ 1971	**Bach,** production quantity 2,000	75.00	75.00
☐ 1971	**Beethoven,** production quantity 2,000	75.00	75.00
☐ 1971	**Mozart,** production quantity 2,000	75.00	75.00
☐ 1971	**Wagner,** production quantity 2,000	75.00	75.00
☐ 1972	**Debussy,** production quantity 2,000	75.00	75.00
☐ 1972	**Gershwin,** production quantity 2,000	75.00	75.00
FOUR SEASONS SERIES			
☐ 1970	**Autumn,** artist: Raymond Corbin, production quantity 2,000	150.00	150.00
☐ 1970	**Winter,** artist: Raymond Corbin, production quantity 2,000	150.00	150.00
☐ 1970	**Spring,** artist: Raymond Corbin, production quantity 2,000	150.00	150.00
☐ 1970	**Summer,** artist: Raymond Corbin, production quantity 2,000	150.00	150.00

		Issue Price	Current Value
NYMPHEA SERIES			
☐ **1979**	**Waterlilies,** production quantity 4,000	**125.00**	**140.00**
☐ **1980**	**Lily Pond,** production quantity 4,000	**150.00**	**170.00**
SALVADOR DALI SERIES			
☐ **1970**	**Ceci N'est Pas Une Assiette,** production quantity 2,000	**475.00**	**475.00**
☐ **1970**	**Triomphale,** production quantity 2,000	**475.00**	**475.00**

DAVENPORT POTTERY

Great Britain

TOBY PLATE COLLECTION			
☐ **1984**	**Toby Fillpot,** artist: Wilfred Blandford	**35.00**	**35.00**
☐ **1984**	**Falstaff,** artist: Douglas Tootle	**35.00**	**35.00**
☐ **1985**	**Jack Tar,** artist: Douglas Tootle	**40.00**	**40.00**
☐ **1986**	**Mr. Pickwick,** artist: Douglas Tootle	**40.00**	**40.00**
☐ **1986**	**Friar Tuck,** artist: Douglas Tootle	**40.00**	**40.00**

DAVID KAPLAN STUDIOS

United States

FIDDLER'S PEOPLE SERIES			
☐ **1978**	**Fiddler on the Roof,** artist: Rik Vig, production quantity 7,500	**60.00**	**60.00**
☐ **1979**	**Tevya,** artist: Rik Vig, production quantity 7,500	**60.00**	**60.00**
☐ **1980**	**Miracle of Love,** artist: Rik Vig, production quantity 7,500	**60.00**	**60.00**
☐ **1981**	**The Wedding,** artist: Rik Vig, production quantity 7,500	**60.00**	**60.00**

DAYBRAKE MARKETING

Canada

SINGLE ISSUE			
☐ **1984**	**Ernie's Farm Friends,** artist: Tammy Laye, production quantity 7,500	**50.00**	**50.00**

DE PAUW STUDIOS

United States

SINGLE RELEASE	Issue Price	Current Value
☐ **1976 Bicentennial Lincoln,** production quantity 2,400	30.00	68.00

DEVONSHIRE USA

United States

SINGLE ISSUE

	Issue Price	Current Value
☐ **1987 A Timeless Tradition,** artist: Carlo Beninati, production: 30-day firing	29.50	30.00

DOMINION CHINA CO.

Canada

WINGS UPON THE WIND SERIES

	Issue Price	Current Value
☐ **1986 The Landing,** artist: Donald Pentz, production quantity: unannounced	21.80	75.00

The Landing, artist: Donald Pentz.

DRESDEN

Germany

CHRISTMAS SERIES	Issue Price	Current Value
☐ **1971 Shepherd Scene,** production quantity 3,500	**15.00**	**50.00**
☐ **1972 Niklas Church,** production quantity 6,000	**15.00**	**25.00**
☐ **1973 Schwanstein Church,** production quantity 6,000	**18.00**	**35.00**
☐ **1974 Village Scene,** production quantity 5,000	**20.00**	**30.00**
☐ **1975 Rothenburg Scene,** production quantity 5,000	**24.00**	**30.00**
☐ **1976 Village Church,** production quantity 5,000	**26.00**	**35.00**
☐ **1977 Old Mill,** production quantity 5,000	**28.00**	**30.00**

MOTHER'S DAY SERIES

	Issue Price	Current Value
☐ **1972 Doe and Fawns,** artist: Hans Waldheimer, production quantity 8,000	**15.00**	**20.00**
☐ **1973 Mare and Colt,** artist: Hans Waldheimer, production quantity 6,000	**16.00**	**25.00**
☐ **1974 Tiger and Cub,** artist: Hans Waldheimer, production quantity 5,000	**20.00**	**25.00**
☐ **1975 Dachshund Family,** artist: Hans Waldheimer, production quantity 5,000	**24.00**	**28.50**
☐ **1976 Mother Owl and Young,** artist: Hans Waldheimer, production quantity 5,000	**26.00**	**30.00**
☐ **1977 Chamois,** artist: Hans Waldheimer, production quantity 5,000	**28.00**	**30.00**

DUNCAN ROYALE

United States

HISTORY OF SANTA CLAUS I

☐ **1985 Medieval,** artist: Susie Morton, production quantity 10,000	**40.00**	**40.00**
☐ **1985 Kris Kringle,** artist: Susie Morton, production quantity 10,000	**40.00**	**40.00**
☐ **1985 Pioneer,** artist: Susie Morton, production quantity 10,000	**40.00**	**40.00**
☐ **1986 Soda Pop,** artist: Susie Morton, production quantity 10,000	**40.00**	**40.00**
☐ **1986 Civil War,** artist: Susie Morton, production quantity 10,000	**40.00**	**40.00**
☐ **1986 Thomas Nast Santa,** artist: Thomas Nast, production quantity 10,000	**40.00**	**40.00**

	Issue Price	Current Value
☐ 1986 **Russian,** artist: Susie Morton, production quantity 10,000	40.00	40.00
☐ 1986 **Wassail,** artist: Susie Morton, production quantity 10,000	40.00	40.00
☐ 1986 **St. Nick,** artist: Susie Morton, production quantity 10,000	40.00	40.00
☐ 1986 **Black Peter,** artist: Susie Morton, production quantity 10,000	40.00	40.00
☐ 1986 **Victorian,** artist: Susie Morton, production quantity 10,000	40.00	40.00
☐ 1986 **Dedt Moroz,** artist: Susie Morton, production quantity 10,000	40.00	40.00

HISTORY OF SANTA CLAUS II SERIES

☐ 1986 **Lord of Misrule,** artist: T. Holter Bruckner, production quantity 10,000	80.00	80.00

EBELING AND REUSS

United States

CHRISTMAS SERIES

☐ 1982 **A Time of Song and Caroling,** artist: Joan Walsh Anglund, production quantity 7,500	15.00	15.00

ELEGANCE OF BRONZE

KNAPP SERIES

☐ 1978 **Navajo Madonna,** production quantity 2,500	250.00	285.00

ENESCO

United States

CHRISTMAS COLLECTION

☐ 1981 **Come Let Us Adore Him,** artist: Biel and Butcher, production quantity 15,000	40.00	60.00
☐ 1982 **Let Heaven and Nature Sing,** artist: Biel and Butcher, production quantity 15,000	40.00	45.00
☐ 1983 **We Three Kings,** artist: Biel and Butcher, production quantity 15,000	40.00	45.00

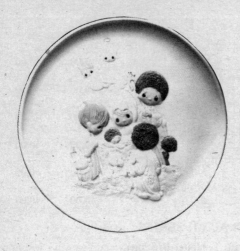

Come Let Us Adore
Him, artist: Biel and
Butcher.

		Issue Price	Current Value
☐ 1984	**Unto Us a Child Is Born,** artist: Sam Butcher, production quantity 15,000	**40.00**	**40.00**

CHRISTMAS LOVE SERIES

		Issue Price	Current Value
☐ 1986	**I'm Sending You a White Christmas,** artist: Sam Butcher, production: one year	**45.00**	**45.00**
☐ 1987	**My Peace I Give Unto Thee,** artist: Sam Butcher, production: one year	**45.00**	**45.00**

ENESCO PRECIOUS MOMENTS COLLECTION

		Issue Price	Current Value
☐ 1980	**The Lord Bless You and Keep You,** artist: Sam Butcher, production: open	**30.00**	**30.00**
☐ 1981	**Rejoicing with You,** artist: Sam Butcher, production: open	**30.00**	**30.00**
☐ 1982	**Our First Christmas Together,** artist: Sam Butcher, production: open	**30.00**	**30.00**
☐ 1982	**Jesus Loves Me—Boy Holding Teddy Bear,** artist: Sam Butcher, production: open	**30.00**	**30.00**
☐ 1982	**Jesus Loves Me—Girl with Teddy Bear,** artist: Sam Butcher, production: open	**30.00**	**30.00**

My Peace I Give Unto Thee, artist: Sam Butcher.

FOUR SEASONS COLLECTION	Issue Price	Current Value
☐ 1985 **Voice of Spring,** artist: Sam Butcher, production: one year	40.00	85.00
☐ 1985 **Summer's Joy,** artist: Sam Butcher, production: one year	40.00	70.00
☐ 1986 **Autumn's Prize,** artist: Sam Butcher, production: one year	40.00	70.00
☐ 1986 **Winter's Song,** artist: Sam Butcher, production: one year	40.00	70.00

INSPIRED THOUGHTS

	Issue Price	Current Value
☐ 1980 **Love One Another,** artist: Samuel Butcher, production quantity 15,000	40.00	60.00
☐ 1981 **Make a Joyful Noise,** artist: Samuel Butcher, production quantity 15,000	40.00	60.00
☐ 1982 **I Believe in Miracles,** artist: Samuel Butcher, production quantity 15,000	40.00	60.00
☐ 1984 **Love Is Kind,** artist: Samuel Butcher, production quantity 15,000	40.00	60.00

JOY OF CHRISTMAS ANNUAL SERIES

	Issue Price	Current Value
☐ 1982 **I'll Play My Drum for Him,** artist: Samuel Butcher, production: one year	40.00	95.00
☐ 1983 **Christmastime Is for Sharing,** artist: Samuel Butcher, production: one year	40.00	80.00

Our First Christmas
Together, artist: Sam
Butcher.

Jesus Loves Me—Boy
Holding Teddy Bear,
artist: Sam Butcher.

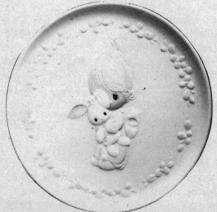

Jesus Loves Me—Girl
With Teddy Bear, artist:
Sam Butcher.

Winter's Song, artist: Sam Butcher.

		Issue Price	Current Value
☐ 1984	The Wonder of Christmas, artist: Samuel Butcher, production: one year	40.00	60.00
☐ 1985	Tell Me the Story of Jesus, artist: Samuel Butcher, production: one year	40.00	90.00

LITTLE BIBLE FRIENDS

		Issue Price	Current Value
☐ 1981	The Nativity, artist: Lucas, production quantity 25,000	40.00	40.00
☐ 1982	Flight into Egypt, artist: Lucas, production quantity 25,000	40.00	40.00
☐ 1982	The Last Supper, artist: Lucas, production quantity 25,000	40.00	40.00

MOTHER'S LOVE

		Issue Price	Current Value
☐ 1980	Mother Sew Dear, artist: Samuel Butcher, production quantity 15,000	40.00	70.00
☐ 1981	The Purr-fect Grandma, artist: Samuel Butcher, production quantity 15,000	40.00	70.00
☐ 1982	The Hand That Rocks the Future, artist: Samuel Butcher, production quantity 15,000	40.00	70.00
☐ 1983	Loving Thy Neighbor, artist: Samuel Butcher, production quantity 15,000	40.00	70.00

Love is Kind, artist: Sam Butcher.

I'll Play My Drum for Him, artist: Samuel Butcher.

Tell Me the Story of Jesus, artist: Samuel Butcher.

R. J. ERNST ENTERPRISES

United States

(See also Viletta China)

		Issue Price	Current Value
BARE INNOCENCE SERIES			
☐ **1986**	**Free at Last,** artist: Glen Banse, production: 10 days	**24.50**	**24.50**
A BEAUTIFUL WORLD SERIES			
☐ **1981**	**Tahitian Dreamer,** artist: Susie Morton, numbered, production quantity 27,500	**27.50**	**27.50**
☐ **1982**	**Flirtation,** artist: Susie Morton, numbered, production quantity 27,500	**27.50**	**27.50**
☐ **1983**	**Elke Of Oslo,** artist: Susie Morton, production quantity 27,500	**27.50**	**27.50**
THE BUSY BEARS SERIES			
☐ **1986**	**Heading South,** artist: Simon Devoche, production: 100 days	**19.50**	**19.50**
☐ **1986**	**Breakfast Break,** artist: Simon Devoche, production: 100 days	**19.50**	**19.50**
☐ **1986**	**Fall Fun,** artist: Simon Devoche, production: 100 days	**19.50**	**19.50**
☐ **1986**	**Flying Low,** artist: Simon Devoche, production: 100 days	**19.50**	**19.50**

Free At Last, artist: Glen Banse.

Heading South, artist:
Simon Devoche.

Flying Low, artist:
Simon Devoche.

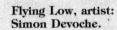

Boy with Hoop, artist:
Peter Quidley.

		Issue Price	Current Value

CHILDREN OF THE PAST SERIES

☐ **1986** **Boy with Hoop,** artist: Peter Quidley, production: 90 days **29.50**   **29.50**

CLASSY CARS

☐ **1982** **The 26T,** artist: Scott Kuhnly, production: 20 days **24.50**   **30.00**

☐ **1982** **The 31A,** artist: Scott Kuhnly, production: 20 days **24.50**   **24.50**

☐ **1983** **The Pickup,** artist: Scott Kuhnly, production: 20 days **24.50**   **24.50**

☐ **1984** **The Panel Van,** artist: Scott Kuhnly, production: 20 days **24.50**   **24.50**

THE COUNTRY COUSINS SERIES

☐ **1986** **Yep That's It,** artist: William Powell, production: 30 days **24.50**   **24.50**

☐ **1986** **She's All Yours,** artist: William Powell, production: 30 days **24.50**   **24.50**

DADDY'S LITTLE GIRL

☐ **1986** **Look at Me, Daddy,** artist: John Letostak, numbered, production: 90 days **29.95**   **29.95**

ELVIRA

☐ **1986** **Night Rose,** artist: Susie Morton, production: 90 days **29.50**   **29.50**

FISHING BOATS

☐ **1983** **Sunset at Monterey,** artist: Scott Kuhnly, production: less than one year **24.50**   **25.50**

FOGG AND STEAM SERIES

☐ **1986** **Pride of the Northwest,** artist: Howard Fogg, hand-numbered, production quantity 7,500   **39.50**   **39.50**

☐ **1986** **Autumn in New England,** artist: Howard Fogg, hand-numbered, production quantity 7,500 . . . .   **39.50**   **39.50**

FONDEST MEMORIES SERIES

☐ **1986** **Mother's Pearls,** artist: Ann Marry-Kenyon, production limited **60.00**   **60.00**

Yep That's It, artist:
William Powell.

She's All Yours, artist:
William Powell.

Look At Me Daddy,
artist: John Letostak.

Autumn in New
England, artist: Howard
Fogg.

		Issue Price	Current Value
☐ **1986**	**A Touching Moment,** artist: Ann Marry-Kenyon, production limited	**60.00**	**60.00**

GO FOR THE GOLD

☐ **1985**	**Valerie,** artist: Susie Morton, production quantity 5,000	**29.50**	**29.50**

HOLLYWOOD GREATS SERIES

☐ **1981**	**John Wayne,** artist: Susie Morton, production quantity 27,500	**29.95**	**50.00**
☐ **1981**	**Gary Cooper,** artist: Susie Morton, production quantity 27,500	**29.95**	**29.95**
☐ **1982**	**Clark Gable,** artist: Susie Morton, production quantity 27,500	**29.95**	**65.00**
☐ **1984**	**Alan Ladd,** artist: Susie Morton, production quantity 27,500	**29.95**	**60.00**

LIEBCHEN

☐ **1983**	**Autumn Liebchen,** artist: Von Ault, production: less than one year	**19.50**	**20.50**
☐ **1983**	**Spring Liebchen,** artist: Von Ault, production: less than one year	**19.50**	**20.50**
☐ **1983**	**Summer Liebchen,** artist: Von Ault, production: less than one year	**19.50**	**20.50**

	Issue Price	Current Value
☐ **1983 Winter Liebchen,** artist: Von Ault, production: less than one year	19.50	20.50

LITTLE MISSES YOUNG AND FAIR SERIES

☐ **1983 Heart of a Child,** artist: Alan Murray, production quantity 29,000	60.00	60.00
☐ **1984 Where Wildflowers Grow,** artist: Alan Murray, production quantity 29,000	60.00	60.00
☐ **1986 Final Touch,** artist: Alan Murray, production quantity 29,000	60.00	60.00

A LOVE STORY

☐ **1982 Chapter I,** artist: Adam Shields, production: less than one year	24.50	25.50
☐ **1983 Chapter II,** artist: Adam Shields, production: less than one year	24.50	25.50

ME AND MOM

☐ **1986 Beach Baby,** artist: Susie Morton, hand-numbered, production quantity 5,000	29.50	29.50
☐ **1986 What's This?,** artist: Susie Morton, hand-numbered, production quantity 5,000	29.50	29.50

Final Touch, artist: Alan Murray.

Beach Baby, artist:
Susie Morton.

		Issue Price	Current Value
MOMMY AND ME			
☐ 1982	**First Tea,** artist: Rusty Money, production: less than one year	**35.00**	**36.00**
☐ 1983	**Baby's Sleeping,** artist: Rusty Money, production: less than one year	**35.00**	**36.00**
MY FAIR LADIES			
☐ 1982	**Lady Sabrina,** artist: Rusty Money, production quantity 29,000	**50.00**	**50.00**
☐ 1983	**Lady Victoria,** artist: Rusty Money, production quantity 29,000	**50.00**	**50.00**
THE NARROW GAUGE			
☐ 1983	**Halfway to Alamosa,** artist: Jack Hamilton, production: less than one year	**29.50**	**31.00**
☐ 1984	**Down from Rico,** artist: Jack Hamilton, production quantity limited	**29.50**	**31.00**
THE PERFORMANCE			
☐ 1980	**Act I,** artist: Bonnie Porter, production quantity 5,000	**65.00**	**65.00**
RUFUS AND ROXANNE			
☐ 1980	**Love Is . . .,** artist: Kelly, production quantity 19,900	**14.95**	**15.50**

	Issue Price	Current Value
SEEMS LIKE YESTERDAY SERIES		
☐ **1981 Stop and Smell the Roses,** artist: Rusty Money, production: 10 days	24.50	35.00
☐ **1982 Home by Lunch,** artist: Rusty Money, numbered, production: 10 days	24.50	30.00
☐ **1982 Lisa's Creek,** artist: Rusty Money, numbered, production: 10 days	24.50	35.00
☐ **1983 It's Got My Name on It,** artist: Rusty Money, production: 10 days	24.50	30.00
☐ **1983 My Magic Hat,** artist: Rusty Money, production: less than one year	24.50	24.50
☐ **1984 Little Prince,** artist: Rusty Money, production quantity limited	24.50	24.50
SHADES OF TIME SERIES		
☐ **1986 Scent and Satin,** artist: Alan Murray, production quantity 5,000	45.00	45.00
STAR TREK		
☐ **1984 Mr. Spock,** artist: Susie Morton, production: 90 days	29.50	29.50
☐ **1984 Dr. McCoy—Medical Officer,** artist: Susie Morton, production: 90 days	29.50	29.50
☐ **1985 Julie,** artist: Susie Morton, production: 90 days	29.50	29.50

Scent and Satin, artist: Alan Murray.

		Issue Price	Current Value

☐ **1985 Scotty,** artist: Susie Morton, production: 90 days **29.50** **29.50**

☐ **1985 Uhura,** artist: Susie Morton, production: 90 days **29.50** **29.50**

☐ **1985 Chekov,** artist: Susie Morton, production: 90 days **29.50** **29.50**

☐ **1985 Captain Kirk,** artist: Susie Morton, production: 90 days **29.50** **29.50**

☐ **1985 Beam Us Down, Scotty,** artist: Susie Morton, production: 90 days **29.50** **29.50**

☐ **1985 The Enterprise,** artist: Susie Morton, production: 90 days **39.50** **39.50**

STAR TREK COMMEMORATIVE SERIES

☐ **1986 The Trouble with Tribbles,** artist: Susie Morton, production quantity limited **29.50** **29.50**

☐ **1987 Mirror, Mirror,** artist: Susie Morton, production quantity limited **29.50** **29.50**

☐ **1987 A Piece of the Action,** artist: Susie Morton, production quantity limited **29.50** **29.50**

☐ **1987 The Devil in the Dark,** artist: Susie Morton, production quantity limited **29.50** **29.50**

☐ **1987 Amok Time,** artist: Susie Morton, production quantity limited **29.50** **29.50**

☐ **1987 The City on the Edge of Forever,** artist: Susie Morton, production quantity limited **29.50** **29.50**

☐ **1987 Journey to Babel,** artist: Susie Morton, production quantity limited **29.50** **29.50**

☐ **1988 The Menagerie,** artist: Susie Morton, production quantity limited **29.50** **29.50**

SO YOUNG, SO SWEET SERIES

☐ **1982 Girl with Straw Hat,** artist: Susie Morton, production: 10 days **39.50** **39.50**

☐ **1983 My Favorite Necklace,** artist: Susie Morton, production: 10 days **39.50** **39.50**

☐ **1983 Breakfast Time,** artist: Susie Morton, production: 10 days **39.50** **39.50**

THIS LAND IS OUR LAND SERIES

☐ **1986 Sand Dunes,** artist: Gage Taylor, production quantity 5,000 .... **29.50** **29.50**

Sand Dunes, artist: Gage Taylor.

		Issue Price	Current Value
TURN OF THE CENTURY SERIES			
☐ 1981	**Riverboat Honeymoon,** artist: Rusty Money, numbered, production: 10 days	35.00	35.00
☐ 1982	**Children's Carousel,** artist: Rusty Money, production: 10 days	35.00	35.00
☐ 1984	**Flower Market,** artist: Rusty Money, production: 10 days	35.00	35.00
☐ 1985	**Balloon Race,** artist: Rusty Money, production: 10 days	35.00	35.00
WOMEN OF THE WEST			
☐ 1979	**Expectations,** artist: Donald Putnam, production quantity 10,000	39.50	39.50
☐ 1981	**Silver Dollar Sal,** artist: Donald Putnam, production quantity 10,000	39.50	39.50
☐ 1982	**School Marm,** artist: Donald Putnam, production quantity 10,000	39.50	39.50
☐ 1983	**Dolly,** artist: Donald Putnam, production quantity 10,000	39.50	39.50
YESTERDAY SERIES			
☐ 1982	**Amber,** artist: Glenice, numbered, production: 10 days	24.50	25.50
☐ 1983	**Elmer,** artist: Glenice, numbered, production: less than one year	24.50	25.50

		Issue Price	Current Value
☐ **1986**	**Katie,** artist: Glenice, numbered, production: 10 days	**24.50**	**25.50**

SINGLE ISSUES

☐ **1978**	**DeGrazia by Marco,** artist: J. Marco, production quantity 5,000	**65.00**	**65.00**
☐ **1983**	**Tribute to Henry Fonda,** artist: Susie Morton, production: 10 days	**45.00**	**45.00**
☐ **1984**	**Marilyn Monroe,** artist: Susie Morton, production: 61 days	**29.50**	**29.50**

SINGLE RELEASES: COMMEMORATIVES

☐ **1981**	**John Lennon,** artist: Susie Morton, numbered, production: 30 days	**39.50**	**60.00**
☐ **1982**	**Elvis Presley,** artist: Susie Morton, numbered, production: 30 days	**39.50**	**85.00**
☐ **1982**	**Marilyn Monroe,** artist: Susie Morton, numbered, production: 30 days	**39.50**	**55.00**
☐ **1983**	**Judy Garland,** artist: Susie Morton, numbered, production: 30 days	**39.50**	**60.00**
☐ **1983**	**John Wayne,** artist: Susie Morton, numbered, production quantity 2,500	**39.50**	**60.00**

Katie, artist: Glenice.

ESCALERA PRODUCTION ART

United States

OLYMPIAD TRIUMPHS COLLECTION	Issue Price	Current Value
☐ **1984 Track,** artist: Rudy Escalera, production quantity 19,500	60.00	60.00
☐ **1984 Field Events,** artist: Rudy Escalera, production quantity 19,500	60.00	60.00
☐ **1984 Basketball,** artist: Rudy Escalera, production quantity 19,500	60.00	60.00
☐ **1984 Swimming,** artist: Rudy Escalera, production quantity 19,500	60.00	60.00
☐ **1984 Soccer,** artist: Rudy Escalera, production quantity 19,500	60.00	60.00
☐ **1984 Baseball and Tennis,** artist: Rudy Escalera, production quantity 19,500	60.00	60.00
☐ **1984 Boxing,** artist: Rudy Escalera, production quantity 19,500	60.00	60.00
☐ **1984 Gymnastics,** artist: Rudy Escalera, production quantity 19,500	60.00	60.00

EVERGREEN PRESS

United States

CATALINA ISLAND SERIES

☐ **1986 Avalon Bay,** artist: Roger Upton, hand-numbered, production quantity 5,000	39.95	39.95
☐ **1986 Pleasure Pier,** artist: Roger Upton, hand-numbered, production quantity 5,000	39.95	39.95
☐ **1987 Catalina Calls,** artist: Frank Loudin, hand-numbered, production quantity: 5,000	39.95	39.95
☐ **1987 Reflections,** artist: Frank Loudin, hand-numbered, production quantity: 5,000	39.95	39.95
☐ **1987 Casino Way,** artist: Frank Loudin, hand-numbered, production quantity: 5,000	39.95	39.95

Pleasure Pier, artist: Roger Upton.

Catalina Calls, artist: Frank Loudin.
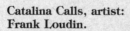

Reflections, artist:
Frank Loudin.

Casino Way, artist:
Frank Loudin.

FAIRMONT CHINA

United States

AMERICA'S MOST BELOVED SERIES	Issue Price	Current Value
☐ **1980 John Wayne**, artist: Clarence Thorpe, production quantity 5,000	**13.95**	**14.50**

		Issue Price	Current Value
☐ 1981	**Portrait of Rockwell,** artist: Clarence Thorpe, production quantity 15,000	40.00	42.00

ANNUAL SERIES

		Issue Price	Current Value
☐ 1984	**Little Ballerina,** artist: Anthony Sidoni, production quantity 5,000	29.95	29.95
☐ 1984	**Organ Grinder,** artist: Anthony Sidoni, production quantity 5,000	29.95	29.95

CHILD OF AMERICA SERIES

		Issue Price	Current Value
☐ 1979	**Eskimo Girl,** artist: Laura Johnson, production quantity 3,000	48.00	48.00

EARLY WORKS SERIES

		Issue Price	Current Value
☐ 1979	**Old Man Winter,** artist: Norman Rockwell, production quantity 15,000	19.95	50.00
☐ 1980	**The Inventor,** artist: Norman Rockwell, production quantity 15,000	19.95	21.00
☐ 1980	**Ready for School,** artist: Norman Rockwell, production quantity 15,000	19.95	21.00
☐ 1980	**Music Maker,** artist: Norman Rockwell, production quantity 15,000	19.95	21.00
☐ 1981	**The Tinkerer,** artist: Norman Rockwell, production quantity 15,000	19.95	21.00

FAMOUS CLOWNS SERIES

		Issue Price	Current Value
☐ 1976	**Freddie the Freeloader,** artist: Red Skelton, production quantity 10,000	55.00	500.00
☐ 1977	**W. C. Fields,** artist: Red Skelton, production quantity 10,000	55.00	75.00
☐ 1978	**Happy,** artist: Red Skelton, production quantity 10,000	55.00	75.00
☐ 1979	**The Pledge,** artist: Red Skelton, production quantity 10,000	55.00	75.00

GNOME FOUR SEASONS SERIES

		Issue Price	Current Value
☐ 1980	**Little Swinger,** artist: Rien Poortvliet, production quantity 15,000	29.50	30.50
☐ 1980	**Gnome de Bloom,** artist: Rien Poortvliet, production quantity 15,000	29.50	30.50
☐ 1980	**The Lookouts,** artist: Rien Poortvliet, production quantity 15,000	29.50	30.50

Freddie the Freeloader, artist: Red Skelton.

The Pledge, artist: Red Skelton.

		Issue Price	Current Value
☐ 1980	**First Skater,** artist: Rien Poortvliet, production quantity 15,000	29.50	30.50
☐ 1981	**Spring Sharing,** artist: Rien Poortvliet, production quantity 15,000	29.95	30.50
☐ 1981	**Fun and Games,** artist: Rien Poortvliet, production quantity 15,000	29.95	30.50

		Issue Price	Current Value
☐ 1981	**Up, Up and Away,** artist: Rien Poortvliet, production quantity 15,000	29.95	30.50
☐ 1981	**First Skier,** artist: Rien Poortvliet, production quantity 15,000	29.95	30.50
☐ 1982	**Gnome Knowledge,** artist: Rien Poortvliet, production quantity 15,000	29.95	30.50
☐ 1982	**The Berry Pickers,** artist: Rien Poortvliet, production quantity 15,000	29.95	30.50
☐ 1982	**Gnome Made,** artist: Rien Poortvliet, production quantity 15,000	29.95	30.50
☐ 1982	**Keep the Gnome Fires Burning,** artist: Rien Poortvliet, production quantity 15,000	29.95	30.50

GNOME HOLIDAY

☐ 1980	**Gnome Blues,** artist: Rien Poortvliet, production quantity 5,000	24.50	25.50
☐ 1981	**Gift of Love,** artist: Rien Poortvliet, production quantity 5,000	29.95	30.50

HOBO JOE SERIES

☐ 1982	**Do Not Disturb,** artist: Ron Lee, numbered, production quantity 7,500	50.00	50.00

ISRAELI COMMEMORATIVE SERIES
(Ghent Collection)

☐ 1978	**The Promised Land,** artist: Tobey, production quantity 5,738	79.00	85.00

LEGEND OF THE GNOMES SERIES

☐ 1984	**Birthday Planting,** artist: Rien Poortvliet, production quantity 15,000	29.95	29.95
☐ 1984	**Forest First Aid,** artist: Rien Poortvliet, production quantity 15,000	29.95	29.95
☐ 1984	**Gnome Home,** artist: Rien Poortvliet, production quantity 15,000	29.95	29.95
☐ 1984	**Gnome Know How,** artist: Rien Poortvliet, production quantity 15,000	29.95	29.95
☐ 1984	**Happy Pastime,** artist: Rien Poortvliet, production quantity 15,000	29.95	29.95
☐ 1984	**Labor of Love,** artist: Rien Poortvliet, production quantity 15,000	29.95	29.95
☐ 1984	**Little Counselor,** artist: Rien Poortvliet, production quantity 15,000	29.95	29.95

		Issue Price	Current Value
☐ **1984**	**Winter Sharing,** artist: Rien Poortvliet, production quantity 15,000	**29.95**	**29.95**

THE LONG ROAD WEST SERIES

☐ **1981**	**The Trailblazers,** artist: Jim Henson, production quantity 20,000	**40.00**	**42.00**
☐ **1981**	**Prairie Schooner Pioneer,** artist: Jim Henson, production quantity 20,000	**40.00**	**42.00**
☐ **1981**	**Pony Express,** artist: Jim Henson, production quantity 20,000	**40.00**	**42.00**
☐ **1981**	**The Peace Makers,** artist: Jim Henson, production quantity 20,000	**40.00**	**42.00**
☐ **1981**	**Cowboys of the West,** artist: Jim Henson, production quantity 20,000	**40.00**	**42.00**
☐ **1981**	**Lawmen of the West,** artist: Jim Henson, production quantity 20,000	**40.00**	**42.00**

LORDS OF THE PLAINS SERIES

☐ **1979**	**Sitting Bull,** artist: Richard Nickerson, production quantity 5,000	**60.00**	**60.00**

MEMORY ANNUAL SERIES
(Ghent Collection)

☐ **1977**	**Memory Plate,** production quantity 1,977	**77.00**	**83.00**
☐ **1978**	**Memory Plate,** production quantity 1,978	**78.00**	**83.00**
☐ **1979**	**Memory Plate,** production quantity 1,979	**79.99**	**85.00**
☐ **1980**	**Memory Plate,** production quantity 1,980	**80.00**	**85.00**

PASSING OF PLAINS INDIANS SERIES
(Collector's Heirlooms)

☐ **1979**	**Cheyenne Chieftain,** artist: Andre Bouche, production quantity 7,500	**65.00**	**70.00**

PLAYFUL MEMORIES SERIES

☐ **1981**	**Renee,** artist: Sue Etem, production quantity 10,000	**39.50**	**75.00**

RUTHVEN BIRDS FEATHERED FRIENDS SERIES

☐ **1978**	**Chickadees,** artist: John Ruthven, production quantity 5,000	**39.50**	**40.50**

	Issue Price	Current Value
☐ **1981 Screech Owls,** artist: John Ruthven, production quantity 5,000	39.50	40.50

SPENCER ANNUAL SERIES

☐ **1977 Patient Ones,** artist: Irene Spencer, production quantity 10,000	42.50	56.00
☐ **1978 Yesterday, Today And Tomorrow,** artist: Irene Spencer, production quantity 10,000	47.50	51.00

SPENCER SPECIAL SERIES

☐ **1978 Hug Me,** artist: Irene Spencer, production quantity 10,000	55.00	95.00
☐ **1978 Sleep Little Baby,** artist: Irene Spencer, production quantity 10,000	65.00	65.00

TIMELESS MOMENTS SERIES

☐ **1978 Tenderness,** artist: Clarence Thorpe, production quantity 5,000	45.00	45.00
☐ **1979 Renaissance,** artist: Clarence Thorpe, production quantity 5,000	45.00	45.00
☐ **1980 Coming in Glory,** artist: Clarence Thorpe, production quantity 5,000	39.95	40.00

VANISHING AMERICANA SERIES

☐ **1984 American Eagle,** artist: Clarence Thorpe, production quantity 15,000	13.50	14.00
☐ **1984 The Country Doctor,** artist: Clarence Thorpe, production quantity 15,000	13.50	14.00

WHEN I GROW UP SERIES

☐ **1981 I'll Be Loved,** artist: Ann Hershenburgh, production quantity 7,500	29.95	30.00
☐ **1981 I'll Be Like Mommy,** artist: Ann Hershenburgh, production quantity 7,500	29.95	30.00
☐ **1981 I'll Be First Lady,** artist: Ann Hershenburgh, production quantity 7,500	29.95	30.00
☐ **1981 I'll Be a Star,** artist: Ann Hershenburgh, production quantity 7,500	29.95	30.00

SINGLE RELEASES

☐ **1978 The Fence,** artist: St. Clair, production quantity 5,000	45.00	45.00

		Issue Price	Current Value
☐ 1978	**Sioux Warrior,** artist: Olaf Wieghorst, production quantity 5,000	65.00	96.00
☐ 1978	**The Scout,** artist: Olaf Wieghorst, production quantity 5,000	65.00	72.00
☐ 1983	**My Little Sheltie,** artist: Clarence Thorpe, production quantity 5,000	39.95	40.00
☐ 1984	**The Organ Grinder,** artist: Anthony Sidoni, production quantity 5,000	29.95	30.00

FENTON ART GLASS

United States

ALLIANCE SERIES

☐ 1975	**Lafayette and Washington,** blue satin glass, production: one year	15.00	28.00
☐ 1975	**Lafayette and Washington,** red satin glass, production: one year	17.50	30.00
☐ 1975	**Lafayette and Washington,** white satin glass, production: one year	15.00	28.00
☐ 1976	**Lafayette and Washington,** blue satin glass, production: one year	15.00	28.00
☐ 1976	**Lafayette and Washington,** chocolate glass, production: one year	17.50	30.00
☐ 1976	**Lafayette and Washington,** white satin glass, production: one year	15.00	28.00

AMERICAN CRAFTSMAN SERIES

☐ 1970	**Glassmaker,** production: one year	10.00	68.00
☐ 1970	**Glassmaker,** black, production quantity 600	10.00	140.00
☐ 1970	**Glassmaker,** production quantity 200	10.00	220.00
☐ 1971	**Printer,** production: one year	10.00	80.00
☐ 1972	**Blacksmith,** production: one year	10.00	150.00
☐ 1973	**Shoemaker,** production: one year	12.50	70.00
☐ 1974	**Cooper,** production: one year	12.50	55.00
☐ 1975	**Silversmith Revere,** production: one year . .	12.50	60.00
☐ 1976	**Gunsmith,** production: one year	15.00	45.00
☐ 1977	**Potter,** production: one year	15.00	35.00
☐ 1978	**Wheelwright,** production: one year	15.00	25.00
☐ 1979	**Cabinetmaker,** production: one year	15.00	23.00
☐ 1980	**Tanner,** production: one year	16.50	20.00
☐ 1981	**Housewright,** production: one year	17.50	18.00

	Issue Price	Current Value
CHILDHOOD TREASURE SERIES		

☐ **1983** **Teddy Bear,** artist: Diane Johnson, production quantity 15,000 . . . . — 45.00 — 45.00

CHRISTMAS IN AMERICA SERIES

☐ **1970** **Little Brown Church in Vale,** carnival glass, production: one year . . . . — 12.50 — 60.00

☐ **1970** **Little Brown Church in Vale,** blue satin glass, production: one year . . . . — 12.50 — 100.00

☐ **1971** **Old Brick Church,** carnival glass, production: one year . . . . — 12.50 — 77.00

☐ **1971** **Old Brick Church,** blue satin glass, production: one year . . . . — 12.50 — 72.00

☐ **1971** **Old Brick Church,** white satin glass, production: one year . . . . — 12.50 — 62.00

☐ **1972** **Two Horned Church,** carnival glass, production: one year . . . . — 12.50 — 68.00

☐ **1972** **Two Horned Church,** blue satin glass, production: one year . . . . — 12.50 — 72.00

☐ **1972** **Two Horned Church,** white satin glass, production: one year . . . . — 12.50 — 52.00

☐ **1973** **Saint Mary's/Mountains,** carnival glass, production: one year . . . . — 12.50 — 62.00

☐ **1973** **Saint Mary's/Mountains,** blue satin glass, production: one year . . . . — 12.50 — 67.00

☐ **1973** **Saint Mary's/Mountains,** white satin glass, production: one year . . . . — 12.50 — 52.00

☐ **1974** **Nation's Church,** carnival glass, production: one year . . . . — 13.50 — 57.00

☐ **1974** **Nation's Church,** blue satin glass, production: one year . . . . — 13.50 — 57.00

☐ **1974** **Nation's Church,** white satin glass, production: one year . . . . — 13.50 — 47.00

☐ **1975** **Birthplace of Liberty,** carnival glass, production: one year . . . . — 13.50 — 67.00

☐ **1975** **Birthplace of Liberty,** blue satin glass, production: one year . . . . — 13.50 — 62.00

☐ **1975** **Birthplace of Liberty,** white satin glass, production: one year . . . . — 13.50 — 52.00

☐ **1976** **Old North Church,** carnival glass, production: one year . . . . — 15.00 — 52.00

☐ **1976** **Old North Church,** blue satin glass, production: one year . . . . — 15.00 — 52.00

☐ **1976** **Old North Church,** white satin glass, production: one year . . . . — 15.00 — 52.00

		Issue Price	Current Value
☐ 1977	**San Carlos Boromeo de Car.,** carnival glass, production: one year	**15.00**	**42.00**
☐ 1977	**San Carlos Boromeo de Car.,** blue satin glass, production: one year	**15.00**	**42.00**
☐ 1977	**San Carlos Boromeo de Car.,** white satin glass, production: one year	**15.00**	**42.00**
☐ 1978	**Church of the Holy Trinity,** carnival glass, production: one year	**15.00**	**37.00**
☐ 1978	**Church of the Holy Trinity,** blue satin glass, production: one year	**15.00**	**37.00**
☐ 1978	**Church of the Holy Trinity,** white satin glass, production: one year	**15.00**	**37.00**
☐ 1979	**San Jose y Miquel de Aquayo,** carnival glass, production: one year	**15.00**	**32.00**
☐ 1979	**San Jose y Miquel de Aquayo,** blue satin glass, production: one year	**15.00**	**32.00**
☐ 1979	**San Jose y Miquel de Aquayo,** white satin glass, production: one year	**15.00**	**32.00**
☐ 1980	**Christ Church, Alexandria, VA,** carnival glass, production: one year	**16.50**	**27.00**
☐ 1980	**Christ Church, Alexandria, VA,** blue satin glass, production: one year	**16.50**	**27.00**
☐ 1980	**Christ Church, Alexandria, VA,** white satin glass, production: one year	**16.50**	**22.00**
☐ 1981	**Mission of San Xavier del Bac,** carnival glass, production: one year	**18.50**	**22.00**
☐ 1981	**Mission of San Xavier del Bac,** blue satin glass, production: one year	**18.50**	**22.00**
☐ 1981	**Mission of San Xavier del Bac,** white satin glass, production: one year	**18.50**	**22.00**

CURRIER & IVES LIMITED EDITION SERIES

☐ 1980	**Winter in the Country—The Old Grist Mill,** artist: Anthony Rosena, production: one year	**25.00**	**26.00**
☐ 1981	**Harvest,** artist: Anthony Rosena, production: one year	**25.00**	**26.00**
☐ 1982	**The Old Homestead in Winter,** artist: Anthony Rosena, production: one year	**25.00**	**26.00**
☐ 1983	**Winter Pastime,** artist: Anthony Rosena, production: one year	**25.00**	**26.00**

		Issue Price	Current Value
DESIGNER SERIES			
☐ 1983	**Down Home,** artist: Gloria Fina, production quantity 1,000	65.00	65.00
☐ 1983	**Lighthouse Point,** artist: Gloria Fina, production quantity 1,000	65.00	65.00

HANDPAINTED CHRISTMAS
CLASSIC SERIES

☐ 1979	**Nature's Christmas,** production: one year ..	35.00	32.00
☐ 1980	**Going Home,** production: one year	38.50	40.00
☐ 1981	**All Is Calm,** production: one year	42.50	45.00
☐ 1982	**Country Christmas,** production: one year ..	42.50	45.00

HANDPAINTED MOTHER'S DAY SERIES

☐ 1980	**New Born,** production: one year	28.50	30.00
☐ 1981	**Gentle Fawn,** production: one year	32.50	35.00
☐ 1982	**Nature's Awakening,** production: one year	35.00	37.00
☐ 1983	**Where's Mom,** production: one year	35.00	37.00

MOTHER'S DAY SERIES

☐ 1971	**Madonna with Sleeping Child,** carnival glass, production: one year	12.50	57.00
☐ 1971	**Madonna with Sleeping Child,** blue satin glass, production: one year	12.50	67.00
☐ 1972	**Madonna of the Goldfinch,** carnival glass, production: one year	12.50	72.00
☐ 1972	**Madonna of the Goldfinch,** blue satin glass, production: one year	12.50	62.00
☐ 1972	**Madonna of the Goldfinch,** white satin glass, production: one year	12.50	48.00
☐ 1973	**Small Cowper Madonna,** carnival glass, production: one year	12.50	62.00
☐ 1973	**Small Cowper Madonna,** blue satin glass, production: one year	12.50	62.00
☐ 1973	**Small Cowper Madonna,** white satin glass, production: one year	12.50	40.00
☐ 1974	**Madonna of the Grotto,** carnival glass, production: one year	13.50	52.00
☐ 1974	**Madonna of the Grotto,** blue satin glass, production: one year	13.50	52.00
☐ 1974	**Madonna of the Grotto,** white satin glass, production: one year	13.50	30.00
☐ 1975	**Taddei Madonna,** carnival glass, production: one year	13.50	62.00

		Issue Price	Current Value
☐ 1975	**Taddei Madonna,** blue satin glass, production: one year	13.50	62.00
☐ 1975	**Taddei Madonna,** white satin glass, production: one year	13.50	47.00
☐ 1976	**Holy Night,** carnival glass, production: one year	13.50	52.00
☐ 1976	**Holy Night,** blue satin glass, production: one year	13.50	18.00
☐ 1976	**Holy Night,** white satin glass, production: one year	13.50	18.00
☐ 1977	**Madonna and Child with Pomegranate,** carnival glass, production: one year	15.00	42.00
☐ 1977	**Madonna and Child with Pomegranate,** blue satin glass, production: one year	15.00	42.00
☐ 1977	**Madonna and Child with Pomegranate,** white satin glass, production: one year	15.00	18.00
☐ 1978	**Madonnina,** carnival glass, production: one year	15.00	30.00
☐ 1978	**Madonnina,** blue satin glass, production: one year	15.00	37.00
☐ 1978	**Madonnina,** white satin glass, production: one year	15.00	18.00
☐ 1979	**Madonna of the Rose Hedge,** carnival glass, production: one year	15.00	32.00
☐ 1979	**Madonna of the Rose Hedge,** blue satin glass, production: one year	15.00	32.00
☐ 1979	**Madonna of the Rose Hedge,** white satin glass, production: one year	15.00	18.00
☐ 1979	**Madonna of the Rose Hedge,** ruby iridescent, production quantity 5,000	15.00	42.00

VALENTINE'S DAY SERIES

		Issue Price	Current Value
☐ 1972	**Romeo and Juliet,** carnival glass, production: one year	15.00	23.00
☐ 1972	**Romeo and Juliet,** blue satin glass, production: one year	15.00	23.00

FINE ARTS MARKETING

Canada

AUTUMN FLIGHTS SERIES

		Issue Price	Current Value
☐ 1986	**Canadian Geese,** artist: Jerold Bishop, hand-numbered, production quantity 5,000	55.00	55.00

Mallard Ducks, artist:
Jerold Bishop.

		Issue Price	Current Value
☐ **1986**	**Mallard Ducks,** artist: Jerold Bishop, hand-numbered, production quantity 5,000	55.00	55.00

TURN, TURN, TURN SERIES

☐ **1986**	**Autumn Back Home,** artist: Jerold Bishop, hand-numbered, production quantity 5,000	50.00	50.00
☐ **1986**	**Winter Memories,** artist: Jerold Bishop, hand-numbered, production quantity 5,000	50.00	50.00

FIREHOUSE COLLECTIBLES

United States

THIS OLE BEAR SERIES

☐ **1984**	**Buster and Sam,** artist: Janet Tuck, production quantity: 5,000	39.50	40.00
☐ **1984**	**Matilda Jane,** artist: Janet Tuck, production quantity: 5,000	39.50	40.00

**Autumn Back Home,
artist: Jerold Bishop.**

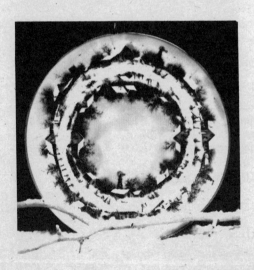

**Winter Memories, artist:
Jerold Bishop.**

FLAMBRO IMPORTS

EMMETT KELLY, JR. PLATES SERIES	Issue Price	Current Value
☐ **1983** **Why Me?** artist: C. Kelly, production quantity 10,000	40.00	100.00
☐ **1984** **Balloons for Sale,** artist: C. Kelly, production quantity 10,000	40.00	80.00

Why Me? Plate I, artist: C. Kelly.

		Issue Price	Current Value
☐ 1985	**Big Business,** artist: C. Kelly, production quantity 10,000	**40.00**	**40.00**
☐ 1986	**And God Bless America,** artist: C. Kelly, production quantity 10,000	**40.00**	**40.00**

THE FLEETWOOD COLLECTION

United States

BIRDS AND FLOWERS OF THE MEADOW AND GARDEN SERIES

☐ 1980	**Baltimore Oriole and Morning Glory,** artist: Don Balke, production limited	**39.00**	**40.00**
☐ 1980	**Goldfinch and Bullthistle,** artist: Don Balke, production limited	**39.00**	**40.00**
☐ 1980	**Cardinal and Lupine,** artist: Don Balke, production limited	**39.00**	**40.00**

		Issue Price	Current Value
☐ 1980	Eastern Blue Bird and Blackeyed Susan, artist: Don Balke, production limited	39.00	40.00
☐ 1980	Capped Chickadee and New England Aster, artist: Don Balke, production limited	39.00	40.00
☐ 1980	Robin and Crabapple, artist: Don Balke, production limited	39.00	40.00
☐ 1980	Painted Bunting and Blackberry, artist: Don Balke, production limited	39.00	40.00
☐ 1980	Golden Crowned Kinglet and Downy Phlox, artist: Don Balke, production limited	39.00	40.00
☐ 1980	Redbreasted Nuthatch and Japanese Honeysuckle, artist: Don Balke, production limited	39.00	40.00
☐ 1980	Magnolia Warbler and Common Day Lily, artist: Don Balke, production limited	39.00	40.00
☐ 1980	Hummingbird and Fire Pink, artist: Don Balke, production limited	39.00	40.00
☐ 1980	Scarlet Tanager and Blue Columbine, artist: Don Balke, production limited	39.00	40.00

BLOSSOMS OF CHINA SERIES

		Issue Price	Current Value
☐ 1982	Peony, artist: Ren Yu, production quantity 7,500	49.50	50.50
☐ 1982	Herbaceous Peony, artist: Ren Yu, production quantity 7,500	49.50	50.50
☐ 1982	Chrysanthemum, artist: Ren Yu, production quantity 7,500	49.50	50.50
☐ 1982	Magnolia, artist: Ren Yu, production quantity 7,500	49.50	50.50
☐ 1982	Plum Blossom, artist: Ren Yu, production quantity 7,500	49.50	50.50
☐ 1983	Narcissus, artist: Ren Yu, production quantity 7,500	49.50	50.50

CHRISTMAS SERIES

		Issue Price	Current Value
☐ 1980	Magi, artist: Fritz Wegner, production quantity 5,000	45.00	75.00
☐ 1981	Holy Child, artist: Fritz Wegner, production quantity 7,500	49.50	58.00
☐ 1982	The Shepherds, artist: Fritz Wegner, production quantity 5,000	50.00	50.00
☐ 1985	Coming Home for Christmas, artist: F. Jacques, production quantity 5,000	50.00	50.00

		Issue Price	Current Value

GOLDEN AGE OF SAIL SERIES

☐ **1981 Flying Cloud,** artist: Charles Lundgren, production quantity 5,000 .... **39.00 40.00**

☐ **1982 New World,** artist: Charles Lundgren, production quantity 5,000 .... **39.00 40.00**

☐ **1982 Young America,** artist: Charles Lundgren, production quantity 5,000 .... **39.00 40.00**

☐ **1982 Courier,** artist: Charles Lundgren, production quantity 5,000 .... **39.00 40.00**

☐ **1982 Sea Witch,** artist: Charles Lundgren, production quantity 5,000 .... **39.00 40.00**

☐ **1983 Great Republic,** artist: Charles Lundgren, production quantity 5,000 .... **39.00 40.00**

MOTHER'S DAY SERIES

☐ **1980 Cottontails,** artist: Don Balke, production quantity 5,000 .... **45.00 75.00**

☐ **1981 Raccoons,** artist: Don Balke, production quantity 5,000 .... **45.00 58.00**

☐ **1982 Whitetail Deer,** artist: Don Balke, production quantity 5,000 .... **50.00 50.00**

☐ **1983 Canada Geese,** artist: Don Balke, production quantity 5,000 .... **50.00 50.00**

PANDAS OF WU ZUOREN SERIES

☐ **1981 Mother and Baby,** artist: Wu Zuoren, production quantity 5,000 .... **39.00 40.00**

☐ **1981 Sleeping Panda,** artist: Wu Zuoren, production quantity 5,000 .... **39.00 40.00**

☐ **1981 Two Pandas,** artist: Wu Zuoren, production quantity 5,000 .... **39.00 40.00**

☐ **1981 Mother and Baby Playing,** artist: Wu Zuoren, production quantity 5,000 .... **39.00 40.00**

☐ **1981 Mother Holding Baby,** artist: Wu Zuoren, production quantity 5,000 .... **39.00 40.00**

☐ **1981 Panda on a Rock,** artist: Wu Zuoren, production quantity 5,000 .... **39.00 40.00**

ROYAL WEDDING SERIES

☐ **1981 Prince Charles/Lady Diana,** artist: Jeffrey Mathews, production quantity 9,500 ...... **49.50 75.00**

☐ **1986 Prince Andrew/Sarah Ferguson,** artist: Jeffrey Mathews, production quantity 10,000 **50.00 50.00**

		Issue Price	Current Value
STATUE OF LIBERTY			
☐ **1986**	**Statue of Liberty Plate,** artist: Jeffrey Mathews, production quantity 10,000	**50.00**	**50.00**

TSAREVICH'S BRIDE SERIES

☐ **1981**	**An Arrow in the Air,** artist: A. M. Kurkin, production quantity 7,500	**50.00**	**60.00**
☐ **1982**	**Boyer's Courtyard,** artist: A. M. Kurkin, production quantity 7,500	**50.00**	**60.00**
☐ **1982**	**Rich Merchant's Yard,** artist: A. M. Kurkin, production quantity 7,500	**50.00**	**60.00**
☐ **1983**	**Mouth of a Frog,** artist: A. M. Kurkin, production quantity 7,500	**50.00**	**60.00**

SINGLE RELEASE

☐ **1982**	**Mom's Apple Pie,** artist: Gene Boyer, production: less than one year . . . . :	**29.00**	**29.00**

FONTANA

CHRISTMAS SERIES

☐ **1972**	**18th Century Couple with Dog,** production quantity 2,000	**35.00**	**25.00**
☐ **1973**	**Sleighing,** production quantity 1,000	**35.00**	**28.00**

MOTHER'S DAY SERIES

☐ **1973**	**Mother and Child,** production quantity 2,000	**35.00**	**25.00**

FOSTORIA GLASS

United States

AMERICAN MILESTONES SERIES

☐ **1971**	**Betsy Ross Flag,** production quantity 5,000	**12.50**	**25.00**
☐ **1972**	**National Anthem,** production quantity 8,000	**12.50**	**15.00**
☐ **1973**	**Washington Crossing Delaware,** production: one year	**12.50**	**18.00**
☐ **1974**	**Spirit of '76,** production: one year	**13.00**	**18.00**
☐ **1975**	**Mount Rushmore,** production: one year . . .	**16.00**	**16.00**

STATE PLATE SERIES

☐ **1971**	**California,** production quantity 6,000	**12.50**	**15.00**
☐ **1971**	**New York,** production quantity 12,000	**12.50**	**15.00**

		Issue Price	Current Value
☐ 1971	**Ohio,** production quantity 3,000	12.50	15.00
☐ 1972	**Florida,** production: one year	12.50	15.00
☐ 1972	**Hawaii,** production: one year	12.50	15.00
☐ 1972	**Pennsylvania,** production: one year	12.50	15.00
☐ 1972	**Massachusetts,** production: one year	13.00	15.00
☐ 1972	**Texas,** production: one year	13.00	15.00
☐ 1973	**Michigan,** production: one year	13.50	15.00

FRANKLIN MINT

United States

AMERICAN REVOLUTION SERIES

☐ 1976–77	**Boston Tea Party,** artist: Steven Dohanos, production quantity 3,596	75.00	80.00
☐ 1976–77	**Patrick Henry Urges Armed Resistance,** artist: Paul Calle, production quantity 3,596	75.00	80.00
☐ 1976–77	**Paul Revere's Ride,** artist: John Falter, production quantity 3,596	75.00	80.00
☐ 1976–77	**The Battle of Concord Bridge,** artist: Paul Rickert, production quantity 3,596	75.00	80.00
☐ 1976–77	**The Capture of Fort Ticonderoga,** artist: Dean Fausett, production quantity 3,596	75.00	80.00
☐ 1976–77	**The Battle of Bunker Hill,** artist: Alton S. Tobey, production quantity 3,596	75.00	80.00
☐ 1976–77	**The Signing of the Declaration,** artist: Gordon Phillips, production quantity 3,596	75.00	80.00
☐ 1976–77	**Washington Crosses the Delaware,** artist: Alexander Farnham, production quantity 3,596	75.00	80.00
☐ 1976–77	**Burgoyne Defeated at Saratoga,** artist: Don Stone, production quantity 3,596 ..	75.00	80.00
☐ 1976–77	**Winter at Valley Forge,** artist: Isa Barratt, production quantity 3,596	75.00	80.00
☐ 1976–77	**Bonhomme Richard Defeats Serapis,** artist: John Pike, production quantity 3,596	75.00	80.00
☐ 1976–77	**Victory at Yorktown,** artist: John Chumley, production quantity 3,596	75.00	80.00

ANNUAL SERIES

☐ 1977	**Tribute to the Arts,** production quantity 1,901	280.00	305.00

		Issue Price	Current Value
☐ 1978	**Tribute to Nature,** production quantity 435	280.00	305.00

ARABIAN NIGHTS SERIES

☐ 1981–82	**Aladdin and His Wonderful Lamp,** artist: Christopher McEwan, production quantity 690	27.50	30.00
☐ 1981–82	**Ali Baba and Forty Thieves,** artist: Christopher McEwan, production quantity 690	27.50	30.00
☐ 1981–82	**The City of Brass,** artist: Christopher McEwan, production quantity 690	27.50	30.00
☐ 1981–82	**The Fair Persian,** artist: Christopher McEwan, production quantity 690	27.50	30.00
☐ 1981–82	**The Fisherman,** artist: Christopher McEwan, production quantity 690	27.50	30.00
☐ 1981–82	**The Magic Horse,** artist: Christopher McEwan, production quantity 690	27.50	30.00
☐ 1981–82	**The Merchant and the Genie,** artist: Christopher McEwan, production quantity 690	27.50	30.00
☐ 1981–82	**Prince Agib,** artist: Christopher McEwan, production quantity 690	27.50	30.00
☐ 1981–82	**Prince Camaralzaman and the Princess Badoura,** artist: Christopher McEwan, production quantity 690	27.50	30.00
☐ 1981–82	**Sinbad the Sailor,** artist: Christopher McEwan, production quantity 690	27.50	30.00
☐ 1981–82	**The Vizier Who Was Punished,** artist: Christopher McEwan, production quantity 690	27.50	30.00
☐ 1981–82	**The Young King of the Ebony Isles,** artist: Christopher McEwan, production quantity 690	27.50	30.00

AUDUBON SOCIETY SERIES

☐ 1972	**The Goldfinch,** artist: James Fenwick Lansdowne, production quantity 10,193	125.00	116.00
☐ 1972	**The Wood Duck,** artist: James Fenwick Lansdowne, production quantity 10,193	125.00	111.00
☐ 1973	**The Cardinal,** artist: James Fenwick Lansdowne, production quantity 10,193	125.00	111.00
☐ 1973	**The Ruffed Grouse,** artist: James Fenwick Lansdowne, production quantity 10,193	125.00	121.00

		Issue Price	Current Value

BERNARD BUFFET SERIES

☐ 1973	**Gazelle,** artist: Bernard Buffet, production quantity 570	**150.00**	**275.00**
☐ 1974	**Panda,** artist: Bernard Buffet, production quantity 408	**150.00**	**250.00**
☐ 1975	**Giraffe,** artist: Bernard Buffet, production quantity 333	**150.00**	**250.00**
☐ 1976	**Lion,** artist: Bernard Buffet, production quantity 263	**150.00**	**250.00**
☐ 1977	**Rhinoceros,** artist: Bernard Buffet, production quantity 200	**150.00**	**250.00**

BICENTENNIAL SERIES

☐ 1973	**Jefferson Drafting the Declaration of Independence,** production quantity 8,556 ..	**175.00**	**210.00**
☐ 1974	**John Adams Champions the Cause of Independence,** production quantity 8,442 ..	**175.00**	**210.00**
☐ 1975	**Caesar Rodney Decides the Vote on Independence,** production quantity 8,319 ...	**175.00**	**210.00**
☐ 1976	**John Hancock Signs the Declaration of Independence,** production quantity 10,166	**175.00**	**210.00**

BIRD SERIES

☐ 1972	**Cardinal,** artist: Richard Evans Younger, production quantity 13,939	**125.00**	**135.00**
☐ 1972	**Bob White,** artist: Richard Evans Younger, production quantity 13,939 ...	**125.00**	**135.00**
☐ 1972	**Mallards,** artist: Richard Evans Younger, production quantity 13,939	**125.00**	**135.00**
☐ 1973	**American Bald Eagle,** artist: Richard Evans Younger, production quantity 13,939	**125.00**	**146.00**

BIRDS AND FLOWERS OF BEAUTIFUL CATHAY SERIES

☐ 1981–82	**Beginning of Winter,** artist: Wei Tseng Yang	**35.00**	**40.00**
☐ 1981–83	**Big Snow,** artist: Wei Tseng Yang	**35.00**	**40.00**
☐ 1981–83	**Ching Che (Awakening of Insects),** artist: Wei Tseng Yang	**35.00**	**40.00**
☐ 1981–83	**Ch'ing Ming (Pure Brightness),** artist: Wei Tseng Yang	**35.00**	**40.00**
☐ 1981–83	**Ch'un Fen (Division of Spring),** artist: Wei Tseng Yang	**35.00**	**40.00**

		Issue Price	Current Value
☐ 1981–83	Cold Dew, artist: Wei Tseng Yang	35.00	40.00
☐ 1981–83	Hsia Chih (Arrival of Summer), artist: Wei Tseng Yang	35.00	40.00
☐ 1981–83	Hsiao Han (Small Cold), artist: Wei Tseng Yang	35.00	40.00
☐ 1981–83	Hsiao Man (Ripening Grain), artist: Wei Tseng Yang	35.00	40.00
☐ 1981–83	Hsiao Shu, artist: Wei Tseng Yang	35.00	40.00
☐ 1981–83	Ku Yu (Corn Rain), artist: Wei Tseng Yang	35.00	40.00
☐ 1981–83	Li Ch'iu (Beginning of Autumn), artist: Wei Tseng Yang	35.00	40.00
☐ 1981–83	Li Ch'un (Beginning of Spring), artist: Wei Tseng Yang	35.00	40.00
☐ 1981–83	Li Hsia (Beginning of Summer), artist: Wei Tseng Yang	35.00	40.00
☐ 1981–83	Limit of Heat, artist: Wei Tseng Yang	35.00	40.00
☐ 1981–83	Mang Chung (Grain in the Ear), artist: Wei Tseng Yang	35.00	40.00
☐ 1981–83	Scarlet Finches and Chrysanthemums, artist: Wei Tseng Yang	35.00	40.00
☐ 1981–83	Small Snow, artist: Wei Tseng Yang . . .	35.00	40.00
☐ 1981–83	Ta Han (Great Cold), artist: Wei Tseng Yang	35.00	40.00
☐ 1981–83	Ta Shus (Great Heat), artist: Wei Tseng Yang	35.00	40.00
☐ 1981–83	White Dew, artist: Wei Tseng Yang	35.00	40.00
☐ 1981–83	Winter Solstice, artist: Wei Tseng Yang	35.00	40.00
☐ 1981–83	Yu Shui (Rain Water), artist: Wei Tseng Yang	35.00	40.00

BIRDS AND FLOWERS OF THE ORIENT SERIES

☐ 1979–80	Rooster and Morning Glory, artist: Naoka Nobata, production quantity 32,373	55.00	60.00
☐ 1979–80	Lotus and Water Fowl, artist: Naoka Nobata, production quantity 32,373	55.00	60.00
☐ 1979–80	Maple Tree and Shrike, artist: Naoka Nobata, production quantity 32,373	55.00	60.00
☐ 1979–80	White Crane and the Pine, artist: Naoka Nobata, production quantity 32,373	55.00	60.00
☐ 1979–80	White Eye and Peach, artist: Naoka Nobata, production quantity 32,373	55.00	60.00
☐ 1979–80	Mandarin Duck and Iris, artist: Naoka Nobata, production quantity 32,373	55.00	60.00

		Issue Price	Current Value
☐ 1979–80	**Egret and Water Lily,** artist: Naoka Nobata, production quantity 32,373	55.00	60.00
☐ 1979–80	**Tree Sparrow and Chrysanthemum,** artist: Naoka Nobata, production quantity 32,373	55.00	60.00
☐ 1979–80	**Wren and Narcissus,** artist: Naoka Nobata, production quantity 32,373	55.00	60.00
☐ 1979–80	**Bush Warbler and Apricot,** artist: Naoka Nobata, production quantity 32,373	55.00	60.00
☐ 1979–80	**Chinese Blue Pie and Cherry,** artist: Naoka Nobata, production quantity 32,373	55.00	60.00
☐ 1979–80	**Peony and Peacock,** artist: Naoka Nobata, production quantity 32,373	55.00	60.00

BUTTERFLIES OF THE WORLD SERIES

☐ 1977–79	**South America,** production quantity 481	240.00	275.00
☐ 1977–79	**Australia,** production quantity 481	240.00	275.00
☐ 1977–79	**North America,** production quantity 481	240.00	275.00
☐ 1977–79	**Europe,** production quantity 481	240.00	275.00
☐ 1977–79	**Africa,** production quantity 481	240.00	275.00
☐ 1977–79	**Asia,** production quantity 481	240.00	275.00

CALENDAR SERIES

☐ 1981	**Turn-of-the-Century Scene,** artist: Deborah Bell Jarratt, production quantity 5,634	55.00	58.00
☐ 1982	**Turn-of-the-Century Children,** artist: Margaret Murphy, production quantity 5,634	58.00	62.00
☐ 1983	**Children Celebrating Victorian Months,** artist: Kate Lloyd Jones	55.00	60.00
☐ 1984	**Children with Teddy Bears,** artist: Margaret Murphy	55.00	60.00

CAROL LAWSON ANNUAL SERIES

☐ 1981	**Storytime,** artist: Carol Lawson, production: one year	35.00	35.00
☐ 1982	**Teacher's Pet,** artist: Carol Lawson, production: one year	35.00	35.00
☐ 1983	**Teatime Surprise,** artist: Carol Lawson, production: one year.................	35.00	35.00

CHRISTMAS—INTERNATIONAL SERIES

☐ 1981	**Christmas in France,** artist: Yves Beaujard	35.00	35.00

		Issue Price	Current Value
☐ 1982	**Christmas in England,** artist: Peter Jackson	35.00	35.00
☐ 1983	**Christmas in America,** artist: William Plummer	35.00	35.00

CHRISTMAS SERIES

☐ 1976	**Silent Night,** production quantity 19,286	65.00	72.00
☐ 1977	**Deck the Halls,** production quantity 9,185	75.00	72.00
☐ 1978	**We Three Kings,** production quantity 6,737	75.00	82.00
☐ 1979	**Hark the Herald Angels Sing,** production quantity 4,784	75.00	82.00
☐ 1980	**Joy to the World,** production: unannounced	125.00	126.00
☐ 1981	**O Holy Night,** production: unannounced	125.00	126.00

CLIPPER SHIPS SERIES

☐ 1982–83	**Ariel,** artist: L. J. Pearce	55.00	58.00
☐ 1982–83	**Challenge,** artist: L. J. Pearce	55.00	58.00
☐ 1982–83	**Cutty Sark,** artist: L. J. Pearce	55.00	58.00
☐ 1982–83	**Flying Cloud,** artist: L. J. Pearce	55.00	58.00
☐ 1982–83	**Great Republic,** artist: L. J. Pearce	55.00	58.00
☐ 1982–83	**Marco Polo,** artist: L. J. Pearce	55.00	58.00
☐ 1982–83	**Nightingale,** artist: L. J. Pearce	55.00	58.00
☐ 1982–83	**Oriental,** artist: L. J. Pearce	55.00	58.00
☐ 1982–83	**Patriarch,** artist: L. J. Pearce	55.00	58.00
☐ 1982–83	**Red Jacket,** artist: L. J. Pearce	55.00	58.00
☐ 1982–83	**Sea Witch,** artist: L. J. Pearce	55.00	58.00
☐ 1982–83	**Thermopylae,** artist: L. J. Pearce	55.00	58.00

COBBLESTONE KIDS SERIES

☐ 1982	**Making Friends,** artist: Debbie Bell Jarratt	65.00	70.00
☐ 1983	**A Stitch in Time,** artist: Debbie Bell Jarratt	65.00	70.00
☐ 1983	**Extra! Extra!,** artist: Debbie Bell Jarratt	65.00	70.00
☐ 1983	**Feeding the Raccoon,** artist: Debbie Bell Jarratt	65.00	70.00
☐ 1983	**Just Ducky,** artist: Debbie Bell Jarratt ..	65.00	70.00

COUNTRY DIARY SERIES

☐ 1984	**January–December,** artist: Geoff Mowery, production limited, set of 12	660.00	660.00

		Issue Price	Current Value

COUNTRY YEAR SERIES

		Issue Price	Current Value
☐ 1980–82	**Country Path in May,** artist: Peter Barratt, production quantity 89,173	**55.00**	**55.00**
☐ 1980–82	**January—Lambing Season,** artist: Peter Barratt, production quantity 89,173	**55.00**	**55.00**
☐ 1980–82	**October—Colours of Autumn,** artist: Peter Barratt, production quantity 89,173	**55.00**	**55.00**
☐ 1980–82	**Wheat Fields in August,** artist: Peter Barratt, production quantity 89,173	**55.00**	**55.00**
☐ 1980–82	**September on the Moors,** artist: Peter Barratt, production quantity 89,173	**55.00**	**55.00**
☐ 1980–82	**June in a Cottage Garden,** artist: Peter Barratt, production quantity 89,173	**55.00**	**55.00**
☐ 1980–82	**Country Church in March,** artist: Peter Barratt, production quantity 89,173	**55.00**	**55.00**
☐ 1980–82	**Secluded Stream in November,** artist: Peter Barratt, production quantity 89,173	**55.00**	**55.00**
☐ 1980–82	**Woodlands in April,** artist: Peter Barratt, production quantity 89,173	**55.00**	**55.00**
☐ 1980–82	**Country Lane in December,** artist: Peter Barratt, production quantity 89,173	**55.00**	**58.00**
☐ 1980–82	**July Beside the River,** artist: Peter Barratt, production quantity 89,173	**55.00**	**58.00**
☐ 1980–82	**February on the Coast,** artist: Peter Barratt, production quantity 89,173	**55.00**	**58.00**

CURRIER & IVES SERIES

		Issue Price	Current Value
☐ 1977–79	**Winter Pastime,** artist: Currier & Ives, production quantity 1,836	**39.50**	**45.00**
☐ 1977–79	**Preparing for Market,** artist: Currier & Ives, production quantity 1,836	**39.50**	**45.00**
☐ 1977–79	**Winter in the Country,** artist: Currier & Ives, production quantity 1,836	**39.50**	**45.00**
☐ 1977–79	**American Homestead—Winter,** artist: Currier & Ives, production quantity 1,836	**39.50**	**45.00**
☐ 1977–79	**American Forest Scene,** artist: Currier & Ives, production quantity 1,836	**39.50**	**45.00**
☐ 1977–79	**American Homestead—Summer,** artist: Currier & Ives, production quantity 1,836	**39.50**	**45.00**
☐ 1977–79	**American Homestead—Autumn,** artist: Currier & Ives, production quantity 1,836	**39.50**	**45.00**
☐ 1977–79	**Haying Time—The Last Load,** artist: Currier & Ives, production quantity 1,836	**39.50**	**45.00**
☐ 1977–79	**Catching a Trout,** artist: Currier & Ives, production quantity 1,836	**39.50**	**45.00**

		Issue Price	Current Value
☐ **1977–79**	**Yosemite Valley,** artist: Currier & Ives, production quantity 1,836	**39.50**	**45.00**

DAYS OF THE WEEK SERIES

		Issue Price	Current Value
☐ **1979–80**	**Monday's Child Is Fair of Face,** artist: Caroline Ebborn, production quantity 1,890	**39.00**	**42.00**
☐ **1979–80**	**Tuesday's Child Is Full of Grace,** artist: Caroline Ebborn, production quantity 1,890	**39.00**	**42.00**
☐ **1979–80**	**Wednesday's Child Is Full of Woe,** artist: Caroline Ebborn, production quantity 1,890	**39.00**	**42.00**
☐ **1979–80**	**Thursday's Child Has Far to Go,** artist: Caroline Ebborn, production quantity 1,890	**39.00**	**42.00**
☐ **1979–80**	**Friday's Child Is Loving and Giving,** artist: Caroline Ebborn, production quantity 1,890	**39.00**	**42.00**
☐ **1979–80**	**Saturday's Child Works Hard for a Living,** artist: Caroline Ebborn, production quantity 1,890	**39.00**	**42.00**
☐ **1979–80**	**Sunday's Child Is Born on the Sabbath Day,** artist: Caroline Ebborn, production quantity 1,890	**39.00**	**42.00**

EASTER SERIES

		Issue Price	Current Value
☐ **1973**	**Resurrection,** artist: Evangelos Frudakis, production quantity 7,116	**175.00**	**185.00**
☐ **1974**	**He Is Risen,** artist: Abram Belski, production quantity 3,719	**185.00**	**195.00**
☐ **1975**	**The Last Supper,** artist: Oriol Sunyer, production quantity 2,004	**200.00**	**225.00**
☐ **1976**	**The Crucifixion,** artist: Marguerite Gaudin, production quantity 3,904	**250.00**	**300.00**
☐ **1977**	**Resurrection,** production quantity 1,206	**250.00**	**300.00**

FAIRY TALES MINIATURES SERIES

		Issue Price	Current Value
☐ **1979–84**	**The Three Bears,** artist: Carol Lawson, production quantity 15,207	**14.50**	**16.00**
☐ **1979–84**	**Little Red Riding Hood,** artist: Carol Lawson, production quantity 15,207	**14.50**	**16.00**
☐ **1979–84**	**The Little Mermaid,** artist: Carol Lawson, production quantity 15,207	**14.50**	**16.00**

		Issue Price	Current Value
☐ 1979–84	**Snow White and the Seven Dwarfs,** artist: Carol Lawson, production quantity 15,207	**14.50**	**16.00**
☐ 1979–84	**Aladdin and the Wonderful Lamp,** artist: Carol Lawson, production quantity 15,207	**14.50**	**16.00**
☐ 1979–84	**The Snow Queen,** artist: Carol Lawson, production quantity 15,207	**14.50**	**16.00**
☐ 1979–84	**Tom Thumb,** artist: Carol Lawson, production quantity 15,207	**14.50**	**16.00**
☐ 1979–84	**Ali Baba,** artist: Carol Lawson, production quantity 15,207	**14.50**	**16.00**
☐ 1979–84	**Jack and the Beanstalk,** artist: Carol Lawson, production quantity 15,207	**14.50**	**16.00**
☐ 1979–84	**Puss in Boots,** artist: Carol Lawson, production quantity 15,207	**14.50**	**16.00**
☐ 1979–84	**The Frog Prince,** artist: Carol Lawson, production quantity 15,207	**14.50**	**16.00**
☐ 1979–84	**Cinderella,** artist: Carol Lawson, production quantity 15,207	**14.50**	**16.00**
☐ 1979–84	**Princess and the Pea,** artist: Carol Lawson, production quantity 15,207	**14.50**	**16.00**
☐ 1979–84	**The Pied Piper,** artist: Carol Lawson, production quantity 15,207	**14.50**	**16.00**
☐ 1979–84	**Valiant Little Tailor,** artist: Carol Lawson, production quantity 15,207	**14.50**	**16.00**
☐ 1979–84	**The Ugly Duckling,** artist: Carol Lawson, production quantity 15,207	**14.50**	**16.00**
☐ 1979–84	**The Three Little Pigs,** artist: Carol Lawson, production quantity 15,207	**14.50**	**16.00**
☐ 1979–84	**Rapunzel,** artist: Carol Lawson, production quantity 15,207	**14.50**	**16.00**
☐ 1979–84	**The Little Match Girl,** artist: Carol Lawson, production quantity 15,207	**14.50**	**16.00**
☐ 1979–84	**Thumbelina,** artist: Carol Lawson, production quantity 15,207	**14.50**	**16.00**
☐ 1979–84	**The Nightingale,** artist: Carol Lawson, production quantity 15,207	**14.50**	**16.00**
☐ 1979–84	**The Steadfast Tin Soldier,** artist: Carol Lawson, production quantity 15,207	**14.50**	**16.00**
☐ 1979–84	**The Goose That Laid the Golden Eggs,** artist: Carol Lawson, production quantity 15,207	**14.50**	**16.00**
☐ 1979–84	**Henny-Penny,** artist: Carol Lawson, production quantity 15,207	**14.50**	**16.00**

		Issue Price	Current Value
☐ 1979–84	**East of the Sun and West of the Moon,** artist: Carol Lawson, production quantity 15,207	**14.50**	**16.00**
☐ 1979–84	**Billy Goat's Gruff,** artist: Carol Lawson, production quantity 15,207	**14.50**	**16.00**
☐ 1979–84	**Sinbad the Sailor,** artist: Carol Lawson, production quantity 15,207	**14.50**	**16.00**
☐ 1979–84	**Beauty and the Beast,** artist: Carol Lawson, production quantity 15,207	**14.50**	**16.00**
☐ 1979–84	**The Red Shoes,** artist: Carol Lawson, production quantity 15,207	**14.50**	**16.00**
☐ 1979–84	**Rumpelstiltskin,** artist: Carol Lawson, production quantity 15,207	**14.50**	**16.00**
☐ 1979–84	**Sleeping Beauty,** artist: Carol Lawson, production quantity 15,207	**14.50**	**16.00**
☐ 1979–84	**The Twelve Dancing Princesses,** artist: Carol Lawson, production quantity 15,207	**14.50**	**16.00**
☐ 1979–84	**Hansel and Gretel,** artist: Carol Lawson, production quantity 15,207	**14.50**	**16.00**
☐ 1979–84	**Snow White and Rose Red,** artist: Carol Lawson, production quantity 15,207	**14.50**	**16.00**
☐ 1979–84	**The Bronze Ring,** artist: Carol Lawson, production quantity 15,207	**14.50**	**16.00**
☐ 1979–84	**Jorinda and Jorindel,** artist: Carol Lawson, production quantity 15,207	**14.50**	**16.00**
☐ 1979–84	**Pinocchio,** artist: Carol Lawson, production quantity 15,207	**14.50**	**16.00**
☐ 1979–84	**The Golden Goose,** artist: Carol Lawson, production quantity 15,207	**14.50**	**16.00**
☐ 1979–84	**The Sorcerer's Apprentice,** artist: Carol Lawson, production quantity 15,207	**14.50**	**16.00**
☐ 1979–84	**Town Mouse and Country Mouse,** artist: Carol Lawson, production quantity 15,207	**14.50**	**16.00**
☐ 1979–84	**Six Swans,** artist: Carol Lawson, production quantity 15,207	**14.50**	**16.00**
☐ 1979–84	**Maid Maleen,** artist: Carol Lawson, production quantity 15,207	**14.50**	**16.00**
☐ 1979–84	**The Gingerbread Boy,** artist: Carol Lawson, production quantity 15,207	**14.50**	**16.00**

FLOWERS OF THE AMERICAN WILDERNESS SERIES

		Issue Price	Current Value
☐ 1978–80	New England, artist: Jeanne Holgate, production quantity 8,759	39.00	42.00
☐ 1978–80	Alaska, artist: Jeanne Holgate, production quantity 8,759	39.00	42.00
☐ 1978–80	Everglades of Florida, artist: Jeanne Holgate, production quantity 8,759	39.00	42.00
☐ 1978–80	Mississippi Delta, artist: Jeanne Holgate, production quantity 8,759	39.00	42.00
☐ 1978–80	California, artist: Jeanne Holgate, production quantity 8,759	39.00	42.00
☐ 1978–80	Rocky Mountains, artist: Jeanne Holgate, production quantity 8,759	39.00	42.00
☐ 1978–80	Cape Cod, artist: Jeanne Holgate, production quantity 8,759	39.00	42.00
☐ 1978–80	Northwest, artist: Jeanne Holgate, production quantity 8,759	39.00	42.00
☐ 1978–80	Southwest, artist: Jeanne Holgate, production quantity 8,759	39.00	42.00
☐ 1978–80	Appalachian Mountains, artist: Jeanne Holgate, production quantity 8,759	39.00	42.00
☐ 1978–80	Prairies, artist: Jeanne Holgate, production quantity 8,759	39.00	42.00
☐ 1978–80	Great Lakes, artist: Jeanne Holgate, production quantity 8,759	39.00	42.00

FLOWERS OF THE YEAR SERIES

		Issue Price	Current Value
☐ 1976	January, artist: Leslie Greenwood, production quantity 27,394	50.00	50.00
☐ 1976	February, artist: Leslie Greenwood, production quantity 27,394	50.00	50.00
☐ 1977	March, artist: Leslie Greenwood, production quantity 27,394	50.00	50.00
☐ 1977	April, artist: Leslie Greenwood, production quantity 27,394	50.00	50.00
☐ 1977	May, artist: Leslie Greenwood, production quantity 27,394	50.00	50.00
☐ 1978	June, artist: Leslie Greenwood, production quantity 27,394	50.00	50.00
☐ 1978	July, artist: Leslie Greenwood, production quantity 27,394	50.00	50.00
☐ 1978	August, artist: Leslie Greenwood, production quantity 27,394	50.00	50.00
☐ 1978	September, artist: Leslie Greenwood, production quantity 27,394	50.00	50.00

		Issue Price	Current Value
☐ **1978**	**October,** artist: Leslie Greenwood, production quantity 27,394	**50.00**	**50.00**
☐ **1978**	**November,** artist: Leslie Greenwood, production quantity 27,394	**50.00**	**50.00**
☐ **1978**	**December,** artist: Leslie Greenwood, production quantity 27,394	**50.00**	**50.00**

FOUR SEASONS CHAMPLEVE SERIES

☐ **1975**	**Spring Blossoms,** artist: Rene Restoueux, production quantity 2,648	**240.00**	**215.00**
☐ **1975**	**Summer Bouquet,** artist: Rene Restoueux, production quantity 2,648	**240.00**	**215.00**
☐ **1976**	**Autumn Garland,** artist: Rene Restoueux, production quantity 2,648	**240.00**	**215.00**
☐ **1976**	**Winter Spray,** artist: Rene Restoueux, production quantity 2,648	**240.00**	**215.00**

GAME BIRDS OF THE WORLD SERIES

☐ **1978–80**	**Chinese Ring-Necked Pheasant,** artist: Basil Ede, production quantity 76,294 ..	**55.00**	**55.00**
☐ **1978–80**	**Red Legged Partridge,** artist: Basil Ede, production quantity 76,294	**55.00**	**55.00**
☐ **1978–80**	**Common Snipe,** artist: Basil Ede, production quantity 76,294	**55.00**	**55.00**
☐ **1978–80**	**Common Partridge,** artist: Basil Ede, production quantity 76,294	**55.00**	**55.00**
☐ **1978–80**	**Rock Ptarmigan,** artist: Basil Ede, production quantity 76,294	**55.00**	**55.00**
☐ **1978–80**	**Woodcock,** artist: Basil Ede, production quantity 76,294	**55.00**	**55.00**
☐ **1978–80**	**Common Pheasant,** artist: Basil Ede, production quantity 76,294	**55.00**	**55.00**
☐ **1978–80**	**Hazel Grouse,** artist: Basil Ede, production quantity 76,294	**55.00**	**55.00**
☐ **1978–80**	**Red Grouse,** artist: Basil Ede, production quantity 76,294	**55.00**	**55.00**
☐ **1978–80**	**Black Grouse,** artist: Basil Ede, production quantity 76,294	**55.00**	**55.00**
☐ **1978–80**	**Capercaillie,** artist: Basil Ede, production quantity 76,294	**55.00**	**55.00**
☐ **1978–80**	**Common Quail,** artist: Basil Ede, production quantity 76,294	**55.00**	**55.00**

		Issue Price	Current Value

GARDEN BIRDS OF THE WORLD SERIES

□ 1984	**American Robin,** artist: Basil Ede, signed, production limited	**55.00**	**55.00**
□ 1984	**Blackbird,** artist: Basil Ede, signed, production limited	**55.00**	**55.00**
□ 1984	**Black-capped Chickadee,** artist: Basil Ede, signed, production limited	**55.00**	**55.00**
□ 1984	**Cardinal,** artist: Basil Ede, signed, production limited	**55.00**	**55.00**
□ 1984	**Eastern Bluebird,** artist: Basil Ede, signed, production limited	**55.00**	**55.00**
□ 1984	**Goldfinch,** artist: Basil Ede, signed, production limited	**55.00**	**55.00**
□ 1984	**Great Titmouse,** artist: Basil Ede, signed, production limited	**55.00**	**55.00**
□ 1984	**Kingfisher,** artist: Basil Ede, signed, production limited	**55.00**	**55.00**
□ 1984	**Mockingbird,** artist: Basil Ede, signed, production limited	**55.00**	**55.00**
□ 1984	**Song Thrush,** artist: Basil Ede, signed, production limited	**55.00**	**55.00**
□ 1984	**Swallow,** artist: Basil Ede, signed, production limited	**55.00**	**55.00**
□ 1984	**White-breasted Nathatch,** artist: Basil Ede, signed, production limited	**55.00**	**55.00**

THE GARDEN YEAR SERIES

| □ 1984 | **January–December,** artist: David Hurrell, signed, production limited, set of 12 .... | **330.00** | **330.00** |

GRIMM'S FAIRY TALES SERIES

□ 1978	**Sleeping Beauty,** artist: Carol Lawson, production quantity 27,006	**42.00**	**43.00**
□ 1978	**Twelve Dancing Princesses,** artist: Carol Lawson, production quantity 27,006	**42.00**	**43.00**
□ 1979	**Bremen Town Musicians,** artist: Carol Lawson, production quantity 27,006	**42.00**	**43.00**
□ 1979	**Golden Goose,** artist: Carol Lawson, production quantity 27,006	**42.00**	**43.00**
□ 1979	**Hansel and Gretel,** artist: Carol Lawson, production quantity 27,006	**42.00**	**43.00**
□ 1979	**Rapunzel,** artist: Carol Lawson, production quantity 27,006	**42.00**	**43.00**

		Issue Price	Current Value
☐ 1979	**Snow White and the Seven Dwarfs,** artist: Carol Lawson, production quantity 27,006	42.00	43.00
☐ 1979	**Frog Prince,** artist: Carol Lawson, production quantity 27,006	42.00	43.00
☐ 1979	**Red Riding Hood,** artist: Carol Lawson, production quantity 27,006	42.00	43.00
☐ 1979	**Rumpelstiltskin,** artist: Carol Lawson, production quantity 27,006	42.00	43.00
☐ 1979	**Cinderella,** artist: Carol Lawson, production quantity 27,006	42.00	43.00
☐ 1979	**Shoemaker and the Elves,** artist: Carol Lawson, production quantity 27,006	42.00	43.00

HANS CHRISTIAN ANDERSEN SERIES

		Issue Price	Current Value
☐ 1976	**The Princess and the Pea,** artist: Pauline Ellison, production quantity 16,875	38.00	70.00
☐ 1976	**The Ugly Duckling,** artist: Pauline Ellison, production quantity 16,875	38.00	70.00
☐ 1976	**The Little Mermaid,** artist: Pauline Ellison, production quantity 16,875	38.00	70.00
☐ 1976	**The Emperor's New Clothes,** artist: Pauline Ellison, production quantity 16,875	38.00	70.00
☐ 1976	**The Steadfast Tin Soldier,** artist: Pauline Ellison, production quantity 16,875	38.00	70.00
☐ 1976	**The Little Match Girl,** artist: Pauline Ellison, production quantity 16,875	38.00	70.00
☐ 1977	**The Snow Queen,** artist: Pauline Ellison, production quantity 16,875	38.00	70.00
☐ 1977	**The Red Shoes,** artist: Pauline Ellison, production quantity 16,875	38.00	70.00
☐ 1977	**The Tinder Box,** artist: Pauline Ellison, production quantity 16,875	38.00	70.00
☐ 1977	**The Nightingale,** artist: Pauline Ellison, production quantity 16,875	38.00	70.00
☐ 1977	**Thumbelina,** artist: Pauline Ellison, production quantity 16,875	38.00	70.00
☐ 1977	**The Shepherdess and the Chimney Sweep,** artist: Pauline Ellison, production quantity 16,875	38.00	70.00

HOMETOWN MEMORIES SERIES

		Issue Price	Current Value
☐ 1979	**Country Fair,** artist: Jo Sickbert, production quantity 4,715	29.00	32.00

		Issue Price	Current Value
☐ 1980	**Red Schoolhouse,** artist: Jo Sickbert, production quantity 4,715	29.00	32.00
☐ 1981	**Sunday Picnic,** artist: Jo Sickbert, production quantity 4,715	29.00	32.00
☐ 1982	**Skating Party,** artist: Jo Sickbert, production quantity 4,715	29.00	32.00

INTERNATIONAL GALLERY OF FLOWERS PLATES SERIES

☐ 1980–81	**Wheat, Black-Eyed Susan, Columbine, Mayflower, California Poppy,** artist: Jeanne Holgate, production quantity 4,294	55.00	60.00
☐ 1980–81	**Orchid,** artist: Marion Ruff Sheehan, production quantity 4,294	55.00	60.00
☐ 1980–81	**Irises,** artist: Claus Caspari, production quantity 4,294	55.00	60.00
☐ 1980–81	**Camelias,** artist: Anne Marie Trechslin, production quantity 4,294	55.00	60.00
☐ 1980–81	**Cherry Blossoms,** artist: Yoai Ohta, production quantity 4,294	55.00	60.00
☐ 1980–81	**English Spring Wild Flowers,** artist: Mary Grierson, production quantity 4,294	55.00	60.00
☐ 1980–81	**Fuchsias,** artist: Raphael Henri/Charles Ghislain, production quantity 4,294	55.00	60.00
☐ 1980–81	**Flame Azaleas,** artist: Martha Prince, production quantity 4,294	55.00	60.00
☐ 1980–81	**Roses,** artist: Gabriele Gossner, production quantity 4,294	55.00	60.00
☐ 1980–81	**English Garden Flowers,** artist: Barbara Everard, production quantity 4,294	55.00	60.00
☐ 1980–81	**Tulips,** artist: Elizabeth Riemer-Gerbardt, production quantity 4,294	55.00	60.00
☐ 1980–81	**Desert Pea,** artist: Paul Jones, production quantity 4,294	55.00	60.00

JAMES WYETH SERIES

☐ 1972	**Along the Brandywine,** artist: James Wyeth, production quantity 19,760	125.00	140.00
☐ 1973	**Winter Fox,** artist: James Wyeth, production quantity 10,394	125.00	130.00
☐ 1974	**Riding to the Hunt,** artist: James Wyeth, production quantity 10,751	150.00	150.00

		Issue Price	Current Value
☐ 1975	**Skating on the Brandywine,** artist: James Wyeth, production quantity 8,058	**175.00**	**160.00**
☐ 1976	**Brandywine Battlefield,** artist: James Wyeth, production quantity 6,968	**180.00**	**185.00**

JOHN JAMES AUDUBON SERIES

☐ 1973	**The Wood Thrush,** artist: John James Audubon, production quantity 5,273	**150.00**	**126.00**
☐ 1973	**The Bald Eagle,** artist: John James Audubon, production quantity 3,040	**150.00**	**126.00**
☐ 1974	**The Night Heron,** artist: John James Audubon, production quantity 3,005	**150.00**	**126.00**
☐ 1974	**Audubon's Warbler,** artist: John James Audubon, production quantity 3,034 ...	**150.00**	**126.00**

JOYS OF THE VICTORIAN YEAR SERIES

☐ 1983	**January–December,** artist: Kate Lloyd-Jones, production limited, set of 12	**660.00**	**660.00**

MARK TWAIN SERIES

☐ 1977	**Whitewashing the Fence,** artist: Yves Beaujard, production quantity 2,645	**38.00**	**56.00**
☐ 1977	**Stealing a Kiss,** artist: Yves Beaujard, production quantity 2,645	**38.00**	**45.00**
☐ 1977	**Traveling the River,** artist: Yves Beaujard, production quantity 2,645	**38.00**	**45.00**
☐ 1977	**Rafting Down the River,** artist: Yves Beaujard, production quantity 2,645	**38.00**	**40.00**
☐ 1978	**Riding a Bronc,** artist: Yves Beaujard, production quantity 2,645	**38.00**	**40.00**
☐ 1978	**Jumping Frog Fence,** artist: Yves Beaujard, production quantity 2,645	**38.00**	**40.00**
☐ 1978	**Facing a Charging Knight,** artist: Yves Beaujard, production quantity 2,645	**38.00**	**40.00**
☐ 1978	**Disguising Huck,** artist: Yves Beaujard, production quantity 2,645	**38.00**	**40.00**
☐ 1978	**Living Along the River,** artist: Yves Beaujard, production quantity 2,645	**38.00**	**40.00**
☐ 1978	**Learning to Smoke,** artist: Yves Beaujard, production quantity 2,645	**38.00**	**40.00**
☐ 1978	**Finger Printing Pays Off,** artist: Yves Beaujard, production quantity 2,645	**38.00**	**40.00**

		Issue Price	Current Value

MOTHER'S DAY SERIES

□ 1977	**A Mother's Love,** artist: Adelaid Sundin, production quantity 12,392	**65.00**	**66.00**
□ 1978	**A Mother's Joy,** artist: Deborah Bell, production quantity unknown	**65.00**	**66.00**
□ 1979	**A Mother's Gift,** artist: Deborah Bell, production: one year	**75.00**	**75.00**

MOTHER'S DAY BY SPENCER SERIES

□ 1972	**Mother and Child,** artist: Irene Spencer, production quantity 21,987	**125.00**	**176.00**
□ 1973	**Mother and Child,** artist: Irene Spencer, production quantity 6,154	**125.00**	**141.00**
□ 1974	**Mother and Child,** artist: Irene Spencer, production quantity 5,116	**150.00**	**160.00**
□ 1975	**Mother and Child,** artist: Irene Spencer, production quantity 2,704	**175.00**	**181.00**
□ 1976	**Mother and Child,** artist: Irene Spencer, production quantity 1,858	**180.00**	**191.00**

POOR RICHARD'S SERIES

□ 1979–81	**Haste Makes Waste,** production quantity 13,133.............................	**12.50**	**16.00**
□ 1979–81	**When the Well's Dry, We Know the Worth of Water,** production quantity 13,133.............................	**12.50**	**16.00**
□ 1979–81	**Love Thy Neighbor, Yet Don't Pull Down Your Hedge,** production quantity 13,133	**12.50**	**16.00**
□ 1979–81	**Diligence Is the Mother of Good Luck,** production quantity 13,133	**12.50**	**16.00**
□ 1979–81	**Who Pleasure Gives, Shall Joy Receive,** production quantity 13,133	**12.50**	**16.00**
□ 1979–81	**The Rotten Apple Spoils His Companion,** production quantity 13,133	**12.50**	**16.00**
□ 1979–81	**A Spoonful of Honey Will Catch More Flies Than a Gallon of Vinegar,** production quantity 13,133	**12.50**	**16.00**
□ 1979–81	**There's a Time to Wink As Well As Time to See,** production quantity 13,133	**12.50**	**16.00**
□ 1979–81	**A True Friend Saved Is a Penny Earned,** production quantity 13,133	**12.50**	**16.00**
□ 1979–81	**Great Talkers, Little Doers,** production quantity 13,133	**12.50**	**16.00**

		Issue Price	Current Value
☐ 1979–81	Early to Bed, and Early to Rise, Makes a Man Healthy, Wealthy and Wise, production quantity 13,133	12.50	16.00
☐ 1979–81	Lost Time Is Never Found Again, production quantity 13,133	12.50	16.00
☐ 1979–81	The Worst Wheel of the Cart Makes the Most Noise, production quantity 13,133	12.50	16.00
☐ 1979–81	Keep Thy Shop and Thy Shop Will Keep Thee, production quantity 13,133	12.50	16.00
☐ 1979–81	An Empty Bag Cannot Stand Upright, production quantity 13,133	12.50	16.00
☐ 1979–81	'Tis Easier to Prevent Bad Habits Than to Break Them, production quantity 13,133	12.50	16.00
☐ 1979–81	The Golden Age Never Was the Present Age, production quantity 13,133	12.50	16.00
☐ 1979–81	No Gains Without Pains, production quantity 13,133	12.50	16.00
☐ 1979–81	You Cannot Pluck Roses Without Fear of Thorns, production quantity 13,133	12.50	16.00
☐ 1979–81	Beware of Little Expenses, A Small Leak Will Sink a Great Ship, production quantity 13,133	12.50	16.00
☐ 1979–81	Now I've a Sheep and a Cow, Every Body Bids Me Good Morning, production quantity 13,133	12.50	16.00
☐ 1979–81	A Quarrelsome Man Has No Good Neighbours, production quantity 13,133	12.50	16.00
☐ 1979–81	Love and Be Loved, production quantity 13,133	12.50	16.00
☐ 1979–81	Look Before, Or You'll Find Yourself Behind, production quantity 13,133	12.50	16.00

PRESIDENTIAL INAUGURAL SERIES

		Issue Price	Current Value
☐ 1973	Nixon/Agnew, artist: Gilroy Roberts, production quantity 10,483	150.00	160.00
☐ 1974	Ford, artist: Mico Kaufman, production quantity 11	3500.00	3600.00
☐ 1974	Ford, artist: Mico Kaufman, production quantity 1,141	200.00	225.00
☐ 1977	Carter, artist: Julian Harris, production quantity 928	225.00	230.00

		Issue Price	Current Value
ROBERT'S ZODIAC SERIES			
☐ 1973–80	**Aries,** artist: Gilroy Roberts	**150.00**	**165.00**
☐ 1973–80	**Taurus,** artist: Gilroy Roberts	**150.00**	**165.00**
☐ 1973–80	**Gemini,** artist: Gilroy Roberts	**150.00**	**165.00**
☐ 1973–80	**Cancer,** artist: Gilroy Roberts	**150.00**	**165.00**
☐ 1973–80	**Leo,** artist: Gilroy Roberts	**150.00**	**165.00**
☐ 1973–80	**Virgo,** artist: Gilroy Roberts	**150.00**	**165.00**
☐ 1973–80	**Libra,** artist: Gilroy Roberts	**150.00**	**165.00**
☐ 1973–80	**Scorpio,** artist: Gilroy Roberts	**150.00**	**165.00**
☐ 1973–80	**Sagittarius,** artist: Gilroy Roberts	**150.00**	**165.00**
☐ 1973–80	**Capricorn,** artist: Gilroy Roberts	**150.00**	**165.00**
☐ 1973–80	**Aquarius,** artist: Gilroy Roberts	**150.00**	**165.00**
☐ 1973–80	**Pisces,** artist: Gilroy Roberts	**150.00**	**165.00**

ROCKWELL AMERICAN SWEETHEARTS SERIES

☐ 1977	**Youngsters at Play,** artist: Norman Rockwell, production quantity 1,004	**120.00**	**161.00**
☐ 1977	**Teenagers Together,** artist: Norman Rockwell, production quantity 1,004 ...	**120.00**	**161.00**
☐ 1978	**Bride and Groom,** artist: Norman Rockwell, production quantity 1,004	**120.00**	**161.00**
☐ 1978	**Proud Parents,** artist: Norman Rockwell, production quantity 1,004	**120.00**	**161.00**
☐ 1978	**Graduation Day,** artist: Norman Rockwell, production quantity 1,004	**120.00**	**161.00**
☐ 1979	**Retirement Kiss,** artist: Norman Rockwell, production quantity 1,004	**120.00**	**161.00**

ROCKWELL CHRISTMAS SERIES

☐ 1970	**Bringing Home the Tree,** artist: Norman Rockwell, production quantity 18,321 ..	**100.00**	**310.00**
☐ 1971	**Under the Mistletoe,** artist: Norman Rockwell, production quantity 24,792 ..	**100.00**	**175.00**
☐ 1972	**The Carolers,** artist: Norman Rockwell, production quantity 29,074	**125.00**	**165.00**
☐ 1973	**Trimming the Tree,** artist: Norman Rockwell, production quantity 18,010	**125.00**	**170.00**
☐ 1974	**Hanging the Wreath,** artist: Norman Rockwell, production quantity 12,822 ..	**175.00**	**160.00**
☐ 1975	**Home for Christmas,** artist: Norman Rockwell, production quantity 11,059 ..	**180.00**	**190.00**

		Issue Price	Current Value
SEVEN SEAS SERIES			
☐ 1976	**Atlantic Ocean,** artist: James Wyeth, production quantity 2,799	120.00	120.00
☐ 1977	**Caribbean Sea,** artist: James Wyeth, production quantity 2,799	120.00	120.00
☐ 1978	**Indian Ocean,** artist: James Wyeth, production quantity 2,799	120.00	120.00
☐ 1979	**Pacific Ocean,** artist: James Wyeth, production quantity 2,799	120.00	120.00
☐ 1980	**Arctic Ocean,** artist: James Wyeth, production quantity 2,799	120.00	120.00
☐ 1981	**Mediterranean Sea,** artist: James Wyeth, production quantity 2,799	120.00	120.00
☐ 1982	**South China Sea,** artist: James Wyeth, production quantity 2,799	120.00	120.00

SONGBIRDS OF THE WORLD SERIES

		Issue Price	Current Value
☐ 1977–81	**Baltimore Oriole,** artist: Arthur Singer, production quantity 20,225	55.00	55.00
☐ 1977–81	**Bohemian Waxwing,** artist: Arthur Singer, production quantity 20,225	55.00	55.00
☐ 1977–81	**Magnolia Warbler,** artist: Arthur Singer, production quantity 20,225	55.00	55.00
☐ 1977–81	**Bobolink,** artist: Arthur Singer, production quantity 20,225	55.00	55.00
☐ 1977–81	**Western Bluebird,** artist: Arthur Singer, production quantity 20,225	55.00	55.00
☐ 1977–81	**Cardinal,** artist: Arthur Singer, production quantity 20,225	55.00	55.00
☐ 1977–81	**European Goldfinch,** artist: Arthur Singer, production quantity 20,225	55.00	55.00
☐ 1977–81	**Wood Thrush,** artist: Arthur Singer, production quantity 20,225	55.00	55.00
☐ 1977–81	**Scarlet Tanager,** artist: Arthur Singer, production quantity 20,225	55.00	55.00
☐ 1977–81	**Barn Swallow,** artist: Arthur Singer, production quantity 20,225	55.00	55.00
☐ 1977–81	**Bluethroat,** artist: Arthur Singer, production quantity 20,225	55.00	55.00
☐ 1977–81	**Turquoise Wren,** artist: Arthur Singer, production quantity 20,225	55.00	55.00

		Issue Price	Current Value

SONGBIRDS OF THE WORLD MINIATURES

		Issue Price	Current Value
☐ 1980–83	Goldfinch, artist: Colin Newman	14.50	18.00
☐ 1980–83	Painted Bunting, artist: Colin Newman	14.50	18.00
☐ 1980–83	Blue Tit, artist: Colin Newman	14.50	18.00
☐ 1980–83	Chaffinch, artist: Colin Newman	14.50	18.00
☐ 1980–83	Yellowhammer, artist: Colin Newman ..	14.50	18.00
☐ 1980–83	European Robin, artist: Colin Newman	14.50	18.00
☐ 1980–83	Cardinal, artist: Colin Newman	14.50	18.00
☐ 1980–83	Golden-fronted Leafbird, artist: Colin Newman	14.50	18.00
☐ 1980–83	Redstart, artist: Colin Newman	14.50	18.00
☐ 1980–83	Rufous Ovenbird, artist: Colin Newman	14.50	18.00
☐ 1980–83	Golden Oriole, artist: Colin Newman ...	14.50	18.00
☐ 1980–83	Diamond Firetail Finch, artist: Colin Newman	14.50	18.00
☐ 1980–83	Rufous Bellied Nitava, artist: Colin Newman	14.50	18.00
☐ 1980–83	Asian Fairy Bluebird, artist: Colin Newman	14.50	18.00
☐ 1980–83	Barn Swallow, artist: Colin Newman ...	14.50	18.00
☐ 1980–83	Western Tanager, artist: Colin Newman	14.50	18.00
☐ 1980–83	Blue Jay, artist: Colin Newman	14.50	18.00

TALES OF ENCHANTMENT SERIES

		Issue Price	Current Value
☐ 1982	Alice in Wonderland, artist: Carol Lawson, production limited	55.00	55.00
☐ 1982	Peter Pan, artist: Carol Lawson, production limited	55.00	55.00
☐ 1982	The Wind in the Willows, artist: Carol Lawson, production limited	55.00	55.00

THANKSGIVING BY DOHANOS SERIES

		Issue Price	Current Value
☐ 1972	The First Thanksgiving, artist: Steven Dohanos, production quantity 10,142	125.00	150.00
☐ 1973	American Wild Turkey, artist: Steven Dohanos, production quantity 3,547	125.00	150.00
☐ 1974	Thanksgiving Prayer, artist: Steven Dohanos, production quantity 5,150	150.00	150.00
☐ 1975	Family Thanksgiving, artist: Steven Dohanos, production quantity 3,025	175.00	200.00
☐ 1976	Home from the Hunt, artist: Steven Dohanos, production quantity 3,474	175.00	200.00

WESTERN SERIES

		Issue Price	Current Value
☐ 1972	**Horizons West,** artist: Richard Baldwin, sterling silver, production quantity 5,860	**150.00**	**160.00**
☐ 1972	**Horizons West,** artist: Richard Baldwin, 22KT gold, production quantity 67	**2200.00**	**2350.00**
☐ 1973	**Mountain Man,** artist: Gordon Phillips, sterling silver, production quantity 5,860	**150.00**	**185.00**
☐ 1973	**Mountain Man,** artist: Gordon Phillips, 22KT gold, production quantity 67	**2200.00**	**2350.00**
☐ 1973	**Prospector,** artist: Gus Shaefer, sterling silver, production quantity 5,860.......	**150.00**	**185.00**
☐ 1973	**Prospector,** artist: Gus Shaefer, 22KT gold, production quantity 69	**150.00**	**185.00**
☐ 1973	**Plains Hunter,** artist: John Weaver, sterling silver, production quantity 5,860 ...	**150.00**	**185.00**
☐ 1973	**Plains Hunter,** artist: John Weaver, 22KT gold, production quantity 67	**2200.00**	**2350.00**

WOODLAND BIRDS OF THE WORLD SERIES

		Issue Price	Current Value
☐ 1980–82	**Blue Jay,** artist: Arthur Singer, production quantity 5,507	**65.00**	**68.00**
☐ 1980–82	**White-Winged Crossbill,** artist: Arthur Singer, production quantity 5,507	**65.00**	**68.00**
☐ 1980–82	**Painted Redstart,** artist: Arthur Singer, production quantity 5,507	**65.00**	**68.00**
☐ 1980–82	**Rivoli's Hummingbird,** artist: Arthur Singer, production quantity 5,507	**65.00**	**68.00**
☐ 1980–82	**Chaffinch,** artist: Arthur Singer, production quantity 5,507	**68.00**	**70.00**
☐ 1980–82	**Collared Trogon,** artist: Arthur Singer, production quantity 5,507	**68.00**	**70.00**
☐ 1980–82	**Evening Grosbeak,** artist: Arthur Singer, production quantity 5,507	**65.00**	**68.00**
☐ 1980–82	**Great Spotted Woodpecker,** artist: Arthur Singer, production quantity 5,507	**65.00**	**68.00**
☐ 1980–82	**Rainbow Lorikeet,** artist: Arthur Singer, production quantity 5,507	**65.00**	**68.00**
☐ 1980–82	**Tawny Owl,** artist: Arthur Singer, production quantity 5,507	**65.00**	**68.00**
☐ 1980–82	**Woodland Kingfisher,** artist: Arthur Singer, production quantity 5,507	**65.00**	**68.00**
☐ 1980–82	**Golden Pheasant,** artist: Arthur Singer, production quantity 5,507	**65.00**	**68.00**

		Issue Price	Current Value

WOODLAND YEAR SERIES

		Issue Price	Current Value
☐ 1981–83	Fawns in the June Meadow, artist: Peter Barratt	55.00	58.00
☐ 1980–83	Butterfly Chase in May, artist: Peter Barratt	55.00	58.00
☐ 1980–83	Rabbits in a July Field, artist: Peter Barratt	55.00	58.00
☐ 1980–83	Striped Skunks at a March Stream, artist: Peter Barratt	55.00	58.00
☐ 1980–83	Squirreling for Nuts in January, artist: Peter Barratt	55.00	58.00
☐ 1980–83	Curious Raccoons at an April Pond, artist: Peter Barratt	55.00	58.00
☐ 1980–83	American Marten in the November Pines, artist: Peter Barratt	55.00	58.00
☐ 1980–83	The Playful Badgers in October, artist: Peter Barratt	55.00	58.00
☐ 1980–83	Cozy Dormouse in the December Woods, artist: Peter Barratt	55.00	58.00
☐ 1980–83	The Friendly Chipmunks in August, artist: Peter Barratt	55.00	58.00
☐ 1980–83	Woodchucks in February Thaw, artist: Peter Barratt	55.00	58.00
☐ 1980–83	Otter at September Waterfall, artist: Peter Barratt	55.00	58.00

WORLD'S GREAT PORCELAIN HOUSES SERIES

		Issue Price	Current Value
☐ 1981–83	Crown Staffordshire	19.50	23.00
☐ 1981–83	Mosa	19.50	23.00
☐ 1981–83	Hutschenreuther	19.50	23.00
☐ 1981–83	Haviland	19.50	23.00
☐ 1981–83	Wedgwood	19.50	23.00
☐ 1981–83	Langenthal	19.50	23.00
☐ 1981–83	Porsgrund	19.50	23.00
☐ 1981–83	Noritake	19.50	23.00
☐ 1981–83	Rostrand	19.50	23.00
☐ 1981–83	Franklin	19.50	23.00
☐ 1981–83	AK Kaiser	19.50	23.00
☐ 1981–83	The Royal Copenhagen	19.50	23.00
☐ 1981–83	Royal Doulton	19.50	23.00
☐ 1981–83	Zsolnay	19.50	23.00
☐ 1981–83	Okura	19.50	23.00
☐ 1981–83	Verbano	19.50	23.00
☐ 1981–83	Lilien Porzelan	19.50	23.00
☐ 1981–83	Royal Worcester	19.50	23.00

		Issue Price	Current Value
☐ 1981–83	Ginory	19.50	23.00
☐ 1981–83	Lladro	19.50	23.00
☐ 1981–83	Franciscan	19.50	23.00
☐ 1981–83	Raynaud	19.50	23.00

SINGLE RELEASES

		Issue Price	Current Value
☐ 1976	**Liberty Tree Crystal,** production quantity 10,927	120.00	130.00
☐ 1976	**Partridge in a Pear Tree,** production quantity 1,453	150.00	185.00
☐ 1977	**Infant,** artist: Abram Belski, production quantity 290	210.00	280.00
☐ 1977	**Lafayette and Washington,** production quantity 546	275.00	330.00
☐ 1977	**Old-Fashioned Thanksgiving,** artist: Norman Rockwell, production quantity 1,361	185.00	230.00
☐ 1977	**The Skating Party,** artist: Vincent Miller, production quantity 908	55.00	40.00
☐ 1978	**Air Force Association**	95.00	105.00
☐ 1978	**Ben Franklin, Printer,** production quantity 281	65.00	70.00
☐ 1978	**Cinderella,** artist: Pauline Ellison, production quantity 29,439	55.00	58.00
☐ 1978	**Oriental**	32.50	35.00
☐ 1979	**Butterfly,** set of 4	38.00	40.00
☐ 1979	**Peter Pan,** artist: Carol Lawson, production quantity 5,391	39.00	42.00
☐ 1979	**Prince and Princess,** artist: T. Okamoto	85.00	90.00
☐ 1979	**University of Pennsylvania,** artist: T. T. McKenzie, production quantity 226	125.00	140.00
☐ 1980	**Angel with Trumpet,** artist: Maureen Jensen, production quantity 8,696	17.50	20.00
☐ 1980	**Great Egrets,** artist: J. Fenwick Lansdowne, production quantity 2,384	65.00	70.00
☐ 1980	**Le Jour des Amoureus,** artist: Raymond Peynet, production quantity 5,332	50.00	53.00
☐ 1981	**Royal Wedding Bouquet,** artist: Mary Grierson	75.00	80.00
☐ 1983	**The Barn Owl,** artist: Basil Ede, production limited	95.00	95.00

FRANKOMA POTTERY

United States

BICENTENNIAL SERIES	Issue Price	Current Value
☐ **1972 Provocations,** artist: John Frank, production: one year	5.00	50.00
☐ **1973 Patriots–Leaders,** artist: John Frank, production: one year	5.00	50.00
☐ **1974 Battles for Independence,** artist: Joniece Frank, production: one year	5.00	50.00
☐ **1975 Victories for Independence,** artist: Joniece Frank, production: one year	5.00	50.00
☐ **1976 Symbols of Freedom,** artist: Joniece Frank, production: one year	6.00	50.00

CHRISTMAS SERIES		
☐ **1965 Goodwill Toward Men,** artist: John Frank, production: one year	3.50	235.00
☐ **1966 Bethlehem Shepherds,** artist: John Frank, production: one year	3.50	100.00
☐ **1967 Gifts for the Christ Child,** artist: John Frank, production: one year	3.50	70.00
☐ **1968 Flight into Egypt,** artist: John Frank, production: one year	3.50	40.00
☐ **1969 Laid in a Manger,** artist: John Frank, production: one year	4.50	35.00
☐ **1970 King of Kings,** artist: John Frank, production: one year	4.50	35.00
☐ **1971 No Room in the Inn,** artist: John Frank, production: one year	4.50	27.00
☐ **1972 Seeking the Christ Child,** artist: John Frank, production: one year	5.00	27.00
☐ **1973 The Annunciation,** artist: John Frank, production: one year	5.00	27.00
☐ **1974 She Loved and Cared,** artist: Joniece Frank, production: one year	5.00	25.00
☐ **1975 Peace on Earth,** artist: Joniece Frank, production: one year	5.00	25.00
☐ **1976 The Gift of Love,** artist: Joniece Frank, production: one year	6.00	25.00
☐ **1977 Birth of Eternal Life,** artist: Joniece Frank, production: one year	6.00	25.00
☐ **1978 All Nature Rejoiced,** artist: Joniece Frank, production: one year	7.50	25.00

		Issue Price	Current Value
☐ 1979	**The Star of Hope,** artist: Joniece Frank, production: one year	7.50	25.00
☐ 1980	**Unto Us a Child Is Born,** artist: Joniece Frank, production: one year	10.00	25.00
☐ 1981	**O Come Let Us Adore Him,** artist: Joniece Frank, production: one year	12.00	20.00
☐ 1982	**The Wise Men Rejoice,** artist: Joniece Frank, production: one year	12.00	20.00
☐ 1983	**The Wise Men Bring Gifts,** artist: Joniece Frank, production: one year	12.00	17.00
☐ 1984	**Faith, Hope and Love,** artist: Joniece Frank, production: one year	12.00	17.00
☐ 1985	**The Angels Watched,** artist: Joniece Frank, production: one year	12.00	17.00
☐ 1986	**For Thee I Play My Drum,** artist: Joniece Frank, production: one year	12.00	17.00
☐ 1987	**God's Chosen Family,** artist: Joniece Frank, production: one year	12.00	17.00

MADONNA PLATES SERIES

☐ 1977	**The Grace Madonna,** artist: Grace Lee Frank, production: one year	12.50	15.00
☐ 1978	**Madonna of Love,** artist: Grace Lee Frank, production: one year	12.50	15.00
☐ 1981	**The Rose Madonna,** artist: Grace Lee Frank, production: one year	15.00	15.00
☐ 1986	**The Youthful Madonna,** artist: Grace Lee Frank, production: one year	15.00	15.00

TEENAGERS OF THE BIBLE SERIES

☐ 1973	**Jesus the Carpenter,** artist: John Frank, production: one year	5.00	40.00
☐ 1974	**David the Musician,** artist: John Frank, production: one year	5.00	30.00
☐ 1975	**Jonathan the Archer,** artist: John Frank, production: one year	5.00	30.00
☐ 1976	**Dorcas the Seamstress,** artist: Joniece Frank, production: one year	6.00	37.00
☐ 1977	**Peter the Fisherman,** artist: Joniece Frank, production: one year	6.00	25.00
☐ 1978	**Martha the Homemaker,** artist: Joniece Frank, production: one year	7.50	25.00
☐ 1979	**Daniel the Courageous,** artist: Joniece Frank, production: one year	7.50	22.00

	Issue Price	Current Value
☐ 1980 **Ruth the Devoted,** artist: Joniece Frank, production: one year	10.00	22.00
☐ 1981 **Joseph the Dreamer,** artist: Joniece Frank, production: one year	12.00	20.00
☐ 1982 **Mary the Mother,** artist: Joniece Frank, production: one year	12.00	20.00

FUKAGAWA

Japan

WARABE NO HAIKU SERIES

☐ 1977 **Beneath Plum Branch,** artist: Suetomi, production: one year	38.00	44.00
☐ 1978 **Child of Straw,** artist: Suetomi, production: one year	42.00	42.00
☐ 1979 **Dragon Dance,** artist: Suetomi, production: one year	42.50	42.00
☐ 1980 **Mask Dancing,** artist: Suetomi, production: one year	42.00	112.00

FURSTENBERG

Germany

CHRISTMAS SERIES

☐ 1971 **Rabbits,** production quantity 7,500	15.00	30.00
☐ 1972 **Snowy Village,** production quantity 6,000	15.00	20.00
☐ 1973 **Christmas Eve,** production quantity 4,000	18.00	35.00
☐ 1974 **Sparrows,** production quantity 4,000	20.00	30.00
☐ 1975 **Deer Family,** production quantity 4,000	22.00	30.00
☐ 1976 **Winter Birds,** production quantity 4,000	25.00	25.00

DELUXE CHRISTMAS SERIES

☐ 1971 **Wise Men,** artist: E. Grossberg, production quantity 1,500	45.00	45.00
☐ 1972 **Holy Family,** artist: E. Grossberg, production quantity 2,000	45.00	45.00
☐ 1973 **Christmas Eve,** artist: E. Grossberg, production quantity 2,000	60.00	65.00

EASTER SERIES

	Issue Price	Current Value
☐ **1971 Sheep,** production quantity 3,500	15.00	75.00
☐ **1972 Chicks,** production quantity 6,000	15.00	22.00
☐ **1973 Bunnies,** production quantity 4,000	16.00	40.00
☐ **1974 Pussywillow,** production quantity 4,000 . . .	20.00	22.00
☐ **1975 Easter Window,** production quantity 4,000	22.00	26.00
☐ **1976 Flower Collecting,** production quantity 4,000	25.00	25.00

MOTHER'S DAY SERIES

☐ **1972 Hummingbirds,** production quantity 6,000	15.00	35.00
☐ **1973 Hedgehogs,** production quantity 5,000	16.00	23.00
☐ **1974 Doe and Fawn,** production quantity 4,000	20.00	20.00
☐ **1975 Swans,** production quantity 4,000	22.00	23.00
☐ **1976 Koala Bears,** production quantity 4,000 . . .	25.00	30.00

OLYMPIC

☐ **1972 Olympics—Munich,** artist: J. Poluszynski, production quantity 5,000	20.00	20.00
☐ **1976 Olympics—Montreal,** artist: J. Poluszynski, production quantity 5,000	37.50	37.50

GARTLAN USA INC.

United States

PLATINUM EDITION

☐ **1985 Pete Rose,** artist: Ted Sizemore, personally signed, production quantity 4,192	100.00	200.00

Pete Rose, artist: Ted Sizemore.

George Brett, artist: John Martin.

	Issue Price	Current Value
GEORGE BRETT GOLD **CROWN COLLECTION**		
☐ **1986 George Brett,** artist: John Martin, personally signed, production quantity 2,000	**100.00**	**100.00**
REGGIE JACKSON "500TH" HOME **RUN EDITION**		
☐ **1986 Reggie Jackson,** artist: John Martin	**12.95**	**12.95**

Roger Staubach, artist:
Charles Soileau.

		Issue Price	Current Value
PERSONALLY AUTOGRAPHED STERLING COLLECTION			
☐ **1986**	**Roger Staubach,** artist: Charles Soileau, personally signed, production quantity 1,979	**100.00**	**100.00**

GEORGE WASHINGTON MINT

United States

INDIAN SERIES

☐ **1972**	**Curley,** artist: Sawyer, gold, production quantity 100	**2000.00**	**2250.00**
☐ **1972**	**Curley,** artist: Sawyer, sterling silver, production quantity 7,300	**150.00**	**110.00**
☐ **1973**	**Two Moons,** artist: Sawyer, gold, production quantity 100	**2000.00**	**2250.00**
☐ **1973**	**Two Moons,** artist: Sawyer, sterling silver, production quantity 7,300	**150.00**	**110.00**

MOTHER'S DAY SERIES

☐ **1972**	**Whistler's Mother,** gold, production quantity 100	**2000.00**	**2250.00**
☐ **1972**	**Whistler's Mother,** sterling silver, production quantity 9,800	**150.00**	**110.00**
☐ **1973**	**Motherhood,** gold, production quantity 100	**2000.00**	**2250.00**
☐ **1972**	**Motherhood,** sterling silver, production quantity 9,800	**175.00**	**110.00**

N. C. WYETH SERIES

		Issue Price	Current Value
☐ 1972	**Uncle Sam's America,** artist: N. C. Wyeth, gold, production quantity 100	2000.00	2250.00
☐ 1972	**Uncle Sam's America,** artist: N. C. Wyeth, sterling silver, production quantity 9,800 ..	150.00	110.00
☐ 1973	**Massed Flags,** artist: N. C. Wyeth, gold, production quantity 100	2000.00	2250.00
☐ 1973	**Massed Flags,** artist: N. C. Wyeth, sterling silver, production quantity 2,300	150.00	110.00

PICASSO SERIES

☐ 1972	**Don Quixote,** gold, production quantity 100	2000.00	2300.00
☐ 1972	**Don Quixote,** sterling silver, production quantity 9,800.........................	125.00	155.00
☐ 1974	**Rites of Spring,** sterling silver, production quantity 9,800.........................	150.00	185.00

REMINGTON SERIES

☐ 1972	**Rattlesnake,** artist: Frederic Remington, production quantity 100	2000.00	2200.00
☐ 1972	**Rattlesnake,** artist: Frederic Remington, production quantity 800	250.00	390.00
☐ 1974	**Coming Through the Rye,** artist: Frederic Remington, production quantity 2,500	300.00	365.00

SINGLE RELEASES

☐ 1972	**Last Supper,** artist: Da Vinci	125.00	140.00
☐ 1973	**Israel Anniversary,** production quantity 10,000	300.00	335.00

GHENT COLLECTION

United States
(See also Bing and Grondahl, Fairmont, Gorham and Villetta)

AMERICAN BICENTENNIAL WILDLIFE SERIES

☐ 1976	**American Bald Eagle,** artist: Harry J. Moeller, production quantity 2,500	95.00	300.00
☐ 1976	**American White-Tailed Deer,** artist: Edward J. Bierly, production quantity 2,500	95.00	300.00

		Issue Price	Current Value
☐ 1976	**American Bison,** artist: Charles Frace, production quantity 2,500	95.00	300.00
☐ 1976	**American Wild Turkey,** artist: Albert Earl Gilbert, production quantity 2,500	95.00	300.00

APRIL FOOL ANNUAL SERIES

☐ 1978	**April Fool,** artist: Norman Rockwell, production quantity 10,000	35.00	60.00
☐ 1979	**April Fool,** artist: Norman Rockwell, production quantity 10,000	35.00	35.00
☐ 1980	**April Fool,** artist: Norman Rockwell, production quantity 10,000	37.50	38.00

CAVERSWALL CHRISTMAS CAROL SERIES

☐ 1979	**Good King Wenceslas,** artist: Holmes Gray, production quantity 2,500	300.00	300.00
☐ 1980	**The First Noel,** artist: Holmes Gray, production quantity 2,500	300.00	300.00

CHRISTMAS WILDLIFE SERIES

☐ 1974	**Cardinals in Snow,** artist: Albert Earl Gray, production quantity 10,030	20.00	53.00
☐ 1975	**We Three Kings,** artist: Harry J. Moeller, production quantity 12,750	29.00	42.00
☐ 1976	**Partridges and Pear Tree,** artist: Guy Tudor, production quantity 12,750	32.00	42.00
☐ 1977	**Foxes and Evergreen,** artist: Edward J. Bierly, production quantity 12,750	32.00	48.00
☐ 1978	**Snowy Owls,** artist: Jay H. Matterness, production quantity 12,750	32.00	35.00

COUNTRY DIARY OF AN EDWARDIAN LADY SERIES

☐ 1979	**April,** artist: Edith Holden, production quantity 10,000	80.00	80.00
☐ 1979	**June,** artist: Edith Holden, production quantity 10,000	80.00	80.00
☐ 1980	**January,** artist: Edith Holden, production quantity 10,000	80.00	80.00
☐ 1980	**May,** artist: Edith Holden, production quantity 10,000	80.00	80.00

			Issue Price	Current Value
☐ 1980	**September,** artist: Edith Holden, production quantity 10,000		80.00	80.00
☐ 1980	**December,** artist: Edith Holden, production quantity 10,000		80.00	85.00
☐ 1981	**July,** artist: Edith Holden, production quantity 10,000		80.00	85.00
☐ 1981	**October,** artist: Edith Holden, production quantity 10,000		80.00	85.00

FAUSETT MURAL PLATES SERIES

☐ 1976	**From Sea to Shining Sea,** production quantity 1,976		76.00	230.00

LANDS OF FABLE SERIES

☐ 1981	**Xanadu,** artist: F. F. Long, production quantity 17,500		55.00	56.00
☐ 1982	**Atlantis,** artist: F. F. Long, production quantity 17,500		55.00	56.00

MOTHER'S DAY SERIES

☐ 1975	**Cotton Tail,** artist: Harry J. Moeller, production quantity 12,750		22.00	42.00
☐ 1976	**Mallard Family,** artist: Guy Tudor, production quantity 12,750		29.00	38.00
☐ 1977	**Chipmunks and Trillium,** artist: Albert Earl Gilbert, production quantity 12,750		32.00	42.00
☐ 1978	**Raccoon Family,** artist: Edward J. Bierly, production quantity 12,750		32.00	35.00
☐ 1979	**Maytime Robins,** artist: Jay H. Matterness, production quantity 12,750		32.00	35.00

SINGLE RELEASES

☐ 1979	**Pilgrim of Peace,** artist: Alton S. Tobey, production: 15 days		29.50	32.00
☐ 1980	**1970s Decade Plate,** artist: Alton S. Tobey, production quantity 5,000		80.00	82.00

GNOMES UNITED

United States

GNOME PATROL	Issue Price	Current Value
☐ **1979** **Number One,** artist: Edith McLennan Choma, production quantity 5,000	45.00	60.00
☐ **1980** **Great Goo Roo Yu-Hoo,** artist: Edith McLennan Choma, production quantity 5,000	48.00	52.00
☐ **1981** **Fleafut,** artist: Edith McLennan Choma, production quantity 5,000	50.00	52.00

SINGLE ISSUE

	Issue Price	Current Value
☐ **1982** **Gnome on the Range,** artist: Rex T. Reed, production quantity 10,000	23.00	26.00

GOEBEL COLLECTION

Germany

AMERICAN HERITAGE SERIES

	Issue Price	Current Value
☐ **1979** **Freedom and Justice Soaring,** artist: Gunther Granget, production quantity 15,000	100.00	105.00
☐ **1980** **Wild and Free,** artist: Gunther Granget, production quantity 10,000	120.00	125.00
☐ **1981** **Where Buffalo Roam,** artist: Gunther Granget, production quantity 5,000	125.00	130.00

ANNUAL CRYSTAL SERIES

	Issue Price	Current Value
☐ **1978** **Praying Girl,** production: one year	45.00	48.00
☐ **1979** **Praying Boy,** production: one year	50.00	54.00
☐ **1980** **Praying Angel,** production quantity 15,000	50.00	54.00
☐ **1981** **Girl with Teddy Bears,** production quantity 10,000	50.00	52.00

BAVARIAN FOREST SERIES

	Issue Price	Current Value
☐ **1980** **Owls,** production quantity 7,500	150.00	170.00
☐ **1981** **Deer,** production quantity 7,500	150.00	155.00

BRATSOFF SERIES

	Issue Price	Current Value
☐ **1979** **Star Steed,** production quantity 15,000	125.00	140.00

		Issue Price	Current Value
CHARLOT BYI SERIES			
☐ **1973**	**Santa at Tree,** production: one year	16.50	18.00
☐ **1974**	**Santa and Girl,** production: one year	22.00	25.00
☐ **1975**	**Up and Away,** production: one year	25.00	28.00
☐ **1976**	**Boy with Teddy Bear,** production: one year	25.00	28.00
☐ **1977**	**Joy to the World,** production: one year ...	25.00	28.00

CHRISTMAS IN KINDERLAND

☐ **1982**	**A Gift of Joy,** production quantity 10,000	49.50	60.00
☐ **1983**	**A Midnight Clear,** production quantity 10,000	49.50	51.00

EXCLUSIVE–CELEBRATION SERIES
(Goebel Collectors Club)

☐ **1986**	**Valentine Gift,** artist: M. I. Hummel, production limited	90.00	90.00
☐ **1987**	**Valentine Joy,** artist: M. I. Hummel, production limited	98.00	98.00
☐ **1988**	**Daisies Don't Tell,** artist: M. I. Hummel, production limited	—	—
☐ **1989**	**It's Cold,** artist: M. I. Hummel, production limited	—	—

HUMMEL ANNIVERSARY SERIES

☐ **1975**	**Stormy Weather,** artist: M. I. Hummel, production: one year	100.00	160.00
☐ **1980**	**Spring Dance,** artist: M. I. Hummel, production: one year	225.00	225.00
☐ **1985**	**Auf Wiedersehen,** artist: M. I. Hummel, production: one year	225.00	225.00

HUMMEL ANNUAL SERIES

☐ **1971**	**Heavenly Angel,** artist: M. I. Hummel, production: one year	25.00	725.00
☐ **1972**	**Hear Ye,** artist: M. I. Hummel, production: one year	30.00	150.00
☐ **1973**	**Globe Trotter,** artist: M. I. Hummel, production: one year	32.50	70.00
☐ **1974**	**Goose Girl,** artist: M. I. Hummel, production: one year	40.00	100.00
☐ **1975**	**Ride into Christmas,** artist: M. I. Hummel, production: one year	50.00	95.00
☐ **1976**	**Apple Tree Girl,** artist: M. I. Hummel, production: one year	50.00	80.00

		Issue Price	Current Value
□ 1977	**Apple Tree Boy,** artist: M. I. Hummel, production: one year	**52.50**	**100.00**
□ 1978	**Happy Pastime,** artist: M. I. Hummel, production: one year	**65.00**	**80.00**
□ 1979	**Singing Lesson,** artist: M. I. Hummel, production: one year	**90.00**	**90.00**
□ 1980	**Schoolgirl,** artist: M. I. Hummel, production: one year	**100.00**	**100.00**
□ 1981	**Umbrella Boy,** artist: M. I. Hummel, production: one year	**100.00**	**100.00**
□ 1982	**Umbrella Girl,** artist: M. I. Hummel, production: one year	**100.00**	**115.00**
□ 1983	**The Postman,** artist: M. I. Hummel, production: one year	**108.00**	**110.00**
□ 1984	**Little Helper,** artist: M. I. Hummel, production: one year	**108.00**	**108.00**
□ 1985	**Chick Girl,** artist: M. I. Hummel, production: one year	**110.00**	**110.00**
□ 1986	**Playmates,** artist: M. I. Hummel, production: one year	**125.00**	**125.00**
□ 1987	**Feeding Time,** artist: M. I. Hummel, production: one year	**135.00**	**135.00**
□ 1988	**Little Goat Herder,** artist: M. I. Hummel, production: one year	**—**	**—**

LITTLE MUSIC MAKER SERIES

□ 1984	**Little Fiddler,** artist: M. I. Hummel, production: one year	**30.00**	**30.00**
□ 1985	**Serenade,** artist: M. I. Hummel, production: one year	**30.00**	**30.00**
□ 1986	**Soloist,** artist: M. I. Hummel, production: one year	**35.00**	**35.00**
□ 1987	**Band Leader,** artist: M. I. Hummel, production: one year	**40.00**	**40.00**

MOTHERS SERIES

□ 1975	**Rabbits,** production: one year	**45.00**	**38.00**
□ 1976	**Cats,** production: one year	**45.00**	**48.00**
□ 1977	**Pandas,** production: one year	**45.00**	**48.00**
□ 1978	**Deer,** production: one year	**50.00**	**53.00**
□ 1979	**Owl,** production: one year 10,000	**65.00**	**68.00**
□ 1980	**Raccoons,** production quantity 10,000	**75.00**	**76.00**

		Issue Price	Current Value

NATIVE COMPANIONS SERIES

☐ **1982 Rachel,** artist: Eddie LePage, production quantity 10,000 . . . . **49.50 50.00**

☐ **1983 Hummingbird,** artist: Eddie LePage, production quantity 10,000 . . . . **49.50 50.00**

☐ **1983 Rabbit Dancer,** artist: Eddie LePage, production quantity 10,000 . . . . **49.50 50.00**

NORTH AMERICAN WILDLIFE SERIES

☐ **1980 Beaver,** artist: Lissa Calvert, production quantity 10,000 . . . . **126.00 125.00**

☐ **1982 Harp Seals,** artist: Lissa Calvert, production quantity 10,000 . . . . **126.00 125.00**

☐ **1983 Polar Bear,** artist: Lissa Calvert, production quantity 10,000 . . . . **126.00 125.00**

OLD TESTAMENT SERIES

☐ **1978 Twelve Tribes of Israel,** production quantity 10,000 . . . . **125.00 125.00**

☐ **1979 Ten Commandments,** production quantity 10,000 . . . . **175.00 175.00**

☐ **1980 Tradition,** production quantity 10,000 . . . . . **225.00 225.00**

ROBSON CHRISTMAS SERIES

☐ **1975 Flight to Egypt,** pewter, production: one year **45.00 48.00**

☐ **1975 Flight to Egypt,** porcelain, production: one year **50.00 55.00**

WILDLIFE SERIES

☐ **1974 Robin,** production: one year **45.00 63.00**

☐ **1975 Blue Titmouse,** production: one year **50.00 48.00**

☐ **1976 Barn Owl,** production: one year **50.00 53.00**

☐ **1977 Bullfinch,** production: one year **50.00 53.00**

☐ **1978 Sea Gull,** production: one year **55.00 53.00**

WINGED FANTASIES SERIES

☐ **1982 Strawberries,** artist: Toller Cranston, production quantity 10,000 . . . . **49.50 50.00**

☐ **1983 Bacchanalia,** artist: Toller Cranston, production quantity 10,000 . . . . **49.50 50.00**

☐ **1984 Cerises,** artist: Toller Cranston, production quantity 10,000 . . . . **49.50 50.00**

☐ **1984 Brambleberries,** artist: Toller Cranston, production quantity 10,000 . . . . **49.50 50.00**

		Issue Price	Current Value
SINGLE RELEASES			
☐ **1979**	**Christmas,** production quantity 200	5,000.00	5,200.00
☐ **1982**	**This Is What It's All About,** artist: Irene Spencer	49.50	53.00

GORHAM COLLECTION

United States

AMERICAN ARTISTS SERIES

☐ **1976**	**Apache Mother and Child,** production quantity 9,800	25.00	56.00

AMERICA'S CUP SERIES

☐ **1975**	**Courageous,** production quantity 5,000	50.00	53.00

AMERICA'S CUP SET SERIES

☐ **1975**	**America, 1861,** production quantity 1,000	200.00	200.00
☐ **1975**	**Puritan,** production quantity 1,000	200.00	200.00
☐ **1975**	**Reliance,** production quantity 1,000	200.00	200.00
☐ **1975**	**Ranger,** production quantity 1,000	200.00	200.00
☐ **1975**	**Courageous,** production quantity 1,000	200.00	200.00

APRIL FOOL ANNUAL SERIES
(Ghent Collection)

☐ **1978**	**April Fool's Day,** artist: Norman Rockwell, production quantity 10,000	35.00	60.00
☐ **1979**	**April Fool's Day,** artist: Norman Rockwell, production quantity 10,000	35.00	35.00
☐ **1980**	**April Fool's Day,** artist: Norman Rockwell, production quantity 10,000	37.50	38.00

AUDUBON AMERICAN WILDLIFE HERITAGE SERIES
(Volair)

☐ **1977**	**House Mouse,** production quantity 2,500 . .	90.00	95.00
☐ **1977**	**Royal Louisiana Heron,** production quantity 2,500	90.00	95.00
☐ **1977**	**Virginia Deer,** production quantity 2,500 . .	90.00	95.00
☐ **1977**	**Snowy Owl,** production quantity 2,500	90.00	95.00

April Fool's Day, artist: Norman Rockwell.

BARRYMORE SERIES	Issue Price	Current Value
☐ **1971 Quiet Waters,** production quantity 15,000	**25.00**	**25.00**
☐ **1972 San Pedro Harbor,** production quantity 15,000	**25.00**	**25.00**
☐ **1972 Nantucket,** production quantity 1,000	**100.00**	**100.00**
☐ **1972 Little Boatyard,** production quantity 1,000	**100.00**	**145.00**

Quiet Waters.

San Pedro Harbor.

		Issue Price	Current Value
BAS RELIEF			
☐ **1981**	**Sweet Song So Young,** artist: Norman Rockwell, production quantity 17,500	**100.00**	**100.00**
☐ **1981**	**Beguiling Buttercup,** artist: Norman Rockwell, production quantity: 17,500	**62.50**	**62.50**
☐ **1982**	**Flowers in Tender Bloom,** artist: Norman Rockwell, production quantity: 17,500	**100.00**	**100.00**
☐ **1982**	**Flying High,** artist: Norman Rockwell, production quantity: 17,500	**62.50**	**62.50**
BEVERLY PORT SERIES			
☐ **1986**	**Miss Emily, Bearing Up,** artist: Beverly Port, production quantity 5,000	**32.50**	**32.50**
☐ **1987**	**Big Bear, The Collector,** artist: Beverly Port, production quantity 5,000	**32.50**	**32.50**
BICENTENNIAL SERIES			
☐ **1971**	**Burning of the Gaspee,** pewter, production quantity 5,000	**35.00**	**35.00**
☐ **1972**	**Burning of the Gaspee,** silver, production quantity 750	**500.00**	**500.00**
☐ **1972**	**The 1776 Plate,** china, production quantity 18,500	**17.50**	**35.00**
☐ **1972**	**The 1776 Plate,** silver, production quantity 750	**500.00**	**500.00**

Flying High, artist:
Norman Rockwell.

Miss Emily, Bearing Up,
artist: Beverly Port.

			Issue Price	Current Value
☐	1972	**The 1776 Plate,** vermeil, production quantity 250	750.00	800.00
☐	1972	**Boston Tea Party,** pewter, production quantity 5,000	35.00	35.00
☐	1973	**Boston Tea Party,** silver, production quantity 750	550.00	575.00
☐	1976	**1776 Bicentennial,** production quantity 8,000	17.50	35.00

Big Bear, The Collector,
artist: Beverly Port.

BOY SCOUT PLATES SERIES	Issue Price	Current Value
☐ 1975 **Our Heritage,** artist: Norman Rockwell, production quantity 18,500	**19.50**	**60.00**
☐ 1976 **A Scout Is Loyal,** artist: Norman Rockwell, production quantity 18,500	**19.50**	**55.00**
☐ 1977 **The Scoutmaster,** artist: Norman Rockwell, production quantity 18,500	**19.50**	**60.00**
☐ 1977 **A Good Sign All Over the World,** artist: Norman Rockwell, production quantity 18,500	**19.50**	**50.00**
☐ 1978 **Pointing the Way,** artist: Norman Rockwell, production quantity 18,500	**19.50**	**50.00**
☐ 1978 **Campfire Story,** artist: Norman Rockwell, production quantity 18,500	**19.50**	**50.00**
☐ 1980 **Beyond the Easel,** artist: Norman Rockwell, production quantity 18,500	**45.00**	**45.00**

CHARLES RUSSELL SERIES		
☐ 1981 **In Without Knocking,** artist: Charles Russell, production quantity 9,800	**38.00**	**50.00**
☐ 1981 **Bronc to Breakfast,** artist: Charles Russell, production quantity 9,800	**38.00**	**38.00**
☐ 1982 **When Ignorance Is Bliss,** artist: Charles Russell, production quantity 9,800	**45.00**	**45.00**
☐ 1983 **Cowboy Life,** artist: Charles Russell, production quantity 9,800	**45.00**	**45.00**

The Scoutmaster, artist:
Norman Rockwell.

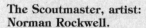

A Good Sign, artist:
Norman Rockwell.

Beyond the Easel,
artist: Norman
Rockwell.

Bronc to Breakfast,
artist: Charles Russell.

When Ignorance is
Bliss, artist: Charles
Russell.

A Cowboy's Life, artist:
Charles Russell.

CHRISTMAS SERIES	Issue Price	Current Value
☐ 1974 **Tiny Tim,** artist: Norman Rockwell, production: one year	**12.50**	**50.00**
☐ 1975 **Good Deeds,** artist: Norman Rockwell, production: one year	**17.50**	**40.00**
☐ 1976 **Christmas Trio,** artist: Norman Rockwell, production: one year	**19.50**	**50.00**
☐ 1977 **Yuletide Reckoning,** artist: Norman Rockwell, production quantity 18,500	**19.50**	**30.00**
☐ 1978 **Planning Christmas Visits,** artist: Norman Rockwell, production: one year	**24.50**	**40.00**
☐ 1979 **Santa's Helpers,** artist: Norman Rockwell, production: one year	**24.50**	**30.00**
☐ 1980 **Letter to Santa,** artist: Norman Rockwell, production: one year	**27.50**	**37.50**
☐ 1981 **Santa Plans His Visit,** artist: Norman Rockwell, production: one year	**29.50**	**35.00**
☐ 1982 **The Jolly Coachman,** artist: Norman Rockwell, production: one year	**29.50**	**32.50**
☐ 1983 **Christmas Dancers,** artist: Norman Rockwell, production: one year	**29.50**	**29.50**
☐ 1984 **Christmas Medley,** artist: Norman Rockwell, production quantity 17,500	**29.95**	**29.95**
☐ 1985 **Home for the Holidays,** artist: Norman Rockwell, production quantity 17,500	**29.95**	**29.95**

Home for the Holidays,
artist: Norman
Rockwell.

		Issue Price	Current Value
☐ 1986	**Merry Christmas Grandma,** artist: Norman Rockwell, production quantity 17,500	29.50	50.00
☐ 1987	**The Homecoming,** artist: Norman Rockwell, production quantity 17,500	35.00	35.00

CLOWN SERIES
(Brown and Bigelow)

☐ 1977	**Runaway,** production quantity 7,500	45.00	52.00
☐ 1978	**It's Your Move,** production quantity 7,500	45.00	52.00
☐ 1979	**Understudy,** production quantity 7,500	45.00	52.00

COWBOY SERIES
(Brown and Bigelow)

☐ 1980	**Sharing an Apple,** production quantity 5,000 —	35.00	40.00
☐ 1980	**Split Decision,** production quantity 5,000 ..	35.00	40.00
☐ 1980	**Hiding Out,** production quantity 5,000	35.00	40.00

ENCOUNTERS, SURVIVAL AND CELEBRATION SERIES

☐ 1982	**A Fine Welcome,** artist: John Clymer, production quantity 7,500	50.00	62.50
☐ 1983	**Winter Trail,** artist: John Clymer, production quantity 7,500	50.00	62.50

Merry Christmas
Grandma, artist:
Norman Rockwell.

The Homecoming,
artist: Norman Rockwell.

		Issue Price	Current Value
☐ **1984**	**Alouette,** artist: John Clymer, production quantity 7,500	**62.50**	**62.50**
☐ **1984**	**The Trader,** artist: John Clymer, production quantity 7,500	**62.50**	**62.50**
☐ **1984**	**Winter Camp,** artist: John Clymer, production quantity 7,500	**62.50**	**62.50**
☐ **1985**	**The Trapper Takes a Wife,** artist: John Clymer, production quantity 7,500	**62.50**	**62.50**

FOUR AGES OF LOVE

		Issue Price	Current Value
☐ **1973**	**Gaily Sharing Vintage Time,** artist: Norman Rockwell, production: one year		
☐ **1973**	**Flowers in Tender Bloom,** artist: Norman Rockwell, production: one year		
☐ **1973**	**Sweet Song So Young,** artist: Norman Rockwell, production: one year		
☐ **1973**	**Fondly We Do Remember,** artist: Norman Rockwell, production: one year		
	Set of four	**60.00**	**200.00**

The Trapper Takes a
Wife, artist: John
Clymer.

Gaily Sharing Vintage
Time, artist: Norman
Rockwell.

	Issue Price	Current Value

FOUR SEASONS SERIES—A BOY AND HIS DOG

☐ 1971 **Boy Meets His Dog,** artist: Norman Rockwell, production: one year . . . .

☐ 1971 **Adventures Between Adventures,** artist: Norman Rockwell, production: one year . . . . . .

☐ 1971 **The Mysterious Malady,** artist: Norman Rockwell, production: one year . . . .

		Issue Price	Current Value
☐ 1971	**Pride of Parenthood,** artist: Norman Rockwell, production: one year		
	Set of four	50.00	230.00

FOUR SEASONS SERIES—DAD'S BOY

		Issue Price	Current Value
☐ 1980	**Ski Skills,** artist: Norman Rockwell, production: one year		
☐ 1980	**In His Spirits,** artist: Norman Rockwell, production: one year		
☐ 1980	**Trout Dinner,** artist: Norman Rockwell, production: one year		
☐ 1980	**Careful Aim,** artist: Norman Rockwell, production: one year		
	Set of four	135.00	135.00

FOUR SEASONS SERIES— GOING ON SIXTEEN

		Issue Price	Current Value
☐ 1977	**Chilling Chore,** artist: Norman Rockwell, production: one year		
☐ 1977	**Sweet Serenade,** artist: Norman Rockwell, production: one year		
☐ 1977	**Shear Agony,** artist: Norman Rockwell, production: one year		
☐ 1977	**Pilgrimage,** artist: Norman Rockwell, production: one year		
	Set of four	75.00	120.00

FOUR SEASONS SERIES—GRAND PALS

		Issue Price	Current Value
☐ 1976	**Snow Sculpturing,** artist: Norman Rockwell, production: one year		
☐ 1976	**Soaring Spirits,** artist: Norman Rockwell, production: one year		
☐ 1976	**Fish Finders,** artist: Norman Rockwell, production: one year		
☐ 1976	**Ghostly Gourds,** artist: Norman Rockwell, production: one year		
	Set of four	70.00	230.00

FOUR SEASONS SERIES—GRANDPA AND ME

		Issue Price	Current Value
☐ 1974	**Gay Blades,** artist: Norman Rockwell, production: one year		

		Issue Price	Current Value
☐ **1974**	**Day Dreamers,** artist: Norman Rockwell, production: one year		
☐ **1974**	**Goin' Fishing,** artist: Norman Rockwell, production: one year		
☐ **1974**	**Pensive Pals,** artist: Norman Rockwell, production: one year		
	Set of four . . . . :	**60.00**	**100.00**

FOUR SEASONS SERIES— A HELPING HAND

		Issue Price	Current Value
☐ **1979**	**Year End Count,** artist: Norman Rockwell, production: one year		
☐ **1979**	**Closed for Business,** artist: Norman Rockwell, production: one year		
☐ **1979**	**Swatter's Rights,** artist: Norman Rockwell, production: one year		
☐ **1979**	**Coal Season's Coming,** artist: Norman Rockwell, production: one year		
	Set of four	**100.00**	**100.00**

FOUR SEASONS SERIES— LANDSCAPE SERIES

		Issue Price	Current Value
☐ **1980**	**Summer Respite,** artist: Norman Rockwell, production: less than one year	**45.00**	**45.00**

Coal Season's Coming, artist: Norman Rockwell.

		Issue Price	Current Value
☐ 1981	**Autumn Reflections,** artist: Norman Rockwell, production: less than one year	**45.00**	**45.00**
☐ 1982	**Winter Delight,** artist: Norman Rockwell, production: less than one year	**50.00**	**50.00**
☐ 1983	**Spring Recess,** artist: Norman Rockwell, production: less than one year	**60.00**	**60.00**

FOUR SEASONS SERIES— LIFE WITH FATHER

		Issue Price	Current Value
☐ 1982	**Big Decision,** artist: Norman Rockwell, production: one year		
☐ 1982	**Blasting Out,** artist: Norman Rockwell, production: one year		
☐ 1982	**Cheering the Champs,** artist: Norman Rockwell, production: one year		
☐ 1982	**A Tough One,** artist: Norman Rockwell, production: one year		
	Set of four	**100.00**	**100.00**

FOUR SEASONS SERIES— ME AND MY PALS

		Issue Price	Current Value
☐ 1975	**A Lickin' Good Bath,** artist: Norman Rockwell, production: one year		
☐ 1975	**Young Man's Fancy,** artist: Norman Rockwell, production: one year		
☐ 1975	**Fisherman's Paradise,** artist: Norman Rockwell, production: one year		
☐ 1975	**Disastrous Daring,** artist: Norman Rockwell, production: one year		
	Set of four	**70.00**	**100.00**

FOUR SEASONS SERIES—OLD BUDDIES

		Issue Price	Current Value
☐ 1983	**Shared Success,** artist: Norman Rockwell, production: one year		
☐ 1983	**Endless Debate,** artist: Norman Rockwell, production: one year		
☐ 1983	**Hasty Retreat,** artist: Norman Rockwell, production: one year		
☐ 1983	**Final Speech,** artist: Norman Rockwell, production: one year		
	Set of four	**115.00**	**115.00**

		Issue Price	Current Value

FOUR SEASONS SERIES—OLD TIMERS

☐ **1981** **Canine Solo,** artist: Norman Rockwell, production: one year . . . .

☐ **1981** **Sweet Surprise,** artist: Norman Rockwell, production: one year . . . .

☐ **1981** **Lazy Days,** artist: Norman Rockwell, production: one year . . . .

☐ **1981** **Fancy Footwork,** artist: Norman Rockwell, production: one year . . . .

Set of four **100.00   100.00**

FOUR SEASONS SERIES— TENDER YEARS

☐ **1978** **New Year Look,** artist: Norman Rockwell, production: one year . . . .

☐ **1978** **Spring Tonic,** artist: Norman Rockwell, production: one year . . . .

☐ **1978** **Cool Aid,** artist: Norman Rockwell, production: one year . . . .

☐ **1978** **Chilly Reception,** artist: Norman Rockwell, production: one year . . . .

Set of four **100.00   100.00**

FOUR SEASONS SERIES— TRAVELING SALESMAN

☐ **1984** **Traveling Salesman,** artist: Norman Rockwell, production: one year . . . .

☐ **1984** **Country Peddler,** artist: Norman Rockwell, production: one year . . . .

☐ **1984** **Expert Salesman,** artist: Norman Rockwell, production: one year . . . .

☐ **1984** **Horse Trader,** artist: Norman Rockwell, production: one year . . . .

Set of four **115.00   115.00**

FOUR SEASONS SERIES—YOUNG LOVE

☐ **1972** **Downhill Daring,** artist: Norman Rockwell, production: one year . . . .

☐ **1972** **Beguiling Buttercup,** artist: Norman Rockwell, production: one year . . . .

☐ **1972** **Flying High,** artist: Norman Rockwell, production: one year . . . .

☐ **1972** **A Scholarly Pace,** artist: Norman Rockwell, production: one year . . . .

Set of four **60.00   50.00**

Downhill Daring, artist:
Norman Rockwell.

Beguiling Buttercup,
artist: Norman
Rockwell.

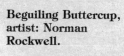

		Issue Price	Current Value
GALLERY OF MASTERS SERIES			
☐ 1971	**Man with a Gift Helmet,** artist: Rembrandt, production quantity 10,000	**50.00**	**50.00**
☐ 1972	**Self Portrait with Saskia,** artist: Rembrandt, production quantity 10,000	**50.00**	**50.00**
☐ 1973	**The Honorable Mrs. Graham,** artist: Gainsborough, production quantity 7,500	**50.00**	**50.00**

Man with a Gift Helmet,
artist: Rembrandt.

Self Portrait with
Saskia, artist:
Rembrandt.

The Honorable Mrs.
Graham, artist:
Gainsborough.

	Issue Price	Current Value

GRANDPA AND ME SERIES
(Brown and Bigelow)

☐ **1977 Gay Blades,** production: one year 55.00 62.00

IRENE SPENCER SERIES

☐ **1975 Dear Child,** artist: Irene Spencer, production quantity 10,000 .... 37.50 110.00
☐ **1976 Promises to Keep,** artist: Irene Spencer, production quantity 10,000 .... 40.00 55.00

JULIAN RITTER SERIES

☐ **1977 Christmas Visit,** artist: Julian Ritter, production quantity 9,800 .... 24.50 29.00
☐ **1978 Valentine, Fluttering Heart,** production quantity 7,500 .... 45.00 45.00

JULIAN RITTER FALL IN LOVE SERIES

☐ **1977 Enchantment,** artist: Julian Ritter, production quantity 5,000 ....
☐ **1977 Frolic,** artist: Julian Ritter, production quantity 5,000 ....
☐ **1977 Gutsy Gal,** artist: Julian Ritter, production quantity 5,000 ....
☐ **1977 Lonely Chill,** artist: Julian Ritter, production quantity 5,000
Set of four 100.00 100.00

JULIAN RITTER TO LOVE A CLOWN SERIES

☐ **1978 Awaited Reunion,** artist: Julian Ritter, production quantity 5,000 .... 120.00 120.00
☐ **1978 Twosome Time,** artist: Julian Ritter, production quantity 5,000 .... 120.00 120.00
☐ **1978 Showtime Beckons,** artist: Julian Ritter, production quantity 5,000 .... 120.00 120.00
☐ **1978 Together in Memories,** artist: Julian Ritter, production quantity 5,000 .... 120.00 120.00

LEADERS OF TOMORROW SERIES
(Kern Collectibles)

☐ **1980 Future Physician,** artist: Leo Jansen, production quantity 9,800 .... 50.00 86.00
☐ **1981 Future Farmer,** artist: Leo Jansen, production quantity 9,800 .... 50.00 51.00

	Issue Price	Current Value
☐ 1982 **Future Florist,** artist: Leo Jansen, production quantity 9,800	55.00	51.00
☐ 1983 **Future Teacher,** artist: Leo Jansen, production quantity 9,800	55.00	51.00

THE LEWIS AND CLARK EXPEDITION SERIES
(The Hamilton Collection)

	Issue Price	Current Value
☐ 1981 **In the Bitterroots,** artist: John Clymer, production: 10 days	55.00	75.00
☐ 1981 **Sacajawea at the Big Water,** artist: John Clymer, production: 10 days	55.00	65.00
☐ 1981 **The Lewis Crossing,** artist: John Clymer, production: 10 days	55.00	55.00
☐ 1981 **Captain Clark and the Buffalo Gang,** artist: John Clymer, production: 10 days	55.00	55.00
☐ 1982 **The Salt Maker,** artist: John Clymer, production: 10 days	55.00	55.00
☐ 1982 **Up the Jefferson,** artist: John Clymer, production: 10 days	55.00	55.00
☐ 1982 **Arrival of Sergeant Pryor,** artist: John Clymer, production: 10 days	55.00	55.00
☐ 1982 **Visitors at Fort Clatsop,** artist: John Clymer, production: 10 days	55.00	55.00

LITTLE MEN SERIES

	Issue Price	Current Value
☐ 1977 **Come Ride with Me,** artist: Lorraine Trester, production: one year	50.00	50.00

MOPPETS ANNIVERSARY SERIES

	Issue Price	Current Value
☐ 1976 **Moppet Couple,** production quantity 20,000	13.00	13.00

MOPPETS CHRISTMAS SERIES

	Issue Price	Current Value
☐ 1973 **Christmas March,** production quantity 20,000	10.00	35.00
☐ 1974 **Decorating the Tree,** production quantity 20,000	12.00	22.00
☐ 1975 **Bringing Home the Tree,** production quantity 20,000	13.00	15.00
☐ 1976 **Christmas Tree,** production quantity 20,000	13.00	15.00
☐ 1977 **Placing the Star,** production quantity 18,500	13.00	14.00
☐ 1978 **The Presents,** production quantity 18,500 ..	10.00	10.00
☐ 1979 **Moppets,** production quantity 18,500	12.00	12.00

			Issue Price	Current Value
☐ 1980	Moppets Christmas, production: one year ..		12.00	12.00
☐ 1981	Moppets Christmas, production: one year ..		12.00	12.00
☐ 1982	Moppets Christmas, production: one year ..		12.00	12.00
☐ 1983	Moppets Christmas, production: one year ..		12.00	12.00

MOPPETS MOTHER'S DAY SERIES

☐ 1973	Mother's Day, production quantity 20,000	10.00	30.00
☐ 1974	Mother's Day, production quantity 20,000	12.00	20.00
☐ 1975	Mother's Day, production quantity 20,000	13.00	15.00
☐ 1976	Mother's Day, production quantity 20,000	13.00	15.00
☐ 1977	Mother's Day, production quantity 18,500	13.00	15.00
☐ 1978	Mother's Day, production quantity 18,500	10.00	10.00

MOTHER'S DAY SERIES
(Brown and Bigelow)

☐ 1980	Family Circus, production quantity 5,000 ..	25.00	27.00

OMNIBUS MURALIS SERIES

☐ 1976	200 Years with Old Glory, production quantity 15,000	60.00	63.00
☐ 1977	Life of Christ, production quantity 15,000	60.00	63.00

MUSEUM DOLL PLATES

☐ 1983	Lydia, artist: Gorham, production quantity 5,000	29.00	125.00
☐ 1984	Belton Bebe, artist: Gorham, production quantity 5,000	29.00	55.00
☐ 1984	Christmas Lady, artist: Gorham, production quantity 7,500	32.50	32.50
☐ 1985	Lucille, artist: Gorham, production quantity 5,000	29.00	35.00
☐ 1985	Jumeau, artist: Gorham, production quantity 5,000	29.00	29.00

PASTORAL SYMPHONY SERIES

☐ 1982	When I Was a Child, artist: Bettie Felder, production quantity 7,500	42.50	50.00
☐ 1983	Gather the Children, artist: Bettie Felder, production quantity 7,500	42.50	50.00
☐ 1984	Sugar and Spice, artist: Bettie Felder, production quantity 7,500	42.50	50.00
☐ 1985	He Loves Me, artist: Bettie Felder, production quantity 7,500	42.50	50.00

Christmas Lady, artist: Gorham.

Lucille, artist: Gorham.

Jumeau, artist: Gorham.

Gather the Children,
artist: Bettie Felder.

Sugar and Spice, artist:
Bettie Felder.

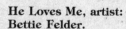
He Loves Me, artist:
Bettie Felder.

		Issue Price	Current Value
PRESIDENTIAL SERIES			
☐ 1976	**Kennedy,** artist: Norman Rockwell, production quantity 9,800	30.00	55.00
☐ 1976	**Eisenhower,** artist: Norman Rockwell, production quantity 9,800	30.00	35.00

REMINGTON WESTERN SERIES

☐ 1973	**New Year on the Cimarron,** artist: Frederic Remington, production: one year	25.00	35.00
☐ 1973	**Aiding a Comrade,** artist: Frederic Remington, production: one year	25.00	30.00
☐ 1973	**The Flight,** artist: Frederic Remington, production: one year	25.00	30.00
☐ 1973	**Fight for the Water Hole,** artist: Frederic Remington, production: one year	25.00	30.00
☐ 1975	**Old Ramond,** artist: Frederic Remington, production: one year	20.00	35.00
☐ 1975	**A Breed,** artist: Frederic Remington, production: one year	20.00	35.00
☐ 1976	**Cavalry Officer,** artist: Frederic Remington, production quantity 5,000	37.50	40.00
☐ 1976	**A Trapper,** artist: Frederic Remington, production quantity 5,000	37.00	40.00

TELEVISION WORKSHOP
CHRISTMAS SERIES

☐ 1981	**Sesame Street Christmas,** artist: unannounced, production: one year	17.50	17.50
☐ 1982	**Sesame Street Christmas,** artist: unannounced, production: one year	17.50	17.50
☐ 1983	**Sesame Street Christmas,** artist: unannounced, production: one year	19.50	19.50

TRAVELING SALESMAN SERIES
(Brown and Bigelow)

☐ 1977	**Traveling Salesman,** production quantity 7,500	35.00	40.00
☐ 1978	**Country Pedlar,** production quantity 7,500	40.00	45.00
☐ 1979	**Horse Trader,** production quantity 7,500	40.00	45.00

WILDERNESS WINGS SERIES
(Brown and Bigelow)

☐ 1978	**Gliding In,** production quantity 5,000	35.00	40.00
☐ 1979	**Taking Off,** production quantity 5,000	40.00	45.00
☐ 1980	**Joining Up,** production quantity 5,000	45.00	47.00

New Year on the
Cimarron, artist:
Frederic Remington.

.Aiding a Comrade,
artist: Frederic
Remington.

The Flight, artist:
Frederic Remington.

SINGLE RELEASES	Issue Price	Current Value
☐ 1970 **American Family Tree,** artist: Norman Rockwell, production quantity 5,000	17.00	105.00
☐ 1974 **Big Three,** artist: Norman Rockwell, production quantity 10,000	17.50	20.00
☐ 1974 **The Golden Rule,** artist: Norman Rockwell, production: one year	12.50	30.00
☐ 1974 **Weighing In,** artist: Norman Rockwell, production quantity 10,000	12.50	50.00
☐ 1975 **Benjamin Franklin,** artist: Norman Rockwell, production quantity 18,500	19.50	40.00
☐ 1976 **The Marriage License,** artist: Norman Rockwell, numbered, production: one year	37.50	40.00
☐ 1976 **Black Regiment,** production quantity 7,500	25.00	58.00
☐ 1976 **Wagon Train,** production: less than one year	19.50	22.50
☐ 1976 **Memorial Plate,** artist: Norman Rockwell, production: one year	37.50	40.00
☐ 1978 **Triple Self-Portrait,** artist: Norman Rockwell, production: one year	37.50	60.00
☐ 1980 **The Annual Visit,** artist: Norman Rockwell, production: one year	32.50	32.50
☐ 1981 **A Day in the Life of a Boy,** artist: Norman Rockwell, production: one year	50.00	80.00

American Family Tree, artist: Norman Rockwell.

The Golden Rule, artist:
Norman Rockwell.

A Day in the Life of a
Boy, artist: Norman
Rockwell.

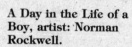

		Issue Price	Current Value
☐ 1981	**A Day in the Life of a Girl,** artist: Norman Rockwell, production: one year	50.00	80.00

A Day in the Life of a Girl, artist: Norman Rockwell.

GRANDE COPENHAGEN

Denmark

CHRISTMAS SERIES	Issue Price	Current Value
☐ **1975 Alone Together,** artist: unannounced, production: one year	24.50	29.50
☐ **1976 Christmas Wreath,** artist: unannounced, production: one year	24.50	29.50
☐ **1977 Fishwives at Gammelstrand,** artist: unannounced, production: one year	26.50	27.00
☐ **1978 Hans Christian Andersen,** artist: unannounced, production: one year	32.50	40.00
☐ **1979 Pheasants,** artist: unannounced, production: one year	34.50	35.00
☐ **1980 Snow Queen in the Tivoli,** artist: Frode Bahnsen, production: less than one year	39.50	40.00
☐ **1981 Little Match Girl in Nyhavn,** artist: Frode Bahnsen, production: one year	42.50	45.00
☐ **1982 Shepherdess/Chimney Sweep,** artist: Frode Bahnsen, production: one year	45.00	60.00
☐ **1983 Little Mermaid near Kronborg,** artist: Frode Bahnsen, production: one year	45.00	140.00
☐ **1984 Sandman at Amalienborg,** artist: Frode Bahnsen, production: one year	45.00	75.00

Shepherdess/Chimney Sweep, artist: Frode Bahnsen.

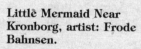

Little Mermaid Near Kronborg, artist: Frode Bahnsen.

	Issue Price	Current Value
SINGLE RELEASE		
□ **1976 Bicentennial—Great Seal,** production: one year	**35.00**	**38.00**

GRANDE DANICA

Denmark

MOTHER'S DAY SERIES	Issue Price	Current Value
☐ 1977 **Dog with Puppies,** production quantity 10,000	25.00	26.00
☐ 1978 **Storks,** production quantity 10,000	25.00	26.00
☐ 1979 **Badgers,** production quantity 10,000	25.00	26.00

MOTHER'S DAY SERIES— KATE GREENAWAY

☐ 1971 Artist: Kate Greenaway	14.95	16.00
☐ 1972 Artist: Kate Greenaway	14.95	16.00
☐ 1973 Artist: Kate Greenaway	16.95	20.00
☐ 1974 Artist: Kate Greenaway	16.95	20.00

GREENTREE POTTERIES

United States

AMERICAN LANDMARKS SERIES

☐ 1970 **Mt. Rushmore,** production quantity: 2,000	10.00	10.00
☐ 1971 **Niagara Falls,** production quantity: 2,000	10.00	10.00

GRANT WOOD SERIES

☐ 1971 **Studio,** production quantity 2,000	10.00	12.00
☐ 1972 **Antioch School,** production quantity 2,000	10.00	12.00
☐ 1973 **At Stone City,** production quantity 2,000	10.00	12.00
☐ 1974 **Adolescence,** production quantity 2,000	10.00	12.00
☐ 1975 **Birthplace,** production quantity 2,000	10.00	12.00
☐ 1976 **American Gothic,** production quantity 2,000	10.00	12.00

KENNEDY SERIES

☐ 1972 **Center for Performing Arts,** production quantity 2,000	20.00	22.50
☐ 1973 **Birthplace, Brookline, Mass.,** production quantity 2,000	12.00	14.00

MISSISSIPPI RIVER SERIES

☐ 1973 **Delta Queen,** production quantity 2,000	20.00	22.50
☐ 1973 **Tri-Centennial,** production quantity 2,000	20.00	22.50

		Issue Price	Current Value
MOTORCAR SERIES			
☐ **1972**	**1929 Packard Dietrich Convertible,** production quantity 2,000	20.00	22.50
☐ **1973**	**Model "A" Ford,** production quantity 2,000	20.00	22.50

GROLIER

United States

SNOW WHITE AND THE SEVEN DWARFS SERIES

☐ **1984**	**At the Wishing Well,** artist: Disney Studios, production quantity 15,000	24.95	25.00

THREE LITTLE PIGS 50TH ANNIVERSARY SERIES

☐ **1984**	**Fifer Pig,** artist: Disney Studios, production quantity 15,000	14.95	14.95

DAVE GROSSMAN DESIGNS

United States

BOY SCOUT ANNUAL SERIES

☐ **1981**	**Can't Wait,** artist: Norman Rockwell, production quantity 10,000	30.00	30.00
☐ **1982**	**A Guiding Hand,** artist: Norman Rockwell, production quantity 10,000	30.00	30.00
☐ **1983**	**Tomorrow's Leader,** artist: Norman Rockwell, production quantity 10,000	30.00	30.00

CHILDREN OF THE WEEK SERIES

☐ **1978**	**Monday's Child,** artist: Barbard, production quantity 5,000	30.00	26.00
☐ **1979**	**Tuesday's Child,** artist: Barbard, production quantity 5,000	30.00	26.00
☐ **1979**	**Wednesday's Child,** artist: Barbard, production quantity 5,000	30.00	28.00
☐ **1980**	**Thursday's Child,** artist: Barbard, production quantity 5,000	30.00	32.00
☐ **1980**	**Friday's Child,** artist: Barbard, production quantity 5,000	30.00	42.00

A Guiding Hand, artist: Norman Rockwell.

Tomorrow's Leader, artist: Norman Rockwell.

		Issue Price	Current Value
☐ 1981	**Saturday's Child,** artist: Barbard, production quantity 5,000	**30.00**	**47.00**
☐ 1981	**Sunday's Child,** artist: Barbard, production quantity 5,000	**30.00**	**52.00**

	Issue Price	Current Value

CHRISTMAS SERIES

☐ **1978 Peace,** artist: Barbard, production quantity 5,000 .... **55.00** **42.00**

☐ **1979 Santa,** artist: Barbard, production quantity 5,000 .... **55.00** **42.00**

EMMETT KELLY CHRISTMAS SERIES

☐ **1986 Christmas Carol,** artist: Barry Leighton-Jones, production quantity N/A **20.00** **20.00**

HUCKLEBERRY FINN SERIES

☐ **1979 The Secret,** artist: Norman Rockwell, production quantity 10,000 .... **40.00** **42.00**

☐ **1980 Listening,** artist: Norman Rockwell, production quantity 10,000 .... **40.00** **42.00**

☐ **1981 No Kings nor Dukes,** artist: Norman Rockwell, production quantity 10,000 .... **40.00** **42.00**

☐ **1981 The Snake Escapes,** artist: Norman Rockwell, production quantity 10,000 .... **40.00** **42.00**

THE MAGIC PEOPLE SERIES

☐ **1982 Music for a Queen,** artist: Lynn Lupetti, hand-numbered, production quantity 10,000 **65.00** **65.00**

☐ **1983 Fantasy Festival,** artist: Lynn Lupetti, hand-numbered, production quantity 10,000 .... **65.00** **65.00**

**Music for a Queen,
artist: Lynn Lupetti.**

Fantasy Festival, artist:
Lynn Lupetti.

		Issue Price	Current Value
☐ 1983	**Bubble Chariot,** artist: Lynn Lupetti, hand-numbered, production quantity 10,000	65.00	65.00

MARGARET KEANE SERIES

☐ 1976	**Balloon Girl,** artist: Margaret Keane, production: one year	25.00	38.00
☐ 1977	**My Kitty,** artist: Margaret Keane, production: one year	25.00	32.00
☐ 1978	**Bedtime,** artist: Margaret Keane, production: one year	25.00	28.00

MINIATURE BAS-RELIEF SERIES

☐ 1981	**No Swimming,** artist: Norman Rockwell, production: unannounced	25.00	40.00

ROCKWELL ANNUAL SERIES

☐ 1979	**Leap Frog,** artist: Norman Rockwell, production: one year	50.00	42.00
☐ 1980	**Lovers,** artist: Norman Rockwell, production: one year	60.00	63.00
☐ 1981	**Dreams of Long Ago,** artist: Norman Rockwell, production: one year	60.00	63.00
☐ 1982	**Doctor and the Doll,** artist: Norman Rockwell, production: one year	65.00	68.00

No Swimming, artist:
Norman Rockwell.

		Issue Price	Current Value
☐ **1984**	**Big Moment,** artist: Norman Rockwell, production: one year	27.00	30.00

ROCKWELL ANNUAL SERIES II

☐ **1983**	**Circus,** artist: Norman Rockwell, production quantity 9,500	65.00	67.00

Circus, artist: Norman
Rockwell.

	Issue Price	Current Value
☐ **1984 Visit with Norman Rockwell,** artist: Norman Rockwell, production quantity 9,500	**65.00**	**67.00**

ROCKWELL CHRISTMAS SERIES

	Issue Price	Current Value
☐ **1980 Christmas Trio,** artist: Norman Rockwell, production: one year	**75.00**	**76.00**
☐ **1981 Santa's Good Boys,** artist: Norman Rockwell, production: one year	**75.00**	**76.00**
☐ **1982 Faces of Christmas,** artist: Norman Rockwell, production: one year	**75.00**	**76.00**

ROCKWELL CHRISTMAS SERIES II

	Issue Price	Current Value
☐ **1983 Christmas Chores,** artist: Norman Rockwell, production quantity 9,500	**75.00**	**77.00**
☐ **1984 Tiny Tim,** artist: Norman Rockwell, production quantity 9,500	**75.00**	**77.00**

TOM SAWYER SERIES

	Issue Price	Current Value
☐ **1976 Whitewashing Fence,** artist: Norman Rockwell, production: one year	**25.00**	**145.00**
☐ **1977 First Smoke,** artist: Norman Rockwell, production: one year	**25.00**	**45.00**
☐ **1977 Take Your Medicine,** artist: Norman Rockwell, production: one year	**25.00**	**50.00**

Visit with Norman Rockwell, artist: Norman Rockwell.

Santa's Good Boys, artist: Norman Rockwell.

Christmas Chores, artist: Norman Rockwell.

Tiny Tim, artist: Norman Rockwell.

Young Doctor, artist: Norman Rockwell.

The American Mother, artist: Norman Rockwell.

	Issue Price	Current Value
☐ 1978 **Lost in Cave**, artist: Norman Rockwell, production: one year	25.00	50.00

SINGLE RELEASES

	Issue Price	Current Value
☐ 1979 **Young Doctor**, artist: Norman Rockwell, production quantity 5,000	50.00	53.00
☐ 1982 **The American Mother**, artist: Norman Rockwell, production quantity 17,500	45.00	47.00

HACKETT AMERICAN

United States

CLASSICAL AMERICAN BEAUTIES SERIES	Issue Price	Current Value
☐ **1978** **Collen,** artist: Vincent, production quantity 7,500	60.00	60.00
☐ **1979** **Heather,** artist: Vincent, production quantity 7,500	60.00	60.00
☐ **1980** **Dawn,** artist: Vincent, production quantity 7,500	60.00	60.00
☐ **1982** **Eve,** artist: Vincent, production quantity 7,500	60.00	60.00

CORITA KENT ANNUAL SERIES

	Issue Price	Current Value
☐ **1983** **Belinda,** artist: Chuck Oberstein, production quantity 7,500	39.50	39.50

CRAZY CATS SERIES

	Issue Price	Current Value
☐ **1982** **Daisy Kitten,** artist: Sadako Mano, production quantity 7,500	42.50	43.00
☐ **1982** **Daisy Cat,** artist: Sadako Mano, production quantity 7,500	42.50	43.00

DAYS REMEMBERED SERIES

	Issue Price	Current Value
☐ **1982** **First Birthday,** artist: David Smith, production quantity 19,500	29.50	30.50
☐ **1983** **First Haircut,** artist: David Smith, production quantity 19,500	35.00	35.00

EARLY DISCOVERIES SERIES

	Issue Price	Current Value
☐ **1982** **Let's Play,** artist: Rudy Escalera, production quantity 7,500	42.50	43.50

ENDANGERED SPECIES SERIES

	Issue Price	Current Value
☐ **1980** **California Sea Otters,** artist: Sadako Mano, production quantity 7,500	35.00	75.00
☐ **1981** **Asian Pandas,** artist: Sadako Mano, production quantity 7,500	37.50	65.00

	Issue Price	Current Value
☐ **1982** **Australian Koalas,** artist: Sadako Mano, production quantity 7,500	37.50	37.50
☐ **1982** **River Otters,** artist: Sadako Mano, production quantity 7,500	39.50	39.50

ESCALERA'S FATHER'S DAY SERIES

☐ **1982** **Daddy's Rose,** artist: Rudy Escalera, production quantity 7,500	42.50	43.50
☐ **1983** **Daddy's Wish,** artist: Rudy Escalera, production quantity 7,500	42.50	43.50

EVERYONE'S FRIENDS SERIES

☐ **1982** **Springtime,** artist: Sadako Mano, production quantity 7,500	42.50	43.00
☐ **1982** **Autumn Bandit,** artist: Sadako Mano, production quantity 7,500	42.50	43.00
☐ **1983** **Snow Bunnies,** artist: Sadako Mano, production quantity 10,000	42.50	43.00
☐ **1984** **Summer's Bandit,** artist: Sadako Mano, production quantity 10,000	42.50	43.00

FAMOUS PLANES OF YESTERDAY SERIES

☐ **1983** **Spirit of St. Louis,** artist: Bob Banks, production quantity 5,000	39.50	40.50
☐ **1984** **Byrd Antarctic,** artist: Bob Banks, production quantity 5,000	39.50	40.50
☐ **1984** **Winnie Mae,** artist: Bob Banks, production quantity 5,000	39.50	40.50

FASHIONS BY IRENE SERIES

☐ **1983** **Elegant Lady,** artist: Virginia Fisher, production quantity 15,000	45.00	45.00

FAVORITE DREAMS SERIES

☐ **1983** **Daddy's Sailor,** artist: Christopher Paluso, production quantity 7,500	39.50	40.50
☐ **1984** **Daddy's Engineer,** artist: Christopher Paluso, production quantity 7,500	39.50	40.50

FRIENDS OF THE FOREST SERIES

☐ **1981** **Forest Alert,** artist: David Smith, production quantity 7,500	50.00	50.00

	Issue Price	Current Value
☐ 1982 **Brookside Protection,** artist: David Smith, production quantity 7,500	50.00	50.00
☐ 1982 **Mountain Guardian,** artist: David Smith, production quantity 7,500	50.00	50.00
☐ 1983 **Friends of the Forest,** artist: David Smith, production quantity 7,500	50.00	50.00

GOLFING GREAT SERIES

	Issue Price	Current Value
☐ 1984 **Gary Player Grand Slam Edition,** artist: Cassidy J. Alexander, production quantity 3,000	125.00	125.00
☐ 1984 **Gary Player Champion Edition,** artist: Cassidy J. Alexander, production: less than one year	45.00	45.00

GRANDPARENTS SERIES

	Issue Price	Current Value
☐ 1984 **Grandpa's Delight,** artist: Greensmith, production quantity 10,000	27.50	28.00

HORSES IN ACTION SERIES

	Issue Price	Current Value
☐ 1981 **The Challenge,** artist: Violet Parkhurst, production quantity 7,500	50.00	50.00
☐ 1982 **Country Days,** artist: Violet Parkhurst, production quantity 7,500	50.00	50.00
☐ 1982 **Family Portrait,** artist: Violet Parkhurst, production quantity 7,500	50.00	50.00
☐ 1983 **All Grown Up,** artist: Violet Parkhurst, production quantity 7,500	50.00	50.00

HUGGABLE MOMENTS SERIES

	Issue Price	Current Value
☐ 1983 **Naptime,** artist: Irish McCalla, production quantity 10,000	39.50	41.00
☐ 1983 **Playtime,** artist: Irish McCalla, production quantity 10,000	39.50	41.00

IMPRESSIONS SERIES

	Issue Price	Current Value
☐ 1982 **Windy Day,** artist: Jo Anne Mix, production quantity 7,500	42.50	43.00
☐ 1982 **Sunny Day,** artist: Jo Anne Mix, production quantity 7,500	42.50	43.00
☐ 1983 **Summer's Day,** artist: Jo Anne Mix, production quantity 7,500	42.50	43.00

		Issue Price	Current Value

KELLY'S STABLE SERIES

☐ 1982	My Champion, artist: Kelly, production quantity 15,000	42.50	43.00
☐ 1983	Glory Bound, artist: Kelly, production quantity 15,000	42.50	43.00
☐ 1983	Arabian Spring, artist: Kelly, production quantity 15,000	42.50	43.00

LANDFALLS SERIES

| ☐ 1982 | San Francisco Bay, artist: Bob Russell, production quantity 7,500 | 39.50 | 40.50 |
| ☐ 1983 | Newport Harbor, artist: Bob Russell, production quantity 7,500 | 39.50 | 40.50 |

LITTLE FRIENDS SERIES

| ☐ 1984 | Tiny Creatures, artist: David Smith, production quantity 5,000 | 35.00 | 35.00 |
| ☐ 1984 | Forest Friends, artist: David Smith, production quantity 5,000 | 35.00 | 35.00 |

LITTLE ORPHANS SERIES

☐ 1982	Surprise Package, artist: Ozz Franca, production quantity 19,500	29.50	30.00
☐ 1983	Castaway, artist: Ozz Franca, production quantity 19,500	32.50	33.00
☐ 1984	Furry Surprise, artist: Ozz Franca, production quantity 19,500	35.00	35.00

MEMORABLE IMPRESSIONS SERIES

| ☐ 1983 | Beachcomber, artist: Ivan Anderson, production quantity 7,500 | 39.50 | 40.50 |
| ☐ 1983 | Beach Girl, artist: Ivan Anderson, production quantity 7,500 | 39.50 | 40.50 |

MILESTONE AUTOMOBILES SERIES

☐ 1983	'57 Chevy, artist: Carl Pape, production quantity 5,000	39.50	40.00
☐ 1984	'57 Thunderbird, artist: Carl Pape, production quantity 5,000	39.50	40.00
☐ 1984	'53 Corvette, artist: Carl Pape, production quantity 5,000	39.50	40.00

MIX ANNUAL CHRISTMAS SERIES	Issue Price	Current Value
☐ **1982 Christmas Love,** artist: Jo Anne Mix, production quantity 7,500	39.50	40.50

MOTHER AND CHILD SERIES

	Issue Price	Current Value
☐ **1981 Mother's Love,** artist: Ozz Franca, production quantity 7,500	42.50	43.50
☐ **1982 Tenderness,** artist: Ozz Franca, production quantity 7,500	42.50	43.50
☐ **1983 Serenity,** artist: Ozz Franca, production quantity 7,500	42.50	43.50
☐ **1984 Navajo Madonna,** artist: Ozz Franca, production quantity 7,500	42.50	43.50

OCEAN MOODS SERIES

	Issue Price	Current Value
☐ **1981 Sunset Tides,** artist: Violet Parkhurst, production quantity 5,000	50.00	50.00
☐ **1981 Moonlight Flight,** artist: Violet Parkhurst, production quantity 5,000	50.00	50.00
☐ **1982 Morning Surf,** artist: Violet Parkhurst, production quantity 5,000	50.00	50.00
☐ **1982 Afternoon Surf,** artist: Violet Parkhurst, production quantity 5,000	50.00	50.00

OCEAN STARS SERIES

	Issue Price	Current Value
☐ **1982 Sea Horse,** artist: Carl Pope, production quantity 7,500	42.50	43.50
☐ **1982 Dolphins,** artist: Carl Pope, production quantity 7,500	42.50	43.50
☐ **1983 Whales,** artist: Carl Pope, production quantity 10,000	42.50	43.50

PARKHURST ANNUAL CHRISTMAS SERIES

	Issue Price	Current Value
☐ **1981 Christmas Tear,** artist: Violet Parkhurst, production quantity 7,500	39.50	40.50
☐ **1982 Christmas Morning,** artist: Violet Parkhurst, production quantity 7,500	39.50	40.50
☐ **1983 Night Before Christmas,** artist: Violet Parkhurst, production quantity 7,500	39.50	40.50

	Issue Price	Current Value

PARKHURST ANNUAL MOTHER'S DAY SERIES

☐ **1981 Daisies for Mother,** artist: Violet Parkhurst, production quantity 7,500 . . . .   **39.50**   **45.00**

PARKHURST DIAMOND COLLECTION

☐ **1982 Chance Encounter,** artist: Violet Parkhurst, production quantity 1,500 . . . .   **300.00**   **300.00**

PEACEFUL RETREAT SERIES

☐ **1982 Refuge,** artist: Joan Horton, production quantity 19,500 . . . .   **29.50**   **30.00**
☐ **1983 Solitude,** artist: Joan Horton, production quantity 19,500 . . . .   **29.50**   **33.50**
☐ **1983 Tranquility,** artist: Joan Horton, production quantity 19,500 . . . .   **35.00**   **35.00**
☐ **1984 Seclusion,** artist: Joan Horton, production quantity 19,500 . . . .   **35.00**   **35.00**

PLAYFUL MEMORIES SERIES

☐ **1981 Renee,** artist: Sue Etem, production quantity 10,000 . . . .   **39.50**   **75.00**
☐ **1982 Jeremy,** artist: Sue Etem, production quantity 10,000 . . . .   **42.50**   **50.00**
☐ **1983 Jamie,** artist: Sue Etem, production quantity 10,000 . . . .   **42.50**   **50.00**
☐ **1983 Randy,** artist: Sue Etem, production quantity 10,000 . . . .   **45.00**   **45.00**

PRAIRIE CHILDREN

☐ **1982 Young Pioneer,** artist: Louise Sigle, production quantity 19,500 . . . .   **32.50**   **33.50**
☐ **1983 Adam,** artist: Louise Sigle, production quantity 19,500 . . . .   **35.00**   **35.00**

PUZZLING MOMENTS SERIES

☐ **1983 The Problem Solver,** artist: William Selden, production quantity 7,500 . . . .   **39.50**   **40.00**
☐ **1983 Practice Makes Perfect,** artist: Louise Sigle, production quantity 19,500 . . . .   **39.50**   **40.00**

REFLECTIONS OF THE SEA SERIES

☐ **1983 Golden Shores,** artist: Violet Parkhurst, production quantity 5,000 . . . .   **42.50**   **43.50**

From 50 cents to $3400, the world's first limited edition plate was "Behind the Frozen Window," issued by Bing and Grøndahl, of Denmark, in 1895. *(Photo courtesy of the Bradford Exchange)*

"Sparrows," issued by Bing and Grøndahl in 1897 for 75 cents; current value is $1000. *(Photo courtesy of the Bradford Exchange)*

"Christmas in Copenhagen," issued in 1956, for $8.50, by Bing and Grøndahl for their "Christmas" series. Current value is $130. *(Photo courtesy of the Bradford Exchange)*

"Dog and Puppies," issued by Bing and Grøndahl in 1969 for $9.75; current value is $400. *(Photo courtesy of the Bradford Exchange)*

"Brave and Free," by artist Gregory Perillo and issued in 1986, was awarded "Plate of the Year" at the California Plate Collectors' Convention in April, 1987. Issue price was $24.50; current value is $24.50. *(Photo courtesy of Artaffects, Ltd.)*

"No Contest," by Christian Bell Age of Canada, was issued in 1983 for $65; current value is $119. *(Photo courtesy of the Bradford Exchange)*

"Symphony in Steam," by Christian Bell Age of Canada, was issued in 1981 for $65; current value is $265. *(Photo courtesy of the Bradford Exchange)*

"Madonna and Child," issued by Royal Copenhagen in 1908 for $1; current value is $1900. *(Photo courtesy of the Bradford Exchange)*

"Flight Into Egypt," issued by Royal Copenhagen in 1943 for $4; current value is $450. *(Photo courtesy of the Bradford Exchange)*

"Maria and Child," issued by Rosenthal in 1971 for $100; current value is $950. *(Photo courtesy of the Bradford Exchange)*

"American Bald Eagle," issued by Pickard in 1974 for $150; current value is $920. *(Photo courtesy of the Bradford Exchange)*

"Toy Maker," from the "Rockwell Heritage" series, was issued in 1977 for $14.50; current value is $160. *(Photo courtesy of the Bradford Exchange)*

"Windsor Castle," by Wedgwood, issued in 1969 for $25; current value is $185. *(Photo courtesy of the Bradford Exchange)*

"Sunday Best" features the children of artist Sandra Kuck, issued in 1983 by Reco for $29.50; current value is $85. *(Photo courtesy of Reco International Corp.)*

Donald Zolan's "Children" series, featuring his son in "Erik and the Dandelion," issued by Viletta in 1978 for $19; current value is $250. *(Photo courtesy of the Bradford Exchange)*

Donald Zolan's daughter, "Sabina in the Grass," issued by Viletta in 1979 for $22; current value is $210. *(Photo courtesy of the Bradford Exchange)*

"Running Free," issued by Royal Doulton in 1977 for $70; current value is $128. *(Photo courtesy of the Bradford Exchange)*

"Sailing With the Tide," issued in 1976 by Royal Doulton for $65; current value is $75. *(Photo courtesy of the Bradford Exchange)*

"Colette and Child," issued in 1973 by Royal Doulton for $40; current value is $285. *(Photo courtesy of the Bradford Exchange)*

Schmid's "Christmas Eve at the Doghouse," from the "Peanuts" series, issued in 1973 for $10; current value is $180. *(Photo courtesy of the Bradford Exchange)*

The Schmid "Disney Christmas" series features "Sleigh Ride," issued in 1973 for $10; current value is $280. *(Photo courtesy of the Bradford Exchange)*

"Decorating the Tree," also in the Schmid "Disney Christmas" series, issued in 1974 for $10; current value is $65. *(Photo courtesy of the Bradford Exchange)*

		Issue Price	Current Value
☐ 1984	**Summer Sands,** artist: Violet Parkhurst, production quantity 5,000	**39.50**	**39.50**
☐ 1984	**Big Sur,** artist: Violet Parkhurst, production quantity 5,000	**39.50**	**39.50**

SADAKO'S HELPERS SERIES

☐ 1983	**Artist's Pal,** artist: Sadako Mano, production quantity 7,500	**39.50**	**40.00**
☐ 1983	**Artist's Helper,** artist: Sadako Mano, production quantity 7,500	**39.50**	**40.00**

SADAKO MANO'S CHRISTMAS SERIES

☐ 1983	**Santa's Special Gift,** artist: Sadako Mano, production quantity 5,000	**39.50**	**40.00**
☐ 1984	**A Gift from Santa,** artist: Sadako Mano, production quantity 5,000	**39.50**	**40.00**

SAVE THE WHALES SERIES

☐ 1980	**Trust and Love,** production quantity 10,000	**30.00**	**32.00**

SENSITIVE MOMENTS SERIES

☐ 1983	**Sharing the Beauty,** artist: Rudy Escalera, production quantity 5,000	**39.50**	**40.50**

SIDE BY SIDE SERIES

☐ 1982	**My Hero,** artist: Jo Anne Mix, production quantity 19,500	**32.50**	**42.00**
☐ 1983	**Sippin' Soda,** artist: Jo Anne Mix, production quantity 19,500	**35.00**	**37.00**

SNOW BABIES SERIES

☐ 1981	**Canadian Harp Seals,** artist: Violet Parkhurst, production quantity 5,000	**39.50**	**65.00**
☐ 1981	**Polar Bear Cubs,** artist: Violet Parkhurst, production quantity 5,000	**39.50**	**40.00**
☐ 1982	**Snow Leopards,** artist: Violet Parkhurst, production quantity 5,000	**42.50**	**43.00**
☐ 1982	**Arctic Foxes,** artist: Violet Parkhurst, production quantity 5,000	**42.50**	**43.00**

SPECIAL MOMENTS SERIES

☐ 1982	**April,** artist: Rudy Escalera, production quantity 7,500	**42.50**	**43.50**

		Issue Price	Current Value
☐ 1983	**Rachael,** artist: Rudy Escalera, production quantity 7,500	42.50	43.50

SUMMER FUN SERIES

		Issue Price	Current Value
☐ 1983	**Fishing Together,** artist: Gina Conche, production quantity 7,500	39.50	40.50
☐ 1984	**Swinging Together,** artist: Gina Conche, production quantity 7,500	39.50	40.50

SUNBONNET BABIES

		Issue Price	Current Value
☐ 1984	**Sunday—Saturday,** artist: Charlotte Gutshall, production limited, set of 7	136.50	140.00

SUNDAY BEST SERIES

		Issue Price	Current Value
☐ 1981	**Stacey,** artist: Jo Anne Mix, production quantity 7,500	42.50	43.50
☐ 1982	**Laurie,** artist: Jo Anne Mix, production quantity 7,500	42.50	43.50

THE OWL AND THE PUSSYCAT SERIES

		Issue Price	Current Value
☐ 1983	**The Owl,** artist: Lenore Béran, production quantity 5,000	40.00	40.00
☐ 1983	**The Pussycat,** artist: Lenore Béran, production quantity 5,000	40.00	40.00

TRUE LOVE SERIES

		Issue Price	Current Value
☐ 1982	**Hog Heaven,** artist: Sadako Mano, production quantity 15,000	42.50	43.00
☐ 1983	**Frog Heaven,** artist: Sadako Mano, production quantity 15,000	39.50	40.00
☐ 1983	**Otter Heaven,** artist: Sadako Mano, production quantity 5,000	39.50	40.00
☐ 1984	**Owl Heaven,** artist: Sadako Mano, production quantity 15,000	39.50	40.00

WATERBIRD FAMILIES SERIES

		Issue Price	Current Value
☐ 1981	**Marsh Venture,** artist: Dave Chapple, production quantity 7,500	42.50	44.00
☐ 1982	**Afternoon Swim,** artist: Dave Chapple, production quantity 7,500	42.50	44.00
☐ 1983	**Nesting Wood Ducks,** artist: Dave Chapple, production quantity 10,000	42.50	44.00

		Issue Price	Current Value

☐ **1983 Returning Home,** artist: Dave Chapple, production quantity 10,000 . . . .   42.50   44.00

WONDERFUL WORLD OF CLOWNS SERIES

☐ **1981 Kiss for a Clown,** artist: Chuck Oberstein, production quantity 5,000 . . . .   39.50   40.00

☐ **1981 Rainbow's End,** artist: Chuck Oberstein, production quantity 5,000 . . . .   39.50   40.00

☐ **1982 Happy Days,** artist: Chuck Oberstein, production quantity 5,000 . . . .   39.50   40.00

☐ **1982 Filling Pop's Shoes,** artist: Chuck Oberstein, production quantity 5,000 . . . .   42.50   43.00

WONDROUS YEARS SERIES

☐ **1981 After the Rains,** artist: Rudy Escalera, production quantity 5,000 . . . .   39.50   40.00

☐ **1982 I Got One,** artist: Rudy Escalera, production quantity 5,000 . . . .   42.50   43.00

WORLD OF OZZ FRANCA SERIES

☐ **1982 Images,** artist: Ozz Franca, production quantity 7,500 . . . .   42.50   43.50

☐ **1982 Lost and Found,** artist: Ozz Franca, production quantity 7,500 . . . .   42.50   43.50

☐ **1983 Best Friends,** artist: Ozz Franca, production quantity 7,500 . . . .   42.50   43.50

YESTERDAY'S IMPRESSIONS SERIES

☐ **1983 Gloria,** artist: Kalan, production quantity 5,000 . . . .   39.50   40.50

SINGLE RELEASES

☐ **1982 John Lennon Tribute,** artist: Violet Parkhurst, production: less than one year . .   25.00   27.00

☐ **1982 John Wayne,** artist: Cassidy Alexander, production quantity 10,000 . . . .   39.50   40.00

☐ **1983 Bill Rogers,** production quantity 7,991 . . . .   42.50   40.00

☐ **1983 Bill Rogers/King of the Road,** production quantity 2,009 . . . .   95.00   95.00

☐ **1983 Henry Fonda,** artist: Cassidy Alexander, production quantity 10,000 . . . .   39.50   40.00

		Issue Price	Current Value
☐ 1983	**John Wayne—Military,** production quantity 10,000	42.50	44.00
☐ 1983	**Laurel and Hardy,** artist: Cassidy Alexander, production quantity 15,000	42.50	44.00
☐ 1983	**Nolan Ryan/Innings Pitched,** production quantity 1,598	100.00	100.00
☐ 1983	**Nolan Ryan,** production quantity 8,402 ...	42.50	44.00
☐ 1983	**Steve Garvey,** artist: Christopher Paluso, production quantity 10,000	60.00	60.00
☐ 1983	**Steve Garvey,** production quantity 1,269 ..	100.00	100.00
☐ 1983	**Reggie Jackson,** artist: Christopher Paluso, production quantity 10,000	60.00	60.00
☐ 1983	**Reggie Jackson,** production quantity 464 ..	100.00	200.00
☐ 1983	**Tom Seaver,** production quantity 6,728	42.50	43.00
☐ 1983	**Tom Seaver/Strike Out,** production quantity 3,272	100.00	100.00
☐ 1984	**Forever Yours,** artist: Cassidy Alexander, production quantity 15,000	42.50	44.00
☐ 1984	**King Remembered (Elvis Presley),** artist: C. J. Alexander, production quantity 10,000 ..	50.00	50.00
☐ 1984	**American Frontier,** artist: C. J. Alexander, production quantity 5,000	39.50	40.50
☐ 1984	**Salvation Army,** artist: William Selden, production quantity 5,000	32.50	33.50

THE HAMILTON COLLECTION

United States
(See also Boehm Studios, Gorham, Heinrich Porzellan, Metal Arts Co., Pickard China, Porcelaine Ariel, Royal Devon, and Viletta China)

AMERICA AT WORK
(River Shore)

		Issue Price	Current Value
☐ 1984	**The School Teacher,** artist: Norman Rockwell, production: 10 days	29.50	29.50
☐ 1984	**The Piano Tuner,** artist: Norman Rockwell, production: 10 days	29.50	29.50
☐ 1984	**The Zoo Keeper,** artist: Norman Rockwell, production: 10 days	29.50	29.50
☐ 1984	**The Cleaning Ladies,** artist: Norman Rockwell, production: 10 days	29.50	29.50
☐ 1984	**The Hatcheck Girl,** artist: Norman Rockwell, production: 10 days	29.50	29.50

		Issue Price	Current Value
☐ 1984	**The Artist,** artist: Norman Rockwell, production: 10 days	**29.50**	**29.50**
☐ 1984	**The Census Taker,** artist: Norman Rockwell, production: 10 days	**29.50**	**29.50**

BUTTERFLY GARDEN

☐ 1987	**Spicebush Swallowtail,** artist: P. Sweany, production: 14 days	**29.50**	**29.50**
☐ 1987	**Common Blue,** artist: P. Sweany, production: 14 days	**29.50**	**29.50**
☐ 1987	**Orange Sulphur,** artist: P. Sweany, production: 14 days	**29.50**	**29.50**
☐ 1987	**Monarch,** artist: P. Sweany, production: 14 days	**29.50**	**29.50**
☐ 1987	**Tiger Swallowtail,** artist: P. Sweany, production: 14 days	**29.50**	**29.50**
☐ 1987	**Crimson Patched Longwing,** artist: P. Sweany, production: 14 days	**29.50**	**29.50**

CHILDREN OF THE AMERICAN FRONTIER

☐ 1986	**In Trouble Again,** artist: D. Crook, production: 10 days	**24.50**	**24.50**
☐ 1986	**Tubs and Suds,** artist: D. Crook, production: 10 days	**24.50**	**24.50**
☐ 1986	**A Lady Needs a Little Privacy,** artist: D. Crook, production: 10 days	**24.50**	**24.50**
☐ 1986	**The Desperadoes,** artist: D. Crook, production: 10 days	**24.50**	**24.50**
☐ 1986	**Riders Wanted,** artist: D. Crook, production: 10 days	**24.50**	**24.50**
☐ 1987	**A Cowboy's Downfall,** artist: D. Crook, production: 10 days	**24.50**	**24.50**
☐ 1987	**Runaway Blues,** artist: D. Crook, production: 10 days	**24.50**	**24.50**
☐ 1987	**A Special Patient,** artist: D. Crook, production: 10 days	**24.50**	**24.50**

A CHILD'S BEST FRIEND

☐ 1985	**In Disgrace,** artist: B. P. Gutmann, production: 14 days	**24.50**	**40.00**
☐ 1985	**The Reward,** artist: B. P. Gutmann, production: 14 days	**24.50**	**24.50**

		Issue Price	Current Value
☐ 1985	**Who's Sleepy,** artist: B. P. Gutmann, production: 14 days	**24.50**	**24.50**
☐ 1985	**Good Morning,** artist: B. P. Gutmann, production: 14 days	**24.50**	**24.50**
☐ 1985	**Sympathy,** artist: B. P. Gutmann, production: 14 days	**24.50**	**24.50**
☐ 1985	**On the Up and Up,** artist: B. P. Gutmann, production: 14 days	**24.50**	**24.50**
☐ 1985	**Mine,** artist: B. P. Gutmann, production: 14 days	**24.50**	**24.50**
☐ 1985	**Going to Town,** artist: B. P. Gutmann, production: 14 days	**24.50**	**24.50**

CHINESE BLOSSOMS OF THE
FOUR SEASONS

☐ 1985	**Spring Peony Blossom,** artist: unannounced, production quantity 9,800	**95.00**	**95.00**
☐ 1985	**Summer Lotus Blossom,** artist: unannounced, production quantity 9,800	**95.00**	**95.00**
☐ 1985	**Autumn Chrysanthemum,** artist: unannounced, production quantity 9,800	**95.00**	**95.00**
☐ 1985	**Winter Plum Blossom,** artist: unannounced, production quantity 9,800	**95.00**	**95.00**

CHINESE SYMBOLS OF THE UNIVERSE

☐ 1984	**The Dragon,** artist: Mou-Sien Tseng, production quantity 7,500	**90.00**	**90.00**
☐ 1984	**The Phoenix,** artist: Mou-Sien Tseng, production quantity 7,500	**90.00**	**90.00**
☐ 1984	**The Tiger,** artist: Mou-Sien Tseng, production quantity 7,500	**90.00**	**90.00**
☐ 1984	**The Tortoise,** artist: Mou-Sien Tseng, production quantity 7,500	**90.00**	**90.00**
☐ 1984	**Man,** artist: Mou-Sien Tseng, production quantity 7,500	**90.00**	**90.00**

COUNTRY GARDEN
CALENDAR COLLECTION
(Bing & Grondahl)

☐ 1984	**September,** artist: Linda Thompson, production quantity 12,500	**55.00**	**57.00**
☐ 1984	**October,** artist: Linda Thompson, production quantity 12,500	**55.00**	**57.00**

September, artist: Linda Thompson.

			Issue Price	Current Value
☐ 1984	**November,** artist: Linda Thompson, production quantity 12,500		55.00	57.00
☐ 1984	**December,** artist: Linda Thompson, production quantity 12,500		55.00	57.00
☐ 1984	**January,** artist: Linda Thompson, production quantity 12,500		55.00	57.00
☐ 1984	**February,** artist: Linda Thompson, production quantity 12,500		55.00	57.00
☐ 1984	**March,** artist: Linda Thompson, production quantity 12,500		55.00	57.00
☐ 1984	**April,** artist: Linda Thompson, production quantity 12,500		55.00	57.00
☐ 1984	**May,** artist: Linda Thompson, production quantity 12,500		55.00	57.00
☐ 1984	**June,** artist: Linda Thompson, production quantity 12,500		55.00	57.00
☐ 1984	**July,** artist: Linda Thompson, production quantity 12,500		55.00	57.00
☐ 1984	**August,** artist: Linda Thompson, production quantity 12,500		55.00	57.00

A COUNTRY SUMMER

☐ 1985	**Butterfly Beauty,** artist: N. Noel, production: 10 days		29.50	29.50
☐ 1985	**The Golden Puppy,** artist: N. Noel, production: 10 days		29.50	29.50

		Issue Price	Current Value
☐ 1985	The Rocking Chair, artist: N. Noel, production: 10 days	29.50	29.50
☐ 1985	My Bunny, artist: N. Noel, production: 10 days	29.50	29.50
☐ 1985	The Brahma Calf, artist: N. Noel, production: 10 days	29.50	29.50
☐ 1985	The Tricycle, artist: N. Noel, production: 10 days	29.50	29.50

ETERNAL WISHES OF GOOD FORTUNE SERIES

		Issue Price	Current Value
☐ 1983	Friendship, artists: Shuho and Senkin Kage, production limited	34.95	37.50
☐ 1983	Love, artists: Shuho and Senkin Kage, production limited	34.95	37.50
☐ 1983	Fertility, artists: Shuho and Senkin Kage, production limited	34.95	37.50
☐ 1983	Purity and Perfection, artists: Shuho and Senkin Kage, production limited	34.95	37.50
☐ 1983	Illustrious Offspring, artists: Shuho and Senkin Kage, production limited	34.95	37.50
☐ 1983	Peace, artists: Shuho and Senkin Kage, production limited	34.95	37.50
☐ 1983	Longevity, artists: Shuho and Senkin Kage, production limited	34.95	37.50
☐ 1983	Immortality, artists: Shuho and Senkin Kage, production limited	34.95	37.50
☐ 1983	Marital Bliss, artists: Shuho and Senkin Kage, production limited	34.95	37.50
☐ 1983	Beauty, artists: Shuho and Senkin Kage, production limited	34.95	37.50
☐ 1983	Fortitude, artists: Shuho and Senkin Kage, production limited	34.95	37.50
☐ 1983	Youth, artists: Shuho and Senkin Kage, production limited	34.95	37.50

FAIRY TALES OF OLD JAPAN

		Issue Price	Current Value
☐ 1984	The Old Man Who Made Cherry Trees Blossom, artist: Shigekasu Hotta, production: 10 days	39.50	41.00
☐ 1984	Little One Inch, artist: Shigekasu Hotta, production: 10 days	39.50	41.00
☐ 1984	My Lord Bag of Rice, artist: Shigekasu Hotta, production: 10 days	39.50	41.00

		Issue Price	Current Value
☐ 1984	**The Tongue-Cut Sparrow,** artist: Shigekasu Hotta, production: 10 days	**39.50**	**41.00**
☐ 1984	**The Bamboo Cutter and the Moon Child,** artist: Shigekasu Hotta, production: 10 days ..	**39.50**	**41.00**
☐ 1984	**The Fisher Lad,** artist: Shigekasu Hotta, production: 10 days	**39.50**	**41.00**
☐ 1984	**The Magic Tea Kettle,** artist: Shigekasu Hotta, production: 10 days	**39.50**	**41.00**

FLOWER FESTIVALS OF JAPAN SERIES

☐ 1985	**Chrysanthemum,** artist: N. Hara, production: 10 days	**45.00**	**55.00**
☐ 1985	**Hollyhock,** artist: N. Hara, production: 10 days	**45.00**	**55.00**
☐ 1985	**Plum Blossom,** artist: N. Hara, production: 10 days	**45.00**	**55.00**
☐ 1985	**Morning Glory,** artist: N. Hara, production: 10 days	**45.00**	**55.00**
☐ 1985	**Cherry Blossom,** artist: N. Hara, production: 10 days	**45.00**	**55.00**
☐ 1985	**Iris,** artist: N. Hara, production: 10 days ..	**45.00**	**55.00**
☐ 1985	**Lily,** artist: N. Hara, production: 10 days ..	**45.00**	**55.00**
☐ 1985	**Peach Blossom,** artist: N. Hara, production: 10 days	**45.00**	**55.00**

GARDENS OF THE ORIENT SERIES

☐ 1983	**Flowering of Spring,** artist: Shunsute Suetomi, production: less than one year	**19.50**	**19.50**
☐ 1983	**Festival of May,** artist: Shunsute Suetomi, production: less than one year	**19.50**	**19.50**
☐ 1983	**Cherry Blossom Brocade,** artist: Shunsute Suetomi, production: less than one year ...	**19.50**	**19.50**
☐ 1983	**A Winter's Repose,** artist: Shunsute Suetomi, production: less than one year	**19.50**	**19.50**
☐ 1983	**The Garden Sanctuary,** artist: Shunsute Suetomi, production: less than one year	**19.50**	**19.50**
☐ 1983	**Summer's Glory,** artist: Shunsute Suetomi, production: less than one year	**19.50**	**19.50**
☐ 1983	**June's Creation,** artist: Shunsute Suetomi, production: less than one year	**19.50**	**19.50**

A GARDEN OF VERSES

☐ 1983	**Picture Books in Winter,** artist: Jessie Wilcox Smith, production: 10 days	**24.50**	**24.50**

		Issue Price	Current Value
☐ 1983	**Little Drops of Water,** artist: Jessie Wilcox Smith, production: 10 days	24.50	24.50
☐ 1983	**A Child's Question,** artist: Jessie Wilcox Smith, production: 10 days	24.50	24.50
☐ 1983	**Looking Glass River,** artist: Jessie Wilcox Smith, production: 10 days	24.50	24.50
☐ 1983	**The Little Busy Bee,** artist: Jessie Wilcox Smith, production: 10 days	24.50	24.50
☐ 1983	**At the Seaside,** artist: Jessie Wilcox Smith, production: 10 days	24.50	24.50
☐ 1983	**The Tea Party,** artist: Jessie Wilcox Smith, production: 10 days	24.50	24.50
☐ 1983	**Foreign Lands,** artist: Jessie Wilcox Smith, production: 10 days	24.50	24.50
☐ 1983	**The Hayloft,** artist: Jessie Wilcox Smith, production: 10 days	24.50	24.50
☐ 1983	**Among the Poppies,** artist: Jessie Wilcox Smith, production: 10 days	24.50	24.50
☐ 1983	**Five O'Clock Tea,** artist: Jessie Wilcox Smith, production: 10 days	24.50	24.50
☐ 1983	**I Love Little Kitty,** artist: Jessie Wilcox Smith, production: 10 days	24.50	24.50

THE GENTLE ARTS OF THE GEISHA SERIES

☐ 1983	**Ikebana,** artist: Yasuhiko Adachi, production limited	21.50	21.50

THE GOLDEN CLASSICS

☐ 1987	**Sleeping Beauty,** artist: C. Larson, production: 14 days	37.50	37.50

THE GREATEST SHOW ON EARTH SERIES

☐ 1981	**Clowns,** artist: F. Moody, production: 10 days	30.00	75.00
☐ 1981	**Elephants,** artist: F. Moody, production: 10 days	30.00	40.00
☐ 1981	**Aerialists,** artist: F. Moody, production: 10 days	30.00	35.00
☐ 1981	**Great Parade,** artist: F. Moody, production: 10 days	30.00	30.00
☐ 1981	**Midway,** artist: F. Moody, production: 10 days	30.00	30.00

		Issue Price	Current Value
☐ 1981	**Equestrians,** artist: F. Moody, production: 10 days	30.00	30.00
☐ 1982	**Lion Tamer,** artist: F. Moody, production: 10 days	30.00	30.00
☐ 1982	**Grande Finale,** artist: F. Moody, production: 10 days	30.00	30.00

THE JAPANESE BLOSSOMS OF AUTUMN

☐ 1985	**Bellflower,** artists: Koseki and Ebihara, production: 10 days	45.00	45.00
☐ 1985	**Arrowroot,** artists: Koseki and Ebihara, production: 10 days	45.00	45.00
☐ 1985	**Wild Carnation,** artists: Koseki and Ebihara, production: 10 days	45.00	45.00
☐ 1985	**Maiden Flower,** artists: Koseki and Ebihara, production: 10 days	45.00	45.00
☐ 1985	**Pampas Grass,** artists: Koseki and Ebihara, production: 10 days	45.00	45.00
☐ 1985	**Bush Clover,** artists: Koseki and Ebihara, production: 10 days	45.00	45.00
☐ 1985	**Purple Trousers,** artists: Koseki and Ebihara, production: 10 days	45.00	45.00

JAPANESE FLORAL CALENDAR

☐ 1981	**New Year's Day,** artists: Shuho and Senkin Kage, production: 10 days	32.50	60.00
☐ 1982	**Early Spring,** artists: Shuho and Senkin Kage, production: 10 days	32.50	40.00
☐ 1982	**Spring,** artists: Shuho and Senkin Kage, production: 10 days	32.50	32.50
☐ 1982	**Girl's Doll Day Festival,** artists: Shuho and Senkin Kage, production: 10 days	32.50	32.50
☐ 1982	**Buddha's Birthday,** artists: Shuho and Senkin Kage, production: 10 days	32.50	32.50
☐ 1982	**Early Summer,** artists: Shuho and Senkin Kage, production: 10 days	32.50	32.50
☐ 1982	**Boy's Doll Day Festival,** artists: Shuho and Senkin Kage, production: 10 days	32.50	32.50
☐ 1982	**Summer,** artists: Shuho and Senkin Kage, production: 10 days	32.50	32.50
☐ 1982	**Autumn,** artists: Shuho and Senkin Kage, production: 10 days	32.50	32.50
☐ 1983	**Festival of the Full Moon,** artists: Shuho and Senkin Kage, production: 10 days	32.50	32.50

		Issue Price	Current Value
☐ 1983	**Late Autumn,** artists: Shuho and Senkin Kage, production: 10 days	**32.50**	**32.50**
☐ 1983	**Winter,** artists: Shuho and Senkin Kage, production: 10 days	**32.50**	**32.50**

LITTLE HOUSE ON THE PRAIRIE
(River Shore)

☐ 1986	**Founder's Day Picnic,** artist: Eugene Christopherson, production: 10 days	**29.50**	**29.50**
☐ 1986	**The Women's Harvest,** artist: Eugene Christopherson, production: 10 days	**29.50**	**29.50**
☐ 1986	**Medicine Show,** artist: Eugene Christopherson, production: 10 days	**29.50**	**29.50**
☐ 1986	**Caroline's Eggs,** artist: Eugene Christopherson, production: 10 days	**29.50**	**29.50**
☐ 1986	**Mary's Gift,** artist: Eugene Christopherson, production: 10 days	**29.50**	**29.50**
☐ 1986	**A Bell for Walnut Grove,** artist: Eugene Christopherson, production: 10 days	**29.50**	**29.50**
☐ 1987	**The Ingalls' Family Christmas,** artist: Eugene Christopherson, production: 10 days	**29.50**	**29.50**
☐ 1987	**The Sweetheart Tree,** artist: Eugene Christopherson, production: 10 days	**29.50**	**29.50**

THE LITTLE RASCALS

☐ 1985	**Three for the Show,** artist: unannounced, production: 10 days	**24.50**	**24.50**
☐ 1985	**My Gal,** artist: unannounced, production: 10 days	**24.50**	**24.50**
☐ 1985	**Skeleton Crew,** artist: unannounced, production: 10 days	**24.50**	**24.50**
☐ 1985	**Roughin' It,** artist: unannounced, production: 10 days	**24.50**	**24.50**
☐ 1985	**Spanky's Pranks,** artist: unannounced, production: 10 days	**24.50**	**24.50**
☐ 1985	**Butch's Challenge,** artist: unannounced, production: 10 days	**24.50**	**24.50**
☐ 1985	**Darla's Debut,** artist: unannounced, production: 10 days	**24.50**	**24.50**
☐ 1985	**Pete's Pal,** artist: unannounced, production: 10 days	**24.50**	**24.50**

	Issue Price	Current Value

MAJESTIC BIRDS OF PREY

☐ **1983** **Golden Eagle,** artist: C. Ford Riley, production quantity 12,500 . . . .   **55.00**   **65.00**

☐ **1983** **Cooper's Hawk,** artist: C. Ford Riley, production quantity 12,500 . . . .   **55.00**   **65.00**

☐ **1983** **Great Horned Owl,** artist: C. Ford Riley, production quantity 12,500 . . . .   **55.00**   **65.00**

☐ **1984** **Bald Eagle,** artist: C. Ford Riley, production quantity 12,500 . . . .   **55.00**   **65.00**

☐ **1984** **Barred Owl,** artist: C. Ford Riley, production quantity 12,500 . . . .   **55.00**   **65.00**

☐ **1984** **Sparrow Hawk,** artist: C. Ford Riley, production quantity 12,500 . . . .   **55.00**   **65.00**

☐ **1984** **Peregrine Falcon,** artist: C. Ford Riley, production quantity 12,500 . . . .   **55.00**   **65.00**

☐ **1984** **Osprey,** artist: C. Ford Riley, production quantity 12,500 . . . .   **55.00**   **65.00**

MOTHER'S DAY SERIES

☐ **1983** **A Gift of Love,** artist: Thornton Utz, production: one year **27.50**   **45.00**

☐ **1983** **Mother's Helping Hand,** artist: Thornton Utz, production: one year **27.50**   **27.50**

☐ **1983** **Mother's Angel,** artist: Thornton Utz, production: one year **27.50**   **27.50**

NOBLE OWLS OF AMERICA

☐ **1986** **Morning Mist,** artist: J. Seerey-Lester, production quantity 15,000 . . . .   **45.00**   **45.00**

☐ **1987** **Prairie Sundown,** artist: J. Seerey-Lester, production quantity 15,000 . . . .   **45.00**   **45.00**

☐ **1987** **Winter Vigil,** artist: J. Seerey-Lester, production quantity 15,000 . . . .   **45.00**   **45.00**

☐ **1987** **Autumn Mist,** artist: J. Seerey-Lester, production quantity 15,000 . . . .   **45.00**   **45.00**

☐ **1987** **Dawn in the Willows,** artist: J. Seerey-Lester, production quantity 15,000 . . . .   **45.00**   **45.00**

PASSAGE TO CHINA

☐ **1983** **Empress of China,** artist: R. Massey, production quantity 15,000 . . . .   **55.00**   **55.00**

☐ **1983** **Alliance,** artist: R. Massey, production quantity 15,000 . . . .   **55.00**   **55.00**

☐ **1985** **Grand Turk,** artist: R. Massey, production quantity 15,000 . . . .   **55.00**   **55.00**

		Issue Price	Current Value
☐ 1985	**Sea Witch,** artist: R. Massey, production quantity 15,000	**55.00**	**55.00**
☐ 1985	**Flying Cloud,** artist: R. Massey, production quantity 15,000	**55.00**	**55.00**
☐ 1985	**Romance of the Seas,** artist: R. Massey, production quantity 15,000	**55.00**	**55.00**
☐ 1985	**Sea Serpent,** artist: R. Massey, production quantity 15,000	**55.00**	**55.00**
☐ 1985	**Challenge,** artist: R. Massey, production quantity 15,000	**55.00**	**55.00**

PORTRAITS OF CHILDHOOD SERIES

☐ 1981	**Butterfly Magic,** artist: Thornton Utz, production: 28 days	**24.95**	**45.00**
☐ 1982	**Sweet Dreams,** artist: Thornton Utz, production: 28 days	**24.95**	**30.00**
☐ 1983	**Turtle Talk,** artist: Thornton Utz, production: 28 days	**24.95**	**24.95**
☐ 1984	**Friends Forever,** artist: Thornton Utz, production: 28 days	**24.95**	**24.95**

PRECIOUS PORTRAITS

☐ 1987	**Sunbeam,** artist: B. P. Gutmann, production: 14 days	**24.50**	**24.50**

SPRINGTIME OF LIFE
(Reco International)

☐ 1985	**Teddy's Bathtime,** artist: Thornton Utz, production: 14 days	**29.50**	**29.50**
☐ 1985	**Just Like Mommy,** artist: Thornton Utz, production: 14 days	**29.50**	**29.50**
☐ 1985	**Among the Daffodils,** artist: Thornton Utz, production: 14 days	**29.50**	**29.50**
☐ 1985	**My Favorite Dolls,** artist: Thornton Utz, production: 14 days	**29.50**	**29.50**
☐ 1985	**Aunt Tillie's Hats,** artist: Thornton Utz, production: 14 days	**29.50**	**29.50**
☐ 1985	**Little Emily,** artist: Thornton Utz, production: 14 days	**29.50**	**29.50**
☐ 1985	**Granny's Boots,** artist: Thornton Utz, production: 14 days	**29.50**	**29.50**
☐ 1985	**My Masterpiece,** artist: Thornton Utz, production: 14 days	**29.50**	**29.50**

	Issue Price	Current Value

STARS OF THE CIRCUS

☐ **1983 Gunther Gebel-Williams,** artist: Franklin Moody, production limited **29.50 29.50**

STAR WARS

☐ **1987 Han Solo,** artist: Thomas Blackshear, production: 14 days **29.50 29.50**

THE STORY OF HEIDI SERIES

		Issue Price	Current Value
☐ 1981	**Heidi,** production quantity 14,750	**45.00**	**48.00**
☐ 1981	**Grandfather,** production quantity 14,750 ..	**45.00**	**48.00**
☐ 1981	**Grandmother,** production quantity 14,750 ..	**45.00**	**48.00**
☐ 1981	**Heidi and Peter,** production quantity 14,750	**45.00**	**48.00**
☐ 1982	**Kittens,** production quantity 14,750	**45.00**	**48.00**
☐ 1982	**Mountain Cure,** production quantity 14,750	**45.00**	**48.00**

THE STORY OF NOAH'S ARK SERIES

		Issue Price	Current Value
☐ 1981	**Two by Two ... Every Living Creature,** artist: Laetitia, production quantity 12,500 ...	**45.00**	**48.00**
☐ 1982	**In Divine Harmony,** artist: Laetitia, production quantity 12,500	**45.00**	**48.00**
☐ 1982	**Finally a Rainbow,** artist: Laetitia, production quantity 12,500	**45.00**	**48.00**
☐ 1982	**The Ark Beckons,** artist: Laetitia, production quantity 12,500	**45.00**	**48.00**

SUMMER DAYS OF CHILDHOOD

		Issue Price	Current Value
☐ 1983	**Mountain Friends,** artist: Thornton Utz, production: 10 days	**29.50**	**29.50**
☐ 1983	**Garden Magic,** artist: Thornton Utz, production: 10 days	**29.50**	**29.50**
☐ 1983	**Little Beachcomber,** artist: Thornton Utz, production: 10 days	**29.50**	**29.50**
☐ 1983	**Blowing Bubbles,** artist: Thornton Utz, production: 10 days	**29.50**	**29.50**
☐ 1983	**The Birthday Party,** artist: Thornton Utz, production: 10 days	**29.50**	**29.50**
☐ 1983	**Playing Doctor,** artist: Thornton Utz, production: 10 days	**29.50**	**29.50**
☐ 1983	**A Stolen Kiss,** artist: Thornton Utz, production: 10 days	**29.50**	**29.50**
☐ 1983	**Kitty's Bathtime,** artist: Thornton Utz, production: 10 days	**29.50**	**29.50**
☐ 1983	**Cooling Off,** artist: Thornton Utz, production: 10 days	**29.50**	**29.50**

		Issue Price	Current Value
☐ 1983	**First Customer,** artist: Thornton Utz, production: 10 days	**29.50**	**29.50**
☐ 1983	**A Jumping Contest,** artist: Thornton Utz, production: 10 days	**29.50**	**29.50**
☐ 1983	**Balloon Carnival,** artist: Thornton Utz, production: 10 days	**29.50**	**29.50**

TALE OF GENJI SERIES

☐ 1985	**Serene Autumn Moon,** artist: Shigekasu Hotta, production: 10 days	**45.00**	**45.00**
☐ 1985	**Dragon and Phoenix Boats,** artist: Shigekasu Hotta, production: 10 days	**45.00**	**45.00**
☐ 1985	**Romantic Duet,** artist: Shigekasu Hotta, production: 10 days	**45.00**	**45.00**
☐ 1985	**Waves of the Blue Ocean Dance,** artist: Shigekasu Hotta, production: 10 days	**45.00**	**45.00**
☐ 1985	**Evening Faces,** artist: Shigekasu Hotta, production: 10 days	**45.00**	**45.00**
☐ 1985	**The Archery Meet,** artist: Shigekasu Hotta, production: 10 days	**45.00**	**45.00**
☐ 1985	**Moon Viewing,** artist: Shigekasu Hotta, production: 10 days	**45.00**	**45.00**
☐ 1985	**The Table Game,** artist: Shigekasu Hotta, production: 10 days	**45.00**	**45.00**

TREASURED DAYS

☐ 1987	**Ashley,** artist: H. Bond, production: 14 days	**24.50**	**24.50**

TREASURES OF THE CHINESE
Mandarins Series

Note: The designs for this series are adaptations of art objects found in the National Palace Museum in Taipei, Taiwan.

☐ 1981	**The Bird of Paradise,** production quantity 2,500	**75.00**	**135.00**
☐ 1982	**The Guardians of Heaven,** production quantity 2,500	**75.00**	**105.00**
☐ 1982	**The Tree of Immortality,** production quantity 2,500	**75.00**	**95.00**
☐ 1982	**The Dragon of Eternity,** production quantity 2,500	**75.00**	**85.00**

SINGLE ISSUES	Issue Price	Current Value
☐ **1983 Princess Grace,** artist: Thornton Utz, production: 21 days	39.50	52.00

HAMILTON MINT

United States

KENNEDY SERIES

☐ **1974** Gold on pewter, production: one year	40.00	40.00
☐ **1974** Pewter, production: one year	25.00	40.00

PICASSO SERIES*
(Sculpted by Alfred Brunettin)

☐ **1972 Le Gourmet,** sterling silver, production quantity 5,000	125.00	125.00
☐ **1972 The Tragedy,** sterling silver, production quantity 5,000	125.00	125.00
☐ **1973 The Lovers,** sterling silver, production quantity 5,000	125.00	125.00

*This series was also produced in 18K gold in editions of only 51. Price: N/A.

SINGLE ISSUE

☐ **1971 St. Patrick,** artist: H. Alvin Sharpe, production quantity: N/A	75.00	75.00

HAMPTON HOUSE STUDIOS

SINGLE ISSUE

☐ **1977 Nancy Ward/Cherokee Nation,** artist: B. Hampton, production quantity 3,000	48.00	300.00

HANTAN PORCELAIN WORKS

China

CHINESE AND AMERICAN HISTORICAL
(China Trade Corporation)

☐ **1982 The Eagle and the Panda,** artist: Zhu Bohua, production quantity 10,000	195.00	215.00

HAVILAND

France

		Issue Price	Current Value
BICENTENNIAL SERIES			
☐ 1972	**Burning of the Gaspee,** artist: Remy Hetreau, production quantity 10,000	39.95	46.00
☐ 1973	**Boston Tea Party,** artist: Remy Hetreau, production quantity 10,000	39.95	42.00
☐ 1974	**Continental Congress,** artist: Remy Hetreau, production quantity 10,000	39.95	42.00
☐ 1975	**Paul Revere,** artist: Remy Hetreau, production quantity 10,000	39.95	51.00
☐ 1976	**The Declaration,** artist: Remy Hetreau, production quantity 10,000	39.95	46.00

CHRISTMAS SERIES

		Issue Price	Current Value
☐ 1970	**Partridge,** artist: Remy Hetreau, production quantity 30,000	25.00	110.00
☐ 1971	**Two Turtle Doves,** artist: Remy Hetreau, production quantity 30,000	25.00	45.00
☐ 1972	**Three French Hens,** artist: Remy Hetreau, production quantity 30,000	27.50	40.00
☐ 1973	**Four Calling Birds,** artist: Remy Hetreau, production quantity 30,000	28.50	40.00
☐ 1974	**Five Golden Rings,** artist: Remy Hetreau, production quantity 30,000	30.00	35.00
☐ 1975	**Six Geese A-Laying,** artist: Remy Hetreau, production quantity 30,000	32.50	30.00
☐ 1976	**Seven Swans,** artist: Remy Hetreau, production quantity 30,000	38.00	30.00
☐ 1977	**Eight Maids,** artist: Remy Hetreau, production quantity 30,000	40.00	45.00
☐ 1978	**Nine Ladies Dancing,** artist: Remy Hetreau, production quantity 30,000	45.00	45.00
☐ 1979	**Ten Lords A-leaping,** artist: Remy Hetreau, production quantity 30,000	50.00	50.00
☐ 1980	**Eleven Pipers Piping,** artist: Remy Hetreau, production quantity 30,000	55.00	55.00
☐ 1981	**Twelve Drummers,** artist: Remy Hetreau, production quantity 30,000	60.00	60.00

FLEURS ET RUBANS SERIES

☐ 1981	**Orchidee,** production quantity 5,000	120.00	120.00
☐ 1981	**Lys,** production quantity 7,500	120.00	120.00

		Issue Price	Current Value
☐ 1981	**Pivoine,** production quantity 7,500	120.00	120.00
☐ 1981	**Pavot (Poppy),** production quantity 7,500 ..	120.00	120.00
☐ 1981	**Ail Sauvage (Wild Garlic),** production quantity 7,500	120.00	120.00
☐ 1982	**Hibiscus,** production quantity 7,500	120.00	120.00

FRENCH COLLECTION
MOTHER'S DAY SERIES

☐ 1973	**Breakfast,** artist: Remy Hetreau, production quantity 10,000	29.95	28.00
☐ 1974	**The Wash,** artist: Remy Hetreau, production quantity 10,000	29.95	22.00
☐ 1975	**In the Park,** artist: Remy Hetreau, production quantity 10,000	30.00	32.00
☐ 1976	**To Market,** artist: Remy Hetreau, production quantity 10,000	38.00	38.00
☐ 1977	**Wash Before Dinner,** artist: Remy Hetreau, production quantity 10,000	38.00	38.00
☐ 1978	**An Evening at Home,** artist: Remy Hetreau, production quantity 10,000	40.00	42.00
☐ 1979	**Happy Mother's Day,** artist: Remy Hetreau, production quantity 10,000	30.00	43.00
☐ 1980	**A Child and His Animals,** artist: Remy Hetreau, production quantity 10,000	55.00	55.00

HISTORICAL SERIES

☐ 1968	**Martha Washington,** production quantity 2,500	35.00	80.00
☐ 1969	**Lincoln,** production quantity 2,500	100.00	70.00
☐ 1970	**Grant,** production quantity 3,000	100.00	70.00
☐ 1971	**Hayes,** production quantity 2,500	100.00	70.00

1001 ARABIAN NIGHTS SERIES

☐ 1979	**Magic Horse,** artist: Liliane Tellier, production quantity 5,000	54.50	60.00
☐ 1980	**Aladdin and His Lamp,** artist: Liliane Tellier, production quantity 5,000	54.50	60.00
☐ 1981	**Scheherazade,** artist: Liliane Tellier, production quantity 5,000	54.50	55.00
☐ 1982	**Sinbad the Sailer,** artist: Liliane Tellier, production quantity 5,000	54.50	55.00

		Issue Price	Current Value

THEATRE DES SAISONS SERIES
(Royal Cornwall)

		Issue Price	Current Value
☐ 1978	**Spring,** production quantity 5,000	120.00	140.00
☐ 1978	**Summer,** production quantity 5,000	120.00	140.00
☐ 1978	**Autumn,** production quantity 5,000	120.00	140.00
☐ 1978	**Winter,** production quantity 5,000	120.00	140.00

TRADITIONAL CHRISTMAS CARDS SERIES

☐ 1986	**Deck the Halls,** artist: Elisa Stone, production: 2,000	75.00	75.00

VISIT FROM SAINT NICHOLAS SERIES

☐ 1980	**Night Before Christmas,** production: one year	55.00	58.00
☐ 1981	**Children Were Nestled,** production quantity 5,000	60.00	63.00
☐ 1982	**For You, Santa,** production quantity 5,000	60.00	62.00
☐ 1982	**When What to My Wondering Eyes . . .,** production quantity 1,500	60.00	65.00
☐ 1985	**Happy Christmas to All,** artist: Loretta Jones, production quantity N/A	60.00	60.00

HAVILAND AND PARLON

France

CHRISTMAS MADONNAS SERIES

☐ 1972	**Madonna and Child,** artist: Raphael, production quantity 5,000	35.00	80.00
☐ 1973	**Madonnina,** artist: Feruzzi, production quantity 5,000	40.00	100.00
☐ 1974	**Cowper Madonna and Child,** artist: Raphael, production quantity 5,000	42.50	60.00
☐ 1975	**Madonna and Child,** artist: Murillo, production quantity 5,000	42.50	45.00
☐ 1976	**Madonna and Child,** artist: Botticelli, production quantity 5,000	45.00	45.00
☐ 1977	**Madonna and Child,** artist: Bellini, production quantity 5,000	48.00	55.00
☐ 1978	**Madonna and Child,** artist: Fra Filippo Lippi, production quantity 7,500	48.00	70.00
☐ 1979	**Madonna of the Eucharist,** artist: Botticelli, production quantity 7,500	49.50	100.00

	Issue Price	Current Value

MOTHER'S DAY SERIES

☐ 1975 **Mother and Child,** production quantity
15,000 .... 37.50 81.00
☐ 1976 **Pinky and Baby,** production quantity 15,000 42.50 32.00
☐ 1977 **Amy and Snoopy,** production quantity 15,000 45.00 38.00

SONGBIRDS SERIES

☐ 1980 **Cardinals,** artist: Patti Canaris, hand-
numbered, production quantity 5,000 ..... 65.00 90.00
☐ 1981 **Blue Birds,** artist: Patti Canaris, hand-
numbered, production quantity 5,000 ..... 70.00 70.00
☐ 1982 **Orioles,** artist: Patti Canaris, hand-
numbered, production quantity 5,000 ..... 70.00 70.00
☐ 1982 **Gold Finches,** artist: Patti Canaris, hand-
numbered, production quantity 5,000 ..... 70.00 70.00

TAPESTRY SERIES I*

☐ 1971 **Unicorn in Captivity,** production quantity
10,000 .... 35.00 130.00
☐ 1972 **Start of the Hunt,** production quantity 10,000 35.00 60.00
☐ 1973 **Chase of the Unicorn,** production quantity
10,000 .... 35.00 100.00
☐ 1974 **End of the Hunt,** production quantity 10,000 37.50 90.00
☐ 1975 **Unicorn Surrounded,** production quantity
10,000 .... 40.00 50.00
☐ 1976 **Brought to the Castle,** production quantity
10,000 .... 42.50 45.00

*These plates are reproductions of medieval tapestries from the collection at The Cloisters in New York City.

TAPESTRY SERIES II

☐ 1977 **Lady and Unicorn,** production quantity
20,000 .... 45.00 60.00
☐ 1978 **Sight,** production quantity 20,000 .... 45.00 55.00
☐ 1979 **Sound,** production quantity 20,000 .... 47.50 55.00
☐ 1980 **Touch,** production quantity 15,000 .... 52.50 60.00
☐ 1981 **Scent,** production quantity 10,000 .... 59.00 60.00
☐ 1982 **Taste,** production quantity 10,000 .... 59.00 60.00

SINGLE RELEASES

☐ 1971 **China Trade Plate** 30.00 20.00
☐ 1971 **Empress** 60.00 66.00

		Issue Price	Current Value
☐ 1972	**Meissen Plate**	30.00	20.00
☐ 1973	**Peaceable Kingdom,** artist: Nan Lee, production quantity 5,000	30.00	63.00
☐ 1977	**Astrological Man,** production quantity 5,000	50.00	53.00
☐ 1978	**Scarab,** production quantity 2,500	100.00	100.00

HEINRICH PORZELLAN

Germany

FAIRIES OF THE FIELDS AND FLOWERS

☐ 1982	**Ragged Robin,** artist: Cicely Mary Barker, production: 10 days	49.50	50.50
☐ 1982	**The Willow Fairy,** artist: Cicely Mary Barker, production: 10 days	49.50	50.50
☐ 1983	**Elderberry Fairy,** artist: Cicely Mary Barker, production: less than one year	49.50	50.50
☐ 1983	**Vetch Fairy,** artist: Cicely Mary Barker, production: less than one year	49.50	50.50
☐ 1984	**Narcissus,** artist: Cicely Mary Barker, production: less than one year	49.50	50.50
☐ 1984	**Nasturtium,** artist: Cicely Mary Barker, production: less than one year	49.50	50.50

FLOWER FAIRY SERIES

☐ 1979	**The Lavender Fairy,** artist: Cicely Mary Barker, production: 21 days	35.00	48.00
☐ 1980	**The Sweet Pea Fairy,** artist: Cicely Mary Barker, production: 21 days	35.00	35.00
☐ 1980	**The Candy Tuft Fairy,** artist: Cicely Mary Barker, production: 21 days	35.00	35.00
☐ 1981	**The Heliotrope Fairy,** artist: Cicely Mary Barker, production: 21 days	35.00	35.00
☐ 1981	**The Blackthorn Fairy,** artist: Cicely Mary Barker, production: 21 days	35.00	35.00
☐ 1981	**The Apple Blossom Fairy,** artist: Cicely Mary Barker, production: 21 days	35.00	35.00

FLOWER FAIRY II

☐ 1985	**Columbine,** artist: Cicely Mary Barker, production: 21 days	35.00	35.00
☐ 1985	**Cornflower,** artist: Cicely Mary Barker, production: 21 days .... / .	35.00	35.00

		Issue Price	Current Value
☐ 1985	**Mallow,** artist: Cicely Mary Barker, production: 21 days	35.00	35.00
☐ 1985	**Black Medick,** artist: Cicely Mary Barker, production: 21 days	35.00	35.00
☐ 1985	**Canterbury Bell,** artist: Cicely Mary Barker, production: 21 days	35.00	35.00
☐ 1985	**Fuchsia,** artist: Cicely Mary Barker, production: 21 days	35.00	35.00

RUSSIAN FAIRY TALES SERIES

		Issue Price	Current Value
☐ 1980	**The Snow Maiden,** artist: Boris Zvorykin, production quantity 27,500	70.00	190.00
☐ 1980	**The Snow Maiden at the Court of the Tsar,** artist: Boris Zvorykin, production quantity 27,500	70.00	125.00
☐ 1980	**The Snow Maiden and Lel the Shepherd Boy,** artist: Boris Zvorykin, production quantity 27,500	70.00	125.00
☐ 1981	**Vassilissa and Her Stepsisters,** artist: Boris Zvorykin, production quantity 27,500	70.00	125.00
☐ 1981	**The Red Knight,** artist: Boris Zvorykin, production quantity 27,500	70.00	85.00
☐ 1981	**Vassilissa Is Presented to the Tsar,** artist: Boris Zvorykin, production quantity 27,500	70.00	85.00
☐ 1982	**In Search of the Firebird,** artist: Boris Zvorykin, production quantity 27,500	70.00	70.00
☐ 1982	**Ivan and Tsarevna on the Grey Wolf,** artist: Boris Zvorykin, production quantity 27,500	70.00	70.00
☐ 1982	**Ivan and Tsarevna Elena the Fair,** artist: Boris Zvorykin, production quantity 27,500	70.00	70.00
☐ 1982	**Maria Morevna and Tsarevich Ivan,** artist: Boris Zvorykin, production quantity 27,500	70.00	70.00
☐ 1983	**Koshchey Carries Off Maria Morevna,** artist: Boris Zvorykin, production quantity 27,500	70.00	70.00
☐ 1983	**Ivan and the Beautiful Castle,** artist: Boris Zvorykin, production quantity 27,500	70.00	70.00

HEIRLOOM TRADITIONS

United States

CINEMA CLASSICS

		Issue Price	Current Value
☐ 1985	**High Noon,** artist: Susan Edison, production quantity 10,000	35.00	35.00

		Issue Price	Current Value
☐ 1986	**Young at Heart,** artist: Susan Edison, production quantity 10,000	**35.00**	**35.00**
☐ 1986	**Rio Grande,** artist: Susan Edison, production quantity 10,000	**35.00**	**35.00**

HOLLYWOOD'S VIEW OF CHRISTMAS

☐ 1986	**Charles Dickens' Christmas Carol,** artist: Susan Edison, production quantity 10,000	**35.00**	**35.00**

SINGLE ISSUES

☐ 1985	**It's a Wonderful Life,** artist: N/A, production quantity: N/A	**35.00**	**35.00**
☐ 1986	**Varga,** artist: Alberto Vargas, production quantity 10,000	**45.00**	**50.00**
☐ 1986	**Barry Manilow,** artist: N/A, production quantity 20,000	**35.00**	**35.00**
☐ 1986	**Miss America, 1927,** artist: Louis Icart, production quantity 7,500	**50.00**	**65.00**

HIBEL STUDIOS

Germany

ARTE OVALE SERIES

☐ 1980	**Cobalt Blue Takara,** artist: Edna Hibel, production quantity 1,000	**595.00**	**1,750.00**
☐ 1980	**Gold Takara,** artist: Edna Hibel, production quantity 300	**1,000.00**	**3,300.00**
☐ 1980	**Porcellana Blanco Takara,** artist: Edna Hibel, production quantity 700	**450.00**	**950.00**
☐ 1984	**Cobalt Blue Tauro-Kun,** artist: Edna Hibel, production quantity 1,000	**595.00**	**650.00**
☐ 1984	**Gold Tauro-Kun,** artist: Edna Hibel, production quantity 300	**1,000.00**	**1,700.00**
☐ 1984	**Porcellana Blanco Tauro-Kun,** artist: Edna Hibel, production quantity 700	**450.00**	**495.00**

CHRISTMAS ANNUAL SERIES

☐ 1985	**Angel's Message,** artist: Edna Hibel, production: one year	**55.00**	**55.00**
☐ 1985	**Gift of the Magi,** artist: Edna Hibel, production: one year	**55.00**	**55.00**

		Issue Price	Current Value
☐ 1987	Flight into Egypt, artist: Edna Hibel, production: one year	55.00	55.00

DAVID SERIES

		Issue Price	Current Value
☐ 1979	The Wedding of David and Bathsheba, artist: Edna Hibel, production quantity 5,000	250.00	300.00
☐ 1980	David, Bathsheba and Solomon, artist: Edna Hibel, production quantity 5,000	275.00	300.00
☐ 1981	David the King, artist: Edna Hibel, production quantity 5,000.....................	275.00	300.00
☐ 1983	Bathsheba, artist: Edna Hibel, production quantity 10,000.........................	275.00	300.00

FAMOUS WOMEN AND CHILDREN SERIES

		Issue Price	Current Value
☐ 1980	Pharaoh's Daughter and Moses, artist: Edna Hibel, production quantity 2,500	350.00	360.00
☐ 1980	Pharaoh's Daughter and Moses, artist: Edna Hibel, production quantity 500	350.00	1000.00
☐ 1982	Cornelia and Her Jewels, artist: Edna Hibel, oriental gold, production quantity 2,500 ...	350.00	350.00
☐ 1982	Cornelia and Her Jewels, artist: Edna Hibel, cobalt blue, production quantity 500	350.00	700.00
☐ 1982	Anna and the Children of the King of Siam, artist: Edna Hibel, oriental gold, production quantity 2,500.........................	450.00	450.00
☐ 1982	Anna and the Children of the King of Siam, artist: Edna Hibel, cobalt blue, production quantity 500	1200.00	1200.00
☐ 1984	Mozart and the Empress Maria Theresa, artist: Edna Hibel, oriental gold, production quantity 2,500.........................	350.00	350.00
☐ 1984	Mozart and the Empress Maria Theresa, artist: Edna Hibel, cobalt blue, production quantity 500	1200.00	1200.00

FLOWER GIRL SERIES

		Issue Price	Current Value
☐ 1986	Lily, artist: Edna Hibel, production quantity 15,000	79.00	79.00
☐ 1986	Iris, artist: Edna Hibel, production quantity 15,000	79.00	79.00
☐ 1987	Rose, artist: Edna Hibel, production quantity 15,000	79.00	79.00

Angel's Message, artist: Edna Hibel.

Gift of the Magi, artist: Edna Hibel.

Flight Into Egypt, artist: Edna Hibel.

Lily, artist: Edna Hibel.

Iris, artist: Edna Hibel.

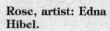Rose, artist: Edna
Hibel.

		Issue Price	Current Value

GERMAN SECTION, INTERNATIONAL MOTHER LOVE SERIES

		Issue Price	Current Value
☐ 1980	**Gesa und Kinder,** artist: Edna Hibel, production quantity 5,000	**195.00**	**195.00**
☐ 1981	**Alexandra und Kinder,** artist: Edna Hibel, production quantity 5,000	**195.00**	**195.00**
☐ 1984	**Yvette avec Ses Infants,** artist: Edna Hibel, production quantity 5,000	**195.00**	**195.00**

MUSEUM COMMEMORATIVE SERIES

		Issue Price	Current Value
☐ 1977	**The Flower Girl of Provence,** artist: Edna Hibel, production quantity 12,750	**375.00**	**400.00**
☐ 1980	**Diana,** artist: Edna Hibel, production quantity 5,000	**350.00**	**375.00**

THE WORLD I LOVE SERIES

		Issue Price	Current Value
☐ 1981	**Leah's Family,** artist: Edna Hibel, production quantity 17,500	**85.00**	**175.00**
☐ 1982	**Kaylin,** artist: Edna Hibel, production quantity 17,500	**85.00**	**175.00**
☐ 1983	**Edna's Music,** artist: Edna Hibel, production quantity 17,500	**85.00**	**125.00**
☐ 1983	**O, Hana,** artist: Edna Hibel, production quantity 17,500	**85.00**	**175.00**

Alexandra und Kinder, artist: Edna Hibel.

Yvette avec Ses Infants,
artist: Edna Hibel.

TO LIFE ANNUAL SERIES	Issue Price	Current Value
☐ 1986 **Golden's Child,** artist: Edna Hibel, production quantity 5,000	**99.00**	**99.00**

Golden's Child, artist:
Edna Hibel.

Giselle, artist: Edna Hibel.

TRIBUTE TO ALL CHILDREN SERIES	Issue Price	Current Value
☐ **1984 Giselle,** artist: Edna Hibel, production quantity 19,500	**55.00**	**55.00**
☐ **1984 Gerard,** artist: Edna Hibel, production quantity 19,500	**55.00**	**55.00**

Gerard, artist: Edna Hibel.

		Issue Price	Current Value
☐ **1984**	**Wendy,** artist: Edna Hibel, production quantity 19,500	55.00	55.00
☐ **1984**	**Todd,** artist: Edna Hibel, production quantity 19,500	55.00	55.00

HISTORIC PROVIDENCE MINT

United States

ALICE IN WONDERLAND SERIES

☐ **1986**	**The Tea Party,** artist: George Terp, production: 45 days	29.50	29.50
☐ **1986**	**The Caterpillar,** artist: George Terp, production: 45 days	29.50	29.50
☐ **1986**	**The White Knight,** artist: George Terp, production: 45 days	29.50	29.50
☐ **1986**	**The Duchess and Cook,** artist: George Terp, production: 45 days	29.50	29.50
☐ **1986**	**Off with Their Heads!,** artist: George Terp, production: 45 days	29.50	29.50
☐ **1986**	**Red and White Queens,** artist: George Terp, production: 45 days	29.50	29.50
☐ **1986**	**The White Rabbit,** artist: George Terp, production: 45 days	29.50	29.50
☐ **1986**	**Talking Flowers,** artist: George Terp, production: 45 days	29.50	29.50
☐ **1986**	**Tweedledee-Tweedledum,** artist: George Terp, production: 45 days	29.50	29.50
☐ **1986**	**Walrus and Carpenter,** artist: George Terp, production: 45 days	29.50	29.50
☐ **1986**	**Lion and Unicorn,** artist: George Terp, production: 45 days	29.50	29.50
☐ **1986**	**Humpty Dumpty,** artist: George Terp, production: 45 days	29.50	29.50

AMERICA THE BEAUTIFUL SERIES

☐ **1981**	**Spacious Skies,** artist: Ben Essenburg, production quantity 17,500	37.50	38.50
☐ **1981**	**Amber Waves of Grain,** artist: Ben Essenburg, production quantity 17,500	37.50	38.50
☐ **1981**	**Purple Mountains Majesty,** artist: Ben Essenburg, production quantity 17,500	37.50	38.50

The White Rabbit,
artist: George Terp.

Talking Flowers, artist:
George Terp.

Tweedledee–
Tweedledum, artist:
George Terp.

Walrus and Carpenter, artist: George Terp.

Lion and Unicorn, artist: George Terp.

Humpty Dumpty, artist: George Terp.

Spacious Skies, artist: Ben Essenburg.

Amber Waves of Grain, artist: Ben Essenburg.

Purple Mountains Majesty, artist: Ben Essenburg.

		Issue Price	Current Value
☐ 1981	**God Shed His Grace,** artist: Ben Essenburg, production quantity 17,500	**37.50**	**38.50**
☐ 1981	**Crown Thy Good with Brotherhood,** artist: Ben Essenburg, production quantity 12,500	**37.50**	**38.50**
☐ 1981	**From Sea to Shining Sea,** artist: Ben Essenburg, production quantity 17,500	**37.50**	**38.50**

CHILDREN OF THE SEASONS SERIES

☐ 1980	**Children of Spring,** production quantity 3,000	**107.50**	**110.00**

LIL' PEDDLERS SERIES

☐ 1986	**Forget Me Nots,** artist: Lee Dubin, production quantity: unannounced	**29.50**	**29.50**
☐ 1986	**Poppin' Corn,** artist: Lee Dubin, production quantity: unannounced	**29.50**	**29.50**
☐ 1986	**Balloons 'n Things,** artist: Lee Dubin, production quantity: unannounced	**29.50**	**29.50**
☐ 1986	**Penny Candy,** artist: Lee Dubin, production quantity: unannounced	**29.50**	**29.50**
☐ 1986	**Today's Catch,** artist: Lee Dubin, production quantity: unannounced	**29.50**	**29.50**
☐ 1986	**Just Picked,** artist: Lee Dubin, production quantity: unannounced	**29.50**	**29.50**
☐ 1986	**Cobblestone Deli,** artist: Lee Dubin, production quantity: unannounced	**29.50**	**29.50**
☐ 1986	**Chimney Sweep,** artist: Lee Dubin, production quantity: unannounced	**29.50**	**29.50**
☐ 1986	**Apple a Day,** artist: Lee Dubin, production quantity: unannounced	**29.50**	**29.50**
☐ 1986	**Extra, Extra,** artist: Lee Dubin, production quantity: unannounced	**29.50**	**29.50**
☐ 1986	**Open Fresh,** artist: Lee Dubin, production quantity: unannounced	**29.50**	**29.50**
☐ 1986	**Coolin' Off,** artist: Lee Dubin, production quantity: unannounced	**29.50**	**29.50**

THE VANISHING AMERICAN BARN SERIES

☐ 1983	**Log Barn,** artist: Harris Hien, production quantity 14,500........................	**39.50**	**39.50**
☐ 1983	**Appalachian Barn,** artist: Harris Hien, production quantity 14,500.................	**39.50**	**39.50**

**God Shed His Grace,
artist: Ben Essenburg.**

**Crown Thy Good with
Brotherhood, artist: Ben
Essenburg.**

**From Sea to Shining
Sea, artist: Ben
Essenburg.**

Forget Me Nots, artist: Lee Dubin.

Poppin' Corn, artist: Lee Dubin.

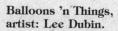

Balloons 'n Things, artist: Lee Dubin.

Extra, Extra, artist: Lee Dubin.

Open Fresh, artist: Lee Dubin.

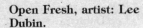

Coolin' Off, artist: Lee Dubin.

Log Barn, artist: Harris
Hien.

		Issue Price	Current Value
☐ 1983	**Bucks County Barn,** artist: Harris Hien, production quantity 14,500	39.50	39.50
☐ 1983	**Round Barn,** artist: Harris Hien, production quantity 14,500	39.50	39.50
☐ 1983	**Lancaster Barn,** artist: Harris Hien, production quantity 14,500	39.50	39.50

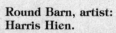

Round Barn, artist:
Harris Hien.

New England Barn,
artist: Harris Hien.

Thatched Barn, artist:
Harris Hien.

Southern Tobacco Farm,
artist: Harris Hien.

		Issue Price	Current Value
☐ 1983	**Victorian Barn,** artist: Harris Hien, production quantity 14,500	39.50	39.50
☐ 1983	**New England Barn,** artist: Harris Hien, production quantity 14,500	39.50	39.50
☐ 1983	**Thatched Barn,** artist: Harris Hien, production quantity 14,500	39.50	39.50
☐ 1983	**Hudson River Barn,** artist: Harris Hien, production quantity 14,500	39.50	39.50
☐ 1983	**Southern Tobacco Farm,** artist: Harris Hien, production quantity 14,500	39.50	39.50
☐ 1983	**Forebay Barn,** artist: Harris Hien, production quantity 14,500	39.50	39.50
☐ 1983	**Connected Barn,** artist: Harris Hien, production quantity 14,500	39.50	39.50

SINGLE RELEASE

☐ 1979	**The Children's Year,** production quantity 3,000	95.00	96.00

HORNSEA

Great Britain

CHRISTMAS SERIES

☐ 1979	**C—Nativity,** production quantity 10,000 ..	24.00	50.50
☐ 1980	**H—Mary and Child,** production quantity 10,000	28.00	50.50
☐ 1981	**R—Three Wisemen,** production quantity 10,000	28.00	50.50

HOUSE OF GLOBAL ART

United States

AMERICAN HERITAGE SERIES

☐ 1979	**Freedom and Justice Soaring,** artist: Gunther Granget, production quantity 15,000	100.00	100.00
☐ 1980	**Wild and Free,** artist: Gunther Granget, production quantity 10,000	120.00	120.00
☐ 1981	**Where Buffalo Roam,** artist: Gunther Granget, production quantity 5,000	125.00	125.00

		Issue Price	Current Value
ANNUAL CRYSTAL SERIES			
☐ 1978	**Praying Girl,** production: one year	45.00	41.00
☐ 1979	**Praying Boy,** production: one year	50.00	30.00
☐ 1980	**Praying Angel,** production quantity 15,000	50.00	54.00
☐ 1981	**Girl with Teddy Bears,** production quantity 10,000	50.00	52.00
BAVARIAN FOREST SERIES			
☐ 1980	**Owls,** production quantity 7,500	150.00	150.00
☐ 1981	**Deer,** production quantity 7,500	150.00	150.00

BLUE-BUTTON TRAINS
CHRISTMAS SERIES

☐ 1983	**By the Fireplace,** artist: Helen Nyce, production quantity 10,000	30.00	30.00
☐ 1983	**Down the Stairs,** artist: Helen Nyce, production quantity 10,000	30.00	30.00

CHRISTMAS MORNING IN DINGLE
DELL SERIES

☐ 1983	**Billie Bump's Christmas,** artist: Grace G. Drayton, production quantity 19,000 ...\...	30.00	30.00
☐ 1983	**Dolly Celebrates Christmas,** artist: Grace G. Drayton, production quantity 10,000	30.00	30.00

DOLLY DINGLE WORLD TRAVELER

☐ 1982	**Dolly Dingle Visits Germany,** artist: Grace G. Drayton, production quantity 10,000 ...	30.00	30.00
☐ 1982	**Dolly Dingle Visits Italy,** artist: Grace G. Drayton, production quantity 10,000	30.00	30.00
☐ 1982	**Dolly Dingle Visits Holland,** artist: Grace G. Drayton, production quantity 10,000	30.00	30.00
☐ 1982	**Dolly Dingle Visits Spain,** artist: Grace G. Drayton, production quantity 10,000	30.00	30.00
☐ 1982	**Dolly Dingle Visits Scotland,** artist: Grace G. Drayton, production quantity 10,000	30.00	30.00
☐ 1982	**Dolly Dingle Visits France,** artist: Grace G. Drayton, production quantity 10,000	30.00	30.00

ENGLISH COUNTRYSIDE
CATS COLLECTION

☐ 1983	**James,** artist: Sharon Jervis, production quantity 10,000	35.00	35.00

		Issue Price	Current Value
☐ 1983	**Henry,** artist: Sharon Jervis, production quantity 10,000	35.00	35.00
☐ 1983	**Lily,** artist: Sharon Jervis, production quantity 10,000	35.00	35.00
☐ 1983	**Lucy,** artist: Sharon Jervis, production quantity 10,000	35.00	35.00

HOYLE PRODUCTS

United States

BYGONE DAYS SERIES

☐ 1983	**Breakfast with Teddy,** artist: Jessie Wilcox Smith, production quantity 12,500	35.00	35.00
☐ 1983	**A Flower Basket,** artist: Jessie Wilcox Smith, production quantity 12,500	35.00	35.00

FAMILY CIRCUS CHRISTMAS SERIES

☐ 1980	**Christmas,** artist: Bil Keane, production quantity 5,000	25.00	25.00
☐ 1981	**Christmas,** artist: Bil Keane, production quantity 5,000	30.00	30.00

GOTHIC ROMANCE SERIES

☐ 1982	**Moonlight Romance,** artist: Jondar, production quantity 5,000	30.00	30.00

HILDA SERIES

☐ 1981	**Toasting Marshmallows,** production quantity 5,000	25.00	25.00

MOTHER'S DAY SERIES

☐ 1980	**Mother's Day,** artist: Bil Keane, production quantity 5,000	25.00	25.00

NORMAN ROCKWELL CLOWNS SERIES

☐ 1977	**The Runaway,** artist: Norman Rockwell, production quantity 7,500	45.00	76.00
☐ 1978	**It's Your Move,** artist: Norman Rockwell, production quantity 7,500	45.00	63.00
☐ 1979	**The Understudy,** artist: Norman Rockwell, production quantity 7,500	45.00	46.00

	Issue Price	Current Value
☐ 1980 **The Idol,** artist: Norman Rockwell, production quantity 7,500	45.00	46.00

NORMAN ROCKWELL
SALESMAN SERIES

	Issue Price	Current Value
☐ 1977 **The Traveling Salesman,** artist: Norman Rockwell, production quantity 7,500	35.00	36.00
☐ 1978 **The Country Pedlar,** artist: Norman Rockwell, production quantity 7,500	40.00	46.00
☐ 1979 **The Horse Trader,** artist: Norman Rockwell, production quantity 7,500	40.00	42.00
☐ 1980 **The Expert Salesman,** artist: Norman Rockwell, production quantity 7,500	45.00	46.00

NOSTALGIA SERIES

	Issue Price	Current Value
☐ 1981 **Pepsi Cola Girl,** production quantity 5,000	25.00	65.00
☐ 1982 **Olympia Girl,** production quantity 5,000 . .	30.00	30.00
☐ 1982 **Savannah Beer Girl,** production quantity 5,000	30.00	30.00
☐ 1982 **Dr. Pepper Girl,** production quantity 5,000	30.00	30.00

NOSTALGIA—CHILDREN SERIES

	Issue Price	Current Value
☐ 1983 **Pear's Soap Ad,** production quantity 12,500	35.00	35.00

NOSTALGIA MAGAZINE
COVERS SERIES

	Issue Price	Current Value
☐ 1983 **Ladies' Home Journal,** artist: H. Hayden, production quantity 12,500	35.00	35.00

RARE ROCKWELL SERIES

	Issue Price	Current Value
☐ 1980 **Mrs. O'Leary's Cow,** artist: Norman Rockwell, production quantity 7,500	30.00	30.00
☐ 1981 **Come and Get It,** artist: Norman Rockwell, production quantity 7,500	30.00	30.00

REMEMBER WHEN SERIES

	Issue Price	Current Value
☐ 1982 **A Surprise for Kitty,** artist: M. Humphrey, production quantity 10,000	30.00	30.00
☐ 1982 **Washday,** artist: M. Humphrey, production quantity 10,000	30.00	30.00
☐ 1983 **Playing Grandmother,** artist: M. Humphrey, production quantity 10,000	30.00	30.00

		Issue Price	Current Value
☐ 1983	**The Physician,** artist: M. Humphrey, production quantity 10,000	30.00	30.00

WESTERN SERIES

☐ 1977	**Sharing an Apple,** production quantity 5,000	35.00	35.00
☐ 1978	**Split Decision,** production quantity 5,000 ..	35.00	35.00
☐ 1979	**Hiding Out,** production quantity 5,000	35.00	35.00
☐ 1980	**In Trouble,** production quantity 5,000	35.00	35.00

WILDERNESS WINGS SERIES

☐ 1978	**Gliding In,** artist: David Maass, production quantity 5,000	35.00	66.00
☐ 1979	**Takeoff,** production quantity 5,000	40.00	53.00
☐ 1980	**Joining Up,** production quantity 5,000	45.00	48.00
☐ 1981	**Canvasbacks,** production quantity 5,000 ...	47.50	50.00
☐ 1982	**Moment of Rest,** artist: David Maass, production quantity 5,000	30.00	30.00
☐ 1983	**Mourning Doves,** artist: David Maass, production quantity 5,000	30.00	30.00

WINGS OF THE WILD SERIES

☐ 1982	**Cinnamon Teal,** artist: David Maass, production quantity 5,000	30.00	32.00
☐ 1982	**Moment of Rest,** artist: David Maass, production quantity 5,000	30.00	32.00
☐ 1983	**Mourning Doves,** artist: David Maass, production quantity 5,000	30.00	32.00

HUDSON PEWTER

United States

A CHILD'S CHRISTMAS SERIES

☐ 1979	**Littlest Angels,** production quantity 10,000	35.00	37.00
☐ 1980	**Heaven's Christmas Tree,** production quantity 10,000	42.50	45.00

AMERICA'S SAILING SHIPS SERIES

☐ 1979	**U.S.S. Constitution,** production quantity 5,000	35.00	36.00

	Issue Price	Current Value
MOTHER'S DAY SERIES		
☐ **1979 Cherished,** production quantity 10,000	**15.00**	**35.00**
SONGBIRDS OF THE FOUR SEASONS SERIES		
☐ **1979 Hummingbird,** production quantity 7,500 ..	**35.00**	**36.00**
SINGLE RELEASE		
☐ **1976 Bicentennial**	**42.00**	**46.00**
'TWAS THE NIGHT BEFORE CHRISTMAS SERIES		
☐ **1982 Not a Creature Was Stirring,** artist: Andrea Hallis, production quantity 10,000	**47.50**	**48.50**

HUTSCHENREUTHER

Germany

ALLEGRO ENSEMBLE		
☐ **1977 Allegro,** artist: Edna Hibel, production quantity 7,500		
☐ **1978 Flutist,** artist: Edna Hibel, production quantity 7,500		
Set of two	**120.00**	**140.00**
ARZBERG		
☐ **1986 Bodo and the Boat,** artist: K. Berger, production: open	**47.50**	**47.50**
BIRDS OF PARADISE SERIES		
☐ **1981 Blue Bird of Paradise,** artist: Ole Winther, production quantity 10,000	**175.00**	**175.00**
☐ **1981 Raggis Great Bird of Paradise,** artist: Ole Winther, production quantity 10,000	**175.00**	**175.00**
BIRTH PLATES SERIES		
☐ **1978 Birth Plate,** artist: Ole Winther, production quantity 10,000	**165.00**	**165.00**

CHRISTMAS SERIES

		Issue Price	Current Value
☐ 1978	**Christmas,** artist: Ole Winther, production quantity 2,000	260.00	260.00
☐ 1979	**Christmas,** artist: Ole Winther, production quantity 2,500	295.00	295.00
☐ 1980	**Christmas,** artist: Ole Winther, production: one year	360.00	360.00
☐ 1981	**Christmas,** artist: Ole Winther, production: one year	400.00	400.00
☐ 1982	**Christmas Concerto,** artist: Ole Winther, production: one year	400.00	400.00
☐ 1983	**The Annunciation,** artist: Ole Winther, production: one year	135.00	135.00
☐ 1984	**Holy Night,** artist: Ole Winther, production: one year	135.00	135.00

COUNTRY BIRDS OF THE YEAR (ARZBERG)

		Issue Price	Current Value
☐ 1983	**Lesser Spotted Woodpecker,** artist: Martin Camm, production: 15 days	29.95	29.95
☐ 1983	**Long Tailed Tit,** artist: Martin Camm, production: 15 days	29.95	29.95
☐ 1986	**January,** artist: Martin Camm, production: open	29.50	29.50
☐ 1986	**February,** artist: Martin Camm, production: open	29.50	29.50
☐ 1986	**March,** artist: Martin Camm, production: open	29.50	29.50
☐ 1986	**April,** artist: Martin Camm, production: open	29.50	29.50
☐ 1986	**May,** artist: Martin Camm, production: open	29.50	29.50
☐ 1986	**June,** artist: Martin Camm, production: open	29.50	29.50
☐ 1986	**July,** artist: Martin Camm, production: open	29.50	29.50
☐ 1986	**August,** artist: Martin Camm, production: open	29.50	29.50
☐ 1986	**September,** artist: Martin Camm, production: open	29.50	29.50
☐ 1986	**October,** artist: Martin Camm, production: open	29.50	29.50
☐ 1986	**November,** artist: Martin Camm, production: open	29.50	29.50
☐ 1986	**December,** artist: Martin Camm, production: open	29.50	29.50

		Issue Price	Current Value

DER RING DES NIBELUNGEN SERIES

		Issue Price	Current Value
☐ 1986	**Motif I—Das Rheingold,** artist: Charlotte and William Hallett, production quantity 5,000	**125.00**	**125.00**
☐ 1986	**Motif II—Die Walkuere,** artist: Charlotte and William Hallett, production quantity 5,000	**125.00**	**125.00**
☐ 1986	**Motif III—Siegfried,** artist: Charlotte and William Hallett, production quantity 5,000	**125.00**	**125.00**
☐ 1986	**Motif IV—Goetterdaemmerung,** artist: Charlotte and William Hallett, production quantity 5,000	**125.00**	**125.00**

EARLY MEMORIES SERIES

☐ 1983	**Do They Bite?,** artist: James Kierstead, production quantity 7,500	**72.50**	**74.00**
☐ 1983	**Tug of War,** artist: James Kierstead, production quantity 7,500	**72.50**	**74.00**
☐ 1983	**The Explorers,** artist: James Kierstead, production quantity 7,500	**72.50**	**74.00**
☐ 1983	**My Turn,** artist: James Kierstead, production quantity 7,500	**72.50**	**74.00**

ENCHANTED SEASONS OF A UNICORN

☐ 1985	**Joyous Spring,** artists: Charlotte and William Hallett, production quantity 12,500	**39.50**	**39.50**
☐ 1985	**Peaceful Summer,** artists: Charlotte and William Hallett, production quantity 12,500	**39.50**	**39.50**
☐ 1985	**Glorious Autumn,** artists: Charlotte and William Hallett, production quantity 12,500	**39.50**	**39.50**
☐ 1985	**Winter's Tranquility,** artists: Charlotte and William Hallett, production quantity 12,500	**39.50**	**39.50**

ENCHANTMENT SERIES

☐ 1979	**Princess Snowflake,** artist: Dolores Valenza, production quantity 5,000	**50.00**	**60.00**
☐ 1979	**Blossom Queen,** artist: Dolores Valenza, production quantity 5,000	**62.50**	**62.50**
☐ 1980	**Princess Marina,** artist: Dolores Valenza, production quantity 5,000	**87.50**	**87.50**
☐ 1981	**Princess Starbright,** artist: Dolores Valenza, production quantity 2,500	**87.50**	**87.50**
☐ 1981	**Harvest Queen,** artist: Dolores Valenza, production quantity 5,000	**87.50**	**87.50**

	Issue Price	Current Value
☐ **1982 Princess Aura,** artist: Dolores Valenza, production quantity 5,000	87.50	87.50

FLOWERS THAT NEVER FADE SERIES

☐ **1982 Annual,** artist: Ole Winther, production: one year	27.50	27.50
☐ **1983 Annual,** artist: Ole Winther, production: one year	27.50	27.50
☐ **1984 Annual,** artist: Ole Winther, production: one year	27.50	27.50

FRIENDSHIP ANNUAL SERIES

☐ **1978 Friendship,** artist: Ole Winther, production: one year	80.00	80.00

THE GLORY OF CHRISTMAS SERIES

☐ **1982 The Nativity,** artists: Charlotte and William Hallett, production quantity 25,000	80.00	100.00
☐ **1983 The Annunciation,** artists: Charlotte and William Hallett, production quantity 25,000 . . .	80.00	90.00
☐ **1984 The Shepherds,** artists: Charlotte and William Hallett, production quantity 25,000 . . .	80.00	80.00
☐ **1985 The Wisemen,** artists: Charlotte and William Hallett, production quantity 25,000	80.00	80.00

GUNTHER GRANGET SERIES

☐ **1972 Sparrows, American,** artist: Gunther Granget, production quantity 5,000	50.00	175.00
☐ **1972 Sparrows, European,** artist: Gunther Granget, production quantity 5,000	30.00	70.00
☐ **1973 Kildeer, American,** artist: Gunther Granget, production quantity 2,500	75.00	100.00
☐ **1973 Squirrel, American,** artist: Gunther Granget, production quantity 2,500	75.00	85.00
☐ **1973 Squirrel, European,** artist: Gunther Granget, production quantity 2,500	35.00	55.00
☐ **1974 Partridge, American,** artist: Gunther Granget, production quantity 2,500	75.00	90.00
☐ **1976 Rabbits, American,** artist: Gunther Granget, production quantity 2,500	90.00	90.00
☐ **1976 Freedom in Flight,** artist: Gunther Granget, production quantity 5000	100.00	50.00
☐ **1976 Freedom in Flight,** gold, artist: Gunther Granget, production quantity 200	200.00	200.00

		Issue Price	Current Value
☐ 1976	**Wrens,** artist: Gunther Granget, production quantity 2,500	**100.00**	**110.00**
☐ 1977	**Bears,** artist: Gunther Granget, production quantity 2,500	**100.00**	**100.00**
☐ 1978	**Spring Journey, Foxes,** artist: Gunther Granget, production quantity 1,000	**125.00**	**200.00**

HANS ACHTZIGER SERIES

		Issue Price	Current Value
☐ 1979	**Heading South,** artist: Hans Achtziger, production quantity 5,000	**150.00**	**150.00**
☐ 1980	**Playful Flight,** artist: Hans Achtziger, production quantity 5,000	**187.50**	**187.50**
☐ 1981	**Tropical Skies,** artist: Hans Achtziger, production quantity 5,000	**245.00**	**245.00**
☐ 1982	**Carried by the Wind,** artist: Hans Achtziger, production quantity 5,000	**250.00**	**250.00**
☐ 1983	**Toward the Sun,** artist: Hans Achtziger, production quantity 5,000	**250.00**	**250.00**
☐ 1985	**Over Land and Sea,** artist: Hans Achtziger, production quantity 5,000	**250.00**	**250.00**

HUMMINGBIRDS SERIES

		Issue Price	Current Value
☐ 1982	**Sword-Billed Hummingbird,** artist: Ole Winther		
☐ 1982	**Train-Bearer,** artist: Ole Winther		
☐ 1982	**Rufous Hummingbird,** artist: Ole Winther		
☐ 1982	**Heliothrix,** artist: Ole Winther		
☐ 1982	**Horned Sungem,** artist: Ole Winther		
☐ 1982	**Vervian Hummingbird,** artist: Ole Winther *Set of six*	**200.00**	**200.00**

KATHIA'S CATS SERIES

		Issue Price	Current Value
☐ 1983	**In a Flower Basket,** artist: Kathia Berger, production quantity: open	**18.50**	**19.00**
☐ 1983	**In the Pasture,** artist: Kathia Berger, production quantity: open	**18.50**	**19.00**
☐ 1983	**Conversation with a Seagull,** artist: Kathia Berger, production quantity: open	**18.50**	**19.00**
☐ 1983	**My Favorite Place,** artist: Kathia Berger, production quantity: open	**18.50**	**19.00**
☐ 1983	**Play in the Snow,** artist: Kathia Berger, production quantity: open	**18.50**	**19.00**
☐ 1983	**Bodo and the Boat,** artist: Kathia Berger, production quantity: open	**47.50**	**48.00**

		Issue Price	Current Value

LEGENDARY ANIMALS

☐ **1982 Griffin,** artists: Charlotte and William Hallett, production quantity 12,500 . . . .

☐ **1982 Unicorn,** artists: Charlotte and William Hallett, production quantity 12,500 . . . .

☐ **1982 Pegasus,** artists: Charlotte and William Hallett, production quantity 12,500 . . . .

☐ **1982 Dragon,** artists: Charlotte and William Hallett, production quantity 12,500 . . . .

Set of four **175.00   175.00**

THE LEGEND OF ST. GEORGE

☐ **1985 The Knight,** artists: Charlotte and William Hallett, production quantity 5,000 . . . .   **100.00   100.00**

☐ **1985 The Lady Knight,** artists: Charlotte and William Hallett, production quantity 5,000 . . . .   **100.00   100.00**

☐ **1985 The Contest,** artists: Charlotte and William Hallett, production quantity 5,000 . . . .   **100.00   100.00**

☐ **1985 The Wedding,** artists: Charlotte and William Hallett, production quantity 5,000 . . . .   **100.00   100.00**

LOVE FOR ALL SEASONS SERIES

☐ **1981 The Ride Out,** artists: Charlotte and William Hallett, production quantity 10,000 . . . .   **125.00   125.00**

☐ **1982 The Minstrel Song,** artists: Charlotte and William Hallett, production quantity 10,000   **125.00   125.00**

☐ **1982 Affection,** artists: Charlotte and William Hallett, production quantity 10,000 . . . .   **125.00   125.00**

☐ **1982 The Tournament,** artists: Charlotte and William Hallett, production quantity 10,000 . . .   **125.00   125.00**

☐ **1983 The Falcon Hunt,** artists: Charlotte and William Hallett, production quantity 10,000 . . .   **125.00   125.00**

☐ **1983 Winter Romance,** artists: Charlotte and William Hallett, production quantity 10,000 . . .   **125.00   125.00**

☐ **1983 The Ride Out,** artists: Charlotte and William Hallett, production quantity 10,000 . . . .   **125.00   125.00**

MOTHER AND CHILD ANNUAL SERIES

☐ **1978 Mother and Child,** artist: Ole Winther, production quantity 2,500 . . . .   **65.00   65.00**

☐ **1979 Mother and Child,** artist: Ole Winther, production quantity 2,500 . . . .   **65.00   65.00**

☐ **1980 Mother and Child,** artist: Ole Winther, production quantity 2,500 . . . .   **87.50   87.50**

		Issue Price	Current Value
☐ 1981	**Mother and Child,** artist: Ole Winther, production quantity 2,500	**87.50**	**87.50**
☐ 1982	**Mother and Child,** artist: Ole Winther, production quantity 2,500	**87.50**	**87.50**
☐ 1983	**Mother and Child,** artist: Ole Winther, production quantity 2,500	**87.50**	**87.50**

MOTHER AND CHILD II

☐ 1983	**Mother and Child,** artist: Ole Winther, production: one year	**47.50**	**47.50**
☐ 1984	**Mother and Child,** artist: Ole Winther, production: one year	**47.50**	**47.50**

MUSEUM COMMEMORATIVE SERIES

☐ 1978	**Flower Girl of Provence,** artist: Edna Hibel, production quantity 12,750	**175.00**	**215.00**

PLATE OF THE MONTH SERIES

☐ 1978	**January—Wren,** artist: Ole Winther, production: open		
☐ 1978	**February—Great Titmouse,** artist: Ole Winther, production: open		
☐ 1978	**March—Peewee,** artist: Ole Winther, production: open		
☐ 1978	**April—Starling,** artist: Ole Winther, production: open		
☐ 1978	**May—Cuckoo,** artist: Ole Winther, production: open		
☐ 1978	**June—Nightingale,** artist: Ole Winther, production: open		
☐ 1978	**July—Lark,** artist: Ole Winther, production: open		
☐ 1978	**August—Swallow,** artist: Ole Winther, production: open		
☐ 1978	**September—Blackbird,** artist: Ole Winther, production: open		
☐ 1978	**October—Pigeon,** artist: Ole Winther, production: open		
☐ 1978	**November—Woodcock,** artist: Ole Winther, production: open		
☐ 1978	**December—Bullfinch,** artist: Ole Winther, production: open		
	Set of 12	**324.00**	**324.00**

		Issue Price	Current Value

RICHARD WAGNER

| ☐ 1986 | **Tannhaeuser,** artists: Charlotte and William Hallett, production quantity 5,000 . . . . | **125.00** | **125.00** |
| ☐ 1986 | **Parsifal,** artists: Charlotte and William Hallett, production quantity 5,000 . . . . | **125.00** | **125.00** |

RUTHVEN SONGBIRDS SERIES

| ☐ 1972 | **Bluebird and Goldfinch,** artist: John Ruthven, production quantity 5,000 . . . . | **100.00** | **81.00** |
| ☐ 1973 | **Mockingbird and Robin,** artist: John Ruthven, production quantity 5,000 . . . . | **100.00** | **81.00** |

SONGBIRDS OF NORTH AMERICA SERIES

☐ 1981	**Rose-Breasted Grosbeak,** artist: Ole Winther, production quantity 12,500	**60.00**	**60.00**
☐ 1981	**Eastern Bluebird,** artist: Ole Winther, production quantity 12,500	**60.00**	**60.00**
☐ 1981	**American Goldfinch,** artist: Ole Winther, production quantity 12,500	**60.00**	**60.00**
☐ 1981	**Mockingbird,** artist: Ole Winther, production quantity 12,500	**60.00**	**60.00**

SPRING IN THE WORLD OF BIRDS

| ☐ 1985 | **The Pheasants,** artist: Hans Achtziger, production quantity 2,500 . . . . | **325.00** | **325.00** |
| ☐ 1986 | **Heron,** artist: Hans Achtziger, production quantity 2,500 . . . . | **350.00** | **350.00** |

UNICORNS IN DREAMER'S GARDEN

☐ 1986	**The Sight of Wonders,** artists: Charlotte and William Hallett, production quantity 12,500		
☐ 1986	**The Smell of Roses,** artists: Charlotte and William Hallett, production quantity 12,500		
☐ 1986	**The Sound of Melodies,** artists: Charlotte and William Hallett, production quantity 12,500		
☐ 1986	**The Taste of Sweetness,** artists: Charlotte and William Hallett, production quantity 12,500		
☐ 1986	**The Touch of a Dream,** artists: Charlotte and William Hallett, production quantity 12,500		
	Set of five	**197.50**	**197.50**

		Issue Price	Current Value

WATERBABIES SERIES

☐ 1983 **Tom and the Dragon Fly** (#1), artist: Sandy Nightingale, production limited **45.00** **45.00**

☐ 1983 **The Fairies Take Care of Tom** (#2), artist: Sandy Nightingale, production limited **45.00** **45.00**

☐ 1983 **Tom and Mrs. Do As You Would Be Done By** (#3), artist: Sandy Nightingale, production limited **45.00** **45.00**

☐ 1983 **Tom and Mrs. Be Done As You Did** (#4), artist: Sandy Nightingale, production limited **45.00** **45.00**

☐ 1984 **Tom and the Sweet-Chest,** artist: Sandy Nightingale, production: 15 days **45.00** **45.00**

☐ 1984 **Ellie Teaches Tom,** artist: Sandy Nightingale, production: 15 days **45.00** **45.00**

☐ 1984 **Tom Takes Care of the Baby,** artist: Sandy Nightingale, production: 15 days **45.00** **45.00**

☐ 1984 **Tom Meets Ellie Again,** artist: Sandy Nightingale, production: 15 days **45.00** **45.00**

WEDDING SERIES

☐ 1979 **Wedding Plate,** artist: Ole Winther, production quantity 10,000 .... **210.00** **235.00**

THE WORLD OF LEGENDS SERIES

☐ 1982 **The Unicorn,** artists: Charlotte and William Hallett, production quantity 12,500 ....

☐ 1982 **The Griffin,** artists: Charlotte and William Hallett, production quantity 12,500 ....

☐ 1982 **The Dragon,** artists: Charlotte and William Hallett, production quantity 12,500 ....

☐ 1982 **The Pegasus,** artists: Charlotte and William Hallett, production quantity 12,500 ....
Set of four **175.00** **195.00**

ZODIAC SERIES

☐ 1978 **Aquarius,** artist: Ole Winther, production quantity 2,000 .... **125.00** **135.00**

☐ 1978 **Aries,** artist: Ole Winther, production quantity 2,000 .... **125.00** **135.00**

☐ 1978 **Cancer,** artist: Ole Winther, production quantity 2,000 .... **125.00** **135.00**

☐ 1978 **Capricorn,** artist: Ole Winther, production quantity 2,000 .... **125.00** **135.00**

☐ 1978 **Gemini,** artist: Ole Winther, production quantity 2,000 .... **125.00** **135.00**

		Issue Price	Current Value
☐ 1978	**Leo,** artist: Ole Winther, production quantity 2,000	**125.00**	**135.00**
☐ 1978	**Libra,** artist: Ole Winther, production quantity 2,000	**125.00**	**135.00**
☐ 1978	**Pisces,** artist: Ole Winther, production quantity 2,000	**125.00**	**135.00**
☐ 1978	**Sagittarius,** artist: Ole Winther, production quantity 2,000	**125.00**	**135.00**
☐ 1978	**Scorpio,** artist: Ole Winther, production quantity 2,000	**125.00**	**135.00**
☐ 1978	**Taurus,** artist: Ole Winther, production quantity 2,000	**125.00**	**135.00**
☐ 1978	**Virgo,** artist: Ole Winther, production quantity 2,000	**125.00**	**135.00**

SINGLE RELEASES

☐ 1970	**UN Commemorative**	**8.00**	**12.00**
☐ 1973	**Christmas**	**37.00**	**42.00**

IMPERIAL

United States

AMERICA THE BEAUTIFUL SERIES
(E. Ward Russell)

☐ 1969	**U.S. Capitol,** production quantity 500	**17.50**	**20.00**
☐ 1970	**Mount Rushmore,** production quantity 500	**17.50**	**20.00**
☐ 1971	**Statue of Liberty,** production quantity 500	**17.50**	**20.00**
☐ 1972	**Monument Valley, Arizona,** production quantity 500	**17.50**	**20.00**
☐ 1973	**Liberty Bell,** production quantity 500	**17.50**	**20.00**
☐ 1974	**Golden Gate,** production quantity 500	**19.95**	**22.50**
☐ 1975	**Mt. Vernon,** production quantity 500	**19.95**	**22.50**

CHRISTMAS SERIES

☐ 1970	**Partridge,** carnival glass, production: one year	**12.00**	**30.00**
☐ 1970	**Partridge,** crystal, production: one year ...	**15.00**	**26.00**
☐ 1971	**Turtledoves,** carnival glass, production: one year	**12.00**	**35.00**
☐ 1971	**Turtledoves,** crystal, production: one year	**16.50**	**30.00**
☐ 1972	**Hens,** carnival glass, production: one year	**12.00**	**30.00**

		Issue Price	Current Value
☐ 1972	**Hens,** crystal, production: one year	**16.50**	**25.00**
☐ 1973	**Colly Birds,** carnival glass, production: one year	**12.00**	**35.00**
☐ 1973	**Colly Birds,** crystal, production: one year ..	**16.50**	**25.00**
☐ 1974	**Golden Rings,** carnival glass, production: one year	**12.00**	**20.00**
☐ 1974	**Golden Rings,** crystal, production: one year	**16.50**	**25.00**
☐ 1975	**Geese,** carnival glass, production: one year	**14.00**	**35.00**
☐ 1975	**Geese,** crystal, production: one year	**19.00**	**25.00**
☐ 1976	**Swans,** carnival glass, production: one year	**16.00**	**20.00**
☐ 1976	**Swans,** crystal, production: one year	**21.00**	**25.00**
☐ 1977	**Maids,** carnival glass, production: one year	**18.00**	**22.50**
☐ 1977	**Maids,** crystal, production: one year	**23.00**	**25.00**
☐ 1978	**Drummers,** carnival glass, production: one year	**20.00**	**28.00**
☐ 1978	**Drummers,** crystal, production: one year ..	**25.00**	**28.00**
☐ 1979	**Pipers,** carnival glass, production: one year	**22.00**	**25.00**
☐ 1979	**Pipers,** crystal, production: one year	**27.00**	**30.00**
☐ 1980	**Ladies,** carnival glass, production: one year	**24.00**	**26.00**
☐ 1980	**Ladies,** crystal, production: one year	**29.00**	**33.00**
☐ 1981	**Lords,** carnival glass, production: one year	**28.00**	**30.00**
☐ 1981	**Lords,** crystal, production: one year	**34.00**	**37.00**

COIN PLATES SERIES

☐ 1971	**Kennedy Coin**	**15.00**	**18.00**
☐ 1972	**Ike Coin**	**15.00**	**18.00**
☐ 1976	**Bicentennial Coin**	**20.00**	**20.00**

INCOLAY STUDIOS

United States

ENCHANTED MOMENTS SERIES

☐ 1984	**Tiffany's World,** artist: Rosemary Calder, production quantity 7,500	**95.00**	**95.00**
☐ 1985	**Jennifer's World,** artist: Rosemary Calder, production quantity 7,500	**95.00**	**95.00**

GREAT ROMANCES OF HISTORY SERIES

☐ 1979	**Antony and Cleopatra,** artist: Carl Romanelli, production: unannounced	**65.00**	**65.00**

Tiffany's World, artist: Rosemary Calder.

Jennifer's World, artist: Rosemary Calder.

		Issue Price	Current Value
☐ 1980	**Taj Mahal Lovers,** artist: Carl Romanelli, production: unannounced	65.00	65.00
☐ 1981	**Lancelot and Guinevere,** artist: Carl Romanelli, production: unannounced	65.00	65.00

**Antony and Cleopatra,
artist: Carl Romanelli.**

**Lancelot and Guinevere,
artist: Carl Romanelli.**

**Uncertain Beginning,
artist: James Roberts.**

		Issue Price	Current Value
☐ 1982	**Lord Nelson and Lady Hamilton,** artist: Carl Romanelli, production: unannounced	70.00	70.00

LIFE'S INTERLUDES SERIES

☐ 1979	**Uncertain Beginning,** artist: James Roberts	95.00	95.00
☐ 1980	**Finally Friends,** artist: James Roberts, production: one year	95.00	95.00

LOVE SONNETS OF SHAKESPEARE SERIES

☐ 1986	**Shall I Compare Thee,** production limited	55.00	55.00

ROMANTIC POETS SERIES

☐ 1977	**She Walks in Beauty,** artist: Gayle Bright Appleby, production: unannounced	60.00	80.00
☐ 1978	**A Thing of Beauty Is a Joy Forever,** artist: Gayle Bright Appleby, production: unannounced	60.00	65.00
☐ 1979	**Ode to A Skylark,** artist: Gayle Bright Appleby, production: unannounced	65.00	65.00
☐ 1980	**She Was a Phantom of Delight,** artist: Gayle Bright Appleby, production: unannounced	65.00	65.00
☐ 1981	**The Kiss,** artist: Roger Akers, production: unannounced	65.00	70.00
☐ 1982	**My Heart Leaps Up,** artist: Roger Akers, production: unannounced	70.00	70.00
☐ 1983	**I Stood Tiptoe,** artist: Roger Akers, production: unannounced	70.00	70.00
☐ 1984	**The Dream,** artist: Roger Akers, production: unannounced	70.00	70.00
☐ 1985	**The Recollection,** artist: Roger Akers, production: unannounced	70.00	70.00

ROMANTIC POETS SERIES PART II

☐ 1981	**The Kiss,** artist: Roger Akers, production: one year	60.00	70.00
☐ 1982	**My Heart Leaps Up When I Behold,** artist: Roger Akers, production: one year	65.00	87.00
☐ 1983	**I Stood Tiptoe,** artist: Roger Akers, production: one year	70.00	72.00
☐ 1984	**The Dream,** artist: Roger Akers, production: one year	70.00	70.00

She was a Phantom of
Delight, artist: Gayle
Bright Appleby.

		Issue Price	Current Value
VOYAGE OF ULYSSES SERIES			
☐ 1984	**The Isle of Circe,** artist: Alan Brunettin, production: one year	**50.00**	**60.00**
☐ 1985	**The Sirens,** artist: Alan Brunettin, production: one year	**50.00**	**50.00**
☐ 1985	**Oygia, Isle of Calypso,** artist: Alan Brunettin, production: one year	**55.00**	**60.00**
☐ 1986	**The Land of Phaecians,** artist: Alan Brunettin, production: one year	**55.00**	**55.00**
☐ 1986	**The Return of Ulysses,** artist: Alan Brunettin, production: one year	**55.00**	**55.00**
☐ 1986	**The Reunion,** artist: Alan Brunettin, production: one year	**55.00**	**55.00**
THE FOUR ELEMENTS MICRO PLATE SERIES			
☐ 1983	**Air,** artisans of Incolay Studios, set of four,	**25.00**	**25.00**
☐ 1983	**Fire,** artisans of Incolay Studios, set of four,	**25.00**	**25.00**
☐ 1983	**Water,** artisans of Incolay Studios, set of four,	**25.00**	**25.00**
☐ 1983	**Earth,** artisans of Incolay Studios, set of four	**25.00**	**25.00**
☐ 1983	Complete set of four	**95.00**	**95.00**

My Heart Leaps Up
When I Behold, artist:
Roger Akers.

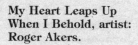

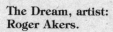

I Stood Tiptoe, artist:
Roger Akers.

The Dream, artist:
Roger Akers.

The Sirens, artist: Alan Brunettin.

Oygia, Isle of Calypso, artist: Alan Brunettin.

The Land of Phaecians,
artist: Alan Brunettin.

The Return of Ulysses,
artist: Alan Brunettin.

Air, Earth, Fire, Water, artisans of Incolay Studios.

INTERNATIONAL

United States

		Issue Price	Current Value
BICENTENNIAL SERIES			
☐ **1972**	**Declaration Signing,** artist: Manuel de Oliveira, production quantity 7,500	**40.00**	**310.00**
☐ **1973**	**Paul Revere,** artist: Manuel de Oliveira, production quantity 7,500	**40.00**	**160.00**
☐ **1974**	**Concord Bridge,** artist: Manuel de Oliveira, production quantity 7,500	**40.00**	**115.00**
☐ **1975**	**Crossing Delaware,** artist: Manuel de Oliveira, production quantity 7,500	**50.00**	**80.00**
☐ **1976**	**Valley Forge,** artist: Manuel de Oliveira, production quantity 7,500	**50.00**	**65.00**
☐ **1977**	**Surrender at Yorktown,** artist: Manuel de Oliveira, production quantity 7,500	**50.00**	**60.00**
CHRISTMAS SERIES			
☐ **1974**	**Tiny Tim,** artist: Carl Sundberg, production quantity 7,500	**75.00**	**75.00**

	Issue Price	Current Value
☐ **1975 Caught,** artist: Beverly Chase, production quantity 7,500	75.00	75.00
☐ **1976 Bringing Home the Tree,** artist: Albert Petitto, production quantity 7,500	75.00	75.00
☐ **1977 Christmas Ball,** artist: Albert Petitto, production quantity 7,500	75.00	85.00
☐ **1978 Alleluia,** artist: Albert Petitto, production quantity 7,500	75.00	75.00
☐ **1979 Rejoice,** artist: Albert Petitto, production quantity 7,500	100.00	110.00

INTERNATIONAL ART SOCIETY LIMITED

United States

ERTE COLLECTION

	Issue Price	Current Value
☐ **1982 Applause,** artist: Erte, production quantity N/A	75.00	90.00

INTERNATIONAL MUSEUM

United States

LETTER WRITER'S SERIES

	Issue Price	Current Value
☐ **1982 Portrait of Michelangelo,** production quantity 15,000	37.50	39.00
☐ **1982 Mrs. John Douglas,** production quantity 15,000	37.50	39.00
☐ **1983 Don Antonio,** production quantity 15,000	37.50	39.00
☐ **1983 Lovely Reader,** production quantity 15,000	37.50	39.00
☐ **1984 Lady Writing Letter,** production quantity 15,000	37.50	39.00

STAMP ART SERIES

	Issue Price	Current Value
☐ **1979 Gingerbread Santa,** production quantity 9,900	29.00	90.00
☐ **1980 Madonna and Child,** production quantity 9,900	37.50	75.00
☐ **1981 Boticelli's Madonna and Child,** production quantity 9,900	45.00	60.00
☐ **1982 Madonna of the Goldfinch,** production quantity 9,900	45.00	50.00

	Issue Price	Current Value
☐ 1983 **Raphael's Madonna,** production quantity 9,900	39.50	41.00

SUPERHEROES

☐ 1983 **Superman,** production limited	29.50	30.00

INTERPACE

United States

ARCHITECTS OF DEMOCRACY

☐ 1974 **George Washington,** production quantity 1,776		
☐ 1974 **John Adams,** production quantity 1,776 ...		
☐ 1974 **Thomas Jefferson,** production quantity 1,776		
☐ 1974 **Alexander Hamilton,** production quantity 1,776		
Set of four	225.00	280.00

MODIGLIANI SERIES

☐ 1972 **Caryatid,** production quantity 10,000	60.00	68.00

ISRAEL CREATIONS
(Naaman Ltd.)

COMMEMORATIVE SERIES

☐ 1967 **Wailing Wall,** production quantity 5,000 ..	7.50	27.00
☐ 1967 **Tower of David,** artist: production quantity 5,000	7.50	27.00
☐ 1968 **Masada,** production quantity 5,000	17.50	22.50
☐ 1969 **Rachel's Tomb,** production quantity 5,000	17.50	22.50
☐ 1970 **Tiberias,** production quantity 5,000	8.00	22.50
☐ 1971 **Nazareth,** production quantity 5,000	9.00	22.50
☐ 1972 **Beer Sheba,** production quantity 5,000	9.00	22.50
☐ 1973 **Acre,** production quantity 5,000	9.00	22.50

ANTHONY C. JACKSON

United States

SINGLE ISSUE	Issue Price	Current Value
☐ **1982 Presidential Plate,** artist: Anthony C. Jackson, quantity 5,000	**195.00**	**195.00**

JENSEN, GEORG

Denmark

CHAGALL SERIES

	Issue Price	Current Value
☐ **1972 The Lovers,** production quantity 12,500 . . .	**50.00**	**120.00**

CHRISTMAS SERIES

	Issue Price	Current Value
☐ **1972 Doves,** production: one year	**15.00**	**53.00**
☐ **1973 Christmas Eve,** production: one year	**15.00**	**42.00**
☐ **1974 Christmas Story,** production: one year	**17.50**	**25.00**
☐ **1975 Winter Scene,** production: one year	**22.50**	**48.00**
☐ **1976 Christmas in the Country,** production: one year	**27.00**	**35.00**

MOTHER'S DAY SERIES

	Issue Price	Current Value
☐ **1973 Mother and Child,** production: one year . . .	**15.00**	**42.00**
☐ **1974 Sweet Dreams,** production: one year	**17.50**	**27.00**
☐ **1975 A Mother's World,** production: one year . .	**22.50**	**27.00**

JENSEN, SVEND

Denmark

ANNIVERSARY SERIES

	Issue Price	Current Value
☐ **1980 Hans Christian Andersen's Home**	**60.00**	**75.00**

CHRISTMAS/ANDERSEN FAIRY TALES SERIES

	Issue Price	Current Value
☐ **1970 Hans Christian Andersen House,** artist: Gerhard Sausmark, production quantity 20,136	**14.50**	**85.00**
☐ **1971 Little Match Girl,** artist: Mads Stage, production quantity 20,000	**15.00**	**40.00**
☐ **1972 Maid of Copenhagen,** artist: Edvard Eriksen, production quantity 22,122	**16.50**	**45.00**

			Issue Price	Current Value
☐ 1973	**The Fir Tree,** artist: Svend Otto, production quantity 11,000		22.00	40.00
☐ 1974	**Chimney Sweep,** artist: Svend Otto, production quantity 11,000		25.00	30.00
☐ 1975	**The Ugly Duckling,** artist: Svend Otto, production: one year		27.50	27.50
☐ 1976	**The Snow Queen,** artist: Mads Stage, production: one year		27.50	39.00
☐ 1977	**The Snowman,** artist: Svend Otto, production: one year		29.50	40.00
☐ 1978	**Last Dream of the Old Oak Tree,** artist: Svend Otto, production: one year		32.00	45.00
☐ 1979	**Old Street Lamp,** artist: Svend Otto, production: one year		36.50	40.50
☐ 1980	**Willie Winkie,** artist: Svend Otto, production: one year		42.50	42.50
☐ 1981	**Uttermost Part of the Sea,** artist: Svend Otto, production: one year		49.50	49.50
☐ 1982	**Twelve by the Mailcoach,** artist: Svend Otto, production: one year		54.50	54.50
☐ 1983	**The Story of the Year,** artist: Svend Otto, production: unknown		54.50	54.50
☐ 1984	**The Nightingale,** artist: Svend Otto, production quantity 10,000		54.50	54.50

MOTHER'S DAY SERIES

			Issue Price	Current Value
☐ 1970	**Bouquet for Mother,** artist: Maggi Baaring, production quantity 13,740		14.50	75.00
☐ 1971	**Mother's Love,** artist: Nulle Oigaard, production quantity 14,310		15.00	40.00
☐ 1972	**Good Night,** artist: Mads Stage, production quantity 11,018		16.50	35.00
☐ 1973	**Flowers for Mother,** artist: Mads Stage, production quantity 11,000		20.00	35.00
☐ 1974	**Daisies for Mother,** artist: Mads Stage, production quantity 11,000		25.00	35.00
☐ 1975	**Surprise for Mother,** artist: Mads Stage, production quantity 15,000		27.50	27.50
☐ 1976	**Complete Gardener,** artist: Mads Stage, production: one year		27.50	27.50
☐ 1977	**Little Friends,** artist: Mads Stage, production: one year		29.50	29.50
☐ 1978	**Dreams,** artist: Mads Stage, production: one year		32.00	32.00

		Issue Price	Current Value
☐ **1979**	**Promenade,** artist: Mads Stage, production: one year	**36.50**	**36.50**
☐ **1980**	**Nursery Scene,** artist: Mads Stage, production: one year	**42.50**	**42.50**
☐ **1981**	**Daily Duties,** artist: Mads Stage, production: one year	**49.50**	**49.50**
☐ **1982**	**My Best Friend,** artist: Mads Stage, production: one year	**54.50**	**54.50**
☐ **1983**	**An Unexpected Meeting,** artist: Mads Stage, production: one year	**54.50**	**54.50**
☐ **1984**	**Who Are You?,** artist: Mads Stage, production: one year	**54.50**	**54.50**

JM COMPANY

United States

COMPETITIVE SPORTS SERIES

☐ **1979**	**Downhill Racing Slalom,** artist: Hal Reed, production quantity 5,000	**30.00**	**30.00**

LOVE SERIES

☐ **1980**	**Love's Serenade,** artist: Hal Reed, production quantity 5,000	**50.00**	**50.00**

ORIENTAL BIRDS SERIES

☐ **1976**	**Window at Tiger Spring Temple,** artist: Hal Reed, production quantity 10,000	**39.00**	**39.00**

JOSAIR

France

BICENTENNIAL SERIES

☐ **1972**	**American Eagle,** production quantity 400	**250.00**	**250.00**
☐ **1973**	**American Flag,** production quantity 400	**250.00**	**250.00**
☐ **1974**	**Abraham Lincoln,** production quantity 400	**250.00**	**250.00**
☐ **1975**	**George Washington,** production quantity 400	**250.00**	**250.00**
☐ **1976**	**Declaration of Independence,** production quantity 400	**250.00**	**250.00**

JUDAIC HERITAGE SOCIETY

United States
(See also Avondale and Villetta China)

GREAT JEWISH WOMEN SERIES	Issue Price	Current Value
☐ 1976 **Golda Meir,** production quantity 4,000	35.00	35.00
☐ 1976 **Henrietta Szold,** production quantity 4,000	35.00	35.00
☐ 1976 **Emma Lazarus,** production quantity 4,000	35.00	35.00

THE HERITAGE PLATES SERIES

☐ 1976 **Rabbi,** production quantity 4,000	35.00	35.00
☐ 1976 **Hasidim,** production quantity 4,000	35.00	35.00
☐ 1976 **Shtetl,** production quantity 4,000	35.00	35.00

ISRAEL'S 30TH ANNIVERSARY COMMEMORATIVE PLATE SERIES

☐ 1979 **L'Chayim to Israel,** production quantity 10,000	59.50	61.00
☐ 1979 **Prophecy of Isaiah,** production quantity 10,000	59.50	61.00

JERUSALEM WEDDING SERIES

☐ 1979 **Bride of Jerusalem,** production quantity 6,000	65.00	58.00
☐ 1979 **Hasidic Dancers,** production quantity 6,000	65.00	58.00

JEWISH HOLIDAYS SERIES

☐ 1972 **Pesach,** gold, production quantity 25	1900.00	1900.00
☐ 1972 **Pesach,** silver, production quantity 2,000 ..	150.00	150.00
☐ 1972 **Purim,** silver, production quantity 2,000 ...	150.00	150.00
☐ 1973 **Chanukah,** gold, production quantity 100 ..	1900.00	1900.00
☐ 1973 **Chanukah,** silver, production quantity 2,000	150.00	150.00
☐ 1974 **Purim,** silver, production quantity 1,000 ...	150.00	150.00
☐ 1979 **Chanukah,** production quantity 2,500	50.00	50.00
☐ 1979 **Purim,** production quantity 2,500	50.00	50.00
☐ 1979 **Shavouth,** production quantity 2,500	50.00	50.00
☐ 1979 **Rosh Hashana,** production quantity 2,500 ..	50.00	50.00
☐ 1979 **Simchat Torah,** production quantity 2,500 ..	50.00	50.00
☐ 1979 **Pesach,** production quantity 2,500	50.00	50.00

	Issue Price	Current Value

SINGLE RELEASES

		Issue Price	Current Value
☐ 1977	**Jacob and Angel,** production quantity 5,000	45.00	45.00
☐ 1977	**Hatikvah,** copper, production quantity 5,000	55.00	55.00
☐ 1977	**Hatikvah,** gold plate, production quantity 1,000	75.00	75.00
☐ 1977	**Hatikvah,** sterling silver, production quantity 500	180.00	180.00
☐ 1980	**Shalom—Peace,** production quantity 6,000	95.00	95.00

KAISER

Germany

ANNIVERSARY SERIES

		Issue Price	Current Value
☐ 1972	**Love Birds,** artist: Toni Schoener, production quantity 12,000	16.50	30.00
☐ 1973	**In the Park,** artist: Toni Schoener, production quantity 7,000	16.50	24.50
☐ 1974	**Canoeing,** artist: Toni Schoener, production quantity 7,000	20.00	30.00
☐ 1975	**Tender Moment,** artist: Kurt Bauer, production quantity 7,000	25.00	27.50
☐ 1976	**Serenade,** artist: Toni Schoener, production quantity 7,000	25.00	25.00
☐ 1977	**Simple Gift,** artist: Toni Schoener, production: one year	25.00	25.00
☐ 1978	**Viking Toast,** artist: Toni Schoener, production: one year	30.00	30.00
☐ 1979	**Romantic Interlude,** artist: Hannelore Blum, production: one year	32.00	32.00
☐ 1980	**Love at Play,** artist: Hannelore Blum, production: one year	40.00	40.00
☐ 1981	**Rendezvous,** artist: Hannelore Blum, production: one year	40.00	40.00
☐ 1982	**Betrothal,** artist: Kurt Bauer, production: one year	40.00	40.00
☐ 1983	**Sunday Afternoon,** artist: Toni Schoener, production: one year	40.00	40.00

BICENTENNIAL

		Issue Price	Current Value
☐ 1976	**Signing Declaration,** artist: J. Trumball, production quantity 1,000	75.00	150.00

		Issue Price	Current Value

BIRD DOG SERIES

☐ XX **Cocker Spaniel,** artist: J. Francis, production quantity 19,500 . . . . **39.50** **39.50**

☐ XX **Beagle,** artist: J. Francis, production quantity 19,500 . . . . **39.50** **39.50**

☐ XX **English Setter,** artist: J. Francis, production quantity 19,500 . . . . **39.50** **39.50**

☐ XX **Black Labrador,** artist: J. Francis, production quantity 19,500 . . . . **39.50** **39.50**

☐ XX **German Short Hair Pointer,** artist: J. Francis, production quantity 19,500 . . . . **39.50** **39.50**

☐ XX **Golden Labrador,** artist: J. Francis, production quantity 19,500 . . . . **39.50** **39.50**

☐ XX **English Pointer,** artist: J. Francis, production quantity 19,500 . . . . **39.50** **39.50**

☐ XX **Irish Setter,** artist: J. Francis, production quantity 19,500 . . . . **39.50** **39.50**

CHILDHOOD MEMORIES

☐ 1985 **Wait a Little,** artist: A. Schlesinger, production quantity 9,800 . . . . **29.00** **29.00**

CHILDREN'S PRAYER SERIES

☐ 1982 **Now I Lay Me Down to Sleep,** artist: Willy Freuner, production quantity 5,000 . . . . **29.50** **29.50**

☐ 1982 **Saying Grace,** artist: Willy Freuner, production quantity 5,000 . . . . **29.50** **29.50**

CHRISTMAS SERIES

☐ 1970 **Waiting for Santa Claus,** artist: Toni Schoener, production: one year **12.50** **50.00**

☐ 1971 **Silent Night,** artist: Kurt Bauer, production quantity 10,000 . . . . **13.50** **15.00**

☐ 1972 **Coming Home for Christmas,** artist: Kurt Bauer, production quantity 10,000 . . . . **16.50** **20.00**

☐ 1973 **Holy Night,** artist: Toni Schoener, production quantity 8,000 . . . . **18.00** **39.00**

☐ 1974 **Christmas Carolers,** artist: Kurt Bauer, production quantity 8,000 . . . . **25.00** **30.00**

☐ 1975 **Bringing Home the Tree,** artist: Joann Northcott, production: one year **25.00** **30.00**

☐ 1976 **Christ the Saviour Is Born,** artist: Carlo Maratti, production: one year **25.00** **36.00**

☐ 1977 **The Three Kings,** artist: Toni Schoener, production: one year **25.00** **30.00**

		Issue Price	Current Value

☐ 1978 **Shepherds in the Field,** artist: Toni Schoener, production: one year **30.00** **30.00**

☐ 1979 **Christmas Eve,** artist: Hannelore Blum, production: one year **32.00** **32.00**

☐ 1980 **Joys of Winter,** artist: Hannelore Blum, production: one year **40.00** **43.00**

☐ 1981 **Adoration of Three Kings,** artist: Kurt Bauer, production: one year **40.00** **41.00**

☐ 1982 **Bringing Home the Tree,** artist: Kurt Bauer, production: one year **40.00** **45.00**

DANCE, BALLERINA, DANCE

☐ 1982 **First Slippers,** artist: Robert Clarke, production quantity 14,500 .... **47.50** **47.50**

☐ 1983 **At the Barre,** artist: Robert Clarke, production quantity 14,500 .... **47.50** **47.50**

☐ XX **The Recital,** artist: Robert Clarke, production quantity 14,500 .... **47.50** **47.50**

☐ XX **Pirouette,** artist: Robert Clarke, production quantity 14,500 .... **47.50** **47.50**

☐ XX **Swan Lake,** artist: Robert Clarke, production quantity 14,500 .... **47.50** **47.50**

☐ XX **Opening Night,** artist: Robert Clarke, production quantity 14,500 .... **47.50** **47.50**

EGYPTIAN SERIES

☐ 1978 **King Tut,** production quantity 15,000 ..... **65.00** **65.00**
☐ 1980 **Nerfertiti,** production quantity 10,000 ..... **275.00** **275.00**
☐ 1980 **Tutankhamen,** production quantity 10,000 **275.00** **275.00**

FAIRY TALE SERIES

☐ 1982 **The Frog King,** artist: Gerda Neubacher, production: 50 days **39.50** **48.00**

☐ 1983 **Puss in Boots,** artist: Gerda Neubacher, production: 50 days **39.50** **42.00**

☐ 1983 **Little Red Riding Hood,** artist: Gerda Neubacher, production: unannounced **39.50** **42.00**

☐ 1984 **Hansel and Gretel,** artist: Gerda Neubacher, production limited **39.50** **40.00**

☐ 1984 **Cinderella,** artist: Gerda Neubacher, production limited **39.50** **40.00**

☐ 1984 **Sleeping Beauty,** artist: Gerda Neubacher, production limited **39.50** **40.00**

The Frog King, artist:
Gerda Neubacher.

		Issue Price	Current Value
FAMOUS HORSES SERIES			
☐ 1983	**Snow Knight,** artist: Adolf Lohmann, production quantity 3,000	95.00	95.00
☐ 1984	**Northern Dancer,** artist: Adolf Lohmann, production quantity 3,000	95.00	95.00
FAMOUS LULLABIES			
☐ 1985	**Sleep Baby Sleep,** artist: Gerda Neubacher, production: unannounced	39.50	48.00
☐ 1986	**Rockabye Baby,** artist: Gerda Neubacher, production: unannounced	39.50	39.50
☐ 1986	**A Mockingbird,** artist: Gerda Neubacher, production: unannounced	39.50	39.50
☐ 1986	**Au Clair de Lune,** artist: Gerda Neubacher, production: unannounced	39.50	39.50
☐ 1987	**Welsh Lullabye,** artist: Gerda Neubacher, production: unannounced	39.50	39.50
☐ 1988	**Brahms' Lullabye,** artist: Gerta Neubacher, production: unannounced	39.50	39.50
FOUR SEASONS SERIES			
☐ 1981	**Spring,** artist: Ivo Cenkovcan, production: one year	50.00	50.00
☐ 1981	**Summer,** artist: Ivo Cenkovcan, production: one year	50.00	50.00

		Issue Price	Current Value
☐ 1981	**Autumn,** artist: Ivo Cenkovcan, production: one year	50.00	50.00
☐ 1981	**Winter,** artist: Ivo Cenkovcan, production: one year	50.00	50.00

GARDEN AND SONGBIRD SERIES

☐ 1973	**Cardinal,** artist: Wolfgang Gawantka, production quantity 2,000	200.00	250.00
☐ 1973	**Blue Titmouse,** artist: Wolfgang Gawantka, production quantity 2,000	200.00	250.00

GLEN LOATES' FEATHERED FRIENDS SERIES

☐ 1978	**Blue Jays,** artist: Glen Loates, production quantity 10,000	70.00	100.00
☐ 1979	**Cardinals,** artist: Glen Loates, production quantity 10,000	80.00	90.00
☐ 1980	**Cedar Waxwings,** artist: Glen Loates, production quantity 10,000	80.00	80.00
☐ 1981	**Gold Finch,** artist: Glen Loates, production quantity 10,000	80.00	80.00

THE GRADUATE

☐ 1986	**Boy,** artist: J. McKernan, production quantity 7,500	39.50	39.50
☐ 1986	**Girl,** artist: J. McKernan, production quantity 7,500	39.50	39.50

HAPPY DAYS SERIES

☐ 1981	**The Aeroplane,** artist: Gerda Neubacher, production quantity 5,000	75.00	75.00
☐ 1982	**Julie,** artist: Gerda Neubacher, production quantity 5,000	75.00	75.00
☐ 1982	**Winter Fun,** artist: Gerda Neubacher, production quantity 5,000	75.00	75.00
☐ 1983	**The Lookout,** artist: Gerda Neubacher, production quantity 5,000	75.00	75.00

HARMONY AND NATURE

☐ 1985	**Spring Encore,** artist: John Littlejohn, production quantity 9,800	39.50	39.50

		Issue Price	Current Value

LITTLE CLOWNS SERIES

☐ 1981	The Red Mask, artist: Lorraine Trester, production quantity 9,500	35.00	38.00
☐ 1982	Pigtails and Puppies, artist: Lorraine Trester, production quantity 9,500	35.00	36.00
☐ 1983	Concertina, artist: Lorraine Trester, production quantity 9,500	35.00	36.00

LITTLE MEN SERIES

☐ 1977	Come Ride with Me, artist: Lorraine Trester, production quantity 9,500	60.00	61.00
☐ 1980	A Magical Moment, artist: Lorraine Trester, production quantity 9,500	60.00	61.00
☐ 1983	Day to Remember, artist: Lorraine Trester, production quantity 9,500	60.00	61.00

MOTHER'S DAY SERIES

☐ 1971	Mare and Foal, artist: Toni Schoener, production: one year	13.00	50.00
☐ 1972	Flowers for Mother, artist: Toni Schoener, production quantity 8,000	16.50	20.00
☐ 1973	Cat and Kittens, artist: Toni Schoener, production quantity 7,000	17.00	67.50
☐ 1974	Fox and Young, artist: Toni Schoener, production quantity 7,000	20.00	50.00
☐ 1975	German Shepherd with Pups, artist: Toni Schoener, production quantity 7,000	25.00	75.00
☐ 1976	Swan and Cygnets, artist: Toni Schoener, production quantity 7,000	25.00	27.50
☐ 1977	Mother Rabbit with Young, artist: Joann Northcott, production: one year	25.00	57.50
☐ 1978	Hen and Chicks, artist: Toni Schoener, production: one year	30.00	55.00
☐ 1979	Mother's Devotion, artist: Nori Peter, production: one year	32.00	52.50
☐ 1980	Raccoon Family, artist: Joann Northcott, production: one year	40.00	50.00
☐ 1981	Safe Near Mother, artist: H. Blum, production: unannounced	40.00	40.00

		Issue Price	Current Value
☐ 1982	**Pheasant Family,** artist: K. Bauer, production: unannounced	40.00	45.00
☐ 1983	**Tender Care,** artist: K. Bauer, production: unannounced	40.00	65.00

ON THE FARM SERIES

☐ 1981	**The Duck,** artist: A. Lohmann, production: one year	50.00	50.00
☐ 1982	**The Rooster,** artist: A. Lohmann, porcelain, production: one year	50.00	50.00
☐ 1983	**The Pond,** artist: A. Lohmann, production: one year	50.00	50.00
☐ 1983	**The Horses,** artist: A. Lohmann, production: one year	50.00	50.00
☐ XX	**White Horse,** artist: A. Lohmann, production: one year	50.00	50.00
☐ XX	**Ducks on the Pond,** artist: A. Lohmann, production: one year	50.00	50.00
☐ XX	**Girl with Goats,** artist: A. Lohmann, production: one year	50.00	50.00
☐ XX	**Girl Feeding Animals,** artist: A. Lohmann, production: one year	50.00	50.00

PASSION PLAY SERIES

☐ 1970	**The Last Supper,** artist: Toni Schoener, production: one year	25.00	30.00
☐ 1980	**The Crucifixion,** artist: Kurt Bauer, production: one year	40.00	42.00

PEOPLE OF THE MIDNIGHT
SUN SERIES

☐ 1978	**Northern Lullaby,** artist: Nori Peter, production quantity 15,000	65.00	70.00
☐ 1979	**Ilaga, My Friend,** artist: Nori Peter, production quantity 15,000	75.00	75.00
☐ 1980	**Motherhood,** artist: Nori Peter, production quantity 15,000	85.00	85.00
☐ 1981	**Odark and Son Samik,** artist: Nori Peter, production quantity 15,000	90.00	90.00
☐ 1982	**Anana with Little Mutak,** artist: Nori Peter, production quantity 15,000	90.00	90.00

	Issue Price	Current Value
☐ **1983** **The Hunter's Reward,** artist: Nori Peter, production quantity 15,000	90.00	90.00

RACING FOR PRIDE AND PROFIT SERIES

	Issue Price	Current Value
☐ **1984** **The Aging Victor,** artist: Roger Horton, production quantity 9,500	50.00	50.00
☐ **1985** **Second Goes Hungry,** artist: Roger Horton, production quantity 9,500	50.00	50.00
☐ **1986** **No Time to Boast,** artist: Roger Horton, production quantity 9,500	50.00	50.00
☐ **1987** **First Fish to Market,** artist: Roger Horton, production quantity 9,500	50.00	50.00
☐ **1988** **Gypsy Traders,** artist: B. Horton, production quantity 9,500	50.00	50.00

ROMANTIC PORTRAITS SERIES

	Issue Price	Current Value
☐ **1981** **Lilie,** artist: Gerda Neubacher, production quantity 5,000	200.00	225.00
☐ **1982** **Camelia,** artist: Gerda Neubacher, production quantity 5,000	175.00	200.00
☐ **1983** **Rose,** artist: Gerda Neubacher, production quantity 5,000	175.00	185.00
☐ **1984** **Daisy,** artist: Gerda Neubacher, production quantity 5,000	175.00	180.00

TRADITIONAL FAIRY TALES SERIES

	Issue Price	Current Value
☐ **1983** **Cinderella,** artist: Dorothea King, production limited	39.50	39.50
☐ **1983** **Jack and the Beanstalk,** artist: Dorothea King, production limited	39.50	39.50
☐ **1984** **Three Little Pigs,** artist: Dorothea King, production limited	39.50	39.50
☐ **1984** **Tom Thumb,** artist: Dorothea King, production limited	39.50	39.50
☐ **1985** **Goldilocks,** artist: Dorothea King, production limited	39.50	39.50
☐ **1985** **Dick Wittington,** artist: Dorothea King, production limited	39.50	39.50

TREASURES OF TUTANKHAMEN SERIES

	Issue Price	Current Value
☐ **1978** **The Golden Mask,** production quantity 3,247	90.00	120.00

		Issue Price	Current Value
☐ 1978	**The Golden Throne,** production quantity 3,247	90.00	120.00
☐ 1978	**The Horus Falcon,** production quantity 3,247	90.00	120.00
☐ 1978	**The Ivory Chest,** production quantity 3,247	90.00	120.00

WILDLIFE SERIES

☐ 1973	**Little Critters,** set of six, production quantity 5,000	100.00	125.00

WATER FOWL

☐ 1985	**Mallard Ducks,** artist: E. Bierly, production quantity 19,500	55.00	55.00
☐ 1985	**Canvas Back Ducks,** artist: E. Bierly, production quantity 19,500	55.00	55.00
☐ 1985	**Wood Ducks,** artist: E. Bierly, production quantity 19,500	55.00	55.00
☐ 1985	**Pintail Ducks,** artist: E. Bierly, production quantity 19,500	55.00	55.00

WILDFLOWERS

☐ 1986	**Trillium,** artist: Gerda Neubacher, production quantity 9,500	39.50	45.00
☐ 1987	**Spring Beauty,** artist: Gerda Neubacher, production quantity 9,500	45.00	45.00
☐ 1988	**Wild Asters,** artist: Gerda Neubacher, production quantity 9,500	45.00	45.00

WOODLAND CREATURES

☐ 1985	**Springtime Frolic,** artist: R. Orr, production: 10 days	37.50	37.50
☐ 1985	**Fishing Trip,** artist: R. Orr, production: 10 days	37.50	37.50
☐ 1985	**Resting in the Glen,** artist: R. Orr, production: 10 days	37.50	37.50
☐ 1985	**Meadowland Vigil,** artist: R. Orr, production: 10 days	37.50	37.50
☐ 1985	**Morning Lesson,** artist: R. Orr, production: 10 days	37.50	37.50
☐ 1985	**First Adventure,** artist: R. Orr, production: 10 days	37.50	37.50
☐ 1985	**The Hiding Place,** artist: R. Orr, production: 10 days	37.50	37.50
☐ 1985	**Startled Sentry,** artist: R. Orr, production: 10 days	37.50	37.50

	Issue Price	Current Value
YACHT SERIES		
☐ **1972 Cetonia,** artist: Kurt Bauer, production quantity 1,000	**50.00**	**50.00**
☐ **1972 Westward,** artist: Kurt Bauer, production quantity 1,000	**50.00**	**50.00**
YESTERDAY'S WORLD SERIES		
☐ **1978 A Time for Dreaming,** artist: Lorraine Trester, production quantity 5,000	**70.00**	**70.00**
☐ **1979 Summer Is Forever,** artist: Lorraine Trester, production quantity 5,000	**75.00**	**75.00**
☐ **1980 Sunday Afternoon,** artist: Lorraine Trester, production quantity 5,000	**80.00**	**80.00**
☐ **1984 Breath of Spring,** artist: Lorraine Trester, production quantity 5,000	**80.00**	**80.00**
SINGLE ISSUES		
☐ **1970 Oberammergau,** artist: Toni Schoener, production: one year	**25.00**	**30.00**
☐ **1970 Oberammergau,** artist: Kurt Bauer, production: one year	**40.00**	**40.00**
☐ **1973 Toronto Horse Show,** production quantity 1,000	**29.00**	**41.00**

DAVID KAPLAN STUDIOS

United States

	Issue Price	Current Value
THE LOVEABLES SERIES		
☐ **1982 Little Angel,** artist: Sol Dember, production quantity 10,000	**40.00**	**40.00**

KEIRSTEAD GALLERY

Canada

	Issue Price	Current Value
THE SISTERS SERIES		
☐ **1987 Brenda's Mill,** artist: James Keirstead, production quantity 4,000	**55.00**	**55.00**
SINGLE ISSUE		
☐ **1985 Dawn, Peggy's Cove,** artist: James Keirstead, production quantity 7,500	**98.00**	**100.00**

KERA

Denmark

CHRISTMAS SERIES	Issue Price	Current Value
☐ 1967 **Kobenhavn,** production: one year	6.00	25.00
☐ 1968 **Forste,** production: one year	6.00	20.00
☐ 1969 **Andersen's House**	6.00	20.00
☐ 1970 **Langelinie,** production: one year	6.00	15.00
☐ 1971 **Little Peter,** production: one year	6.00	14.00

MOON SERIES

	Issue Price	Current Value
☐ 1969 **Apollo II,** production: one year	6.00	6.00
☐ 1970 **Apollo 13,** production: one year	6.00	6.00

MOTHER'S DAY SERIES

	Issue Price	Current Value
☐ 1970 **Mother's Day,** production: one year	6.00	6.00
☐ 1971 **Mother's Day,** production: one year	6.00	6.00

KERN COLLECTIBLES

United States
(See also Gorham, Haviland & Parlon and Pickard)

ADVENTURES OF THE OLD WEST SERIES

	Issue Price	Current Value
☐ 1981 **Grizzly Ambush,** artist: Harland Young, hand-numbered, production quantity 7,500	65.00	65.00
☐ 1982 **The Train Robbers,** artist: Harland Young, hand-numbered, production quantity 7,500	65.00	65.00
☐ 1983 **Bank Holdup,** artist: Harland Young, hand-numbered, production quantity 7,500	65.00	65.00
☐ 1985 **Nature Strikes,** artist: Harland Young, production quantity 7,500	75.00	75.00

BUTTERFLIES SERIES

	Issue Price	Current Value
☐ 1983 **Monarchs,** artist: Patti Canaris, production quantity 7,500	75.00	75.00

CHILDREN OF THE SOUTHWEST SERIES

	Issue Price	Current Value
☐ 1984 **Navajo Pixie,** artist: Jay Schmidt, production quantity 7,500	36.00	36.00
☐ 1984 **Morning Sun,** artist: Jay Schmidt, production quantity 7,500	36.00	36.00

CHILD'S WORLD SERIES

		Issue Price	Current Value
☐ 1983	**Kathie,** artist: Leo Jansen, production quantity 9,800	**45.00**	**45.00**
☐ 1983	**Meredith,** artist: Leo Jansen, production quantity 9,800	**45.00**	**45.00**
☐ 1984	**Freddie,** artist: Leo Jansen, production quantity 9,800	**45.00**	**45.00**
☐ 1984	**Jamie,** artist: Leo Jansen, production quantity 9,800	**45.00**	**45.00**

CHRISTMAS OF YESTERDAY SERIES

		Issue Price	Current Value
☐ 1978	**Christmas Call,** artist: Marvin Nye, production quantity 5,000	**45.00**	**45.00**
☐ 1979	**Woodcutter's Christmas,** artist: Marvin Nye, production quantity 5,000	**50.00**	**50.00**
☐ 1980	**Baking Christmas Goodies,** artist: Marvin Nye, production quantity 5,000	**65.00**	**65.00**
☐ 1981	**Singing Christmas Carols,** artist: Marvin Nye, production quantity 5,000	**55.00**	**55.00**

COMPANIONS SERIES

		Issue Price	Current Value
☐ 1978	**Cubs,** artist: Gregory Perillo, production quantity 5,000	**40.00**	**90.00**
☐ 1978	**Mighty Sioux,** artist: Gregory Perillo, production quantity 5,000	**40.00**	**70.00**
☐ 1979	**Nature Girl,** artist: Gregory Perillo, production quantity 5,000	**50.00**	**50.00**
☐ 1980	**Buffalo Boy,** artist: Gregory Perillo, production quantity 5,000	**50.00**	**65.00**
☐ 1981	**Shepherds,** artist: Gregory Perillo, production quantity 5,000	**55.00**	**55.00**

COUNTRY FRIENDS SERIES

		Issue Price	Current Value
☐ 1984	**Elizabeth,** artist: Leesa Hoffman, production quantity 7,500	**35.00**	**35.00**

FAVORITE PETS SERIES

		Issue Price	Current Value
☐ 1981	**Schnauzers,** artist: Leo Jansen, production quantity 7,500	**39.95**	**85.00**
☐ 1982	**Cocker Spaniels,** artist: Leo Jansen, production quantity 7,500	**39.95**	**40.00**
☐ 1983	**Pointers,** artist: Leo Jansen, production quantity 7,500	**39.95**	**40.00**

		Issue Price	Current Value

GREAT ACHIEVEMENTS IN ART SERIES

| ☐ 1980 | The Arabian, artist: Harland Young, production quantity 3,000 | 65.00 | 170.00 |
| ☐ 1981 | The Longhorns, artist: T. Young, production quantity 3,000 | 60.00 | 60.00 |

THE HORSES OF HARLAND YOUNG SERIES

☐ 1982	Quarterhorses, artist: Harland Young, hand-numbered, production quantity 10,000	55.00	55.00
☐ 1983	Arabians, artist: Harland Young, hand-numbered, production quantity 10,000	55.00	55.00
☐ 1984	Mustangs, artist: Harland Young, hand-numbered, production quantity 10,000	55.00	55.00

KITTY CATS SERIES

| ☐ 1983 | Morrie, artist: Leo Jansen, production quantity 7,500 | 39.00 | 39.00 |
| ☐ 1984 | Tattoo, artist: Leo Jansen, production quantity 7,500 | 39.00 | 39.00 |

LEADERS OF TOMORROW SERIES

☐ 1980	Future Physician, artist: Leo Jansen, production quantity 9,800	50.00	50.00
☐ 1981	Future Farmer, artist: Leo Jansen, production quantity 9,800	50.00	50.00
☐ 1982	Future Florist, artist: Leo Jansen, production quantity 9,800	50.00	50.00
☐ 1983	Future Teacher, artist: Leo Jansen, production quantity 9,800	50.00	50.00

LINDA'S LITTLE LOVEABLE SERIES

☐ 1978	The Blessing, artist: Linda Avey, production quantity 7,500	30.00	40.00
☐ 1978	Appreciation, artist: Linda Avey, production quantity 7,500	37.50	38.50
☐ 1979	Adopted Burro, artist: Linda Avey, production quantity 7,500	42.50	43.00

MOTHER'S DAY SERIES

| ☐ 1976 | Mother and Children, artist: Leslie De Mille, production quantity 7,500 | 40.00 | 41.00 |
| ☐ 1977 | Darcy, artist: Edward Runci, production quantity 7,500 | 50.00 | 48.50 |

		Issue Price	Current Value
☐ 1978	**A Moment to Reflect,** artist: Edward Runci, production quantity 5,000	**55.00**	**50.50**
☐ 1979	**Fulfillment,** artist: Edward Runci, production quantity 5,000	**45.00**	**48.50**
☐ 1980	**A Renewal of Faith,** artist: Edward Runci, production quantity 5,000	**45.00**	**45.50**

NORTH AMERICAN GAME BIRDS SERIES

☐ 1983	**Canadian Geese,** artist: Derk Hansen, production quantity 7,500	**60.00**	**60.00**
☐ 1984	**Mallards,** artist: Derk Hansen, production quantity 7,500	**60.00**	**60.00**
☐ 1984	**Pheasants,** artist: Derk Hansen, production quantity 7,500	**60.00**	**60.00**

PORTRAIT OF INNOCENCE SERIES

☐ 1977	**Johnnie and Duke,** artist: Leo Jansen, production quantity 7,500	**40.00**	**55.00**
☐ 1978	**Randy and Rex,** artist: Leo Jansen, production quantity 7,500	**42.50**	**65.00**
☐ 1979	**Furry Friends,** artist: Leo Jansen, production quantity 7,500	**47.50**	**50.50**
☐ 1980	**Benji's Burro,** artist: Leo Jansen, production quantity 7,500	**50.00**	**115.00**

SCHOOL DAYS SERIES

☐ 1982	**Apple for My Teacher,** artist: Marvin Nye, production quantity 7,500	**65.00**	**60.00**
☐ 1983	**The Arithmetic Lesson,** artist: Marvin Nye, production quantity 7,500	**65.00**	**60.00**

SUGAR AND SPICE SERIES

☐ 1976	**Dana and Debbie,** artist: Leo Jansen, production quantity 7,500	**40.00**	**130.00**
☐ 1977	**Becky and Baby,** artist: Leo Jansen, production quantity 7,500	**42.50**	**75.00**
☐ 1978	**Jeannette and Julie,** artist: Leo Jansen, production quantity 7,500	**47.50**	**60.00**
☐ 1980	**Ramona and Rachel,** artist: Leo Jansen, production quantity 7,500	**50.00**	**100.00**

		Issue Price	Current Value

THIS LITTLE PIG WENT TO MARKET SERIES

☐ **1982** **This Little Pig Went To Market,** artist: Linda Nye, production quantity 9,800 . . . . **39.95** **40.00**

☐ **1983** **This Little Pig Stayed Home,** artist: Linda Nye, production quantity 9,800 . . . . **42.50** **43.00**

☐ **1984** **This Little Pig Had Roast Beef,** artist: Linda Nye, production quantity 9,800 . . . . **45.00** **45.00**

☐ **1985** **This Little Pig Had None,** artist: Linda Nye, production quantity 9,800 . . . . **45.00** **45.00**

TRIBAL COMPANIONS SERIES

☐ **1984** **My Best Friend,** artist: Derk Hansen, production quantity 6,000 . . . . : **35.00** **35.00**

ZOOLOGICAL GARDEN SERIES

☐ **1983** **Elephants,** artist: Mike Carroll, production quantity 5,000 . . . . **55.00** **55.00**

☐ **1984** **Tigers,** artist: Mike Carroll, production quantity 5,000 . . . . **55.00** **55.00**

SINGLE ISSUE

☐ **1984** **Champ,** artist: Leo Jansen, production quantity 7,500 . . . . **39.50** **40.00**

KING'S

Italy

CHRISTMAS SERIES

☐ **1973** **Adoration,** artist: Merli, production quantity 1,500 . . . . **100.00** **180.00**

☐ **1974** **Madonna,** artist: Merli, production quantity 1,500 . . . . **150.00** **160.00**

☐ **1975** **Heavenly Choir,** artist: Merli, production quantity 1,500 . . . . **160.00** **200.00**

☐ **1976** **Siblings,** artist: Merli, production quantity 1,500 . . . . **200.00** **240.00**

FLOWERS SERIES

☐ **1973** **Carnation,** artist: Aldo Falchi, production quantity 1,000 . . . . **85.00** **130.00**

		Issue Price	Current Value
☐ 1974	**Red Rose,** artist: Aldo Falchi, production quantity 1,000	**100.00**	**145.00**
☐ 1975	**Yellow Dahlia,** artist: Aldo Falchi, production quantity 1,000	**110.00**	**162.00**
☐ 1976	**Bluebells,** artist: Aldo Falchi, production quantity 1,000	**130.00**	**165.00**
☐ 1977	**Anemones,** artist: Aldo Falchi, production quantity 1,000	**130.00**	**175.00**

MOTHER'S DAY SERIES

☐ 1973	**Dancing Girl,** production quantity 1,500 . . .	**100.00**	**150.00**
☐ 1974	**Dancing Boy,** production quantity 1,500 . . .	**115.00**	**120.00**
☐ 1975	**Motherly Love,** production quantity 1,500	**140.00**	**180.00**
☐ 1976	**Maiden,** production quantity 1,500	**180.00**	**200.00**

KIRK

United States

BICENTENNIAL SERIES

☐ 1972	**Washington,** production quantity 5,000	**75.00**	**75.00**
☐ 1972	**Constellation,** production quantity 825	**75.00**	**75.00**

CHRISTMAS SERIES

☐ 1972	**Flight into Egypt,** production quantity 3,500	**150.00**	**150.00**

MOTHER'S DAY SERIES

☐ 1972	**Mother and Child,** production quantity 3,500	**75.00**	**75.00**
☐ 1973	**Mother and Child,** production quantity 2,500	**80.00**	**80.00**

THANKSGIVING SERIES

☐ 1972	**Thanksgiving Ways and Means,** production quantity 3,500	**150.00**	**155.00**

KIRK, JODI

United States

DEGRAZIA SERIES

☐ 1972	**Heavenly Blessing,** production quantity 200	**75.00**	**85.00**

KNOWLES, EDWIN M.

United States

A FATHER'S LOVE SERIES	Issue Price	Current Value
☐ **1985 Open Wide,** artist: Betsey Bradley, production limited	**19.50**	**22.00**
☐ **1985 Batter Up,** artist: Betsey Bradley, production limited	**19.50**	**25.00**
☐ **1985 Little Shaver,** artist: Betsey Bradley, production limited	**19.50**	**26.00**
☐ **1985 Swing Time,** artist: Betsey Bradley, production limited	**22.50**	**27.00**

AMERICANA HOLIDAYS SERIES

	Issue Price	Current Value
☐ **1978 The Fourth of July,** artist: Don Spaulding, production: one year	**26.00**	**35.00**
☐ **1979 Thanksgiving,** artist: Don Spaulding, production: one year	**26.00**	**35.00**
☐ **1980 Easter,** artist: Don Spaulding, production: one year	**26.00**	**28.00**
☐ **1981 Valentine's Day** artist: Don Spaulding, production: one year	**26.00**	**26.00**
☐ **1982 Father's Day,** artist: Don Spaulding, production: one year	**26.00**	**26.00**
☐ **1983 Christmas,** artist: Don Spaulding, production: one year	**26.00**	**26.00**

Little Shaver, artist: Betsey Bradley.

		Issue Price	Current Value
☐ 1984	**Mother's Day,** artist: Don Spaulding, production: one year	26.00	26.00

AMERICAN INNOCENTS SERIES

☐ 1986	**Abigail in the Rose Garden,** artists: Barbara Marsten and Valentin Mandrajji, production: 150 firing days	19.50	19.50
☐ 1986	**Ann by the Terrace,** artists: Marsten and Mandrajji, production: 150 firing days	19.50	19.50

ANNIE SERIES

☐ 1983	**Annie and Sandy,** artist: William Chambers, production limited	19.00	25.00
☐ 1983	**Daddy Warbucks,** artist: William Chambers, production limited	19.00	26.00
☐ 1983	**Annie and Grace,** artist: William Chambers, production limited	19.00	35.00
☐ 1984	**Annie and the Orphans,** artist: William Chambers, production limited	21.00	29.00
☐ 1985	**Tomorrow,** artist: William Chambers, production limited	21.00	30.00
☐ 1986	**Annie and Miss Hannigan,** artist: William Chambers, production limited	21.00	24.00
☐ 1986	**Annie, Lily and Rooster,** artist: William Chambers, production limited	24.00	25.00

Annie and Sandy, artist: William Chambers.

Daddy Warbucks, artist:
William Chambers.

	Issue Price	Current Value
☐ **1986 Grand Finale,** artist: William Chambers, production limited	24.00	24.00

BAND'S SONGBIRDS OF EUROPE SERIES

☐ **1987 The Chaffinch,** artist: Ursula Band, production: 100 days	24.50	24.50

BIBLICAL MOTHERS SERIES

☐ **1983 Bathsheba and Solomon,** artist: Eve Licea, production: one year	39.50	100.00
☐ **1984 Judgment of Solomon,** artist: Eve Licea, production: one year	39.50	75.00
☐ **1984 Pharaoh's Daughter and Moses,** artist: Eve Licea, production: one year	39.50	60.00
☐ **1984 Mary and Jesus,** artist: Eve Licea, production: one year	39.50	50.00
☐ **1985 Sarah and Isaac,** artist: Eve Licea, production: one year	44.50	55.00
☐ **1986 Rebekah, Jacob and Esau,** artist: Eve Licea, production: one year	44.50	46.00

The Chaffinch, artist:
Ursula Band.

BIRDS OF YOUR GARDEN SERIES	Issue Price	Current Value
☐ **1985 Cardinal,** artist: Kevin Daniel, production: 100 days	**19.50**	**33.00**
☐ **1985 Blue Jay,** artist: Kevin Daniel, production: 100 days	**19.50**	**19.50**
☐ **1985 Oriole,** artist: Kevin Daniel, production: 100 days	**22.50**	**22.50**
☐ **1986 Chickadees,** artist: Kevin Daniel, production: 100 days	**22.50**	**22.50**
☐ **1986 Robin,** artist: Kevin Daniel, production: 100 days	**22.50**	**22.50**
☐ **1986 Bluebird,** artist: Kevin Daniel, production: 100 days	**22.50**	**22.50**
☐ **1986 Hummingbird,** artist: Kevin Daniel, production: 100 days	**24.50**	**24.50**
☐ **1987 Goldfinch,** artist: Kevin Daniel, production: 100 days	**24.50**	**24.50**

CAT TALES SERIES

☐ **1987 A Chance Meeting,** artist: Amy Brackenbury, production quantity: N/A	**21.50**	**21.50**

CHRISTMAS SERIES

☐ **1985 The Angel's Message,** artist: Edna Hibel, production quantity: N/A	**45.00**	**50.00**

Pharaoh's Daughter and Moses, artist: Eve Licea.

Mary and Jesus, artist: Eve Licea.

Sarah and Isaac, artist: Eve Licea.

Goldfinch, artist: Kevin Daniel.

	Issue Price	Current Value
☐ **1986** **Gifts of the Magi,** artist: Edna Hibel, production quantity: N/A	45.00	45.00

CSATARI GRANDPARENT SERIES

	Issue Price	Current Value
☐ **1980** **Bedtime Story,** artist: Joseph Csatari, production: one year	18.00	28.00
☐ **1981** **Skating Lesson,** artist: Joseph Csatari, production: one year	20.00	25.00
☐ **1982** **Cookie Tasting,** artist: Joseph Csatari, production: one year	20.00	28.00
☐ **1983** **Swinger,** artist: Joseph Csatari, production: one year	20.00	20.00
☐ **1984** **The Skating Queen,** artist: Joseph Csatari, production: one year	20.00	25.00
☐ **1985** **Patriot's Parade,** artist: Joseph Csatari, production: one year	22.00	22.00
☐ **1986** **The Home Run,** artist: Joseph Csatari, production: one year	22.00	22.00

FOUR ANCIENT ELEMENTS SERIES

	Issue Price	Current Value
☐ **1984** **Earth,** artist: Georgia Lambert, production limited	27.50	33.00
☐ **1984** **Water,** artist: Georgia Lambert, production limited	27.50	32.00

		Issue Price	Current Value
☐ 1985	**Air,** artist: Georgia Lambert, production limited	29.50	35.00
☐ 1985	**Fire,** artist: Georgia Lambert, production limited	29.50	38.00

FRIENDS I REMEMBER SERIES

		Issue Price	Current Value
☐ 1984	**Fish Story,** artist: Jeanne Down, production limited	17.50	32.00
☐ 1984	**Office Hours,** artist: Jeanne Down, production limited	17.50	25.00
☐ 1984	**A Coat of Paint,** artist: Jeanne Down, production limited	17.50	25.00
☐ 1985	**Here Comes the Bride,** artist: Jeanne Down, production limited	19.50	29.00
☐ 1985	**Fringe Benefits,** artist: Jeanne Down, production limited	19.50	30.00
☐ 1985	**High Society,** artist: Jeanne Down, production limited	19.50	28.00
☐ 1986	**Flower Arrangement,** artist: Jeanne Down, production limited	21.50	22.00
☐ 1986	**Taste Test,** artist: Jeanne Down, production limited	21.50	44.00

Fish Story, artist: Jeanne Down.

Office Hours, artist:
Jeanne Down.

GONE WITH THE WIND SERIES	Issue Price	Current Value
☐ 1978 **Scarlet,** artist: Raymond Kursar, production: one year	**21.50**	**300.00**
☐ 1979 **Ashley,** artist: Raymond Kursar, production: one year	**21.50**	**230.00**
☐ 1980 **Melanie,** artist: Raymond Kursar, production: one year	**21.50**	**75.00**

Melanie, artist:
Raymond Kursar.

		Issue Price	Current Value
☐ 1981	**Rhett,** artist: Raymond Kursar, production: one year	23.50	50.00
☐ 1982	**Mammy Lacing Scarlett,** artist: Raymond Kursar, production: one year	23.50	64.00
☐ 1983	**Melanie Gives Birth,** artist: Raymond Kursar, production: one year	23.50	90.00
☐ 1984	**Scarlett's Green Dress,** artist: Raymond Kursar, production: one year	25.00	50.00
☐ 1985	**Rhett and Bonnie,** artist: Raymond Kursar, production: one year	25.50	38.00
☐ 1985	**Scarlett and Rhett: The Finale,** artist: Raymond Kursar, production: one year	29.50	30.00

HIBEL MOTHER'S DAY SERIES

		Issue Price	Current Value
☐ 1984	**Abby and Lisa,** artist: Edna Hibel, production: one year	29.50	50.00
☐ 1985	**Erica and Jamie,** artist: Edna Hibel, production: one year	29.50	33.00
☐ 1986	**Emily and Jennifer,** artist: Edna Hibel, production: one year	29.50	35.00
☐ 1987	**Catherine and Heather,** artist: Edna Hibel, production: one year	34.50	34.00

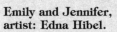

Emily and Jennifer, artist: Edna Hibel.

Catherine and Heather,
artist: Edna Hibel.

		Issue Price	Current Value
HOOK LEGACY SERIES			
☐ 1985	**Fascination,** artist: Frances Hook, production limited	**19.50**	**21.00**
☐ 1985	**Daydreaming,** artist: Frances Hook, production limited	**19.50**	**25.00**
☐ 1986	**Discovery,** artist: Frances Hook, production limited	**22.50**	**22.50**
☐ 1986	**Disappointment,** artist: Frances Hook, production limited	**22.50**	**22.50**
☐ 1986	**Wonderment,** artist: Frances Hook, production limited	**22.50**	**22.50**
☐ 1987	**Expectation,** artist: Frances Hook, production limited	**22.50**	**22.50**

JESSIE WILLCOX SMITH HOLIDAY SERIES

☐ 1986	**Easter,** artist: Jessie Willcox Smith, production quantity: N/A	**19.50**	**19.50**
☐ 1986	**Thanksgiving,** artist: Jessie Willcox Smith, production quantity: N/A	**19.50**	**19.50**
☐ 1986	**Christmas,** artist: Jessie Willcox Smith, production quantity: N/A	**19.50**	**19.50**
☐ 1986	**Valentine's Day,** artist: Jessie Willcox Smith, production quantity: N/A	**22.50**	**22.50**
☐ 1987	**Mother's Day,** artist: Jessie Willcox Smith, production quantity: N/A	**22.50**	**22.50**

Fascination, artist:
Frances Hook.

Daydreaming, artist:
Frances Hook.

Discovery, artist:
Frances Hook.

Disappointment, artist:
Frances Hook.

KING AND I SERIES	Issue Price	Current Value
☐ 1984 **A Puzzlement,** artist: William Chambers, production: one year	19.50	55.00
☐ 1984 **Shall We Dance?,** artist: William Chambers, production: one year	19.50	40.00
☐ 1985 **Getting to Know You,** artist: William Chambers, production: one year	19.50	29.00

A Puzzlement, artist:
William Chambers.

Shall We Dance?, artist:
William Chambers.

		Issue Price	Current Value
☐ 1985	**We Kiss in a Shadow,** artist: William Chambers, production: one year	**19.50**	**19.50**

LINCOLN, MAN OF AMERICA SERIES

☐ 1986	**The Gettysburg Address,** artist: Mort Kunstler, production: 150 firing days	**24.50**	**24.50**
☐ 1987	**The Lincoln–Douglas Debates,** artist: Mort Kunstler, production: 150 firing days	**24.50**	**24.50**

LIVING WITH NATURE SERIES

☐ 1986	**The Pintail,** artist: Bart Jerner, production: 150 days	**19.50**	**19.50**
☐ 1986	**The Mallard,** artist: Bart Jerner, production: 150 days	**19.50**	**19.50**
☐ 1987	**The Wood Duck,** artist: Bart Jerner, production: 150 days	**22.50**	**23.00**

OKLAHOMA SERIES

☐ 1985	**Oh, What a Beautiful Mornin',** artist: Mort Kunstler, production quantity: N/A	**19.50**	**19.50**
☐ 1986	**Surrey with the Fringe on Top,** artist: Mort Kunstler, production quantity: N/A	**19.50**	**19.50**
☐ 1986	**I Can't Say No,** artist: Mort Kunstler, production quantity: N/A	**19.50**	**19.50**

The Wood Duck, artist:
Bart Jerner.

		Issue Price	Current Value
☐ 1987	Oklahoma, artist: Mort Kunstler, production quantity: N/A	19.50	19.50

PORTRAITS OF MOTHERHOOD

		Issue Price	Current Value
☐ 1987	Mother's Here, artist: William Chambers, production: 150 days	29.50	29.50

Mother's Here, artist:
William Chambers.

	Issue Price	Current Value
SOUND OF MUSIC SERIES		
☐ 1986 **Sound of Music,** artist: Tony Crnkovich, production quantity: N/A	**19.50**	**19.50**
☐ 1986 **Do-Re-Mi,** artist: Tony Crnkovich, production quantity: N/A	**19.50**	**19.50**
☐ 1986 **My Favorite Things,** artist: Tony Crnkovich, production quantity: N/A	**22.50**	**22.50**
☐ 1986 **Laendler Waltz,** artist: Tony Crnkovich, production quantity: N/A	**22.50**	**22.50**
☐ 1987 **Edelweiss,** artist: Tony Crnkovich, production quantity: N/A	**22.50**	**22.50**
UPLAND BIRDS OF NORTH AMERICA SERIES		
☐ 1986 **The Pheasant,** artist: Wayne Anderson, production: 150 days	**24.50**	**24.50**
☐ 1986 **The Grouse,** artist: Wayne Anderson, production: 150 days	**24.50**	**24.50**
☐ 1987 **The Quail,** artist: Wayne Anderson, production: 150 days	**27.50**	**27.50**
WINGS UPON THE WIND SERIES		
☐ 1987 **The Family,** artist: Donald Pentz, production: 150 days	**24.80**	**24.80**

The Quail, artist: Wayne Anderson.

The Family, artist: Donald Pentz.

WIZARD OF OZ SERIES	Issue Price	Current Value
☐ 1977 **Over the Rainbow,** artist: James Auckland, production: one year	**19.00**	**68.00**
☐ 1978 **If I Only Had a Brain,** artist: James Auckland, production: one year	**19.00**	**30.00**
☐ 1978 **If I Only Had a Heart,** artist: James Auckland, production: one year	**19.00**	**35.00**
☐ 1978 **If I Were King of the Forest,** artist: James Auckland, production: one year	**19.00**	**30.00**
☐ 1979 **Wicked Witch of the West,** artist: James Auckland, production: one year	**19.00**	**40.00**
☐ 1979 **Follow the Yellow Brick Road,** artist: James Auckland, production: one year	**19.00**	**35.00**
☐ 1979 **Wonderful Wizard of Oz,** artist: James Auckland, production: one year	**19.00**	**50.00**
☐ 1980 **Grand Finale,** artist: James Auckland, production: one year	**24.00**	**60.00**

KONIGSZELT BAVARIA

Germany

CHRISTMAS SERIES

	Issue Price	Current Value
☐ 1985 **The Angel's Vigil,** artist: Sulamith Wulfing, production quantity: N/A	**35.00**	**40.00**

		Issue Price	Current Value
☐ 1986	**Christmas Child,** artist: Sulamith Wulfing, production quantity: N/A	35.00	45.00

DEUTCHES FACHWERK SERIES

☐ 1984	**Bauernhaus,** artist: Karl Bedal, production quantity: N/A	24.00	24.00
☐ 1984	**Niedersachsenhaus,** artist: Karl Bedal, production quantity: N/A.	24.00	24.00
☐ 1985	**Moselhaus,** artist: Karl Bedal, production quantity: N/A	27.00	30.00
☐ 1985	**Westfalenhaus,** artist: Karl Bedal, production quantity: N/A	27.00	30.00
☐ 1985	**Mittelfrankenhaus,** artist: Karl Bedal, production quantity: N/A	27.00	35.00
☐ 1986	**Bodenseehaus,** artist: Karl Bedal, production quantity: N/A	27.00	45.00

GRIMM'S FAIRY TALES SERIES

☐ 1981	**Rumpelstilzchen,** artist: Charles Gehm, production: one year	23.00	23.00
☐ 1982	**Rapunzel,** artist: Charles Gehm, production: one year	25.50	40.00
☐ 1983	**Hansel and Gretel,** artist: Charles Gehm, production: one year	25.00	25.00
☐ 1983	**Rest on the Flight,** artist: Hedi Keller, production: one year	29.50	30.00
☐ 1984	**Shoemaker and Elves,** artist: Charles Gehm, production: one year	25.00	25.00
☐ 1984	**Golden Goose,** artist: Charles Gehm production: one year	29.00	29.00
☐ 1985	**Shoes That Were Danced,** artist: Charles Gehm production: one year	29.00	29.00
☐ 1986	**Sleeping Beauty,** artist: Charles Gehm, production: one year	29.00	29.00
☐ 1987	**Snow White,** artist: Charles Gehm production: one year	29.00	29.00

HEDI KELLER CHRISTMAS SERIES

☐ 1979	**The Adoration,** artist: Hedi Keller, production: 90 days	29.50	38.00
☐ 1980	**Flight into Egypt,** artist: Hedi Keller, production: 90 days	29.50	35.00
☐ 1981	**Return into Galilee,** artist: Hedi Keller, production: 90 days	29.50	35.00

		Issue Price	Current Value
☐ 1982	**Following the Star,** artist: Hedi Keller, production: 90 days	**29.50**	**35.00**
☐ 1983	**Rest on the Flight,** artist: Hedi Keller, production: 90 days	**29.50**	**35.00**
☐ 1984	**The Nativity,** artist: Hedi Keller, production: 90 days	**29.50**	**45.00**
☐ 1985	**Gift of the Magi,** artist: Hedi Keller, production: 90 days	**34.50**	**42.00**
☐ 1986	**Annunciation,** artist: Hedi Keller, production: 90 days	**34.50**	**50.00**

LOVE AND LIFE SERIES

☐ 1986	**Since I First Saw Him,** artist: Sulamith Wulfing, production quantity limited	**29.85**	**29.85**
☐ 1986	**He, Noblest of All,** artist: Sulamith Wulfing, production quantity limited	**29.85**	**29.85**
☐ 1987	**I Can't Understand It,** artist: Sulamith Wulfing, production quantity limited	**29.85**	**29.85**

SULAMITH'S LOVE SONG SERIES

☐ 1982	**Music,** artist: Sulamith Wulfing, production limited	**29.00**	**35.00**
☐ 1983	**Pledge,** artist: Sulamith Wulfing, production limited	**29.00**	**29.00**

Following the Star, artist: Hedi Keller.

		Issue Price	Current Value
☐ 1983	**Vision,** artist: Sulamith Wulfing, production limited	**29.00**	**29.00**
☐ 1983	**Gift,** artist: Sulamith Wulfing, production limited	**29.00**	**29.00**
☐ 1984	**The Circle,** artist: Sulamith Wulfing, production limited	**29.00**	**29.00**

KOSCHERAK BROTHERS

Czechoslovakia

CHRISTMAS SERIES

☐ 1973	**Christmas,** artist: Mary Gregory, production quantity 1,000	**55.00**	**55.00**
☐ 1974	**Christmas,** artist: Mary Gregory, production quantity 1,000	**60.00**	**60.00**
☐ 1975	**Christmas,** artist: Mary Gregory, production quantity 1,000	**60.00**	**60.00**
☐ 1976	**Christmas,** artist: Mary Gregory, production quantity 1,000	**60.00**	**60.00**

MOTHER'S DAY SERIES

☐ 1973	**Mother's Day,** artist: Mary Gregory, production quantity 500	**55.00**	**55.00**
☐ 1974	**Mother's Day,** artist: Mary Gregory, production quantity 300	**60.00**	**60.00**
☐ 1975	**Mother's Day,** artist: Mary Gregory, production quantity 300	**60.00**	**60.00**
☐ 1976	**Mother's Day,** artist: Mary Gregory, production quantity 500	**65.00**	**65.00**

KPM—ROYAL BERLIN

Germany

CHRISTMAS SERIES

☐ 1969	**Christmas Star,** production quantity 5,000	**28.00**	**380.00**
☐ 1970	**Three Kings,** production quantity 5,000 . . .	**28.00**	**300.00**
☐ 1971	**Christmas Tree,** production quantity 5,000	**28.00**	**290.00**
☐ 1972	**Christmas Angel,** production quantity 5,000	**31.00**	**300.00**
☐ 1973	**Christ Child on Sled,** production quantity 5,000	**33.00**	**280.00**
☐ 1974	**Angel and Horn,** production quantity 5,000	**35.00**	**180.00**

		Issue Price	Current Value
☐ 1975	**Shepherds,** production quantity 5,000	40.00	165.00
☐ 1976	**Star of Bethlehem,** production quantity 5,000	43.00	140.00
☐ 1977	**Mary at Crib,** production quantity 5,000 ..	46.00	100.00
☐ 1978	**Three Wise Men,** production quantity 5,000	49.00	54.00
☐ 1979	**The Manger,** production quantity 5,000 ...	55.00	55.00
☐ 1980	**Shepherds in Fields,** production quantity 5,000	55.00	55.00

LAKE SHORE PRINTS

United States

ROCKWELL SERIES

☐ 1973	**Butter Girls,** artist: Norman Rockwell, production quantity 9,433	14.95	142.00
☐ 1974	**Truth About Santa,** artist: Norman Rockwell, production quantity 15,141	19.50	77.00
☐ 1975	**Home from Fields,** artist: Norman Rockwell, production quantity 8,500	24.50	60.00
☐ 1976	**A President's Wife,** artist: Norman Rockwell, production quantity 2,500	70.00	80.00

LALIQUE

France

ANNUAL SERIES

☐ 1965	**Two Birds,** artist: Marie-Claude Lalique, production quantity 2,000	25.00	100.00
☐ 1966	**Dreamrose,** artist: Marie-Claude Lalique, production quantity 5,000	25.00	200.00
☐ 1967	**Fish Ballet,** artist: Marie-Claude Lalique, production quantity 5,000	25.00	125.00
☐ 1968	**Gazeller Fantasie,** artist: Marie-Claude Lalique, production quantity 6,000	25.00	70.00
☐ 1969	**Papillon,** artist: Marie-Claude Lalique, production quantity 6,000	30.00	80.00
☐ 1970	**Peacock,** artist: Marie-Claude Lalique, production quantity 6,000	30.00	45.00
☐ 1971	**Hibou,** artist: Marie-Claude Lalique, production quantity 6,000	35.00	60.00
☐ 1972	**Coquillage,** artist: Marie-Claude Lalique, production quantity 7,000	40.00	55.00

	Issue Price	Current Value
☐ **1973 Jayling,** artist: Marie-Claude Lalique, production quantity 7,500	**42.50**	**66.00**
☐ **1974 Silver Pennies,** artist: Marie-Claude Lalique, production quantity 7,500	**47.50**	**70.00**
☐ **1975 Fish Duet,** artist: Marie-Claude Lalique, production quantity 8,000	**50.00**	**75.00**
☐ **1976 Eagle,** artist: Marie-Claude Lalique, production quantity 7,500	**60.00**	**100.00**

LANCE INTERNATIONAL

United States

TWAS THE NIGHT BEFORE CHRISTMAS SERIES

☐ **1985 Happy Christmas to All,** artist: Andrea Hollis, production quantity 10,000	**47.50**	**48.00**

LANGENTHAL CHINA WORKS

Switzerland

ANKER'S HERITAGE SERIES

☐ **1986 The First Smile,** artist: Albert Anker, production quantity: N/A	**34.86**	**35.00**
☐ **1986 Grandfather Tells a Story,** artist: Albert Anker, production quantity: N/A	**34.86**	**35.00**
☐ **1987 Girl Feeding the Chickens,** artist: Albert Anker, production quantity: N/A	**34.86**	**35.00**

LAPSYS

United States

CRYSTAL SERIES

☐ **1977 Snowflake,** crystal, production quantity 5,000	**47.50**	**75.00**
☐ **1978 Peace on Earth,** crystal, production quantity 5,000	**47.50**	**48.00**

LEGACY LIMITED

United States

CHRISTMAS SERIES	Issue Price	Current Value
☐ **1986 Christmas 1986,** artist: Les Kouba, production quantity 5,000	39.50	40.00

LENOX

United States

AMERICAN WILDLIFE SERIES

	Issue Price	Current Value
☐ **1983 Red Foxes,** artist: N. Adams, production quantity 9,500	65.00	65.00
☐ **1983 Ocelots,** artist: N. Adams, production quantity 9,500	65.00	65.00
☐ **1983 Sea Lions,** artist: N. Adams, production quantity 9,500	65.00	65.00
☐ **1983 Raccoons,** artist: N. Adams, production quantity 9,500	65.00	65.00
☐ **1983 Dall Sheep,** artist: N. Adams, production quantity 9,500	65.00	65.00

BOEHM BIRD SERIES

	Issue Price	Current Value
☐ **1970 Wood Thrush,** artist: Edward Marshall Boehm, production: one year	35.00	225.00
☐ **1971 Goldfinch,** artist: Edward Marshall Boehm, production: one year	35.00	65.00
☐ **1972 Mountain Bluebird,** artist: Edward Marshall Boehm, production: one year	37.50	60.00
☐ **1973 Meadowlark,** artist: Edward Marshall Boehm, production: one year	50.00	55.00
☐ **1974 Rufous Hummingbird,** artist: Edward Marshall Boehm, production: one year	45.00	55.00
☐ **1975 American Redstart,** artist: Edward Marshall Boehm, production: one year	50.00	50.00
☐ **1976 Cardinals,** artist: Edward Marshall Boehm, production: one year	53.00	55.00
☐ **1977 Robins,** artist: Edward Marshall Boehm, production: one year	55.00	55.00
☐ **1978 Mockingbirds,** artist: Edward Marshall Boehm, production: one year	58.00	58.00
☐ **1979 Golden-Crowned Kinglets,** artist: Edward Marshall Boehm, production: one year . . . :	65.00	65.00

		Issue Price	Current Value
☐ 1980	**Black-Throated Blue Warbler,** artist: Edward Marshall Boehm, production: one year	**80.00**	**80.00**
☐ 1981	**Eastern Phoebes,** artist: Edward Marshall Boehm, production: one year	**92.50**	**92.50**

BOEHM BIRDS/
YOUNG AMERICA SERIES

☐ 1972	**Eaglet,** artist: Edward Marshall Boehm, production quantity 5,000	**175.00**	**175.00**
☐ 1973	**Eaglet,** artist: Edward Marshall Boehm, production quantity 6,000	**175.00**	**175.00**
☐ 1975	**Eaglet,** artist: Edward Marshall Boehm, production quantity 6,000	**175.00**	**175.00**

BOEHM WOODLAND WILDLIFE SERIES

☐ 1973	**Raccoons,** production: one year	**50.00**	**80.00**
☐ 1974	**Red Foxes,** production: one year	**52.50**	**52.50**
☐ 1975	**Cottontail Rabbits,** production: one year . .	**58.50**	**58.50**
☐ 1976	**Eastern Chipmunks,** production: one year . .	**62.50**	**62.50**
☐ 1977	**Beavers,** production: one year	**67.50**	**67.50**
☐ 1978	**Whitetail Deer,** production: one year	**70.00**	**70.00**
☐ 1979	**Squirrels,** production: one year	**76.00**	**76.00**
☐ 1980	**Bobcats,** production: one year	**82.50**	**82.50**
☐ 1981	**Martens,** production: one year	**100.00**	**100.00**
☐ 1982	**River Otters,** production: one year	**100.00**	**120.00**

BUTTERFLIES AND FLOWERS SERIES

☐ 1982	**Question Mark Butterfly and New England Aster,** artist: Val Roy Gerischer, production quantity 25,000	**60.00**	**60.00**
☐ 1983	**Sonoran Blue Butterfly and Mariposa Lily,** artist: Val Roy Gerischer, production quantity 25,000	**65.00**	**65.00**
☐ 1983	**Malachite Butterfly and Orchid,** artist: Val Roy Gerischer, production quantity 25,000	**65.00**	**65.00**
☐ 1984	**American Painted Lady and Virginia Rose,** artist: Val Roy Gerischer, production quantity 25,000	**70.00**	**70.00**
☐ 1984	**Ruddy Daggerwing Butterfly and Lantana,** artist: Val Roy Gerischer, production quantity 25,000	**70.00**	**70.00**
☐ 1985	**Buckeye Butterfly and Bluebells,** artist: Val Roy Gerischer, production quantity 25,000	**75.00**	**75.00**

Golden-Crowned Kinglets, artist: Edward Marshall Boehm.

Black-Throated Blue Warbler, artist: Edward Marshall Boehm.

Eastern Phoebes, artist: Edward Marshall Boehm.

**Red Foxes, artist:
Edward Marshall
Boehm.**

**Beavers, artist: Edward
Marshall Boehm.**

**Martens, artist: Edward
Marshall Boehm.**

Ruddy Daggerwing
Butterfly and Lantana,
artist: Val Roy
Gerischer.

Buckeye Butterfly and
Bluebells, artist: Val
Roy Gerischer.

	Issue Price	Current Value
COLONIAL CHRISTMAS WREATH SERIES		
☐ **1981 Colonial Virginia,** production: one year . . .	65.00	100.00
☐ **1982 Massachusetts,** production: one year	70.00	90.00

	Issue Price	Current Value
☐ **1983 Maryland,** production: one year	70.00	80.00
☐ **1984 Rhode Island,** production quantity: unannounced	70.00	70.00

Maryland, Colonial Christmas Wreath Series.

Rhode Island, Colonial Christmas Wreath Series.

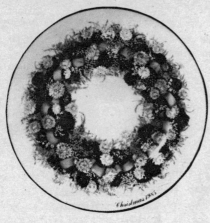

Connecticut, Colonial Christmas Wreath Series.

	Issue Price	Current Value
☐ **1985 Connecticut,** production quantity: unannounced	70.00	70.00

THE CONFEDERACY COLLECTION

	Issue Price	Current Value
☐ **1971 The White House of the Confederacy,** artist: W. Schiener, production quantity 1,201 ...		
☐ **1971 The Great Seal of the Confederacy,** artist: W. Schiener, production quantity 1,201 ...		
☐ **1971 A Call to Arms,** artist: W. Schiener, production quantity 1,201		
☐ **1971 The General,** artist: W. Schiener, production quantity 1,201		
☐ **1971 Lee and Jackson,** artist: W. Schiener, production quantity 1,201		
☐ **1971 The Merrimac,** artist: W. Schiener, production quantity 1,201		
☐ **1971 J. E. B. Stuart,** artist: W. Schiener, production quantity 1,201		
☐ **1971 Confederate Camp,** artist: W. Schiener, production quantity 1,201		
☐ **1971 Blockade Runner,** artist: W. Schiener, production quantity 1,201		
☐ **1971 Fort Sumter,** artist: W. Schiener, production quantity 1,201		
Set of 10	900.00	900.00

THE CONFEDERACY PLATES

	Issue Price	Current Value
☐ **1972 States of the Confederacy,** artist: unannounced, production: unannounced	900.00	900.00

LENOX CHRISTMAS TREE SERIES

		Issue Price	Current Value
☐ 1976	**Douglas Fir,** production: one year	50.00	50.00
☐ 1977	**Scotch Pine,** production: one year	55.00	55.00
☐ 1978	**Blue Spruce,** production: one year	65.00	65.00
☐ 1979	**Balsam Fir,** production: one year	65.00	65.00
☐ 1980	**Brewer's Spruce,** production: one year	75.00	75.00
☐ 1981	**China Fir,** production: one year	75.00	75.00
☐ 1982	**Aleppo Pine,** production: one year	80.00	80.00

NATURE'S NURSERY SERIES

☐ 1982	**Snow Leopards,** artist: Lynn Chase, production quantity 15,000	65.00	65.00
☐ 1983	**Koalas,** artist: Lynn Chase, production quantity 15,000	65.00	65.00
☐ 1983	**Llamas,** artist: Lynn Chase, production quantity 15,000	70.00	70.00

Snow Leopards, artist: Lynn Chase.

Koalas, artist: Lynn Chase.

Emperor Penguins, artist: Lynn Chase.

Zebras, artist: Lynn Chase.

		Issue Price	Current Value
☐ **1984**	**Bengal Tigers,** artist: Lynn Chase, production quantity 15,000	70.00	70.00
☐ **1985**	**Emperor Penguins,** artist: Lynn Chase, production quantity 15,000	75.00	75.00
☐ **1985**	**Polar Bears,** artist: Lynn Chase, production quantity 15,000	75.00	75.00
☐ **1986**	**Zebras,** artist: Lynn Chase, production quantity 15,000	80.00	80.00

LIHS LINDER

Germany

	Issue Price	Current Value

AMERICA THE BEAUTIFUL

	Issue Price	Current Value
☐ **1975 Independence Hall,** production quantity 1,500	42.00	45.00
☐ **1975 Statue of Liberty,** production quantity 1,500	42.00	45.00
☐ **1975 Niagara Falls,** production quantity 1,500 ..	42.00	45.00
☐ **1975 Grand Canyon,** production quantity 1,500	42.00	45.00
☐ **1975 Golden Gate,** production quantity 1,500 ...	42.00	45.00
☐ **1975 Capitol,** production quantity 1,500	42.00	45.00

CHILD'S CHRISTMAS SERIES

	Issue Price	Current Value
☐ **1978 Holy Night,** artist: Ferner, production quantity 5,000	40.00	40.00
☐ **1979 Shepherds in the Field,** artist: Ferner, production quantity 5,000	40.00	40.00

CHRISTMAS SERIES

	Issue Price	Current Value
☐ **1972 Little Drummer Boy,** artist: Josef Neubauer, production quantity 6,000	25.00	50.00
☐ **1973 Carolers,** artist: Josef Neubauer, production quantity 6,000	25.00	25.00
☐ **1974 Peace,** artist: Josef Neubauer, production quantity 6,000	25.00	31.00
☐ **1975 Christmas Cheer,** artist: Josef Neubauer, production quantity 6,000	30.00	31.00
☐ **1976 Joy of Christmas,** artist: Josef Neubauer, production quantity 6,000	30.00	30.00
☐ **1977 Holly Jolly Christmas,** artist: Josef Neubauer, production quantity 6,000	30.00	30.00
☐ **1978 Holy Night,** artist: Josef Neubauer, production quantity 5,000	40.00	40.00

EASTER SERIES

	Issue Price	Current Value
☐ **1973 Happy Easter,** production quantity 1,500 ..	22.00	45.00
☐ **1974 Springtime,** production quantity 1,500	25.00	30.00
☐ **1975 With Love,** production quantity 1,500	28.00	30.00

GOLDEN SPIKE CENTENNIAL SERIES

	Issue Price	Current Value
☐ **1977 Central Pacific Jupiter,** production quantity 1,500	25.00	25.00
☐ **1977 Union Pacific 119,** production quantity 1,500	25.00	25.00

		Issue Price	Current Value
HISTORY SERIES			
☐ 1973	**Tribute to Flag,** production quantity 3,000	60.00	120.00
☐ 1974	**Golden Spike Centennial,** production quantity 1,500	40.00	42.00
MOTHER'S DAY SERIES			
☐ 1972	**Mother and Child,** production quantity 1,000	20.00	90.00
☐ 1973	**Mother and Child,** production quantity 2,000	24.00	18.00
☐ 1974	**Bouquet,** production quantity 2,000	25.00	30.00
☐ 1975	**Happiness,** production quantity 2,000	28.00	30.00
PLAYMATES SERIES			
☐ 1976	**Timmy and Friend**	45.00	55.00
☐ 1977	**Heidi and Friend**	45.00	45.00
SINGLE RELEASES			
☐ 1972	**Union Pacific Railroad,** production quantity 1,500	22.00	25.00
☐ 1973	**Union Pacific Big Boy,** production quantity 1,500	25.00	28.00
☐ 1973	**Flag,** production quantity 3,000	60.00	140.00
☐ 1976	**Drummer Boy,** production quantity 1,500 . .	45.00	55.00
☐ 1976	**Freedom Train,** production quantity 1,500	45.00	60.00
☐ 1978	**Union Pacific 8444,** production quantity 1,500	27.50	30.00
☐ 1979	**Union Pacific Challenger,** production quantity 1,500	30.00	30.00

LIMOGES-TURGOT

France

DURAND'S CHILDREN SERIES			
☐ 1978	**Marie-Ange,** artist: Paul Durand, numbered, production: one year	36.40	35.00
☐ 1979	**Emilie et Philippe,** artist: Paul Durand, numbered, production: one year	36.40	35.00
☐ 1980	**Christiane et Fifi,** artist: Paul Durand, numbered, production: one year	36.40	35.00
☐ 1980	**Cecile et Raoul,** artist: Paul Durand, numbered, production: one year	36.40	35.00

LES ENFANTS DE LA FIN DU SIECLE	Issue Price	Current Value
☐ 1984 **Patinage au Trocadero,** artist: Bernard Peltriauz, production limited	**24.82**	**25.00**
☐ 1985 **Petits Voiliers au Bassin des Tuileries,** artist: Bernard Peltriauz, production limited	**29.82**	**40.00**
☐ 1985 **Guignol au Luxembourg,** artist: Bernard Peltriauz, production limited	**29.82**	**40.00**
☐ 1986 **Manage aux Champs-Elysees,** artist: Bernard Peltriauz, production limited	**29.82**	**30.00**

QUELLIER'S MORALS OF PERRAULT SERIES

	Issue Price	Current Value
☐ 1983 **Cinderella** artist: Andre Quellier, production limited	**28.67**	**30.00**
☐ 1984 **Little Tom Thumb,** artist: Andre Quellier, production limited	**28.67**	**30.00**
☐ 1984 **Little Red Riding Hood,** artist: Andre Quellier, production limited	**28.67**	**29.00**
☐ 1985 **Sleeping Beauty,** artist: Andre Quellier, production limited	**28.67**	**35.00**

Patinage au Trocadero,
artist: Bernard
Peltriauz.

LINCOLN MINT

United States

ARTISTS SERIES	Issue Price	Current Value
☐ 1971 **Dali Unicorn,** gold, production quantity 100	1500.00	1600.00
☐ 1971 **Dali Unicorn,** silver, production quantity 5,000	100.00	100.00
☐ 1972 **Dali Athena,** gold, production quantity 300	2000.00	2000.00
☐ 1972 **Dali Athena,** vermeil, production quantity 2,500	1150.00	150.00
☐ 1972 **Dali Athena,** silver, production quantity 7,500	125.00	125.00

CHRISTMAS SERIES		
☐ 1978 **Santa Belongs to All Children,** production quantity 7,500	29.50	30.00

EASTER SERIES		
☐ 1972 **Dali,** gold, production quantity 10,000	200.00	215.00
☐ 1972 **Dali,** silver, production quantity 20,000 . . .	150.00	130.00
☐ 1974 **Dali,** pewter	45.00	45.00

MOTHER'S DAY SERIES		
☐ 1972 **Collies,** gold on silver	90.00	102.00
☐ 1972 **Collies,** silver	125.00	87.00

MADONNAS SERIES		
☐ 1972 **Madonna della Seggiola,** production quantity 3,000	125.00	110.00

LIONSHEAD MINT

IDITAROD RACE CHAMPS SERIES

☐ 1984 **Rick Mackey,** artist: George Rodgers, production quantity 5,000	35.00	35.00

LITT

United States

	Issue Price	Current Value

ANNUAL SERIES

☐ **1979 Apache Sunset,** enamel, production quantity
1,250 .... **275.00** **275.00**

CHRISTMAS SERIES

☐ **1978 Madonna and Child,** enamel, production
quantity 1,000 .... **200.00** **200.00**
☐ **1979 O Holy Night,** production quantity 1,000 .. **200.00** **200.00**

LLADRO

Spain

CHRISTMAS SERIES

☐ **1971 Caroling,** artist: unannounced, production:
one year **27.50** **30.00**
☐ **1972 Carolers,** artist: unannounced, production:
one year **35.00** **35.00**
☐ **1973 Boy and Girl,** artist: unannounced, production: one year **45.00** **50.00**
☐ **1974 Carolers,** artist: unannounced, production:
one year **55.00** **75.00**
☐ **1975 Cherubs,** artist: unannounced, production:
one year **60.00** **60.00**
☐ **1976 Christ Child,** artist: unannounced, production: one year **60.00** **50.00**
☐ **1977 Nativity,** artist: unannounced, production:
one year **80.00** **70.00**
☐ **1978 Caroling Child,** artist: unannounced, production: one year **80.00** **60.00**
☐ **1979 Snow Dance,** artist: unannounced, production: one year **90.00** **80.00**

MOTHER'S DAY SERIES

☐ **1971 Kiss of the Child,** artist: unannounced, production quantity 800 .... **27.50** **75.00**
☐ **1972 Birds and Chicks,** artist: unannounced, production quantity 3,500 .... **27.50** **30.00**
☐ **1973 Mother and Children,** artist: unannounced, production quantity 2,000 .... **35.00** **35.00**

		Issue Price	Current Value
☐ 1974	**Nursing Mother,** artist: unannounced, production: one year	45.00	135.00
☐ 1975	**Mother and Children,** artist: unannounced, production: one year	60.00	55.00
☐ 1976	**Vigil,** artist: unannounced, production: one year	60.00	51.00
☐ 1977	**Mother and Daughter,** artist: unannounced, production: one year	67.50	60.00
☐ 1978	**New Arrival,** artist: unannounced, production: one year	80.00	55.00
☐ 1979	**Off to School,** artist: unannounced, production: one year	90.00	90.00

LONGTON CROWN POTTERY

Great Britain

THE CANTERBURY TALES SERIES

☐ 1980	**The Man of Law's Tale,** artist: G. A. Hoover, production: unannounced	29.80	30.00
☐ 1982	**The Franklin's Tale,** artist: G. A. Hoover, production: unannounced	29.80	30.00
☐ 1982	**Knight's Tale,** artist: G. A. Hoover, production: unannounced	31.80	32.00

Knight's Tale, artist: G. A. Hoover.

	Issue Price	Current Value
☐ **1982** **Wife of Bath's Tale,** artist: G. A. Hoover, production: unannounced	31.80	35.00

LOUISIANA HERITAGE ART GALLERIES

United States

SOUTHERN BACKROADS SERIES

☐ **1985** **Morning Mystique,** artist: Barrie Van Osdell, production quantity: N/A	39.50	40.00

LOUP, JEAN-PAUL

CHRISTMAS SERIES

☐ **1971** **Noel,** production quantity 300	125.00	1100.00
☐ **1972** **Noel,** production quantity 500	150.00	650.00
☐ **1973** **Noel,** production quantity 500	175.00	500.00
☐ **1974** **Noel,** production quantity 400	200.00	500.00
☐ **1975** **Noel,** production quantity 250	250.00	500.00
☐ **1976** **Noel,** production quantity 150	300.00	600.00

MOTHER'S DAY SERIES

☐ **1974** **Mother and Child,** champleve, production quantity 500	250.00	1100.00
☐ **1975** **Mother and Child,** enamel, production quantity 400	285.00	550.00
☐ **1976** **Mother and Child,** enamel, production quantity 150	300.00	600.00

LUND AND CLAUSEN

Denmark

CHRISTMAS SERIES

☐ **1971** **Deer,** production: one year	13.50	15.00
☐ **1972** **Stave Church,** production: one year	13.50	15.00
☐ **1973** **Christmas Scene,** production: one year	13.50	17.50

MOON SERIES

☐ **1969** **Moon Landing,** production: one year	10.00	12.00
☐ **1971** **Apollo 13,** production: one year	15.00	18.00

	Issue Price	Current Value

MOTHER'S DAY SERIES

		Issue Price	Current Value
☐ 1979	Rose, production: one year	10.00	18.00
☐ 1971	Forget-Me-Nots, production: one year	10.00	15.00
☐ 1972	Bluebell, production: one year	15.00	15.00
☐ 1973	Lily of the Valley, production: one year . . .	16.00	15.00

LYNELL

United States

AMERICAN ADVENTURE SERIES

☐ 1979	The Whaler, artist: Endre Szabo, production quantity 7,500	50.00	60.00
☐ 1980	The Trapper, artist: Endre Szabo, production quantity 7,500	50.00	55.00
☐ 1980	The Forty-Niner, production quantity 7,500	50.00	50.00
☐ 1981	The Pioneer Woman, production quantity 7,500	50.00	50.00
☐ 1981	The Wagon Master, production quantity 7,500	50.00	50.00
☐ 1982	Wagon Ho!, production quantity 7,500	50.00	50.00

BEST OF TIMES SERIES

☐ 1982	The Candy Shop, artist: Shirley Brinegar, production quantity 15,000	38.50	38.50

BETSY BATES ANNUAL SERIES

☐ 1979	Olde Country Inn, production quantity 7,500	38.50	45.00
☐ 1980	Village Schoolhouse, production quantity 7,500	38.50	39.00
☐ 1981	Village Blacksmith, production quantity 7,500	38.50	39.00
☐ 1982	Christmas Village, artist: Betsy Bates, production quantity 15,000	24.50	24.50

CHILDREN'S MOMENTS SERIES

☐ 1981	Official Babysitter, artist: Mike Hagel, production quantity 15,000	24.50	25.00
☐ 1981	Cowboy Capers, artist: Mike Hagel, production quantity 15,000	24.50	25.00
☐ 1982	Nurse Nancy, artist: Mike Hagel, production quantity 15,000	24.50	25.00

	Issue Price	Current Value

CIRCUS DREAMS SERIES

☐ **1982 Two for the Show,** artist: Susan Neelon, production quantity 19,500 . . . .   **24.50**   **25.00**

FAMOUS CLOWNS OF THE CIRCUS SERIES

☐ **1982 Emmett,** artist: Robert Weaver, production: one year **38.50**   **39.00**

☐ **1982 Lou Jacobs,** artist: Robert Weaver, production: one year **38.50**   **39.00**

☐ **1982 Felix Adler,** artist: Robert Weaver, production: one year **38.50**   **39.00**

☐ **1982 Otto Griebling,** artist: Robert Weaver, production: one year **38.50**   **39.00**

GREAT CHIEFS OF CANADA SERIES

☐ **1980 Chief Joseph Brant,** artist: Murray Killman, production quantity 7,500 . . . .   **65.00**   **65.00**

☐ **1981 Chief Crowfoot,** artist: Murray Killman, production quantity 7,500 . . . .   **65.00**   **65.00**

☐ **1982 Tecumseh,** artist: Murray Killman, production quantity 7,500 . . . .   **65.00**   **65.00**

HAGEL CELEBRITY SERIES

☐ **1982 Bob Hope/Thanks for the Memories,** artist: Mike Hagel, production limited **45.00**   **45.00**

☐ **1982 George Burns,** artist: Mike Hagel, production: 100 days **45.00**   **46.00**

☐ **1982 I Love Lucy,** artist: Mike Hagel, production limited **45.00**   **45.00**

HAGEL CHRISTMAS SERIES

☐ **1981 Sh-h-h!,** artist: Mike Hagel, production quantity 17,500 . . . .   **25.90**   **30.00**

☐ **1982 A Kiss for Santa,** artist: Mike Hagel, production quantity 17,500 . . . .   **25.90**   **35.00**

HAGEL MOTHER'S DAY SERIES

☐ **1982 Once upon a Time,** artist: Mike Hagel, production: 60 days **29.50**   **30.00**

HOBO JOE SERIES

☐ **1982 Hold the Onions,** artist: Ron Lee, production quantity 10,000 . . . .   **50.00**   **50.00**

		Issue Price	Current Value
☐ 1982	**Traveling in Style,** artist: Ron Lee, production quantity 10,000	50.00	50.00

HOW THE WEST WAS WON SERIES

		Issue Price	Current Value
☐ 1981	**Pony Express,** artist: Gayle Gibson, production quantity 19,500	38.50	40.00
☐ 1981	**The Oregon Trail,** artist: Gayle Gibson, production quantity 19,500	38.50	40.00
☐ 1982	**California Gold Rush,** artist: Gayle Gibson, production quantity 19,500	38.50	40.00
☐ 1982	**Driving the Golden Spike,** artist: Gayle Gibson, production quantity 19,500	38.50	40.00
☐ 1982	**Cattle Drive,** artist: Gayle Gibson, production quantity 19,500	38.50	40.00
☐ 1982	**Peace Pipe,** artist: Gayle Gibson, production quantity 19,500	38.50	40.00

LITTLE HOUSE ON THE
PRAIRIE SERIES

		Issue Price	Current Value
☐ 1982	**Welcome to Walnut Creek,** artist: Eugene Christopherson, production: one year	45.00	45.00
☐ 1982	**Country Girls,** artist: Eugene Christopherson, production: one year	45.00	45.00

LITTLE TRAVELER SERIES

		Issue Price	Current Value
☐ 1978	**On His Way,** artist: Malick, production quantity 4,000	45.00	35.00
☐ 1979	**On Her Way,** artist: Malick, production quantity 4,000	45.00	35.00

NORMAN ROCKWELL
CHRISTMAS SERIES

		Issue Price	Current Value
☐ 1979	**Snow Queen,** artist: Norman Rockwell, production: 60 days	29.50	30.00
☐ 1980	**Surprises for All,** artist: Norman Rockwell, production: 60 days	29.50	30.00
☐ 1982	**Grandpop and Me,** artist: Norman Rockwell, production: 60 days	29.50	30.00

NORMAN ROCKWELL COLLECTION OF
LEGENDARY ART SPECIAL ISSUE

		Issue Price	Current Value
☐ 1980	**Artist's Daughter,** artist: Norman Rockwell, production: one year	65.00	65.00

		Issue Price	Current Value
☐ 1980	**Poor Richard's Almanack,** artist: Norman Rockwell, production quantity 17,500	**45.00**	**45.00**
☐ 1981	**A Daily Prayer,** artist: Norman Rockwell, production: less than one year	**29.50**	**30.00**

NORMAN ROCKWELL
MOTHER'S DAY SERIES

☐ 1980	**Cradle of Love,** artist: Norman Rockwell, production: 60 days	**29.50**	**40.00**
☐ 1981	**A Mother's Blessing,** artist: Norman Rockwell, production: 30 days	**29.50**	**30.00**
☐ 1982	**Memories,** artist: Norman Rockwell, production: 60 days	**29.50**	**30.00**

NORTH AMERICAN WILDLIFE SERIES

☐ 1982	**Snuggling Cougars,** artist: Murray Killman, production quantity 7,500	**65.00**	**65.00**

POPEYE'S 50TH ANNIVERSARY SERIES

☐ 1980	**Happy Birthday Popeye,** production: one year	**22.50**	**23.00**

ROCKWELL'S SCOTTY SERIES

☐ 1981	**Scotty's Stowaway,** artist: Norman Rockwell, production quantity 17,500	**45.00**	**45.00**
☐ 1982	**Scotty Strikes a Bargain,** artist: Norman Rockwell, production quantity 17,500	**35.00**	**35.00**

SOAP BOX DERBY SERIES

☐ 1979	**Last Minute Changes,** artist: Norman Rockwell, production: one year	**24.50**	**30.00**
☐ 1980	**At the Gate,** artist: Norman Rockwell, production: one year	**24.50**	**25.00**
☐ 1982	**In the Stretch,** artist: Norman Rockwell, production: one year	**24.50**	**30.00**

SPECIAL CELEBRITY SERIES

☐ 1981	**Reagan/Bush,** artist: Mike Hagel, production quantity 17,500	**45.00**	**45.00**
☐ 1982	**Hope/Thanks for the Memories,** artist: Mike Hagel, production limited	**45.00**	**45.00**
☐ 1982	**Burns/Young at Heart,** artist: Mike Hagel, production limited	**45.00**	**45.00**

		Issue Price	Current Value
☐ **1982**	**I Love Lucy,** artist: Mike Hagel, production limited	45.00	45.00

SINGLE RELEASES

		Issue Price	Current Value
☐ **1979**	**John Wayne Tribute,** artist: Endre Szabo, production quantity 7,500	45.00	46.00
☐ **1980**	**His Master's Voice,** production: less than one year	24.50	28.00
☐ **1981**	**Eyes of the Seasons,** set of four, production quantity 19,500	154.00	160.00
☐ **1982**	**Norman Rockwell Tribute,** artist: George Malik, production quantity 5,000	55.00	55.00
☐ **1982**	**Betty Boop,** artist: N/A, production quantity 15,000	24.50	25.00
☐ **1982**	**White House Panda,** artist: Bogdan Grom, production quantity 15,000	38.50	38.50

MANJUNDO

Japan

CHINESE LUNAR CALENDAR SERIES

		Issue Price	Current Value
☐ **1972**	**Year of the Rat,** production quantity 5,000	15.00	15.00
☐ **1973**	**Year of the Ox,** production quantity 5,000	15.00	15.00
☐ **1974**	**Year of the Monkey,** production quantity 5,000	15.00	15.00

MARIGOLD

PICASSO SERIES

		Issue Price	Current Value
☐ **1984**	**Tete Appuyee sur les Mains,** production quantity 7,777	50.00	50.00

WORLD STAR SERIES

		Issue Price	Current Value
☐ **1984**	**Mickey Mantle,** artist: Pablo Carreno, production quantity 10,000	60.00	60.00
☐ **1984**	**Mickey Mantle,** artist: Pablo Carreno, signed, production quantity 1,000	100.00	100.00

MARMOT

Germany

CHRISTMAS SERIES	Issue Price	Current Value
☐ 1970 **Polar Bear,** production quantity 5,000	13.00	35.00
☐ 1971 **Buffalo Bill,** production quantity 6,000	16.00	16.00
☐ 1972 **Boy and Grandfather,** production quantity 5,000................................	20.00	30.00
☐ 1973 **Snowman,** production quantity 3,000	22.00	35.00
☐ 1974 **Dancing,** production quantity 2,000	24.00	30.00
☐ 1975 **Quail,** production quantity 2,000	30.00	30.00
☐ 1976 **Windmill,** production quantity 2,000	40.00	40.00

FATHER'S DAY SERIES

	Issue Price	Current Value
☐ 1970 **Stag,** production quantity 3,500	12.00	100.00
☐ 1971 **Horse,** production quantity 3,500	12.50	40.00

MOTHER'S DAY SERIES

	Issue Price	Current Value
☐ 1972 **Seal,** production quantity 6,000	16.00	30.00
☐ 1973 **Polar Bear,** production quantity 3,000	20.00	140.00
☐ 1974 **Penguins,** production quantity 2,000	24.00	25.00
☐ 1975 **Raccoons,** production quantity 2,000	30.00	30.00
☐ 1976 **Ducks,** production quantity 2,000	40.00	40.00

PRESIDENTS SERIES

	Issue Price	Current Value
☐ 1971 **Washington,** production quantity 1,500	25.00	30.00
☐ 1972 **Jefferson,** production quantity 1,500	25.00	30.00
☐ 1973 **John Adams,** production quantity 1,500 ...	25.00	25.00

MARURI USA

United States

EAGLE SERIES

	Issue Price	Current Value
☐ 1984 **Free Flight,** artist: W. Gaither, production quantity 995	150.00	150.00

MARY ENGELBREIT SOCIETY

United States

BELIEVE SERIES	Issue Price	Current Value
☐ 1986 Santa's Treasure, artist: Mary Engelbreit, production quantity 10,000	29.95	30.00

MASON

Great Britain

CHRISTMAS SERIES

	Issue Price	Current Value
☐ 1975 Windsor Castle, production: one year	75.00	75.00
☐ 1976 Holyrood House, production: one year	75.00	75.00
☐ 1977 Buckingham Palace, production: one year	75.00	75.00
☐ 1978 Balmoral Castle, production: one year	75.00	75.00
☐ 1979 Hampton Court, production: one year	75.00	75.00
☐ 1980 Sandringham House, production: one year	75.00	75.00

MASTER ENGRAVERS OF AMERICA

United States

INDIAN DANCERS SERIES

	Issue Price	Current Value
☐ 1979 Eagle Dancer, production quantity 2,500 . .	300.00	340.00
☐ 1980 Hoop Dancer, production quantity 2,500 . .	300.00	340.00

MEISSEN

Germany

ANNUAL SERIES

	Issue Price	Current Value
☐ 1973 Winter Countryside by Sleigh, production quantity 5,000	71.00	71.00
☐ 1974 Sleeping Beauty, production quantity 5,000	75.00	75.00
☐ 1975 Archway to Albrecht's Castle, production quantity 5,500	92.00	92.00
☐ 1976 Doge's Palace in Venice, production quantity 5,000	92.00	92.00
☐ 1977 Fra Holle, production quantity 5,000	114.00	114.00
☐ 1978 Ice Crystal with Children, production quantity 7,000	123.00	123.00
☐ 1979 Winter Fairy Tale, production quantity 7,000	151.00	151.00
☐ 1980 Booted Cat	155.00	155.00

METAL ARTS COMPANY

United States

		Issue Price	Current Value

CHILDREN OF NORMAN ROCKWELL SERIES
(The Hamilton Collection)

		Issue Price	Current Value
☐ 1979	**Doctor and Doll,** artist: Norman Rockwell, production quantity 19,750	21.00	24.00
☐ 1979	**Knuckles Down,** artist: Norman Rockwell, production quantity 19,750	21.00	24.00
☐ 1979	**Grandpa's Girl,** artist: Norman Rockwell, production quantity 19,750	21.00	24.00
☐ 1979	**Leapfrog,** artist: Norman Rockwell, production quantity 19,750	21.00	24.00
☐ 1980	**Dog Gone It,** artist: Norman Rockwell, production quantity 19,750	21.00	24.00
☐ 1980	**Look Out Below,** artist: Norman Rockwell, production quantity 19,750	21.00	24.00
☐ 1980	**Batter Up,** artist: Norman Rockwell, production quantity 19,750	21.00	24.00
☐ 1980	**No Peeking,** artist: Norman Rockwell, production quantity 19,750	21.00	24.00

NORMAN ROCKWELL CHRISTMAS
(The Hamilton Collection)

		Issue Price	Current Value
☐ 1978	**The Christmas Gift,** artist: Norman Rockwell, production: one year	48.00	49.00
☐ 1979	**The Big Moment,** artist: Norman Rockwell, production: one year	48.00	49.00
☐ 1980	**Santa's Helpers,** artist: Norman Rockwell, production: one year	48.00	49.00
☐ 1981	**Santa,** artist: Norman Rockwell, production: one year	48.00	49.00

NORMAN ROCKWELL MAN'S BEST FRIEND
(The Hamilton Collection)

		Issue Price	Current Value
☐ 1979	**The Hobo,** artist: Norman Rockwell, production quantity 9,500	40.00	60.00
☐ 1979	**The Doctor,** artist: Norman Rockwell, production quantity 9,500	40.00	40.00
☐ 1979	**Making Friends,** artist: Norman Rockwell, production quantity 9,500	40.00	40.00

		Issue Price	Current Value
☐ 1979	**Gone Fishing,** artist: Norman Rockwell, production quantity 9,500	40.00	40.00
☐ 1980	**The Thief,** artist: Norman Rockwell, production quantity 9,500	40.00	40.00
☐ 1980	**Puppy Love,** artist: Norman Rockwell, production quantity 9,500	40.00	40.00

WINSLOW HOMER'S THE SEA SERIES

☐ 1977	**Breezing Up,** production quantity 9,500 . . .	29.95	35.00

SINGLE RELEASES

☐ 1977	**America's First Family—Carters,** production quantity 9,500	40.00	42.00
☐ 1977	**Washington at Valley Forge,** pewter, production quantity 9,500	95.00	105.00
☐ 1977	**Washington at Valley Forge,** sterling silver, production quantity 500	225.00	250.00

METAWA

Netherlands

CHRISTMAS SERIES

☐ 1972	**Iceskaters,** production quantity 3,000	30.00	35.00
☐ 1973	**One-Horse Sleigh,** production quantity 1,500	30.00	30.00
☐ 1974	**Sailboat,** production: one year	35.00	35.00

METROPOLITAN MUSEUM OF ART

United States

METROPOLITAN CAT SERIES

☐ 1986	**Two Cats,** artist: Felix Vallotton, production quantity: N/A	12.00	15.00

TREASURES OF TUTANKHAMEN SERIES

☐ 1977	**King Tut,** production quantity 2,500	150.00	170.00

METTLACH

Germany

CHRISTMAS SERIES	Issue Price	Current Value
☐ **1978** **Christmas,** production quantity 20,000	**175.00**	**150.00**
☐ **1979** **Mother with Child,** production quantity 10,000	**198.00**	**198.00**
☐ **1980** **Madonna in Glory,** production quantity 10,000	**210.00**	**210.00**

COLLECTORS SOCIETY SERIES

	Issue Price	Current Value
☐ **1980** **Snow White and Seven Dwarfs,** production: one year	**60.00**	**60.00**

MOTHER'S DAY PLAQUE SERIES

	Issue Price	Current Value
☐ **1978** **Mother's Day,** production quantity 15,000	**100.00**	**100.00**

MICHELON ENTERPRISES

QUIET PLACES SERIES

	Issue Price	Current Value
☐ **1981** **Day Dreaming,** artist: Tom Heflin, production quantity 5,000	**75.00**	**75.00**
☐ **1981** **Try to Remember,** artist: Tom Heflin, production quantity 5,000	**75.00**	**75.00**
☐ **1981** **Emmert's Gate,** artist: Tom Heflin, production quantity 5,000	**77.00**	**75.00**

MICHIGAN NATURAL RESOURCES

United States

NATURE'S HERITAGE SERIES

	Issue Price	Current Value
☐ **1982** **White Tailed Fawn,** artist: Richard Timm, production quantity 14,500	**37.50**	**38.00**

MINGOLLA/HOME PLATES

United States

	Issue Price	Current Value
CHRISTMAS SERIES (Enamel on Copper)		
☐ **1973 Christmas,** production quantity 1,000	**95.00**	**165.00**
☐ **1974 Christmas,** production quantity 1,000	**110.00**	**145.00**
☐ **1975 Christmas,** production quantity 1,000	**125.00**	**145.00**
☐ **1976 Christmas,** production quantity 1,000	**125.00**	**125.00**
☐ **1977 Winter Wonderland,** production quantity 2,000	**200.00**	**200.00**
CHRISTMAS SERIES (Porcelain)		
☐ **1974 Christmas,** production quantity 5,000	**35.00**	**65.00**
☐ **1975 Christmas,** production quantity 5,000	**35.00**	**45.00**
☐ **1976 Christmas,** production quantity 5,000	**35.00**	**30.00**
FOUR SEASONS SERIES		
☐ **1978 Dashing Through the Snow,** production quantity 2,000	**150.00**	**150.00**
☐ **1978 Spring Flowers,** production quantity 2,000	**150.00**	**150.00**
☐ **1978 Beach Fun,** production quantity 2,000	**150.00**	**150.00**
☐ **1978 Balloon Breezes,** production quantity 2,000	**150.00**	**150.00**

MISTWOOD DESIGNS

United States

	Issue Price	Current Value
AMERICAN WILDLIFE SERIES		
☐ **1981 Desperado at the Waterhole,** artist: Skipper Kendricks, production quantity 5,000	**45.00**	**46.00**
☐ **1982 Bayou Bunnies,** artist: Skipper Kendricks, production quantity 5,000	**45.00**	**46.00**

MODERN CONCEPTS LIMITED

United States

	Issue Price	Current Value
MAGIC OF THE SEA SERIES		
☐ **1983 Future Miss,** artist: Lucelle Raad, production limited	**25.00**	**25.00**

		Issue Price	Current Value
☐ 1984	**One, Two, Three,** artist: Lucelle Raad, production limited	26.50	26.50

NURSERY RHYME FAVORITE SERIES

☐ 1984	**Sugar and Spice,** artist: Lucelle Raad, production quantity 7,500	38.50	38.50
☐ 1985	**Snips and Snails,** artist: Lucelle Raad, production quantity 7,500	38.50	38.50

SIGNS OF LOVE SERIES

☐ 1983	**When Hearts Touch,** artist: Lucelle Raad, production quantity 19,500	39.50	40.00
☐ 1984	**My Very Own,** artist: Lucelle Raad, production quantity 19,500	39.50	40.00

SPECIAL MOMENTS SERIES

☐ 1982	**David's Dilemma,** artist: Lucelle Raad, numbered, production quantity 12,500	35.00	50.00
☐ 1983	**Secrets,** artist: Lucelle Raad, numbered, production quantity 12,500	35.00	35.00
☐ 1983	**Enough for Two,** artist: Lucelle Raad, numbered, production quantity 12,500	38.50	39.50
☐ 1984	**Chatterbox,** artist: Lucelle Raad, numbered, production quantity 12,500	38.50	39.00

MODERN MASTERS

United States

A CHILD'S BEST FRIEND SERIES

☐ 1982	**Christi's Kitty,** artist: Richard Zolan, production: 15 days	29.50	30.50
☐ 1982	**Patrick's Puppy,** artist: Richard Zolan, production: 15 days	29.50	30.50

BABES IN THE WOODS SERIES

☐ 1982	**Newborn Fawn,** artist: Sally Miller, production quantity 9,500	45.00	46.00
☐ 1983	**First Outing,** artist: Sally Miller, production quantity 9,500	45.00	45.00
☐ 1983	**Bandy Bandit,** artist: Sally Miller, production quantity 9,500	50.00	50.00

	Issue Price	Current Value
☐ **1984 Moment's Rest,** artist: Sally Miller, production quantity 9,500	50.00	35.00

FAMILY TREASURES SERIES

	Issue Price	Current Value
☐ **1981 Cora's Recital,** artist: Richard Zolan, production quantity 18,500	39.50	45.00
☐ **1982 Cora's Tea Party,** artist: Richard Zolan, production quantity 18,500	39.50	40.50
☐ **1983 Cora's Garden Party,** artist: Richard Zolan, production quantity 18,500	39.50	40.00

FLORAL FELINES SERIES

	Issue Price	Current Value
☐ **1983 The Baron,** artist: Julie Shearer, production quantity 9,500	55.00	55.00
☐ **1984 Her Majesty,** artist: Julie Shearer, production quantity 9,500	55.00	55.00
☐ **1984 Duchess,** artist: Julie Shearer, production quantity 9,500	55.00	55.00
☐ **1984 His Lordship,** artist: Julie Shearer, production quantity 9,500	55.00	55.00

HORSES OF FRED STONE SERIES

	Issue Price	Current Value
☐ **1981 Patience,** artist: Fred Stone, production quantity 9,500	55.00	70.00

The Baron, artist: Julie Shearer.

	Issue Price	Current Value
☐ **1982 Arabian Mare and Foal,** artist: Fred Stone, production quantity 9,500	55.00	56.00
☐ **1982 Safe and Sound,** artist: Fred Stone, production quantity 9,500	55.00	55.00
☐ **1983 Contentment,** artist: Fred Stone, production quantity 9,500	55.00	55.00

LITTER BASKET SERIES

☐ **1983 Last of the Litter,** artist: Sally Miller, production limited	35.00	35.00
☐ **1984 Double Delight,** artist: Sally Miller, production limited	35.00	35.00
☐ **1984 Tender Trio,** artist: Sally Miller, production limited	35.00	35.00
☐ **1985 Litter Bug,** artist: Sally Miller, production limited	35.00	35.00
☐ **1985 Hide and Seek,** artist: Sally Miller, production limited	35.00	35.00
☐ **1985 Poodle Picnic,** artist: Sally Miller, production limited	35.00	35.00

LITTLE LADIES SERIES

☐ **1983 When Mommy's Away,** artist: Claire Freedman, production quantity limited	29.50	30.00
☐ **1984 Before the Show Begins,** artist: Claire Freedman, production quantity limited	29.50	30.00

SALLY MILLER CHRISTMAS

☐ **1985 They Came to Adore Him,** artist: Sally Miller, production quantity 5,000	39.50	40.00

THROUGH THE EYES OF LOVE SERIES

☐ **1981 Enchanted Eyes,** artist: Karin Schaefers, production quantity 9,500	55.00	55.00
☐ **1982 Summer Secrets,** artist: Karin Schaefers, production quantity 9,500	55.00	55.00
☐ **1983 Garden Gathering,** artist: Karin Schaefers, production quantity 9,500	55.00	55.00

WILL MOSES' AMERICA SERIES

☐ **1982 September Fair,** artist: Will Moses, production quantity 7,500	45.00	45.00

		Issue Price	Current Value
□ **1983**	**Spring Recess,** artist: Will Moses, production quantity 7,500	**45.00**	**45.00**

WINGS OF NOBILITY SERIES

		Issue Price	Current Value
□ **1984**	**American Bald Eagle,** production quantity 7,500	**49.50**	**50.00**
□ **1984**	**Peregrine Falcon,** production quantity 7,500	**49.50**	**50.00**
□ **1984**	**Red-Shouldered Hawk,** production quantity 7,500	**49.50**	**50.00**

SINGLE ISSUE

		Issue Price	Current Value
□ **1983**	**Twelve Days of Christmas,** artist: Will Moses, production limited to 12 days	**45.00**	**45.00**

MONACO PORCELAIN FACTORY

Monaco

DAY AND NIGHT

		Issue Price	Current Value
□ **1983**	**Le Nuit,** artist: Erich Rozewicz, production quantity 600		
□ **1983**	**Le Jour,** artist: Erich Rozewicz, production quantity 600		
	Set of two	**200.00**	**200.00**

MORGANTOWN CRYSTAL

United States

COUNTRY LADIES SERIES

		Issue Price	Current Value
□ **1981**	**Angelica,** artist: Michael Yates, production quantity 30,000	**75.00**	**75.00**
□ **1982**	**Violet,** artist: Michael Yates, production quantity 30,000	**75.00**	**75.00**
□ **1983**	**Heather,** artist: Michael Yates, production quantity 30,000	**75.00**	**100.00**
□ **1984**	**Laurel,** artist: Michael Yates, production quantity 30,000	**75.00**	**100.00**

**Laurel, artist: Michael
Yates.**

MOSER

Czechoslovakia

CHRISTMAS SERIES	Issue Price	Current Value
☐ 1970 **Hradcany Castle,** production quantity 400	75.00	170.00
☐ 1971 **Karlstein Castle,** production quantity 1,365	75.00	80.00
☐ 1972 **Old Town Hall,** production quantity 1,000	85.00	85.00
☐ 1983 **Karlovy Vary Castle,** production quantity 500	90.00	100.00

MOTHER'S DAY SERIES

	Issue Price	Current Value
☐ 1971 **Peacocks,** production quantity 350	75.00	100.00
☐ 1972 **Butterflies,** production quantity 750	85.00	90.00
☐ 1973 **Squirrels,** production quantity 500	90.00	95.00

MOUSSALLI

United States

BIRDS OF FOUR SEASONS SERIES

☐ 1977 **Cedar Waxwing,** production quantity 1,000	375.00	450.00
☐ 1978 **The Cardinal,** production quantity 1,000 . . .	375.00	425.00
☐ 1978 **Wren,** production quantity 1,000	375.00	380.00
☐ 1979 **Hummingbird,** production quantity 1,000 . .	375.00	380.00
☐ 1979 **Indigo Bunting,** production quantity 1,000	375.00	380.00

	Issue Price	Current Value
MOTHER'S DAY SERIES		
☐ **1979 Chickadee,** production quantity 500	**450.00**	**450.00**

NASSAU ART GALLERY

Bahamas

COLLECTOR PLATES OF THE BAHAMAS SERIES

☐ **1982 Bahamas 1982,** artist: Elyse Wasile, production quantity 5,000	**35.00**	**35.00**
☐ **1982 Gregory's Arch,** artist: Elyse Wasile, production quantity 5,000	**35.00**	**35.00**

NEWELL POTTERY COMPANY

United States

CALENDAR SERIES

☐ **1984 June,** artist: Sarah Stilwell Weber, production limited	**19.00**	**19.00**
☐ **1985 July,** artist: Sarah Stilwell Weber, production limited	**19.00**	**19.00**
☐ **1985 August,** artist: Sarah Stilwell Weber, production limited	**19.00**	**19.00**
☐ **1985 September,** artist: Sarah Stilwell Weber, production limited	**19.00**	**30.00**
☐ **1985 October,** artist: Sarah Stilwell Weber, production limited	**19.00**	**25.00**
☐ **1985 November,** artist: Sarah Stilwell Weber, production limited	**19.00**	**19.00**
☐ **1986 December,** artist: Sarah Stilwell Weber, production limited	**19.00**	**30.00**
☐ **1986 January,** artist: Sarah Stilwell Weber, production limited	**19.00**	**19.00**
☐ **1986 February,** artist: Sarah Stilwell Weber, production limited	**19.00**	**19.00**
☐ **1986 March,** artist: Sarah Stilwell Weber, production limited	**19.00**	**19.00**
☐ **1986 April,** artist: Sarah Stilwell Weber, production limited	**19.00**	**19.00**

NORITAKE

Japan

ANNUAL SERIES	Issue Price	Current Value
☐ 1977 **Paradise Birds,** production quantity 3,000	**380.00**	**390.00**
☐ 1978 **Chrysanthemums,** production quantity 3,000	**494.00**	**500.00**
☐ 1979 **Cranes,** production quantity 3,000	**556.00**	**560.00**
☐ 1980 **Water Lilies and Butterflies,** production quantity 3,000	**575.00**	**580.00**

CHRISTMAS SERIES

	Issue Price	Current Value
☐ 1975 **Madonna with Child,** production quantity 3,000	**42.00**	**43.00**
☐ 1975 **Gratia Hoso Kawa,** production quantity 3,000	**54.00**	**55.00**
☐ 1977 **Julia Otaa,** production quantity 3,000	**83.00**	**84.00**
☐ 1978 **Amakusa Shiro,** production quantity 3,000	**109.00**	**110.00**
☐ 1979 **Munzio Ito,** production quantity 3,000	**124.00**	**125.00**
☐ 1980 **Furst Takayana,** production quantity 3,000	**125.00**	**125.00**

NOSTALGIA COLLECTIBLES

United States

ELVIS PRESLEY COLLECTION
(Rockwell Museum)

☐ 1985 **Hound Dog,** production limited	**15.00**	**15.00**
☐ 1985 **Lonesome Tonight,** production limited	**15.00**	**15.00**
☐ 1985 **Teddy Bear,** production limited	**15.00**	**15.00**
☐ 1985 **Don't Be Cruel,** production limited	**15.00**	**15.00**
☐ 1985 Complete set of four	**60.00**	**60.00**

JAMES DEAN COLLECTION
(Rockwell Museum)

☐ 1985 **East of Eden,** production limited	**15.00**	**15.00**
☐ 1985 **Rebel Without a Cause,** production limited	**15.00**	**15.00**
☐ 1985 **Giant,** production limited	**15.00**	**15.00**
☐ 1985 **Jim and Spyder,** production limited	**15.00**	**15.00**
☐ 1985 Complete set of four	**60.00**	**60.00**

		Issue Price	Current Value
SHIRLEY TEMPLE COLLECTION (Rockwell Museum)			
□ 1983	**Captain January,** artist: Bill Jacobson, production quantity 25,000	**35.00**	**35.00**
□ 1984	**Heidi,** artist: Bill Jacobson, production quantity 25,000	**35.00**	**35.00**
□ 1984	**Little Miss Marker,** artist: Bill Jacobson, production quantity 25,000	**35.00**	**35.00**
□ 1984	**Bright Eyes,** artist: Bill Jacobson, production quantity 25,000	**35.00**	**35.00**
□ 1985	**The Little Colonel,** artist: Bill Jacobson, production quantity 25,000	**35.00**	**35.00**
□ 1985	**Rebecca of Sunnybrook Farm,** artist: Bill Jacobson, production quantity 25,000	**35.00**	**35.00**
□ 1986	**Poor Little Rich Girl,** artist: Bill Jacobson, production quantity 25,000	**35.00**	**35.00**
□ 1986	**Wee Willie Winkie,** artist: Bill Jacobson, production quantity 25,000	**35.00**	**35.00**
SHIRLEY TEMPLE COLLECTIBLES SERIES			
□ 1982	**Baby Take a Bow,** production quantity 22,500	**75.00**	**100.00**
□ 1983	**Baby Take a Bow,** autographed, production quantity 2,500	**100.00**	**160.00**
□ 1983	**Curly Top,** production quantity 22,500	**75.00**	**100.00**
□ 1983	**Curly Top,** autographed, production quantity 2,500	**100.00**	**150.00**
□ 1982	**Stand Up and Cheer,** production quantity 22,500	**75.00**	**100.00**
□ 1983	**Stand Up and Cheer,** autographed, production quantity 2,500	**100.00**	**100.00**
SPECIAL COMMEMORATIVE ISSUES (Rockwell Museum)			
□ 1985	**James Dean—America's Rebel,** artist: William Jacobson, production quantity 10,000	**45.00**	**45.00**
□ 1985	**Elvis Presley—The Once and Forever King,** artist: William Jacobson, production quantity 10,000	**45.00**	**45.00**

OHIO ARTS

United States

		Issue Price	Current Value
NORMAN ROCKWELL SERIES			
□ **1979**	**Looking Out to Sea,** artist: Norman Rockwell, production quantity 20,000	**19.50**	**21.00**

O.K. COLLECTIBLES

FANTASY FARM SERIES

□ **1984**	**Lowena,** artist: Louise Sigle, production quantity 3,000.........................	**39.95**	**40.00**

SINGLE RELEASES

□ **1984**	**Chester,** artist: Ralph Waterhouse, production quantity 5,000.....................	**55.00**	**55.00**
□ **1984**	**Midwestern Summer,** artist: Jeanne Horak, production quantity 4,500	**50.00**	**50.00**
□ **1984**	**Morning in the Marshland,** artist: Evel Knievel, production quantity 15,000	**50.00**	**50.00**

OPA'S HAUS

Germany

ANNUAL GERMAN CHRISTMAS
(Weihnachten)

□ **1978**	**Annual Christmas Plate,** production quantity 2,500	**58.00**	**58.00**
□ **1979**	**Annual Christmas Plate,** production quantity 2,500	**58.00**	**58.00**
□ **1980**	**Annual Christmas Plate,** production quantity 2,500	**58.00**	**58.00**
□ **1981**	**Annual Christmas Plate,** production quantity 2,500	**58.00**	**58.00**
□ **1982**	**Annual Christmas Plate,** production quantity 2,500	**58.00**	**58.00**
□ **1983**	**Annual Christmas Plate,** production quantity 2,500	**58.00**	**58.00**
□ **1984**	**Annual Christmas Plate,** production quantity 2,500	**58.00**	**58.00**

ORREFORS

Sweden

ANNUAL CATHEDRAL SERIES

		Issue Price	Current Value
☐ 1970	**Notre Dame,** production quantity 5,000 ...	**50.00**	**65.00**
☐ 1971	**Westminster Abbey,** production quantity 5,000	**45.00**	**41.00**
☐ 1972	**Basilica di San Marco,** production quantity 5,000	**50.00**	**60.00**
☐ 1973	**Cologne Cathedral,** production quantity 5,000	**50.00**	**65.00**
☐ 1974	**Rue de la Victoire,** production quantity 5,000	**60.00**	**71.00**
☐ 1975	**Basilica di San Pietro,** production quantity 5,000	**85.00**	**110.00**
☐ 1976	**Christ Church,** production quantity 3,000 ..	**85.00**	**85.00**
☐ 1977	**Masjid-I-Shah,** production quantity 3,000	**90.00**	**100.00**
☐ 1978	**Santiago de Compostela,** production quantity 3,000	**95.00**	**100.00**

MOTHER'S DAY SERIES

		Issue Price	Current Value
☐ 1971	**Flowers for Mother,** production: one year	**45.00**	**61.00**
☐ 1972	**Mother and Children,** production: one year	**45.00**	**46.00**
☐ 1973	**Mother and Child,** production: one year ...	**50.00**	**51.00**
☐ 1974	**Mother and Child,** production: one year ...	**50.00**	**51.00**
☐ 1975	**Mother and Child,** production: one year ...	**60.00**	**61.00**
☐ 1976	**Children and Puppy,** production: one year	**75.00**	**61.00**
☐ 1977	**Child and Dove,** production quantity 1,500	**85.00**	**86.00**
☐ 1978	**Mother and Child,** production quantity 1,500	**90.00**	**91.00**

PACIFIC ART LIMITED

United States

JUST LIKE DADDY'S HATS SERIES

		Issue Price	Current Value
☐ 1983	**Jessica,** artist: Franklin Moody, production quantity 10,000	**29.00**	**30.00**

VICTORIA AND JASON

		Issue Price	Current Value
☐ 1983	**Victoria,** artist: Lee Dubin, production quantity 7,500		
☐ 1983	**Jason,** artist: Lee Dubin, production quantity 7,500		
	Set of two	**65.00**	**65.00**

	Issue Price	Current Value
SINGLE ISSUES		

☐ **1983 Mae West,** artist: Bob Harman, production quantity 5,000 . . . .   **42.50**   **42.50**

☐ **1983 Guardian Angel,** artist: Lily Cavell, production quantity 7,500 . . . .   **29.50**   **30.00**

PALISANDER

Denmark

CHRISTMAS SERIES

☐ **1971 Red Robin,** production quantity 1,200 . . . . .   **50.00**   **63.00**
☐ **1972 Flying Geese,** production quantity 1,200 . . .   **50.00**   **58.00**
☐ **1973 Christmas,** production quantity 1,200 . . . . .   **50.00**   **53.00**

PRESIDENTIAL SERIES

☐ **1971 Washington,** production quantity 1,000 . . . .   **50.00**   **53.00**
☐ **1972 Jefferson,** production quantity 1,000 . . . . . .   **50.00**   **53.00**
☐ **1973 John Adams,** production quantity 1,000 . . .   **50.00**   **53.00**

SINGLE RELEASE

☐ **1973 Bicentennial,** production quantity 250 . . . . .   **50.00**   **53.00**

PAPEL

OLYMPICS

☐ **1984 Sports Plate,** production: one year **30.00**   **30.00**
☐ **1984 Star in Motion,** production quantity 25,000   **17.00**   **17.50**
☐ **1984 Sam the Olympic Eagle,** production quantity 25,000 . . . .   **17.00**   **17.50**

PARKHURST ENTERPRISES

United States

INTERNATIONAL WILDLIFE FOUNDATION SERIES

☐ **1984 Pandas,** artist: Violet Parkhurst, production quantity 1,000 . . . .   **60.00**   **60.00**

☐ **1984 Grizzlies,** artist: Violet Parkhurst, production quantity 1,000 . . . .   **60.00**   **60.00**

	Issue Price	Current Value
☐ **1984 Elephants,** artist: Violet Parkhurst, production quantity 1,000	60.00	60.00
☐ **1984 Bengal Tigers,** artist: Violet Parkhurst, production quantity 1,000	60.00	60.00
☐ **1984 Polar Bears,** artist: Violet Parkhurst, production quantity 1,000	60.00	60.00
☐ **1984 Snow Leopards,** artist: Violet Parkhurst, production quantity 1,000	60.00	60.00
☐ **1984 Harp Seals,** artist: Violet Parkhurst, production quantity 1,000	60.00	60.00
☐ **1984 Giraffes,** artist: Violet Parkhurst, production quantity 1,000	60.00	60.00
☐ **1984 Bactrian Camel,** artist: Violet Parkhurst, production quantity 1,000	60.00	60.00
☐ **1984 Hippos,** artist: Violet Parkhurst, production quantity 1,000	60.00	60.00
☐ **1984 Lions,** artist: Violet Parkhurst, production quantity 1,000	60.00	60.00
☐ **1984 Cheetahs,** artist: Violet Parkhurst, production quantity 1,000	60.00	60.00

PARKHURST & BOWER

United States

SINGLE ISSUE

☐ **1984 I Love Teddy Bears,** artist: Violet Parkhurst, production quantity N/A	39.50	40.00

PAWNEE CREEK PRESS

CHRISTMAS CLASSICS SERIES

☐ **1984 Cardinals and Mistletoe,** artist: James Landenberger, production quantity 2,000	50.00	50.00

PEMBERTON AND OAKES

United States

CHILDHOOD FRIENDSHIP SERIES

☐ **1987 Beach Break,** artist: Donald Zolan, production: unannounced	19.00	25.00

		Issue Price	Current Value
☐ **1987**	**Little Engineers,** artist: Donald Zolan, production: unannounced	19.00	19.00
☐ **1988**	**Tiny Treasures,** artist: Donald Zolan, production: unannounced	19.00	19.00

Beach Break, artist: Donald Zolan.

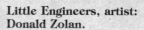

Little Engineers, artist: Donald Zolan.

Tiny Treasures, artist: Donald Zolan.

CHILDREN AT CHRISTMAS SERIES	Issue Price	Current Value
☐ **1981** **A Gift for Laurie,** artist: Donald Zolan, production quantity 15,000	**48.00**	**86.00**
☐ **1987** **A Gift for Laurie,** artist: Donald Zolan, miniature	**12.50**	**25.00**
☐ **1982** **A Christmas Prayer,** artist: Donald Zolan, production quantity 15,000	**48.00**	**99.00**
☐ **1983** **Erik's Delight,** artist: Donald Zolan, production quantity 15,000	**48.00**	**62.00**
☐ **1984** **Christmas Secret,** artist: Donald Zolan, production quantity 15,000	**48.00**	**65.00**
☐ **1985** **Christmas Kitten,** artist: Donald Zolan, production quantity 15,000	**48.00**	**62.00**
☐ **1986** **Laurie and the Creche,** artist: Donald Zolan, production quantity 15,000	**48.00**	**65.00**

A Gift for Laurie, artist: Donald Zolan.

A Christmas Prayer, artist: Donald Zolan.

Erik's Delight, artist:
Donald Zolan.

Christmas Secret, artist:
Donald Zolan.

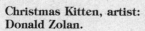
Christmas Kitten, artist:
Donald Zolan.

Laurie and the Creche, artist: Donald Zolan.

FATHER'S DAY SERIES	Issue Price	Current Value
☐ 1986 **Daddy's Home,** artist: Donald Zolan, production: unannounced	19.00	80.00
☐ 1986 **Daddy's Home,** artist: Donald Zolan, miniature, production: unannounced	12.50	84.00

Daddy's Home, artist: Donald Zolan.

LITTLE GIRLS SERIES	Issue Price	Current Value
☐ **1985 Curious Kitten,** artist: Robert Anderson, production: unannounced	**29.00**	**83.00**
☐ **1986 Making Magic,** artist: Robert Anderson, production: unannounced	**29.00**	**56.00**
☐ **1986 Sunny Umbrella,** artist: Robert Anderson, production: unannounced	**29.00**	**32.00**
☐ **1987 Apple Blossom Time,** artist: Robert Anderson, production: unannounced	**29.00**	**29.00**

Curious Kitten, artist: Robert Anderson.

Making Magic, artist: Robert Anderson.

Sunny Umbrella, artist:
Robert Anderson.

Apple Blossom Time,
artist: Robert Anderson.

MOMENTS ALONE SERIES	Issue Price	Current Value
□ 1980 **The Dreamer,** artist: Robert Bentley, production: less than one year	28.80	45.00
□ 1981 **Reverie,** artist: Robert Bentley, production: less than one year	28.80	30.00
□ 1982 **Gentle Thoughts,** artist: Robert Bentley, production: less than one year	28.80	35.00
□ 1983 **Wheatfields,** artist: Robert Bentley, production: less than one year	28.80	28.80

MOTHER'S DAY

	Issue Price	Current Value
□ 1988 **Mother's Angels,** artist: Donald Zolan, production quantity: unannounced	19.00	19.00

Mother's Angels, artist:
Donald Zolan.

NUTCRACKER II COLLECTION (Viletta)	Issue Price	Current Value
☐ 1981 **Grande Finale,** artist: Shell Fisher, production: less than one year	24.40	56.00
☐ 1982 **The Arabian Dancers,** artist: Shell Fisher, production: less than one year	24.40	69.00
☐ 1983 **Dew Drop Fairy,** artist: Shell Fisher, production limited	24.40	210.00
☐ 1984 **Clara's Delight,** artist: Shell Fisher, production limited	24.40	70.00
☐ 1985 **Bedtime for Nutcracker,** artist: Shell Fisher, production limited	24.40	51.00

Bedtime for Nutcracker,
artist: Shell Fisher.

Crowning of Clara,
artist: Shell Fisher.

Dance of the
Snowflakes, artist:
Donald Zolan.

		Issue Price	Current Value
☐ 1986	**Crowning of Clara,** artist: Shell Fisher, production limited	24.40	30.00
☐ 1987	**Dance of the Snowflakes,** artist: Donald Zolan, production limited	24.40	24.40

SPECIAL MOMENTS

		Issue Price	Current Value
☐ 1988	**Brotherly Love,** artist: Donald Zolan, production quantity: unannounced	19.00	19.00

Brotherly Love, artist:
Donald Zolan.

SWAN LAKE COLLECTION (Viletta)	Issue Price	Current Value
☐ 1983 **Swan Queen,** artist: Shell Fisher, production quantity 15,000	35.00	65.00
☐ 1984 **Swan Maidens,** artist: Shell Fisher, production quantity 15,000	35.00	45.00
☐ 1984 **Swan Lake Adagio,** artist: Shell Fisher, production quantity 15,000	35.00	45.00
☐ 1984 **The Black Swan,** artist: Shell Fisher, production quantity 15,000	35.00	45.00

Swan Lake Adagio,
artist: Shell Fisher.

The Black Swan, artist: Shell Fisher.

The Dying Swan, artist: Shell Fisher.

		Issue Price	Current Value
☐ 1985	**The Dying Swan,** artist: Shell Fisher, production quantity 15,000	**35.00**	**65.00**

THANKSGIVING DAY

☐ 1987	**I'm Thankful, Too,** artist: Donald Zolan, production quantity: unannounced	**19.00**	**19.00**

WONDER OF CHILDHOOD SERIES

☐ 1982	**Touching the Sky,** artist: Donald Zolan ...	**19.00**	**35.00**
☐ 1986	**Touching the Sky,** artist: Donald Zolan miniature	**12.50**	**28.00**
☐ 1983	**Spring Innocence,** artist: Donald Zolan	**19.00**	**43.00**
☐ 1984	**Winter Angel,** artist: Donald Zolan	**22.00**	**52.00**
☐ 1985	**Small Wonder,** artist: Donald Zolan	**22.00**	**35.00**

I'm Thankful, Too,
artist: Donald Zolan.

Touching the Sky, artist:
Donald Zolan.

Spring Innocence, artist:
Donald Zolan.

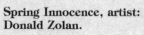

Grandma's Garden,
artist: Donald Zolan.

Day Dreamer, artist:
Donald Zolan.

		Issue Price	Current Value
☐ 1987	Small Wonder, artist: Donald Zolan, miniature	12.50	12.50
☐ 1986	Grandma's Garden, artist: Donald Zolan ..	22.00	33.00
☐ 1987	Day Dreamer, artist: Donald Zolan	22.00	28.00

ZOLAN'S CHILDREN SERIES

		Issue Price	Current Value
☐ 1978	Erik and the Dandelion, artist: Donald Zolan, production: one year	19.00	239.00
☐ 1986	Erik and the Dandelion, artist: Donald Zolan, miniature production: one year	12.50	63.00
☐ 1979	Sabina in the Grass, artist: Donald Zolan, production: one year	22.00	200.00
☐ 1985	Sabina in the Grass, artist: Donald Zolan, miniature, production: one year	12.50	96.00

		Issue Price	Current Value
☐ **1980**	**By Myself,** artist: Donald Zolan, production: one year	**24.00**	**45.00**
☐ **1981**	**For You,** artist: Donald Zolan, production: one year	**24.00**	**37.00**
☐ **1987**	**For You,** artist: Donald Zolan, miniature ..	**12.50**	**12.50**

ZOLAN'S CHILDREN AND PETS SERIES

☐ **1984**	**Tender Moment,** artist: Donald Zolan, production limited	**19.00**	**84.00**
☐ **1986**	**Tender Moment,** artist: Donald Zolan, miniature, production limited	**12.50**	**43.00**
☐ **1984**	**Golden Moment,** artist: Donald Zolan, production limited	**19.00**	**35.00**
☐ **1985**	**Making Friends,** artist: Donald Zolan, production limited	**19.00**	**37.00**

Tender Moment, artist: Donald Zolan.

Golden Moment, artist: Donald Zolan.

**Making Friends, artist:
Donald Zolan.**

**Tender Beginning,
artist: Donald Zolan.**

**Backyard Discovery,
artist: Donald Zolan.**

Waiting to Play, artist:
Donald Zolan.

		Issue Price	Current Value
☐ 1985	**Tender Beginning,** artist: Donald Zolan, production limited	**19.00**	**49.00**
☐ 1986	**Backyard Discovery,** artist: Donald Zolan, production limited	**19.00**	**34.00**
☐ 1986	**Backyard Discovery,** artist: Donald Zolan, miniature.............................	**12.50**	**62.00**
☐ 1986	**Waiting to Play,** artist: Donald Zolan, production limited	**19.00**	**37.00**

PFAFF

HERITAGE SERIES

☐ 1977	**Germany,** production quantity 2,500	**40.00**	**53.00**
☐ 1978	**Holland,** production quantity 2,500	**40.00**	**42.00**
☐ 1979	**Switzerland,** production quantity 2,500	**40.00**	**42.00**
☐ 1980	**Norway,** production quantity 2,500	**40.00**	**42.00**

PICKARD

United States

ANNUAL CHRISTMAS PLATE SERIES

☐ 1976	**Alba Madonna,** artist: Raphael, production quantity 7,500........................	**60.00**	**90.00**
☐ 1977	**Nativity,** artist: L. Lotto, production quantity 7,500	**65.00**	**65.00**
☐ 1978	**Rest on the Flight into Egypt,** artist: G. David, production quantity 10,000	**65.00**	**65.00**
☐ 1979	**Adoration of the Magi,** artist: Botticelli, production quantity 10,000	**70.00**	**70.00**

		Issue Price	Current Value
☐ 1980	**Madonna and Child,** artist: Sodoma, production quantity 10,000	80.00	80.00
☐ 1981	**Madonna and Child with Angels,** artist: Memling, production quantity 10,000	90.00	90.00

CHILDREN OF CHRISTMAS PAST SERIES

☐ 1983	**Sledding on Christmas Day,** production quantity 7,500	60.00	60.00

CHILDREN OF MARY CASSATT SERIES

☐ 1983	**Simone in White Bonnet,** artist: Mary Cassatt, production quantity 7,500	60.00	60.00
☐ 1983	**Children Playing on Beach,** artist: Mary Cassatt, production quantity 7,500	60.00	60.00
☐ 1984	**Girl in a Straw Hat,** artist: Mary Cassatt, production quantity 7,500	60.00	60.00
☐ 1984	**Young Girls,** artist: Mary Cassatt, production quantity 7,500	60.00	60.00

CHILDREN OF MEXICO SERIES

☐ 1981	**Maria,** artist: J. Sanchez, production quantity 5,000	85.00	190.00
☐ 1981	**Miguel,** artist: J. Sanchez, production quantity 5,000	85.00	110.00
☐ 1982	**Regina,** artist: J. Sanchez, production quantity 5,000	90.00	95.00
☐ 1983	**Raphael,** artist: J. Sanchez, production quantity 5,000	90.00	90.00

CHILDREN OF RENOIR SERIES

☐ 1978	**Girl with Watering Can,** artist: Auguste Renoir, production quantity 5,000	50.00	125.00
☐ 1978	**Child in White,** artist: Auguste Renoir, production quantity 5,000	50.00	125.00
☐ 1979	**Girl with Hoop,** artist: Auguste Renoir, production quantity 5,000	55.00	75.00
☐ 1979	**At the Piano,** artist: Auguste Renoir, production quantity 5,000	55.00	75.00
☐ 1980	**Circus Girls,** artist: Auguste Renoir, production quantity 5,000	60.00	70.00
☐ 1980	**Artist's Son Jean,** artist: Auguste Renoir, production quantity 5,000	60.00	65.00

		Issue Price	Current Value

THE LEGENDS OF CAMELOT SERIES
(The Hamilton Collection)

☐ **1982 Merlin the Magician,** artist: David Palladini, hand-numbered, production quantity 12,500 — **62.50 63.60**

☐ **1982 The Secret Romance,** artist: David Palladini, hand-numbered, production quantity 12,500 — **62.50 63.60**

☐ **1982 I Knight Thee Sir Lancelot,** artist: David Palladini, hand-numbered, production quantity 12,500 .... **62.50 63.60**

☐ **1982 King Arthur and His Queen,** artist: David Palladini, hand-numbered, production quantity 12,500 .... **62.50 63.60**

LET'S PRETEND SERIES

☐ **1984 Cleopatra,** artist: Irene Spencer, production quantity 5,000 .... **80.00 80.00**

☐ **1984 Mark Antony,** artist: Irene Spencer, production quantity 5,000 .... **80.00 80.00**

☐ **1985 Maid Marian,** artist: Irene Spencer, production quantity 5,000 .... **80.00 80.00**

☐ **1985 Robin Hood,** artist: Irene Spencer, production quantity 5,000 .... **80.00 80.00**

LOCKHART WILDLIFE SERIES

☐ **1970 Woodcock and Grouse,** artist: James Lockhart, pair, production quantity 2,000 ...... **150.00 290.00**

☐ **1971 Teal and Mallard,** artist: James Lockhart, pair, production quantity 2,000 .... **150.00 198.00**

☐ **1972 Cardinal and Mockingbird,** artist: James Lockhart, pair, production quantity 2,000 **162.50 190.00**

☐ **1973 Pheasant and Wild Turkey,** artist: James Lockhart, pair, production quantity 2,000 **162.50 162.50**

☐ **1974 American Bald Eagle,** artist: James Lockhart, production quantity 2,000 .... **150.00 850.00**

☐ **1975 White-Tailed Deer,** artist: James Lockhart, production quantity 2,500 .... **100.00 100.00**

☐ **1976 American Buffalo,** artist: James Lockhart, production quantity 2,500 .... **165.00 165.00**

☐ **1977 Great Horned Owl,** artist: James Lockhart, production quantity 2,500 .... **100.00 100.00**

☐ **1978 Panther,** artist: James Lockhart, production quantity 2,500 .... **175.00 175.00**

☐ **1979 Red Foxes,** artist: James Lockhart, production quantity 2,500 .... **120.00 120.00**

☐ **1980 Trumpeter Swan,** artist: James Lockhart, production quantity 2,500 .... **200.00 200.00**

		Issue Price	Current Value
THE MOST BEAUTIFUL WOMEN OF ALL TIME SERIES			
☐ **1981**	**Helen of Troy,** artist: Oleg Cassini	**75.00**	**75.00**
☐ **1982**	**Marie Antoinette,** artist: Oleg Cassini	**75.00**	**75.00**
☐ **1983**	**Lillie Langtry,** artist: Oleg Cassini	**75.00**	**75.00**
☐ **1984**	**Salome,** artist: Oleg Cassini	**75.00**	**75.00**
MOTHER'S LOVE SERIES			
☐ **1980**	**Miracle,** artist: Irene Spencer, production quantity 7,500	**95.00**	**150.00**
☐ **1981**	**Story Time,** artist: Irene Spencer, production quantity 7,500	**110.00**	**130.00**
☐ **1982**	**First Edition,** artist: Irene Spencer, production quantity 7,500	**115.00**	**125.00**
☐ **1983**	**Precious Moment,** artist: Irene Spencer, production quantity 7,500	**120.00**	**140.00**
NATIVITY TRIPTYCH SERIES			
☐ **1986**	**Unto Us a Child Is Born,** artist: John Lawson, production quantity 3,500	**95.00**	**100.00**
PICKARD COMMEMORATIVE SERIES			
☐ **1982**	**Great Seal of United States,** production quantity 10,000	**95.00**	**95.00**
☐ **1984**	**Statue of Liberty,** production quantity: unannounced	**150.00**	**150.00**
PRESIDENTIAL SERIES			
☐ **1972**	**Truman,** production quantity 3,000	**35.00**	**35.00**
☐ **1973**	**Lincoln,** production quantity 5,000	**35.00**	**35.00**
SANCHEZ MINIATURES SERIES			
☐ **1985**	**Carmen,** artist: Sanchez, production quantity 3,500	**50.00**	**50.00**
☐ **1985**	**Felipe,** artist: Sanchez, production quantity 3,500	**50.00**	**50.00**
SYMPHONY OF ROSES SERIES			
☐ **1982**	**Wild Irish Rose,** artist: Irene Spencer, production quantity 10,000	**85.00**	**95.00**
☐ **1983**	**Yellow Rose of Texas,** artist: Irene Spencer, production quantity 10,000	**90.00**	**95.00**
☐ **1984**	**Honeysuckle Rose,** artist: Irene Spencer, production quantity 10,000	**95.00**	**95.00**

		Issue Price	Current Value
□ 1985	**Rose of Washington Square,** artist: Irene Spencer, production quantity 10,000	95.00	95.00

SINGLE RELEASES
(Paramount Classics)

□ 1977	**Coronation Plate,** production quantity 5,000	95.00	105.00
□ 1977	**King George III,** production quantity 5,000	95.00	105.00
□ 1977	**Queen Elizabeth,** production quantity 5,000	375.00	425.00
□ 1977	**Queen Victoria,** production quantity 5,000	95.00	105.00
□ 1977	**Queen of England,** production quantity 5,000	95.00	105.00

POILLERAT

France

CALENDAR SERIES

□ 1972	**January,** production quantity 1,000	100.00	115.00
□ 1972	**February,** production quantity 1,000	100.00	115.00
□ 1973	**March,** production quantity 1,000	125.00	145.00
□ 1973	**April,** production quantity 1,000	125.00	145.00

CHRISTMAS SERIES

□ 1972	**Three Kings,** production quantity 500	350.00	380.00
□ 1973	**Rose,** production quantity 500	350.00	380.00

POOLE POTTERY

Great Britain

BIRDS OF NORTH AMERICA SERIES

□ 1979	**Great Horned Owl,** production quantity 11,000	37.50	38.00

CATHEDRAL SERIES

□ 1973	**Christ on Cross,** production quantity 11,000	125.00	125.00

CHRISTMAS SERIES

□ 1973	**Adoration of Magi,** production quantity 10,000	37.50	38.00
□ 1979	**Three Wisemen,** production quantity 10,000	37.50	38.00

	Issue Price	Current Value
MEDIEVAL CALENDAR SERIES		
☐ **1972 January—Drinking Wine by Fire,** production quantity 1,000	**100.00**	**105.00**
☐ **1972 February—Chopping Wood,** production quantity 1,000	**100.00**	**105.00**
☐ **1973 March—Digging in Fields and Setting Seeds,** production quantity 1,000	**125.00**	**125.00**
☐ **1973 April—Carrying Flowering Branch,** production quantity 1,000	**125.00**	**125.00**
☐ **1974 May—Hawking,** production quantity 1,000	**125.00**	**125.00**
☐ **1974 June—Mowing Hay,** production quantity 1,000	**125.00**	**125.00**
☐ **1975 July—Cutting Corn with Sickle,** production quantity 1,000	**125.00**	**125.00**
☐ **1975 August—Threshing with Flail,** production quantity 1,000	**125.00**	**125.00**
☐ **1976 September—Picking Grapes,** production quantity 1,000	**125.00**	**125.00**
☐ **1976 October—Sowing Winter Corn,** production quantity 1,000	**125.00**	**125.00**
☐ **1977 November—Gathering Acorns to Feed Pigs,** production quantity 1,000	**125.00**	**125.00**
☐ **1977 December—Pig Killing,** production quantity 1,000	**125.00**	**125.00**
MOTHER'S DAY SERIES		
☐ **1979 Tenderness,** production quantity 10,000	**37.50**	**38.00**

PORCELAINE ARIEL

United States

A TRIBUTE TO LOVE—THE RUBAIYAT OF OMAR KHAYYAM
(The Hamilton Collection)

	Issue Price	Current Value
☐ **1980 A Shaft of Light,** artist: Mossan Eskandar, production quantity 17,500	**45.00**	**46.00**
☐ **1981 A Jug of Wine,** artist: Mossan Eskandar, production quantity 17,500	**45.00**	**46.00**
☐ **1981 Sultan After Sultan,** artist: Mossan Eskandar, production quantity 17,500	**45.00**	**46.00**
☐ **1982 The Bird Is on the Wing,** artist: Mossan Eskandar, production quantity 17,500	**45.00**	**46.00**

	Issue Price	Current Value
☐ **1982** **If Today Be Sweet,** artist: Mossan Eskandar, production quantity 17,500	**45.00**	**46.00**
☐ **1982** **The Flower That Once Has Blown,** artist: Mossan Eskandar, production quantity 17,500	**45.00**	**46.00**
☐ **1982** **The Door to Which We Have No Key,** artist: Mossan Eskandar, production quantity 17,500	**45.00**	**46.00**
☐ **1982** **Ah, My Beloved Fill the Cup,** artist: Mossan Eskandar, production quantity 17,500	**45.00**	**46.00**
☐ **1982** **The Moving Finger Writes,** artist: Mossan Eskandar, production quantity 17,500	**45.00**	**46.00**

THE GREATEST SHOW ON EARTH SERIES
(The Hamilton Collection)

	Issue Price	Current Value
☐ **1981** **The Clowns,** artist: Franklin Moody, hand-numbered, initialed and dated, production: 10 days	**30.00**	**60.00**
☐ **1981** **The Elephants,** artist: Franklin Moody, hand-numbered, initialed and dated, production: 10 days	**30.00**	**31.00**
☐ **1981** **The Aerialists,** artist: Franklin Moody, hand-numbered, initialed and dated, production: 10 days	**30.00**	**31.00**
☐ **1981** **The Great Parade,** artist: Franklin Moody, hand-numbered, initialed and dated, production: 10 days	**30.00**	**31.00**
☐ **1981** **The Midway,** artist: Franklin Moody, hand-numbered, initialed and dated, production: 10 days	**30.00**	**31.00**
☐ **1981** **The Equestrians,** artist: Franklin Moody, hand-numbered, initialed and dated, production: 10 days	**30.00**	**31.00**
☐ **1982** **The Lion Tamer,** artist: Franklin Moody, hand-numbered, initialed and dated, production: 10 days	**30.00**	**31.00**
☐ **1982** **The Grand Finale,** artist: Franklin Moody, hand-numbered, initialed and dated, production: 10 days	**30.00**	**31.00**

		Issue Price	Current Value
THE WALTZES OF JOHANN STRAUSS SERIES (The Hamilton Collection)			
☐ 1981	**The Emperor's Waltz,** artist: Marca America, hand-numbered, initialed and dated, production: 10 days	25.00	26.00
☐ 1981	**The Blue Danube,** artist: Marca America, hand-numbered, initialed and dated, production: 10 days	25.00	26.00
☐ 1981	**Voices of Spring,** artist: Marca America, hand-numbered, initialed and dated, production: 10 days	25.00	26.00
☐ 1981	**Vienna Life,** artist: Marca America, hand-numbered, initialed and dated, production: 10 days ....,.............	25.00	26.00
☐ 1981	**Roses of the South,** artist: Marca America, hand-numbered, initialed and dated, production: 10 days	25.00	26.00
☐ 1982	**Wine, Women and Song,** artist: Marca America, hand-numbered, initialed and dated, production: 10 days	25.00	26.00
☐ 1982	**Artist's Life,** artist: Marca America, hand-numbered, initialed and dated, production: 10 days	25.00	26.00
☐ 1982	**Tales of the Vienna Woods,** artist: Marca America, hand-numbered, initialed and dated, production: 10 days	25.00	26.00

PORCELANA GRANADA

Argentina

CHRISTMAS SERIES

☐ 1971	**The Annunciation,** artist: Tom Fennell Jr., production quantity 5,000	12.00	16.00
☐ 1972	**Mary and Elizabeth,** artist: Tom Fennell Jr., production quantity 5,000	12.00	16.00
☐ 1973	**Road to Bethlehem,** artist: Tom Fennell Jr., production quantity 5,000	14.00	16.00
☐ 1974	**No Room,** artist: Tom Fennell Jr., production quantity 5,000	16.00	16.00
☐ 1975	**Shepherds in the Fields,** artist: Tom Fennell Jr., production quantity 5,000	16.50	21.00
☐ 1976	**Nativity,** artist: Tom Fennell Jr., production quantity 5,000	17.50	21.00

		Issue Price	Current Value
☐ 1977	**Three Kings,** artist: Tom Fennell Jr., production quantity 5,000	18.00	19.00
☐ 1978	**Young Carpenter,** artist: Tom Fennell Jr., production quantity 5,000	18.00	19.00
☐ 1979	**Calling of the Disciples,** artist: Tom Fennell Jr., production quantity 5,000	19.50	20.00
☐ 1980	**Loaves and Fishes,** artist: Tom Fennell Jr., production quantity 5,000	20.00	21.00
☐ 1981	**Suffer the Little Children,** artist: Tom Fennell Jr., production quantity 5,000	20.00	21.00
☐ 1982	**Triumphal Entry,** artist: Tom Fennell Jr., production quantity 5,000	20.00	21.00

PORSGRUND

Norway

CASTLE SERIES

☐ 1970	**Hamlet**	13.00	17.00
☐ 1971	**Rosenborg**	13.00	17.00

CHRISTMAS SERIES

☐ 1968	**Church Scene,** artist: Gunnar Bratile, production: one year	12.00	115.00
☐ 1969	**Three Kings,** artist: Gunnar Bratile, production: one year	12.00	20.00
☐ 1970	**Road to Bethlehem,** artist: Gunnar Bratile, production: one year	12.00	13.00
☐ 1971	**A Child Is Born,** artist: Gunnar Bratile, production: one year	12.00	16.00
☐ 1972	**Hark, the Herald Angels Sing,** artist: Gunnar Bratile, production: one year	12.00	24.00
☐ 1973	**Promise of the Savior,** artist: Gunnar Bratile, production: one year	12.00	32.00
☐ 1974	**The Shepherds,** artist: Gunnar Bratile, production: one year	15.00	43.00
☐ 1975	**Road to the Temple,** artist: Gunnar Bratile, production: one year	19.50	22.00
☐ 1976	**Jesus and the Elders,** artist: Gunnar Bratile, production: one year	22.00	22.00
☐ 1977	**Draught of the Fish,** artist: Gunnar Bratile, production: one year	24.00	24.00

		Issue Price	Current Value

CHRISTMAS SERIES

		Issue Price	Current Value
☐ 1983	**Christmas Night,** artist: Thorstein Rittun, production quantity: unannounced	42.00	42.00

CHRISTMAS DELUXE SERIES

☐ 1970	**Road to Bethlehem,** production quantity 3,000	50.00	50.00
☐ 1971	**A Child Is Born,** production quantity 3,000	50.00	50.00
☐ 1972	**Hark, the Herald Angels Sing,** production quantity 3,000.........................	50.00	50.00
☐ 1973	**Promise of the Savior,** production quantity 3,000	50.00	53.00

EASTER SERIES

☐ 1972	**Ducks,** production: one year	12.00	15.00
☐ 1973	**Birds,** production: one year	12.00	14.00
☐ 1974	**Bunnies,** production: one year	15.00	20.00
☐ 1975	**Chicks,** production: one year	19.50	20.00
☐ 1976	**Sheep,** production: one year	22.00	25.00
☐ 1977	**Butterflies,** production: one year	24.00	24.00

FATHER'S DAY SERIES

☐ 1971	**Fishing,** production: one year	7.50	15.00
☐ 1972	**Cookout,** production: one year	8.00	14.00
☐ 1973	**Sledding,** production: one year	8.00	13.00
☐ 1974	**Father and Son,** production: one year	10.00	13.00
☐ 1975	**Skating,** production: one year	12.50	14.00
☐ 1976	**Skiing,** production: one year	15.00	16.00
☐ 1977	**Soccer,** production: one year	16.50	17.00
☐ 1978	**Canoeing,** production: one year	17.50	22.00
☐ 1979	**Father and Daughter,** production: one year	19.50	20.00
☐ 1980	**Sailing,** production: one year	21.50	22.00

JUBILEE SERIES

☐ 1970	**Femboringer,** production: one year	25.00	30.00

MOTHER'S DAY SERIES

☐ 1970	**Mare and Foal,** artist: Gunnar Bratile, production: one year	7.50	15.00
☐ 1971	**Boy and Geese,** artist: Gunnar Bratile, production: one year	7.50	11.00
☐ 1972	**Doe and Fawn,** artist: Gunnar Bratile, production: one year	10.00	10.00

	Issue Price	Current Value
☐ 1973 **Cat and Kittens,** artist: Gunnar Bratile, production: one year	10.00	12.00
☐ 1974 **Boy and Goats,** artist: Gunnar Bratile, production: one year	10.00	15.00
☐ 1975 **Dog and Puppies,** artist: Gunnar Bratile, production: one year	12.50	19.00
☐ 1976 **Girl and Calf,** artist: Gunnar Bratile, production: one year	15.00	18.00
☐ 1977 **Boy and Chickens,** artist: Gunnar Bratile, production: one year	16.50	20.50
☐ 1978 **Girls and Pigs,** artist: Gunnar Bratile, production: one year	17.50	20.00
☐ 1979 **Boy and Reindeer,** artist: Gunnar Bratile, production: one year	19.50	20.00
☐ 1980 **Girl and Sheep,** artist: Gunnar Bratile, production: one year	21.50	22.00
☐ 1981 **Boy and Birds,** artist: Gunnar Bratile, production: one year	24.00	24.00
☐ 1982 **Child with Rabbit,** artist: Gunnar Bratile, production: one year	26.00	26.00
☐ 1983 **Mother and Kittens,** artist: Gunnar Bratile, production: one year	26.00	26.00
☐ 1984 **By the Pond,** artist: Gunnar Bratile, production: one year	25.00	25.00

TRADITIONAL NORWEGIAN
CHRISTMAS SERIES

	Issue Price	Current Value
☐ 1978 **Guests Are Coming,** artist: Gunnar Bratile, production: one year	27.00	30.00
☐ 1979 **Home for Christmas,** artist: Gunnar Bratile, production: one year	30.00	30.00
☐ 1980 **Preparing for Christmas,** artist: Gunnar Bratile, production: one year	34.00	35.00
☐ 1981 **Christmas Skating,** artist: Gunnar Bratile, production: one year	38.00	39.00
☐ 1982 **White Christmas,** artist: Gunnar Bratile, production: one year	42.00	43.00

SINGLE RELEASE

	Issue Price	Current Value
☐ 1909 **Christmas Flowers,** rare	—	1,150.00

POVERTY BAY PORCELAIN

HENRY'S LOVEABLE MODEL T SERIES	Issue Price	Current Value
☐ **1984 Papa's New Ford,** artist: Randy Giovenale, production quantity 5,000	**29.95**	**30.00**

Tea Party, artist: John Sloane.

RAINBOW TREASURY

GAMES WE USED TO PLAY SERIES

	Issue Price	Current Value
☐ **1984 Tea Party,** artist: John Sloane, production limited	**29.50**	**29.50**

RAM

United States

BOSTON 500 SERIES

	Issue Price	Current Value
☐ **1973 Easter,** production quantity 500	**30.00**	**35.00**
☐ **1973 Mother's Day,** production quantity 500 ...	**30.00**	**35.00**
☐ **1973 Father's Day,** production quantity 500	**30.00**	**35.00**
☐ **1973 Christmas,** production quantity 500	**30.00**	**35.00**

GREAT BIRD HEROES SERIES

	Issue Price	Current Value
☐ **1973 Cher Ami,** production quantity 1,000	**7.95**	**10.00**
☐ **1973 Mocker,** production quantity 1,000	**7.95**	**10.00**

RARE BIRD

Canada

		Issue Price	Current Value
THE CANADIAN DREAM SERIES			
☐ **1983**	**Going to the Rink,** artist: Joan Healey, production quantity 7,500	**45.00**	**50.00**
☐ **1984**	**Lacing Up,** artist: Joan Healey, production quantity 7,500	**45.00**	**50.00**
CHRISTMAS IN CANADA SERIES			
☐ **1986**	**The Windmill,** artist: Joan Healey, production quantity 5,000	**45.00**	**45.00**

RAYNAUD—LIMOGES

France

CASTLE SERIES			
☐ **1979**	**Bodiam Castle,** production quantity 5,000	**48.00**	**50.00**
☐ **1979**	**Glamis Castle,** production quantity 5,000	**48.00**	**50.00**
☐ **1979**	**Tower of London,** production quantity 5,000	**48.00**	**50.00**
CHILDREN OF THE SEASON SERIES			
☐ **1985**	**The Hiker,** artist: Michael Vincent, production quantity 7,500	**40.00**	**40.00**
WILDLIFE COLLECTION			
☐ **1978**	**Tiger Bouquet,** artist: Cowles, production: one year	**50.00**	**53.00**

RECO INTERNATIONAL

United States

A CHILDHOOD ALMANAC SERIES			
☐ **1985**	**Fireside Dreams—January,** artist: Sandra Kuck, production: 14 days	**29.50**	**29.50**
☐ **1985**	**Be Mine—February,** artist: Sandra Kuck, production: 14 days	**29.50**	**29.50**
☐ **1985**	**Winds of March—March,** artist: Sandra Kuck, production: 14 days	**29.50**	**29.50**
☐ **1985**	**Easter Morning—April,** artist: Sandra Kuck, production: 14 days	**29.50**	**29.50**

		Issue Price	Current Value
☐ 1985	**For Mom—May,** artist: Sandra Kuck, production: 14 days	**29.50**	**29.50**
☐ 1985	**Just Daydreaming—June,** artist: Sandra Kuck, production: 14 days	**29.50**	**29.50**
☐ 1985	**Star Spangled Sky—July,** artist: Sandra Kuck, production: 14 days	**29.50**	**29.50**
☐ 1985	**Summer Secrets—August** artist: Sandra Kuck, production: 14 days	**29.50**	**29.50**
☐ 1985	**School Days—September,** artist: Sandra Kuck, production: 14 days	**29.50**	**35.00**
☐ 1985	**Indian Summer—October,** artist: Sandra Kuck, production: 14 days	**29.50**	**29.50**
☐ 1985	**Giving Thanks—November,** artist: Sandra Kuck, production: 14 days	**29.50**	**40.00**
☐ 1985	**Christmas Magic—December,** artist: Sandra Kuck, production: 14 days	**29.50**	**29.50**

A CHILDREN'S CHRISTMAS PAGEANT

☐ 1986	**Silent Night,** artist: Sandra Kuck, production: one year	**32.50**	**32.50**
☐ 1987	**Hark, the Herald Angels Sing,** artist: Sandra Kuck, production: one year	**32.50**	**32.50**

AMERICANA

☐ 1972	**Gaspee Incident,** artist: S. Devlin, production quantity 1,500	**200.00**	**325.00**

ARABELLE AND FRIENDS SERIES

☐ 1982	**Ice Delight,** artist: Carol Greunke, production quantity 15,000	**35.00**	**35.00**
☐ 1983	**First Love,** artist: Carol Greunke, production quantity 15,000	**35.00**	**35.00**

ARTA CHRISTMAS

☐ 1973	**Nativity,** production quantity 220	**50.00**	**70.00**

ARTA MOTHER'S DAY

☐ 1973	**Family with Puppy,** production quantity 300	**50.00**	**70.00**

THE BAREFOOT CHILDREN SERIES

☐ 1987	**Night-Time Story,** artist: Sandra Kuck, production: 14 days	**29.50**	**29.50**

Night-Time Story, artist:
Sandra Kuck.

		Issue Price	Current Value
☐ 1987	**Golden Afternoon,** artist: Sandra Kuck, production: 14 days	29.50	29.50
☐ 1987	**Little Sweethearts,** artist: Sandra Kuck, production: 14 days	29.50	29.50

BECKY'S DAY SERIES

		Issue Price	Current Value
☐ 1985	**Awakening,** artist: John McClelland, production: 90 days	24.50	30.00
☐ 1985	**Getting Dressed,** artist: John McClelland, production: 90 days	24.50	28.50
☐ 1985	**Breakfast,** artist: John McClelland, production: 90 days	27.50	27.50
☐ 1986	**Learning Is Fun,** artist: John McClelland, production: 90 days	27.50	27.50
☐ 1986	**Muffin Making,** artist: John McClelland, production: 90 days	27.50	27.50
☐ 1986	**Tub Time,** artist: John McClelland, production: 90 days	27.50	27.50
☐ 1986	**Evening Prayer,** artist: John McClelland, production: 90 days	27.50	27.50

BOHEMIAN ANNUAL SERIES

		Issue Price	Current Value
☐ 1974	**1974,** artist: unannounced, production quantity 500	130.00	155.00

Awakening, artist: John
McClelland.

Getting Dressed, artist:
John McClelland.

Breakfast, artist: John
McClelland.

		Issue Price	Current Value
☐ 1975	**1975,** artist: unannounced, production quantity 500	**140.00**	**160.00**
☐ 1976	**1976,** artist: unannounced, production quantity 500	**150.00**	**160.00**

DAYS GONE BY COLLECTION

☐ 1983	**Amy's Magic Horse,** artist: Sandra Kuck, production: 14 days	**29.50**	**60.00**
☐ 1983	**Sunday Best,** artist: Sandra Kuck, production: 14 days	**29.50**	**120.00**
☐ 1984	**Little Tudor,** artist: Sandra Kuck, production: 14 days	**29.50**	**38.00**
☐ 1984	**Little Anglers,** artist: Sandra Kuck, production: 14 days	**29.50**	**54.00**
☐ 1985	**Afternoon Recital,** artist: Sandra Kuck, production: 14 days	**29.50**	**52.00**
☐ 1985	**Easter at Grandma's,** artist: Sandra Kuck, production: 14 days	**29.50**	**36.00**
☐ 1985	**Morning Song,** artist: Sandra Kuck, production: 14 days	**29.50**	**32.50**
☐ 1985	**The Surrey Ride,** artist: Sandra Kuck, production: 14 days	**29.50**	**39.00**

DRESDEN CHRISTMAS SERIES

☐ 1971	**Shepherd Scene,** artist: unannounced, production quantity 3,500	**15.00**	**50.00**
☐ 1972	**Niklas Church,** artist: unannounced, production quantity 6,000	**15.00**	**25.00**
☐ 1973	**Schwanstein Church,** artist: unannounced, production quantity 6,000	**18.00**	**35.00**
☐ 1974	**Village Scene,** artist: unannounced, production quantity 5,000	**20.00**	**30.00**
☐ 1975	**Rothenburg Scene,** artist: unannounced, production quantity 5,000	**24.00**	**30.00**
☐ 1976	**Village Church,** artist: unannounced, production quantity 5,000	**26.00**	**35.00**
☐ 1977	**Old Mill,** artist: unannounced, production quantity 5,000	**28.00**	**30.00**

DRESDEN MOTHER'S DAY

☐ 1972	**Doe and Fawn,** artist: unannounced, production quantity 8,000	**15.00**	**20.00**
☐ 1973	**Mare and Colt,** artist: unannounced, production quantity 6,000	**16.00**	**25.00**

		Issue Price	Current Value
☐ 1974	**Tiger and Cub,** artist: unannounced, production quantity 5,000	20.00	23.00
☐ 1975	**Dachshunds,** artist: unannounced, production quantity 5,000	24.00	28.00
☐ 1976	**Owl and Offspring,** artist: unannounced, production quantity 5,000	26.00	30.00
☐ 1977	**Chamois,** artist: unannounced, production quantity 5,000	28.00	30.00

FOUR SEASONS SERIES

☐ 1973	**Spring,** artist: J. Poluszynski, production quantity 2,500	50.00	75.00
☐ 1973	**Summer,** artist: J. Poluszynski, production quantity 2,500	50.00	75.00
☐ 1973	**Fall,** artist: J. Poluszynski, production quantity 2,500	50.00	75.00
☐ 1973	**Winter,** artist: J. Poluszynski, production quantity 2,500	50.00	75.00

GAMES CHILDREN PLAY SERIES

☐ 1979	**Me First,** artist: Sandra Kuck, production quantity 10,000	45.00	52.00
☐ 1980	**Forever Bubbles,** artist: Sandra Kuck, production quantity 10,000	45.00	50.00
☐ 1981	**Skating Pals,** artist: Sandra Kuck, production quantity 10,000	45.00	47.50
☐ 1982	**Join Me,** artist: Sandra Kuck, production quantity 10,000	45.00	45.00

GRANDPARENT SERIES

☐ 1981	**Grandma's Cookie Jar,** artist: Sandra Kuck, production: one year	37.50	37.50
☐ 1981	**Grandpa and the Dollhouse,** artist: Sandra Kuck, production: one year	37.50	37.50

GREAT STORIES FROM THE BIBLE SERIES

☐ 1987	**Moses in the Bulrushes,** artist: Garri Katz, production: 14 days	29.50	29.50
☐ 1987	**King David and Saul,** artist: Garri Katz, production: 14 days	29.50	29.50
☐ 1987	**Joseph's Coat of Many Colors,** artist: Garri Katz, production: 14 days	29.50	29.50

Moses in the Bulrushes,
artist: Garri Katz.

		Issue Price	Current Value
☐ 1987	**Moses and the Ten Commandments,** artist: Garri Katz, production: 14 days	29.50	29.50
☐ 1987	**Rebekah at the Well,** artist: Garri Katz, production: 14 days	29.50	29.50
☐ 1987	**Daniel Reads the Writing on the Wall,** artist: Garri Katz, production: 14 days	29.50	29.50
☐ 1987	**King Solomon,** artist: Garri Katz, production: 14 days	29.50	29.50
☐ 1987	**The Story of Ruth,** artist: Garri Katz, production: 14 days	29.50	29.50

LITTLE PROFESSIONALS SERIES

☐ 1982	**All Is Well,** artist: Sandra Kuck, production quantity 10,000	39.50	47.50
☐ 1983	**Tender Loving Care,** artist: Sandra Kuck, production quantity 10,000	39.50	55.00
☐ 1984	**Lost and Found,** artist: Sandra Kuck, production quantity 10,000	39.50	42.50
☐ 1985	**Reading, Writing And ... ,** artist: Sandra Kuck, production quantity 10,000	39.50	39.50

McCLELLAND CHILDREN'S
CIRCUS COLLECTION

☐ 1982	**Tommy, the Clown,** artist: John McClelland, production: 100 days	29.50	30.00

		Issue Price	Current Value
☐ 1982	**Katie, the Tightrope Walker,** artist: John McClelland, production: 100 days	29.50	35.00
☐ 1983	**Johnny, the Strongman,** artist: John McClelland, production: 100 days	29.50	32.50
☐ 1984	**Maggie, the Animal Trainer,** artist: John McClelland, production limited	29.50	36.00

MOTHER'S DAY SERIES

☐ 1985	**Once upon a Time,** artist: Sandra Kuck, production: less than one year	29.50	50.00
☐ 1986	**Times Remembered,** artist: Sandra Kuck, production: less than one year	29.50	36.00
☐ 1987	**A Cherished Time,** artist: Sandra Kuck, production: less than one year	29.50	29.50

MOTHER GOOSE SERIES

☐ 1979	**Mary, Mary,** artist: John McClelland, production: less than one year	22.50	315.00
☐ 1980	**Little Boy Blue,** artist: John McClelland, production: less than one year	22.50	130.00
☐ 1981	**Little Miss Muffet,** artist: John McClelland, production: less than one year	24.50	45.00
☐ 1982	**Little Jack Horner,** artist: John McClelland, production: one year	24.50	42.50
☐ 1983	**Little Bo Peep,** artist: John McClelland, production: one year	24.50	45.00
☐ 1984	**Diddle Diddle Dumpling,** artist: John McClelland, production: one year	24.50	33.00
☐ 1985	**Mary Had a Little Lamb,** artist: John McClelland, production: one year	27.50	42.00
☐ 1986	**Jack and Jill,** artist: John McClelland, production: one year	27.50	27.50

THE SOPHISTICATED LADIES SERIES

☐ 1985	**Felicia,** artist: Aldo Fazio, production: 21 days	29.50	31.50
☐ 1985	**Samantha,** artist: Aldo Fazio, production: 21 days	29.50	29.50
☐ 1985	**Phoebe,** artist: Aldo Fazio, production: 21 days	29.50	29.50
☐ 1985	**Cleo,** artist: Aldo Fazio, production: 21 days	29.50	29.50
☐ 1986	**Cerissa,** artist: Aldo Fazio, production: 21 days	29.50	29.50

Mary Had a Little Lamb, artist: John McClelland.

		Issue Price	Current Value
☐ 1986	**Natasha,** artist: Aldo Fazio, production: 21 days	29.50	29.50
☐ 1986	**Bianka,** artist: Aldo Fazio, production: 21 days	29.50	29.50
☐ 1986	**Chelsea,** artist: Aldo Fazio, production: 21 days	29.50	29.50

SPRINGTIME OF LIFE SERIES

		Issue Price	Current Value
☐ 1985	**Teddy's Bathtime,** artist: Thornton Utz, production quantity: N/A	29.50	29.50
☐ 1986	**Just Like Mommy,** artist: Thornton Utz, production: 14 days	29.50	29.50
☐ 1986	**Among the Daffodils,** artist: Thornton Utz, production: 14 days	29.50	29.50
☐ 1986	**My Favorite Dolls,** artist: Thornton Utz, production: 14 days	29.50	29.50
☐ 1986	**Aunt Tillie's Hats,** artist: Thornton Utz, production: 14 days	29.50	29.50
☐ 1986	**Little Emily,** artist: Thornton Utz, production: 14 days	29.50	29.50
☐ 1986	**Granny's Boots,** artist: Thornton Utz, production: 14 days	29.50	29.50
☐ 1986	**My Masterpiece,** artist: Thornton Utz, production: 14 days	29.50	29.50

		Issue Price	Current Value
VANISHING ANIMAL KINGDOMS SERIES			
☐ 1986	**Rama the Tiger,** artists: Dot and Sy Barlowe, production quantity 21,500	35.00	35.00
☐ 1986	**Olepi the Buffalo,** artists: Dot and Sy Barlowe, production quantity 21,500	35.00	35.00
☐ 1987	**Coolibah the Koala,** artist: Sy Barlowe, production quantity 21,500	35.00	35.00
☐ 1987	**Ortwin the Deer,** artist: Sy Barlowe, production quantity 21,500	35.00	35.00
☐ 1987	**Yen-Poh the Panda,** artist: Sy Barlowe, production quantity 21,500	35.00	35.00
WESTERN SERIES			
☐ 1974	**Mountain Man,** artist: E. Berke, production quantity 1,000	165.00	165.00
THE WORLD OF CHILDREN SERIES			
☐ 1977	**Rainy Day Fun,** artist: John McClelland, production quantity 10,000	50.00	130.00
☐ 1978	**When I Grow Up ... ,** artist: John McClelland, production quantity 15,000	50.00	95.00
☐ 1979	**You're Invited,** artist: John McClelland, production quantity 15,000	50.00	55.00
☐ 1980	**Kittens for Sale,** artist: John McClelland, production quantity 15,000	50.00	60.00

Rama the Tiger, artists: Dot and Sy Barlowe.

REECE, MAYNARD

WATERFOWL SERIES	Issue Price	Current Value
☐ 1973 **Mallards and Wood Ducks,** set, production quantity 900	250.00	375.00
☐ 1974 **Canvasback and Canadian Geese,** set, production quantity 900	250.00	375.00
☐ 1975 **Pintails and Teal,** set, production quantity 900	250.00	425.00

REED AND BARTON

United States

AMERICAN CHRISTMAS SERIES

	Issue Price	Current Value
☐ 1976 **Morning Train,** production quantity 7,500	65.00	75.00
☐ 1977 **Decorating the Church,** production quantity 7,500	65.00	65.00
☐ 1978 **General Store at Christmas Time,** production quantity 7,500	65.00	65.00

ANNUAL SERIES

☐ 1972 **Free Trapper,** production quantity 2,500	65.00	65.00
☐ 1973 **Outpost,** production quantity 2,500	65.00	65.00
☐ 1974 **Toll Collector,** production quantity 2,500	65.00	65.00
☐ 1975 **Indians Discovering Lewis and Clark,** production quantity 2,500	65.00	65.00

AUDUBON SERIES

☐ 1970 **Pine Siskin,** production quantity 5,000	60.00	175.00
☐ 1971 **Red-Shouldered Hawk,** production quantity 5,000	60.00	75.00
☐ 1972 **Stilt Sandpiper,** production quantity 5,000	60.00	70.00
☐ 1973 **Red Cardinal,** production quantity 5,000	60.00	65.00
☐ 1974 **Boreal Chickadee,** production quantity 5,000	65.00	65.00
☐ 1975 **Yellow-Breasted Chat,** production quantity 5,000	65.00	65.00
☐ 1976 **Bay-Breasted Warbler,** production quantity 5,000	65.00	65.00
☐ 1977 **Purple Finch,** production quantity 5,000	65.00	65.00

		Issue Price	Current Value
BICENTENNIAL SERIES (Keller and George)			
☐ 1972	**Monticello,** damascene silver, production quantity 1,000	75.00	80.00
☐ 1972	**Monticello,** silver plate, production quantity 200	200.00	225.00
☐ 1973	**Mt. Vernon,** production: one year	75.00	80.00

CHRISTMAS SERIES

☐ 1973	**Adoration of the Kings,** artist: Roger van der Weyden, production quantity 7,500	60.00	65.00
☐ 1974	**The Adoration of the Magi,** artist: Fra Angelico and Fra Lippi, production quantity 7,500	65.00	65.00
☐ 1975	**Adoration of the Kings,** artist: Steven Lochner, production quantity 7,500	65.00	65.00
☐ 1976	**Morning Train,** artist: Maxwell Mays, production quantity 7,500	65.00	66.00

CHRISTMAS CAROLS SERIES

☐ 1970	**A Partridge in a Pear Tree,** artist: Robert Johnson, production quantity 2,500	55.00	210.00
☐ 1971	**We Three King of Orient Are,** artist: Robert Johnson, production quantity 7,500	60.00	75.00
☐ 1972	**Hark! The Herald Angels Sing,** artist: Robert Johnson, production quantity 7,500	60.00	65.00

CHRISTMAS—OLD FASHIONED SERIES

☐ 1977	**Decorating the Church,** artist: Maxwell Mays, production quantity 7,500	65.00	65.00
☐ 1978	**The General Store at Christmas Time,** artist: Maxwell Mays, production quantity 7,500	65.00	56.00
☐ 1979	**Merry Old Santa Claus,** artist: Thomas Nast, production quantity 2,500	55.00	56.00
☐ 1980	**Gathering Christmas Greens,** artist: unknown, production quantity 2,500	65.00	65.00
☐ 1981	**The Shopkeeper at Christmas,** artist: W. L. Sheppard, production quantity 2,500	75.00	66.00

CURRIER & IVES SERIES

☐ 1972	**Village Blacksmith,** production quantity 1,500	85.00	85.00
☐ 1972	**Wester Migration,** production quantity 1,500	85.00	85.00
☐ 1973	**Oaken Bucket,** production quantity 1,500	85.00	85.00

		Issue Price	Current Value
☐ 1973	**Winter in Country,** production quantity 1,500	**85.00**	**85.00**
☐ 1974	**Preparing for Market,** production quantity 1,500	**85.00**	**85.00**

FOUNDING FATHERS SERIES

		Issue Price	Current Value
☐ 1974	**George Washington,** production quantity 2,500	**65.00**	**65.00**
☐ 1975	**Thomas Jefferson,** production quantity 2,500	**65.00**	**65.00**
☐ 1976	**Ben Franklin,** production quantity 2,500 ..	**65.00**	**65.00**
☐ 1976	**Patrick Henry,** production quantity 2,500	**65.00**	**65.00**
☐ 1976	**John Hancock,** production quantity 2,500	**65.00**	**65.00**
☐ 1976	**John Adams,** production quantity 2,500 ...	**65.00**	**65.00**

KENTUCKY DERBY SERIES

		Issue Price	Current Value
☐ 1972	**Nearing Finish,** production quantity 1,000	**75.00**	**85.00**
☐ 1973	**Riva Ridge,** production quantity 1,500	**75.00**	**85.00**
☐ 1974	**100th Running,** production quantity 1,500	**75.00**	**85.00**

MISSIONS OF CALIFORNIA SERIES

		Issue Price	Current Value
☐ 1971	**San Diego,** production quantity 1,500	**75.00**	**75.00**
☐ 1972	**Carmel,** production quantity 1,500	**75.00**	**75.00**
☐ 1973	**Santa Barbara,** production quantity 1,500	**60.00**	**60.00**
☐ 1974	**Santa Clara,** production quantity 1,500	**60.00**	**60.00**
☐ 1976	**San Gabriel,** production quantity 1,500	**65.00**	**65.00**

THOMAS NAST CHRISTMAS SERIES
(Collector Creations)

		Issue Price	Current Value
☐ 1973	**Christmas,** production quantity 750	**100.00**	**110.00**

SINGLE RELEASES

		Issue Price	Current Value
☐ 1970	**Zodiac,** production quantity 1,500	**75.00**	**75.00**
☐ 1972	**Road Runner,** production quantity 1,500 ..	**65.00**	**65.00**
☐ 1972	**Delta Queen,** production quantity 2,500 ...	**75.00**	**75.00**
☐ 1973	**Alice in Wonderland** (Collector Creations), production quantity 750	**100.00**	**110.00**
☐ 1973	**Chicago Fire,** production: one year	**60.00**	**60.00**
☐ 1975	**Mississippi Queen,** production quantity 2,500	**75.00**	**75.00**

RHEA SILVA PORCELAIN COLLECTION

United States

		Issue Price	Current Value
CHILD'S GARDEN OF VERSE SERIES			
☐ **1983**	**Land of Counterpane,** artist: Tom Bharnson, production quantity 17,500	39.00	40.00
ENDANGERED BIRDS SERIES			
☐ **1983**	**Whooping Cranes,** artist: Frank DeMatteis, production quantity 5,000	60.00	60.00
FELINE FAVORITES SERIES			
☐ **1982**	**Long-haired Ladies,** artist: Patrick Oxenham, production quantity 10,000	47.00	47.00
☐ **1983**	**Siamese and Apple Blossoms,** artist: Patrick Oxenham, production quantity 10,000	47.00	47.00

RICKER-BARTLETT CASTING STUDIOS

United States

		Issue Price	Current Value
AMERICA'S CHILDREN SERIES			
☐ **1981**	**Del,** artist: Anthony Ricker, production quantity 5,000	20.00	20.00
SINGLE ISSUE			
☐ **1982**	**Mother's Day,** artist: Michael Ricker, production quantity 5,250	65.00	65.00

RIDGEWOOD

United States

		Issue Price	Current Value
BICENTENNIAL SERIES			
☐ **1974**	**First in War,** production quantity 12,500 . .	40.00	40.00
CHRISTMAS SERIES			
☐ **1975**	**Christmas Morning,** artist: J. C. Leyendecker, production quantity 10,000	24.50	37.00
☐ **1976**	**Christmas Surprise,** production quantity 10,000	26.50	37.00

		Issue Price	Current Value

LITTLE WOMEN SERIES

☐ **1976 Sweet Long Ago,** artist: Lorraine Trester, production quantity 5,000 . . . . 45.00 / 65.00

☐ **1976 Song of Spring,** artist: Lorraine Trester, production quantity 5,000 . . . . 45.00 / 75.00

☐ **1977 Joy in the Morning,** artist: Lorraine Trester, production quantity 5,000 . . . . 45.00 / 46.00

MOTHER'S DAY SERIES

☐ **1976 Grandma's Apple Pie,** artist: J. C. Leyendecker, production quantity 5,000 . . . . 24.50 / 26.00

☐ **1977 Tenderness,** artist: J. C. Leyendecker, production quantity 10,000 . . . . 35.00 / 36.00

TOM SAWYER SERIES

☐ **1974 Trying a Pipe,** artist: Norman Rockwell, production quantity 3,000 . . . . 9.98 / 10.00

☐ **1974 Lost in Cave,** artist: Norman Rockwell, production quantity 3,000 . . . . 9.98 / 10.00

☐ **1974 Painting Fence,** artist: Norman Rockwell, production quantity 3,000 . . . . 9.98 / 10.00

☐ **1974 Taking Medicine,** artist: Norman Rockwell, production quantity 3,000 . . . . 9.98 / 10.00

VASILS SERIES

☐ **1976 All Hallows Eve,** production quantity 5,000 38.50 / 40.00

WILD WEST SERIES

☐ **1975 Discovery of Last Chance Gulch,** production quantity 15,000 . . . . 16.25 / 17.00

☐ **1975 Doubtful Visitor,** production quantity 15,000 16.25 / 17.00

☐ **1975 Bad One,** production quantity 15,000 . . . . . 16.25 / 17.00

☐ **1975 Cattleman,** production quantity 15,000 . . . . 16.25 / 17.00

RIVER SHORE

United States

BABY ANIMALS COLLECTION

☐ **1979 Akiku,** artist: Roger Brown, production quantity 20,000 . . . . 50.00 / 105.00

☐ **1980 Roosevelt,** artist: Roger Brown, production quantity 20,000 . . . . 50.00 / 90.00

		Issue Price	Current Value
☐ **1981**	**Clover,** artist: Roger Brown, production quantity 20,000	50.00	70.00
☐ **1982**	**Zuela,** artist: Roger Brown, production quantity 20,000	50.00	65.00

DELLA ROBBIA ANNUAL SERIES

☐ **1979**	**Adoration,** artist: Roger Brown, production quantity 5,000	550.00	550.00
☐ **1980**	**Virgin and Child,** artist: Roger Brown, production quantity 5,000	450.00	450.00

FAMOUS AMERICANS SERIES

☐ **1976**	**Lincoln,** artist: Norman Rockwell, production quantity 9,500	40.00	250.00
☐ **1977**	**Triple Self-Portrait,** artist: Norman Rockwell, production quantity 9,500	45.00	55.00
☐ **1978**	**Peace Corps,** artist: Norman Rockwell, production quantity 9,500	45.00	75.00
☐ **1978**	**Spirit of Lindbergh,** artist: Norman Rockwell, production quantity 9,500	50.00	50.00

FAVORITE AMERICAN SONGBIRDS SERIES

☐ **1985**	**Western Tanager,** artist: L. Thompson, production: 14 days	19.50	19.50
☐ **1985**	**Purple Finches,** artist: L. Thompson, production: 14 days	19.50	19.50
☐ **1985**	**Mountain Bluebirds,** artist: L. Thompson, production: 14 days	19.50	19.50
☐ **1985**	**Cardinal,** artist: L. Thompson, production: 14 days	19.50	19.50
☐ **1985**	**Barn Swallow,** artist: L. Thompson, production: 14 days	19.50	19.50
☐ **1985**	**Canyon Wren,** artist: L. Thompson, production: 14 days	19.50	19.50
☐ **1985**	**Mockingbird,** artist: L. Thompson, production: 14 days	19.50	19.50
☐ **1985**	**Wood Thrush,** artist: L. Thompson, production: 14 days	19.50	19.50

GRANT WOOD SINGLE ISSUE

☐ **1982**	**American Gothic,** artist: Grant Wood, production quantity 17,500	80.00	80.00

LOVABLE TEDDIES SERIES

	Issue Price	Current Value
□ 1985 **Bedtime Blues,** artist: M. Hague, production: 10 days	21.50	21.50
□ 1985 **Bearly Frightful,** artist: M. Hague, production: 10 days	21.50	21.50
□ 1985 **Caught in the Act,** artist: M. Hague, production: 10 days	21.50	21.50
□ 1985 **Fireside Friends,** artist: M. Hague, production: 10 days	21.50	21.50
□ 1985 **Harvest Time,** artist: M. Hague, production: 10 days	21.50	21.50
□ 1985 **Missed a Button,** artist: M. Hague, production: 10 days	21.50	21.50
□ 1985 **Tender Loving Bear,** artist: M. Hague, production: 10 days	21.50	21.50
□ 1985 **Sunday Stroll,** artist: M. Hague, production: 10 days	21.50	21.50

REMINGTON BRONZE SERIES

	Issue Price	Current Value
□ 1977 **Bronco Buster,** artist: Roger Brown, production quantity 15,000	55.00	70.00
□ 1978 **Coming Through the Rye,** artist: Roger Brown, production quantity 15,000	60.00	60.00
□ 1980 **Cheyenne,** artist: Roger Brown, production quantity 15,000	60.00	60.00
□ 1981 **The Mountain Man,** artist: Roger Brown, production quantity 15,000	60.00	60.00

ROCKWELL CATS SERIES

	Issue Price	Current Value
□ 1982 **Jennie and Tina,** artist: Norman Rockwell, production quantity 9,500	39.50	39.50

ROCKWELL FOUR FREEDOMS SERIES

	Issue Price	Current Value
□ 1981 **Freedom of Speech,** artist: Norman Rockwell, production quantity 17,000	65.00	65.00
□ 1982 **Freedom of Worship,** artist: Norman Rockwell, production quantity 17,000	65.00	65.00
□ 1982 **Freedom from Fear,** artist: Norman Rockwell, production quantity 17,000	65.00	65.00
□ 1982 **Freedom from Want,** artist: Norman Rockwell, production quantity 17,000	65.00	65.00

ROCKWELL/GOOD OLD DAYS SERIES

	Issue Price	Current Value
□ 1982 **Old Oaken Bucket,** artist: Norman Rockwell, production: unannounced	24.50	24.50

		Issue Price	Current Value
☐ 1982	**Boy Fishing,** artist: Norman Rockwell, production: unannounced	24.50	24.50
☐ 1982	**Barefoot Boy,** artist: Norman Rockwell, production: unannounced	24.50	24.50

ROCKWELL SINGLE RELEASES

☐ 1979	**Spring Flowers,** artist: Norman Rockwell, production quantity 17,000	75.00	145.00
☐ 1980	**Looking Out to Sea,** artist: Norman Rockwell, production quantity 17,000	75.00	130.00
☐ 1982	**Grandpa's Guardian,** artist: Norman Rockwell, production quantity 17,000	80.00	80.00
☐ 1982	**Grandpa's Treasures,** artist: Norman Rockwell, production quantity 17,000	80.00	80.00

SIGNS OF LOVE SERIES

☐ 1981	**A Kiss for Mother,** artist: Yin-Rei Hicks, production: less than one year	18.50	19.00
☐ 1981	**A Watchful Eye,** artist: Yin-Rei Hicks, production: less than one year	21.50	22.00
☐ 1982	**A Gentle Persuasion,** artist: Yin-Rei Hicks, production: less than one year	21.50	22.00
☐ 1983	**A Protective Embrace,** artist: Yin-Rei Hicks, production: less than one year	23.50	24.50
☐ 1983	**A Tender Coaxing,** artist: Yin-Rei Hicks, production: less than one year	23.50	24.50

TIMBERLAKE'S CHRISTMAS AFTER CHRISTMAS SERIES

☐ 1982	**Kay's Doll,** artist: Bob Timberlake, production quantity 9,500	75.00	75.00

VIGNETTE SERIES

☐ 1981	**The Broken Window,** artist: Norman Rockwell, production quantity 22,500	19.50	19.50
☐ 1982	**Sunday Best,** artist: Norman Rockwell, production quantity 22,500	19.50	19.50

ROCKFORD EDITIONS

United States

LITTLE MOTHERS SERIES	Issue Price	Current Value
☐ **1985 Love Is Blind,** artist: Bessie Pease Gutman, production quantity: N/A	**29.95**	**30.00**
☐ **1985 First Step,** artist: Bessie Pease Gutman, production quantity: N/A	**29.95**	**30.00**

ROCKWELL COLLECTORS CLUB

United States

CHRISTMAS SERIES

☐ **1978 Christmas Story,** artist: Norman Rockwell, production quantity 15,000	**24.50**	**26.00**

ROCKWELL MUSEUM

United States

AMERICAN FAMILY SERIES I

☐ **1979 Baby's First Step,** artist: Norman Rockwell, production quantity 9,900	**28.50**	**135.00**
☐ **1979 Happy Birthday, Dear Mother,** artist: Norman Rockwell, production quantity 9,900 ..	**28.50**	**60.00**
☐ **1979 Sweet Sixteen,** artist: Norman Rockwell, production quantity 9,900	**28.50**	**45.00**
☐ **1979 First Haircut,** artist: Norman Rockwell, production quantity 9,900	**28.50**	**45.00**
☐ **1979 First Prom,** artist: Norman Rockwell, production quantity 9,900	**28.50**	**35.00**
☐ **1979 Wrapping Christmas Presents,** artist: Norman Rockwell, production quantity 9,900 ..	**28.50**	**35.00**
☐ **1979 The Student,** artist: Norman Rockwell, production quantity 9,900	**28.50**	**35.00**
☐ **1979 The Birthday Party,** artist: Norman Rockwell, production quantity 9,900	**28.50**	**35.00**
☐ **1979 Little Mother,** artist: Norman Rockwell, production quantity 9,900	**28.50**	**35.00**
☐ **1979 Washing Our Dog,** artist: Norman Rockwell, production quantity 9,900	**28.50**	**35.00**
☐ **1979 Mother's Little Helpers,** artist: Norman Rockwell, production quantity 9,900	**28.50**	**35.00**

		Issue Price	Current Value
☐ 1979	**Bride and Groom,** artist: Norman Rockwell, production quantity 9,900	**28.50**	**35.00**

AMERICAN FAMILY SERIES II

		Issue Price	Current Value
☐ 1980	**New Arrival,** artist: Norman Rockwell, production quantity 22,500	**35.00**	**55.00**
☐ 1980	**Sweet Dreams,** artist: Norman Rockwell, production quantity 22,500	**35.00**	**37.50**
☐ 1980	**Little Shaver,** artist: Norman Rockwell, production quantity 22,500	**35.00**	**37.50**
☐ 1980	**We Missed You, Daddy,** artist: Norman Rockwell, production quantity 22,500	**35.00**	**37.50**
☐ 1981	**Home Run Slugger,** artist: Norman Rockwell, production quantity 22,500	**35.00**	**37.50**
☐ 1981	**Giving Thanks,** artist: Norman Rockwell, production quantity 22,500	**35.00**	**37.50**
☐ 1981	**Little Salesman,** artist: Norman Rockwell, production quantity 22,500	**35.00**	**37.50**
☐ 1981	**Almost Grown Up,** artist: Norman Rockwell, production quantity 22,500	**35.00**	**37.50**
☐ 1981	**Courageous Hero,** artist: Norman Rockwell, production quantity 22,500	**35.00**	**37.50**
☐ 1981	**At the Circus,** artist: Norman Rockwell, production quantity 22,500	**35.00**	**37.50**
☐ 1981	**Good Food, Good Friends,** artist: Norman Rockwell, production quantity 22,500	**35.00**	**37.50**

CHRISTMAS COLLECTIBLES SERIES

		Issue Price	Current Value
☐ 1979	**The Day After Christmas,** artist: Norman Rockwell, production: one year	**75.00**	**87.50**
☐ 1980	**Checking His List,** artist: Norman Rockwell, production: one year	**75.00**	**85.00**
☐ 1981	**Ringing in Good Cheer,** artist: Norman Rockwell, production: one year	**75.00**	**85.00**
☐ 1982	**Waiting for Santa,** artist: Norman Rockwell, production: one year	**75.00**	**75.00**
☐ 1983	**High Hopes,** artist: Norman Rockwell, production: one year	**75.00**	**75.00**
☐ 1984	**Space Age Santa,** artist: Norman Rockwell, production: one year	**55.00**	**55.00**

CLASSIC PLATE SERIES

		Issue Price	Current Value
☐ 1981	**Puppy Love,** artist: Norman Rockwell, production: 60 days	**24.50**	**26.00**

Space Age Santa, artist: Norman Rockwell.

		Issue Price	Current Value
☐ 1981	**While the Audience Waits,** artist: Norman Rockwell, production: 60 days	24.50	26.00
☐ 1981	**Off to School,** artist: Norman Rockwell, production: 60 days	24.50	26.00
☐ 1982	**Country Doctor,** artist: Norman Rockwell, production: 60 days	24.50	26.00
☐ 1982	**Spring Fever,** artist: Norman Rockwell, production: 60 days	24.50	26.00
☐ 1982	**A Dollhouse for Sis,** artist: Norman Rockwell, production: 60 days	24.50	26.00

ELVIS PRESLEY COLLECTION
(Nostalgia Collectibles)

☐ 1985	**Hound Dog,** production limited	15.00	15.00
☐ 1985	**Lonesome Tonight,** production limited	15.00	15.00
☐ 1985	**Teddy Bear,** production limited	15.00	15.00
☐ 1985	**Don't Be Cruel,** production limited	15.00	15.00
	Complete set of four	60.00	60.00

GENE AUTRY COLLECTION SERIES
(Nostalgia Collectibles)

☐ 1984	**America's Favorite Cowboy,** artist: Norman Rockwell, production quantity 25,000	45.00	45.00

		Issue Price	Current Value

JAMES DEAN COLLECTION
(Nostalgia Collectibles)

			Issue Price	Current Value
☐	1985	**East of Eden,** production limited	15.00	15.00
☐	1985	**Rebel Without a Cause,** production limited	15.00	15.00
☐	1985	**Giant,** production limited	15.00	15.00
☐	1985	**Jim and Spyder,** production limited	15.00	15.00
		Complete set of four	60.00	60.00

MOTHER'S DAY

			Issue Price	Current Value
☐	1982	**A Tender Moment,** artist: Norman Rockwell, production quantity 5,000	70.00	75.00

SHIRLEY TEMPLE CLASSICS
(Nostalgia Collectibles)

			Issue Price	Current Value
☐	1983	**Captain January,** artist: Bill Jacobson, production quantity 25,000	35.00	42.50
☐	1984	**Heidi,** artist: Bill Jacobson, production quantity 25,000	35.00	35.00
☐	1984	**Little Miss Marker,** artist: Bill Jacobson, production quantity 25,000	35.00	40.00
☐	1984	**Bright Eyes,** artist: Bill Jacobson, production quantity 25,000	35.00	35.00
☐	1985	**The Little Colonel,** artist: Bill Jacobson, production quantity 25,000	35.00	35.00
☐	1985	**Rebecca of Sunnybrook Farm,** artist: Bill Jacobson, production quantity 25,000	35.00	35.00
☐	1986	**Poor Little Rich Girl,** artist: Bill Jacobson, production quantity 25,000	35.00	35.00
☐	1986	**Wee Willie Winkie,** artist: Bill Jacobson, production quantity 25,000	35.00	35.00

SHIRLEY TEMPLE
COLLECTIBLES SERIES
(Nostalgia Collectibles)

			Issue Price	Current Value
☐	1982	**Baby Take a Bow,** production quantity 22,500	75.00	75.00
☐	1983	**Baby Take a Bow,** autographed, production quantity 2,500	100.00	160.00
☐	1983	**Curly Top,** production quantity 22,500	75.00	75.00
☐	1983	**Curly Top,** autographed, production quantity 2,500	100.00	150.00
☐	1982	**Stand Up and Cheer,** production quantity 22,500	75.00	100.00

Baby Take a Bow.

		Issue Price	Current Value
☐ 1983	**Stand Up and Cheer,** autographed, production quantity 2,500	100.00	100.00

A TOUCH OF ROCKWELL SERIES

		Issue Price	Current Value
☐ 1984	**Songs of Praise,** artist: Norman Rockwell, production: one year	14.95	15.00
☐ 1984	**Bedtime Prayers,** artist: Norman Rockwell, production: one year	14.95	15.00
☐ 1984	**First Day of School,** artist: Norman Rockwell, production: one year	14.95	15.00
☐ 1984	**Surprise Treat,** artist: Norman Rockwell, production: one year	14.95	15.00
☐ 1984	**The Runaway,** artist: Norman Rockwell, production: one year	14.95	30.00

WORLD OF CHILDREN
BAS-RELIEF SERIES

		Issue Price	Current Value
☐ 1982	**Downhill Racer,** artist: Norman Rockwell, production quantity 15,000	45.00	45.00
☐ 1982	**Vacation Over,** artist: Norman Rockwell, production quantity 15,000	45.00	45.00
☐ 1982	**Little Patient,** artist: Norman Rockwell, production quantity 15,000	45.00	45.00
☐ 1982	**Bicycle Boys,** artist: Norman Rockwell, production quantity 15,000	45.00	45.00

SPECIAL COMMEMORATIVE ISSUES	Issue Price	Current Value
☐ **1985 Elvis Presley—The Once and Forever King,** artist: William Jacobson, production quantity 10,000	**40.00**	**45.00**
☐ **1985 James Dean—America's Rebel,** artist: William Jacobson, production quantity 10,000	**45.00**	**45.00**

SINGLE RELEASES

☐ **1979 Rockwell Remembered,** artist: Norman Rockwell, production: 30 days	**45.00**	**45.00**
☐ **1982 Celebration,** artist: Norman Rockwell, production quantity 9,900	**55.00**	**55.00**
☐ **1983 A Tribute to John F. Kennedy,** artist: Norman Rockwell, production: unannounced ..	**39.50**	**40.00**
☐ **1983 With This Ring,** artist: Norman Rockwell, production: one year	**50.00**	**50.00**

ROCKWELL SOCIETY

United States

AMERICAN DREAM SERIES

☐ **1985 A Young Girl's Dream,** artist: Norman Rockwell, production limited	**19.90**	**19.90**
☐ **1985 A Couple's Commitment,** artist: Norman Rockwell, production limited	**19.90**	**19.90**
☐ **1985 A Family's Full Measure,** artist: Norman Rockwell, production limited	**22.90**	**22.90**
☐ **1986 A Mother's Welcome,** artist: Norman Rockwell, production limited	**22.90**	**22.90**
☐ **1986 A Young Man's Dream,** artist: Norman Rockwell, production limited	**22.90**	**22.90**
☐ **1986 The Musician's Magic,** artist: Norman Rockwell, production limited	**22.90**	**22.90**
☐ **1987 An Orphan's Hope,** artist: Norman Rockwell, production limited	**24.90**	**24.90**
☐ **1987 Love's Reward,** artist: Norman Rockwell, production limited	**24.90**	**24.90**

A MIND OF HER OWN SERIES

☐ **1986 Sitting Pretty,** artist: Norman Rockwell, production limited	**24.90**	**24.90**

CHRISTMAS SERIES	Issue Price	Current Value
☐ 1974 **Scotty Gets His Tree,** artist: Norman Rockwell, production: one year	24.50	120.00
☐ 1975 **Angel with a Black Eye,** artist: Norman Rockwell, production: one year	24.50	61.00
☐ 1976 **Golden Christmas,** artist: Norman Rockwell, production: one year	24.50	60.00
☐ 1977 **Toy Shop Window,** artist: Norman Rockwell, production: one year	24.50	40.00
☐ 1978 **Christmas Dream,** artist: Norman Rockwell, production: one year	24.50	40.00
☐ 1979 **Somebody's Up There,** artist: Norman Rockwell, production: one year	24.50	26.00
☐ 1980 **Scotty Plays Santa,** artist: Norman Rockwell, production: one year	24.50	26.00
☐ 1981 **Wrapped Up in Christmas,** artist: Norman Rockwell, production: one year	25.50	30.00
☐ 1982 **Christmas Courtship,** artist: Norman Rockwell, production: one year	25.50	30.00
☐ 1983 **Santa in the Subway,** artist: Norman Rockwell, production: one year	25.50	30.00
☐ 1984 **Santa in His Workshop,** artist: Norman Rockwell, production: one year	27.50	45.00

COLONIALS—THE RAREST ROCKWELL SERIES
(see also Edwin M. Knowles)

	Issue Price	Current Value
☐ 1985 **Unexpected Proposal,** artist: Norman Rockwell, production limited	27.90	27.90
☐ 1986 **Words of Comfort,** artist: Norman Rockwell, production limited	27.90	27.90
☐ 1986 **Light for the Winter,** artist: Norman Rockwell, production limited	30.90	30.90
☐ 1987 **Portrait for a Bridegroom,** artist: Norman Rockwell, production limited	30.90	30.90

HERITAGE SERIES

	Issue Price	Current Value
☐ 1977 **Toy Maker,** artist: Norman Rockwell, production: one year	14.50	160.00
☐ 1978 **The Cobbler,** artist: Norman Rockwell, production: one year	19.50	130.00
☐ 1979 **The Lighthouse Keeper's Daughter,** artist: Norman Rockwell, production: one year	19.50	55.00
☐ 1980 **The Ship Builder,** artist: Norman Rockwell, production: one year	19.50	40.00

Portrait for a
Bridegroom, artist:
Norman Rockwell.

		Issue Price	Current Value
☐ 1981	**The Music Maker,** artist: Norman Rockwell, production: one year	**19.50**	**24.00**
☐ 1982	**The Tycoon,** artist: Norman Rockwell, production: one year	**19.50**	**25.00**
☐ 1983	**The Painter,** artist: Norman Rockwell, production: one year	**19.50**	**28.00**
☐ 1984	**The Storyteller,** artist: Norman Rockwell, production: one year	**19.50**	**35.00**
☐ 1985	**The Gourmet,** artist: Norman Rockwell, production: one year	**19.50**	**40.00**

MOTHER'S DAY SERIES

		Issue Price	Current Value
☐ 1976	**A Mother's Love,** artist: Norman Rockwell, production: one year	**24.50**	**110.00**
☐ 1977	**Faith,** artist: Norman Rockwell, production: one year	**24.50**	**80.00**
☐ 1978	**Bedtime,** artist: Norman Rockwell, production: one year	**24.50**	**90.00**
☐ 1979	**Reflections,** artist: Norman Rockwell, production: one year	**24.50**	**35.00**
☐ 1980	**A Mother's Pride,** artist: Norman Rockwell, production: one year	**24.50**	**30.00**
☐ 1981	**After the Party,** artist: Norman Rockwell, production: one year	**24.50**	**30.00**
☐ 1982	**The Cooking Lesson,** artist: Norman Rockwell, production: one year	**25.50**	**30.00**

		Issue Price	Current Value
☐ 1983	**Add Two Cups and a Measure of Love,** artist: Norman Rockwell, production: one year ...	**25.50**	**37.00**
☐ 1984	**Grandma's Courting Dress,** artist: Norman Rockwell, production: one year	**25.50**	**28.00**
☐ 1985	**Mending Time,** artist: Norman Rockwell, production: one year	**27.50**	**35.00**
☐ 1986	**Pantry Raid,** artist: Norman Rockwell, production: one year	**27.90**	**28.00**
☐ 1987	**Grandma's Surprise,** artist: Norman Rockwell, production: one year	**29.90**	**29.90**

ROCKWELL'S LIGHT CAMPAIGN SERIES

		Issue Price	Current Value
☐ 1983	**This Is the Room That Light Made,** artist: Norman Rockwell, production limited	**19.50**	**65.00**
☐ 1984	**Grandpa's Treasure Chest,** artist: Norman Rockwell, production limited	**19.50**	**20.00**
☐ 1984	**Father's Help,** artist: Norman Rockwell, production limited	**19.50**	**19.50**
☐ 1984	**Evening's Ease,** artist: Norman Rockwell, production limited	**19.50**	**23.00**
☐ 1984	**Close Harmony,** artist: Norman Rockwell, production limited	**21.50**	**22.00**

Grandma's Surprise, artist: Norman Rockwell.

		Issue Price	Current Value
☐ 1984	**The Birthday Wish,** artist: Norman Rockwell, production limited	21.50	21.50

ROCKWELL ON TOUR SERIES

☐ 1983	**Walking Through Merrie Englande,** artist: Norman Rockwell, production limited	16.00	38.00
☐ 1983	**Promenade a Paris,** artist: Norman Rockwell, production limited	16.00	17.00
☐ 1983	**When in Rome—,** artist: Norman Rockwell, production limited	16.00	16.00
☐ 1984	**Die Walk am Rhein,** artist: Norman Rockwell, production limited	16.00	20.00

ROCKWELL'S REDISCOVERED WOMEN SERIES

☐ 1982	**Dreaming in the Attic,** artist: Norman Rockwell, production limited	19.50	33.00
☐ 1982	**Waiting on the Shore,** artist: Norman Rockwell, production limited	22.50	27.00
☐ 1982	**Pondering on the Porch,** artist: Norman Rockwell, production limited	22.50	30.00
☐ 1982	**Making Believe at the Mirror,** artist: Norman Rockwell, production limited	22.50	32.00
☐ 1983	**Waiting at the Dance,** artist: Norman Rockwell, production limited	22.50	35.00

Making Believe at the Mirror, artist: Norman Rockwell.

		Issue Price	Current Value
☐ 1983	**Gossiping in the Alcove,** artist: Norman Rockwell, production limited	**22.50**	**29.00**
☐ 1983	**Standing in the Doorway,** artist: Norman Rockwell, production limited	**22.50**	**44.00**
☐ 1983	**Flirting in the Parlor,** artist: Norman Rockwell, production limited	**22.50**	**30.00**
☐ 1983	**Working in the Kitchen,** artist: Norman Rockwell, production limited	**22.50**	**27.50**
☐ 1984	**Meeting on the Path,** artist: Norman Rockwell, production limited	**22.50**	**25.00**
☐ 1984	**Confiding in the Den,** artist: Norman Rockwell, production limited	**22.50**	**22.50**
☐ 1984	**Reminiscing in the Quiet,** artist: Norman Rockwell, production limited	**22.50**	**35.00**
☐ 1984	**Reminiscing 'Neath the Eaves,** artist: Norman Rockwell, production limited	**22.50**	**22.50**

ROMAN, INC.

United States

CATS SERIES

☐ 1984	**Grizabella,** production: 30 days	**29.50**	**29.50**
☐ 1984	**Mr. Mistoffelees,** production: 30 days	**29.50**	**29.50**
☐ 1984	**Rum Tum Tugger,** production: 30 days	**29.50**	**29.50**
☐ 1985	**Growltiger,** production: 30 days	**29.50**	**29.50**
☐ 1985	**Skimbleshanks,** production: 30 days	**29.50**	**29.50**
☐ 1985	**Mungojerrie and Rumpelteazer,** production: 30 days	**29.50**	**29.50**

CERAMICA EXCELSIS SERIES

☐ 1980	**Little Children Come to Me,** production quantity 15,000	**45.00**	**45.00**

A CHILD'S PLAY SERIES
(Knowles China Co.)

☐ 1982	**Breezy Day,** artist: Frances Hook, production: 30 days	**29.95**	**35.00**
☐ 1982	**Kite Flying,** artist: Frances Hook, production: 30 days	**29.95**	**35.00**
☐ 1984	**Bathtub Sailor,** artist: Frances Hook, production: 30 days	**29.95**	**35.00**

		Issue Price	Current Value
☐ 1984	**The First Snow,** artist: Frances Hook, production: 30 days	29.95	35.00

A CHILD'S WORLD SERIES

☐ 1980	**Little Children, Come to Me,** artist: Frances Hook, production quantity 15,000	45.00	45.00

FONTANINI ANNUAL SERIES

☐ 1986	**A King Is Born,** artist: E. Simonetti, production: one year	60.00	60.00
☐ 1987	**O Come, Let Us Adore Him,** artist: E. Simonetti, production: one year	60.00	60.00

FRANCES HOOK COLLECTION

☐ 1982	**I Wish, I Wish,** artist: Frances Hook, numbered, production quantity 15,000	24.95	75.00
☐ 1982	**Baby Blossoms,** artist: Frances Hook, numbered, production quantity 15,000	24.95	75.00
☐ 1982	**Daisy Dreamer,** artist: Frances Hook, numbered, production quantity 15,000	24.95	75.00
☐ 1982	**Trees So Tall,** artist: Frances Hook, numbered, production quantity 15,000	24.95	75.00
☐ 1983	**Caught It Myself,** artist: Frances Hook, numbered, production quantity 15,000	24.95	50.00

Little Children, Come to Me, artist: Frances Hook.

		Issue Price	Current Value
☐ 1983	**Winter Wrappings,** artist: Frances Hook, numbered, production quantity 15,000	24.95	50.00
☐ 1983	**So Cuddly,** artist: Frances Hook, numbered, production quantity 15,000	24.95	50.00
☐ 1983	**Can I Keep Him?,** artist: Frances Hook, numbered, production quantity 15,000	24.95	50.00

FRANCES HOOK LEGACY
(see Knowles China Co.)

THE ICE CAPADES CLOWN SERIES

☐ 1983	**Presenting Freddie Trenkler,** artist: George B. Petty, production: 30 days	24.50	24.50

THE LORD'S PRAYER SERIES

☐ 1986	**Our Father,** artist: Abbie Williams, production: 10 days	24.50	24.50
☐ 1986	**Thy Kingdom Come,** artist: Abbie Williams, production: 10 days	24.50	24.50
☐ 1986	**Give Us This Day,** artist: Abbie Williams, production: 10 days	24.50	24.50
☐ 1986	**Forgive Our Trespasses,** artist: Abbie Williams, production: 10 days	24.50	24.50
☐ 1986	**As We Forgive,** artist: Abbie Williams, production: 10 days	24.50	24.50
☐ 1986	**Lead Us Not,** artist: Abbie Williams, production: 10 days	24.50	24.50
☐ 1986	**Deliver Us from Evil,** artist: Abbie Williams, production: 10 days	24.50	24.50
☐ 1986	**Thine Is the Kingdom,** artist: Abbie Williams, production: 10 days	24.50	24.50

THE MAGIC OF CHILDHOOD SERIES

☐ 1984	**Special Friends,** artist: Abbie Williams, production: 10 days	24.50	24.50
☐ 1985	**Feeding Time,** artist: Abbie Williams, production: 10 days	24.50	24.50
☐ 1985	**Best Buddies,** artist: Abbie Williams, production: 10 days	24.50	24.50
☐ 1985	**Getting Acquainted,** artist: Abbie Williams, production: 10 days	24.50	24.50
☐ 1985	**Look Alikes,** artist: Abbie Williams, production: 10 days	24.50	24.50

		Issue Price	Current Value
☐ 1985	**Last One In,** artist: Abbie Williams, production: 10 days	**24.50**	**24.50**
☐ 1985	**A Handful of Love,** artist: Abbie Williams, production: 10 days	**24.50**	**24.50**
☐ 1985	**No Fair Peeking,** artist: Abbie Williams, production: 10 days	**24.50**	**24.50**

MASTERPIECE COLLECTION

☐ 1979	**Adoration,** artist: Fra Lippi, production quantity 5,000	**65.00**	**65.00**
☐ 1980	**Madonna with Grapes,** artist: P. Mignard, production quantity 5,000	**87.50**	**87.50**
☐ 1981	**The Holy Family,** artist: G. Delle Notti, production quantity 5,000	**95.00**	**95.00**
☐ 1982	**Madonna of the Streets,** artist: Robert Ferruzzi, production quantity 5,000	**85.00**	**85.00**

PETTY GIRLS OF THE ICE CAPADES SERIES

☐ 1983	**Ice Princess,** artist: George B. Petty, production: 30 days	**24.50**	**24.50**

ROMAN MEMORIAL SERIES
(Pickard China)

☐ 1984	**The Carpenter,** artist: Frances Hook, production quantity: 1984	**100.00**	**300.00**

THE SWEETEST SONGS SERIES

☐ 1986	**A Baby's Prayer,** artist: Irene Spencer, production: 30 days	**39.50**	**45.00**
☐ 1986	**This Little Piggie,** artist: Irene Spencer, production: 30 days	**39.50**	**39.50**

SINGLE ISSUES

☐ 1983	**The Kneeling Santa,** production limited ...	**29.50**	**29.50**
☐ 1985	**Fairest Flower of Paradise,** artist: Mary Jean Dorcy, production quantity: unannounced	**45.00**	**45.00**

The Carpenter, artist:
Frances Hook.

This Little Piggie, artist:
Irene Spencer.

RORSTRAND

Sweden

CHRISTMAS SERIES	Issue Price	Current Value
☐ 1968 **Bringing Home the Tree**, artist: Gunner Nylund, production: one year	12.00	425.00

		Issue Price	Current Value
☐ 1969	**Fishermen Sailing Home,** artist: Gunner Nylund, production: one year	13.50	50.00
☐ 1970	**Nils with His Geese,** artist: Gunner Nylund, production: one year	13.50	20.00
☐ 1971	**Nils in Lapland,** artist: Gunner Nylund, production: one year	15.00	15.00
☐ 1972	**Dalecarlian Fiddler,** artist: Gunner Nylund, production: one year	15.00	28.00
☐ 1973	**Farm in Smaland,** artist: Gunner Nylund, production: one year	16.00	70.00
☐ 1974	**Vadslena,** artist: Gunner Nylund, production: one year	19.00	50.00
☐ 1975	**Nils in Vastmanland,** artist: Gunner Nylund, production: one year	20.00	25.00
☐ 1976	**Nils in Uppland,** artist: Gunner Nylund, production: one year	20.00	28.00
☐ 1977	**Nils in Varmland,** artist: Gunner Nylund, production: one year	29.50	29.50
☐ 1978	**Nils in Fjallbacka,** artist: Gunner Nylund, production: one year	32.50	32.50
☐ 1979	**Nils in Vaestergoetland,** artist: Gunner Nylund, production: one year	38.50	38.50
☐ 1980	**Nils in Halland,** artist: Gunner Nylund, production: one year	55.00	55.00
☐ 1981	**Nils in Gotland,** artist: Gunner Nylund, production: one year	55.00	55.00
☐ 1982	**Nils at Skansen,** artist: Gunner Nylund, production: one year	47.50	50.00
☐ 1983	**Nils in Oland,** artist: Gunner Nylund, production: one year	42.50	54.00
☐ 1984	**Nils in Angermanland,** artist: Gunner Nylund, production: one year	42.50	42.50
☐ 1985	**Christmas,** artist: Gunner Nylund, production: one year	42.50	43.00
☐ 1986	**Nils in Karlskrona,** artist: Gunner Nylund, production: one year	42.50	45.00

FATHER'S DAY SERIES

		Issue Price	Current Value
☐ 1971	**Father and Child,** production: one year	15.00	21.00
☐ 1972	**Meal at Home,** production: one year	15.00	23.00
☐ 1973	**Tilling the Fields,** production: one year . . .	16.00	23.00
☐ 1974	**Fishing,** production: one year	18.00	26.00
☐ 1975	**Painting,** production: one year	20.00	26.00
☐ 1976	**Plowing,** production: one year	20.00	26.00

		Issue Price	Current Value
☐ 1977	Sawing, production: one year	27.50	29.00
☐ 1978	In the Studio, production: one year	27.50	29.00
☐ 1979	Riding in the Buggy, production: one year	27.50	29.00
☐ 1980	My Etch-Nook, production: one year	27.50	29.00
☐ 1981	Esbjorn with Playmate, production: one year	27.50	29.00
☐ 1982	House Servants, production: one year	36.00	36.00
☐ 1983	Father Painting, production: one year	42.50	42.50
☐ 1984	Father Working, production: one year	42.50	42.50

JUBILEE SERIES

☐ 1980	1980, production: one year	47.50	50.00

JULPOESI SERIES

☐ 1979	Silent Night, production: one year	38.50	40.00
☐ 1980	Adoration, production: one year	47.50	50.00

MOTHER'S DAY SERIES

☐ 1971	Mother and Child, production: one year ...	15.00	26.00
☐ 1972	Shelling Peas, production: one year	15.00	26.00
☐ 1973	Old-Fashioned Picnic, production: one year	16.00	31.00
☐ 1974	Candle Lighting, production: one year	18.00	26.00
☐ 1975	Pontius on the Floor, production: one year	20.00	26.00
☐ 1976	Apple Picking, production: one year	20.00	26.00
☐ 1977	Kitchen, production: one year	27.50	31.00
☐ 1978	Azalea, production: one year	27.50	29.00
☐ 1989	Studio Idyll, production: one year	27.50	29.00
☐ 1980	Lisbeth, production: one year	27.50	29.00
☐ 1981	Karin with Brita, production: one year	27.50	29.00
☐ 1982	Brita, production: one year	36.00	36.00
☐ 1983	Little Girl, production: one year	42.50	42.50
☐ 1984	Mother Sewing, production: one year	42.50	42.50

ROSENTHAL

Germany

CHRISTMAS SERIES

☐ 1910	Winter Peace	—	550.00
☐ 1911	Three Wise Men	—	325.00
☐ 1912	Stardust	—	255.00
☐ 1913	Christmas Lights	—	235.00
☐ 1914	Christmas Song	—	350.00
☐ 1915	Walking to Church	—	180.00

			Issue Price	Current Value
☐ 1916	Christmas During War	....	—	240.00
☐ 1917	Angel of Peace	....	—	200.00
☐ 1918	Peace on Earth	....	—	200.00
☐ 1919	St. Christopher with the Christ Child	.....	—	225.00
☐ 1920	The Manger in Bethlehem	....	—	325.00
☐ 1921	Christmas in the Mountains	....	—	200.00
☐ 1922	Advent Branch	....	—	200.00
☐ 1923	Children in the Winter Woods	....	—	200.00
☐ 1924	Deer in the Woods	....	—	200.00
☐ 1925	The Three Wise Men	....	—	200.00
☐ 1926	Christmas in the Mountains	....	—	195.00
☐ 1927	Station on the Way	....	—	200.00
☐ 1928	Chalet Christmas	....	—	185.00
☐ 1929	Christmas in the Alps	....	—	225.00
☐ 1930	Group of Deer Under the Pines	....	—	225.00
☐ 1931	Path of the Magi	....	—	225.00
☐ 1932	Christ Child	....	—	185.00
☐ 1933	Through the Night to Light	....	—	190.00
☐ 1934	Christmas Peace	....	—	190.00
☐ 1935	Christmas by the Sea	....	—	200.00
☐ 1936	Nurnberg Angel	....	—	195.00
☐ 1937	Berchtesgaden	....	—	195.00
☐ 1938	Christmas in the Alps	....	—	195.00
☐ 1939	Schneekoppe Mountain	....	—	195.00
☐ 1940	Marien Church in Danzig	....	—	250.00
☐ 1941	Strassburg Cathedral	....	—	250.00
☐ 1942	Marianburg Castle	....	—	300.00
☐ 1943	Winter Idyll	....	—	300.00
☐ 1944	Wood Scape	....	—	300.00
☐ 1945	Christmas Peace	....	—	400.00
☐ 1946	Christmas in an Alpine Valley	....	—	240.00
☐ 1947	The Dillingen Madonna	....	—	985.00
☐ 1948	Message to the Shepherds	....	—	875.00
☐ 1949	The Holy Family	....	—	185.00
☐ 1950	Christmas in the Forest	....	—	185.00
☐ 1951	Star of Bethlehem	....	—	450.00
☐ 1952	Christmas in the Alps	....	—	195.00
☐ 1953	The Holy Light	....	—	195.00
☐ 1954	Christmas Eve	....	—	195.00
☐ 1955	Christmas in a Village	....	—	195.00
☐ 1956	Christmas in the Alps	....	—	195.00
☐ 1957	Christmas by the Sea	....	—	195.00
☐ 1958	Christmas Eve	....	—	195.00
☐ 1959	Midnight Mass	....	—	195.00

		Issue Price	Current Value
☐ 1960	Christmas in a Small Village	—	195.00
☐ 1961	Solitary Christmas	—	225.00
☐ 1962	Christmas Eve	—	195.00
☐ 1963	Silent Night	—	195.00
☐ 1964	Christmas Market in Nurnberg	—	225.00
☐ 1965	Christmas in Munich	—	185.00
☐ 1966	Christmas in Ulm	—	275.00
☐ 1967	Christmas in Reginburg	—	185.00
☐ 1968	Christmas in Bremen	—	195.00
☐ 1969	Christmas in Rothenburg	—	220.00
☐ 1970	Christmas in Cologne	—	175.00
☐ 1971	Christmas in Garmisch	42.00	100.00
☐ 1972	Christmas in Franconia	50.00	95.00
☐ 1973	Lubeck-Holstein	77.00	105.00
☐ 1974	Wurzburg	85.00	100.00

CLASSIC ROSE CHRISTMAS SERIES

		Issue Price	Current Value
☐ 1974	**Memorial Church in Berlin,** artist: Helmut Drexel, production: unannounced	84.00	160.00
☐ 1975	**Freiburg Cathedral,** artist: Helmut Drexel, production: unannounced	75.00	80.00
☐ 1976	**Castle of Cochem,** artist: Helmut Drexel, production: unannounced	95.00	85.00
☐ 1977	**Hanover Town Hall,** artist: Helmut Drexel, production: unannounced	125.00	125.00
☐ 1978	**Cathedral at Aachen,** artist: Helmut Drexel, production: unannounced	150.00	150.00
☐ 1979	**Cathedral in Luxembourg,** artist: Helmut Drexel, production: unannounced	165.00	165.00
☐ 1980	**Christmas in Brussels,** artist: Helmut Drexel, production: unannounced	190.00	190.00
☐ 1981	**Christmas in Trier,** artist: Helmut Drexel, production: unannounced	190.00	190.00
☐ 1982	**Milan Cathedral,** artist: Helmut Drexel, production: unannounced	190.00	190.00
☐ 1983	**Church at Castle Wittenberg,** artist: Helmut Drexel, production: unannounced	195.00	195.00
☐ 1984	**City Hall of Stockholm,** artist: Helmut Drexel, production: unannounced	195.00	195.00
☐ 1985	**Christmas in Augsburg,** artist: Helmut Drexel, production: unannounced	195.00	195.00

		Issue Price	Current Value

FAMOUS WOMEN AND CHILDREN SERIES

		Issue Price	Current Value
☐ 1980	**Pharaoh's Daughter and Moses,** artist: Edna Hibel, gold, production quantity 2,500	350.00	390.00
☐ 1980	**Pharaoh's Daughter and Moses,** artist: Edna Hibel, cobalt blue, production quantity 500	350.00	560.00
☐ 1981	**Cornelia and Jewels,** artist: Edna Hibel, gold, production quantity 2,500	350.00	350.00
☐ 1981	**Cornelia and Jewels,** artist: Edna Hibel, cobalt blue, production quantity 500	350.00	350.00
☐ 1982	**Anna and Children of King of Siam,** artist: Edna Hibel, gold, production quantity 2,500	350.00	350.00
☐ 1982	**Anna and Children of King of Siam,** artist: Edna Hibel, cobalt blue, production quantity 500	350.00	350.00

FANTASIES AND FABLES SERIES

		Issue Price	Current Value
☐ 1976	**Oriental Night Music,** production quantity 10,000	50.00	53.00
☐ 1977	**Mandolin Players,** production: one year ...	75.00	75.00

HARVEST TIME SERIES

		Issue Price	Current Value
☐ 1976	**Pumpkins,** artist: John Falter, production quantity 5,000	70.00	71.00
☐ 1977	**Honest Day's Work,** artist: John Falter, production quantity 4,000	70.00	71.00

LORRAINE TRESTER SERIES

		Issue Price	Current Value
☐ 1975	**Summertime,** artist: Lorraine Trester, production quantity 5,000	60.00	135.00
☐ 1977	**One Lovely Yesterday,** artist: Lorraine Trester, production quantity 5,000	70.00	92.00

NOBILITY OF CHILDREN SERIES

		Issue Price	Current Value
☐ 1976	**La Contessa Isabella,** artist: Edna Hibel, production quantity 12,750	120.00	150.00
☐ 1977	**Le Marquis Maurice-Pierre,** artist: Edna Hibel, production quantity 12,750	120.00	120.00
☐ 1978	**Baronesse Johanna,** artist: Edna Hibel, production quantity 12,750	130.00	140.00
☐ 1979	**Chief Red Feather,** artist: Edna Hibel, production quantity 12,750	140.00	140.00

		Issue Price	Current Value

ORIENTAL GOLD SERIES

☐ **1973 Yasuko,** artist: Edna Hibel, production quantity 2,000 .... **275.00** **850.00**

☐ **1976 Mr. Obata,** artist: Edna Hibel, production quantity 2,000 .... **275.00** **550.00**

☐ **1978 Sakura,** artist: Edna Hibel, production quantity 2,000 .... **295.00** **425.00**

☐ **1979 Michio,** artist: Edna Hibel, production quantity 2,000 .... **325.00** **375.00**

RUNCI CLASSIC SERIES

☐ **1977 Summertime,** artist: Edward Runci, production quantity 5,000 .... **95.00** **100.00**

☐ **1978 Springtime,** artist: Edward Runci, production quantity 5,000 .... **95.00** **100.00**

TRIBUTE TO CLASSICAL GREEK BEAUTY SERIES

☐ **1980 Diana,** artist: Edna Hibel, production quantity 3,000 .... **350.00** **360.00**

WIINBLAD CHRISTMAS SERIES

☐ **1971 Maria and Child,** artist: Bjorn Wiinblad, production quantity 8,000 .... **100.00** **1250.00**

☐ **1972 Caspar,** artist: Bjorn Wiinblad, production quantity 10,000 .... **100.00** **540.00**

☐ **1973 Melchior,** artist: Bjorn Wiinblad, production quantity 10,000 .... **125.00** **450.00**

☐ **1974 Balthazar,** artist: Bjorn Wiinblad, production quantity 10,000 .... **125.00** **520.00**

☐ **1975 The Annunciation,** artist: Bjorn Wiinblad, production: one year **195.00** **195.00**

☐ **1976 Angel with Trumpet,** artist: Bjorn Wiinblad, production: one year **195.00** **195.00**

☐ **1977 Adoration of Shepherds,** artist: Bjorn Wiinblad, production: one year **225.00** **250.00**

☐ **1978 Angel with Harp,** artist: Bjorn Wiinblad, production: one year **275.00** **278.00**

☐ **1979 Exodus from Egypt,** artist: Bjorn Wiinblad, production: one year **310.00** **310.00**

☐ **1980 Angel with Glockenspiel,** artist: Bjorn Wiinblad, production: one year **360.00** **360.00**

☐ **1981 The Christ Child Visits the Temple,** artist: Bjorn Wiinblad, production: one year **375.00** **375.00**

		Issue Price	Current Value

☐ **1982** **Christening of Christ,** artist: Bjorn Wiinblad, production: one year 375.00   400.00

WIINBLAD CRYSTAL SERIES

☐ **1976** **The Madonna,** artist: Bjorn Wiinblad, production quantity 2,000 ....   150.00   400.00
☐ **1977** **The Annunciation,** artist: Bjorn Wiinblad, production quantity 2,000 ....   195.00   285.00
☐ **1978** **Three Kings,** artist: Bjorn Wiinblad, production quantity 2,000 ....   225.00   270.00
☐ **1980** **Angel with Shepherds,** artist: Bjorn Wiinblad, production: one year 290.00   300.00
☐ **1981** **Adoration of the Shepherds,** artist: Bjorn Wiinblad, production: one year 295.00   300.00

ROYAL BAYREUTH

Germany

ANNIVERSARY SERIES

☐ **1980** **Young Americans,** artist: Leo Jansen, production quantity 5,000 ....   125.00   130.00

ANTIQUE AMERICAN ART SERIES

☐ **1976** **Farmyard Tranquility,** production quantity 3,000 ....   50.00   71.00
☐ **1977** **Half Dome,** production quantity 3,000 ....   55.00   63.00
☐ **1978** **Down Memory Lane,** production quantity 3,000 ....   65.00   66.00

CHRISTMAS SERIES

☐ **1972** **Carriage in the Village,** production quantity 4,000 ....   15.00   80.00
☐ **1973** **Snow Scene,** production quantity 4,000 ....   16.50   20.00
☐ **1974** **The Old Mill,** production quantity 4,000 ..   24.00   24.00
☐ **1975** **Forest Chalet "Serenity,"** production quantity 4,000 ....   27.50   27.50
☐ **1976** **Christmas in the Country,** production quantity 5,000 ....   40.00   40.00
☐ **1977** **Peace on Earth,** production quantity 5,000   40.00   40.00
☐ **1978** **Peaceful Interlude,** production quantity 5,000 ....   45.00   45.00
☐ **1979** **Homeward Bound,** production quantity 5,000   50.00   50.00

		Issue Price	Current Value

L. HENRY SERIES

☐ 1976	**Just Friends,** production quantity 5,000 ...	**50.00**	**60.00**
☐ 1977	**Interruption,** production quantity 5,000 ...	**55.00**	**55.00**

MOTHER'S DAY SERIES

☐ 1973	**Consolation,** artist: Leo Jansen, production quantity 4,000	**16.50**	**50.00**
☐ 1974	**Young Americans,** artist: Leo Jansen, production quantity 4,000	**25.00**	**130.00**
☐ 1975	**Young Americans II,** artist: Leo Jansen, production quantity 5,000	**25.00**	**105.00**
☐ 1976	**Young Americans III,** artist: Leo Jansen, production quantity 5,000	**30.00**	**70.00**
☐ 1977	**Young Americans IV,** artist: Leo Jansen, production quantity 5,000	**40.00**	**60.00**
☐ 1978	**Young Americans V,** artist: Leo Jansen, production quantity 5,000	**45.00**	**50.00**
☐ 1979	**Young Americans VI,** artist: Leo Jansen, production quantity 5,000	**60.00**	**62.00**
☐ 1980	**Young Americans VII,** artist: Leo Jansen, production quantity 5,000	**65.00**	**75.00**
☐ 1981	**Young Americans VIII,** artist: Leo Jansen, production quantity 5,000	**65.00**	**66.00**
☐ 1982	**Young Americans IX,** artist: Leo Jansen, production quantity 5,000	**65.00**	**66.00**

SUN BONNET BABIES SERIES

☐ 1974	**Monday—Washing Day,** production quantity 15,000		
☐ 1974	**Tuesday—Ironing Day,** production quantity 15,000		
☐ 1974	**Wednesday—Mending Day,** production quantity 15,000		
☐ 1974	**Thursday—Scrubbing Day,** production quantity 15,000		
☐ 1974	**Friday—Sweeping Day,** production quantity 15,000		
☐ 1974	**Saturday—Baking Day,** production quantity 15,000		
☐ 1974	**Sunday—Fishing Day,** production quantity 15,000		
	Set of seven	**120.00**	**230.00**

SUN BONNET BABIES
PLAYTIME SERIES

		Issue Price	Current Value
☐ 1981	**Swinging,** production quantity 5,000	60.00	60.00
☐ 1981	**Round Dance,** production quantity 5,000 ..	60.00	60.00
☐ 1982	**Marbles,** production quantity 5,000	60.00	60.00
☐ 1982	**Playing Catch,** production quantity 5,000 ..	60.00	60.00

ROYAL COPENHAGEN

Denmark

CHRISTMAS SERIES

☐ 1908	**Madonna and Child,** artist: Christian Thomsen, production: one year	1.00	1800.00
☐ 1909	**Danish Landscape,** artist: Stephan Ussing, production: one year	1.00	144.00
☐ 1910	**The Magi,** artist: Christian Thomsen, production: one year	1.00	120.00
☐ 1911	**Danish Landscape,** artist: Oluf Jensen, production: one year	1.00	150.00
☐ 1912	**Elderly Couple by the Christmas Tree,** artist: Christian Thomsen, production: one year ..	1.00	120.00
☐ 1913	**Spire of Frederik Church,** artist: Arthur Boesen, production: one year	1.50	128.00
☐ 1914	**Holy Spirit Church,** artist: Arthur Boesen, production: one year	1.50	113.00
☐ 1915	**Danish Landscape,** artist: Arnold Krog, production: one year	1.50	128.00
☐ 1916	**The Shepherds in the Field,** artist: Richard Bocher, production: one year	1.50	84.00
☐ 1917	**The Tower of Our Saviour's Church,** artist: Oluf Jensen, production: one year	2.00	90.00
☐ 1918	**The Shepherds and Sheep,** artist: Oluf Jensen, production: one year	2.00	84.00
☐ 1919	**In the Park,** artist: Oluf Jensen, production: one year	2.00	95.00
☐ 1920	**Mary with the Child Jesus,** artist: Oluf Jensen, production: one year	2.00	78.00
☐ 1921	**Aabenraa Marketplace,** artist: Oluf Jensen, production: one year	2.00	80.00
☐ 1922	**Three Singing Angels,** artist: Ellinor Selschau, production: one year	2.00	54.00
☐ 1923	**Danish Landscape,** artist: Oluf Jensen, production: one year	2.00	68.00

		Issue Price	Current Value
☐ 1924	**Christmas Star over the Sea,** artist: Benjamin Olsen, production: one year	**2.00**	**105.00**
☐ 1925	**Street Scene from Christianshavn,** artist: Oluf Jensen, production: one year	**2.00**	**84.00**
☐ 1926	**Christianshavn Canal,** artist: Richard Bocher, production: one year	**2.00**	**101.00**
☐ 1927	**The Ship's Boy at the Tiller Christmas Night,** artist: Benjamin Olsen, production: one year	**2.00**	**165.00**
☐ 1928	**The Vicar—Family on the Way to Church,** artist: Gotfred Rode, production: one year	**2.00**	**75.00**
☐ 1929	**The Grundtvig Church, Copenhagen,** artist: Oluf Jensen, production: one year	**2.00**	**90.00**
☐ 1930	**Fishing Boats,** artist: Benjamin Olsen, production: one year	**2.50**	**96.00**
☐ 1931	**Mother and Child,** artist: Gotfred Rode, production: one year	**2.50**	**96.00**
☐ 1932	**Frederiksberg Gardens with Statue of Frederik VI,** artist: Oluf Jensen, production: one year	**2.50**	**110.00**
☐ 1933	**The Ferry and the Great Belt,** artist: Benjamin Olsen, production: one year	**2.50**	**113.00**
☐ 1934	**The Hermitage Castle,** artist: Oluf Jensen, production: one year	**2.50**	**95.00**
☐ 1935	**Fishing Boat off Kronborg Castle,** artist: Benjamin Olsen, production: one year	**2.50**	**147.00**
☐ 1936	**Roskilde Cathedral,** artist: Ricard Bocher, production: one year	**2.50**	**138.00**
☐ 1937	**Christmas Scene in Copenhagen,** artist: Nils Thorsson, production: one year	**2.50**	**150.00**
☐ 1938	**The Round Church in Osterlars,** artist: Herne Nielsen, production: one year	**3.00**	**195.00**
☐ 1939	**Expeditionary Ship in the Pack Ice of Greenland,** artist: Svend Nicolai Nielsen, production: one year	**3.00**	**180.00**
☐ 1940	**The Good Shepherd,** artist: Kai Lange, production: one year	**3.00**	**300.00**
☐ 1941	**Danish Village Church,** artist: Theodor Kjolner, production: one year	**3.00**	**315.00**
☐ 1942	**Bell Tower of Old Church in Jutland,** artist: Nils Thorsson, production: one year	**4.00**	**290.00**
☐ 1943	**The Flight of the Holy Family to Egypt,** artist: Nils Thorsson, production: one year ...	**4.00**	**510.00**
☐ 1944	**Typical Danish Winter Scene,** artist: Viggo Olsen, production: one year	**4.00**	**185.00**

		Issue Price	Current Value
☐ 1945	**A Peaceful Motif,** artist: Richard Bocher, production: one year	4.00	300.00
☐ 1946	**Zealand Village Church,** artist: Nils Thorsson, production: one year	4.00	162.00
☐ 1947	**The Good Shepherd,** artist: Kai Lange, production: one year	4.50	215.00
☐ 1948	**Nodebo Church,** artist: Theodor Kjolner, production: one year	4.50	150.00
☐ 1949	**Our Lady's Cathedral, Copenhagen,** artist: Hans H. Hansen, production: one year	5.00	140.00
☐ 1950	**Boeslunde Church,** artist: Viggo Olsen, production: one year	5.00	195.00
☐ 1951	**Christmas Angel,** artist: Richard Bocher, production: one year	5.00	300.00
☐ 1952	**Christmas in the Forest,** artist: Kai Lange, production: one year	5.00	120.00
☐ 1953	**Frederiksberg Castle,** artist: Theodor Kjolner, production: one year	6.00	125.00
☐ 1954	**Amalienborg Palace, Copenhagen,** artist: Kai Lange, production: one year	6.00	148.00
☐ 1955	**Fano Girl,** artist: Kai Lange, production: one year	7.00	195.00
☐ 1956	**Rosenborg Castle,** artist: Kai Lange, production: one year	7.00	140.00
☐ 1957	**The Good Shepherd,** artist: Hans H. Hansen, production: one year	8.00	90.00
☐ 1958	**Sunshine over Greenland,** artist: Hans H. Hansen, production: one year	9.00	120.00
☐ 1959	**Christmas Night,** artist: Hans H. Hansen, production: one year	9.00	110.00
☐ 1960	**The Stag,** artist: Hans H. Hansen, production: one year	10.00	135.00
☐ 1961	**The Training Ship Danmark,** artist: Kai Lange, production: one year	10.00	140.00
☐ 1962	**The Little Mermaid at Wintertime,** artist: Kai Lange, production: one year	11.00	200.00
☐ 1963	**Hojsager Mill,** artist: Kai Lange, production: one year	11.00	63.00
☐ 1964	**Fetching the Christmas Tree,** artist: Kai Lange, production: one year	11.00	66.00
☐ 1965	**Little Skaters,** artist: Kai Lange, production: one year	12.00	125.00
☐ 1966	**Blackbird and Church,** artist: Kai Lange, production: one year	12.00	125.00

		Issue Price	Current Value
☐ 1967	**The Royal Oak,** artist: Kai Lange, production: one year	13.00	107.50
☐ 1968	**The Lost Umiak,** artist: Kai Lange, production: one year	13.00	105.00
☐ 1969	**The Old Farmyard,** artist: Kai Lange, production: one year	14.00	102.50
☐ 1970	**Christmas Rose and Cat,** artist: Kai Lange, production: one year	14.00	100.00
☐ 1971	**Hare in Winter,** artist: Kai Lange, production: one year	15.00	97.50
☐ 1972	**In the Desert,** artist: Kai Lange, production: one year	16.00	97.50
☐ 1973	**Train Homeward Bound,** artist: Kai Lange, production: one year	22.00	87.50
☐ 1974	**Winter Twilight,** artist: Kai Lange, production: one year	22.00	87.50
☐ 1975	**Queen's Palace,** artist: Kai Lange, production: one year	27.50	87.50
☐ 1976	**Danish Watermill,** artist: Sven Vestergaard, production: one year	27.50	80.00
☐ 1977	**Immervad Bridge,** artist: Kai Lange, production: one year	32.50	80.00
☐ 1978	**Greenland Scenery,** artist: Kai Lange, production: one year	35.00	80.00
☐ 1979	**Choosing a Christmas Tree,** artist: Kai Lange, production: one year	42.50	77.50
☐ 1980	**Bringing Home the Christmas Tree,** artist: Kai Lange, production: one year	49.50	75.50
☐ 1981	**Admiring the Christmas Tree,** artist: Kai Lange, production: one year	52.50	72.00
☐ 1982	**Waiting for Christmas,** artist: Kai Lange, production: one year	54.50	70.00
☐ 1983	**Merry Christmas,** artist: Kai Lange, production: one year	54.50	67.50
☐ 1984	**Jingle Bells,** artist: Kai Lange, production: one year	54.50	65.00

CHRISTMAS JUBILEE SERIES

☐ 1983	**Christmas Memories,** production: one year	95.00	95.00

HANS CHRISTIAN ANDERSEN
FAIRY TALES SERIES

☐ 1983	**Shepherdess and Chimney Sweep,** artist: Sven Vestergaard, production: one year	39.50	40.00

		Issue Price	Current Value
☐ 1984	**Thumbelina,** artist: Sven Vestergaard, production: one year	39.50	40.00
☐ 1985	**Mermaid,** artist: Sven Vestergaard, production: one year	44.50	45.00

HISTORICAL SERIES

☐ 1975	**R. C. Bicentennial,** production: one year ..	30.00	32.00
☐ 1976	**U. S. Bicentennial,** production: one year ..	35.00	37.00
☐ 1977	**Electromagnetism,** production: one year ...	35.00	37.00
☐ 1978	**Captain Cook,** production: one year	37.50	37.00
☐ 1979	**Adam Oehlenschleger,** production: one year	42.00	37.00
☐ 1980	**Amagetorv,** production: one year	57.50	55.00
☐ 1983	**Royal Copenhagen 75th Anniversary,** production: one year	95.00	95.00

THE MOTHERHOOD COLLECTION

☐ 1982	**Mother Robin with Babies,** artist: Sven Vestergaard, production: one year	29.50	47.50
☐ 1983	**Mother Cat and Kittens,** artist: Sven Vestergaard, production: one year	29.50	45.00
☐ 1984	**Mare and Foal,** artist: Sven Vestergaard, production: one year	29.50	42.50
☐ 1985	**Mother and Baby Rabbit,** artist: Sven Vestergaard, production: one year	32.00	32.00

MOTHER'S DAY SERIES

☐ 1971	**American Mother,** artist: Kamma Svensson, production: one year	12.50	130.00
☐ 1972	**Oriental Mother,** artist: Kamma Svensson, production: one year	14.00	65.00
☐ 1973	**Danish Mother,** artist: Arne Ungermann, production: one year	16.00	62.50
☐ 1974	**Greenland Mother,** artist: Arne Ungermann, production: one year	16.00	60.00
☐ 1975	**Bird in Nest,** artist: Arne Ungermann, production: one year	20.00	57.50
☐ 1976	**Mermaids,** artist: Arne Ungermann, production: one year	20.00	55.00
☐ 1977	**Twins,** artist: Arne Ungermann, production: one year	24.00	52.50
☐ 1978	**Mother and Child,** artist: Ib Spang Olsen, production: one year	26.00	26.00
☐ 1979	**A Loving Mother,** artist: Ib Spang Olsen, production: one year	29.50	29.50

		Issue Price	Current Value
☐ 1980	**An Outing with Mother,** artist: Ib Spang Olsen, production: one year	37.50	47.50
☐ 1981	**Reunion,** artist: Ib Spang Olsen, production: one year	37.50	45.00
☐ 1982	**Children's Hour,** artist: Ib Spang Olsen, production: one year	37.50	42.50

NATIONAL PARKS OF AMERICA SERIES

☐ 1978	**Yellowstone,** production quantity 5,000 ...	75.00	75.00
☐ 1979	**Shenandoah,** production quantity 5,000	75.00	75.00
☐ 1981	**Mt. McKinley,** production quantity 5,000	75.00	75.00
☐ 1981	**The Everglades,** production quantity 5,000	75.00	75.00
☐ 1981	**Grand Canyon,** production quantity 5,000	75.00	75.00
☐ 1981	**Yosemite,** production quantity 5,000	75.00	75.00

SPECIAL ISSUES

☐ 1967	**Virgin Islands,** production: one year	12.00	25.00
☐ 1969	**Danish Flag,** production: one year	12.00	25.00
☐ 1969	**Apollo II,** production: one year	15.00	15.00
☐ 1970	**Reunion,** production: one year	12.00	22.00
☐ 1970	**Statue of Liberty**	15.00	24.00
☐ 1972	**Munich Olympiad**	25.00	25.00
☐ 1972	**King Frederik IX**	25.00	25.00

ROYAL CORNWALL

United States
(See Haviland, Schumann, Wedgwood and Woodmere)

ALICE IN WONDERLAND SERIES

☐ 1979	**Alice and the White Rabbit,** artist: Lawrence W. Whittaker, production quantity 27,500	45.00	45.00
☐ 1979	**Advice from a Caterpillar,** artist: Lawrence W. Whittaker, production quantity 27,500	45.00	45.00
☐ 1980	**The Cheshire Cat's Grin,** artist: Lawrence W. Whittaker, production quantity 27,500	45.00	45.00
☐ 1980	**Mad Hatter's Tea Party,** artist: Lawrence W. Whittaker, production quantity 27,500	45.00	45.00
☐ 1980	**Queen's Croquet Match,** artist: Lawrence W. Whittaker, production quantity 27,500	45.00	45.00
☐ 1980	**Who Stole the Tarts?,** artist: Lawrence W. Whittaker, production quantity 27,500	45.00	45.00

		Issue Price	Current Value

BEAUTY OF BOUGUEREAU SERIES

☐ **1979 Lucie,** artist: William A. Bouguereau, production quantity 19,500 . . . . — 35.00 — 45.00

☐ **1980 Madelaine,** artist: William A. Bouguereau, production quantity 19,500 . . . . — 35.00 — 35.00

☐ **1980 Frere et Soeur,** artist: William A. Bouguereau, production quantity 19,500 . . . — 35.00 — 35.00

☐ **1980 Solange et Enfant,** artist: William A. Bouguereau, production quantity 19,500 . . . — 35.00 — 35.00

☐ **1980 Colette,** artist: William A. Bouguereau, production quantity 19,500 . . . . — 35.00 — 65.00

☐ **1980 Jean et Jeanette,** artist: William A. Bouguereau, production quantity 19,500 . . . — 35.00 — 35.00

BETHLEHEM CHRISTMAS SERIES

☐ **1977 First Christmas Eve,** artist: Gerald R. Miller, production quantity 10,000 . . . . — 29.50 — 85.00

☐ **1978 Glad Tidings,** artist: Robert Ahlcrona, production quantity 10,000 . . . . — 34.50 — 75.00

☐ **1979 The Gift Bearers,** artist: Higgins Bond, production quantity 10,000 . . . . — 34.50 — 35.00

☐ **1980 Great Joy,** artist: David McCall Johnson, production quantity 10,000 . . . . — 39.95 — 40.00

CLASSIC CHRISTMAS COLLECTION

☐ **1978 Child of Peace,** production quantity 10,000 — 55.00 — 85.00

☐ **1978 Silent Night,** production quantity 10,000 . . — 55.00 — 68.00

☐ **1978 Most Precious Gift,** production quantity 10,000 . . . . — 55.00 — 65.00

☐ **1978 We Three Kings,** production quantity 10,000 — 55.00 — 65.00

CLASSIC COLLECTION

☐ **1980 Romeo and Juliet,** artist: J. C. Leyendecker, production quantity 17,500 . . . . — 55.00 — 65.00

☐ **1980 Young Galahad,** artist: J. C. Leyendecker, production quantity 17,500 . . . . — 55.00 — 65.00

☐ **1980 At Locksley Hall,** artist: J. C. Leyendecker, production quantity 17,500 . . . . — 55.00 — 55.00

☐ **1980 St. Agnes Eve,** artist: J. C. Leyendecker, production quantity 17,500 . . . . — 55.00 — 55.00

COURAGEOUS FEW SERIES

☐ **1982 The Fall of Jericho,** artist: Yiannis Koutsis, production quantity 19,500 . . . . — 59.50 — 63.00

		Issue Price	Current Value
☐ 1982	**Gideon's Five Hundred,** artist: Yiannis Koutsis, production quantity 19,500	59.50	63.00
☐ 1982	**Destruction of the Temple,** artist: Yiannis Koutsis, production quantity 19,500	59.50	63.00
☐ 1982	**Ruth at the Harvest,** artist: Yiannis Koutsis, production quantity 19,500	59.50	60.00
☐ 1982	**David and Goliath,** artist: Yiannis Koutsis, production quantity 19,500	59.50	60.00
☐ 1982	**Solomon's Decision,** artist: Yiannis Koutsis, production quantity 19,500	59.50	60.00
☐ 1982	**Building of the Temple,** artist: Yiannis Koutsis, production quantity 19,500	59.50	60.00
☐ 1982	**Elijah and Heaven's Chariot,** artist: Yiannis Koutsis, production quantity 19,500	59.50	60.00
☐ 1982	**Job's Reward,** artist: Yiannis Koutsis, production quantity 19,500	59.50	60.00
☐ 1983	**Psalm of David,** artist: Yiannis Koutsis, production quantity 19,500	59.50	60.00
☐ 1983	**Daniel and the Lions,** artist: Yiannis Koutsis, production quantity 19,500	59.50	60.00
☐ 1983	**Jonah and the Whale,** artist: Yiannis Koutsis, production quantity 19,500	59.50	60.00

THE CREATION SERIES
(First Release)

		Issue Price	Current Value
☐ 1977	**In the Beginning,** artist: Yiannis Koutsis, production quantity 10,000	37.50	90.00
☐ 1977	**In His Image,** artist: Yiannis Koutsis, production quantity 10,000	45.00	130.00
☐ 1978	**Adam's Rib,** artist: Yiannis Koutsis, production quantity 10,000	45.00	125.00
☐ 1978	**Banished from Eden,** artist: Yiannis Koutsis, production quantity 10,000	45.00	125.00
☐ 1978	**Noah and the Ark,** artist: Yiannis Koutsis, production quantity 10,000	45.00	120.00
☐ 1980	**Tower of Babel,** artist: Yiannis Koutsis, production quantity 10,000	45.00	75.00
☐ 1980	**Sodom and Gomorrah,** artist: Yiannis Koutsis, production quantity 10,000	45.00	75.00
☐ 1980	**Jacob's Wedding,** artist: Yiannis Koutsis, production quantity 10,000	45.00	75.00
☐ 1980	**Rebekah at the Well,** artist: Yiannis Koutsis, production quantity 10,000	45.00	75.00
☐ 1980	**Jacob's Ladder,** artist: Yiannis Koutsis, production quantity 10,000	45.00	75.00

		Issue Price	Current Value
☐ 1980	**Joseph's Coat of Many Colors,** artist: Yiannis Koutsis, production quantity 10,000	**45.00**	**75.00**
☐ 1980	**Joseph Interprets Pharaoh's Dream,** artist: Yiannis Koutsis, production quantity 10,000	**45.00**	**75.00**

THE CREATION SERIES
(Charter Release For Calhoun's Collector's Society)

		Issue Price	Current Value
☐ 1977	**In the Beginning,** artist: Yiannis Koutsis, production quantity 19,500	**29.50**	**152.00**
☐ 1977	**In His Image,** artist: Yiannis Koutsis, production quantity 19,500	**29.50**	**120.00**
☐ 1978	**Adam's Rib,** artist: Yiannis Koutsis, production quantity 19,500	**29.50**	**100.00**
☐ 1978	**Banished from Eden,** artist: Yiannis Koutsis, production quantity 19,500	**29.50**	**90.00**
☐ 1978	**Noah and the Ark,** artist: Yiannis Koutsis, production quantity 19,500	**29.50**	**90.00**
☐ 1980	**Tower of Babel,** artist: Yiannis Koutsis, production quantity 19,500	**29.50**	**80.00**
☐ 1980	**Sodom and Gomorrah,** artist: Yiannis Koutsis, production quantity 19,500	**29.50**	**80.00**
☐ 1980	**Jacob's Wedding,** artist: Yiannis Koutsis, production quantity 19,500	**29.50**	**80.00**
☐ 1980	**Rebekah at the Well,** artist: Yiannis Koutsis, production quantity 19,500	**29.50**	**80.00**
☐ 1980	**Jacob's Ladder,** artist: Yiannis Koutsis, production quantity 19,500	**29.50**	**80.00**
☐ 1980	**Joseph's Coat of Many Colors,** artist: Yiannis Koutsis, production quantity 19,500	**29.50**	**80.00**
☐ 1980	**Joseph Interprets Pharaoh's Dream,** artist: Yiannis Koutsis, production quantity 19,500	**29.50**	**80.00**

CRYSTAL MAIDENS SERIES

		Issue Price	Current Value
☐ 1979	**Strawberry Season (Spring),** production quantity 2,500	**57.50**	**80.00**
☐ 1979	**Sunshine Season (Summer),** production quantity 2,500	**57.50**	**80.00**
☐ 1979	**Scenic Season (Fall),** production quantity 2,500	**57.50**	**80.00**
☐ 1979	**Snowflake Season (Winter),** production quantity 2,500	**57.50**	**80.00**

		Issue Price	Current Value
DOROTHY'S DAY PLATES SERIES			

☐ **1980 Brand-New Day,** artist: Bill Mack, production quantity 15,000 .... **55.00 55.00**

☐ **1980 All by Myself,** artist: Bill Mack, production quantity 15,000 .... **55.00 55.00**

☐ **1981 Off to School,** artist: Bill Mack, production quantity 15,000 .... **55.00 55.00**

☐ **1981 Best Friends,** artist: Bill Mack, production quantity 15,000 .... **55.00 55.00**

☐ **1981 Helping Mammy,** artist: Bill Mack, production quantity 15,000 .... **55.00 55.00**

☐ **1981 Bless Me Too!,** artist: Bill Mack, production quantity 15,000 .... **55.00 55.00**

EXOTIC BIRDS OF TROPIQUE SERIES

☐ **1981 Scarlett Macaws,** artist: Konrad Hack, production quantity 19,500 .... **49.50 50.00**

☐ **1981 Toco Toucan,** artist: Konrad Hack, production quantity 19,500 .... **49.50 50.00**

☐ **1981 Greater Sulfur-Crested Cockatoo,** artist: Konrad Hack, production quantity 19,500 **49.50 50.00**

☐ **1981 Rosy Flamingos,** artist: Konrad Hack, production quantity 19,500 .... **49.50 50.00**

☐ **1982 Ultramarine King,** artist: Konrad Hack, production quantity 19,500 .... **49.50 50.00**

☐ **1982 Red-Fan Parrot,** artist: Konrad Hack, production quantity 19,500 .... **49.50 50.00**

☐ **1982 Goldie's Bird of Paradise,** artist: Konrad Hack, production quantity 19,500 .... **49.50 50.00**

☐ **1982 Andean Cock-of-the-Rock,** artist: Konrad Hack, production quantity 19,500 .... **49.50 50.00**

☐ **1982 Seven-Colored Tanager,** artist: Konrad Hack, production quantity 19,500 .... **49.50 50.00**

☐ **1982 Scarlet Ibis,** artist: Konrad Hack, production quantity 19,500 .... **49.50 50.00**

☐ **1982 Quetzal,** artist: Konrad Hack, production quantity 19,500 .... **49.50 50.00**

☐ **1982 Long-Tailed Sylph,** artist: Konrad Hack, production quantity 19,500 .... **49.50 50.00**

FIVE PERCEPTIONS OF WEO CHO SERIES

☐ **1979 Sense of Touch,** production quantity 19,500 **55.00 125.00**

☐ **1979 Sense of Sight,** production quantity 19,500 **55.00 85.00**

☐ **1980 Sense of Taste,** production quantity 19,500 **55.00 75.00**

		Issue Price	Current Value
☐ 1980	**Sense of Hearing,** production quantity 19,500	**55.00**	**75.00**
☐ 1980	**Sense of Smell,** production quantity 19,500	**55.00**	**75.00**

FOUR SEASONS (First Release)

☐ 1978	**Warmth (Winter),** artist: Gunther Granget, production quantity 5,000	**60.00**	**60.00**
☐ 1978	**Voices of Spring (Spring),** artist: Gunther Granget, production quantity 5,000	**60.00**	**60.00**
☐ 1978	**The Fledgling (Summer),** artist: Gunther Granget, production quantity 5,000	**60.00**	**60.00**
☐ 1978	**We Survive (Fall),** artist: Gunther Granget, production quantity 5,000	**60.00**	**60.00**

FOUR SEASONS
(Charter Release For Calhoun
Collector's Society)

☐ 1978	**Warmth (Winter),** artist: Gunther Granget, production quantity 17,500	**60.00**	**60.00**
☐ 1978	**Voices of Spring (Spring),** artist: Gunther Granget, production quantity 17,500	**60.00**	**60.00**
☐ 1978	**The Fledgling (Summer),** artist: Gunther Granget, production quantity 17,500	**60.00**	**60.00**
☐ 1978	**We Survive (Fall),** artist: Gunther Granget, production quantity 17,500	**60.00**	**60.00**

THE GOLDEN AGE OF CINEMA SERIES

☐ 1978	**The King and His Ladies,** artist: Lawrence W. Whittaker, production quantity 22,500	**45.00**	**45.00**
☐ 1978	**Fred and Ginger,** artist: Lawrence W. Whittaker, production quantity 22,500	**45.00**	**45.00**
☐ 1978	**Judy and Mickey,** artist: Lawrence W. Whittaker, production quantity 22,500	**45.00**	**45.00**
☐ 1978	**The Philadelphia Story,** artist: Lawrence W. Whittaker, production quantity 22,500	**45.00**	**45.00**
☐ 1979	**The Thin Man,** artist: Lawrence W. Whittaker, production quantity 22,500	**45.00**	**45.00**
☐ 1979	**Gigi,** artist: Lawrence W. Whittaker, production quantity 22,500	**45.00**	**45.00**

GOLDEN PLATES OF THE NOBLE
FLOWER MAIDENS SERIES

☐ 1982	**Iris Maiden,** artist: Kitagawa Utamaro, production quantity 19,500	**65.00**	**65.00**

		Issue Price	Current Value
☐ 1982	**Plum Blossom,** artist: Kitagawa Utamaro, production quantity 19,500	65.00	65.00
☐ 1982	**Quince Maiden,** artist: Kitagawa Utamaro, production quantity 19,500	65.00	65.00
☐ 1982	**Cherry Blossom Maiden,** artist: Kitagawa Utamaro, production quantity 19,500	65.00	65.00
☐ 1982	**Crysanthemum Maiden,** artist: Kitagawa Utamaro, production quantity 19,500	65.00	65.00
☐ 1982	**August Lily Maiden,** artist: Kitagawa Utamaro, production quantity 19,500	65.00	65.00

IMPRESSIONS OF YESTERYEAR SERIES

		Issue Price	Current Value
☐ 1982	**Moon Mist,** artist: Dominic Mingolla, production quantity 19,500	59.50	60.00
☐ 1982	**Fall Flowers,** artist: Dominic Mingolla, production quantity 19,500	59.50	60.00
☐ 1982	**Wishing Well,** artist: Dominic Mingolla, production quantity 19,500	59.50	60.00
☐ 1982	**The Letter,** artist: Dominic Mingolla, production quantity 19,500	59.50	60.00
☐ 1982	**Sledding,** artist: Dominic Mingolla, production quantity 19,500	59.50	60.00
☐ 1982	**Red Tree,** artist: Dominic Mingolla, production quantity 19,500	59.50	60.00
☐ 1982	**Swans,** artist: Dominic Mingolla, production quantity 19,500	59.50	60.00
☐ 1982	**Sailboat,** artist: Dominic Mingolla, production quantity 19,500	59.50	60.00
☐ 1982	**Winter Park,** artist: Dominic Mingolla, production quantity 19,500	59.50	60.00
☐ 1983	**Seashore,** artist: Dominic Mingolla, production quantity 19,500	59.50	60.00
☐ 1983	**Red Balloon,** artist: Dominic Mingolla, production quantity 19,500	59.50	60.00
☐ 1983	**Snowman,** artist: Dominic Mingolla, production quantity 19,500	59.50	60.00

KITTEN'S WORLD SERIES

		Issue Price	Current Value
☐ 1979	**Just Curious,** artist: Rudy Droguett, production quantity 27,500	45.00	80.00
☐ 1979	**Hello, World,** artist: Rudy Droguett, production quantity 27,500	45.00	50.00
☐ 1979	**Are You a Flower?,** artist: Rudy Droguett, production quantity 27,500	45.00	50.00

		Issue Price	Current Value
☐ 1980	**Talk to Me,** artist: Rudy Droguett, production quantity 27,500	**45.00**	**50.00**
☐ 1980	**My Favorite Toy,** artist: Rudy Droguett, production quantity 27,500	**45.00**	**50.00**
☐ 1980	**Purr-fect Pleasure,** artist: Rudy Droguett, production quantity 27,500	**45.00**	**50.00**

LEGEND OF THE PEACOCK MAIDENS SERIES

☐ 1982	**Dance of the Peacock Maidens,** production quantity 19,500	**69.50**	**70.00**
☐ 1982	**Promise of Love,** production quantity 19,500	**69.50**	**70.00**
☐ 1982	**The Betrayal,** production quantity 19,500 ..	**69.50**	**70.00**
☐ 1982	**The Prince and the Python,** production quantity 19,500	**69.50**	**70.00**
☐ 1982	**Return of the Bracelet,** production quantity 19,500	**69.50**	**70.00**
☐ 1982	**The Marriage,** production quantity 19,500	**69.50**	**70.00**

LEGENDARY SHIPS OF THE SEA SERIES

☐ 1980	**The Flying Dutchman,** artist: Alan D'Estrehan, production quantity 19,500 ...	**49.50**	**90.00**
☐ 1981	**The Refanu,** artist: Alan D'Estrehan, production quantity 19,500	**49.50**	**50.00**
☐ 1981	**The Gaspe Bay,** artist: Alan D'Estrehan, production quantity 19,500	**49.50**	**50.00**
☐ 1981	**The Rescue,** artist: Alan D'Estrehan, production quantity 19,500	**49.50**	**50.00**
☐ 1981	**The Copenhagen,** artist: Alan D'Estrehan, production quantity 19,500	**49.50**	**50.00**
☐ 1981	**The Palatine,** artist: Alan D'Estrehan, production quantity 19,500	**49.50**	**50.00**
☐ 1981	**The Pride,** artist: Alan D'Estrehan, production quantity 19,500	**49.50**	**50.00**
☐ 1981	**The Foochow Sea Junk,** artist: Alan D'Estrehan, production quantity 19,500 ...	**49.50**	**50.00**
☐ 1981	**The Roth Ramhach,** artist: Alan D'Estrehan, production quantity 19,500	**49.50**	**50.00**
☐ 1981	**The Frigorifique,** artist: Alan D'Estrehan, production quantity 19,500	**49.50**	**50.00**

THE LITTLE PEOPLE SERIES

☐ 1980	**Off to the Picnic,** artist: Seima, production quantity 19,500	**34.50**	**35.00**

		Issue Price	Current Value
☐ 1981	**Decorating the Tree,** artist: Seima, production quantity 19,500	**34.50**	**35.00**
☐ 1981	**Cruising Down the River,** artist: Seima, production quantity 19,500	**34.50**	**35.00**
☐ 1981	**The Sweetest Harvest,** artist: Seima, production quantity 19,500	**34.50**	**35.00**
☐ 1981	**The Happy Chorus,** artist: Seima, production quantity 19,500	**34.50**	**35.00**
☐ 1981	**Painting the Leaves,** artist: Seima, production quantity 19,500	**34.50**	**35.00**

LOVE'S PRECIOUS MOMENTS SERIES

☐ 1981	**Love's Sweet Vow,** artist: Robert Gunn, production quantity 17,500	**55.00**	**55.00**
☐ 1981	**Love's Sweet Verse,** artist: Robert Gunn, production quantity 17,500	**55.00**	**55.00**
☐ 1981	**Love's Sweet Offering,** artist: Robert Gunn, production quantity 17,500	**55.00**	**55.00**
☐ 1981	**Love's Sweet Embrace,** artist: Robert Gunn, production quantity 17,500	**55.00**	**55.00**
☐ 1981	**Love's Sweet Melody,** artist: Robert Gunn, production quantity 17,500	**55.00**	**55.00**
☐ 1981	**Love's Sweet Kiss,** artist: Robert Gunn, production quantity 17,500	**55.00**	**55.00**

MEMORIES OF AMERICA BY GRANDMA MOSES SERIES

☐ 1980	**Bringing in the Maple Sugar,** artist: Grandma Moses, production quantity 5,000	**120.00**	**120.00**
☐ 1980	**The Old Automobile,** artist: Grandma Moses, production quantity 5,000	**120.00**	**120.00**
☐ 1981	**Halloween,** artist: Grandma Moses, production quantity 5,000	**120.00**	**120.00**
☐ 1981	**The Rainbow,** artist: Grandma Moses, production quantity 5,000	**120.00**	**120.00**

MEMORIES OF THE WESTERN PRAIRIES SERIES

☐ 1983	**Picking Daisies,** artist: Rosemary Calder, production: one year	**49.50**	**50.00**
☐ 1984	**Feeding the Colt,** artist: Rosemary Calder, production: one year	**49.50**	**50.00**

	Issue Price	Current Value

MINGOLLA CHRISTMAS SERIES

☐ **1977   Winter Wonderland,** artist: Dominic Mingolla, production quantity 5,000 .... | 65.00 | 66.00 |

MOST PRECIOUS GIFTS OF
SHEN LUNG SERIES

☐ **1981 Fire,** artist: Sharleen Pederson, production quantity 19,500	49.00	50.00
☐ **1981 Water,** artist: Sharleen Pederson, production quantity 19,500	49.00	50.00
☐ **1981 Sun,** artist: Sharleen Pederson, production quantity 19,500	49.00	50.00
☐ **1981 Moon,** artist: Sharleen Pederson, production quantity 19,500	49.00	50.00
☐ **1981 Earth,** artist: Sharleen Pederson, production quantity 19,500	49.00	50.00
☐ **1981 Sky,** artist: Sharleen Pederson, production quantity 19,500	49.00	50.00

THE PROMISED LAND SERIES

☐ **1979 Pharaoh's Daughter Finds Moses,** artist: Yiannis Koutsis, production quantity 24,500	45.00	50.00
☐ **1979 The Burning Bush,** artist: Yiannis Koutsis, production quantity 24,500	45.00	50.00
☐ **1979 Let My People Go,** artist: Yiannis Koutsis, production quantity 24,500	45.00	45.00
☐ **1979 The Parting of the Red Sea,** artist: Yiannis Koutsis, production quantity 24,500	45.00	45.00
☐ **1980 Miriam's Song of Thanksgiving,** artist: Yiannis Koutsis, production quantity 24,500 ...	45.00	45.00
☐ **1980 Manna from Heaven,** artist: Yiannis Koutsis, production quantity 24,500	45.00	45.00
☐ **1980 Water from the Rock,** artist: Yiannis Koutsis, production quantity 24,500	45.00	45.00
☐ **1980 The Battle of Amalek,** artist: Yiannis Koutsis, production quantity 24,500	45.00	45.00
☐ **1980 The Ten Commandments,** artist: Yiannis Koutsis, production quantity 24,500	45.00	45.00
☐ **1980 The Golden Calf,** artist: Yiannis Koutsis, production quantity 24,500	45.00	45.00
☐ **1980 Moses Smashes the Tablet,** artist: Yiannis Koutsis, production quantity 24,500	45.00	45.00
☐ **1980 The Glorious Tabernacle,** artist: Yiannis Koutsis, production quantity 24,500	45.00	45.00

	Issue Price	Current Value

PUPPY'S WORLD SERIES

☐ 1982	**First Birthday,** artist: Rudy Droguett, production quantity 19,500	49.50	50.00
☐ 1982	**Beware of Dog,** artist: Rudy Droguett, production quantity 19,500	49.50	50.00
☐ 1982	**Top Dog,** artist: Rudy Droguett, production quantity 19,500	49.50	50.00
☐ 1982	**Need a Friend?,** artist: Rudy Droguett, production quantity 19,500	49.50	50.00
☐ 1982	**Double Trouble,** artist: Rudy Droguett, production quantity 19,500	49.50	50.00
☐ 1982	**Just Clowning,** artist: Rudy Droguett, production quantity 19,500	49.50	50.00
☐ 1982	**Guest for Dinner,** artist: Rudy Droguett, production quantity 19,500	49.50	50.00
☐ 1982	**Gift Wrapped,** artist: Rudy Droguett, production quantity 19,500	49.50	50.00

THE REMARKABLE WORLD OF CHARLES DICKENS SERIES

☐ 1980	**Oliver Twist and Fagin,** artist: Konrad Hack, production quantity 19,500	60.00	65.00
☐ 1980	**Scrooge and Marley's Ghost,** artist: Konrad Hack, production quantity 19,500	60.00	65.00
☐ 1980	**Bob Cratchit and Tiny Tim,** artist: Konrad Hack, production quantity 19,500	60.00	65.00
☐ 1980	**David Copperfield and Great-Aunt Betsy Trotwood,** artist: Konrad Hack, production quantity 19,500	60.00	65.00
☐ 1980	**Micawber Denouncing Uriah Heep,** artist: Konrad Hack, production quantity 19,500	60.00	65.00
☐ 1980	**Little Nell,** artist: Konrad Hack, production quantity 19,500	60.00	60.00
☐ 1981	**Madame Defarge,** artist: Konrad Hack, production quantity 19,500	60.00	60.00
☐ 1981	**Mr. Pickwick and Friends,** artist: Konrad Hack, production quantity 19,500	60.00	60.00
☐ 1981	**Nicholas Nickleby,** artist: Konrad Hack, production quantity 19,500	60.00	60.00
☐ 1982	**Little Dorrit,** artist: Konrad Hack, production quantity 19,500	60.00	60.00
☐ 1982	**Barkis and Peggotty,** artist: Konrad Hack, production quantity 19,500	60.00	60.00
☐ 1982	**Pip and Miss Havisham,** artist: Konrad Hack, production quantity 19,500	60.00	60.00

		Issue Price	Current Value
TREASURES OF CHILDHOOD SERIES			
☐ 1979	**My Cuddlies Collection,** artist: Charlotte Jackson, production quantity 19,500	45.00	50.00
☐ 1980	**My Coin Collection,** artist: Charlotte Jackson, production quantity 19,500	45.00	45.00
☐ 1980	**My Shell Collection,** artist: Charlotte Jackson, production quantity 19,500	45.00	45.00
☐ 1980	**My Stamp Collection,** artist: Charlotte Jackson, production quantity 19,500	45.00	45.00
☐ 1980	**My Doll Collection,** artist: Charlotte Jackson, production quantity 19,500	45.00	45.00
☐ 1980	**My Rock Collection,** artist: Charlotte Jackson, production quantity 19,500	45.00	45.00

TWO THOUSAND YEARS OF SHIPS SERIES

		Issue Price	Current Value
☐ 1982	**USS Constitution,** artist: Alan D'Estrehan, production limited	39.50	40.00
☐ 1982	**Santa Maria,** artist: Alan D'Estrehan, production limited	39.50	40.00
☐ 1983	**Mayflower,** artist: Alan D'Estrehan, production limited	39.50	40.00
☐ 1983	**Drakar,** artist: Alan D'Estrehan, production limited	39.50	40.00
☐ 1983	**Cutty Sark Thermopylae,** artist: Alan D'Estrehan, production limited	39.50	40.00
☐ 1983	**HMS Royal Sovereign,** artist: Alan D'Estrehan, production limited	39.50	40.00
☐ 1983	**Vasa,** artist: Alan D'Estrehan, production limited	39.50	40.00
☐ 1983	**HMS Victory,** artist: Alan D'Estrehan, production limited	39.50	40.00
☐ 1983	**Royal Barge,** artist: Alan D'Estrehan, production limited	39.50	40.00
☐ 1984	**America,** artist: Alan D'Estrehan, production limited	39.50	40.00
☐ 1984	**Golden Hind,** artist: Alan D'Estrehan, production limited	39.50	40.00

WINDOWS ON THE WORLD SERIES

		Issue Price	Current Value
☐ 1980	**The Golden Gate of San Francisco,** artist: Higgins Bond, production quantity 19,500	45.00	45.00
☐ 1981	**The Snow Village of Madulain,** artist: Higgins Bond, production quantity 19,500	45.00	45.00

		Issue Price	Current Value
☐ 1981	**Rainy Day in London,** artist: Higgins Bond, production quantity 19,500	45.00	45.00
☐ 1981	**Water Festival in Venice,** artist: Higgins Bond, production quantity 19,500	45.00	45.00
☐ 1981	**Springtime in Paris,** artist: Higgins Bond, production quantity 19,500	45.00	45.00
☐ 1981	**Harvestime in the Ukraine,** artist: Higgins Bond, production quantity 19,500	45.00	45.00
☐ 1981	**Lunchtime in Michelstadt,** artist: Higgins Bond, production quantity 19,500	45.00	45.00
☐ 1981	**Flamenco of Madrid,** artist: Higgins Bond, production quantity 19,500	45.00	45.00
☐ 1981	**Great Tusks of the Serengeti,** artist: Higgins Bond, production quantity 19,500	45.00	45.00
☐ 1981	**Carnival Time in Rio,** artist: Higgins Bond, production quantity 19,500	45.00	45.00
☐ 1981	**Tokyo at Cherry Blossom Time,** artist: Higgins Bond, production quantity 19,500	45.00	45.00
☐ 1981	**Palace of the Winds, Jaipur,** artist: Higgins Bond, production quantity 19,500	45.00	45.00
☐ 1982	**Carnival Time in Rio,** artist: Higgins Bond, production quantity 19,500	45.00	45.00

ROYAL DELFT

Netherlands

CHRISTMAS SERIES
(Large)

☐ 1915	**Christmas Bells,** production: one year	2.25	6250.00
☐ 1916	**Star-Floral Design,** production: one year . .	4.25	720.00
☐ 1916	**Cradle with Child,** production: one year . . .	4.25	370.00
☐ 1917	**Shepherd,** production: one year	6.00	450.00
☐ 1917	**Christmas Star,** production: one year	4.25	288.00
☐ 1918	**Shepherd,** production: one year	7.50	375.00
☐ 1918	**Christmas Star,** production: one year	5.50	275.00
☐ 1919	**Church,** production: one year	12.50	400.00
☐ 1920	**Church Tower,** production: one year	12.50	388.00
☐ 1920	**Holly Wreath,** production: one year	7.50	288.00
☐ 1921	**Canal Boatman,** production: one year	12.50	425.00
☐ 1921	**Christmas Star,** production: one year	6.25	315.00
☐ 1922	**Landscape,** production: one year	10.00	425.00
☐ 1922	**Christmas Wreath,** production: one year . . .	6.25	288.00

		Issue Price	Current Value
☐ 1923	**Shepherd,** production: one year	10.00	438.00
☐ 1924	**Christmas Star,** production: one year	6.25	290.00
☐ 1924	**Shepherd,** production: one year	10.00	415.00
☐ 1925	**Towngate in Delft,** production: one year ...	10.00	465.00
☐ 1925	**Christmas Star,** production: one year	6.25	265.00
☐ 1926	**Windmill Landscape,** production: one year	12.50	465.00
☐ 1926	**Christmas Star,** production: one year	6.25	290.00
☐ 1927	**Christmas Star,** production: one year	6.25	300.00
☐ 1927	**Sailboat,** production: one year	10.00	475.00
☐ 1928	**Lighthouse,** production: one year	10.00	375.00
☐ 1928	**Christmas Poinsettia,** production: one year	6.25	315.00
☐ 1929	**Christmas Bell,** production: one year	6.25	388.00
☐ 1929	**Small Dutch Town,** production: one year ..	10.00	390.00
☐ 1930	**Church Entrance,** production: one year	10.00	350.00
☐ 1930	**Christmas Rose,** production: one year	6.25	325.00
☐ 1931	**Christmas Star,** production: one year	5.00	300.00
☐ 1931	**Snow Landscape,** production: one year	8.00	375.00
☐ 1932	**Fireplace,** production: one year	8.00	440.00
☐ 1932	**Christmas Star,** production: one year	5.00	388.00
☐ 1933	**Interior Scene,** production: one year	7.88	450.00
☐ 1934	**Interior Scene,** production: one year	7.75	475.00
☐ 1935	**Interior Scene,** production: one year	8.25	475.00
☐ 1936	**Interior Scene,** production: one year	8.25	490.00
☐ 1937	**Interior Scene,** production: one year	8.25	490.00
☐ 1938	**Interior Scene,** production: one year	8.25	485.00
☐ 1939	**Interior Scene,** production: one year	8.25	490.00
☐ 1940	**Christmas Tree,** production: one year	8.75	490.00
☐ 1941	**Interior Scene,** production: one year	8.75	440.00
☐ 1955	**Church Tower,** production quantity 200 ...	24.00	440.00
☐ 1956	**Landscape,** production quantity 200	27.50	325.00
☐ 1957	**Landscape,** production quantity 225	23.50	325.00
☐ 1958	**Landscape,** production quantity 225	25.00	325.00
☐ 1959	**Landscape,** production quantity 250	26.25	325.00
☐ 1960	**Street in Delft,** production quantity 250 ...	25.00	350.00
☐ 1961	**Village Scene,** production quantity 260	30.00	370.00
☐ 1962	**Tower in Leeuwarden,** production quantity 275	30.00	370.00
☐ 1963	**Tower in Enkhuisen,** production quantity 275	35.00	370.00
☐ 1964	**Tower in Hoorn,** production quantity 300	35.00	370.00
☐ 1965	**Corn Mill in Rhoon,** production quantity 300	35.00	370.00
☐ 1966	**Snuff Mill in Rotterdam,** production quantity 325	40.00	370.00
☐ 1967	**Tower in Amsterdam,** production quantity 350	45.00	370.00

		Issue Price	Current Value
☐ 1968	Tower in Amsterdam, production quantity 350	60.00	365.00
☐ 1969	Church in Utrecht, production quantity 400	60.00	340.00
☐ 1970	Cathedral in Veere, production quantity 500	60.00	340.00
☐ 1971	"Dom" Tower in Utrecht, production quantity 550	60.00	340.00
☐ 1972	Church in Edam, production quantity 1,500	70.00	340.00
☐ 1973	"De Waag" in Alkamar, production quantity 1,500	75.00	415.00
☐ 1974	Kitchen in Hindeloopen, production quantity 1,500	160.00	400.00
☐ 1975	Farmer in Laren, production quantity 1,500	250.00	390.00
☐ 1976	Farm in Staphorst, production quantity 1,500	220.00	375.00
☐ 1977	Farm in Spakenburg, production quantity 1,500	277.00	370.00
☐ 1978	Winter Skating Scene, production quantity 1,000	277.00	300.00
☐ 1979	Christmas Rhenen, production quantity 500	260.00	270.00
☐ 1980	Winter Scene, production quantity 500	245.00	260.00
☐ 1981	Winter Scene, production quantity 500	245.00	260.00
☐ 1982	Winter Scene, production quantity 500	245.00	245.00
☐ 1983	Evening Twilight, production quantity 500	230.00	230.00
☐ 1984	The Homecoming, artist: Jan Dessens, production quantity 500	230.00	230.00
☐ 1985	Church at T'Woudt, artist: Mar de Bruijn, production quantity 500.	270.00	270.00
☐ 1986	St. Dionysius, artist: Mar de Bruijn, production quantity 500	324.00	324.00

CHRISTMAS SERIES
(9")

		Issue Price	Current Value
☐ 1955	Christmas Star, production: one year	11.75	175.00
☐ 1956	Christmas Bells, production: one year	11.75	340.00
☐ 1956	Flower Design, production: one year	11.75	140.00
☐ 1957	Christmas Star, production: one year	12.25	140.00
☐ 1958	Christmas Star, production: one year	12.25	140.00

CHRISTMAS SERIES
(Small)

		Issue Price	Current Value
☐ 1915	Christmas Star, production: one year	1.50	3630.00
☐ 1926	Bell Tower, production: one year	3.00	225.00
☐ 1927	Church Tower, 7", production: one year ...	3.00	300.00
☐ 1928	Mill, production: one year	3.00	325.00

		Issue Price	Current Value
☐ 1929	Church Spire, production: one year	3.00	325.00
☐ 1930	Sailing Boat, production: one year	3.00	225.00
☐ 1931	Church Tower, production: one year	3.00	300.00
☐ 1932	Bell Tower, production: one year	3.00	300.00
☐ 1959	Landscape with Mill, production quantity 400	9.50	140.00
☐ 1960	Landscape, production quantity 400	11.25	170.00
☐ 1961	Snow Landscape, production quantity 500	12.00	165.00
☐ 1962	Town View, production quantity 500	12.00	165.00
☐ 1963	Mill in Zeddam, production quantity 500 ..	12.25	165.00
☐ 1964	Mill in Poelenburg, production quantity 600	13.75	165.00
☐ 1965	Towngate in Kampen, production quantity 600	14.75	165.00
☐ 1966	Towngate in Medemblik, production quantity 600	16.75	165.00
☐ 1967	Mill in Hazerswoude, production quantity 700	16.75	165.00
☐ 1968	Mill in Schiedam, production quantity 700	18.00	165.00
☐ 1969	Mill near Gorkum, production quantity 800	26.25	140.00
☐ 1970	Mill near Haarlem, production quantity 1,500	26.25	140.00
☐ 1971	Towngate at Zierikzee, production quantity 3,500	30.00	140.00
☐ 1972	Towngate at Elburg, production quantity 3,500	42.50	125.00
☐ 1973	Towngate at Amersfoort, production quantity 4,500	47.50	125.00
☐ 1974	Watergate at Sneek, production quantity 4,500	52.50	165.00
☐ 1975	Towngate at Amsterdam, production quantity 1,000	65.00	165.00
☐ 1976	Towngate in Gorinchem, production quantity 4,500	72.50	165.00
☐ 1977	Dromedaris Tower, production quantity 4,500	77.50	150.00
☐ 1978	Christmas Fisherman, production quantity 1,500	77.50	140.00
☐ 1978	Christmas Angels, production quantity 1,500	77.50	140.00
☐ 1979	Golf Players on the Ice, production quantity 1,000	97.50	130.00
☐ 1980	Ice Sailing, production quantity 1,000	117.50	130.00
☐ 1981	Horse Sledding, production quantity 1,000	117.50	130.00
☐ 1982	Ice Skating, production quantity 1,000	125.00	125.00
☐ 1983	Cake and Something to Drink, production quantity 1,000	120.00	120.00

		Issue Price	Current Value
☐ 1984	**Figure Skating,** artist: Jan Dessens, production quantity 1,000	120.00	120.00
☐ 1985	**The Farmhouse,** artist: Mar de Bruijn, production quantity 1,000	140.00	140.00
☐ 1986	**Farmhouse,** artist: Mar de Bruijn, production quantity 1,000	168.00	168.00

EASTER SERIES

☐ 1973	**Dutch Easter Palm,** production quantity 3,500	75.00	150.00
☐ 1974	**Dutch Easter Palm,** production quantity 1,000	110.00	145.00
☐ 1975	**Dutch Easter Palm,** production quantity 1,000	125.00	180.00
☐ 1976	**Dutch Easter Palm,** production quantity 1,000	175.00	205.00

FATHER'S DAY SERIES

☐ 1972	**Father and Son, Volendam,** production quantity 1,500	40.00	75.00
☐ 1973	**Father and Son, Hindeloopen,** production quantity 2,000	40.00	70.00
☐ 1974	**Father and Son, Marken,** production quantity 1,000	80.00	90.00
☐ 1975	**Father and Son, Zuid-Beveland,** production: one year	80.00	105.00
☐ 1976	**Father and Son, Spakenburg,** production: one year	140.00	120.00

MOTHER'S DAY SERIES

☐ 1971	**Mother and Daughter, Volendam,** production quantity 2,500	50.00	75.00
☐ 1972	**Mother and Daughter, Hindeloopen,** production quantity 2,500	40.00	80.00
☐ 1973	**Mother and Daughter, Marken,** production quantity 3,000	50.00	75.00
☐ 1974	**Mother and Daughter, Zuid-Bevaland,** production: one year	80.00	100.00
☐ 1975	**Mother and Daughter, Spakenburg,** production: one year	100.00	120.00
☐ 1976	**Mother and Daughter, Scheveningen,** production: one year	115.00	125.00

		Issue Price	Current Value
SPECIAL BICENTENARY SERIES			
☐ 1976	George Washington, production quantity 2,500	350.00	350.00
☐ 1976	Eagle Plate, production quantity 5,000	150.00	150.00

STARS, SATELLITES AND SPACE SERIES

☐ 1910	Halley's Comet	22.50	750.00
☐ 1957	First Earth Satellite	22.50	90.00
☐ 1968	Apollo 8	22.50	40.00
☐ 1969	Apollo II	22.50	40.00
☐ 1974	Skylab and Comet Kohoutek, production quantity 1,000.........................	80.00	65.00
☐ 1975	Apollo Soyuz	140.00	115.00
☐ 1972	Olympiad	70.00	60.00

VALENTINE SERIES

☐ 1973	Valentine "Enduring Beauty," production quantity 1,500.........................	75.00	150.00
☐ 1974	Valentine, production quantity 1,000	125.00	135.00
☐ 1975	Valentine, production quantity 1,000	125.00	130.00
☐ 1976	Valentine, production quantity 1,000	175.00	175.00

SINGLE ISSUE

☐ 1987	50th Wedding Anniversary of Princess Juliana and Prince Bernhard, artist: Mar de Bruijn, production quantity 500	337.50	350.00

ROYAL DEVON

United States

NORMAN ROCKWELL CHRISTMAS SERIES

☐ 1975	Downhill Daring, artist: Norman Rockwell, production: one year	24.50	30.00
☐ 1976	The Christmas Gift, artist: Norman Rockwell, production: one year...............	24.50	55.00
☐ 1977	The Big Moment, artist: Norman Rockwell, production: one year	27.50	85.00
☐ 1978	Puppets for Christmas, artist: Norman Rockwell, production: one year	27.50	27.50
☐ 1979	One Present Too Many, artist: Norman Rockwell, production: one year	31.50	31.50
☐ 1980	Gramps Meets Gramps, artist: Norman Rockwell, production: one year	33.00	33.00

		Issue Price	Current Value
NORMAN ROCKWELL HOME OF THE BRAVE SERIES			
☐ 1981	**Reminiscing,** artist: Norman Rockwell, production quantity 18,000	35.00	75.00
☐ 1981	**Hero's Welcome,** artist: Norman Rockwell, production quantity 18,000	35.00	50.00
☐ 1981	**The War Hero,** artist: Norman Rockwell, production quantity 18,000	35.00	40.00
☐ 1981	**Back to His Old Job,** artist: Norman Rockwell, production quantity 18,000	35.00	35.00
☐ 1982	**Willie Gillis in Church,** artist: Norman Rockwell, production quantity 18,000	35.00	35.00
☐ 1982	**War Bond,** artist: Norman Rockwell, production quantity 18,000	35.00	35.00
☐ 1982	**Uncle Sam Takes Wings,** artist: Norman Rockwell, production quantity 18,000	35.00	35.00
☐ 1982	**Taking Mother over the Top,** artist: Norman Rockwell, production quantity 18,000	35.00	35.00
NORMAN ROCKWELL MOTHER'S DAY SERIES (The Hamilton Collection)			
☐ 1975	**Doctor and Doll,** artist: Norman Rockwell, production: one year	23.50	60.00
☐ 1976	**Puppy Love,** artist: Norman Rockwell, production: one year	24.50	50.00
☐ 1977	**The Family,** artist: Norman Rockwell, production: one year	24.50	95.00
☐ 1978	**Mother's Day Off,** artist: Norman Rockwell, production: one year	27.00	65.00
☐ 1979	**Mother's Evening Out,** artist: Norman Rockwell, production: one year	30.00	31.00
☐ 1980	**Mother's Treat,** artist: Norman Rockwell, production: one year	32.50	32.50

ROYAL DOULTON

Great Britain

ALL GOD'S CHILDREN SERIES			
☐ 1979	**A Brighter Day,** artist: Lisette DeWinne, production quantity 10,000	60.00	75.00
☐ 1980	**Village Children,** artist: Lisette DeWinne, production quantity 10,000	65.00	65.00

A Brighter Day, artist:
Lisette DeWinne.

		Issue Price	Current Value
☐ 1981	**Noble Heritage,** artist: Lisette DeWinne, production quantity 10,000	85.00	85.00
☐ 1982	**Buddies,** artist: Lisette DeWinne, production quantity 10,000	85.00	85.00
☐ 1983	**My Little Brother,** artist: Lisette DeWinne, production quantity 10,000	95.00	95.00
☐ 1984	**Sisterly Love,** artist: Lisette DeWinne, production quantity 10,000	95.00	95.00

AMERICAN TAPESTRIES SERIES

☐ 1978	**Sleigh Bells,** artist: C. A. Brown, production quantity 10,000	70.00	70.00
☐ 1979	**Pumpkin Patch,** artist: C. A. Brown, production quantity 10,000	70.00	70.00
☐ 1980	**General Store,** artist: C. A. Brown, production quantity 10,000	95.00	95.00
☐ 1981	**Fourth of July,** artist: C. A. Brown, production quantity 10,000	95.00	95.00

ANNUAL CHRISTMAS SERIES

☐ 1983	**Silent Night,** artist: Neil Faulkner, production quantity: unannounced	39.95	39.95

Sisterly Love, artist: Lisette DeWinne.

		Issue Price	Current Value
☐ 1984	**While Shepherds Watched Their Flocks by Night,** artist: Neil Faulkner, production quantity: unannounced	39.95	39.95
☐ 1985	**O, Little Town of Bethlehem,** artist: Neil Faulkner, production quantity: unannounced	39.95	39.95
☐ 1986	**We Saw Three Ships A-Sailing,** artist: Neil Faulkner, production quantity: unannounced	39.95	39.95
☐ 1987	**The Holly and the Ivy,** artist: Neil Faulkner, production quantity: unannounced	39.95	39.95

BEHIND THE PAINTED MASQUE SERIES

☐ 1982	**Painted Feelings,** artist: Ben Black, numbered, production quantity 10,000	95.00	100.00
☐ 1983	**Make Me Laugh,** artist: Ben Black, numbered, production quantity 10,000	95.00	95.00

BESWICK CHRISTMAS SERIES

☐ 1972	**Christmas in Old England,** production quantity 15,000	35.00	47.00
☐ 1973	**Christmas in Mexico,** production quantity 15,000	35.00	40.00
☐ 1974	**Christmas in Bulgaria,** production quantity 15,000	37.50	45.00
☐ 1975	**Christmas in Norway,** production quantity 15,000	45.00	50.00

Painted Feelings, artist:
Ben Black.

		Issue Price	Current Value
☐ 1976	**Christmas in Holland,** production quantity 15,000	**50.00**	**41.00**
☐ 1977	**Christmas in Poland,** production quantity 15,000	**50.00**	**70.00**
☐ 1978	**Christmas in America,** production quantity 15,000	**55.00**	**56.00**

CELEBRATION OF FAITH SERIES

☐ 1982	**Rosh Hashanah,** artist: James Woods, production quantity 7,500	**250.00**	**250.00**

CHILDREN OF THE PUEBLO SERIES

☐ 1983	**Apple Flower,** artist: Mimi Jungbluth ("She Cloud"), production quantity 10,000	**60.00**	**60.00**
☐ 1983	**Morning Star,** artist: Mimi Jungbluth ("She Cloud"), production quantity 10,000	**60.00**	**60.00**

COMMEDIA DELL' ARTE SERIES

☐ 1974	**Harlequin,** artist: LeRoy Neiman, production quantity 15,000	**50.00**	**80.00**
☐ 1975	**Pierrot,** artist: LeRoy Neiman, production quantity 15,000	**60.00**	**75.00**
☐ 1977	**Columbine,** artist: LeRoy Neiman, production quantity 15,000	**70.00**	**70.00**

		Issue Price	Current Value
☐ **1978**	**Punchinello,** artist: LeRoy Neiman, production quantity 15,000	70.00	75.00

FESTIVAL CHILDREN OF THE WORLD SERIES

☐ **1983**	**Mariani,** artist: Brenda Burke, production quantity 15,000	65.00	65.00
☐ **1983**	**Michico,** artist: Brenda Burke, production quantity 15,000	65.00	65.00
☐ **1983**	**Magdalena,** artist: Brenda Burke, production quantity 15,000	65.00	65.00
☐ **1983**	**Monika,** artist: Brenda Burke, production quantity 15,000	65.00	65.00

FLOWER GARDEN SERIES

☐ **1975**	**Spring Harmony,** artist: Hahn Vidal, production quantity 15,000	60.00	80.00
☐ **1976**	**Dreaming Lotus,** artist: Hahn Vidal, production quantity 15,000	65.00	90.00
☐ **1977**	**From the Poet's Garden,** artist: Hahn Vidal, production quantity 15,000	70.00	75.00
☐ **1978**	**Country Bouquet,** artist: Hahn Vidal, production quantity 15,000	70.00	75.00
☐ **1979**	**From My Mother's Garden,** artist: Hahn Vidal, production quantity 15,000	85.00	85.00

THE GRANDEST GIFT SERIES

☐ **1984**	**Reunion,** artist: MaGo, production quantity 10,000	75.00	75.00

I REMEMBER AMERICA SERIES

☐ **1977**	**Pennsylvania Pastorale,** artist: Eric Sloane, production quantity 15,000	70.00	90.00
☐ **1978**	**Lovejoy Bridge,** artist: Eric Sloane, production quantity 15,000	70.00	80.00
☐ **1979**	**Four Corners,** artist: Eric Sloane, production quantity 15,000	75.00	75.00
☐ **1980**	**Marshlands,** artist: Eric Sloane, production quantity 15,000	95.00	80.00

JUNGLE FANTASY SERIES

☐ **1980**	**The Ark,** artist: Gustavo Novoa, production quantity 10,000	75.00	80.00

Mariani, artist: Brenda Burke.

Michico, artist: Brenda Burke.

Magdalena, artist: Brenda Burke.

Reunion, artist: MaGo.

		Issue Price	Current Value
☐ 1981	**Compassion,** artist: Gustavo Novoa, production quantity 10,000	**95.00**	**80.00**
☐ 1982	**Patience,** artist: Gustavo Novoa, production quantity 10,000	**95.00**	**100.00**
☐ 1983	**Refuge,** artist: Gustavo Novoa, production quantity 10,000	**95.00**	**95.00**

LEROY NEIMAN SPECIAL SERIES

☐ 1980	**Winning Colors,** artist: LeRoy Neiman, production quantity 10,000	**85.00**	**85.00**

LOG OF THE DASHING WAVE SERIES

☐ 1976	**Sailing with the Tide,** artist: John Stobart, production quantity 15,000	**65.00**	**120.00**
☐ 1977	**Running Free,** artist: John Stobart, production quantity 15,000	**70.00**	**120.00**
☐ 1978	**Rounding the Horn,** artist: John Stobart, production quantity 15,000	**70.00**	**90.00**
☐ 1979	**Hong Kong,** artist: John Stobart, production quantity 15,000	**75.00**	**90.00**
☐ 1980	**Bora Bora,** artist: John Stobart, production quantity 15,000	**95.00**	**95.00**
☐ 1984	**Journey's End,** artist: John Stobart, production quantity 15,000	**95.00**	**95.00**

		Issue Price	Current Value

MOTHER AND CHILD SERIES

		Issue Price	Current Value
☐ 1973	**Colette and Child,** artist: Edna Hibel, production quantity 15,000	40.00	460.00
☐ 1974	**Sayuri and Child,** artist: Edna Hibel, production quantity 15,000	40.00	165.00
☐ 1975	**Kristina and Child,** artist: Edna Hibel, production quantity 15,000	50.00	125.00
☐ 1976	**Marilyn and Child,** artist: Edna Hibel, production quantity 15,000	55.00	115.00
☐ 1977	**Lucia and Child,** artist: Edna Hibel, production quantity 15,000	70.00	92.00
☐ 1982	**Kathleen and Child,** artist: Edna Hibel, production quantity 15,000	85.00	90.00

PORTRAITS OF INNOCENCE SERIES

		Issue Price	Current Value
☐ 1980	**Panchito,** artist: Francisco Masseria, production quantity 15,000	75.00	200.00
☐ 1981	**Adrien,** artist: Francisco Masseria, production quantity 15,000	85.00	125.00
☐ 1982	**Angelica,** artist: Francisco Masseria, production quantity 15,000	95.00	110.00
☐ 1983	**Juliana,** artist: Francisco Masseria, production quantity 15,000	95.00	95.00

PORTS OF CALL SERIES

		Issue Price	Current Value
☐ 1975	**San Francisco,** artist: Dong Kingman, production quantity 15,000	60.00	90.00
☐ 1976	**New Orleans,** artist: Dong Kingman, production quantity 15,000	65.00	80.00
☐ 1977	**Venice,** artist: Dong Kingman, production quantity 15,000	70.00	65.00
☐ 1978	**Paris,** artist: Dong Kingman, production quantity 15,000	70.00	70.00

REFLECTIONS ON CHINA SERIES

		Issue Price	Current Value
☐ 1976	**Garden of Tranquility,** artist: Chen Chi, production quantity 15,000	70.00	90.00
☐ 1977	**Imperial Palace,** artist: Chen Chi, production quantity 15,000	70.00	80.00
☐ 1978	**Temple of Heaven,** artist: Chen Chi, production quantity 15,000	75.00	70.00
☐ 1979	**Lake of Mists,** artist: Chen Chi, production quantity 15,000	85.00	85.00

	Issue Price	Current Value

VICTORIAN CHRISTMAS SERIES

		Issue Price	Current Value
☐ 1977	Winter Fun, production: one year	25.00	55.00
☐ 1978	Christmas Day, production: one year	25.00	25.00
☐ 1979	Sleigh Ride, production: one year	29.95	30.00
☐ 1980	Santa's Visit, production: one year	42.00	42.00
☐ 1981	Christmas Carolers, production: one year ..	37.50	40.00
☐ 1982	Christmas, production: one year	39.95	40.00

VICTORIAN VALENTINE SERIES

		Issue Price	Current Value
☐ 1976	Victorian Boy and Girl, production: one year	25.00	65.00
☐ 1977	My Sweetest Friend, production: one year	25.00	40.00
☐ 1978	If I Loved You, production: one year	25.00	40.00
☐ 1979	My Valentine, production: one year	29.95	40.00
☐ 1980	On a Swing, production: one year	32.95	40.00
☐ 1981	Sweet Music, production: one year	35.00	35.00
☐ 1982	From My Heart, production: one year	40.00	40.00
☐ 1983	Cherub's Song, production: one year	40.00	45.00
☐ 1984	Accept These Flowers, production: one year	39.95	40.00

SINGLE ISSUE

		Issue Price	Current Value
☐ 1981	Commemorative Wedding of the Prince of Wales and Lady Diana Spencer, production quantity 1,500	195.00	225.00

ROYAL GRAFTON

Great Britian

TWELVE DAYS OF CHRISTMAS SERIES

		Issue Price	Current Value
☐ 1976	Partridge on Pear Tree, production quantity 3,000	17.50	18.00
☐ 1977	Two Turtle Doves, production quantity 3,000	17.50	18.00
☐ 1978	Three French Hens, production quantity 3,000	21.50	22.00
☐ 1979	Four Colly Birds, production quantity 3,000	26.50	27.00
☐ 1980	Five Golden Rings, production quantity 3,000	35.00	35.00

ROYAL LIMOGES

France

		Issue Price	Current Value
CHRISTMAS SERIES			
☐ **1972**	**Nativity,** production quantity 5,000	**25.00**	**40.00**
☐ **1973**	**Three Wise Men,** production quantity 5,000	**27.50**	**40.00**

ROYAL OAKS LIMITED

United States

LOVE'S LABOR SERIES

☐ **1983**	**The Intruder,** artist: James Landenberger, production quantity 15,000	**50.00**	**50.00**

ROYAL ORLEANS

United States

COCA-COLA: THE CLASSIC SANTA CLAUS SERIES

☐ **1983**	**Good Boys and Girls,** artist: Haddon Sundblom, production quantity 15,000	**55.00**	**55.00**
☐ **1984**	**A Gift for Santa,** artist: Haddon Sundblom, production quantity 15,000	**65.00**	**65.00**
☐ **1985**	**Santa, Please Pause Here,** artist: Haddon Sundblom, production quantity 15,000	**65.00**	**65.00**

DYNASTY SERIES

☐ **1986**	**Krystle,** artist: Shell Fischer, production quantity N/A	**35.00**	**35.00**

ELVIS IN CONCERT SERIES

☐ **1984**	**Aloha from Hawaii** artist: Rick Grimes, production quantity 20,000	**35.00**	**35.00**
☐ **1985**	**Las Vegas,** artist: Rick Grimes, production quantity 20,000	**35.00**	**35.00**

FAMOUS MOVIES

☐ **1985**	**Cat on a Hot tin Roof,** artist: Rick Grimes, production quantity 20,000	**35.00**	**35.00**

Las Vegas, artist: Rick
Grimes.

		Issue Price	Current Value
MARILYN—AN AMERICAN CLASSIC SERIES			
☐ 1983	**The Seven Year Itch,** artist: Twentieth Century–Fox, production quantity 20,000	35.00	35.00
☐ 1984	**Gentlemen Prefer Blondes,** artist: Twentieth Century–Fox, production quantity 20,000 . .	35.00	35.00
☐ 1985	**Niagara,** artist: Rick Grimes, production quantity 20,000	35.00	35.00
NOSTALGIC MAGAZINE COVERS SERIES			
☐ 1983	**Ladies' Home Journal,** artist: Hayden Hayden, production quantity 12,500	35.00	35.00
PINK PANTHER CHRISTMAS COLLECTION SERIES			
☐ 1982	**Sleigh Ride,** artist: D. DePatie, production quantity 10,000	18.50	18.50
☐ 1983	**Happy Landings,** artist: D. DePatie, production quantity 10,000	18.50	18.50
☐ 1984	**Down the Chimney,** artist: D. DePatie, production quantity 10,000	18.50	18.50
☐ 1985	**Pass the Blast,** artist: D. DePatie, production quantity 10,000	18.50	18.50

	Issue Price	Current Value
IN TROMPE L'OEIL SERIES		
☐ **1984 Up to Mischief,** artist: Carol Eytinge, production quantity 10,000	25.00	25.00
TV SERIES		
☐ **1983 The M*A*S*H Plate,** artist: J. LaBonte, production: one year	25.00	30.00
☐ **1983 Dynasty,** Shell Fischer, production: one year	35.00	35.00
YORKSHIRE BRONTES		
☐ **1984 Wuthering Heights,** production: 30 days ...	35.00	35.00
☐ **1985 Jane Eyre,** production: 30 days	35.00	35.00

ROYAL PRINCESS

CHRISTMAS SERIES		
☐ **1973 Three Wise Men**	10.00	10.00

ROYAL TETTAU

Germany

CHRISTMAS SERIES		
☐ **1972 Carriage in the Village**	12.50	15.00

The M*A*S*H Plate,
artist: J. LaBonte.

Dynasty, artist: Shell Fischer.

PAPAL SERIES		Issue Price	Current Value
☐ **1971**	**Pope Paul VI,** production quantity 5,000 ..	**100.00**	**175.00**
☐ **1972**	**Pope John XXIII,** production quantity 5,000	**100.00**	**150.00**
☐ **1973**	**Pope Pius XII,** production quantity 5,000	**100.00**	**125.00**

ROYALWOOD

United States

LEYENDECKER SERIES

☐ **1978**	**Cornflake Boy,** artist: J. C. Leyendecker, production quantity 10,000	**25.00**	**25.00**
☐ **1978**	**Cornflake Girl,** artist: J. C. Leyendecker, production quantity 10,000	**25.00**	**25.00**

SINGLE RELEASE

☐ **1977**	**Doctor and Doll,** artist: Norman Rockwell, production: one year	**21.50**	**22.00**

ROYAL WORCESTER

Great Britain

	Issue Price	Current Value

AMERICAN HISTORY SERIES

		Issue Price	Current Value
☐ 1977	**Washington's Inauguration,** production quantity 1,250	65.00	300.00

AUDUBON BIRDS SERIES

		Issue Price	Current Value
☐ 1977	**Warbler and Jay,** set of two, production quantity 5,000	150.00	150.00
☐ 1978	**Kingbird and Sparrow,** set of two, production quantity 10,000	150.00	150.00

BICENTENNIAL SERIES

		Issue Price	Current Value
☐ 1972	**Boston Tea Party,** artist: P. Baston, production quantity 10,000	45.00	45.00
☐ 1973	**Paul Revere,** artist: P. Baston, production quantity 10,000	45.00	45.00
☐ 1974	**Concord Bridge,** artist: P. Baston, production quantity 10,000	50.00	80.00
☐ 1975	**Signing Declaration,** artist: P. Baston, production quantity 10,000	65.00	65.00
☐ 1976	**Crossing Delaware,** artist: P. Baston, production quantity 10,000	65.00	65.00

CURRIER & IVES SERIES

		Issue Price	Current Value
☐ 1974	**Road in Winter,** artist: P. W. Baston, production closed	59.50	125.00
☐ 1975	**Old Grist Mill,** artist: P. W. Baston, production closed	59.50	125.00
☐ 1976	**Winter Pastime,** artist: P. W. Baston, production closed	59.50	150.00
☐ 1977	**Home to Thanksgiving,** artist: P. W. Baston, production quantity 500	59.50	200.00

DOUGHTY BIRDS SERIES

		Issue Price	Current Value
☐ 1972	**Redstart and Beech,** artist: D. Doughty, production quantity 2,750	150.00	150.00
☐ 1973	**Myrtle Warbler and Cherry,** artist: D. Doughty, production quantity 3,000	175.00	175.00
☐ 1974	**Blue-Grey Gnatcatchers,** artist: D. Doughty, production quantity 3,000	195.00	210.00
☐ 1975	**Blackburnian Warbler,** artist: D. Doughty, production quantity 3,000	195.00	195.00

		Issue Price	Current Value
☐ 1976	**Blue-Winged Sivas and Bamboo,** artist: D. Doughty, production quantity 3,000	**195.00**	**195.00**
☐ 1977	**Paradise Wydah,** artist: D. Doughty, production quantity 3,000	**195.00**	**200.00**
☐ 1978	**Bluetits and Witch Hazel,** artist: D. Doughty, production quantity 3,000	**195.00**	**195.00**
☐ 1979	**Mountain Bluebird and Pine,** artist: D. Doughty, production quantity 3,000	**195.00**	**195.00**
☐ 1980	**Cerulean Warblers and Beech,** artist: D. Doughty, production quantity 3,000	**315.00**	**315.00**
☐ 1981	**Willow Warbler,** artist: D. Doughty, production quantity 3,000	**315.00**	**315.00**
☐ 1982	**Ruby-Crowned Kinglets,** artist: D. Doughty, production quantity 3,000	**330.00**	**330.00**
☐ 1983	**Wren and Jasmine,** artist: D. Doughty, production quantity 3,000	**330.00**	**330.00**

ENGLISH CHRISTMAS SERIES

☐ 1979	**Christmas Eve,** production: one year	**60.00**	**60.00**
☐ 1980	**Christmas Morning,** artist: Ewnece, production: one year	**65.00**	**65.00**
☐ 1980	**Christmas Day,** production quantity unannounced	**70.00**	**70.00**

FABULOUS BIRDS SERIES

☐ 1976	**Peacocks,** production quantity 10,000	**65.00**	**65.00**
☐ 1978	**Peacocks II,** production quantity 10,000 . .	**65.00**	**65.00**

KITTEN CLASSICS SERIES

☐ 1985	**Cat Nap,** artist: P. Cooper, production: 14 days	**29.50**	**29.50**
☐ 1985	**Purrfect Treasure,** artist: P. Cooper, production: 14 days	**29.50**	**29.50**
☐ 1985	**Wild Flower,** artist: P. Cooper, production: 14 days	**29.50**	**29.50**
☐ 1985	**Birdwatcher,** artist: P. Cooper, production: 14 days	**29.50**	**29.50**
☐ 1985	**Tiger's Fancy,** artist: P. Cooper, production: 14 days	**29.50**	**29.50**
☐ 1985	**Country Kitty,** artist: P. Cooper, production: 14 days	**29.50**	**29.50**
☐ 1985	**Little Rascal,** artist: P. Cooper, production: 14 days	**29.50**	**29.50**

		Issue Price	Current Value
☐ **1985**	**First Prize,** artist: P. Cooper, production: 14 days	**29.50**	**29.50**

SINGLE RELEASE

☐ **1976**	**Independence 1776,** production quantity 10,000	**65.00**	**65.00**

WATER BIRDS OF NORTH AMERICA SERIES

☐ **1985**	**Mallards,** artist: J. Cooke, production quantity 15,000	**55.00**	**55.00**
☐ **1985**	**Canvas Backs,** artist: J. Cooke, production quantity 15,000	**55.00**	**55.00**
☐ **1985**	**Wood Ducks,** artist: J. Cooke, production quantity 15,000	**55.00**	**55.00**
☐ **1985**	**Snow Geese,** artist: J. Cooke, production quantity 15,000	**55.00**	**55.00**
☐ **1985**	**American Pintails,** artist: J. Cooke, production quantity 15,000	**55.00**	**55.00**
☐ **1985**	**Green Winged Teals,** artist: J. Cooke, production quantity 15,000	**55.00**	**55.00**
☐ **1985**	**Hooded Mergansers,** artist: J. Cooke, production quantity 15,000	**55.00**	**55.00**
☐ **1985**	**Canada Geese,** artist: J. Cooke, production quantity 15,000	**55.00**	**55.00**

ROYAL WORCESTER

United States

BIRTH OF A NATION SERIES

☐ **1972**	**Boston Tea Party,** artist: Prescott Baston, production quantity 10,000	**45.00**	**250.00**
☐ **1973**	**The Ride of Paul Revere,** artist: Prescott Baston, production quantity 10,000	**45.00**	**230.00**
☐ **1974**	**Incident at Concord Bridge,** artist: Prescott Baston, production quantity 10,000	**50.00**	**80.00**
☐ **1975**	**Signing the Declaration of Independence,** artist: Prescott Baston, production quantity 10,000	**65.00**	**65.00**
☐ **1976**	**Washington Crossing the Delaware,** artist: Prescott Baston, production quantity 10,000	**65.00**	**75.00**

	Issue Price	Current Value
CURRIER & IVES SERIES		
□ **1974 Road in Winter,** production quantity 10,000	59.50	60.00
□ **1975 Old Grist Mill,** production quantity 10,000	59.50	60.00
□ **1976 Winter Pastime,** production quantity 10,000	59.50	60.00
SINGLE RELEASE		
□ **1976 Spirit of 1776,** production quantity 10,000	—	150.00

ROYALE

Germany

	Issue Price	Current Value
CHRISTMAS SERIES		
□ **1969 Christmas Fair,** production quantity 6,000	12.00	60.00
□ **1970 Vigil Mass,** production quantity 10,000 ...	13.00	30.00
□ **1971 Christmas Night,** production quantity 8,000	14.00	35.00
□ **1972 Elks,** production quantity 8,000	16.00	40.00
□ **1973 Christmas Dawn,** production quantity 6,000	20.00	30.00
□ **1974 Village Christmas,** production quantity 5,000	22.00	60.00
□ **1975 Feeding Time,** production quantity 5,000 ..	26.00	30.00
□ **1976 Seaport Christmas,** production quantity 5,000	27.50	30.00
□ **1977 Sledding,** production quantity 5,000	30.00	30.00
FATHER'S DAY SERIES		
□ **1970 United States Frigate Constitution,** production quantity 5,000	13.00	60.00
□ **1971 Man Fishing,** production quantity 5,000 ...	13.00	35.00
□ **1972 Mountaineer,** production quantity 5,000 ...	16.00	50.00
□ **1973 Camping,** production quantity 4,000	18.00	25.00
□ **1974 Eagle,** production quantity 2,500	22.00	35.00
□ **1975 Regatta,** production quantity 2,500	26.00	30.00
□ **1976 Hunting,** production quantity 2,500	30.00	30.00
□ **1977 Fishing,** production quantity 2,500	30.00	30.00
GAME PLATES SERIES		
□ **1972 Setters,** production quantity 500	180.00	200.00
□ **1973 Fox,** production quantity 500	200.00	250.00
□ **1974 Osprey,** production quantity 250	250.00	250.00
□ **1975 California Quail,** production quantity 250	265.00	265.00
MOTHER'S DAY SERIES		
□ **1970 Swan and Young,** production quantity 6,000	12.00	80.00
□ **1971 Doe and Fawn,** production quantity 9,000	13.00	55.00

		Issue Price	Current Value
☐ 1972	**Rabbits,** production quantity 9,000	16.00	40.00
☐ 1973	**Owl Family,** production quantity 6,000	18.00	80.00
☐ 1974	**Duck and Young,** production quantity 5,000	22.00	30.00
☐ 1975	**Lynx and Cubs,** production quantity 5,000	26.00	30.00
☐ 1976	**Woodcock and Young,** production quantity 5,000	27.50	30.00
☐ 1977	**Koala Bear,** production quantity 5,000	30.00	30.00

SINGLE RELEASE

☐ 1969	**Apollo Moon Landing,** production quantity 2,000	30.00	80.00

ROYALE GERMANIA

Germany

ANNUAL SERIES

☐ 1970	**Orchid,** production quantity 600	200.00	650.00
☐ 1971	**Cyclamen,** production quantity 1,000	200.00	325.00
☐ 1972	**Silver Thistle,** production quantity 1,000 . .	250.00	290.00
☐ 1973	**Tulips,** production quantity 600	275.00	310.00
☐ 1974	**Sunflowers,** production quantity 500	300.00	320.00
☐ 1975	**Snowdrops,** production quantity 350	450.00	500.00
☐ 1976	**Flaming Heart,** production quantity 350 . . .	450.00	450.00

MOTHER'S DAY CRYSTAL SERIES

☐ 1971	**Roses,** production quantity 250	135.00	650.00
☐ 1972	**Elephant and Youngster,** production quantity 750	180.00	250.00
☐ 1973	**Koala Bear and Cub,** production quantity 600	200.00	225.00
☐ 1974	**Squirrels,** production quantity 500	240.00	250.00
☐ 1975	**Swan and Young,** production quantity 350	350.00	360.00

RUTHVEN, JOHN A.

United States

MOMENTS OF NATURE SERIES

☐ 1977	**Screech Owls,** production quantity 5,000 . .	37.50	40.00
☐ 1979	**Chickadees,** production quantity 5,000	39.50	40.00
☐ 1980	**California Quail,** production quantity 5,000	39.50	40.00

SABINO

France

ANNUAL CRYSTAL SERIES	Issue Price	Current Value
☐ 1970 **King Henry IV and Maria de Medici,** production quantity 1,500	65.00	75.00
☐ 1971 **Milo and the Beasts,** production quantity 1,500	65.00	75.00

SANGO

Japan

CHRISTMAS SERIES

☐ 1974 **Spark of Christmas,** artist: Marvin Nye, production quantity 5,000	25.00	25.00
☐ 1975 **Christmas Eve in Country,** artist: Marvin Nye, production quantity 5,000	27.50	28.00
☐ 1976 **Madonna and Child,** artist: Marvin Nye, production quantity 5,000	25.00	25.00
☐ 1976 **Undesired Slumber,** artist: Marvin Nye, production quantity 7,500	25.00	55.00
☐ 1977 **Togetherness,** artist: Marvin Nye, production quantity 7,500	25.00	40.00

LIVING AMERICAN ARTISTS SERIES

☐ 1976 **Sweethearts,** artist: Norman Rockwell, production quantity 10,000	30.00	60.00
☐ 1977 **Apache Girl,** artist: Gregory Perillo, production quantity 5,000	35.00	290.00
☐ 1978 **Natural Habitat,** production quantity 5,000	40.00	40.00

MOTHER'S DAY

☐ 1976 **Spring Delight,** artist: Leslie De Mille, production quantity 7,500	20.00	20.00
☐ 1977 **Broken Wings,** artist: Leslie De Mille, production quantity 5,000	22.50	23.00

SANTA CLARA

Spain

			Issue Price	Current Value
CHRISTMAS SERIES				
☐ 1970	**Christmas Message,** production quantity 10,000		**18.00**	**40.00**
☐ 1971	**Three Wise Men,** production quantity 10,000		**18.00**	**35.00**
☐ 1972	**Children on Woods Path,** production quantity 10,000		**20.00**	**40.00**
☐ 1974	**Archangel,** production quantity 5,000		**25.00**	**50.00**
☐ 1974	**Spirit of Christmas,** production quantity 5,000		**25.00**	**25.00**
☐ 1975	**Christmas Eve,** production quantity 5,000		**27.50**	**33.00**
☐ 1976	**Madonna and Child,** production quantity 5,000		**25.00**	**35.00**
☐ 1977	**Mother and Child,** production quantity 10,000		**27.50**	**32.00**
☐ 1978	**Angel with Flowers,** production quantity 10,000		**32.00**	**32.00**
☐ 1979	**Madonna and Angels,** production quantity 10,000		**34.50**	**35.00**

MOTHER'S DAY SERIES

☐ 1971	**Mother and Child,** production quantity 10,000		**12.00**	**30.00**
☐ 1972	**Mother and Children,** production quantity 12,000		**12.00**	**40.00**

SARNA

India

CHRISTMAS SERIES

☐ 1975	**Holy Family,** production quantity 4,000		**17.50**	**18.50**

SCHMID

Germany

BEATRIX POTTER SERIES

☐ 1978	**Peter Rabbit,** artist: Beatrix Potter, production quantity 5,000		**50.00**	**50.00**

		Issue Price	Current Value
☐ 1979	**Jemima Puddleduck,** artist: Beatrix Potter, production quantity 5,000	50.00	50.00
☐ 1980	**Tale of Benjamin Bunny,** artist: Beatrix Potter, production quantity 5,000	50.00	50.00

BERTA HUMMEL CHRISTMAS SERIES

		Issue Price	Current Value
☐ 1971	**Angel,** artist: Berta Hummel, production: one year	15.00	85.00
☐ 1972	**Angel with Flute,** artist: Berta Hummel, production: one year	15.00	75.00
☐ 1973	**Nativity,** artist: Berta Hummel, production: one year	15.00	450.00
☐ 1974	**Guardian Angel,** artist: Berta Hummel, production: one year	18.50	70.00
☐ 1975	**Christmas Child,** artist: Berta Hummel, production: one year	25.00	67.50
☐ 1976	**Sacred Journey,** artist: Berta Hummel, production: one year	27.50	65.00
☐ 1977	**Herald Angel,** artist: Berta Hummel, production: one year	27.50	57.50
☐ 1978	**Heavenly Trio,** artist: Berta Hummel, production: one year	32.50	60.00
☐ 1979	**Starlight Angel,** artist: Berta Hummel, production: one year	38.00	60.00
☐ 1980	**Parade into Toyland,** artist: Berta Hummel, production: one year	45.00	57.50
☐ 1981	**A Time to Remember,** artist: Berta Hummel, production: one year	45.00	55.00
☐ 1982	**Angelic Procession,** artist: Berta Hummel, production: one year	45.00	52.00
☐ 1983	**Angelic Messenger,** artist: Berta Hummel, production: one year	45.00	50.00
☐ 1984	**A Gift from Heaven,** artist: Berta Hummel, production: one year	45.00	47.50
☐ 1985	**Heavenly Light,** artist: Berta Hummel, production: one year	45.00	45.00
☐ 1986	**Tell the Heavens,** artist: Berta Hummel, production: one year	45.00	45.00
☐ 1987	**Angelic Gifts,** artist: Berta Hummel, production: one year	47.50	47.50

		Issue Price	Current Value
BERTA HUMMEL			
MOTHER'S DAY SERIES			
☐ **1972**	**Playing Hooky,** artist: Berta Hummel, production: one year	15.00	25.00
☐ **1973**	**Little Fishermen,** artist: Berta Hummel, production: one year	15.00	54.00
☐ **1974**	**Bumblebee,** artist: Berta Hummel, production: one year	18.50	72.50
☐ **1975**	**Message of Love,** artist: Berta Hummel, production: one year	25.00	25.00
☐ **1976**	**Devotion to Mother,** artist: Berta Hummel, production: one year	27.50	30.00
☐ **1977**	**Moonlight Return,** artist: Berta Hummel, production: one year	27.50	62.50
☐ **1978**	**Afternoon Stroll,** artist: Berta Hummel, production: one year	32.50	60.00
☐ **1979**	**Cherub's Gift,** artist: Berta Hummel, production: one year	38.00	38.00
☐ **1980**	**Mother's Little Helpers,** artist: Berta Hummel, production: one year	45.00	52.00
☐ **1981**	**Playtime,** artist: Berta Hummel, production: one year	45.00	52.00
☐ **1982**	**The Flower Basket,** artist: Berta Hummel, production: one year	45.00	47.50
☐ **1983**	**Spring Bouquet,** artist: Berta Hummel, production: one year	45.00	54.00
☐ **1984**	**A Joy to Share,** artist: Berta Hummel, production: one year	45.00	45.00
☐ **1985**	**A Mother's Journey,** artist: Berta Hummel, production: one year	45.00	45.00
☐ **1986**	**Home from School,** artist: Berta Hummel, production: one year	45.00	55.00
☐ **1987**	**Mother's Little Learner,** artist: Berta Hummel, production: one year	47.50	47.50

CAROUSEL FANTASIES SERIES

☐ **1983**	**A Fairy Tale Princess,** artist: Jessica Zemsky and Jack Hines, production quantity 7,500	50.00	50.00

CAT TALES SERIES

☐ **1982**	**Right Church, Wrong Pew,** artist: Lowell Davis, numbered, production quantity 12,500	37.50	55.00
☐ **1982**	**Company's Coming,** artist: Lowell Davis, numbered, production quantity 12,500	37.50	50.00

		Issue Price	Current Value
☐ 1983	**On the Move,** artist: Lowell Davis, numbered, production quantity 12,500	37.50	42.00
☐ 1983	**Flew the Coop,** artist: Lowell Davis, numbered, production quantity 12,500	37.50	40.00

COUNTRY CHRISTMAS ANNUAL SERIES

☐ 1983	**Country Christmas,** artist: Lowell Davis, production quantity 7,500	45.00	50.00
☐ 1984	**Country Christmas,** artist: Lowell Davis, production quantity 7,500	45.00	50.00
☐ 1985	**Christmas at Foxfire Farm,** artist: Lowell Davis, production quantity 7,500	45.00	45.00
☐ 1986	**Christmas at Red Oak,** artist: Lowell Davis, production quantity 7,500	45.00	45.00
☐ 1987	**Blossom's Gift,** artist: Lowell Davis, production quantity 7,500	47.50	47.50

COUNTRY PRIDE SERIES

☐ 1980	**Surprise in the Cellar,** artist: Lowell Davis, production quantity 7,500	35.00	125.00
☐ 1981	**Plum Tuckered Out,** artist: Lowell Davis, production quantity 7,500	35.00	40.00
☐ 1981	**Duke's Mixture,** artist: Lowell Davis, production quantity 7,500	35.00	65.00
☐ 1981	**Bustin' with Pride,** artist: Lowell Davis, production quantity 7,500	35.00	45.00

FERRANDIZ BEAUTIFUL BOUNTY PORCELAIN SERIES

☐ 1982	**Summer's Golden Harvest,** artist: Juan Ferrandiz, production quantity 10,000	40.00	47.50
☐ 1982	**Autumn Blessing,** artist: Juan Ferrandiz, production quantity 10,000	40.00	45.00
☐ 1982	**A Midwinter's Dream,** artist: Juan Ferrandiz, production quantity 10,000	40.00	42.50
☐ 1982	**Spring Blossoms,** artist: Juan Ferrandiz, production quantity 10,000	40.00	40.00

FERRANDIZ MOTHER AND CHILD SERIES

☐ 1977	**Orchard Mother and Child,** artist: Juan Ferrandiz, production quantity 10,000	65.00	65.00

		Issue Price	Current Value
☐ 1978	**Pastoral Mother and Child,** artist: Juan Ferrandiz, production quantity 10,000	75.00	75.00
☐ 1979	**Floral Mother,** artist: Juan Ferrandiz, production quantity 10,000	95.00	95.00
☐ 1979	**Avian Mother and Child,** artist: Juan Ferrandiz, production quantity 10,000	100.00	100.00

FERRANDIZ WOODEN JUBILEE SERIES

☐ 1978	**Spring Dance,** artist: Juan Ferrandiz, production quantity 2,500	500.00	500.00
☐ 1982	**Riding thru the Rain,** artist: Juan Ferrandiz, production quantity 2,500	550.00	550.00

GIFT OF HAPPINESS SERIES

☐ 1984	**Lilies of the Field,** artist: Pati Bannister, production quantity 7,500	125.00	125.00
☐ 1984	**Morning Glories,** artist: Pati Bannister, production quantity 7,500	125.00	125.00

GOLDEN ANNIVERSARY SERIES

☐ 1987	**Snow White and the Seven Dwarfs,** artist: Disney Studio, production quantity 5,000 ..	47.50	47.50

GOLDEN MOMENTS SERIES

☐ 1978	**Tranquility,** production quantity 15,000 ...	250.00	250.00
☐ 1981	**Serenity,** production quantity 15,000	250.00	250.00

GOOD OL' DAYS SERIES

☐ 1984	**When Minutes Seem Like Hours,** artist: L. Davis, production quantity 5,000		
☐ 1984	**Waiting for His Master,** artist: L. Davis, production quantity 5,000		
	Set of two	60.00	60.00

THE MUSIC MAKERS SERIES

☐ 1981	**The Flutist,** artist: Juan Ferrandiz, production quantity 10,000	25.00	25.00
☐ 1981	**The Entertainer,** artist: Juan Ferrandiz, production quantity 10,000	25.00	25.00
☐ 1981	**Magical Medley,** artist: Juan Ferrandiz, production quantity 10,000	25.00	27.50
☐ 1982	**Sweet Serenade,** artist: Juan Ferrandiz, production quantity 10,000	25.00	25.00

		Issue Price	Current Value

MY NAME IS STAR SERIES

☐ **1981** **Star's Spring,** artist: Jessica Zemsky, numbered, production quantity 10,000 .... **30.00** **30.00**

☐ **1981** **Star's Summer,** artist: Jessica Zemsky, numbered, production quantity 10,000 .... **30.00** **30.00**

☐ **1982** **Star's Autumn,** artist: Jessica Zemsky, numbered, production quantity 10,000 .... **30.00** **30.00**

☐ **1982** **Star's Winter,** artist: Jessica Zemsky, numbered, production quantity 10,000 .... **30.00** **30.00**

PRAIRIE WOMAN SERIES

☐ **1982** **The Maiden,** artist: Jack Hines, production quantity 12,500 .... **35.00** **35.00**

☐ **1982** **The Courtship Blanket,** artist: Jack Hines, production quantity 12,500 .... **35.00** **35.00**

☐ **1982** **Mother Now,** artist: Jack Hines, production quantity 12,500 .... **35.00** **35.00**

☐ **1982** **The Passing of the Moons,** artist: Jack Hines, production quantity 12,500 .... **35.00** **35.00**

RED OAK SAMPLER SERIES

☐ **1986** **General Store,** artist: L. Davis, production quantity 5,000 .... **45.00** **45.00**

☐ **1987** **Country Wedding,** artist: L. Davis, production quantity 5,000 .... **47.00** **47.00**

REFLECTIONS OF LIFE SERIES

☐ **1980** **Quiet Reflections,** artist: Juan Ferrandiz, production quantity 10,000 .... **85.00** **85.00**

☐ **1981** **Tree of Life,** artist: Juan Ferrandiz, production quantity 10,000 .... **85.00** **85.00**

SCHMID CRYSTAL DESEVRES SERIES

☐ **1978** **The Sea,** artist: unannounced, production quantity 1,500 .... **60.00** **60.00**

☐ **1979** **The Sky,** artist: unannounced, production quantity 1,500 .... **80.00** **80.00**

☐ **1980** **The Earth,** artist: unannounced, production quantity 1,500 .... **90.00** **90.00**

SCHMID DESIGN SERIES

☐ **1971** **Family Portrait,** artist: unannounced, production quantity 5,000 .... **13.00** **13.00**

		Issue Price	Current Value
☐ 1972	**On Horseback,** artist: unannounced, production quantity 5,000	15.00	15.00
☐ 1973	**Bringing Home Tree,** artist: unannounced, production quantity 5,000	20.00	20.00
☐ 1974	**Decorating Tree,** artist: unannounced, production quantity 5,000 :	25.00	25.00
☐ 1975	**Opening Presents,** artist: unannounced, production quantity 5,000	27.00	27.00
☐ 1976	**By Fireside,** artist: unannounced, production quantity 5,000	28.50	28.50
☐ 1977	**Skating,** artist: unannounced, production quantity 5,000	28.50	28.50
☐ 1978	**Family Picking Tree,** artist: unannounced, production quantity 5,000	36.00	36.00
☐ 1979	**Breakfast by Tree,** artist: unannounced, production quantity 5,000	45.00	45.00
☐ 1980	**Feeding Animals,** artist: unannounced, production quantity 5,000	55.00	55.00

SCHMID FATHER'S DAY SERIES

		Issue Price	Current Value
☐ 1975	**Bavarian Father's Day,** artist: unannounced, production: unannounced	27.50	27.50

SCHMID PEWTER CHRISTMAS PLATES

		Issue Price	Current Value
☐ 1977	**Santa,** artist: unannounced, production quantity 6,000	50.00	50.00
☐ 1978	**Beautiful Snow,** artist: unannounced, production quantity 6,000	50.00	50.00
☐ 1979	**I Hear America Sing,** artist: unannounced, production quantity 6,000	50.00	50.00
☐ 1980	**A Country Sleigh Ride,** artist: unannounced, production quantity 6,000	50.00	50.00

SINGLE RELEASES

		Issue Price	Current Value
☐ 1983	**The Critics,** artist: Lowell Davis, production quantity 12,500	45.00	65.00
☐ 1983	**Christmas Kingdom,** artist: Juan Ferrandiz, production quantity 10,000	45.00	45.00
☐ 1986	**Home from Market,** artist: Lowell Davis, production quantity 7,000	55.00	55.00

SCHMID

Japan

	Issue Price	Current Value
DISNEY ANNUAL SERIES		
☐ **1983 Sneak Preview,** artist: Disney Studio, production quantity 20,000	22.50	22.50
☐ **1984 Command Performance,** artist: Disney Studio, production quantity 20,000	22.50	22.50
☐ **1985 Snow Biz,** artist: Disney Studio, production quantity 20,000	22.50	22.50
☐ **1986 Merry Mouse Medley,** artist: Disney Studio, production quantity 20,000	25.00	25.00
DISNEY BICENTENNIAL SERIES		
☐ **1976 Bicentennial Plate,** artist: Disney Studio, production: unannounced	13.00	13.00
DISNEY CHRISTMAS SERIES		
☐ **1973 Sleigh Ride,** artist: Disney Studio, production: one year	10.00	450.00
☐ **1974 Trimming the Tree,** artist: Disney Studio, production: one year	10.00	200.00
☐ **1975 Caroling,** artist: Disney Studio, production: one year	12.50	13.00
☐ **1976 Building a Snowman,** artist: Disney Studio, production: one year	13.00	32.50
☐ **1977 Down the Chimney,** artist: Disney Studio, production: one year	13.00	30.00
☐ **1978 Night Before Christmas,** artist: Disney Studio, production: one year	15.00	21.00
☐ **1979 Santa's Surprise,** artist: Disney Studio, production quantity 15,000	17.50	25.00
☐ **1980 Sleigh Ride,** artist: Disney Studio, production quantity 15,000	17.50	22.50
☐ **1981 Happy Holidays,** artist: Disney Studio, production quantity 15,000	17.50	20.00
☐ **1982 Winter Games,** artist: Disney Studio, production quantity 15,000	18.50	18.50
DISNEY FOUR SEASONS OF LOVE SERIES		
☐ **1983 Tickets on the Fifty Yard Line,** artist: Disney Studio, production quantity 10,000	17.50	17.50

		Issue Price	Current Value
☐ 1983	Let It Snow, artist: Disney Studio, production quantity 10,000	17.50	17.50
☐ 1983	Spring Bouquet, artist: Disney Studio, production quantity 10,000	17.50	17.50
☐ 1983	Shades of Summer, artist: Disney Studio, production quantity 10,000	17.50	17.50

DISNEY'S MOTHER'S DAY SERIES

☐ 1974	Flowers for Mother, artist: Disney Studio, production: one year	10.00	60.00
☐ 1975	Snow White, artist: Disney Studio, production: one year	12.50	45.00
☐ 1976	Minnie Mouse and Friends, artist: Disney Studio, production: one year	13.00	15.00
☐ 1977	Pluto's Pals, artist: Disney Studio, production: one year	13.00	25.00
☐ 1978	Flowers for Bambi, artist: Disney Studio, production: one year	15.00	30.00
☐ 1979	Happy Feet, artist: Disney Studio, production quantity 10,000	17.50	30.00
☐ 1980	Minnie's Surprise, artist: Disney Studio, production quantity 10,000	17.50	25.00
☐ 1981	Playmates, artist: Disney Studio, production quantity 10,000	17.50	20.00
☐ 1982	A Dream Come True, artist: Disney Studio, production quantity 10,000	18.50	18.50

DISNEY SPECIAL SERIES

☐ 1978	Mickey at 50, artist: Disney Studio, production quantity 15,000	25.00	45.00
☐ 1980	Happy Birthday, Pinocchio, artist: Disney Studio, production quantity 7,500	17.50	25.00
☐ 1981	Alice in Wonderland, artist: Disney Studio, production quantity 7,500	17.50	17.50
☐ 1982	Goofy's Golden Jubilee, artist: Disney Studio, production quantity 7,500	18.50	18.50
☐ 1982	Happy Birthday, Pluto, artist: Disney Studio, production quantity 7,500	17.50	17.50

DISNEY VALENTINE'S DAY SERIES

☐ 1979	Hands and Heart, artist: Disney Studio, production: one year	17.50	17.50
☐ 1980	Mickey's I Love You, artist: Disney Studio, production: one year	17.50	17.50

		Issue Price	Current Value
☐ 1981	**Be Mine,** artist: Disney Studio, production: one year	**17.50**	**17.50**
☐ 1982	**Picnic for Two,** artist: Disney Studio, production quantity 7,500	**17.50**	**17.50**

NATURE'S TREASURES SERIES

☐ 1984	**Tulip Nest—Robin,** artist: Mitsuko Gerhart, production quantity 5,000	**45.00**	**45.00**
☐ 1984	**Rose Haven—Chipping Sparrow,** artist: Mitsuko Gerhart, production quantity 5,000	**45.00**	**45.00**
☐ 1984	**Leafy Bower—Spotted Oriole,** artist: Mitsuko Gerhart, production quantity 5,000	**45.00**	**45.00**
☐ 1984	**Nesting Companion—Mockingbird,** artist: Mitsuko Gerhart, production quantity 5,000	**45.00**	**45.00**

PADDINGTON BEAR ANNUAL SERIES

☐ 1979	**Pyramid of Presents,** artist: unannounced, production quantity 25,000	**12.50**	**27.50**
☐ 1980	**Springtime,** artist: unannounced, production quantity 25,000	**12.50**	**25.00**
☐ 1981	**Sandcastles,** artist: unannounced, production quantity 25,000	**12.50**	**22.50**
☐ 1981	**Back to School,** artist: unannounced, production quantity 25,000	**12.50**	**12.50**

PADDINGTON BEAR ANNUAL CHRISTMAS SERIES

☐ 1983	**A Bear's Noel,** artist: unannounced, production quantity 10,000	**22.50**	**22.50**
☐ 1984	**How Sweet It Is,** artist: unannounced, production quantity 10,000	**22.50**	**22.50**

PADDINGTON BEAR MUSICIAN'S DREAM SERIES

☐ 1982	**The Beat Goes On,** artist: unannounced, production quantity 10,000	**17.50**	**22.50**
☐ 1982	**Knowing the Score,** artist: unannounced, production quantity 10,000	**17.50**	**20.00**
☐ 1983	**Perfect Harmony,** artist: unannounced, production quantity 10,000	**17.50**	**17.50**
☐ 1983	**Tickling the Ivory,** artist: unannounced, production quantity 10,000	**17.50**	**17.50**

		Issue Price	Current Value

PEANUTS ANNUAL SERIES

		Issue Price	Current Value
☐ 1983	**Peanuts in Concert,** artist: Charles Schulz, production quantity 20,000	**22.50**	**22.50**
☐ 1984	**Snoopy and the Beaglescouts,** artist: Charles Schulz, production quantity 20,000	**22.50**	**22.50**
☐ 1985	**Clown Capers,** artist: Charles Schulz, production quantity 20,000	**22.50**	**22.50**
☐ 1986	**Lion Tamer Snoopy,** artist: Charles Schulz, production quantity 20,000	**22.50**	**22.50**
☐ 1987	**Big Top Blast Off,** artist: Charles Schulz, production quantity 20,000	**17.50**	**17.50**

PEANUTS CHRISTMAS SERIES

		Issue Price	Current Value
☐ 1972	**Snoopy Guides the Sleigh,** artist: Charles Schulz, production quantity 20,000	**10.00**	**90.00**
☐ 1973	**Christmas Eve at the Doghouse,** artist: Charles Schulz, production: one year	**10.00**	**120.00**
☐ 1974	**Christmas Eve at the Fireplace,** artist: Charles Schulz, production: one year	**10.00**	**65.00**
☐ 1975	**Woodstock, Santa Claus,** artist: Charles Schulz, production: one year	**12.50**	**12.50**
☐ 1976	**Woodstock's Christmas,** artist: Charles Schulz, production: one year	**13.00**	**32.50**
☐ 1977	**Deck the Doghouse,** artist: Charles Schulz, production: one year	**13.00**	**15.00**
☐ 1978	**Filling the Stocking,** artist: Charles Schulz, production: one year	**15.00**	**27.50**
☐ 1979	**Christmas at Hand,** artist: Charles Schulz, production quantity 15,000	**17.50**	**15.00**
☐ 1980	**Waiting for Santa,** artist: Charles Schulz, production quantity 15,000	**17.50**	**52.00**
☐ 1981	**A Christmas Wish,** artist: Charles Schulz, production quantity 15,000	**17.50**	**25.00**
☐ 1982	**Perfect Performance,** artist: Charles Schulz, production quantity 15,000	**18.50**	**33.00**

PEANUTS MOTHER'S DAY SERIES

		Issue Price	Current Value
☐ 1972	**Linus,** artist: Charles Schulz, production quantity 15,000	**10.00**	**55.00**
☐ 1973	**Mom?,** artist: Charles Schulz, production quantity 8,000	**10.00**	**50.00**
☐ 1974	**Snoopy and Woodstock on Parade,** artist: Charles Schulz, production: one year	**10.00**	**45.00**
☐ 1975	**A Kiss for Lucy,** artist: Charles Schulz, production: one year	**12.50**	**40.00**

	Issue Price	Current Value
☐ 1976 **Linus and Snoopy,** artist: Charles Schulz, production: one year	13.00	35.00
☐ 1977 **Dear Mom,** artist: Charles Schulz, production: one year	13.00	30.00
☐ 1978 **Thoughts That Count,** artist: Charles Schulz, production: one year	15.00	25.00
☐ 1979 **A Special Letter,** artist: Charles Schulz, production quantity 10,000	17.50	22.50
☐ 1980 **A Tribute to Mom,** artist: Charles Schulz, production quantity 10,000	17.50	22.50
☐ 1981 **Mission for Mom,** artist: Charles Schulz, production quantity 10,000	17.50	20.00
☐ 1982 **Which Way to Mother,** artist: Charles Schulz, production quantity 10,000	18.50	18.50

PEANUTS SPECIAL SERIES

☐ 1976 **Bicentennial,** artist: Charles Schulz, production: one year	13.00	30.00
☐ 1980 **Peanuts 30th Birthday,** artist: Charles Schulz, production quantity 15,000	27.50	27.50

PEANUTS VALENTINE SERIES

☐ 1977 **Home Is Where the Heart Is,** artist: Charles Schulz, production: one year	13.00	32.50
☐ 1978 **Heavenly Bliss,** artist: Charles Schulz, production: one year	13.00	30.00
☐ 1979 **Love Match,** artist: Charles Schulz, production: one year	17.50	27.50
☐ 1980 **From Snoopy, with Love,** artist: Charles Schulz, production: one year	17.50	25.00
☐ 1981 **Hearts-a-Flutter,** artist: Charles Schulz, production: one year	17.50	20.00
☐ 1982 **Love Patch,** artist: Charles Schulz, production: one year	17.50	17.50

PEANUTS WORLD'S GREATEST ATHLETE SERIES

☐ 1983 **Go Deep,** artist: Charles Schulz, production quantity 10,000	17.50	25.00
☐ 1983 **The Puck Stops Here,** artist: Charles Schulz, production quantity 10,000	17.50	22.50
☐ 1983 **The Way You Play the Game,** artist: Charles Schulz, production quantity 10,000	17.50	20.00

		Issue Price	Current Value
☐ 1983	The Crowd Went Wild, artist: Charles Schulz, production quantity 10,000 . . . . , ...	17.50	17.50

PRIME TIME SERIES

| ☐ 1984 | Love Boat, artist: Shelly Mathers, production limited . . . . | 30.00 | 30.00 |
| ☐ 1984 | Dallas, artist: Shelly Mathers, production limited . . . . | 30.00 | 30.00 |

RAGGEDY ANN ANNUAL SERIES

☐ 1980	Sunshine Wagon, production quantity 10,000	17.50	80.00
☐ 1981	The Raggedy Shuffle, production quantity 10,000 . . . . , . .	17.50	27.50
☐ 1982	Flying High, production quantity 10,000 . .	18.50	18.50
☐ 1983	Winning Streak, production quantity 10,000	22.50	22.50
☐ 1984	Rocking Rodeo, production quantity 10,000	22.50	22.50

RAGGEDY ANN BICENTENNIAL SERIES

| ☐ 1976 | Bicentennial Plate, production: one year . . | 13.00 | 30.00 |

RAGGEDY ANN CHRISTMAS SERIES

☐ 1975	Gifts of Love, production: one year	12.50	45.00
☐ 1976	Merry Blades, production: one year	13.00	37.50
☐ 1977	Christmas Morning, production: one year . .	13.00	22.50
☐ 1978	Checking the List, production: one year . . .	15.00	20.00
☐ 1979	Little Helper, production quantity 15,000	17.50	19.50

RAGGEDY ANN
MOTHER'S DAY SERIES

☐ 1976	Motherhood, production: one year	13.00	13.00
☐ 1977	Bouquet of Love, production: one year	13.00	13.00
☐ 1978	Hello Mom, production: one year	15.00	15.00
☐ 1979	High Spirits, production: one year	17.50	17.50

RAGGEDY ANN
VALENTINE'S DAY SERIES

| ☐ 1978 | As Time Goes By, production: one year . . . | 13.00 | 25.00 |
| ☐ 1979 | Daisies Do Tell, production: one year . . . . . | 17.50 | 20.00 |

SINGLE ISSUE

| ☐ 1987 | Snow White and the Seven Dwarfs, artist: Disney Studio, production quantity 5,000 . . | 47.50 | 50.00 |

SCHOFIELD GALLERY

United States

CLOWNS, KLOWNS, KLONZ SERIES	Issue Price	Current Value
☐ 1986 **Painting on a Smile,** artist: Mildred Schofield, production quantity 7,500	47.50	48.00
☐ 1986 **Keystone Kop,** artist: Mildred Schofield, production quantity 7,500	47.50	48.00

SCHUMANN

Germany

CHRISTMAS SERIES

☐ 1971 **Snow Scene,** production quantity 10,000 ...	12.00	15.00
☐ 1972 **Deer in Snow,** production quantity 15,000	12.00	15.00
☐ 1973 **Weihnachten,** production quantity 5,000 ...	12.00	15.00
☐ 1974 **Church in Snow,** production quantity 5,000	12.00	15.00
☐ 1975 **Fountain,** production quantity 5,000	12.00	15.00

COMPOSERS SERIES

☐ 1970 **Beethoven**	12.00	15.00
☐ 1972 **Mozart**	12.00	15.00

IMPERIAL CHRISTMAS SERIES
(Royal Cornwall)

☐ 1979 **Liebling,** artist: Marianne Stuwe, production quantity 10,000	65.00	100.00
☐ 1980 **Hallelujah,** artist: Marianne Stuwe, production quantity 10,000	65.00	80.00
☐ 1981 **Stille Nacht,** artist: Marianne Stuwe, production quantity 10,000	75.00	80.00
☐ 1982 **Winter Melodie,** artist: Marianne Stuwe, production quantity 10,000	75.00	80.00

SEBASTIAN

United States

AMERICA'S FAVORITE SCENES

☐ 1978 **Motif #1,** production quantity 10,000	75.00	75.00
☐ 1979 **Grand Canyon,** production quantity 10,000	75.00	75.00

SEELEY'S CERAMIC SERVICE

United States

	Issue Price	Current Value

ANTIQUE FRENCH DOLL COLLECTION

		Issue Price	Current Value
☐ 1979	**The Bru,** artist: Mildred Seely, production quantity 5,000	**39.00**	**200.00**
☐ 1979	**The E. J.,** artist: Mildred Seely, production quantity 5,000	**39.00**	**75.00**
☐ 1979	**The A. T.,** artist: Mildred Seely, production quantity 5,000	**39.00**	**55.00**
☐ 1980	**Alexandre,** artist: Mildred Seely, production quantity 5,000	**39.00**	**45.00**
☐ 1981	**The Schmitt,** artist: Mildred Seeley, production quantity 5,000	**39.00**	**43.00**
☐ 1981	**The Marque,** artist: Mildred Seeley, production quantity 5,000	**39.00**	**43.00**
☐ 1983	**Bebe Halo,** artist: Mildred Seeley, production quantity 5,000	**39.00**	**39.00**
☐ 1984	**Bru's Faith,** artist: Mildred Seeley, production quantity 5,000 . . . . '. . . .	**39.00**	**39.00**
☐ 1984	**Steiner's Easter,** artist: Mildred Seeley, production quantity 5,000	**39.00**	**39.00**

ANTIQUE FRENCH DOLL COLLECTION II

		Issue Price	Current Value
☐ 1983	**The Snow Angel,** artist: Mildred Seeley, production quantity 5,000	**39.00**	**39.00**
☐ 1984	**Marque's Alyce,** artist: Mildred Seeley, production quantity 5,000	**39.00**	**39.00**
☐ 1984	**Jumeau's Gaynell,** artist: Mildred Seeley, production quantity 5,000	**39.00**	**39.00**

THE OLD BABY DOLL COLLECTION

		Issue Price	Current Value
☐ 1982	**JDK Hilda,** artist: Mildred Seeley, numbered, production quantity 9,500	**43.00**	**43.00**
☐ 1982	**Goldie,** artist: Mildred Seeley, numbered, production quantity 9,500	**43.00**	**43.00**
☐ 1983	**Lori,** artist: Mildred Seeley, numbered, production quantity 9,500	**43.00**	**43.00**
☐ 1983	**Bye-lo,** artist: Mildred Seeley, numbered, production quantity 9,500	**43.00**	**43.00**
☐ 1983	**Laughing Baby,** artist: Mildred Seeley, numbered, production quantity 9,500	**43.00**	**43.00**

		Issue Price	Current Value

OLD GERMAN DOLL
COLLECTION SERIES

☐ **1981 Dear Googly,** artist: Mildred Seeley, production quantity 7,500 .... **39.00 39.00**

☐ **1981 Lucy,** artist: Mildred Seeley, production quantity 7,500 .... **39.00 39.00**

☐ **1981 The Whistler,** artist: Mildred Seeley, production quantity 7,500 .... **39.00 39.00**

☐ **1982 April,** artist: Mildred Seeley, production quantity 7,500 .... **39.00 39.00**

☐ **1982 Elise,** artist: Mildred Seeley, production quantity 7,500 .... **39.00 39.00**

SELANDIA

CHRISTMAS SERIES

☐ **1972 Way to Bethlehem,** signed, production quantity 250 .... **100.00 100.00**

☐ **1972 Way to Bethlehem,** unsigned, production quantity 4,750 .... **30.00 50.00**

☐ **1973 Three Wise Men,** signed, production quantity 200 .... **100.00 100.00**

☐ **1973 Three Wise Men,** unsigned, production quantity 4,750 .... **35.00 35.00**

SEVEN SEAS

United States

CHRISTMAS CAROLS SERIES

☐ **1970 I Heard the Bells,** production quantity 4,000 **15.00 25.00**

☐ **1971 Oh Tannenbaum,** production quantity 4,000 **15.00 20.00**

☐ **1972 Deck the Halls,** production quantity 1,500 **18.00 25.00**

☐ **1973 O Holy Night,** production quantity 2,000 .. **18.00 25.00**

☐ **1974 Jingle Bells,** production quantity 1,200 .... **25.00 25.00**

☐ **1975 Winter Wonderland,** production quantity 1,500 .... **25.00 25.00**

☐ **1976 Twelve Days of Christmas,** production quantity 1,500 .... **25.00 25.00**

☐ **1977 Up on the Housetop,** production quantity 1,500 .... **25.00 25.00**

☐ **1978 Little Town of Bethlehem,** production quantity 1,500 .... **25.00 25.00**

		Issue Price	Current Value
☐ 1979	**Santa Claus Is Coming to Town,** production quantity 1,500	**25.00**	**25.00**
☐ 1980	**Frosty the Snowman,** production quantity 1,500	**25.00**	**25.00**

HISTORICAL EVENT SERIES

☐ 1969	**Moon Landing—No Flag,** production quantity 2,000	**13.50**	**175.00**
☐ 1969	**Moon Landing—with Flag,** production quantity 2,000	**13.50**	**70.00**
☐ 1970	**Year of Crisis,** production quantity 4,000	**15.00**	**20.00**
☐ 1971	**First Vehicular Travel,** production quantity 3,000	**15.00**	**35.00**
☐ 1972	**Last Moon Journey,** production quantity 2,000	**15.00**	**35.00**
☐ 1973	**Peace,** production quantity 3,000	**15.00**	**35.00**

MOTHER'S DAY SERIES

☐ 1970	**Girl of All Nations,** production quantity 5,000	**15.00**	**20.00**
☐ 1971	**Sharing Confidences,** production quantity 1,400	**15.00**	**20.00**
☐ 1972	**Scandinavian Girl,** production quantity 1,600	**15.00**	**20.00**
☐ 1973	**All-American Girl,** production quantity 1,500	**15.00**	**30.00**

NEW WORLD SERIES

☐ 1970	**Holy Family,** production quantity 3,500	**15.00**	**20.00**
☐ 1971	**Three Wise Men,** production quantity 1,500	**15.00**	**30.00**
☐ 1972	**Shepherds Watched,** production quantity 1,500	**18.00**	**20.00**

SINGLE RELEASE

☐ 1970	**Oberammergau,** production quantity 2,500	**18.00**	**25.00**

SIGNATURE COLLECTION

ANGLER'S DREAM SERIES

☐ 1983	**Brook Trout,** artist: John Eggert, production quantity 9,800	**55.00**	**55.00**
☐ 1983	**Chinook Salmon,** artist: John Eggert, production quantity 9,800	**55.00**	**55.00**
☐ 1983	**Largemouth Bass,** artist: John Eggert, production quantity 9,800	**55.00**	**55.00**

	Issue Price	Current Value
☐ **1983** Striped Bass, artist: John Eggert, production quantity 9,800	**55.00**	**55.00**

BAKER STREET SERIES

	Issue Price	Current Value
☐ **1983** Sherlock Holmes, artist: Mitchell Hooks, production quantity 9,800	**55.00**	**55.00**
☐ **1983** Dr. Watson, artist: Mitchell Hooks, production quantity 9,800	**55.00**	**55.00**

CARNIVAL SERIES

	Issue Price	Current Value
☐ **1983** Knock 'Em Down, artist: Tom Newsom, production quantity 19,500	**39.95**	**39.95**
☐ **1983** Carousel, artist: Tom Newsom, production quantity 19,500	**39.95**	**39.95**
☐ **1983** Fortune Teller, artist: Tom Newsom, production quantity 19,500	**39.95**	**39.95**
☐ **1983** Ring the Bell, artist: Tom Newsom, production quantity 19,500	**39.95**	**39.95**

CHILDHOOD DELIGHTS

	Issue Price	Current Value
☐ **1983** Amanda, artist: Rob Sauber, production quantity 7,500	**45.00**	**45.00**

GRANDMA'S SCRAPBOOK

	Issue Price	Current Value
☐ **1983** Courting, artist: Robert Berran, production quantity 12,500	**45.00**	**45.00**

HOW DO I LOVE THEE SERIES

	Issue Price	Current Value
☐ **1983** Alaina, artist: Rob Sauber, production quantity 14,000	**39.95**	**41.00**
☐ **1983** Taylor, artist: Rob Sauber, production quantity 14,000	**39.95**	**41.00**
☐ **1983** Rendezvous, artist: Rob Sauber, production quantity 14,000	**39.95**	**41.00**
☐ **1983** Embrace, artist: Rob Sauber, production quantity 14,000	**39.95**	**41.00**

LEGENDS SERIES

	Issue Price	Current Value
☐ **1983** Paul Bunyan, artist: Carl Cassler, production quantity 10,000	**45.00**	**45.00**
☐ **1983** Rip Van Winkle, artist: Carl Cassler, production quantity 10,000	**45.00**	**45.00**

	Issue Price	Current Value

MELODIES OF CHILDHOOD

☐ 1983 **Twinkle, Twinkle, Little Star,** artist: Hector Girrado, production quantity 19,500	35.00	35.00
☐ 1983 **Row, Row, Row Your Boat,** artist: Hector Girrado, production quantity 19,500	39.95	39.95
☐ 1984 **Mary Had a Lamb,** artist: Hector Girrado, production quantity 19,500	35.00	35.00

SONGS OF STEPHEN FOSTER SERIES

☐ 1984 **Oh! Susannah,** artist: Rob Sauber, production quantity 3,500	60.00	60.00
☐ 1984 **I Dream of Jeanie with the Light Brown Hair,** artist: Rob Sauber, production quantity 3,500	60.00	60.00
☐ 1984 **Beautiful Dreamer,** artist: Rob Sauber, production quantity 3,500	60.00	60.00

UNICORN MAGIC SERIES

☐ 1983 **Morning Encounter,** artist: Jeffrey Ferreson, production quantity 10,000	50.00	50.00
☐ 1983 **Afternoon Offering,** artist: Jeffrey Ferreson, production quantity 10,000	50.00	50.00

VERY SPECIAL EDITION

☐ 1984 **The Wedding,** artist: Rob Sauber, production: unannounced	50.00	50.00
☐ 1984 **Happy Birthday,** artist: Rob Sauber, production: unannounced	50.00	50.00

SILVER CITY

CHRISTMAS SERIES

☐ 1969 **Winter Scene**	37.00	37.00
☐ 1970 **Water Mill**	25.00	27.00
☐ 1971 **Skating Scene**	25.00	27.00
☐ 1972 **Logging in Winter**	30.00	33.00
☐ 1973 **St. Claudens**	20.00	23.00

SINGLE RELEASE

☐ 1972 **Independence Hall**	13.50	16.00

SILVER CREATIONS

United States

AMERICANA SERIES	Issue Price	Current Value
☐ 1973 Clydesdales	150.00	150.00

HISTORY SERIES

☐ 1972 Churchillian Heritage, proof	550.00	575.00
☐ 1972 Churchillian Heritage	150.00	200.00
☐ 1973 Yalta Conference, proof	550.00	575.00
☐ 1973 Yalta Conference	150.00	150.00

SMITH GLASS

United States

AMERICANA SERIES

☐ 1971 Morgan Silver Dollar, production quantity 5,000	10.00	10.00

CHRISTMAS SERIES

☐ 1971 Family at Christmas	10.00	10.00
☐ 1972 Flying Angel	10.00	10.00
☐ 1973 St. Mary's in Mountains	10.00	10.00

FAMOUS AMERICANS SERIES

☐ 1971 Kennedy, production quantity 2,500	10.00	10.00
☐ 1971 Lincoln, production quantity 2,500	10.00	10.00
☐ 1972 Davis, production quantity 5,000	11.00	10.00
☐ 1972 Lee, production quantity 5,000	11.00	11.00

SOUTHERN LIVING GALLERY

United States

GAME BIRDS OF THE SOUTH SERIES

☐ 1983 Bobwhite Quail, artist: Antony Heritage, production quantity 19,500	39.95	39.95
☐ 1983 Mourning Dove, artist: Antony Heritage, production quantity 19,500	39.95	39.95
☐ 1983 Green-Winged Teal, artist: Antony Heritage, production quantity 19,500	39.95	39.95

		Issue Price	Current Value
☐ 1983	**Ring-Necked Pheasant,** artist: Antony Heritage, production quantity 19,500	39.95	39.95
☐ 1983	**Mallard Duck,** artist: Antony Heritage, production quantity 19,500	39.95	39.95
☐ 1983	**American Coot,** artist: Antony Heritage, production quantity 19,500	39.95	39.95
☐ 1983	**Ruffed Grouse,** artist: Antony Heritage, production quantity 19,500	39.95	39.95
☐ 1983	**Pintail Duck,** artist: Antony Heritage, production quantity 19,500	39.95	39.95
☐ 1983	**American Woodcock,** artist: Antony Heritage, production quantity 19,500	39.95	39.95
☐ 1983	**Canada Goose,** artist: Antony Heritage, production quantity 19,500	39.95	39.95
☐ 1983	**Wild Turkey,** artist: Antony Heritage, production quantity 19,500	39.95	39.95
☐ 1983	**Wood Duck,** artist: Antony Heritage, production quantity 19,500	39.95	39.95

SONGBIRDS OF THE SOUTH SERIES

		Issue Price	Current Value
☐ XX	**American Goldfinch,** artist: A. E. Ruffing, production quantity 19,500	39.95	39.95
☐ XX	**Tufted Titmouse,** artist: A. E. Ruffing, production quantity 19,500	39.95	39.95
☐ XX	**Red-Winged Blackbird,** artist: A. E. Ruffing, production quantity 19,500	39.95	39.95
☐ XX	**Mockingbird,** artist: A. E. Ruffing, production quantity 19,500	39.95	39.95
☐ XX	**Cardinal,** artist: A. E. Ruffing, production quantity 19,500	39.95	39.95
☐ XX	**Bluejay,** artist: A. E. Ruffing, production quantity 19,500	39.95	39.95
☐ XX	**Robin,** artist: A. E. Ruffing, production quantity 19,500	39.95	39.95

SOUTHERN FOREST FAMILIES SERIES

		Issue Price	Current Value
☐ XX	**Eastern Cottontail Rabbit,** artists: S./D. Barlowe, production quantity 19,500	39.95	39.95
☐ XX	**White-Tailed Deer,** artists: S./D. Barlowe, production quantity 19,500	39.95	39.95
☐ XX	**Raccoon,** artists: S./D. Barlowe, production quantity 19,500	39.95	39.95
☐ XX	**Striped Skunk,** artists: S./D. Barlowe, production quantity 19,500	39.95	39.95

		Issue Price	Current Value
☐ XX	**Bobcat,** artists: S./D. Barlowe, production quantity 19,500	39.95	39.95
☐ XX	**Fox Squirrel,** artists: S./D. Barlowe, production quantity 19,500	39.95	39.95
☐ XX	**Red Fox,** artists: S./D. Barlowe, production quantity 19,500	39.95	39.95
☐ XX	**Black Bear,** artists: S./D. Barlowe, production quantity 19,500	39.95	39.95
☐ XX	**Opossum,** artists: S./D. Barlowe, production quantity 19,500	39.95	39.95
☐ XX	**Chipmunk,** artists: S./D. Barlowe, production quantity 19,500	39.95	39.95
☐ XX	**Beaver,** artists: S./D. Barlowe, production quantity 19,500	39.95	39.95
☐ XX	**Mink,** artists: S./D. Barlowe, production quantity 19,500	39.95	39.95

WILDFLOWERS OF THE SOUTH SERIES

		Issue Price	Current Value
☐ XX	**Wild Honeysuckle,** artist: R. Mark, production quantity 19,500	39.95	39.95
☐ XX	**Frost Aster,** artist: R. Mark, production quantity 19,500	39.95	39.95
☐ XX	**Flowering Dogwood,** artist: R. Mark, production quantity 19,500	39.95	39.95
☐ XX	**Bee Balm,** artist: R. Mark, production quantity 19,500	39.95	39.95
☐ XX	**Queen Anne's Lace,** artist: R. Mark, production quantity 19,500	39.95	39.95
☐ XX	**Bluebonnet,** artist: R. Mark, production quantity 19,500	39.95	39.95
☐ XX	**Southern Magnolia,** artist: R. Mark, production quantity 19,500	39.95	39.95
☐ XX	**Birdsfoot Violet,** artist: R. Mark, production quantity 19,500	39.95	39.95
☐ XX	**Regal Lily,** artist: R. Mark, production quantity 19,500	39.95	39.95
☐ XX	**Lady Slipper Orchid,** artist: R. Mark, production quantity 19,500	39.95	39.95
☐ XX	**Black-Eyed Susan,** artist: R. Mark, production quantity 19,500	39.95	39.95
☐ XX	**Buttercup,** artist: R. Mark, production quantity 19,500	39.95	39.95

SPODE

Great Britain

	Issue Price	Current Value

AMERICAN SONGBIRDS SERIES

☐ **1970 Rufus-Sided Towhee,** artist: Ray Harm, production quantity 5,000 . . . .

☐ **1970 Winter Wren,** artist: Ray Harm, production quantity 5,000 . . . .

☐ **1971 Eastern Bluebird,** artist: Ray Harm, production quantity 5,000 . . . .

☐ **1971 Stellar's Jay,** artist: Ray Harm, production quantity 5,000 . . . .

☐ **1971 Eastern Mockingbird,** artist: Ray Harm, production quantity 5,000 . . . .

☐ **1971 Barn Swallow,** artist: Ray Harm, production quantity 5,000 . . . .

☐ **1971 Rose-Breasted Grosbeak,** artist: Ray Harm, production quantity 5,000 . . . .

☐ **1971 Cardinal,** artist: Ray Harm, production quantity 5,000 . . . .

☐ **1972 Western Tanager,** artist: Ray Harm, production quantity 5,000 . . . .

☐ **1972 Woodpecker,** artist: Ray Harm, production quantity 5,000 . . . .

☐ **1972 Chickadee,** artist: Ray Harm, production quantity 5,000 . . . .

☐ **1972 American Goldfinch,** artist: Ray Harm, production quantity 5,000 . . . .

Set of 12 . . . . **350.00**   **765.00**

CHRISTMAS SERIES

		Issue Price	Current Value
☐ 1970	**Partridge,** artist: Gillian West, production: one year	35.00	35.00
☐ 1971	**Angels Singing,** artist: Gillian West, production: one year	35.00	35.00
☐ 1972	**Three Ships A-sailing,** artist: Gillian West, production: one year	35.00	35.00
☐ 1973	**We Three Kings of Orient,** artist: Gillian West, production: one year	35.00	60.00
☐ 1974	**Deck the Halls,** artist: Gillian West, production: one year	35.00	45.00
☐ 1975	**Christbaum,** artist: Gillian West, production: one year	45.00	40.00
☐ 1976	**Good King Wenceslas,** artist: Gillian West, production: one year	45.00	40.00

		Issue Price	Current Value
☐ 1977	**Holly and Ivy,** artist: Gillian West, production: one year	**45.00**	**40.00**
☐ 1978	**While Shepherds Watched,** artist: Gillian West, production: one year	**45.00**	**45.00**
☐ 1979	**Away in a Manger,** artist: Gillian West, production: one year	**50.00**	**45.00**
☐ 1980	**Bringing in the Boar's Head,** artist: P. Wood, production: one year	**60.00**	**35.00**
☐ 1981	**Make We Merry,** artist: P. Wood, production: one year	**65.00**	**55.00**

CHRISTMAS PASTIMES SERIES

		Issue Price	Current Value
☐ 1982	**Sleigh Ride,** artist: unannounced, production: unannounced	**75.00**	**75.00**

MARITIME SERIES

		Issue Price	Current Value
☐ 1980	**USS United States and HMS Macedonian,** production quantity 2,000	**150.00**	**150.00**
☐ 1980	**USS President and HMS Little Belt,** production quantity 2,000	**150.00**	**150.00**
☐ 1980	**HMS Shannon and USS Chesapeake,** production quantity 2,000	**150.00**	**150.00**
☐ 1980	**USS Constitution and HMS Guerriere,** production quantity 2,000	**150.00**	**150.00**
☐ 1980	**USS Constitution and HMS Java,** production quantity 2,000	**150.00**	**150.00**
☐ 1980	**HMS Pelican and USS Argus,** production quantity 2,000	**150.00**	**150.00**

SINGLE RELEASES

		Issue Price	Current Value
☐ 1969	**Prince of Wales,** production quantity 1,500	**65.00**	**65.00**
☐ 1970	**Dickens**	**70.00**	**80.00**
☐ 1970	**Mayflower,** production quantity 2,500	**70.00**	**130.00**
☐ 1970	**Lowestoft**	**70.00**	**25.00**
☐ 1971	**Imperial Persia,** production quantity 10,000	**125.00**	**130.00**
☐ 1971	**Churchill,** production quantity 5,000	**110.00**	**120.00**
☐ 1972	**Passover,** production quantity 5,000	**59.00**	**45.00**
☐ 1972	**Cutty Sark**	**59.00**	**80.00**
☐ 1973	**Dickens's London**	**70.00**	**40.00**

SPORTS IMPRESSIONS

United States

BASEBALL SERIES	Issue Price	Current Value
☐ 1987 **Wade Boggs,** artist: Brian Johnson, production quantity 2,000	60.00	60.00
☐ 1987 **Wade Boggs,** artist: Brian Johnson, signed, production quantity 1,000	100.00	100.00
☐ 1987 **Darryl Strawberry,** artist: Robert Stephen Simon, production quantity 2,000	60.00	60.00
☐ 1987 **Darryl Strawberry,** artist: Robert Stephen Simon, signed, production quantity 1,000 . .	100.00	100.00
☐ 1987 **Keith Hernandez,** artist: Robert Stephen Simon, production quantity 2,000	60.00	60.00
☐ 1987 **Keith Hernandez,** artist: Robert Stephen Simon, signed, production quantity 1,000 . .	100.00	100.00
☐ 1987 **Gary Carter "The Kid,"** artist: Robert Stephen Simon, production quantity 2,000	60.00	60.00
☐ 1987 **Gary Carter "The Kid,"** artist: Robert Stephen Simon, signed, production quantity 1,000	125.00	125.00
☐ 1987 **Lenny Dykstra,** artist: Robert Stephen Simon, production quantity 1,000	60.00	60.00
☐ 1987 **Lenny Dykstra,** artist: Robert Stephen Simon, signed, production quantity 1,000 . .	100.00	100.00
☐ 1987 **Carl Yastremski,** artist: Robert Stephen Simon, production quantity 3,000	60.00	60.00
☐ 1987 **Carl Yastremski,** artist: Robert Stephen Simon, signed, production quantity 1,500 . .	125.00	125.00
☐ 1987 **Mantle, "Mickey at Night,"** artist: Robert Stephen Simon, production quantity 3,500	60.00	60.00
☐ 1987 **Mantle, "Mickey at Night,"** artist: Robert Stephen Simon, signed, production quantity 1,500	100.00	100.00

BASKETBALL SERIES

	Issue Price	Current Value
☐ 1987 **Larry Bird,** artist: Robert Stephen Simon, production quantity 5,000	60.00	60.00
☐ 1987 **Larry Bird,** artist: Robert Stephen Simon, signed, production quantity 2,000	125.00	125.00

DON MATTINGLY SERIES

	Issue Price	Current Value
☐ 1987 **Player of the Year,** artist: Brian Johnson, production quantity 5,000	60.00	60.00

Wade Boggs, artist:
Brian Johnson.

Darryl Strawberry,
artist: Robert Stephen
Simon.

Keith Hernandez, artist:
Robert Stephen Simon.

Gary Carter "The Kid,"
artist: Robert Stephen
Simon.

Lenny Dykstra, artist:
Robert Stephen Simon.

Carl Yastremski, artist:
Robert Stephen Simon.

Mantle, "Mickey At Night," artist: Robert Stephen Simon.

Larry Bird, artist: Robert Stephen Simon.

		Issue Price	Current Value
☐ 1987	**Player of the Year,** artist: Brian Johnson, signed, production quantity 5,000	**125.00**	**125.00**

Player of the Year,
artist: Brian Johnson.

STANEK, FRANZ

SINGLE RELEASES	Issue Price	Current Value
☐ 1969 **Moon Landing,** production quantity 150 ...	250.00	1100.00
☐ 1972 **Mayflower,** production quantity 60	250.00	650.00
☐ 1972 **Santa Maria,** production quantity 60	250.00	600.00
☐ 1973 **Eagle,** production quantity 400	250.00	250.00

STERLING AMERICA

United States

CHRISTMAS CUSTOMS SERIES

	Issue Price	Current Value
☐ 1970 **Yule Log,** production quantity 2,500	18.00	30.00
☐ 1971 **Holland,** production quantity 2,500	18.00	28.00
☐ 1972 **Norway,** production quantity 2,500	18.00	20.00
☐ 1973 **Germany,** production quantity 2,500	20.00	23.00
☐ 1974 **Mexico,** production quantity 2,500	24.00	27.00

MOTHER'S DAY SERIES

	Issue Price	Current Value
☐ 1971 **Mare and Foal,** production quantity 2,500	18.00	25.00
☐ 1972 **Horned Owl,** production quantity 2,500 ...	18.00	25.00
☐ 1973 **Raccoons,** production quantity 2,500	20.00	20.00
☐ 1974 **Deer,** production quantity 2,500	24.00	25.00
☐ 1975 **Quail,** production quantity 2,500	24.00	25.00

	Issue Price	Current Value

TWELVE DAYS OF CHRISTMAS SERIES

		Issue Price	Current Value
☐ 1970	**Partridge,** production quantity 2,500	**18.00**	**25.00**
☐ 1971	**Turtle Doves,** production quantity 2,500 . . .	**18.00**	**25.00**
☐ 1972	**French Hens,** production quantity 2,500 . . .	**18.00**	**25.00**
☐ 1973	**Colly Birds,** production quantity 2,500	**18.00**	**25.00**
☐ 1974	**Five Rings,** production quantity 2,500	**24.00**	**25.00**
☐ 1975	**Six Geese,** production quantity 2,500	**24.00**	**25.00**
☐ 1976	**Seven Swans,** production quantity 2,500 . . .	**24.00**	**25.00**
☐ 1977	**Eight Maids,** production quantity 2,500 . . .	**28.00**	**25.00**

STIEFF

United States

BICENTENNIAL SERIES

☐ 1972	**Declaration of Independence,** production quantity 10,000	**50.00**	**50.00**
☐ 1974	**Betsy Ross,** production quantity 10,000 . . .	**50.00**	**50.00**
☐ 1975	**Crossing Delaware,** production quantity 10,000	**50.00**	**50.00**
☐ 1976	**Serapio and Bon Homme,** production quantity 10,000	**50.00**	**50.00**

STRATFORD COLLECTION

United States

FAMOUS CLOWNS SERIES

☐ 1982	**Emmett Looking Out to See,** artist: Robert Blottiaux, production quantity 10,000	**35.00**	**35.00**
☐ 1982	**Jack Thum and Child,** artist: Robert Blottiaux, production quantity 10,000	**35.00**	**35.00**

FOUR SEASONS OF THE UNICORN SERIES

☐ 1983	**Unicorn in Winter,** artist: Michele Livingstone, production quantity 10,000	**45.00**	**45.00**

REAL CHILDREN SERIES

☐ 1982	**Michael's Miracle,** artist: Nancy Turner, production quantity 19,500	**39.50**	**45.00**
☐ 1983	**Susan's World,** artist: Nancy Turner, production quantity 19,500	**45.00**	**45.00**

		Issue Price	Current Value
YOUNG WILDLIFE SERIES			
☐ 1982	**Siberian Cub at Play,** artist: Robert Blottiaux, production quantity 15,000	35.00	35.00
☐ 1982	**Curious Raccoon,** artist: Robert Blottiaux, production quantity 15,000	35.00	35.00

STUART DEVLIN SILVER

United States

AMERICANA SERIES

☐ 1972	**Gaspee Incident,** production quantity 1,000	130.00	145.00

STUART INTERNATIONAL

United States

CHILDHOOD SECRETS SERIES

☐ 1983	Billy's Treasure, artist: Nancy Turner, production quantity 19,500	39.50	40.00

STUDIO DANTE DI VOLTERADICI

Italy

BENVENUTI'S MUSES SERIES

☐ 1985	**Erato,** artist: Sergio Benvenuti, production: unannounced	50.00	50.00
☐ 1985	**Clio,** artist: Sergio Benvenuti, production: unannounced	50.00	50.00
☐ 1986	**Terpsichore,** artist: Sergio Benvenuti, production: unannounced	55.00	55.00
☐ 1986	**Euterpe,** artist: Sergio Benvenuti, production: unannounced	55.00	55.00

GHIBERTI DOORS

☐ 1983	**Adoration of the Magi,** artist: Alberto Santangela, production: unannounced	50.00	100.00
☐ 1984	**The Nativity,** artist: Alberto Santangela, production: unannounced	50.00	50.00
☐ 1985	**The Annunciation,** artist: Alberto Santangela, production: unannounced	50.00	55.00

		Issue Price	Current Value
☐ 1985	**Christ Among the Doctors,** artist: Alberto Santangela, production: unannounced	55.00	55.00
☐ 1986	**Christ Walks on the Water,** artist: Alberto Santangela, production: unannounced	55.00	55.00
☐ 1986	**The Expulsion of the Money Changers,** artist: Alberto Santangela, production: unannounced	55.00	55.00

GRAND OPERA SERIES

☐ 1976	**Rigoletto,** artist: Gino Ruggeri, production: one year	35.00	38.00
☐ 1977	**Madam Butterfly,** artist: Gino Ruggeri, production: one year	35.00	38.00
☐ 1978	**Carmen,** artist: Gino Ruggeri, production: one year	40.00	40.00
☐ 1979	**Aida,** artist: Gino Ruggeri, production: one year	40.00	40.00
☐ 1980	**Barber of Seville,** artist: Franco Ingargiola, production: one year	40.00	40.00
☐ 1981	**Tosca,** artist: Franco Ingargiola, production: one year	40.00	40.00
☐ 1982	**I Pagliacci,** artist: Franco Ingargiola, production: one year	40.00	100.00

MADONNE VIVENTI
(Living Madonnas Series)

☐ 1978	**Madonna Pensosa (The Pensive Madonna),** artist: Ado Santini, production: unannounced	45.00	45.00
☐ 1979	**Madonna Serena (The Serene Madonna),** artist: Alberto Santangela, production: unannounced	45.00	45.00
☐ 1980	**Madonna Beata (The Beatific Madonna),** artist: Alberto Santangela, production: unannounced	45.00	45.00
☐ 1981	**Madonna Profetica (The Prophetic Madonna),** artist: Alberto Santangela, production: unannounced	45.00	45.00
☐ 1982	**Madonna Modesta (The Demure Madonna),** artist: Alberto Santangela, production: unannounced	45.00	60.00
☐ 1983	**Madonna Saggio (The Wise Madonna),** artist: Alberto Santangela, production: unannounced	45.00	90.00

The Nativity, artist: Alberto Santangela.

The Annunciation, artist: Alberto Santangela.

Christ Among the Doctors, artist: Alberto Santangela.

		Issue Price	Current Value
☐ 1984	**Madonna Tenera (The Tender Madonna),** artist: Alberto Santangela, production: unannounced	**45.00**	**55.00**

STUMAR

Germany

CHRISTMAS SERIES

☐ 1970	**Angel,** production quantity 10,000	**8.00**	**35.00**
☐ 1971	**The Old Canal,** production quantity 10,000	**8.00**	**25.00**
☐ 1972	**Countryside,** production quantity 10,000 ...	**10.00**	**23.00**
☐ 1973	**Friendship,** production quantity 10,000 ...	**10.00**	**20.00**
☐ 1974	**Making Fancy,** production quantity 10,000	**10.00**	**20.00**
☐ 1975	**Christmas,** production quantity 10,000	**10.00**	**20.00**
☐ 1976	**Christmas,** production quantity 10,000	**15.00**	**20.00**
☐ 1977	**Joyful Expectations,** production quantity 10,000	**15.00**	**20.00**
☐ 1978	**Christmas,** production quantity 10,000	**19.50**	**20.00**

EGYPTIAN SERIES

☐ 1977	**Ancient Egyptian Trilogy,** production quantity 5,000	**45.00**	**45.00**
☐ 1978	**Charioteer,** production quantity 5,000	**54.00**	**54.00**

MOTHER'S DAY SERIES

☐ 1971	**Amish Mother and Daughter,** production quantity 10,000	**8.00**	**35.00**
☐ 1972	**Children,** production quantity 10,000	**8.00**	**22.00**
☐ 1973	**Mother Sewing,** production quantity 10,000	**10.00**	**21.00**
☐ 1974	**Mother, Cradle,** production quantity 10,000	**10.00**	**20.00**
☐ 1975	**Baking,** production quantity 10,000	**10.00**	**20.00**
☐ 1976	**Reading to Children,** production quantity 10,000	**15.00**	**15.00**
☐ 1977	**Comforting Child,** production quantity 10,000	**15.00**	**20.00**
☐ 1978	**Tranquility,** production quantity 10,000 ...	**19.50**	**20.00**

TIRSCHENREUTH

Germany

CHRISTMAS SERIES	Issue Price	Current Value
☐ 1969 **Homestead,** production quantity 3,500	12.00	25.00
☐ 1970 **Church,** production quantity 3,500	12.00	15.00
☐ 1971 **Star of Bethlehem,** production quantity 3,500	12.00	15.00
☐ 1972 **Elk,** production quantity 3,500	13.00	15.00
☐ 1973 **Christmas,** production quantity 3,500	14.00	15.00

SONGBIRDS OF EUROPE SERIES

☐ 1985 **Blue Titmouse,** artist: Ursula Band, production: 100 firing days	19.50	20.00
☐ 1985 **Firecrest,** artist: Ursula Band, production: 100 firing days	19.50	20.00
☐ 1986 **Corsican Nuthatch,** artist: Ursula Band, production: 100 firing days	22.50	23.00
☐ 1986 **Golden Oriole,** artist: Ursula Band, production: 100 firing days	22.50	23.00
☐ 1986 **Great Titmouse,** artist: Ursula Band, production: 100 firing days	22.50	23.00
☐ 1986 **Red Robin,** artist: Ursula Band, production: 100 firing days	22.50	23.00
☐ 1987 **Chaffinch,** artist: Ursula Band, production: 100 firing days	24.50	25.00

TOPSY TURVY

United States

STORYBOOK SERIES
(From illustrations in antique storybooks)

☐ 1982 **Hares and Hounds,** production quantity 10,000	19.50	20.00
☐ 1982 **Ostrich and Elephant,** production quantity 10,000	19.50	20.00

TOWLE SILVERSMITHS

United States

CHRISTMAS SERIES

☐ 1972 **Wise Men,** production quantity 2,500	250.00	250.00

	Issue Price	Current Value
VALENTINES		
☐ 1972 **Single Heart,** production: one year	**10.00**	**10.00**
☐ 1973 **Entwined Hearts,** production: one year	**10.00**	**10.00**

UNITED STATES GALLERY OF ART

United States

SINGLE ISSUE

☐ 1984 **Innocence,** artist: Jack Woodson, production quantity N/A	**24.50**	**25.00**

U.S. HISTORICAL SOCIETY

United States

ANNUAL HISTORICAL SERIES

☐ 1977 **Great Events,** production quantity 5,000 ...	**60.00**	**65.00**
☐ 1978 **Great Events,** production quantity 10,000 ..	**75.00**	**80.00**

ANNUAL SPRING FLOWERS SERIES

☐ 1983 **Flowers in a Blue Vase,** artist: J. Clark, production quantity 10,000	**135.00**	**150.00**
☐ 1984 **Spring Flowers,** artist: M. Wampler, production quantity	**135.00**	**135.00**

ANNUAL STAINED GLASS AND PEWTER CHRISTMAS SERIES

☐ 1978 **The Nativity—Canterbury Cathedral,** production quantity 10,000	**97.00**	**175.00**
☐ 1979 **Flight into Egypt—St. John's, New York,** production quantity 10,000	**97.00**	**175.00**
☐ 1980 **Madonna and Child—Washington Cathedral,** production quantity 10,000	**125.00**	**175.00**
☐ 1981 **The Magi—St. Paul's, San Francisco,** production quantity 10,000	**125.00**	**175.00**
☐ 1982 **Flight into Egypt—Los Angeles Cathedral,** production quantity 10,000	**135.00**	**175.00**
☐ 1983 **The Shepherds at Bethlehem—St. John's, New Orleans,** production quantity 10,000 ..	**135.00**	**150.00**
☐ 1984 **The Nativity—St. Anthony's, St. Louis,** production quantity 10,000	**135.00**	**135.00**

		Issue Price	Current Value
☐ 1985	**Good Tidings of Great Joy—Boston,** production quantity 10,000	160.00	160.00
☐ 1986	**The Nativity—Old St. Mary's Church, Philadelphia,** production quantity 10,000	160.00	160.00
☐ 1987	**O Come, Little Children,** production quantity 10,000	160.00	—

AUDUBON'S BIRDS SERIES

☐ 1986	**Audubon and the Bluejay,** artist: J. Woodson, production quantity 10,000	135.00	135.00

BUFFALO BILL'S WILD WEST SERIES

☐ 1984	**Pony Express,** artist: Jack Woodson, production quantity 5,000	55.00	55.00
☐ 1984	**Annie Oakley,** artist: Jack Woodson, production quantity 5,000	55.00	55.00
☐ 1984	**Sitting Bull,** artist: Jack Woodson, production quantity 5,000	55.00	55.00
☐ XX	**Buffalo Hunter,** artist: Jack Woodson, production quantity 5,000	55.00	55.00
☐ XX	**Farewell Appearance,** artist: Jack Woodson, production quantity 5,000	55.00	55.00
☐ XX	**Deadwood Stage,** artist: Jack Woodson, production quantity 5,000	55.00	55.00
☐ XX	**Congress of the Rough Riders,** artist: Jack Woodson, production quantity 5,000	55.00	55.00
☐ XX	**Royal Visit,** artist: Jack Woodson, production quantity 5,000	55.00	55.00

CHRISTMAS CAROL SERIES

☐ 1982	**Deck the Halls with Boughs of Holly,** artist: J. Landis, production quantity 10,000	55.00	65.00
☐ 1983	**O Christmas Tree,** artist: J. Woodson, production quantity 10,000	55.00	65.00
☐ 1984	**Winter Wonderland,** artist: J. Woodson, production quantity 10,000	55.00	55.00
☐ 1985	**Here We Come A-Caroling,** artist: J. Woodson, production quantity 10,000	55.00	55.00
☐ 1986	**The Christmas Song,** artist: J. Woodson, production quantity 10,000	55.00	55.00
☐ 1987	**I Heard the Bells on Christmas Day,** artist: J. Landis, production quantity 10,000	55.00	55.00

	Issue Price	Current Value
DACEY SERIES		
☐ **1984** **Melodies of Stephen Foster,** artist: Robert Dacey, production: unannounced	**19.50**	**20.00**
EASTER SERIES		
☐ **1987** **The Good Shepherd,** artist: Jack Woodson, production quantity 5,000	**160.00**	**160.00**
GREAT AMERICAN SAILING SHIPS SERIES		
☐ **1983** **Old Ironsides,** artist: Jack Woodson, production quantity 10,000	**135.00**	**150.00**
☐ **1984** **Charles W. Morgan,** artist: Jack Woodson, production quantity 10,000	**135.00**	**135.00**
☐ **1985** **Flying Cloud,** artist: Jack Woodson, production quantity 10,000	**135.00**	**135.00**
STAINED GLASS CATHEDRAL CHRISTMAS SERIES		
☐ **1978** **Canterbury Cathedral,** production quantity 10,000	**87.00**	**95.00**
☐ **1979** **Flight into Egypt,** production quantity 10,000	**97.00**	**97.00**
☐ **1980** **Madonna and Child,** production quantity 10,000	**125.00**	**150.00**
☐ **1981** **The Magi,** production quantity 10,000	**125.00**	**125.00**
☐ **1982** **Flight into Egypt,** production quantity 10,000	**125.00**	**125.00**
☐ **1983** **Shepherds at Bethlehem,** production quantity 10,000	**150.00**	**150.00**
STAINED GLASS MOTHER'S DAY		
☐ **1987** **A Mother's Love,** artist: Nancy Noel, production quantity 5,000	**160.00**	**160.00**
STAINED GLASS AND PEWTER SPECIAL ISSUES		
☐ **1986** **Texas Sesquicentennial Commemorative,** artist: Jack Woodson, production quantity 10,000	**135.00**	**135.00**
☐ **1986** **Statue of Liberty,** artist: Jack Woodson, production quantity 10,000	**135.00**	**135.00**

	Issue Price	Current Value

TWO HUNDRED YEARS OF FLIGHT SERIES

☐ **1984 Man's First Flight,** artist: Jack Woodson, production quantity 5,000 . . . . 48.75 49.00

☐ **1984 Miracle at Kitty Hawk,** artist: Jack Woodson, production quantity 5,000 . . . . 48.75 49.00

☐ **1984 China Clipper,** artist: Jack Woodson, production quantity 5,000 . . . . 48.75 49.00

☐ **1984 Man in Space,** artist: Jack Woodson, production quantity 5,000 . . . . 48.75 49.00

YOUNG AMERICA SERIES

☐ **1972 Young America of Winslow Homer,** artist: Winslow Homer, production quantity 2,500 (Set of six) 425.00 1100.00

D. H. USSHER LTD.

Canada

THE MASTERWORKS OF BENJAMIN CHEE CHEE SERIES

☐ **1986 Friends,** artist: Benjamin Chee Chee, production: ten days 32.50 32.50

☐ **1986 Good Morning,** artist: Benjamin Chee Chee, production: ten days 32.50 32.50

VAGUE SHADOWS

United States

THE ARABIANS SERIES

☐ **1987 Silver Streak,** artist: Gregory Perillo, production quantity 3,500 . . . . 95.00 95.00

ARCTIC FRIENDS SERIES

☐ **1982 Siberian Love and Snow Pals,** artist: Gregory Perillo, production quantity 7,500 (Set of two) 100.00 180.00

Silver Streak, artist:
Gregory Perillo.

		Issue Price	Current Value
CHIEFTAIN SERIES			
□ 1979	**Chief Sitting Bull,** artist: Gregory Perillo, production quantity 7,500	65.00	550.00
□ 1979	**Chief Joseph,** artist: Gregory Perillo, production quantity 7,500	65.00	100.00
□ 1980	**Chief Red Cloud,** artist: Gregory Perillo, production quantity 7,500	65.00	140.00
□ 1980	**Geronimo,** artist: Gregory Perillo, production quantity 7,500	65.00	90.00
□ 1981	**Chief Crazy Horse,** artist: Gregory Perillo, production quantity 7,500	65.00	150.00
CHIEFTAIN II SERIES			
□ 1983	**Chief Pontiac,** artist: Gregory Perillo, production quantity 7,500	70.00	70.00
□ 1984	**Chief Victorio,** artist: Gregory Perillo, production quantity 7,500	70.00	70.00
□ 1984	**Chief Tecumseh,** artist: Gregory Perillo, production quantity 7,500	70.00	70.00
□ 1984	**Chief Cochise,** artist: Gregory Perillo, production quantity 7,500	70.00	70.00
□ 1984	**Chief Black Kettle,** artist: Gregory Perillo, production quantity 7,500	70.00	70.00

		Issue Price	Current Value

CHILDLIFE SERIES

☐ **1983** **Siesta,** artist: Gregory Perillo, production quantity 10,000 .... **45.00** **45.00**

☐ **1984** **Sweet Dreams,** artist: Gregory Perillo, production quantity 10,000 .... **45.00** **45.00**

INDIAN NATIONS SERIES

☐ **1983** **Blackfoot,** artist: Gregory Perillo, production quantity 7,500 .... **35.00** **50.00**

☐ **1983** **Cheyenne,** artist: Gregory Perillo, production quantity 7,500 .... **35.00** **50.00**

☐ **1983** **Apache,** artist: Gregory Perillo, production quantity 7,500 .... **35.00** **50.00**

☐ **1983** **Sioux,** artist: Gregory Perillo, production quantity 7,500 .... **35.00** **50.00**

LEGENDS OF THE WEST SERIES

☐ **1982** **Daniel Boone,** artist: Gregory Perillo, production quantity 10,000 .... **65.00** **65.00**

☐ **1983** **Davy Crockett,** artist: Gregory Perillo, production quantity 10,000 .... **65.00** **65.00**

☐ **1984** **Kit Carson,** artist: Gregory Perillo, production quantity 10,000 .... **65.00** **65.00**

☐ **1984** **Buffalo Bill,** artist: Gregory Perillo, production quantity 10,000 .... **65.00** **65.00**

MASTERWORKS OF IMPRESSIONISM SERIES

☐ **1980** **Woman with a Parasol,** production quantity 17,500 .... **35.00** **35.00**

☐ **1981** **Young Mother Sewing,** production quantity 17,500 .... **35.00** **35.00**

MASTERWORKS OF ROCKWELL SERIES

☐ **1980** **After Prom,** production quantity 17,500 .... **35.00** **38.00**

☐ **1981** **Challenger,** production quantity 17,500 .... **42.50** **45.00**

MASTERWORKS OF THE WEST SERIES

☐ **1980** **Texas Night Herder,** production quantity 17,500 .... **35.00** **38.00**

☐ **1981** **Indian Scout,** production quantity 17,500 .. **35.00** **38.00**

		Issue Price	Current Value

MOTHERHOOD ANNUAL SERIES

☐ **1983** **Madre,** artist: Gregory Perillo, production quantity 10,000 ... **50.00** **100.00**
☐ **1984** **Madonna of Plains,** artist: Gregory Perillo, production quantity 3,500 ... **50.00** **75.00**

NATURE'S HARMONY SERIES

☐ **1982** **Peaceable Kingdom,** artist: Gregory Perillo, production quantity 12,500 ... **100.00** **100.00**
☐ **1982** **Zebra,** artist: Gregory Perillo, production quantity 12,500 ... **50.00** **50.00**
☐ **1982** **Bengal Tiger,** artist: Gregory Perillo, production quantity 12,500 ... **50.00** **50.00**
☐ **1982** **Black Panther,** artist: Gregory Perillo, production quantity 12,500 ... **50.00** **50.00**
☐ **1982** **Elephant,** artist: Gregory Perillo, production quantity 12,500 ... **50.00** **50.00**

PERILLO'S SANTA SERIES

☐ **1980** **Santa's Joy,** artist: Gregory Perillo, production: one year ... **29.95** **29.95**
☐ **1981** **Santa's Bundle,** artist: Gregory Perillo, production: one year ... **29.95** **29.95**

THE PLAINSMEN SERIES

☐ **1978** **Buffalo Hunt,** artist: Gregory Perillo, production quantity 2,500 ... **300.00** **350.00**
☐ **1979** **The Proud One,** artist: Gregory Perillo, production quantity 2,500 ... **300.00** **350.00**

PRIDE OF AMERICA'S INDIANS SERIES

☐ **1986** **Brave and Free,** artist: Gregory Perillo, production: 10 days ... **24.50** **24.50**
☐ **1986** **Dark-Eyed Friends,** artist: Gregory Perillo, production: 10 days ... **24.50** **24.50**
☐ **1986** **Noble Companions,** artist: Gregory Perillo, production: 10 days ... **24.50** **24.50**
☐ **1987** **Kindred Spirits,** artist: Gregory Perillo, production: 10 days ... **24.50** **24.50**
☐ **1987** **Loyal Alliance,** artist: Gregory Perillo, production: 10 days ... **24.50** **24.50**
☐ **1987** **Small and Wise,** artist: Gregory Perillo, production: 10 days ... **24.50** **24.50**
☐ **1987** **Winter Scouts,** artist: Gregory Perillo, production: 10 days ... **24.50** **24.50**

**Dark-Eyed Friends,
artist: Gregory Perillo.**

**Noble Companions,
artist: Gregory Perillo.**

**Kindred Spirits, artist:
Gregory Perillo.**

**Loyal Alliance, artist:
Gregory Perillo.**

**Small and Wise, artist:
Gregory Perillo.**

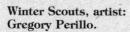

**Winter Scouts, artist:
Gregory Perillo.**

		Issue Price	Current Value
☐ 1987	**Peaceful Comrades,** artist: Gregory Perillo, production: 10 days	24.50	24.50

THE PRINCESSES SERIES

☐ 1981	**Lily of the Mohawks,** artist: Gregory Perillo, production quantity 7,500	50.00	100.00
☐ 1981	**Pocahontas,** artist: Gregory Perillo, production quantity 7,500	50.00	80.00
☐ 1982	**Minnehaha,** artist: Gregory Perillo, production quantity 7,500	50.00	75.00
☐ 1982	**Sacajawea,** artist: Gregory Perillo, production quantity 7,500	50.00	75.00

THE PROFESSIONALS SERIES

☐ 1979	**The Big Leaguer,** artist: Gregory Perillo, production quantity 15,000	29.95	135.00
☐ 1980	**Ballerina's Dilemma,** artist: Gregory Perillo, production quantity 15,000	32.50	60.00
☐ 1981	**Quarterback,** artist: Gregory Perillo, production quantity 15,000	32.50	35.00
☐ 1981	**Rodeo Joe,** artist: Gregory Perillo, production quantity 15,000	35.00	35.00
☐ 1982	**Major Leaguer,** artist: Gregory Perillo, production quantity 15,000	35.00	45.00

Peaceful Comrades,
artist: Gregory Perillo.

		Issue Price	Current Value
□ 1983	**The Hockey Player,** artist: Gregory Perillo, production quantity 15,000	35.00	35.00

THE STORYBOOK COLLECTION

		Issue Price	Current Value
□ 1980	**Little Red Riding Hood,** artist: Gregory Perillo, production: less than one year	45.00	45.00
□ 1981	**Cinderella,** artist: Gregory Perillo, production: less than one year	45.00	45.00
□ 1981	**Hansel and Gretel,** artist: Gregory Perillo, production: less than one year	45.00	45.00
□ 1982	**Goldilocks and the Three Bears,** artist: Gregory Perillo, production: 18 days	45.00	45.00

THE THOROUGHBREDS SERIES

		Issue Price	Current Value
□ 1984	**Man-o-War,** artist: Gregory Perillo, production quantity 9,500	50.00	50.00
□ 1984	**Seabiscuit,** artist: Gregory Perillo, production quantity 9,500	50.00	50.00
□ 1984	**Secretariat,** artist: Gregory Perillo, production quantity 9,500	50.00	80.00
□ 1984	**Whirlaway,** artist: Gregory Perillo, production quantity 9,500	50.00	90.00

TRIBAL PONIES SERIES

		Issue Price	Current Value
□ 1984	**Arapaho,** artist: Gregory Perillo, production quantity 3,500	65.00	65.00
□ 1984	**Comanche,** artist: Gregory Perillo, production quantity 3,500	65.00	65.00
□ 1984	**Crow,** artist: Gregory Perillo, production quantity 3,500	65.00	90.00

WAR PONIES SERIES

		Issue Price	Current Value
□ 1983	**Sioux,** artist: Gregory Perillo, production quantity 7,500	60.00	120.00
□ 1984	**Nez Perce,** artist: Gregory Perillo, production quantity 7,500	60.00	100.00
□ 1984	**Apache,** artist: Gregory Perillo, production quantity 7,500	60.00	100.00

SINGLE RELEASES

		Issue Price	Current Value
□ 1981	**Apache Boy,** artist: Gregory Perillo, production quantity 5,000	95.00	175.00

		Issue Price	Current Value
☐ 1981	**Perillo Litho Book,** artist: Gregory Perillo, production quantity 3,000	95.00	95.00
☐ 1983	**Papoose,** artist: Gregory Perillo, production quantity 3,000	100.00	100.00
☐ 1987	**Navajo Boy,** artist: Gregory Perillo, production quantity 3,500	95.00	95.00

VAL ST. LAMBERT

Belgium

AMERICAN HERITAGE SERIES

☐ 1969	**Pilgrim Fathers,** production quantity 500 ..	200.00	450.00
☐ 1970	**Paul Revere's Ride,** production quantity 500	200.00	225.00
☐ 1971	**Washington on Delaware,** production quantity 500	200.00	225.00

ANNUAL OLD MASTERS SERIES

☐ 1969	**Reubens and Rembrandt,** pair, production quantity 5,000	50.00	90.00
☐ 1969	**Van Gogh and Van Dyck,** pair, production quantity 5,000	50.00	85.00
☐ 1970	**Da Vinci and Michelangelo,** pair, production quantity 5,000	50.00	90.00
☐ 1971	**El Greco and Goya,** pair, production quantity 5,000	50.00	85.00
☐ 1972	**Reynolds and Gainsborough,** pair, production quantity 5,000	50.00	70.00

SINGLE RELEASE

☐ 1970	**Rembrandt**	25.00	40.00

VENETO FLAIR

Italy

AMERICAN LANDSCAPE SERIES

☐ 1979	**Hudson Valley,** production quantity 7,500	75.00	75.00
☐ 1980	**Northwest Cascade,** production quantity 7,500	75.00	80.00

	Issue Price	Current Value

BELLINI SERIES

☐ 1971 **Madonna,** artist: Vincente Tiziano, production quantity 500 .... **45.00** **425.00**

BIRDS SERIES

☐ 1972 **Owl,** production quantity 2,000 .... **37.50** **100.00**
☐ 1973 **Falcon,** production quantity 2,000 .... **37.50** **37.50**
☐ 1974 **Mallard,** production quantity 2,000 .... **45.00** **45.00**

CATS SERIES

☐ 1974 **Persian,** production quantity 2,000 .... **40.00** **55.00**
☐ 1975 **Siamese,** production quantity 2,000 .... **45.00** **55.00**
☐ 1976 **Tabby,** production quantity 2,000 .... **45.00** **55.00**

CHILDREN'S CHRISTMAS SERIES

☐ 1979 **The Carolers,** artist: Vincente Tiziano, production quantity 7,500 .... **60.00** **60.00**
☐ 1980 **Heading Home,** artist: Vincente Tiziano, production quantity 7,500 .... **75.00** **75.00**
☐ 1981 **The Night Before,** artist: Vincente Tiziano, production quantity 7,500 .... **95.00** **95.00**
☐ 1982 **A Visit to Santa,** artist: Vincente Tiziano, production quantity 7,500 .... **95.00** **95.00**

CHRISTMAS SERIES

☐ 1971 **Three Kings,** artist: Vincente Tiziano, production quantity 1,500 .... **55.00** **160.00**
☐ 1972 **Shepherds,** artist: Vincente Tiziano, production quantity 2,000 .... **55.00** **90.00**
☐ 1973 **Christ Child,** artist: Vincente Tiziano, production quantity 2,000 .... **55.00** **55.00**
☐ 1974 **Angel,** artist: Vincente Tiziano, production quantity 2,000 .... **55.00** **55.00**

CHRISTMAS CARD SERIES

☐ 1975 **Christmas Eve,** artist: Vincente Tiziano, production quantity 5,000 .... **37.50** **40.00**
☐ 1976 **Old North Church,** artist: Vincente Tiziano, production quantity 5,000 .... **37.50** **40.00**
☐ 1977 **Log Cabin Christmas,** artist: Vincente Tiziano, production quantity 5,000 .... **37.50** **40.00**
☐ 1978 **Dutch Christmas,** artist: Vincente Tiziano, production quantity 5,000 .... **40.00** **50.00**

		Issue Price	Current Value

DOG SERIES

		Issue Price	Current Value
□ 1972	**German Shepherd,** artist: Vincente Tiziano, production quantity 2,000	37.50	75.00
□ 1973	**Poodle,** artist: Vincente Tiziano, production quantity 2,000	37.50	45.00
□ 1974	**Doberman,** artist: Vincente Tiziano, production quantity 2,000	37.50	35.00
□ 1975	**Collie,** artist: Vincente Tiziano, production quantity 2,000	40.00	45.00
□ 1976	**Dachshund,** artist: Vincente Tiziano, production quantity 2,000	45.00	45.00

EASTER SERIES

□ 1973	**Rabbits,** production quantity 2,000	50.00	90.00
□ 1974	**Chicks,** production quantity 2,000	50.00	55.00
□ 1975	**Lamb,** production quantity 2,000	50.00	55.00
□ 1976	**Composite,** production quantity 2,000	50.00	55.00

FLOWER CHILDREN SERIES

□ 1978	**Rose,** production quantity 3,000	45.00	45.00
□ 1979	**Orchid,** production quantity 3,000	60.00	60.00
□ 1980	**Camelia,** production quantity 3,000	65.00	65.00

FOUR SEASONS SERIES

□ 1972	**Fall,** sterling, production quantity 2,000 ...	125.00	130.00
□ 1972	**Fall,** silver plate, production quantity 2,000	75.00	100.00
□ 1973	**Winter,** sterling, production quantity 250 ..	125.00	125.00
□ 1973	**Winter,** silver plate, production quantity 2,000	75.00	90.00
□ 1973	**Spring,** sterling, production quantity 750 ..	125.00	125.00
□ 1973	**Spring,** silver plate, production quantity 300	75.00	75.00
□ 1974	**Summer,** sterling, production quantity 750	125.00	125.00
□ 1974	**Summer,** silver plate, production quantity 300	75.00	75.00

GODDESS SERIES

□ 1973	**Pomona,** production quantity 1,500	75.00	125.00
□ 1974	**Diana,** production quantity 1,500	75.00	75.00

LA BELLE FEMME SERIES

□ 1978	**Lily,** production quantity 9,500	70.00	70.00
□ 1979	**Gigi,** production quantity 9,500	76.50	77.00
□ 1980	**Dominique,** production quantity 9,500	76.50	77.00
□ 1980	**Gabrielle,** production quantity 9,500	76.50	77.00

		Issue Price	Current Value

LAMINCIA ANNUAL SERIES

□ 1981 **Young Love,** artist: Lamincia, production quantity 7,500 .... — 95.00 — 95.00

LAST SUPPER SERIES

□ 1972 **Three Apostles,** artist: Vincente Tiziano, production quantity 2,000 .... 100.00 — 100.00
□ 1973 **Three Apostles,** artist: Vincente Tiziano, production quantity 2,000 .... 70.00 — 75.00
□ 1974 **Three Apostles,** artist: Vincente Tiziano, production quantity 2,000 .... 70.00 — 70.00
□ 1975 **Three Apostles,** artist: Vincente Tiziano, production quantity 2,000 .... 70.00 — 70.00
□ 1976 **Jesus Christ,** artist: Vincente Tiziano, production quantity 2,000 .... 70.00 — 85.00

MOSAIC SERIES

□ 1973 **Justinian,** artist: Vincente Tiziano, production quantity 500 .... 50.00 — 75.00
□ 1974 **Pelican,** artist: Vincente Tiziano, production quantity 1,000 .... 50.00 — 45.00
□ 1977 **Theodora,** artist: Vincente Tiziano, production quantity 500 .... 50.00 — 45.00

MOTHER AND CHILD SERIES

□ 1981 **Loons,** artist: Guilio Gialletti and Franco Lamincia, production quantity 5,000 ...... 95.00 — 95.00
□ 1981 **Polar Bear,** artist: Guilio Gialletti and Franco Lamincia, production quantity 5,000 95.00 — 95.00
□ 1981 **Koalas,** artist: Guilio Gialletti and Franco Lamincia, production quantity 5,000 ...... 95.00 — 95.00
□ 1981 **Buffalos,** artist: Guilio Gialletti and Franco Lamincia, production quantity 5,000 ...... 95.00 — 95.00
□ 1981 **Lions,** artist: Guilio Gialletti and Franco Lamincia, production quantity 5,000 ...... 95.00 — 95.00
□ 1981 **Elephants,** artist: Guilio Gialletti and Franco Lamincia, production quantity 5,000 ...... 95.00 — 95.00

MOTHER'S DAY SERIES

□ 1972 **Madonna and Child,** artist: Vincente Tiziano, production quantity 2,000 .... 55.00 — 85.00
□ 1973 **Madonna and Child,** artist: Vincente Tiziano, production quantity 2,000 .... 55.00 — 55.00
□ 1974 **Mother and Son,** artist: Vincente Tiziano, production quantity 2,000 .... 55.00 — 55.00

		Issue Price	Current Value
☐ 1975	**Daughter and Doll,** artist: Vincente Tiziano, production quantity 2,000	45.00	45.00
☐ 1976	**Son and Daughter,** artist: Vincente Tiziano, production quantity 2,000	55.00	55.00
☐ 1977	**Mother and Child,** artist: Vincente Tiziano, production quantity 2,000	50.00	50.00

VALENTINE'S DAY SERIES

☐ 1977	**Valentine Boy,** production quantity 3,000 ..	45.00	60.00
☐ 1978	**Valentine Girl,** production quantity 3,000 ..	45.00	55.00
☐ 1979	**Hansel,** production quantity 3,000	60.00	60.00
☐ 1980	**Gretel,** production quantity 5,000	67.50	70.00

WILDLIFE SERIES

☐ 1971	**Deer,** production quantity 500	37.50	450.00
☐ 1972	**Elephant,** production quantity 1,000	37.50	275.00
☐ 1973	**Puma,** production quantity 2,000	37.50	65.00
☐ 1974	**Tiger,** production quantity 2,000	40.00	50.00

VERNONWARE

United States

CHRISTMAS SERIES

☐ 1971	**Partridge,** production: one year	15.00	60.00
☐ 1972	**Jingle Bells,** production: one year	17.50	30.00
☐ 1973	**The First Noel,** production: one year	20.00	35.00
☐ 1974	**Upon a Midnight Clear,** production: one year	20.00	30.00
☐ 1975	**O Holy Night,** production: one year	20.00	30.00
☐ 1976	**Hark! The Herald Angels,** production: one year	20.00	30.00
☐ 1977	**Away in the Manger,** production: one year	30.00	35.00
☐ 1978	**White Christmas,** production quantity 10,000	30.00	35.00
☐ 1979	**Little Drummer Boy,** production quantity 10,000	30.00	35.00

CORVETTE COLLECTOR SERIES

☐ 1986	**Pace Car Convertible,** artist: Bill Seitz, production quantity 2,000	29.95	30.00
☐ 1987	**'63 Split Window Coupe,** artist: Bill Seitz, production quantity 2,000	29.95	30.00

VILETTA CHINA

United States
(See also Pemberton & Oakes)

		Issue Price	Current Value
ALICE IN WONDERLAND SERIES			
☐ **1980**	**Alice and the White Rabbit,** artist: Robert Blitzer, hand-numbered, initialed, and dated, production: 28 days	**25.00**	**25.00**
☐ **1980**	**Advice from a Caterpillar,** artist: Robert Blitzer, hand-numbered, initialed, and dated, production: 28 days	**25.00**	**25.00**
☐ **1980**	**End of a Dream,** artist: Robert Blitzer, hand-numbered, initialed, and dated, production: 28 days	**25.00**	**25.00**
☐ **1981**	**Mad Hatter's Tea Party,** artist: Robert Blitzer, hand-numbered, initialed, and dated, production: 28 days	**25.00**	**25.00**
☐ **1981**	**Alice and Cheshire Cat,** artist: Robert Blitzer, hand-numbered, initialed, and dated, production: 28 days	**25.00**	**25.00**
☐ **1981**	**Alice and Croquet Match,** artist: Robert Blitzer, hand-numbered, initialed, and dated, production: 28 days	**25.00**	**25.00**

THE CAREFREE DAYS SERIES
(The Hamilton Collection)

		Issue Price	Current Value
☐ **1982**	**Autumn Wanderer,** artist: Thornton Utz, hand-numbered, production: 10 days	**24.50**	**24.50**
☐ **1982**	**Best Friends,** artist: Thornton Utz, hand-numbered, production: 10 days	**24.50**	**24.50**
☐ **1982**	**Feeding Time,** artist: Thornton Utz, hand-numbered, production: 10 days	**24.50**	**24.50**
☐ **1982**	**First Catch,** artist: Thornton Utz, hand-numbered, production: 10 days	**24.50**	**24.50**
☐ **1982**	**Bathtime Visitor,** artist: Thornton Utz, hand-numbered, production: 10 days	**24.50**	**24.50**
☐ **1982**	**Monkey Business,** artist: Thornton Utz, hand-numbered, production: 10 days	**24.50**	**24.50**

CHILDHOOD MEMORIES SERIES
(Collector's Heirlooms)

		Issue Price	Current Value
☐ **1978**	**Jennifer by Candlelight,** artist: William Bruckner, production quantity 5,000	**60.00**	**60.00**

	Issue Price	Current Value
☐ **1979 Brian's Birthday,** artist: William Bruckner, production quantity 5,000	60.00	60.00

CHILDREN'S SERIES

☐ **1979 Last of the Ninth,** production quantity 5,000	45.00	45.00

CHRISTMAS ANNUAL SERIES

☐ **1978 Expression of Faith,** production quantity 7,400	49.95	50.00
☐ **1979 Skating Lesson,** production quantity 7,400	49.95	50.00
☐ **1980 Bringing Home the Tree,** production quantity 7,400	49.95	50.00

THE COPPELIA BALLET
PLATE COLLECTION
(The Hamilton Collection)

☐ **1980 Franz's Fantasy Love,** artist: Renee Faure, hand-numbered, production: 28 days	25.00	28.00
☐ **1980 The Creation of a Doll,** artist: Renee Faure, hand-numbered, production: 28 days	25.00	28.00
☐ **1981 The Secret Is Unlocked,** artist: Renee Faure, hand-numbered, production: 28 days	25.00	28.00
☐ **1981 Swanilda's Deception,** artist: Renee Faure, hand-numbered, production: 28 days	25.00	28.00
☐ **1981 An Uneasy Sleep,** artist: Renee Faure, hand-numbered, production: 28 days	25.00	28.00
☐ **1981 Coppelia Awakens,** artist: Renee Faure, hand-numbered, production: 28 days	25.00	28.00
☐ **1982 A Shattered Dream,** artist: Renee Faure, hand-numbered, production: 28 days	25.00	28.00
☐ **1982 The Wedding,** artist: Renee Faure, hand-numbered, production: 28 days	25.00	28.00

DAYS OF THE WEST SERIES

☐ **1978 Cowboy Christmas,** production quantity 5,000	50.00	60.00

DISNEYLAND SERIES

☐ **1976 Signing the Declaration,** production quantity 3,000	15.00	100.00
☐ **1976 Crossing the Delaware,** production quantity 3,000	15.00	100.00

		Issue Price	Current Value
☐ 1976	**Betsy Ross,** production quantity 3,000	**15.00**	**100.00**
☐ 1976	**Spirit of 76,** production quantity 3,000	**15.00**	**100.00**
☐ 1979	**Mickey's 50th Anniversary,** production quantity 5,000	**37.00**	**50.00**

GREAT COMEDIANS SERIES
(Warwick)

☐ 1978	**The Little Tramp,** production quantity 7,500	**35.00**	**35.00**
☐ 1978	**Outrageous Groucho,** production quantity 7,500	**35.00**	**35.00**

IN TRIBUTE TO AMERICA'S GREAT ARTISTS SERIES

☐ 1978	**DeGrazia,** artist: Marco, production quantity 5,000	**65.00**	**65.00**

ISRAEL'S 30TH ANNIVERSARY SERIES
(Judaic Heritage Society)

☐ 1979	**L'Chayim to Israel,** production quantity 10,000	**59.50**	**60.00**
☐ 1979	**Prophecy of Isaiah,** production quantity 4,000	**59.50**	**60.00**

JOYS OF MOTHERHOOD SERIES
(Collector's Heirlooms)

☐ 1978	**Crystal's Joy,** artist: William Bruckner, production quantity 7,500	**60.00**	**40.00**

MAKING FRIENDS SERIES

☐ 1978	**Feeding the Neighbor's Pony,** artist: Irish McCalla, production quantity 5,000	**45.00**	**40.00**
☐ 1979	**Cowboys 'n Indians,** artist: Irish McCalla, production quantity 5,000	**47.50**	**50.00**
☐ 1980	**Surprise for Christy,** artist: Irish McCalla, production quantity 5,000	**47.50**	**50.00**

THE NUTCRACKER BALLET SERIES
(The Hamilton Collection)

☐ 1978	**Clara and the Nutcracker,** artist: Shell Fisher, hand-numbered, initialed, and dated, production: 28 days	**19.50**	**75.00**

		Issue Price	Current Value
☐ **1979**	**Gift from Godfather,** artist: Shell Fisher, hand-numbered, initialed, and dated, production: 28 days	19.50	65.00
☐ **1979**	**Sugarplum Fairy,** artist: Shell Fisher, hand-numbered, initialed, and dated, production: 28 days	19.50	55.00
☐ **1979**	**Snow King and Queen,** artist: Shell Fisher, hand-numbered, initialed, and dated, production: 28 days	19.50	47.00
☐ **1979**	**Waltz of Flowers,** artist: Shell Fisher, hand-numbered, initialed, and dated, production: 28 days	19.50	47.00
☐ **1980**	**Clara and the Prince,** artist: Shell Fisher, hand-numbered, initialed, and dated, production: 28 days	19.50	47.00

OLYMPIC SERIES
(Ghent Collection)

☐ **1980**	**Winter Olympics,** production: 13 days	24.50	25.00
☐ **1980**	**Summer Olympics,** production: less than one year	29.50	30.00

THE PERFORMANCE
(R. J. Ernst Enterprises)

☐ **1979**	**Act I,** artist: Bonnie Porter, production quantity 5,000	65.00	65.00

PORTRAITS OF CHILDHOOD SERIES
(The Hamilton Collection)

☐ **1981**	**Butterfly Magic,** artist: Thornton Utz, production: one year	24.95	25.00
☐ **1982**	**Sweet Dreams,** artist: Thornton Utz, production: one year	24.95	24.95
☐ **1983**	**Turtle Falk,** artist: Thornton Utz, production: one year	24.95	24.95

PRECIOUS MOMENTS SERIES
(The Hamilton Collection)

☐ **1979**	**A Friend in the Sky,** artist: Thornton Utz, hand-numbered, initialed, and dated, production: 28 days	21.50	50.00

		Issue Price	Current Value
☐ 1980	**Sand in Her Shoe,** artist: Thornton Utz, hand-numbered, initialed, and dated, production: 28 days	**21.50**	**40.00**
☐ 1980	**Snow Bunny,** artist: Thornton Utz, hand-numbered, initialed, and dated, production: 28 days	**21.50**	**40.00**
☐ 1980	**Seashells,** artist: Thornton Utz, hand-numbered, initialed, and dated, production: 28 days	**21.50**	**27.00**
☐ 1981	**Dawn,** artist: Thornton Utz, hand-numbered, initialed, and dated, production: 28 days . . .	**21.50**	**27.00**
☐ 1981	**My Kitty,** artist: Thornton Utz, hand-numbered, initialed, and dated, production: 28 days	**21.50**	**27.00**

RUFUS AND ROXANNE
(R. J. Ernst Enterprises)

☐ 1980	**Love Is . . . ,** artist: Kelly, production quantity 19,000	**14.95**	**15.00**

SEASONS OF THE OAK SERIES

☐ 1979	**Lazy Days,** artist: Ralph Homan, production quantity 5,000	**55.00**	**55.00**
☐ 1980	**Come Fly with Me,** artist: Ralph Homan, production quantity 5,000	**55.00**	**55.00**

TENDER MOMENTS SERIES

☐ 1978	**Old-Fashioned Persuasion,** artist: Eugene Christopherson, production quantity 7,500	**40.00**	**40.00**
☐ 1980	**Dandelions,** artist: Eugene Christopherson, production quantity 7,500	**40.00**	**45.00**

UNICORN FANTASIES SERIES

☐ 1979	**Followers of Dreams,** artist: K. Chin, production quantity 5,000	**55.00**	**55.00**
☐ 1980	**Twice upon a Time,** artist: K. Chin, production quantity 5,000	**55.00**	**55.00**
☐ 1981	**Familiar Spirit,** artist: K. Chin, production quantity 5,000	**55.00**	**55.00**
☐ 1982	**Noble Gathering,** artist: K. Chin, production quantity 5,000	**55.00**	**55.00**

		Issue Price	Current Value

WEDDINGS AROUND THE WORLD SERIES

		Issue Price	Current Value
☐ 1979	**Hawaiian Wedding,** artist: Elke Sommer, production quantity 5,000	75.00	75.00
☐ 1980	**Dutch Wedding,** artist: Elke Sommer, production quantity 5,000	75.00	75.00

WOMEN OF THE WEST SERIES
(R. J. Ernst Enterprises)

☐ 1979	**Expectation,** artist: Donald Putnam, production quantity 10,000	39.50	42.00
☐ 1979	**Silver Dollar Sal,** artist: Donald Putnam, production quantity 10,000	39.50	42.00
☐ 1980	**First Day,** artist: Donald Putnam, production quantity 10,000	39.50	42.00
☐ 1980	**Dolly,** artist: Donald Putnam, production quantity 10,000	39.50	42.00

SINGLE RELEASES

☐ 1980	**Mail Order Bride,** artist: Irish McCalla, production quantity 5,000	60.00	60.00
☐ 1980	**The Duke** (R. J. Ernst Enterprises), production quantity 27,500	29.75	30.00
☐ 1983	**Princess Grace,** artist: Thornton Utz, production: 21 days	75.00	75.00

VILLEROY AND BOCH

Germany
(See also Heinrich Porzellan)

CHRISTMAS SERIES

☐ 1977	**Holy Family,** production quantity 10,000 ..	175.00	200.00
☐ 1978	**Three Holy Kings,** production quantity 20,000	175.00	200.00
☐ 1979	**Mary with Child,** production quantity 10,000	198.00	200.00
☐ 1980	**Madonna in Glory,** production quantity 10,000	200.00	200.00

WALDENBURG PORCELAIN

Canada

		Issue Price	Current Value
PUNKINHEAD, THE HAPPY LITTLE BEAR SERIES			
☐ 1983	**Punkinhead and His Friends,** production quantity 4,000	**34.50**	**35.00**
☐ 1983	**Punkinhead and Santa Claus,** production quantity 4,000	**34.50**	**35.00**

WEDGWOOD, ENOCH

Great Britain

AVON AMERICANA SERIES

☐ 1973	**Betsy Ross,** production: one year	**15.00**	**25.00**
☐ 1974	**Freedom,** production: one year	**15.00**	**25.00**

AVON CHRISTMAS SERIES

☐ 1973	**Christmas on the Farm,** production: one year	**15.00**	**40.00**
☐ 1974	**Country Church,** production: one year	**16.00**	**30.00**
☐ 1975	**Skaters on Pond,** production: one year	**18.00**	**25.00**
☐ 1976	**Bringing Home the Tree,** production: one year	**18.00**	**22.00**
☐ 1977	**Carolers in the Snow,** production: one year	**19.50**	**22.00**
☐ 1978	**Trimming the Tree,** production: one year . .	**21.50**	**24.00**
☐ 1979	**Dashing Through the Snow,** production: one year	**24.00**	**24.00**

AVON MOTHER'S DAY SERIES

☐ 1974	**Tenderness,** production: one year	**15.00**	**22.00**
☐ 1975	**Gentle Moments,** production: one year	**17.00**	**30.00**

AVON NORTH AMERICAN SONGBIRD SERIES

☐ 1974	**Cardinals,** artist: D. Eckelberry, production: one year	**18.00**	**22.00**

BICENTENNIAL SERIES

☐ 1972	**Boston Tea Party,** production: one year . . .	**40.00**	**40.00**
☐ 1973	**Paul Revere's Ride,** production: one year . .	**40.00**	**115.00**
☐ 1974	**Battle of Concord,** production: one year . . .	**40.00**	**55.00**
☐ 1975	**Across the Delaware,** production: one year	**40.00**	**105.00**

Declaration
Signed.

		Issue Price	Current Value
☐ 1975	**Victory at Yorktown,** production: one year	**45.00**	**53.00**
☐ 1976	**Declaration Signed,** production: one year ..	**45.00**	**45.00**

BLOSSOMING OF SUZANNE SERIES

☐ 1977	**Innocence,** artist: Mary Vickers, production quantity 7,000	**60.00**	**60.00**
☐ 1978	**Cherish,** artist: Mary Vickers, production quantity 7,000	**60.00**	**60.00**
☐ 1979	**Daydream,** artist: Mary Vickers, production quantity 24,000	**65.00**	**65.00**

Innocence, artist: Mary Vickers.

		Issue Price	Current Value
☐ **1980**	**Wistful,** artist: Mary Vickers, production quantity 24,000	**70.00**	**70.00**

CALENDAR SERIES

		Issue Price	Current Value
☐ **1971**	**Victorian Almanac,** production: one year . .	**12.00**	**12.00**
☐ **1972**	**The Carousel,** production: one year	**12.95**	**12.95**

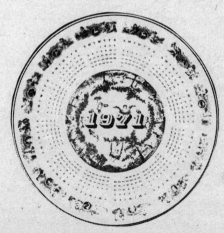

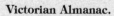
Victorian Almanac.

		Issue Price	Current Value
☐ 1973	**Bountiful Butterfly,** production: one year ..	12.95	12.95
☐ 1974	**Camelot,** production: one year	14.00	75.00
☐ 1975	**Children's Games,** production: one year ...	15.00	15.00
☐ 1976	**Robin,** production: one year	25.00	25.00
☐ 1977	**Tonatiuh,** production: one year	30.00	30.00
☐ 1978	**Samurai,** production: one year	30.00	30.00
☐ 1979	**Sacred Scarab,** production: one year	35.00	35.00
☐ 1980	**Safari,** production: one year	42.50	42.50
☐ 1981	**Horses,** production: one year	47.50	47.50
☐ 1982	**Wild West,** production: one year	52.00	52.00
☐ 1983	**The Age of the Reptiles,** production: one year	54.00	54.00
☐ 1984	**Dogs,** production: one year	54.00	54.00
☐ 1985	**Cats,** production: one year	54.00	54.00
☐ 1986	**British Birds,** production: one year	54.00	54.00
☐ 1987	**Water Birds,** production: one year	54.00	54.00
☐ 1988	**Sea Birds,** production: one year	54.00	54.00

CATHEDRALS CHRISTMAS SERIES

☐ 1986	**Canterbury Cathedral,** production: one year	40.00	40.00

CHILD'S BIRTHDAY SERIES

☐ 1981	**Peter Rabbit,** artist: Beatrix Potter, production: one year	24.00	24.00
☐ 1982	**Mrs. Tiggy-Winkle,** artist: Beatrix Potter, production: one year	27.00	27.00

Water Birds.

		Issue Price	Current Value
☐ 1983	**Peter Rabbit and Benjamin Bunny,** artist: Beatrix Potter, production: one year	29.00	29.00
☐ 1984	**Peter Rabbit,** artist: Beatrix Potter, production: one year	29.00	29.00
☐ 1985	**Peter Rabbit,** artist: Beatrix Potter, production: one year	29.00	29.00
☐ 1986	**Peter Rabbit,** artist: Beatrix Potter, production: one year	29.00	29.00
☐ 1987	**Oakapple Wood,** artist: J. Partridge, production: one year	29.00	29.00
☐ 1988	**Oakapple Wood,** artist: J. Partridge, production: one year	29.00	29.00

CHILD'S CHRISTMAS SERIES

☐ 1979	**Children and Snowman,** production: one year	35.00	35.00
☐ 1980	**Collecting the Christmas Tree,** production: one year	37.50	37.50
☐ 1981	**Children Sledding,** production: one year ...	40.00	40.00
☐ 1982	**Skaters,** production: one year	40.00	40.00
☐ 1983	**Carol Singing,** production: one year	40.00	40.00
☐ 1984	**Mixing the Christmas Pudding,** production: one year	40.00	40.00

CHILDREN'S STORY SERIES

☐ 1971	**The Sandman,** production: one year	7.95	23.00
☐ 1972	**The Tinder Box,** production: one year	7.95	9.00
☐ 1973	**The Emperor's New Clothes,** production: one year	9.00	9.00
☐ 1974	**The Ugly Duckling,** production: one year ..	10.00	10.00
☐ 1975	**The Little Mermaid,** production: one year	11.00	12.00
☐ 1976	**Hansel and Gretel,** production: one year ..	12.00	12.00
☐ 1977	**Rumplestiltskin,** production: one year	15.00	15.00
☐ 1978	**The Frog Prince,** production: one year	15.00	24.00
☐ 1979	**The Golden Goose,** production: one year ..	15.00	15.00
☐ 1980	**Rapunzel,** production: one year	16.00	16.00
☐ 1981	**Tom Thumb,** production: one year	18.00	18.00
☐ 1982	**The Lady and the Lion,** production: one year	20.00	20.00
☐ 1983	**The Elves and the Shoemaker,** production: one year	20.00	20.00
☐ 1984	**King Roughbeard,** production: one year ...	20.00	20.00
☐ 1985	**The Brave Little Tailor,** production: one year	20.00	20.00

		Issue Price	Current Value
CHRISTMAS SERIES			
☐ 1969	**Windsor Castle,** artist: Tom Harper, production: one year	25.00	225.00
☐ 1970	**Trafalgar Square,** artist: Tom Harper, production: one year	30.00	30.00
☐ 1971	**Piccadilly Circus,** artist: Tom Harper, production: one year	30.00	40.00
☐ 1972	**St. Paul's Cathedral,** artist: Tom Harper, production: one year	35.00	40.00
☐ 1973	**Tower of London,** artist: Tom Harper, production: one year	40.00	42.00
☐ 1974	**Houses of Parliament,** artist: Tom Harper, production: one year	40.00	40.00
☐ 1975	**Tower Bridge,** artist: Tom Harper, production: one year	45.00	45.00
☐ 1976	**Hampton Court,** artist: Tom Harper, production: one year	50.00	50.00
☐ 1977	**Westminster Abbey,** artist: Tom Harper, production: one year	55.00	55.00
☐ 1978	**Horse Guards,** artist: Tom Harper, production: one year	60.00	60.00
☐ 1979	**Buckingham Palace,** production: one year	65.00	65.00
☐ 1980	**St. James's Palace,** production: one year	70.00	70.00
☐ 1981	**Marble Arch,** production: one year	75.00	75.00
☐ 1982	**Lambeth Palace,** production: one year	80.00	80.00
☐ 1983	**All Souls, Langham Palace,** production: one year	80.00	80.00
☐ 1984	**Constitution Hill,** production: one year	80.00	80.00
☐ 1985	**The Tate Gallery,** production: one year	80.00	80.00
☐ 1986	**The Albert Memorial,** production: one year	80.00	80.00
☐ 1987	**Guildhall,** production: one year	80.00	80.00
EYES OF THE CHILD SERIES			
☐ XX	**Little Lady Love,** artist: Fromme-Douglas, production quantity 15,000	65.00	65.00
☐ XX	**My Best Friend,** artist: Fromme-Douglas, production quantity 15,000	65.00	65.00
☐ XX	**I Wish upon a Star,** artist: Fromme-Douglas, production quantity 15,000	65.00	65.00
☐ XX	**In a Child's Thought,** artist: Fromme-Douglas, production quantity 15,000	65.00	65.00
☐ XX	**Puppy Love,** artist: Fromme-Douglas, production quantity 15,000	65.00	65.00

	Issue Price	Current Value
THE LEGEND OF KING ARTHUR SERIES		
☐ **1986 Arthur Draws the Sword,** artist: Richard Hook, production: unannounced	39.00	39.00

MOTHER'S DAY SERIES

	Issue Price	Current Value
☐ **1971 Sportive Love,** artist: unannounced, production: one year	20.00	20.00
☐ **1972 The Sewing Lesson,** artist: unannounced, production: one year	20.00	20.00
☐ **1973 The Baptism of Achilles,** artist: unannounced, production: one year	20.00	25.00
☐ **1974 Domestic Employment,** artist: unannounced, production: one year	30.00	33.00
☐ **1975 Mother and Child,** artist: unannounced, production: one year	35.00	37.00
☐ **1976 The Spinner,** artist: unannounced, production: one year	35.00	35.00
☐ **1977 Leisure Time,** artist: unannounced, production: one year	35.00	35.00
☐ **1978 Swan and Cygnets,** artist: unannounced, production: one year	40.00	40.00
☐ **1979 Deer and Fawn,** artist: unannounced, production: one year	45.00	45.00
☐ **1980 Birds,** artist: unannounced, production: one year	47.50	47.50
☐ **1981 Mare and Foal,** artist: unannounced, production: one year	50.00	50.00
☐ **1982 Cherubs and Swing,** artist: unannounced, production: one year	55.00	55.00
☐ **1983 Cupid and Butterfly,** artist: unannounced, production: one year	55.00	55.00
☐ **1984 Musical Cupids,** artist: unannounced, production: one year	55.00	55.00
☐ **1985 Cupids and Doves,** artist: unannounced, production: one year	55.00	55.00
☐ **1986 Cupids Fishing,** artist: unannounced, production: one year	55.00	55.00
☐ **1987 Anemones,** artist: unannounced, production: one year	55.00	55.00
☐ **1988 Tiger Lily,** artist: unannounced, production: one year	55.00	55.00

	Issue Price	Current Value

MY MEMORIES SERIES

☐ **1981 Be My Friend,** artist: Mary Vickers, production limited .... 27.00 / 27.00

☐ **1982 Playtime,** artist: Mary Vickers, production limited .... 27.00 / 27.00

☐ **1983 Our Garden,** artist: Mary Vickers, production limited .... 27.00 / 50.00

☐ **1984 The Recital,** artist: Mary Vickers, production limited .... 27.00 / 48.00

☐ **1985 Mother's Treasures,** artist: Mary Vickers, production limited .... 27.00 / 35.00

☐ **1986 Riding High,** artist: Mary Vickers, production limited .... 29.00 / 29.00

PETER RABBIT CHRISTMAS SERIES

☐ **1981 Peter Rabbit,** artist: Beatrix Potter, production: one year .... 27.00 / 27.00

☐ **1982 Peter Rabbit,** artist: Beatrix Potter, production: one year .... 27.00 / 27.00

☐ **1983 Peter Rabbit,** artist: Beatrix Potter, production: one year .... 29.00 / 29.00

☐ **1984 Peter Rabbit,** artist: Beatrix Potter, production: one year .... 29.00 / 29.00

☐ **1985 Peter Rabbit,** artist: Beatrix Potter, production: one year .... 29.00 / 29.00

☐ **1986 Peter Rabbit,** artist: Beatrix Potter, production: one year .... 29.00 / 29.00

☐ **1987 Peter Rabbit,** artist: Beatrix Potter, production: one year .... 29.00 / 29.00

PORTRAITS OF FIRST LOVE SERIES

☐ **1986 The Love Letter,** artist: Mary Vickers, production: unannounced .... 27.00 / 27.00

QUEEN'S CHRISTMAS SERIES

☐ **1980 Windsor Castle,** artist: A. Price, production: one year .... 24.95 / 24.95

☐ **1981 Trafalgar Square,** artist: A. Price, production: one year .... 24.95 / 24.95

☐ **1982 Piccadilly Circus,** artist: A. Price, production: one year .... 32.50 / 32.50

☐ **1983 St. Paul's,** artist: A. Price, production: one year .... 32.50 / 32.50

☐ **1984 Tower of London,** artist: A. Price, production: one year .... 35.00 / 35.00

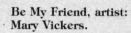
Be My Friend, artist: Mary Vickers.

Playtime, artist: Mary Vickers.

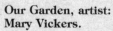
Our Garden, artist: Mary Vickers.

	Issue Price	Current Value
☐ **1985 Palace of Westminster,** artist: A. Price, production: one year	35.00	35.00
☐ **1986 Tower Bridge,** artist: A. Price, production: one year	35.00	35.00

STREET SELLERS OF LONDON SERIES

☐ **1986 The Baked Potato Man,** artist: John Finnie, production: unannounced	25.00	25.00

WENDELL AUGUSTE FORGE

United States

CHRISTMAS SERIES

☐ **1974 Caroler,** bronze, production quantity 2,500	25.00	25.00
☐ **1974 Caroler,** pewter, production quantity 2,500	30.00	35.00
☐ **1975 Christmas in Country,** bronze, production quantity 2,500........................	30.00	35.00
☐ **1975 Christmas in Country,** pewter, production quantity 2,500........................	35.00	35.00
☐ **1976 Lamplighter,** bronze, production quantity 2,500	35.00	35.00
☐ **1976 Lamplighter,** pewter, production quantity 2,500	40.00	40.00
☐ **1977 Covered Bridge,** bronze, production quantity 2,500	40.00	40.00
☐ **1977 Covered Bridge,** pewter, production quantity 2,500	45.00	45.00

GREAT AMERICANS SERIES

☐ **1971 Kennedy,** pewter, production quantity 500	40.00	35.00
☐ **1971 Kennedy,** silver, production quantity 500 ..	200.00	200.00
☐ **1972 Lincoln,** pewter, production quantity 500 ..	40.00	40.00
☐ **1972 Lincoln,** silver, production quantity 500 ...	200.00	200.00

GREAT MOMENTS SERIES

☐ **1972 Landing of Pilgrims,** pewter, production quantity 5,000........................	40.00	40.00
☐ **1972 Landing of Pilgrims,** silver, production quantity 500	200.00	200.00
☐ **1973 First Thanksgiving,** pewter, production quantity 5,000.............................	40.00	40.00

		Issue Price	Current Value
☐ **1972**	**First Thanksgiving,** silver, production quantity 500	200.00	200.00
☐ **1974**	**Patrick Henry,** pewter, production quantity 5,000	40.00	40.00
☐ **1974**	**Patrick Henry,** silver, production quantity 500..................................	200.00	200.00
☐ **1975**	**Paul Revere,** pewter, production quantity 5,000	45.00	45.00
☐ **1975**	**Paul Revere,** silver, production quantity 500	200.00	200.00
☐ **1976**	**Signing of Declaration,** pewter, production quantity 5,000.........................	45.00	45.00
☐ **1976**	**Signing of Declaration,** silver, production quantity 500	200.00	200.00

PEACE SERIES

		Issue Price	Current Value
☐ **1973**	**Peace Doves,** production quantity 2,500 ...	250.00	275.00

WILDLIFE SERIES

		Issue Price	Current Value
☐ **1977**	**On Guard,** aluminum, production quantity 1,900	35.00	35.00
☐ **1977**	**On Guard,** bronze, production quantity 1,500	45.00	45.00
☐ **1977**	**On Guard,** pewter, production quantity 1,500	55.00	55.00
☐ **1977**	**On Guard,** silver, production quantity 100	250.00	250.00
☐ **1978**	**Thunderbird,** aluminum, production quantity 1,900	40.00	40.00
☐ **1978**	**Thunderbird,** bronze, production quantity 1,500	50.00	50.00
☐ **1978**	**Thunderbird,** pewter, production quantity 1,500	60.00	60.00
☐ **1978**	**Thunderbird,** silver, production quantity 100	250.00	250.00

WINGS OF MAN SERIES

		Issue Price	Current Value
☐ **1971**	**Columbus's Ships,** pewter, production quantity 5,000..............................	40.00	40.00
☐ **1971**	**Columbus's Ships,** silver, production quantity 500..................................	200.00	200.00
☐ **1972**	**Conestoga Wagon,** pewter, production quantity 5,000..............................	40.00	40.00
☐ **1972**	**Conestoga Wagon,** silver, production quantity 500	200.00	200.00

WESTERN AUTHENTICS

Canada

GUNS AT SEA SERIES	Issue Price	Current Value
☐ 1986 **H.M.C.S. Haida,** artist: Robert Banks, production quantity 5,000	39.95	40.00
☐ 1986 **H.M.C.S. Bonaventure,** artist: Robert Banks, production quantity 5,000	39.95	40.00

IRON PIONEERS SERIES

	Issue Price	Current Value
☐ 1986 **CPR No. 374,** artist: Robert Banks, production quantity 15,000	39.95	40.00
☐ 1986 **Countess of Dufferin,** artist: Robert Banks, production quantity 15,000	39.95	40.00

TUNES OF GLORY SERIES

	Issue Price	Current Value
☐ 1986 **The Piper,** artist: Robert Banks, production quantity 15,000	42.50	42.50
☐ 1986 **Piper & Drummer,** artist: Robert Banks, production quantity 15,000	42.50	42.50

SINGLE ISSUE

	Issue Price	Current Value
☐ 1986 **Douglass DC-3,** artist: Robert Banks, production quantity 7,500	39.95	40.00
☐ 1986 **Scarlet and Gold,** artist: Robert Banks, production quantity 19,500	49.95	50.00

WESTMINSTER COLLECTIBLES

United States

HOLIDAYS SERIES

☐ 1976 **All Hallows Eve,** production quantity 5,000		38.50	39.00
☐ 1977 **Christmas,** production quantity 5,000		38.50	39.00

WEXFORD GROUP

United States

GRANDMOTHER'S WORLD SERIES

	Issue Price	Current Value
☐ 1982 **Little Toy Friends,** artist: Cynthia Knapton, production quantity 12,500	45.00	50.00

		Issue Price	Current Value
☐ 1983	**The Promenade,** artist: Cynthia Knapton, production quantity 12,500	**45.00**	**45.00**
☐ 1983	**Afternoon Tea,** artist: Cynthia Knapton, production quantity 12,500	**45.00**	**45.00**

STORYLAND DOLLS SERIES

☐ 1984	**Mary Had a Little Lamb,** artist: Cynthia Knapton, production quantity 5,000	**39.50**	**40.00**

WILDLIFE INTERNATIONALE

United States

OWL FAMILY SERIES

☐ 1983	**Saw-Whet Owl Family,** artist: John Ruthven, production quantity 5,000	**55.00**	**55.00**
☐ 1983	**Great Horned Owl Family,** artist: John Ruthven, production quantity 5,000	**55.00**	**55.00**
☐ 1983	**Snowy Owl Family,** artist: John Ruthven, production quantity 5,000	**55.00**	**55.00**
☐ 1983	**Barred Owl Family,** artist: John Ruthven, production quantity 5,000	**55.00**	**55.00**

SPORTING DOG SERIES

☐ 1985	**Decoy (Labrador Retriever),** artist: John Ruthven, production quantity 5,000	**55.00**	**110.00**
☐ 1985	**Rummy (English Setter),** artist: John Ruthven, production quantity 5,000	**55.00**	**55.00**
☐ 1985	**Dusty (Golden Retriever),** artist: John Ruthven, production quantity 5,000	**55.00**	**80.00**
☐ 1985	**Scarlett (Irish Setter),** artist: John Ruthven, production quantity 5,000	**55.00**	**110.00**

WATERFOWL SERIES

☐ 1983	**Wood Ducks,** artist: John Ruthven, production quantity 5,000	**65.00**	**65.00**

WINDEMERE COLLECTION

United States

		Issue Price	Current Value

SINGLE ISSUE

☐ **1984 Piano Moods,** artist: Robert Olson, production quantity 7,500 . . . . **60.00 60.00**

WOODMERE CHINA

United States

CHILDREN OF THE AMERICAN FRONTIER SERIES

☐ **1986 In Trouble Again,** artist: Don Crook, production quantity N/A **24.50 25.00**

ZANOBIA

AFRICAN VIOLET MINIATURES SERIES

☐ **1985 Half Pint,** artist: Zanobia, production quantity 5,000 . . . . **29.50 30.00**

☐ **1985 Luvkins,** artist: Zanobia, production quantity 5,000 . . . . **29.50 30.00**

VIOLET PORTRAITS SERIES

☐ **1987 Canadian Sunset,** artist: Zanobia, production quantity 5,000 . . . . **34.50 35.00**

☐ **1987 Kiss't,** artist: Zanobia, production quantity 5,000 . . . . **34.50 35.00**

Index

Aarestrup, Bing & Grondahl,
   168, 173
Achtziger, Hans,
   Hutschenreuther, 386,
   389
Adachi, Yasuhiko, Hamilton
   Collection, 346
Adams, Allen, American
   Heritage, 121, 122
Adams, N., Lenox, 444
Ahlcrona, Robert, Royal
   Cornwall, 556
Akers, Roger
   biographical information, 69
   Incolay Studios, 395
Alexander, Cassidy J., Hackett
   American, 333, 339, 340
Allison, Betty, Allison and
   Company, 116
Almazetta, Avondale, 157
America, Marca, Porcelaine
   Ariel, 504
Anderson, Ivan, Hackett
   American, 334
Anderson, Robert, Pemberton
   and Oakes, 487
Anderson, Susan, Carson Mint,
   192

Anderson, Wayne, Knowles,
   Edwin M., 437
Angelico, Fra, Reed and
   Barton, 520
Anglund, Joan Walsh, Ebeling
   and Reuss, 221
Anguiano, Raul, Bonita,
   185
Anker, Albert, Langenthal
   China Works, 443
Anna-Perenna, history of, 81,
   82
Appleby, Gayle Bright, Incolay
   Studios, 395
Appleby, Gregg, Avondale,
   156
Appleton, Jack, Braymer Hall,
   187
Ard, Kurt, Bing & Grondahl,
   173, 174
Auckland, James, Knowles,
   Edwin M., 438
Audubon, John James, Franklin
   Mint, 272
Ault, Von, Ernst Enterprises,
   R.J., 231, 232
Avey, Linda, Kern Collectibles,
   419

Baaring, Maggi, Svend, Jensen,
    404
Bahnsen, Frode, Grande
    Copenhagen, 320
Baldwin, Richard, Franklin
    Mint, 278
Balke, Don, Fleetwood
    Collection, 253–255
Band, Ursula
    Knowles, Edwin M., 425
    Tirschenreuth, 626
Banks, Bob, Hackett American,
    332
Banks, Robert, Western
    Authentics, 660
Bannister, Patti, Schmid
    (Germany), 596
Barbard, Dave Grossman
    Designs, 323–325
Bareuther, 158–162
    history of, 82, 83
Barker, Cicely Mary, Heinrich
    Porzellan, 358, 359
Barlowe, Dorothea, biographical
    information, 69, 70
Barlowe, Dot, Reco
    International, 518
Barlowe, S./D., Southern Living
    Gallery, 612, 613
Barlowe, Sy
    biographical information,
        69
    Reco International, 518
Barratt, Isa, Franklin Mint,
    257
Barratt, Peter, Franklin Mint,
    263, 279
Barrer, Gertrude,
    Anna-Perenna, 129
Baston, P., Royal Worcester,
    586
Baston, Prescott, Royal
    Worcester, 588
Bates, Betsy, Lynell, 460

Bauer, Kurt, Kaiser, 407, 408,
    412, 413, 416
Beaujard, Yves, Franklin Mint,
    261, 272
Becker, Charlotte, Curator
    Collection, 206, 210
Bedal, Karl, Konigszelt Bavaria,
    439
Bell, Deborah, Franklin Mint,
    273
Bellini, Haviland and Parlon,
    356
Bell Jarratt, Debbie, Franklin
    Mint, 262
Belski, Abram, Franklin Mint,
    264, 280
Bentley, Robert, Pemberton and
    Oakes, 488
Benvenuti, Sergio, Studio Dante
    di Volteradici, 622
Béran, Lenore
    biographical information,
        70
    Brindle Fine Arts, 188
    Hackett American, 338
Berger, K., Hutschenreuther,
    382
Berger, Kathia,
    Hutschenreuther, 386
Berke, E., Reco International,
    518
Bernadotte, Count Lennart,
    Anna-Perenna, 127
Berran, Robert, Signature
    Collection, 609
Bharnson, Tom, Rhea Silva
    Porcelain Collection,
    522
Biel and Butcher, Enesco, 221
Bierly, E., Kaiser, 415
Bierly, Edward J., Ghent
    Collection, 287–289
Bing and Grondahl, history of,
    83, 84

Bishop, Jerold, Fine Arts
        Marketing, 250, 251
Black, Ben
    biographical information, 71
    Royal Doulton, 575
Blackshear, Thomas, Hamilton
        Collection, 351
Blandford, Wilfred, Davenport
        Pottery, 218
Blish, Carolyn, California
        Porcelain, Inc., 189
Blitzer, Robert, Viletta China,
        643
Blottiaux, Robert, Stratford
        Collection, 621, 622
Blum, Hannelore, Kaiser, 407,
        409, 412
Bocher, Richard, Royal
        Copenhagen, 550–552
Boehm, Edward Marshall,
        Lenox, 444, 445
Boehm, Linda, 178
Boehm Studio Artists, 178–185
Boesen, Arthur, Royal
        Copenhagen, 550
Bond, A., Hamilton Collection,
        352
Bond, Higgins, Royal Cornwall,
        556, 566, 567
Bonfils, Kjeld, Bing &
        Grondahl, 170, 171
Botticelli
    Haviland and Parlon, 356
    Pickard, 497
Bouche, Andre, Fairmont
        China, 244
Bouguereau, William A., Royal
        Cornwall, 556
Bourgeault, Robert, Art World
        of Bourgeault, 155, 156
Boyer, Gene
    Armstrong's/Crown Parian,
        138
    Fleetwood Collection, 256

Boys Town, 186
Brackenbury, Amy, Knowles,
        Edwin M., 426
Bradley, Betsey, Knowles,
        Edwin M., 423
Brastoff, Sascha, California
        Porcelain, Inc., 189
Bratile, Gunnar, Porsgrund,
        505–507
Brennan, Walter, Jr., American
        Legacy, 123
Briant, Paul and Sons, 187
Brinegar, Shirley, Lynell, 460
Brown, C.A., Royal Doulton,
        574
Brown, Roger
    Creative World, 204, 205
    River Shore, 523–525
Bruckner, T. Holter, Duncan
        Royale, 221
Bruckner, William, Viletta
        China, 643–645
Brunettin, Alan
    biographical information, 71,
        72
    Incolay Studios, 396
Buffet, Bernard, Franklin Mint,
        259
Burgues, Carol, Anna-Perenna,
        127
Burgues, Dr. Irving,
        Anna-Perenna, 126, 128
Burke, Brenda, Royal Doulton,
        577
Butcher, Sam, Enesco, 222–226

Calder, Rosemary
    Armstrong's/Crown Parian,
        149
    Incolay Studios, 392
    Royal Cornwall, 563
Calle, Paul, Franklin Mint,
        257

Calvert, Lissa, Ghent
    Collection, 293
Cambier, Guy, D'Arceau
    Limoge, 214
Camm, Martin,
    Hutschenreuther, 383
Canaris, Patti
  Haviland and Parlon, 357
  Kern Collectibles, 417
Carreno, Pablo, Marigold, 464
Carroll, Mike, Kern
    Collectibles, 421
Caspari, Claus, Franklin Mint,
    271
Cassatt, Mary
  Curator Collection, 209
  Pickard, 498
Cassini, Oleg, Pickard, 500
Cassler, Carl, Signature
    Collection, 609
Casson, A.J., Canadian
    Collector Plates, 190
Cavell, Lily, Pacific Art
    Limited, 481
Cenkovcan, Ivo, Kaiser, 410,
    411
Chambers, William, Knowles,
    Edwin M., 424, 425,
    434–436
Chapple, Dave, Hackett
    American, 338, 339
Chase, Beverly, Incolay Studios,
    401
Chase, Lynn, Lenox, 451, 452
Chee Chee, Benjamin, Ussher,
    D.H., Ltd., 630
Chi, Chen, Royal Doulton, 580
Chin, K., Viletta China, 647
Christopherson, Eugene
  Hamilton Collection, 348
  Lynell, 462
  Viletta China, 647
Christy, Howard Chandler,
    Curator Collection, 212

Chumley, John, Franklin Mint,
    257
Clark, J., U.S. Historical
    Society, 627
Clark, Terry, Briant, Paul and
    Sons, 187
Clarke, Robert, Kaiser, 409
Cleary, Fergus, Belleek Pottery,
    163
Clymer, John, Gorham
    Collection, 302, 303, 312
Colbert, June, Carson Mint, 193
Collector plates (Introduction)
  artist interviews
    Zolan, Donald, 65–68
    Kuck, Sandra, 58–60
    McClelland, John, 61–63
    Perillo, Gregory, 63–65
  artists
    Akers, Roger, 69
    Barlowe, Dorothea, 69, 70
    Barlowe, Sy, 69
    Béran, Lenore, 70
    Black, Ben, 71
    Brunettin, Alan, 71, 72
    De Grazia, Ted, 73
    Hibel, Edna, 74, 75
    Money, Rusty, 75
    Moss, P. Buckley, 76
    Romanelli, Carl, 72, 73
    Ruffin, Don, 76, 77
    Rust, D.L. "Rusty," 77
    Skelton, Red, 77
    Spencer, Irene, 78, 79
    Williams, Abigail, 79, 80
  dealers
    Canadian dealers, 109–113
    NALED list (1987), 96–108
  manufacturers
    Anna-Perenna, 81, 82
    Bareuther, 82, 83
    Bing and Grondahl, 83, 84
    Fenton Art Glass
      Company, 84, 85

Frankoma Pottery, 85, 86
Pemberton & Oakes, 86
Rockwell Museum, 86, 87
Royal Copenhagen, 87, 88
publications related to, 94–96
terms related to, 89–93
Collector's Weekly, 203
Conche, Gina, Hackett
American, 338
Cooke, J., Royal Worcester, 588
Cooper, A.H., Bing &
Grondahl, 172
Cooper, P., Royal Worcester,
587, 588
Corbin, Raymond, Daum, 217
Cowles, Raynaud-Limoges, 509
Cranston, Toller, Ghent
Collection, 293
Crnkovich, Tony, Knowles,
Edwin M., 437
Crook, D., Hamilton Collection,
341
Crook, Don, Woodmere China,
662
Cross, Penni Anne,
Armstrong's/Crown
Parian, 149, 150
Crouch, Linda, American
Artists, 117
Csatari, Joseph, Knowles,
Edwin M., 428
Currier & Ives, Franklin Mint,
263, 264

Dacey, Robert, U.S. Historical
Society, 629
Dali, Louis, D'Arceau Limoge,
216
Daly, James,
Armstrong's/Crown
Parian, 149
Danby, Ken, Anna-Perenna,
129

Daniel, Kevin, Knowles, Edwin
M., 426
David, G., Pickard, 497
Davies, Will, Canadian
Collector Plates, 190
Da Vinci, Leonardo, George
Washington Mint, 287
Davis, Lowell, Schmid
(Germany), 594–596,
598
Dealers
Canadian dealers, 109–113
NALED list (1987), 96–108
de Bruijn, Mar, Royal Delft,
569, 571, 572
De Grazia, Ted
Armstrong's/Crown Parian,
152–155
biographical information, 73
Delle Notti, G., Roman, Inc.,
540
De Matteis, Frank, Rhea Silva
Porcelain Collection, 522
Dember, Sol, David Kaplan
Studios, 416
De Mille, Leslie
Kern Collectibles, 419
Sango, 591
Deneen, Jim, Curator
Collection, 208
de Oliveira, Manuel, Incolay
Studios, 400
De Patie, D., Royal Orleans,
583
Dessens, Jan, Royal Delft, 569,
571
D'Estrehan, Alan
Armstrong's/Crown Parian,
148
Royal Cornwall, 562, 566
Devlin, S., Reco International,
510
Devoche, Simon, Ernst
Enterprises, R.J., 227

Devonshire USA, 219

De Winne, Lisette, Royal
    Doulton, 573, 574

Dieckhoner, Gene, California
    Porcelain, Inc., 189, 190

Disney Studios
  Grolier, 323
  Schmid (Germany), 596
  Schmid (Japan), 599–601,
    604

Dohanos, Steven, Franklin
    Mint, 257, 277

Dolph, John Henry, Curator
    Collection, 210

Dorcy, Mary Jean, Roman,
    Inc., 540

Doughty, D., Royal Worcester,
    586, 587

Down, Jeanne, Knowles, Edwin
    M., 429

Doyle, Nancy, Contemporary
    Originals, Inc., 189

Drayton, Grace G., House of
    Global Art, 378

Drexel, Helmut, Roman, Inc.,
    545

Droguette, Rudy, Royal
    Cornwall, 561, 562, 565

Dubin, Lee
  Historic Providence Mint,
    371
  Pacific Art Limited, 480

Durand, Paul, Limoges-Turgot,
    454

Dutheil, Jean, D'Arceau
    Limoge, 216

Ebborn, Caroline, Franklin
    Mint, 264

Eckelberry, D., Wedgwood,
    Enoch, 649

Ede, Basil, Franklin Mint, 268,
    269, 280

Edison, Susan, Heirloom
    Traditions, 359, 360

Eggert, John
  Curator Collection, 210
  Signature Collection, 608, 609

Ellison, Pauline, Franklin Mint,
    270, 280

Engelbreit, Mary, Mary
    Engelbreit Society, 466

Engstrom, Michael, Boys Town,
    186

Eriksen, Edvard, Svend, Jensen,
    403

Ersgaard, C., Bing & Grondahl,
    168, 173

Erte, International Art Society
    Limited, 401

Escalera, Rudy
  Catalina Porcelain, 195
  Escalera Production Art, 238
  Hackett American, 331,
    337–339

Eskandar, Mossan, Porcelaine
    Ariel, 502, 503

Essenburg, Ben, Historic
    Providence Mint, 367,
    371

Etem, Sue
  American Legacy, 122, 123
  Fairmont China, 244
  Hackett American, 336

Everard, Barbara, Franklin
    Mint, 271

Ewnece, Royal Worcester,
    587

Eytinge, Carol, Royal Orleans,
    584

Falchi, Aldo, King's, 421, 422

Falter, John
  Brantwood Collection, 186
  Franklin Mint, 257
  Roman, Inc., 546

Farnham, Alexander, Franklin
    Mint, 257
Faulkner, Neil, Royal Doulton,
    574, 575
Faure, Renee, Viletta China,
    644
Fausett, Dean, Franklin Mint,
    257
Fazio, Aldo, Reco International,
    516, 517
Felder, Bettie, Gorham
    Collection, 313
Fennell, Tom, Jr., Porcelana
    Granada, 504, 505
Fenton Art Glass Company,
    history of, 84, 85
Ferner, Lihs Linder, 453
Ferrandiz, Juan
    Anri, 133–135
    Schmid (Germany), 595–
        598
Ferreson, Jeffrey, Signature
    Collection, 610
Feruzzi, Haviland and Parlon,
    356
Fina, Gloria, Fenton Art Glass,
    249
Finnie, John, Wedgwood,
    Enoch, 658
Fisher, Shell
    Pemberton and Oakes,
        489–492
    Royal Orleans, 582, 584
    Viletta China, 645, 646
Fisher, Virginia, Hackett
    American, 332
Flugenring, H., Bing &
    Grondahl, 169, 173
Fogg, Howard, Ernst
    Enterprises, R.J., 229
Frace, Charles, Ghent
    Collection, 288
Franca, Ozz, Hackett American,
    334, 335, 339

Francis, J., Kaiser, 408
Frank, Grace Lee, Franklin
    Mint, 282
Frank, John, Franklin Mint,
    281, 282
Frank, Joniece, Franklin Mint,
    281–283
Frankoma Pottery, history of,
    85, 86
Freedman, Claire, Modern
    Masters, 473
Freuner, Willy, Kaiser, 408
Friis, Achton, Bing &
    Grondahl, 169, 173
Fromme-Douglas, Wedgwood,
    Enoch, 654
Frudakis, Evangelos, Franklin
    Mint, 264
Fukagawa, Suetomi, 283

Gainsborough, Gorham
    Collection, 309
Gaither, W., Maruri USA, 465
Galli, Stanley, Certified Rarities,
    196
Ganeau, Francois, D'Arceau
    Limoge, 214, 215
Garavani, Valentino,
    Armstrong's/Crown
    Parian, 149
Garde, Fanny, Bing &
    Grondahl, 168, 173
Gaudin, Marguerite, Franklin
    Mint, 264
Gawantka, Wolfgang, Kaiser,
    411
Gehm, Charles, Konigszelt
    Bavaria, 439
Gerhart, Mitsuko, Schmid
    (Japan), 601
Gerischer, Val Roy, Lenox, 445
Ghislain, Charles, Franklin
    Mint, 271

Gialletti, Guilio, Veneto Flair, 641

Gibson, Gayle, Lynell, 462

Gilbert, Albert Earl, Ghent Collection, 288, 289

Giovenale, Randy, Poverty Bay Porcelain, 508

Girrado, Hector, Signature Collection, 610

Glenice, Ernst Enterprises, R.J., 236, 237

Gomez, Ignacio, American Legacy, 122

Gossner, Gabriele, Franklin Mint, 271

Grandma Moses, Royal Cornwall, 563

Granget, Gunther
  Ghent Collection, 290
  House of Global Art, 377
  Hutschenreuther, 385, 386
  Royal Cornwall, 560

Graves, Oscar, Accent on Art, 115

Gray, Albert Earl, Ghent Collection, 288

Gray, Holmes, Ghent Collection, 288

Greensmith, Hackett American, 333

Greenaway, Kate, Grande Danica, 322

Greenwood, Leslie, Franklin Mint, 267, 268

Gregory, Mary, Koscherak Brothers, 441

Greunke, Carol, Reco International, 510

Grierson, Mary, Franklin Mint, 271, 280

Grimes, Rick, Royal Orleans, 582, 583

Grossberg, E., Furstenberg, 283

Guidou, Jean-Claude, D'Arceau Limoge, 216

Gunn, Robert, Royal Cornwall, 563

Gustafson, Scott, American Artists, 118

Gutmann, Bessie Pease
  Curator Collection, 209
  Hamilton Collection, 341, 342
  Rockford Editions, 527

Gutshall, Charlotte, Hackett American, 338

Hack, Konrad, Royal Cornwall, 559, 565

Hagara, Jan
  B & J Art Designs, 157, 158
  Carson Mint, 192

Hagel, Mike, Lynell, 460, 461, 463, 464

Hague, M., River Shore, 525

Hallett, Charlotte, Hutschenreuther, 384, 385, 387, 389

Hallett, William, Hutschenreuther, 384, 385, 387, 389

Hallin, Franz August, Bing & Grondahl, 168, 173

Hallis, Andrea, Hudson Pewter, 382

Hamilton, Jack, Ernst Enterprises, R.J., 233

Hampler, M., U.S. Historical Society, 627

Hansen, Derk, Kern Collectibles, 420

Hansen, Einar, Bing & Grondahl, 168

Hansen, Hans H., Royal Copenhagen, 552

Hara, N., Hamilton Collection, 345

Harm, Ray, Spode, 614
Harman, Bob, Pacific Art
    Limited, 481
Harper, Tom, Wedgwood,
    Enoch, 654
Harris, Julian, Franklin Mint,
    274
Hayden, Hayden
  Hoyle Products, 380
  Royal Orleans, 583
Healey, Joan, Rare Bird, 509
Helland, John, American
    Heritage, 121, 122
Henri, Ralph, Franklin Mint,
    271
Henson, Jim, Fairmont China,
    244
Heritage, Antony, Southern
    Living Gallery, 611, 612
Hershenburgh, Ann, Fairmont
    China, 245
Hetreau, Remy, Hampton
    House Studios, 354, 355
Hibel, Edna
  Anna-Perenna, 128
  biographical information, 74,
    75
  Hibel Studios, 360–366
  Hutschenreuther, 382
  Knowles, Edwin M., 426,
    428, 431
  Roman, Inc., 546, 547
  Royal Doulton, 580
Hicks, Yin-Rei, River Shore,
    526
Hien, Harris, Historic
    Providence Mint, 377
Hildebrandt, Tim, Christian
    Fantasy Collectibles,
    198–202
Hines, Jack, Schmid (Germany),
    597
Hirschfeld, Al, Anna-Perenna,
    129

Hoffman, Leesa, Kern
    Collectibles, 418
Holden, Edith, Ghent
    Collection, 288, 289
Holgate, Jeanne, Franklin Mint,
    267, 271
Hollands-Robinson, Phyllis,
    American Artists, 118
Hollis, Andrea, Lance
    International, 443
Homan, Ralph, Viletta China,
    647
Homer, Winslow, U.S.
    Historical Society, 630
Hook, Frances
  Knowles, Edwin M., 432
  Roman, Inc., 537–540
Hook, Richard, Wedgwood,
    Enoch, 655
Hooks, Mitchell, Signature
    Collection, 609
Hoover, G.A., Longton
    Crown Pottery, 458,
    459
Horak, Jeanne, O.K.
    Collectibles, 479
Horton, Joan, Hackett
    American, 336
Horton, Robert, Kaiser, 414
Hotta, Shigekasu, Hamilton
    Collection, 344, 345,
    352
Hulce, Claude, Brindle Fine
    Arts, 188
Hummel, Berta, Schmid
    (Germany), 593, 594
Hummel, M.I., Ghent
    Collection, 291, 292
Humphrey, M., Hoyle Products,
    380, 381
Hunter, Frances Tipton,
    Curator Collection, 211
Hyldahl, Margarethe, Bing &
    Grondahl, 168, 170, 173

Icart, Louis, Heirloom
    Traditions, 360
Ingargiola, Franco, Studio
    Dante di Volteradici, 623

Jackson, Anthony C., 403
Jackson, Charlotte, Royal
    Cornwall, 566
Jackson, Peter, Franklin Mint,
    262
Jacobson, Bill
  Nostalgia Collectibles, 478
  Rockwell Museum, 530, 532
Jacques, F., Fleetwood
    Collection, 254
Jansen, Leo
  Gorham Collection, 311, 312
  Kern Collectibles, 418–420
  Royal Bayreuth, 548, 549
Jarratt, Deborah Bell, Franklin
    Mint, 261
Jensen, Dahl, Bing & Grondahl,
    168, 173
Jensen, Edward, Bing &
    Grondahl, 172
Jensen, Maureen, Franklin
    Mint, 280
Jensen, Oluf, Royal
    Copenhagen, 550, 551
Jerner, Bart, Knowles, Edwin
    M., 435
Jervis, Sharon, House of Global
    Art, 378, 379
Johnson, Brian, Sports
    Impressions, 616, 619
Johnson, David McCall, Royal
    Cornwall, 556
Johnson, Diane, Fenton Art
    Glass, 247
Johnson, Laura, Fairmont
    China, 241
Johnson, Robert, Reed and
    Barton, 520

Jondar, Hoyle Products, 379
Jones, Kate Lloyd, Franklin
    Mint, 261
Jones, Loretta, Hampton House
    Studios, 356
Jones, Paul, Franklin Mint, 271
Jorgensen, J. Bloch, Bing &
    Grondahl, 168
Jorgensen, Povi, Bing &
    Grondahl, 168
Jungbluth, Mimi, Royal
    Doulton, 576

Kage, Senkin, Hamilton
    Collection, 344, 347,
    348
Kage, Shuho, Hamilton
    Collection, 344, 347,
    348
Kalan, Hackett American, 339
Kane, Margaret, Anna-Perenna,
    126, 128
Karn, Murray, Creative World,
    205
Katz, Garri, Reco International,
    514, 515
Kaufman, Mico, Franklin Mint,
    274
Kay, Sarah, Anri, 135
Keane, Bil, Hoyle Products,
    379
Keane, Margaret, Dave
    Grossman Designs, 326
Keirstead, Canadian Collector
    Plates, 190
Keirstead, James, Keirstead
    Gallery, 416
Keller, Hedi, Konigszelt
    Bavaria, 439, 440
Kelly, C., Flambro Imports,
    252, 253
Kelly
  Ernst Enterprises, R.J., 233

Hackett American, 334
Viletta China, 647
Kendricks, Skipper, Mistwood
    Designs, 470
Kent, Melanie Taylor, Carmel
    Collection, 191
Kierstead, James,
    Hutschenreuther, 384
Killman, Murray, Lynell, 461,
    463
King, Dorothea, Kaiser, 414
Kingman, Don, Royal Doulton,
    580
Kirk, Jodi, 422
Kjolner, Theodor, Royal
    Copenhagen, 551, 552
Knapton, Cynthia
    Carson Mint, 194
    Wexford Group, 660, 661
Knievel, Evel, O.K. Collectibles,
    479
Knowles, Edwin M., 423–428
Koseki and Ebihara, Hamilton
    Collection, 347
Kouba, Les, Legacy Unlimited,
    444
Koutsis, Yiannis, Royal
    Cornwall, 556–558, 564
KPM–Royal Berlin, 441, 442
Krog, Arnold, Royal
    Copenhagen, 550
Krumeich, Thaddeus,
    Anna-Perenna, 127,
    129–132
Kuck, Sandra
    interview with, 58–60
    Reco International, 509–511,
    513–516
Kuhnly, Scott, Ernst
    Enterprises, R.J., 229
Kurkin, A.M., Fleetwood
    Collection, 256
Kursar, Raymond, Knowles,
    Edwin M., 430, 431

La Bonte, J., Royal Orleans,
    584
Laetitia, Hamilton Collection,
    351
Lalique, Marie-Claude, 442, 443
Lamb, R., Chilmark, 196
Lambert, Georgia, Knowles,
    Edwin M., 428, 429
Lamincia, Franco, Veneto Flair,
    641
Landenberger, James, Pawnee
    Creek Press, 482
Landis, J., U.S. Historical
    Society, 628
Lange, Kai, Royal Copenhagen,
    551–553
Lansdowne, James Fenwick,
    Franklin Mint, 258,
    280
Lanz, Walter,
    Armstrong's/Crown
    Parian, 140
Larsen, Ove, Bing & Grondahl,
    169, 170, 173
Larsen, T., Bing & Grondahl,
    168, 173
Larson, C., Hamilton
    Collection, 346
Lawrence, Sir Thomas,
    Armstrong's/Crown
    Parian, 145, 146
Lawson, Carol, Franklin Mint,
    261, 264–266, 269–270,
    277, 280
Lawson, John, Pickard, 500
Laye, Tammy, Daybrake
    Marketing, 218
Lee, Nan, Haviland and Parlon,
    358
Lee, Ron
    Fairmont China, 243
    Lynell, 461, 462
Leigh, Susan, American Artists,
    117

Leigh, William R., Curator
    Collection, 209
Le Page, Eddie, Ghent
    Collection, 293
Letostak, John, Ernst
    Enterprises, R.J., 229
Leyendecker, J.C.
  Ridgewood, 522, 523
  Royal Cornwall, 556
  Royalwood, 585
Licea, Eve, Knowles, Edwin M.,
    425
Lihs Linder, 451–454
Limoges-Turgot, 454, 455
Lippi, Fra Filippo
  Haviland and Parlon, 356
  Reed and Barton, 520
  Roman, Inc., 540
Littlejohn, John, Kaiser, 411
Livingstone, Michele, Stratford
    Collection, 621
Lloyd-Jones, Kate, Franklin
    Mint, 272
Loates, Glen, Kaiser, 411
Lochner, Steven, Reed and
    Barton, 520
Lockhart, James, Pickard, 499
Lohmann, Adolf, Kaiser, 410,
    413
Long, F.F., Ghent Collection,
    289
Lotto, L., Pickard, 497
Loudin, Frank, Evergreen Press,
    238
Loup, Jean-Paul, 459
Lundgren, Charles, Fleetwood
    Collection, 255
Lupetti, Lynn, Dave Grossman
    Designs, 325, 326

Maass, David, Hoyle Products,
    381

McCalla, Irish
  Hackett American, 333
  Viletta China, 645, 648
McCarty, Armstrong's/Crown
    Parian, 148, 149
McClelland, John
  interview with, 61–63
  Reco International, 511,
    515–516, 518
McEwan, Christopher, Franklin
    Mint, 257
Mack, Bill, Royal Cornwall,
    559
McKenzie, T.T., Franklin Mint,
    280
McKernan, J., Kaiser, 411
McLennan, Edith, Ghent
    Collection, 290
Malfertheiner, J., Anri, 132,
    133
Mandrajji, Valentin, Knowles,
    Edwin M., 424
Manning, Douglas, Christian
    Bell Porcelain, 198
Mano, Sadaka, Hackett
    American, 331, 332, 337,
    338
Maratti, Carlo, Kaiser, 408
Marco, J., Ernst Enterprises,
    R.J., 237
Marco, Viletta China, 645
Mark, R., Southern Living
    Gallery, 613
Marry-Kenyon, Ann, Ernst
    Enterprises, R.J., 229,
    231
Marsten, Barbara, Knowles,
    Edwin M., 424
Martin, John, Gartlan USA
    Inc., 284
Masseria, Francisco, Royal
    Doulton, 580
Massey, R., Hamilton
    Collection, 349, 350

Mathers, Shelly, Schmid
(Japan), 604
Matterness, Jay H., Ghent
Collection, 288, 289
Matthews, Jeffrey, Fleetwood
Collection, 255, 256
Maxwell, Elizabeth, Carmel
Collection, 191
Mays, Maxwell, Reed and
Barton, 520
Memling, Pickard, 498
Merli, King's, 421
Mignard, P., Roman, Inc.,
540
Miller, David, American
Heritage, 122
Miller, Gerald R., Royal
Cornwall, 556
Miller, Sally, Modern Masters,
471–473
Miller, Vel, Armstrong's/Crown
Parian, 155
Miller, Vincent, Franklin Mint,
280
Mingolla, Dominic, Royal
Cornwall, 561, 564
Mitchell, James, Bing &
Grondahl, 176
Mix, Jo Anne
Carson Mint, 193
Hackett American, 333, 335,
337, 338
Moeller, Harry J., Ghent
Collection, 287–289
Moltke, H., Bing & Grondahl,
168
Monet, Claude, Curator
Collection, 209
Money, Rusty
Armstrong's/Crown Parian,
154
biographical information, 75
Ernst Enterprises, R.J., 233,
234, 236

Montgomery, James, Curator
Collection, 212
Moody, Franklin
Hamilton Collection, 346,
347, 351
Pacific Art Limited, 480
Porcelaine Ariel, 503
Morrisseau, Norval,
Anna-Perenna, 126
Morton, Susie
Duncan Royale, 220, 221
Ernst Enterprises, R.J., 227,
229, 231, 232, 234, 235,
237
Moses, Will, Modern Masters,
473, 474
Moss, P. Buckley
Anna-Perenna, 124, 125
biographical information, 76
Mowrey, Geoff, Franklin Mint,
262
Mueller, Hans, Bareuther,
158–162
Munch, Verner, Bing &
Grondahl, 175, 176
Murillo, Haviland and Parlon,
356
Murphy, Margaret, Franklin
Mint, 261
Murray, Alan, Ernst
Enterprises, R.J., 232,
234

Nast, Thomas
Duncan Royale, 220
Reed and Barton, 520
Neelon, Susan, Lynell, 461
Neiman, LeRoy, Royal
Doulton, 576, 577, 579
Neubacher, Gerda, Kaiser, 409,
411, 414, 415
Neubauer, Josef, Lihs Linder,
453

Newman, Colin, Franklin Mint, 277

Newsom, Tom, Signature Collection, 609

Ng, Kee Fung, Armstrong's/Crown Parian, 151

Nickerson, Richard, Fairmont China, 244

Nielsen, Herne, Royal Copenhagen, 551

Nielsen, Svend Nicolai, Royal Copenhagen, 551

Nightingale, Sandy, Hutschenreuther, 390

Nitschke, Detlev, Berlin Design, 165

Nobata, Naika, Franklin Mint, 260, 261

Noel, N., Hamilton Collection, 343, 344

Noel, Nancy, U.S. Historical Society, 629

Northcott, Joann, Kaiser, 408, 412

Novoa, Gustavo, Royal Doulton, 577, 579

Nussbaum, J., Chilmark, 196

Nyce, Helen, House of Global Art, 378

Nye, Linda, Kern Collectibles, 421

Nye, Marvin
 Kern Collectibles, 418, 420
 Sango, 591

Nylund, Gunner, Roman, Inc., 541, 542

Oberstein, Chuck, Hackett American, 331, 339

Ohta, Yoai, Franklin Mint, 271

Okamoto, T., Franklin Mint, 280

Olsen, Benjamin, Royal Copenhagen, 551

Olsen, Centhinka, Bing & Grondahl, 168

Olsen, Ib Spang, Royal Copenhagen, 554, 555

Olsen, Viggo, Royal Copenhagen, 551, 552

Olson, Robert, Windmere Collection, 662

Orosz, Ray, American Heritage, 121

Orr, Robert, Kaiser, 415

Osdell, Barrie Van, Louisiana Heritage Art Galleries, 459

Otto, Svend, Svend, Jensen, 404

Oxenham, Patrick, Rhea Silva Porcelain Collection, 522

Palladini, David, Pickard, 499

Palmieri, Frank, Braymer Hall, 187

Paluso, Christopher, Hackett American, 332, 340

Pape, Carl, Hackett American, 334, 335

Paredes, Miguel, Armstrong's/Crown Parian, 146

Parkhurst, Violet
 Hackett American, 333, 335–337, 339
 Parkhurst & Bower, 482
 Parkhurst Enterprises, 481, 482

Pearce, L.J., Franklin Mint, 262

Pearcy, Robert, Armstrong's/Crown Parian, 138, 139, 141

Pederson, Sharleen, Royal Cornwall, 564

Peel, Paul, Canadian Collector
    Plates, 190
Peltriauz, Bernard,
    Limoges-Turgot, 455
Pemberton & Oakes, history of,
    86
Pentz, Donald
    Dominion China Co., 219
    Knowles, Edwin M., 437
Perham, Michael,
    Armstrong's/Crown
    Parian, 148
Perillo, Gregory
    Curator Collection, 209
    interview with, 63–65
    Kern Collectibles, 418
    Ussher, D.H., Ltd., 630–633,
        636–638
Peter, Nori
    Anador Trading Company,
        124
    Anna-Perenna, 125
    Kaiser, 412–414
Petitto, Albert, Incolay Studios,
    401
Petty, George B., Roman, Inc.,
    539, 540
Peynet, Raymond, Franklin
    Mint, 280
Phillips, Gordon, Franklin
    Mint, 257, 278
Pike, John, Franklin Mint, 257
Plates (Collector)
    approaches to collecting,
        20–25
        collecting by artist, 24, 25
        collecting by manufacturer,
            23, 24
        series collecting, 22
        specializing, 21, 22
    budget-conscious buyers, 7
    buying plates, 29–43
        at auctions, 38–41
        at flea markets, 52

    at secondhand shops, 52
    Bradford Exchange, 42, 43
    by mail order, 35–37
    from manufacturer, 32, 33
    from other collectors, 41
    from plate dealers, 33–35
caring for plates, 54–57
    packing for shipment, 55,
        56
    washing, 70
displaying plates, 50–53
fakes, 30, 31, 47–49
history of, 13–19
insurance, 56, 57
investing in plates, 26–28
    buying for profit, 26, 27
    future price forecasting, 27,
        28
limited-edition plates, 6, 12,
    18
market overview, 3–5
    top artists, 4, 5
production of plates,
    processes of, 8–12
selling plates, 43–45
    at auctions, 46
Plockross, E., Bing & Grondahl,
    168, 173
Plummer, William, Franklin
    Mint, 262
Poluszynski, J.
    Furstenberg, 284
    Reco International, 514
Poortvliet, Rien, Fairmont
    China, 241–244
Port, Beverly, Gorham
    Collection, 296
Porter, Bonnie
    Ernst Enterprises, R.J., 233
    Viletta China, 646
Potter, Beatrix
    Schmid (Germany), 592, 593
    Wedgwood, Enoch, 652, 653,
        656

Powell, William, Ernst
        Enterprises, R.J., 229
Pramvig, Borge, Bing &
        Grondahl, 170
Price, A., Wedgwood, Enoch,
        656, 658
Price, Don, Carson Mint, 194
Prince, Martha, Franklin Mint,
        271
Putnam, Donald
    Ernst Enterprises, R.J., 236
    Viletta China, 648

Quellier, Andre,
        Limoges-Turgot, 455
Quidley, Peter, Ernst
        Enterprises, R.J., 229

Raad, Lucelle, Modern
        Concepts Limited, 470,
        471
Rampel, Helen, Carmel
        Collection, 191
Raphael
    Haviland and Parlon, 356
    Pickard, 497
Reed, Hal
    JM Company, 405
    Svend, Jensen, 405
Reed, Rex T., Ghent Collection,
        290
Rembrandt, Gorham Collection,
        309
Remington, Frederic
    Curator Collection, 209
    George Washington Mint,
        287
    Gorham Collection, 316
Renoir, Auguste, Pickard,
        498
Restieau, Andre, D'Arceau
        Limoge, 214–216

Restoueux, Rene, Franklin
        Mint, 268
Richter, Ludwig, Bareuther,
        160, 161
Ricker, Anthony,
        Ricker-Bartlett Casting
        Studios, 522
Ricker, Michael, Ricker-Bartlett
        Casting Studios, 522
Rickert, Paul, Franklin Mint,
        257
Riemer-Gerbardt, Elizabeth,
        Franklin Mint, 271
Ries, Edward, American
        Heritage, 121
Riley, C. Ford, Hamilton
        Collection, 349
Ritter, John,
        Armstrong's/Crown
        Parian, 149
Ritter, Julian, Gorham
        Collection, 311
Rittun, Thorstein, Porsgrund,
        506
Roberton, John,
        Armstrong's/Crown
        Parian, 145
Roberts, Gilroy, Franklin Mint,
        274, 275
Roberts, James, Incolay Studios,
        395
Rockwell Museum, 527–541
    history of, 86, 87
Rockwell, Norman
    Curator Collection, 209–212
    Dave Grossman Designs, 323,
        325–330
    Fairmont China, 241
    Franklin Mint, 275, 280
    Ghent Collection, 288
    Gorham Collection, 294, 296,
        298, 301–308, 316, 318
    Hamilton Collection, 340, 341
    Hoyle Products, 379, 380

Lake Shore Prints, 442
Lynell, 462, 463
Metal Arts Company, 467, 468
Ohio Arts, 479
Ridgewood, 523
River Shore, 524–526
Rockwell Collectors Club, 527
Rockwell Museum, 527–537
Royal Devon, 572, 573
Royalwood, 585
Sango, 591
Rode, Gottfred, Royal Copenhagen, 551
Rodgers, George, Lionshead Mint, 456
Rohn, Edward J., Carson Mint, 192, 193
Roller, C., Bing & Grondahl, 167
Romanelli, Carl
  biographical information, 72, 73
  Incolay Studios, 395
Rosena, Anthony, Fenton Art Glass, 248
Rossel Waugh, Carol-Lynn, Brimark Ltd., 188
Royal Copenhagen, history of, 87, 88
Rozewicz, Erich, Monaco Porcelain Factory, 474
Ruffin, Don
  Armstrong's/Crown Parian, 152, 153, 155
  biographical information, 76, 77
  Certified Rarities, 195
Ruffing, A.E., Southern Living Gallery, 612
Ruggeri, Gino, Studio Dante di Volteradici, 623

Runci, Edward, Kern Collectibles, 419, 420
Russell, Bob, Hackett American, 334
Russell, Charles, Gorham Collection, 298
Russell, Frank, Anna-Perenna, 129
Rust, D.L. "Rusty,"
  biographical information, 77
Ruthven, John
  Armstrong's/Crown Parian, 141, 144, 146
  Fairmont China, 244, 245
  Hutschenreuther, 389
  Wildlife Internationale, 661

Sabra, S., Bing & Grondahl, 168, 173
St. Clair, Fairmont China, 245
Sanchez, J., Pickard, 498, 500
Santangela, Alberto, Studio Dante di Volteradici, 622, 623, 625
Santini, Ado, Studio Dante di Volteradici, 623
Sauber, Rob
  Braymer Hall, 187
  Curator Collection, 206, 207, 210
  Signature Collection, 609, 610
Sayer, Angela, Bing & Grondahl, 167
Schaefers, Karin, Modern Masters, 473
Schenken, Rod, Armstrong's/Crown Parian, 150
Schiener, W., Lenox, 450
Schlesinger, A., Kaiser, 408
Schmidt, Jay, Kern Collectibles, 417

Schoener, Toni, Kaiser,
407–409, 412, 413,
416

Schofield, Mildred, Schofield
Gallery, 605

Schultz, Charles, Schmid
(Japan), 602–604

Seeley, Mildred, Seeley's
Ceramic Service, 606,
607

Seerey-Lester, J., Hamilton
Collection, 349

Seima, Royal Cornwall, 562,
563

Seitz, Bill, Vernonware, 642

Selden, William, Hackett
American, 336, 340

Selschau, Ellinor, Royal
Copenhagen, 550

Shaefer, Gus, Franklin Mint,
278

Sharpe, H. Alvin, Hamilton
Mint, 353

Shearer, Julie, Modern Masters,
472

Sheehan, Marion Ruff, Franklin
Mint, 271

Sheppard, L.L., Reed and
Barton, 520

Shields, Adam, Ernst
Enterprises, R.J., 232

Sickbert, Jo, Franklin Mint,
270, 271

Sidoni, Anthony,
Armstrong's/Crown Parian,
151
Fairmont China, 241, 246

Sigle, Louise
Hackett American, 336
O.K. Collectibles, 479

Simon, Robert Stephen, Sports
Impressions, 616

Singer, Arthur, Franklin Mint,
276, 278

Sizemore, Ted, Gartlan USA
Inc., 284

Skelton, Red
Armstrong's/Crown Parian,
139, 140, 149, 150
biographical information, 77
Fairmont China, 241

Sloane, Eric, Royal Doulton,
577

Sloane, John, Rainbow
Treasury, 508

Smith, David, Hackett
American, 331–333

Smith, Jessie Wilcox, Knowles,
Edwin M., 432

Smiton, David, Creative World,
204

Snyder, Peter Etril, Christian
Bell Porcelain, 197, 198

Sodoma, Pickard, 498

Soileau, Charles, Gartlan USA
Inc., 286

Soldwedel, Kipp, Curator
Collection, 211

Sommer, Elke
Anna-Perenna, 127
Viletta China, 648

Spaulding, Don, Knowles,
Edwin M., 423, 424

Spencer, Irene
biographical information, 78,
79
Fairmont China, 245
Franklin Mint, 273
Gorham Collection, 311
Pickard, 499–501
Roman, Inc., 540

Stage, Mads, Svend, Jensen,
403–405

Stanek, Franz, 620

Stobart, John, Royal Doulton,
579

Stokes, Zoe, American Artists,
118

Stone, Don, Franklin Mint, 257

Stone, Elisa, Hampton House Studios, 356

Stone, Fred
American Artists, 117, 118
Modern Masters, 472, 473

Stuwe, Marianne, Schumann, 605

Suetomi, Shunsute, Hamilton Collection, 345

Sundberg, Carl, Incolay Studios, 400

Sundblom, Haddon, Royal Orleans, 582

Sundin, Adelaid, Franklin Mint, 273

Sunyer, Oriol, Franklin Mint, 264

Svend, Jensen, 403–405

Svensson, Kamma, Royal Copenhagen, 554

Sweany, P., Hamilton Collection, 341

Szabo, Endre, Lynell, 460, 464

Taylor, Gage, Ernst Enterprises, R.J., 235

Tellier, Liliane, Hampton House Studios, 355

Tenny, Frank, Curator Collection, 209

Terp, George, Historic Providence Mint, 367

Thelander, Henry, Bing & Grondahl, 171, 172, 174, 175

Thompson, L., River Shore, 524

Thompson, Linda, Hamilton Collection, 342, 343

Thomsen, Christian, Royal Copenhagen, 550

Thorpe, Clarence, Fairmont China, 238, 241, 245, 246

Thorsson, Nils, Royal Copenhagen, 551, 552

Timberlake, Bob, River Shore, 526

Timm, Richard, Michigan Natural Resources, 469

Tiziano, Vincente, Veneto Flair, 639–642

Tjerne, Immanuel, Bing & Grondahl, 169, 170

Tobey, Alton S.
Franklin Mint, 257
Ghent Collection, 289

Tobey, Fairmont China, 243

Tootle, Douglas, Davenport Pottery, 218

Toschik, Larry, Armstrong's/Crown Parian, 154, 155

Trechslin, Anne Marie, Franklin Mint, 271

Trester, Lorraine
Gorham Collection, 312
Kaiser, 412, 416
Ridgewood, 523
Roman, Inc., 546

Tseng, Mou-Sien, Hamilton Collection, 342

Tuck, Janet
Briarcrest, 188
Firehouse Collectibles, 251

Tudor, Guy, Ghent Collection, 288, 289

Turner, Nancy
Stratford Collection, 621
Stuart International, 622

Ungermann, Arne, Royal Copenhagen, 554

Upton, Roger, Evergreen Press, 238

Ussher, D.H., Ltd., 630–638

Ussing, Stephan, Royal Copenhagen, 550

Utamaro, Kitagawa, Royal Cornwall, 560, 561

Utz, Thornton
  Hamilton Collection, 349–353
  Reco International, 517
  Viletta China, 643, 646, 647

Valenza, Dolores, Hutschenreuther, 384, 385

Vallotton, Felix, Metropolitan Museum of Art, 468

Val St. Lambert, 638

Van der Weyden, Roger, Reed and Barton, 520

Van Howd, Douglas, American Heritage, 121

van Howd, Douglas, Armstrong's/Crown Parian, 138

Vargas, Alberto, Heirloom Traditions, 360

Vestergaard, Sven, Royal Copenhagen, 553, 554

Vickers, Mary, Wedgwood, Enoch, 650, 651

Vidal, Hahn, Royal Doulton, 577

Vig, Rik, David Kaplin Studios, 218

Vincent, Hackett American, 331

Vincent, Michael, Raynaud-Limoges, 509

Vosikkinen, Raija, Arabia of Finland, 137

Walczak, Jerome, Carmel Collection, 191

Waldheimer, Hans, Dresden, 220

Wallin, Fred, Braymer Hall, 186

Wasile, Elyse, Nassau Art Gallery, 476

Waterhouse, Ralph, O.K. Collectibles, 479

Weaver, John, Franklin Mint, 278

Weaver, Robert, Lynell, 461

Weber, Sarah Stilwell, Newell Pottery Company, 476

Wegner, Fritz, Fleetwood Collection, 254

Wehrli, Mary Ellen, Anna-Perenna, 125, 126

Weidhorst, Olaf, Armstrong's/Crown Parian, 149

Wendell Auguste Forge, 658, 659

West, Gillian, Spode, 614, 615

Whittaker, Lawrence W., Royal Cornwall, 555, 560

Wieghorst, Olaf, Fairmont China, 246

Wiinblad, Bjorn, Roman, Inc., 547, 548

Wilcox, Jessie
  Hamilton Collection, 345, 346
  Hoyle Products, 379

Williams, Abbie, Roman, Inc., 539, 540

Williams, Abigail, biographical information, 79, 80

Williams, Frances Taylor, Avondale, 156

Winther, Ole, Hutschenreuther, 382, 383, 385–388, 390, 391

Wood, Grant, River Shore, 524
Wood, P., Spode, 615
Woods, James, Royal Doulton, 576
Woodson, J.
  Bing & Grondahl, 167
  U.S. Historical Society, 628–630
Wulfing, Sulamith, Konigszelt Bavaria, 438–441
Wyeth, James, Franklin Mint, 271, 272, 276
Wyeth, N.C., George Washington Mint, 287

Xaras, Theodore, Christian Bell Porcelain, 196, 197

Yang, Wei Tseng, Franklin Mint, 259, 260
Yates, Michael, Morgantown Crystal, 474
Young, Harland, Kern Collectibles, 417, 419

Young, T., Kern Collectibles, 419
Younger, Richard Evans, Franklin Mint, 259
Yu, Ren, Fleetwood Collection, 254

Zanobia, 662
Zapp, Marilyn, Braymer Hall, 187
Zemsky, Jessica, Schmid (Germany), 594, 597
Zolan, Donald
  interview with, 65–68
  Pemberton and Oakes, 482–484, 486, 488, 490, 492, 494, 495, 497
Zolan, R., American Artists, 117, 118
Zolan, Richard, Modern Masters, 471, 472
Zuoren, Wu, Fleetwood Collection, 255
Zvorykin, Boris, Heinrich Porzellan, 359

The HOUSE OF COLLECTIBLES Series

☐ Please send me the following price guides—
☐ I would like the most current edition of the books listed below.

THE OFFICIAL PRICE GUIDES TO:

☐ 753-3	American Folk Art (ID) 1st Ed.	$14.95
☐ 199-3	American Silver & Silver Plate 5th Ed.	11.95
☐ 513-1	Antique Clocks 3rd Ed.	10.95
☐ 283-3	Antique & Modern Dolls 3rd Ed.	10.95
☐ 287-6	Antique & Modern Firearms 6th Ed.	11.95
☐ 755-X	Antiques & Collectibles 9th Ed.	11.95
☐ 289-2	Antique Jewelry 5th Ed.	11.95
☐ 362-7	Art Deco (ID) 1st Ed.	14.95
☐ 447-X	Arts and Crafts: American Decorative Arts, 1894–1923 (ID) 1st Ed.	12.95
☐ 539-5	Beer Cans & Collectibles 4th Ed.	7.95
☐ 521-2	Bottles Old & New 10th Ed.	10.95
☐ 532-8	Carnival Glass 2nd Ed.	10.95
☐ 295-7	Collectible Cameras 2nd Ed.	10.95
☐ 548-4	Collectibles of the '50s & '60s 1st Ed.	9.95
☐ 740-1	Collectible Toys 4th Ed.	10.95
☐ 531-X	Collector Cars 7th Ed.	12.95
☐ 538-7	Collector Handguns 4th Ed.	14.95
☐ 748-7	Collector Knives 9th Ed.	12.95
☐ 361-9	Collector Plates 5th Ed.	11.95
☐ 296-5	Collector Prints 7th Ed.	12.95
☐ 001-6	Depression Glass 2nd Ed.	9.95
☐ 589-1	Fine Art 1st Ed.	19.95
☐ 311-2	Glassware 3rd Ed.	10.95
☐ 243-4	Hummel Figurines & Plates 6th Ed.	10.95
☐ 523-9	Kitchen Collectibles 2nd Ed.	10.95
☐ 080-6	Memorabilia of Elvis Presley and The Beatles 1st Ed.	10.95
☐ 291-4	Military Collectibles 5th Ed.	11.95
☐ 525-5	Music Collectibles 6th Ed.	11.95
☐ 313-9	Old Books & Autographs 7th Ed.	11.95
☐ 298-1	Oriental Collectibles 3rd Ed.	11.95
☐ 761-4	Overstreet Comic Book 18th Ed.	12.95
☐ 522-0	Paperbacks & Magazines 1st Ed.	10.95
☐ 297-3	Paper Collectibles 5th Ed.	10.95
☐ 744-4	Political Memorabilia 1st Ed.	10.95
☐ 529-8	Pottery & Porcelain 6th Ed.	11.95
☐ 524-7	Radio, TV & Movie Memorabilia 3rd Ed.	11.95
☐ 081-4	Records 8th Ed.	16.95
☐ 763-0	Royal Doulton 6th Ed.	12.95
☐ 280-9	Science Fiction & Fantasy Collectibles 2nd Ed.	10.95
☐ 747-9	Sewing Collectibles 1st Ed.	8.95
☐ 358-9	Star Trek/Star Wars Collectibles 2nd Ed.	8.95
☐ 086-5	Watches 8th Ed.	12.95
☐ 248-5	Wicker 3rd Ed.	10.95

THE OFFICIAL:

☐ 760-6	Directory to U.S. Flea Markets 2nd Ed.	5.95
☐ 365-1	Encyclopedia of Antiques 1st Ed.	9.95
☐ 369-4	Guide to Buying and Selling Antiques 1st Ed.	9.95
☐ 414-3	Identification Guide to Early American Furniture 1st Ed.	9.95
☐ 413-5	Identification Guide to Glassware 1st Ed.	9.95
☐ 412-7	Identification Guide to Pottery & Porcelain 1st Ed.	$9.95
☐ 415-1	Identification Guide to Victorian Furniture 1st Ed.	9.95

THE OFFICIAL (SMALL SIZE) PRICE GUIDES TO:

☐ 309-0	Antiques & Flea Markets 4th Ed.	4.95
☐ 269-8	Antique Jewelry 3rd Ed.	4.95
☐ 085-7	Baseball Cards 8th Ed.	4.95
☐ 647-2	Bottles 3rd Ed.	4.95
☐ 544-1	Cars & Trucks 3rd Ed.	5.95
☐ 519-0	Collectible Americana 2nd Ed.	4.95
☐ 294-9	Collectible Records 3rd Ed.	4.95
☐ 306-6	Dolls 4th Ed.	4.95
☐ 762-2	Football Cards 8th Ed.	4.95
☐ 540-9	Glassware 3rd Ed.	4.95
☐ 526-3	Hummels 4th Ed.	4.95
☐ 279-5	Military Collectibles 3rd Ed.	4.95
☐ 764-9	Overstreet Comic Book Companion 2nd Ed.	4.95
☐ 278-7	Pocket Knives 3rd Ed.	4.95
☐ 527-1	Scouting Collectibles 4th Ed.	4.95
☐ 494-1	Star Trek/Star Wars Collectibles 3rd Ed.	3.95
☐ 088-1	Toys 5th Ed.	4.95

THE OFFICIAL BLACKBOOK PRICE GUIDES OF:

☐ 092-X	U.S. Coins 27th Ed.	4.95
☐ 095-4	U.S. Paper Money 21st Ed.	4.95
☐ 098-9	U.S. Postage Stamps 11th Ed.	4.95

THE OFFICIAL INVESTORS GUIDE TO BUYING & SELLING:

☐ 534-4	Gold, Silver & Diamonds 2nd Ed.	12.95
☐ 535-2	Gold Coins 2nd Ed.	12.95
☐ 536-0	Silver Coins 2nd Ed.	12.95
☐ 537-9	Silver Dollars 2nd Ed.	12.95

THE OFFICIAL NUMISMATIC GUIDE SERIES:

☐ 254-X	The Official Guide to Detecting Counterfeit Money 2nd Ed.	7.95
☐ 257-4	The Official Guide to Mint Errors 4th Ed.	7.95

SPECIAL INTEREST SERIES:

☐ 506-9	From Hearth to Cookstove 3rd Ed.	17.95
☐ 504-2	On Method Acting 8th Printing	6.95

TOTAL	

SEE REVERSE SIDE FOR ORDERING INSTRUCTIONS

☐ FOR IMMEDIATE DELIVERY ☐

VISA & MASTER CARD CUSTOMERS

ORDER TOLL FREE!
1-800-733-3000

This number is for orders only; it is not tied into the customer service or business office. Customers not using charge cards must use mail for ordering since payment is required with the order—sorry, no C.O.D's.

OR SEND ORDERS TO

THE HOUSE OF COLLECTIBLES
201 East 50th Street
New York, New York 10022

——— POSTAGE & HANDLING RATES ———

First Book	$1.00
Each Additional Copy or Title	$0.50

Total from columns on order form. Quantity_____ $_____

☐ Check or money order enclosed $_____ (include postage and handling)

☐ Please charge $_____ to my: ☐ MASTERCARD ☐ VISA

Charge Card Customers Not Using Our Toll Free Number
Please Fill Out The Information Below

Account No. _____ (All Digits) _____ Expiration Date_____

Signature_____

NAME (please print)_____ PHONE_____

ADDRESS_____ APT. #_____

CITY_____ STATE_____ ZIP_____